THE MEDITERRANEAN

THE MEDITERRANEAN

SAGA OF A SEA

by Emil Ludwig

WHITTLESEY HOUSE

New York MCGRAW-HILL BOOK COMPANY · INC *London*

THE MEDITERRANEAN

COPYRIGHT, 1942, BY EMIL LUDWIG

Translated from the German by Barrows Mussey

Illustrations by Rafaello Busoni

Maps and End Papers by Stephen J. Voorhies

PUBLISHED BY WHITTLESEY HOUSE
A division of the McGraw-Hill Book Company, Inc.

Printed in the United States of America

To the

Columns of the Parthenon

PREFACE

THE DESTINIES OF AN OCEAN are played out on the water and along the coast. But the barren expanse has little history; the struggle develops ashore, only occasionally invading the sea. Yet through all the struggles, deeds, and creations, we shall hear the roar of the sea and catch sight of its blueness; storms and clouds will steer the doings of men toward prosperous voyages or shipwreck; oars and sails, anchors and lighthouses will keep bringing the reader back to the element that holds all together. Cliffs and trees, winds and fish will animate this island-dotted book.

The history of an ocean demands another style than that of a stream. The Nile was comparable to a human life from birth to death, an epic course. The sea, which all the adjacent inhabitants hope to dominate, is a prize being striven for in a drama. As against the masculine river, pushing its way downward through rocks and deserts, we have here the feminine sea, like Helen of old, which everyone would possess, so that it passes from one master to another.

Among all the seas the Mediterranean is unique, as an element and as a center. By nature it is almost a lake, and yet it is not; for Gibraltar, the Dardanelles, and Suez, which confine its freedom, are dramatic in their causes and effects. The third of these, the canal, has influenced the life of the sea in most recent times.

Throughout civilized times the Mediterranean has been the center of the cultural history that developed the western barbarians into human beings. All our religions and philosophies, our sciences and arts, were born, transformed, disputed, perfected here. Here the souls and minds of the Europeans found their political, intellectual, and artistic patterns, and every dogma, constitution, and pillar in America likewise comes from the Mediterranean. It is only since the great discoveries that the imagination of the peoples has turned to other oceans as well. For that reason the color of our treatment changes about 1500, that is, from Book Four on, and follows trade and traffic rather than the intellect. For this long cultural history does not increase with the centuries, but declines with each era. The history of antiquity in the Mediterranean should have been three times as long, and in its original form it actually was far longer than it is here.

Completeness is impossible in any case, for to tell the mere history of the coast countries would have taken three volumes. Many kings' names are missing, and no doubt readers will often look in vain for their favorites. Like *The Nile,* such a book as this can be written only in aphorisms; it is intended to start the reader studying special periods in other books. Objectivity too you will find in them or in the encyclopedia, not here. The likes and dislikes displayed here depend on the personality, philosophy, and background of the author. I have spent many years on the Mediterranean, seeing all its shores and peoples, and I can give only my own Mediterranean, with which other Mediterraneans may be contrasted. This is not a travel book; it is nature and history as I see them. The best historians have always written subjectively, only they have not said so aloud in the preface. My picture is fixed by the Greeks, to whose gods, art, and wisdom I owe everything.

Since Mediterranean history practically constituted the history of Europe up to the Middle Ages, I have been able to present here at some length a new form of history writing that I have long been moving toward in detail. When I began the modern form of biography in 1919, the simple basic idea was that the human traits alone really counted—that private and public life determined and explained each other. To discover the man behind his actions seems to me more interesting than the actions. Kings receive deeper study than laborers not only because they produce great effects but because there are no documents concerning the workmen.

It is useless to study history unless we seek the parable in everything that comes to pass. The symbol alone is significant, for it reflects the passions of the warring mortals, the forces of destiny, and thus demands comparison with our time, with our own victories and defeats in national life without and in our hearts within. He that does not discover himself in the mortals whose shadows we conjure up will merely learn facts; his own development will be forwarded not at all.

If the reader can feel how heroes, so called, are impelled by the same passions that move him in his own intimate life, then he is mirroring himself in the historical figure, and secretly testing himself to see how he would have behaved in the other's shoes. But he can put himself in the hero's place only if the author has previously metamorphosed himself into that character. If in this fashion the reader can learn a lesson for his own life from the destinies of men and nations, comparing his personal destiny with that of historic figures, history becomes his counselor.

This style of treatment, putting the human element in the foreground, I have here tried to apply to the life of nations, following three fundamental rules: All intellectual movements are significant; prophets and lawgivers, thinkers and artists are the true backbone of history. Furthermore, anything that agitates our own era is important, for "Politics without history has no root, history without politics bears no fruit." Thirdly, characters are significant. Actions belong in the museum of history; characters, the substance of action and intellect, approach the heart and brain of every individual.

The works of the mind and of art outlive their creators, but the deeds of the kings and statesmen, of the popes, presidents, and generals for whom periods are named, perish with or soon after the doers. None of the foreign kingdoms whose dates burden the memory of schoolboys has survived; all the treaties and alliances have turned to mere paper. Only the spirit they sprang from, only the symbol that they connote, has remained. The Greek influence carried to Asia by Alexander is important; so is the Christian influence carried there by the crusaders, or the Arabic influence in Europe. The battles, on the other hand, are merely comical as shown in old pictures; not even a soldier can learn anything from them. The solemnly signed and sealed treaties of peace refer to provinces and seaports that have long since changed hands or been destroyed.

What, then, deserves to be treated? Not so much the battles
fought in and on the Mediterranean by Themistocles, Agrippa,
Mohammed, Solyman, Nelson, or Garibaldi; not the peace treaties
concluded by Dionysius, Theodoric, Gregory, Philip, or Cavour.
The importance of an era depends solely on what it leaves behind—
whether wisdom, art, the memory of an outstanding generation,
or the character of a great man. To the life of the Mediterranean,
the Acropolis is more important than the whole history of Morocco.
If there can be any other than cultural history, everything must depend on the human traits revealed in the actors. This was the secret
of Plutarch my master, and it made him one of the greatest teachers
of the human race. Surely it must be possible to write world history
in the same style—with no pretension to being definitive, but with
one's eyes on the thousand human hearts asking to be moved.

Like my earlier books, this one makes plain my belief in individual personalities, which fix the course of human events. Without the murder of Caesar or Henry IV, or with a premature death
for Attila, Charles V, or Louis XIV, whole ages might have had
a different history. Economic statistics were not available; only
at the outset of the nineteenth century could trade and commerce
in the Mediterranean be enlarged upon more clearly. On the other
hand the climate, rivers, and products have been treated as factors
that shape character.

A definite political philosophy underlies the book. It is written
from the point of view of an individualist who has always believed
in the predominance of the intellect over force, yet has realized that
the advanced mind makes itself felt but slowly. A thinker cannot
guide the state in his own time; in the Mediterranean a few such
men as Pericles, Marcus Aurelius, and Saladin have been exceptions to this rule. Only political thinkers who, like Mohammed,
accepted their given circumstances have been successful during
their lifetimes; Plato and Dante, much greater brains, were not.
Conquerors without intellect, like Attila, have been forgotten. In
this book conquerors are studied closely only if, like Alexander,
they brought ideas to the conquered, or, like certain Roman and

Arab rulers, received ideas from them; if they made laws, like Justinian or Napoleon, or forwarded civilization, like some of the Ptolemies, Byzantines, Popes, and doges. "The men I call great," said Voltaire, "are those who have distinguished themselves as useful or constructive; the others, who ravage and conquer provinces, are only so-called heroes."

This treatment of history constantly challenges comparison with our present world crisis. We can indeed learn nothing from the old revolutions, whose development was different; but the way the dictators of former times built up their parties is enlightening.

Above all, the problem of democracy confronts us everywhere. In every age a corrupt democracy has been followed by dictatorship, which in turn has perished of its own natural consequences. In all democracies there have been canny secret dictators, and often uncanny open ones too; some of the greatest ancient statesmen were called tyrants. The value of democracy has lain not so much in universal suffrage; it lies—today as in the time of Pericles—in the opportunity it affords to every talent and in supervision and control of those who hold power. Genius, which alone matters, is brought forth by democracy today as it was in the republics of Athens and Rome. But democracy weakens it too, and often winds up by defeating it entirely.

Thanks to the abundance of authenticated events during twenty-five centuries, I have passed over all unattested prehistory and all questions of race. The reader will not find here the problems of early earth and oceanic movements or any treatment of the aboriginal Mediterranean races—fashions in which change as they do in Mediterranean beach wear. What races once dwelt on the Mediterranean, and which peoples belonged to them, is at present a party game of professors in the service of dictators. For instance: "On the Ibero-Pelasgians, Satem-peoples of semi-Indo-Germanic character, and Hamito-Iberians"—nothing but funny names from the laboratory of our modern race investigators. Instead I have tried to show that the races were nowhere more mixed than on the Mediterranean—hence their genius.

My vision of the Mediterranean derives not at all from races, but from the landscape, from light, air, and water. For that reason I began the book on the Mediterranean itself, close to the Hyères Islands, before the war.* Later, under the protection of an unknown god, I came in my exile to a land like paradise. Here a garden was opened to me, a garden that was laid out half a century ago in the style of the Villa d'Este near Rome by a great lover of the Mediterranean and had slowly flowered into the loveliest garden in America. Here, with the Pacific spread before me I went on and finished my book, six thousand miles away from the Mediteranean.

This book is a sort of tapestry in which the reader will see beasts and men, trees and mountains, migrations of peoples and of fish, priests and warriors, prophets and poets, and sailors constantly at work among them. Sitting before it he can choose what he pleases. It has always been my effort to transmute gray or even golden ideas into colorful pictures, and the present book is made up almost wholly of these pictures.

With such promises and warnings of the weather awaiting him at sea, I invite the reader to come aboard my vessel, which will grow from a rowboat into a galley, then into a sailing vessel, and finally into a turbine steamer. Amid this wealth of history he will certainly not find tedious his journey hither and thither from Genoa to Jaffa, from the Black Sea to Gibraltar, through the ages from Odysseus to Mussolini, cruising the loveliest of all seas.

EMIL LUDWIG.

Santa Barbara, California.

---

* Owing to circumstances attendant on the war, three of the author's books have appeared in rapid succession. *Bolívar* and *The Germans* were finished as early as 1938 and 1940.

CONTENTS

THE MEDITERRANEAN

AT THE LIGHTHOUSE

THE OLIVE TREE *was losing its shadow, and the man on the bench below, who had been shading his eyes under the peak of his cap, now looked straight into the pink glitter across the surface of the western sea. Only the topmost branches of the tree, a fresh, greenish gray, still glinted in the declining sun. The man's face was already marked with heavy lines. He was in his middle years, a robust seaman who had looked often into the sinking sun, and always over the sea.*

The tree was old; it had probably survived some three centuries. In this half wilderness it had once sprouted out of a seed brought from shore by the west wind; high above the precipitous abyss it had struck root in cracks between the limestone ribs, splitting them slightly in the course of time, to find nourishment below and room above. Now the trunk, cracked a hundred ways, its grayish wood stained green with moss, leaned steeply over the high cliff. But with the steadfastness of a great character the unwavering trunk in its deep cleft stood firm against storms and thunderbolts, while its newest branches and twigs, reaching far out, bent over the rock.

The bench, too, set perhaps by his grandfather, against one side of the mighty tree, facing inland, seemed just as secure and perma-

3

nent as the aged tree. The man who had been sitting looking across the sea, his shoulders turned half about, his elbows on the back of the bench, seemed as solid as tree and bench. Standing up, with the slow, angular movement of a seaman, he walked past his little white house toward the high tower. Yonder, at the end of an irregular avenue of storm-twisted stone pines, the lighthouse loomed against the surface of the sea, sunlit still. It was white like the house, but solid and massive, and at the same time odd with its long lines and its staircase windows, built expressly for what it carried in place of a spire—a round glass structure of fantastic shape, crowning the tall hexagonal tower, and capped in turn by an umbrellalike copper roof that had probably gleamed red long ago, in the days when tower and stone pines were young.

The keeper slowly mounted the lighthouse stairs. First he looked at the light, the soul of it all. The keeper could have recognized the sound of his feet in a deep sleep, for it was more than twenty years ago that he took this job after the seafaring adventures of the Great War.

Upstairs an iron spiral staircase with sixteen treads led to the glass chamber. It was still bathed in the burning red and yellow radiance of the evening sky, a thousand times refracted by the lenses of the light, narrowing at top and bottom like a gigantic pear of many-faceted glass. The keeper had only to stoop slightly to get his head and arms into the inner glass chamber, in the center of which a single large electric light, pointing upward, was mounted on glass rings—pale, cold, waiting for duty. By itself the light was no stronger than a highway lamp, but the lenses magnified its brilliance to 150,000 candle power. Instead of sending its rays a quarter mile, the light beamed forth more than ten miles.

But apparently the day was refusing to surrender its rights, was trying to multiply its luminosity a hundredfold. The thousand facets of the gigantic lens flashed glorious rainbow colors on the keeper's face. And as he lifted his hand to test a ring below the lamp, it became a spectral hand in magic hues. Carefully withdrawing his head from the crystal interior, he cast a precautionary glance at the brilliance and spotlessness of the curved glasses, blew away a thread, and took a final turn around the catwalk between the lamp and the outside panes.

The man he was relieving had compared his entries with the clock and with light, foghorn, and radio indicators. The log sheets were in their accustomed place, and the sequence of slow movements and sparse words was a habit of months and years.

We are at the lighthouse on one of the Hyères Islands, which stand guard over the French coast east of Toulon. A wild, romantic countryside.

The day man picks up the book he has been reading. The title catches the eye of his companion, who reaches for it and looks up inquiringly; the other merely nods and leaves the book for the night watchman. Departing steps echo in the stone entrance and crunch faintly along the avenue of pines. Then there is silence.

The night man looks at the clock, looks and feels for the four or five sheets lying on the table, scrutinizes lever, indicator, clocks, telephone, radio. Then he makes a notation to record his going on duty at 19:23. Weather clear, wind light. The summer night falls soundless over the sea.

He turns on the electric stove, for the night will be cool, he knows; taking off his coat, he picks up a knitted jacket from the open drawer. Then he takes off his heavy shoes and reaches for his lined slippers. One more look at the instruments, and he goes to the big desk and throws a little switch. The next instant a strong shaft of light, circling slowly, travels overhead across a landscape still in almost broad daylight. The pressure of a finger has turned on the lamp above. The piercing beams revolve red, white, and blue at four-second intervals. This is the beacon of the island, which all ships at sea know or can find in their lists when they are taking their bearings.

The keeper has made himself comfortable; his little reading lamp lights up the table, from which he can hear, see, and supervise everything. In this gentle night there seems nothing special to do. What shall it be? Reading is the way lighthouse keepers of all seas and shores spend their nights. But they seldom read novels or history. They are all from the sea, have all been seamen, and never *weary of reading and dreaming about the ocean, even when they have exchanged it for shore. Our Frenchman has sailed all the oceans, but he was born here on the south coast; his fathers were Provençals.*

Today he reaches for the volume his companion has left for him. He turns it about deliberately, seeming to measure the length and even the weight, and skims over the pictures. Then he opens to the title page, leans back, and begins to read the story of his own sea: the Mediterranean.

BOOK ONE

THE DISCOVERY OF THE OCEAN

"We Athenians enjoy a form of government different from that of our neighbors; and because we rule the State not for the few but for the many, we call it Democracy. The citizens, on an equal footing in private life, are selected for the higher positions in the State according to merits, not party, and still less according to property."

PERICLES

I

BY THE SEASHORE a powerful, bearded man sits on a stone, his elbow on his knee, his chin leaning upon a massive fist. He stares fixedly into the west. A few great tears trickle from his eyes to drop upon his beard; upon his lips both the tears and the spray from the leaping breakers have a bitter, salty taste, and bitter and salty is his heart.

What ails this grieving man by the seashore? Where are we?

On the strand of an island—probably Malta, in legend called Ogygia. This bearded man is Odysseus. All his life has been bound to the Mediterranean; on an island he was born, to islands he has sailed in spruce-wood ships. An ocean flowing from island to island bore him with the other heroes to Troy, and even there they stayed close to their ships. A goddess nymph to whose realm his ship was carried away has now long detained him; she thirsts insatiably for the strength of this mortal man. Calypso offers him the life of a god, and yet Homer has him sit weeping on the beach—him, the craftiest and boldest, the great adventurer. For what he dreams of is another isle, an isle yet smaller than this, and like it in trees and beasts— Ithaca, where he was born, where he has house, wife, and son. Odysseus is weeping for home.

His great protectress, Athena, has made up her mind to save him, and now Calypso, who groaned aloud when she heard this divine decree and bewailed to Hermes the envy and cruelty of the gods, comes forth from her grotto. She goes down to the shore, where Odysseus is moping away the days, and offers to help him build a ship to take him home. She brings him an ax and leads him to cloud-capped pines on another shore; she shows him trees withered with age, already dry, and thus more readily fit for planks. He follows her full of hope. The nymph leads him to another shore. Odysseus fells twenty trunks, measures the planks, makes timbers with an iron tool fetched by the nymph, and fastens them together with nails and clamps into the form of a great raft.

9

He places uprights all around, attaches braces, puts on a deck of boards, shapes the mast, puts on the crossyards, and finally the rudder. Then he covers it all with willow wattles and puts stones in the bottom for ballast. Now Calypso, still wavering between rage and grief, brings woven stuffs for him to cut sails of; she watches while he fixes ropes and lines to the mast to turn the sail, and finally builds a slip to launch the raft.

All this Odysseus, who could not have had much help, finished in four days. On the fifth morning the nymph came to the new ship carrying a skin of wine and one of water and viands in a woven basket. Then she raised a gentle breeze ahead of him. Thus Homer pictured the scene in the Fifth Book of the *Odyssey*.

For eighteen days and nights Odysseus' ship sailed the stormy seas: it rose on high, and it plunged into the depths, hurling the man into the waves. Finally tossed by the storm upon the reefs, and nearly torn to pieces, he managed to swim to the mouth of a river; there, murmuring prayers, he collapsed half dead among trees and bushes.

The new island where Odysseus landed, probably Cephalonia, was the land of the Phaeacians; and once again it was a woman who saved the Divine Sufferer, and would have held him fast. She was Nausicaa, who never wearied of listening to him as he told tales of Troy and of his wanderings, which carried him from isle to isle, far to westward, round about Sicily.

At last, laden with gifts, he was brought by the Phaeacians to a ship, this time with rowers, which was to take him home. On this last journey Odysseus lay stretched out in the ship, on cushions and rugs, and after all his years of struggle and suffering he fell into a sleep "sweet and past awakening, almost like unto death." It was a voyage of but a day and a night. Then the rowers put in to the harbor of Ithaca; but still Odysseus slept. They picked him up, sleeping, and laid him, together with rugs and cushions, on the shore beneath an olive tree, at the mouth of a grotto.

Such were the first two sea voyages that legend has lifted from the clouds and billows of the Mediterranean into the emotional consciousness of posterity. They show storm and calm, shore and reef, raft and ship; they show grottoes and gardens, the struggles of peoples, merchandise, hospitality, and the favor of women; but above all they show the blessings and the terrors of destiny, which rises, under many gods' names, above the blue ocean, and manifests itself in adventures forever new.

For the Mediterranean is the loveliest of all seas, favored by situation, shape, and climate above all others, and likewise before all others discovered and sailed. This is the Helen among oceans; like her it was desired by all that saw it, and captured by the boldest. But it was fought over not for ten but for two thousand years. Then it was half forsaken, obscured by the fame of new and distant oceans; rediscovered, as it were, after three hundred years; and today, before our eyes, it is fought over anew.

Why?

Is it not smaller than the great oceans beyond? Have not these been conquered by great vessels? Can they not be spanned in a few days on the new wings, straight through space? Why then is the Mediterranean fought for again?

Because it is the home of mankind. Because all men feel that beauty, knowledge, and accomplishment once had their source here. Men return to the Mediterranean as they would to their mothers.

II

MEN SELDOM REALIZE that they are all islanders. Born on islands that they choose to call continents, they inhabit but a quarter of their planet, for almost three-fourths of its surface is an element impossible of habitation and impossible to tame wholly, even in fleeting passage. For that reason the conquest of the sea was mankind's greatest achievement. It is unequaled even by the conquest of the air, for amid the waves there are islands to be explored and conquered, while amid the clouds there is nothing.

He who was born by the sea, he who in childhood fell asleep to the beat of the surf and awoke each morning to the same note, remains somehow mysteriously favored above other men, though he himself remain a land dweller and seldom put foot on a ship. These are the few million islanders who recognize one another as brothers from one coast to another; they are set apart from the two billions who believe that firm, fertile soil, forest and meadow, mountain and stream, cities and houses, are alone the true home of man.

Anyone who lives by the seashore, whose gaze is constantly turned upon the vast, unwieldy distance, will apprehend more deeply the great experiences—God, love, music—because he is not in the habit of diverting his eyes toward trifles. From the loud and colorful abundance of the earth, which he has long loved, he will turn back some day to the mute expanse, from the individually conceivable to the inconceivably universal. This is why all philosophers have been islanders, even though they lived inland, and the apostles of all religions have sought the sea. The ancients said of the Eleatics that the same spirit which led them upon the Western Ocean had guided them into the waters of pure thinking. Fear and attraction alternate, but both show that the larger element, the shapelessly vast surface with its invisible animals, plants, and mountains beneath, is stronger than the myriad life of the islands, which developed so proudly and brilliantly from the coast line inward, begetting and rearing the riders of the sea.

Again, the sea is not unlike death, which receives all living beings and makes them equal, and the great streams that carry men's loads might serve them as a parable when at last they see the waters pour out and mingle with the greater universe, the sea. The vast cemetery that forms unexplored new layers at the bottom of the ocean, immortalizing the vital energy of dead creatures and too daring islanders, has remained unsung and unmarked. The people who scatter flowers on the waves at the scene of a marine disaster have not grasped the true pathos of the watery element. Only the diver (who, like the man at the microscope, discovers the invisible) could speak: but by habit he is silent.

And yet it was not the wise man nor the desperate man who conquered the sea from the islands; these have only watched it, with a look of renunciation. The first to adventure upon the sea, those who yield to its allure even today, are men full of daring and curiosity, boldness and joy in life, who stand on the coast, shading their eyes with their hands, searching for the nearest island, and then measuring the ship in the harbor to see if she will withstand storm and wave. At first a man wanted to cross from the shore of some little island to the next island, hoping there perhaps to catch other fish and see other nets and boats, of which tales had reached him. One islander sought another—that was all.

And then he saw to his astonishment that after a hundred strokes of the oars, perhaps with a favoring wind astern, he was already on the high sea. He began to realize how every narrow bit of coast borders on the great ocean, just as even the humblest character fringes the universal human destiny. A first, tiny curiosity, not even greed, carried the voyager out on the open sea. With the discovery of new islands and shores he recognized new possibilities, built bigger ships, then fitted them with arms, since strange islanders had tried to keep the unknown sailor from landing. This monotonous element that offered neither frontiers nor roads, that belonged to no one and therefore to everyone, attracted the bold and the reflective alike, and soon mingled their traits.

For while courage and ambition broke away from the solid earth, from safe homes and fields, to steer in hazardous vessels to unknown shores, at the same time the urge to power grew in the very people ashore who had been unable to develop in face of their neighbors. Across the sea, which owns no ruler, you could trade with strange islands; from the sea assault and plunder are to be feared, but there is gain too. Here is an element that subjugates no one; it suffers everything, only occasionally rising in storm against the foolhardy men who seek to master it. But afar, on alien shores, anything can be seized—the longer the coast, the easier. The far-seeing mariners of a little people on an insignificant island conquer broad countries whose own powerful neighbors could not down them. The slightest access, narrow and forbidding—Athens, Venice, or Lübeck—sufficed for the founding of a sea power, even when no deep hinterland protected the conquering seafarer.

In this sense the sea has always been free, for no one can draw boundaries or pretend to monopolies on the waters. When Carthage forbade the Latins to sail west of the Lacinian foothills, she was cheated, and finally beaten. In vain Genoa tried by decree to keep the Provençals away from Sicily. The Venetians wanted the Adriatic, the Turks the Black Sea, the United States the Bering Sea, for themselves, for shipping or fishing—in vain. The ocean cannot be bought; neither by labor nor by war can it be divided up and broken into zones, as nations have succeeded in doing ashore.

No world power has ever endured on land; but at sea Rome founded a long dominion after the fall of Carthage, England after that of Napoleon. The victory of a fleet has decided the fate of world powers, sometimes in a single day—far more swiftly than any battle on land, for a land victory, after all, must be repeated on other fronts. Conversely, the process of developing a land power into a sea power succeeded in Rome; in France it did not. England during the War of the Spanish Succession was divided between the Tories' desire to rest at ease on their estates and the bourgeois shippers' and merchants' push toward the sea. It was not until later that the whole nation strove for sea power.

There is so much to be gained at sea—so much that land with its variety, its thousand barriers of river and mountain, canal, fort, and fortification, cannot offer! Did not little Athens defeat the mighty Persians? Did not England, even before her expansion, did not little Holland vanquish the mighty trinity of Spain, Portugal, and France? Did not luxurious Venice humble the terrible Turk? And yet the great decisions at sea have almost always taken place in a small space.

Most astonishing of all, each sea power begets a new one, and stirs, if not curiosity and thirst for glory, at least the remote defiance of peoples across the sea, eager to rival it. Rome, outmatched by Sicily, was forced to become a sea power. The Persians, likewise, went to sea only that they might vanquish the Ionian sea state. So mighty a port as Syracuse only learned real seafaring from the Corinthians, but, like a prosperous France of later times, the Sicilians had too much fertile land ever to become a great sea power.

Yet amid all the struggles and victories, even of nations whose sole wish is conquest, the mute, infertile element offers a means of connecting remote peoples, and it spreads civilizations, which advance far more slowly on land. Just as currents and temperatures blend in its depths, so ideas and goods are brought to the ends of the world in the holds of ships, in the behavior of seamen, in the hands and heads of those who plow the ocean. Much as he wants to plunder and rule, still the seaman loves to trade and bargain, to talk and throw dice with strangers, and above all to know and to carry away (not always by force) the women of alien races, with their strange eyes and hair, their astonishing clothes and jewels.

Not mercenaries but free men sailed the seas: and even the brutal Crusades brought amazing harmonies of distant peoples. Seafaring became an irresistible torrent of worldly understanding. There have been engendered on the sea associations and friendships among men such as the narrowness, defiance, and mistrust of continents have never achieved. The wind that blew the seeds of Egyptian plants to Italy has filled a thousand sails beneath which men of all ages have borne thoughts and products to distant shores.

III

MANKIND TRAVELS WESTWARD. The while we seek the light and its message of morning in faith and understanding, our travels take us ever farther from it. The swiftness with which we can span the Pacific today, and arrive again in the East, is not symbolic: civilization does not fly, and if it does, it falls. The advance of mankind, on the contrary, has progressed from the smallest sea to a larger one: from the eastern Mediterranean to the western, then to the Atlantic, then to the Pacific. The Greeks regarded only the Aegean and what lay east of it as their sea. An old saying warns the mariner, "When you round the Cape of Sparta, forget home!" Odysseus scarcely knew the north Adriatic, and what lay west of Sicily, full of strange winds and currents, was at first the hostile universe. Only a scattered few, Carthaginians and Greeks, ventured out to find the shores of the Atlantic.

But what these shores meant—that there lay yonder an ocean

infinitely greater than the Mediterranean—remained unknown to everyone, even to the Normans, who sailed parts of it five hundred years before Columbus. The Mediterranean surrendered to the assaults of the early mariners far more easily, because it offers so many gateways deep into terra firma. No sea abounds more in islands, neither is there any richer in gulfs and bays. The narrow Gulf of Patras opens up all of central Greece, the Bosporus all eastern Europe.

What we call the Mediterranean, the Middle Sea, repeats itself in curiously similar situations in two other middle seas. As the Mediterranean unites Europe and Africa, the South China Sea joins Asia and Australia; the two are similar in their wealth of islands and their involute coast lines. The Caribbean Sea cuts America through in the center, down to one small strip.

But in its main feature our Mediterranean, let us say our hero, is quite unlike the other two: it is a lake, held together by three sets of straits as if it were a pond.

The basic lake-like character of the Mediterranean has so strongly influenced its history, and thus the civilization of mankind, as well as the character of the coast peoples, that we may wonder how its strange shape came to be. Here begins an old game of the geologists, who have hurled whole volumes of imprecations and threats at one another's heads—arguments as fruitless as historical novels, because there is no certain ground to stand on. This prehistory is as hypothetical as that of the peoples. The things that can be tangibly read from the documents of 2,500 years, on the other hand, concerning what has happened on and close by the Mediterranean, are so dazzling with rich scenes of human life that we are not tempted to dwell in the mists of prehistory. Any Greek temple means more to us than the famous rocks of Dordogne, whose antiquity is variously argued at from fifteen to twenty thousand years. Omitting all technical terms, we merely recapitulate here the best explanation of the Mediterranean that we can offer to the intelligent layman.

In the ice age it is supposed that the area of the Mediterranean was occupied by a lowland containing two great lakes, one in the west and one in the east, deep down like the Dead Sea, but much bigger. When the glaciers melted, the lakes spread over the land into one large inland sea. Whether it was the land that rose or the sea that fell in later millenniums, at any rate the dams which formed the last thin barriers against other seas, at the Dardanelles and Gibraltar, gave way. This monstrous inundation, recurring in all mythologies as the Flood, left certain pieces of mountainous terrain standing as islands, so that the Aegean archipelago of today represents the peaks of a mountain range ending in Crete.

But before or after this catastrophe other breaches must have occurred—crumplings of the earth's crust, volcanic disturbances, and lowerings of the new inland sea. In the north one great arm of the Mediterranean seems to have gone along the outer edges of the Alps and Carpathians, reaching Vienna, Hungary, and even the Caucasus. The so-called Syrian Fault, continuing halfway through east Africa, bears witness to later eruptions, as do a Greek Fault and a number of precipitous abysses, among them one of the deepest underwater abysses on our planet, in the Ionian Sea.

The surest proof of an ancient connection between Africa and the land and islands of the present-day Mediterranean is offered by animal bones, which no theory can invent or suppress. On the islands of the Aegean, formerly joined to the mainland, have been found bones proving that bears and wolves went south across the mountains while jackals and leopards turned north. There are lions' bones near Florence, elephants on Malta, hippopotamuses on Crete; and we who connect the names of Crete and Malta with the red thread of Ariadne are surprised and amused to see these sons of the Sudan slinking across the square in front of the Palazzo Vecchio, the daughters of the Nile bathing at the great theater at Cnossus, and an elephant patiently doing the work of a crane over in the harbor at Malta.

And is it not a comforting feeling to live as part of an endless chain? When we find shells on the slopes of Etna at an altitude of 2,300 feet, proving the former presence of the sea, when we see ancient Greek buildings standing in the water today, we are inclined to agree with the mayor of a coast city in Thessaly, who is reported recently to have forbidden the building of the town hall on the shore, arguing that in a thousand years it would all be ocean.

Everywhere, along the coast and among the islands, traces of ruptures point to the universal catastrophe that created the coast line and islands of the Mediterranean. These convulsions have never actually ceased, and they still produce new variations. Soundings along the Gulf of Gabès (Syrtis Minor) have indicated the outlines of the mainland that plunged into the sea there, probably within historic times. The island of Pantelleria rose from 3,250 feet beneath the sea to a height of 2,600 feet above it, perhaps in a single hour. This was the work of a volcano that suddenly awoke in 1891 after thousands of years beneath the sea and heaved up the north coast of the island. The Nile once poured into the ocean farther east, draining Palestine; and south of Carmel there are crocodiles, now a rarity on the lower Nile. Only yesterday the cables west of Calabria were parted by invisible forces.

The speech of the volcanoes on shore was even more ominous. By comparison with recent eruptions we can guess what they must once have destroyed. But the eruptions had their advantages, too, for the hot springs and the fertile soil on which olives and grapes flourish all around the Mediterranean today come from the volcanic soil, and fruits have arisen here from the ashes as new ideas arise from revolutions. When the ancient chronicles begin, we can read out the dates. At the same spot, in the channel of Euboea, we find the first seaquake in 425 B.C., the latest in A.D. 1894. How strongly this recent repetition brings to mind the recurrence of uprisings that we are now witnessing in that same country! When volcanoes create whole islands, lifting them from the sea, as an eruption in 1831 did south of Sicily, and sinking them again at once, our minds are turned from the mortality of man to the elements, and thus somehow reassured.

The elements have remained the same through scores of centuries. Probably the gods laugh as they read in the writings of the academies certain explanations from the old days; perhaps they decide to revive the theories tomorrow. Ancient sources tell us of many inundations—how the city of Helike near Corinth was plunged beneath the sea with all its inhabitants, as was the eastern coast of Lemnos—and how Stromboli, an eternally ruminant volcano, was never at rest. With its unwavering pine-shaped cloud of smoke and its almost daily grumblings, it has been growing since ancient times. It is the dean of volcanoes, so to speak, and its continual futile growling makes it seem like an old gentleman who wants to deliver a speech and cannot find the words. Andalusia and Calabria, too, and the southern slope of Parnassus, have suffered severe shocks, but the beauty of Athens remained almost immune. There the hand of man has destroyed with cannon what even the elements had spared.

All this roaring and quaking through thousands of years has produced in the men of the Mediterranean a fatalism that turns to gods and destinies. Poseidon was most worshiped in the ravaged countrysides, and once when the Spartans invaded Argolis, and an earthquake visited enemy territory, they struck up a mighty chorus of praise to Poseidon. The prehistoric separation of Sicily into an island, the cleaving of the straits, the rending of the ground at the foot of Olympus—all this lent equanimity of spirit to the inhabitants, made them ready to endure the changes of fortune, more skeptical, wiser, more philosophical. These people had in their bones a feeling for the shifts of peak and abyss that have taken place in the natural history of their sea and its shores.

If the floor of the Ionian Sea reaches at 15,200 feet one of the greatest ocean depths, and Atlas, yonder on the African coast, towers to an equal height, the great-grandsons feel these contrasts, even if they know no figures. For the figures are in their blood. The articulation of the Aegean, the cleavage of the bays, the abundance of the islands, are unique and have played their part in shaping men's souls.

If, then, we regard the landlocked sea of the Mediterranean as an old, tried and true character, which finds itself forever confined to its own bounds and has but one narrow gate to freedom, our curiosity leads us to ask how this gate works and how it makes use of the great ocean beyond.

Here is the fateful point in the Mediterranean.

The sea gate is set up here, at Gibraltar, where a bridge of land once lured African elephants to Spain. When we see it narrowing down to a width of less than nine miles, we might almost think it was a canal dug by the hand of man, as at Suez, only much wider. And indeed there was an ancient de Lesseps. His name was Hercules, and he is supposed to have broken through the land and set up two pillars in memory of his deed. That breaches have occurred here as they did at the Bosporus is shown by the name of Deucalion and a few passages in the Bible; Aristotle, Seneca, and Buffon also agree. Edrisi, the great Arab, who was born close to Gibraltar, found a truly Voltairian solution of the question. According to him, Alexander, hearing of the endless struggles between Spaniards and Africans, finally had these hostile tribes separated by making slaves cut through the land according to careful measurements, until the great ocean poured into the lesser one.

The decisive fact at Gibraltar, however, is not the narrowness but the shallowness. A thousand feet is much too little depth to allow a proper exchange between the waters of the two oceans. It is like the relation of two brothers, one of them rich and powerful but niggardly, the other delicate and highly gifted. The powerful brother ought to support the delicate one but always gives him too little. So the mighty Atlantic holds back; the access to its strangely whimsical brother, the half lake beyond, is too small. The Arabs called it Bab-el-Zaka, Gate of the Narrow Entrance; the English even termed it The Gut. All signs distinguish the two oceans at Cape Spartel—salt content, specific gravity, temperature. Flanked on both sides by mountains rising to 6,500 feet, yet very narrow, Gibraltar was bound to be one of the worst draught holes on earth. At the same time the depth of the Atlantic and the shallowness of the underwater threshold had an important effect on temperature and fauna. As the temperature of all the great oceans is lower in the depths, the Atlantic along the Spanish coast has a temperature of but 37 degrees in the lower depths, whereas the Mediterranean runs between 53 and 55. Thus the mild climate of Provence and Greece, and all the beautiful things it produces, are possible only because Gibraltar is so shallow.

Just as a really dominant personality is born to shape itself from within the influence of the world, this fascinating ocean is destined to solitude by a second circumstance: it has but few feeders. For the moment we disregard the Black Sea, whose many large feeders do not affect the economy of the Mediterranean. To the Mediterranean only one stream of first rank, the Nile, brings its waters; this particular river has but little flow left at its mouth. Only fourteen hundredths of one per cent of the river water in Europe flows into the Mediterranean, and of the fifty rivers forty are so small as to be exceedingly obscure. And what the three big ones, the Rhone, the Po, and the Nile, contribute amounts to but a third of what the heavy evaporation takes away. The evaporation is also far heavier than the rainfall, and so the level of the Mediterranean always remains lower than that of the Atlantic.

The Atlantic is forced to discharge tremendous streams of water into this lower basin, and to do it swiftly, but this is not enough to equalize the water level or the salt content.

Thus the water of the Mediterranean becomes richer in salt, and consequently heavier, than that of the Atlantic in the same latitude. Both qualities increase with the distance from Gibraltar, that is, eastward, into the Mediterranean. As the water is heavier, pressure even at slight depths is greater, which produces an undercurrent of water that flows off at Gibraltar. Nevertheless there is always more flowing in than out.

The second strait, the Dardanelles, is also called the Hellespont. With this are connected the loveliest legends that the Greeks told, they who worshiped love and not suffering, they whose imaginations lived in many gods and were unchained by a single or invisible God.

There was Dardanus, a son of love, whom Zeus begot with the Pleiad Electra. There was Hero, a priestess, who nightly received Leander. There were Phrixos and Helle, the demigod brother and sister who fled for their lives on the back of a golden-fleeced flying ram—but alas! Helle fell off and was drowned in the strait. There was the perilous voyage of the Argonauts to steal the golden fleece which Phrixos had dedicated in a temple at Colchis. What a won-

derful world it was when pantheism invented symbols for all the elements and the gods lived visibly and actively with men! They were patterned after great mortals in those days; hero, demigod, and god represented, in the eyes of the Greeks, different stages of the same striving.

The Dardanelles decide the hydrographic fate of the Mediterranean to northeastward; here it flows and breathes according to different laws. The two bottlenecks that terminate the sea correspond in a marvelous balance: here at Byzantium (later Constantinople, now Istanbul) civilization issued from the old Asiatic world, while yonder at Gibraltar it went out to the new.

As the Black Sea, which flows in at the Bosporus, is landlocked, it cannot intervene with such definite effect as the Atlantic at Gibraltar. It is rather like a third, quiet brother, who lives in retirement after his own fashion, but can hold his own where he touches the middle one, and even suddenly make demands. Formed from a fresh-water lake, it sends into the Mediterranean an upper current lacking in salt, receiving salty Mediterranean water through the undercurrent in exchange.

This adjustment between two very different characters that have the look of friendly neighbors is what determines the inner life of both. The speeds of the water, you might even say the temperaments, are so different, and the influx from the Mediterranean northward so slow, that if the Black Sea were an empty basin, it

would take 3,000 years to fill. The lack of oxygen in the Black Sea, with its shortage of salt, allows but scant marine life; even in Homer's day this darkened the reputation of the Euxine. In addition the narrowness and shallowness of the strait increases the speed of the upper current flowing into the Mediterranean. In the Bosporus, often less than a hundred feet deep, rapids become so fierce that the fishermen drag their boats upstream on cables from shore, lest the current should smash them.

The nervous character of the Mediterranean, which makes it so interesting, is especially pronounced at the straits. As the sea is almost entirely landlocked, the natural tidal wave of the great oceans is checked here, without wholly disappearing. The tide is visible at only a few points. This marvelous breathing of the oceans, connecting them with the influence of the moon, puts the watery element above the inertness of dry ground. But in the Mediterranean the phenomenon is subdued in a way that suggests chamber music as opposed to the vast symphony of the great oceans. Only the expert can detect ebb and flow along all coasts; at the straits the tide is visible to anyone. Mariners recognize it anywhere, and at Leghorn they even say "Aqua piena di luna." At the end of the longer gulfs the tide influences navigation, as we can see with our own eyes in Venice, in the Gulf of Corinth, and in the Syrtes. In some intricate bays there is even high tide on one side, while the ebb is still sinking on the other; this produces dangerous differences of level that make tide races. All this the ancient authors had already observed.

If the Greeks are often quoted in the following pages, it is because their intuition and keen observation without the help of instruments productively combined seeing with thinking and thus made them the philosophic nation par excellence. Homer called the ocean "gently flowing," and saw that certain reefs now rose above the sea, now were drowned in it. Plato has the sea sometimes pouring more swiftly from the caverns of earth, and then again retiring into them, and Herodotus even gives a name to the Wise Man of Samos who was cast into the ocean by the gods, and there became the first witness of the tides. Later Caesar describes the moon as the cause of the spring tides, and Pliny in his interpretation forecasts half of Kepler and Newton.

Modern physics, offering other explanations for the same phenomena, points to the narrowness of the passage at Gibraltar and to its westerly situation, which makes the sea run counter to the Atlantic flood tide. Naval officers have often been infuriated by the independent behavior of this element. An English admiral commanding a gunboat in 1810 cursed and swore because flood tide arrived two hours earlier than it should have according to the almanac.

Among the straits that necessarily produce not merely tides but currents of all sorts, the Strait of Messina nearly cost even Odysseus his life, and down to our own day many ships have been wrecked there, between Scylla and Charybdis. Even the ancients, giving credit to the strength of Orion for this breach between Italy and Sicily, recognized that this strait was of late origin, just like Gibraltar and the Dardanelles. What Diodorus ascribed to Orion, the son of Poseidon, the geologists call an early eruption of Etna, which might have opened up the straits there. If an old fable of the gods is thus easily explained by the professors, we may hope that some day our cynical actuality, with all its arithmeticians' rows of figures, may be transformed into fables again, so that our engineers will be fabulously introduced to their great-grandchildren as demigods.

The whirlpool of Charybdis off the peninsula of Messina, a mere hundred feet wide and a thousand feet from the shore, is capable during an ebb tide of turning ships end for end. When the earth is nearest the sun, and the moon is close to it, on March 21, the tide there rises twenty inches. All the surprises offered by this whirlpool were known to the ancient captains, and used in sea fights. It is untrue that Nelson was the first to venture into the Strait of Messina.

In the straits between the island of Euboea and the Greek mainland, too, where the sea is no more than 115 feet wide, ships can steal through only in the brief interval during the change of currents. Since great tempests do not blow here as they do in the open ocean, there are more whirlpools, currents, and sudden eddies. In the capricious Mediterranean the height of the waves is never more than fifteen feet, but the surf is heavier than that of the Atlantic, whose waves are sometimes fifty feet high. Its motion is made up of short, abrupt, choppy waves rather than long, steady swells. When in addition a vessel passing amid the islands encounters a roaring wind coming down from the mountainous coasts and a wicked whistling from the rocky narrows, the mariner grows seasick sooner than on the great oceans. At the mouths of certain rivers, particularly on the south coast of Sicily, the sirocco may lash the sea so high that fish are hurled ashore, and men with them.

IV

NOTHING, PERHAPS, has spread the fame of the Mediterranean throughout the earth so much as its color. A deep blue, it is pleasing to eyes unaccustomed to oceans of such color—and indeed blue is rarer throughout nature than green. No doubt a blue sky casts blue reflections on bays and lakes the world over, and gray winter days go racing even across the Mediterranean. The weather, painting light and shade across the landscape of earth, setting the general mood that decides and keeps forever changing the color of nature, as it does of mortal character, also fixes the destinies of seas and mountains, transforming them overnight. One cloud, a breeze, the mere shadow of a shadow may blot out the splendor of a heavenly afternoon, like Death brushing a happy mortal pair.

But still there is a basic hue of soul that bestows light or darkness upon the elements in human bosom and nature alike. It keeps
gleaming through everywhere, and though it be at times wholly
enshrouded, the observer knows it will return.

It is this basic hue that ennobles the Mediterranean. When did
the infinite, unislanded expanses of Atlantic and Pacific ever stir
a poet to sing idyllic lays? When, if we except Gauguin, have the
vast oceans out beyond ever tempted a painter to use his most delicate tones? Only the Mediterranean has this suggestive power:
when we describe the hue of its soul, we say it is a blue, a smiling
ocean.

When storms sweep over it, when the sea quakes, when Scylla
boils and the winds from Crete come howling around Cape
Matapan, we are reminded that a thunderstorm interrupted even
Beethoven's *Pastoral Symphony*. Despite all the warlike voyages
and naval battles, despite all the drowned vessels and men, the
Mediterranean heavens always brighten again, returning to their
natural state. Yes, it is a pastoral sea—if only because its thousand
coasts teem with vistas and hidden nooks, with an unending
series of azure bays, framed in crags, thorny tufts of stone pine, and
the gray, silken leaves of the olive.

And yet even the blue color has been disputed since the earliest
days. The sea darkens like a man's heart when it is stirred, and thus
we find Homer calling the tempestuous ocean now purple, now
wine-dark, fading, violet. Some of the Greeks called it the White
Sea, contrasting it with the Black Sea; many modern scholars say
it is colorless, not realizing that to appear blue it must be seen
from afar and in the large. The sailor catches signs of storm in the
darkening of the water. To him a greenish tinge means an anchor-
age, a blue, great depth. But all of them, ancient and modern, singers
and voyagers, praise the crystal clearness of the Mediterranean. Indeed the physicist explains the blue itself by the clearness and the
depth, for blue light rays are the most highly refractable in such
an element. The famous Blue Grotto of Capri is but one of the
marvels of light and liquid motion.

From the limpid, uniform blue the eye returns to the frame

whose thousand transformations enclose the ageless and unchanging portrait. One glance at the map makes clear that all the islands and all the coasts are mountainous, except for the southern fringe of lowland that reaches from Tunis to Jerusalem. There monotonous deserts and steppes seem to project the ocean in an endless yellow line. All the other shores rise up before the passing vessel, giving promise of mountains and valleys, bays and rivers, forests and flocks, fruit and wine, and a year without winter.

To all this the romantic aura of the old names gives life. If somewhere in the world there were an island that looked exactly like Delos, we would pass it carelessly by because it bore some indifferent name and jutted up somewhere or other in, for example, the unimaginative desert of the Pacific. If a simple country house can speak to us because Washington lived there, how deeply must we be moved as we sail an ocean whose history belongs to all nations, and whose basin collects the currents of all the civilizations that have shaped our inner life! It is history that gives life to geography. And here history is stronger than elsewhere, for everything that raises us above the savages sprang from the Mediterranean.

The ideas, the creations wrought by the brains and imaginations of the Mediterranean people could never have come into being under pressure of the tropical sun, nor in combat with the cold. The forms and standards of mankind could not develop in the jungles at the equator or in the primeval forests of the ancient Teutons, where constant resistance to glare or ice makes men either lax or warlike. Genius is bred by a temperate zone, which is why the great Europeans of the north—artists, thinkers, sometimes even emperors —have always been drawn to the Mediterranean.

"Mediterranean climate" has become a concept by itself; people claim it for California, for central Chile, for the Cape of Good Hope, for southwest Australia. But all these places lack a sea that pushes deep into the masses of solid land.

Only in the Mediterranean do all the factors combine to perpetuate the mild, even climate that begets sunny, harmonious characters and, through them, culture and art. Here we must not count the northernmost points, such as northern Italy, or the rare exceptions.

There is more skating at Milan than at Cologne, and there have been times when children have snowballed each other in the streets of Athens and Jerusalem and when people could even stroll across the frozen Bosporus to Asia.

But considered in the large the situation of the Mediterranean, as the very name indicates, inevitably makes it the golden mean between two extremes of climate. While sea winds bring rain the year round to the north, to central Europe, the Sahara in north Africa remains dry the whole year under the constant trade winds. The Mediterranean mediates between the two: in summer the trade winds rule the sea, and in winter rain comes from the northwest. Alexandria knows seven dry months. Byzantium has but two, and if three-quarters of a hundredth of an inch of rain falls in Malta, it is three-fifths of an inch in Rome, and three inches in Trieste. In general December brings the most rain, and July the least, even in the north. The atmosphere, with its sharply varying temperature, is at the same time more tumultuous than that of the two bordering climate zones. Indeed the summer winds in the Greek archipelago are too strong to let any trees grow very high.

Nothing about the Mediterranean is so deeply embedded in the popular mind as the winds, whose names change with the changing tongues, creating utter confusion. What people dread as far as the Caucasus under the name of bora is the mistral of France, cold, usually dry and dusty, arising from cold and high-pressure areas in the back country, which offset the low pressure over the warm sea. Thus the wind plunges down from the Alps, particularly along the Rhone valley, to the warm coast, and disturbs life there. Out of a blue sky it comes raging at Marseille every other day, an uncanny monster, fond of a nap at night but ready to break loose in the morning. Augustus tried to placate it with a temple. Today tall cypress hedges ward it off the gardens of Provence. Symbol and messenger of the barbarous north, it issues from the foothills of the Alps and, colliding with the warm, moist south wind from the sea, produces storms equal in violence to the assault of the barbarians; but like them the storms swiftly disappear—the same old vandals, today and long ago.

Quite otherwise the sirocco, properly called the samum, simoom, or khamsin, whose name is given to many other winds as well. A hot south wind, which the Arabs term the rain of blood and milk, it washes all color from the sky, turns everything yellow, darkens the sun, irritates the skin, ruins whole harvests of olives and wine.

Parts of the Mediterranean, particularly the Adriatic, are so stormy that rules were once established for sailing vessels, and the city council of Venice forbade boats to return home between November and January.

The nature of the true sirocco accords with that of the Arabs, who, like it, pushed forward from Africa into the Mediterranean. If the northerly mistral, as envoy of the cold barbarian lands, can tip over railway cars, the southerly sirocco shows its nature by splitting furniture, drying out barrels, ruining everything with dust, enervating men by heat that lasts all night.

Along with the blasts, the ancient Tower of the Winds upon which the Athenians once carved such splendid symbols has survived the ages. On top a revolving iron Triton plays conductor of the windy orchestra, pointing his staff in the direction of the prevailing wind. Winged figures, carved in relief all around, show the cold north winds as bearded barbarians and the kindlier breezes as young, lightly clad figures. Chiron, the northwest wind, warmly garbed and even booted, pours water from a vessel, because he sometimes brings rain. Zephyr, a half naked youth, glides serene-faced, carrying flowers, since he is good to the garden. Boreas muffles nose and mouth in his cloak, and seems, like certain misanthropes, to be shivering in cold of his own making. Thus the winds looked down on the Athenians even in the days of the black-figured vases. Two thousand years later Turkish dervishes danced about the foot of the tower. Not long ago a fashionable Athenian lady, waiting to receive an admirer not far from the Tower of the Winds, looked up at Zephyr from her car, winked slightly, and smiled.

The even warmth of the Mediterranean is promoted by the great length and narrowness of the sea. At the same time, the cold north is more sheltered by the wall of the Alps, while the Black Sea receives the cold of the Russian steppes in full measure. These factors explain the contrast between the salubrious climate of Naples and the dangerous one of Istanbul, two cities in the same latitude.

The Mediterranean is healthful in almost every quarter. The long, wearying general rains are quite absent here, and even on the worst day there will be an hour of sun. Cloudbursts match the suddenness of the earthquakes and whirlpools, but with equal speed the air grows lucid again and the distant view becomes clear. Sultriness is a total stranger to this part of the world; if the physicist did not prove it to us, we could read the facts from the pure lines of the Greek vase paintings or the dry serenity of Homer and Horace. A territory whose highest mountains, Etna, Olympus, and Sierra Nevada, rising to ten thousand feet, gather but little snow and hold it but a short time, a sea whose surface almost the year round is warmer than the air above it—we shall scarcely see their likes elsewhere. Only in the glare of the tropics can the earth show another zone that knows but forty-four cloudy days in the year.

The peasant sings the praises of such a climate, even though he may sometimes want rain, and the seafarer praises the brightness of the stars by night. Winter is not deprived of its own, and the eternally blue sky of Italy that our fathers spoke of seems so blue because it is not really eternal. There is snow, but it inspires no fear; nor does the cold. The man of the Mediterranean shows his serenity of spirit in the very fact that he does not fear extremes but tries to control the expected by staying in the shade when the heat is greatest and taking his coat along at night.

How could any peasant from the north, forced to spend part of his life in a stuffy workshop, stable, or kitchen, keep the easy carriage and clear eye that distinguish the men of the Mediterranean, who live almost wholly out of doors? Your Mediterranean peasant does not pluck his fruits effortlessly, like the Negro in Uganda, and the lack of rain that lets him live outdoors often forces upon him the toil of irrigation. Nor does he live longer than the northerner; but he has a better life. If the warmth protects him, no blazing heat saps his strength. He need not sweat and slave, and the little that grows for him is enough; grain and olives, wine and tobacco are almost all he needs. He does not go naked like the Negro, he loves to adorn himself and his women; but for everyday wear in the country he hardly needs more than a smock and a hat: since the time of his remote ancestors, men's feet have suited themselves to the stony ground.

Thus he has shaped from his climate a form of life that proclaims itself in the similarity of his history, in the recurrence of the same features across the ages and frontiers, unchanging even among airplanes and radios. For though he and his friends may sit over their wine in the pergola, rolling cigarettes, spitting, and grousing at the government, still every now and then he looks with a glance of reassurance at the bright blueness of the clear air above, and the dark blueness of the sea below.

V

THE MEDITERRANEAN abuts on three continents, but it does not divide them, it joins them. If some ancient god had taken a notion to drain this ocean through the Strait of Gibraltar, and to fertilize and populate the dry basin by magic, the ancient world would have been the poorer for it. Would the modern world be the richer if an engineer, as successor to the gods, were by some magic to dry up and conjure this great area into the midst of a supposedly overpopulated Europe?

Europe would never have come into being if an immobile African mass had remained united in a single whole to the jutting little corner of Asia that we call Europe. The ocean created the movement by which men emerged into the sunlight of thought. The little, whimsical genius of Europe could come forth from Asia and Africa, those two massive colossi, only because the long inland sea first cut it off, then sent its thousand vessels flying to and fro like love letters after separation.

A mere glance at the maps that bring the symbols of the world so marvelously before our eyes will suffice to show what the Mediterranean has made of the two sleeping monsters. Their shapeless masses suddenly begin to take form. Peninsulas, mountain chains, and a host of islands are gathered around the gulfs. The resultant mingling of land and water, the profusion of messengers to shorten distance, make it appear as if the three continents meant to exchange civilizations, and were sending them to the ocean that lies in the middle. Deserts and mountains cut off the coast territories to south and east, and so we have a unit that lives by itself. Today the Mediterranean territory embraces three-quarters of Europe, and as much of its history. Yet Europe has received almost everything from the Mediterranean, and given almost nothing; of Asia the reverse is true.

Here too our scrutiny returns to the elements and finds the history of peoples predetermined, or at least affected, by nature. Every current in the tides, every shift in the struggle between land and sea, the world of fish and the world of trees, has its importance for the bodily nourishment and mental guidance of people who know nothing about it, or thrust it aside if it touches their lives. Generals and dictators, who seldom study or understand the elements, are often surprised too late at the intervention of nature. Napoleon said he was beaten not by man but by the elements: he had simply underestimated the Russian snowfall. We cannot understand what we shall see roaming along the shores of our ocean unless we begin by knowing what dwells and works in the tides and what grows along the shore.

As wars and rivalries of peoples stir the coast cities, as the winds determine the effect of the atmosphere, so too the currents belong to the economy of oceanic life. The nature of the Mediterranean, as an almost landlocked sea, renders these struggles more varied than anywhere else. The specific gravity of its water, the differences in levels and temperature, the profusion of islands and bays, here multiply a hundredfold the currents that determine the lives of sea creatures and plants, as the ever billowing currents of thought determine the life of the mortals on its shores.

The straits regulate these currents in many ways. Thus the Dardanelles work like a huge spillway between two seas: more and more water keeps pouring from the Black Sea, because the evaporation there is less than the influx from the great rivers, while the outgo from the Mediterranean is considerably slower. Along the southern coast of Sicily the Marobbio, that is, the Mad Sea, a suddenly boiling whirlpool-like current, has been known to swallow not merely boats but even large steamers.

Along with these somber forces bursting unexpectedly from the depths, this problematic ocean, like some human characters, is capable of sudden tender surprises, veiling its menace like a smile: fresh-water springs that do not mix with the sea water. Most of these were familiar to the ancients—one in the Gulf of Spezia and one near Taranto, where thirsty fishermen can dip up drinking water in the midst of the gulf, and one in Syracuse—Arethusa— of which the poets sang.

The roaring battle of land and sea drowns out these idyllic asides. The work of currents and winds upon the coast is twofold: the assaults that tumbled great stretches of land into the water were mostly in prehistoric times. But the filling in that we can read from the remnants of shells and sea creatures on the shore has continued in historic times, now and then even compelling the early inhabitants to move a harbor closer to the sea, because it had silted up.

For here, on the fringe of the coast, is the great battleground of land and sea, alternate attack and defense. The sea beats vainly against the rocky cliffs; anything that breaks off goes to the bottom. It eats slowly at sloping banks of rubble, and a swollen mountain brook, rushing like a young warrior to help, will often bring home in a few hours what the slowly advancing sea has gained through the course of months. In the Mediterranean the jagged line of the rocky coast alternates with the far-flung and usually elliptical curve of the sandy beaches. The sea is victorious over sunken valley bottoms and river deltas when the main stream leaves them to seek other channels.

In this war between sea and land the land is defeated in any case, no matter whether it sees fragments vanishing in the ocean or new pieces being washed ashore and building out to sea. In either case the land is dominated by the other element, and it was not until late in history that human brains began to protect it against the sea. The advantage found by modern engineers in reclaiming parts of the Zuider Zee, the old desire of statesmen and reformers to win new land from the sea, have tempted man to impossible engineering feats. But in the Mediterranean region the water, aided by peculiar climatic conditions, has caused the shore to disintegrate more and more ever since ancient times.

First we have old Father Nile, whose deposits have so filled out the Syrian coast that the ancient ports of Tyre and Sidon are far inland today. Alexander built a roadway from the island of Tyre to the coast, and alluvial deposits broadened it, as if the elements approved of the king's idea. Modern travelers between Port Said and Gaza, smoking cigarettes on deck after lunch, have been horrified to see huge black layers of mud suddenly come floating like islands toward the ship, only to be cut and dissolved after all by the ship's prow. When the stream finally wearies after a long life, it dumps the shattered rock at its mouth, making a morass of the coast. Thus shipping is hampered, the country grows unhealthy, and the port becomes an inland town.

Ravenna was probably once on an island. The proverbial windings of the Maeander once led to a gulf that has now become a marsh. When it overflowed the country, the lessees of the lighthouses had to pay for the damage—an astounding revenge of man upon man, while nature delighted in toying with both.

Miletus and Ephesus, famed old commercial seaports, moved again and again after the fleeing ocean, and even the Piraeus, the harbor of Athens, is said to have been upon an island at one time. The ruins of old Smyrna are now far inland, yet formerly they were on the sea. Even Troy is further inshore now than it used to be, which shows us that even Homer could not command the elements. Mooring rings fastened to the walls of Syrian sea castles no more than a thousand years ago, in the days of the Saracens, now hitch in their stalls the cattle that plow the fields.

In other phases of the struggle, the sea has advanced upon the earth. At Beyrouth it has put an old tower under water, and parts of Jaffa have sunk. Roman buildings in Algiers have been shattered by the surf, and French structures are endangered even now. In Tripoli and Malta the beach has narrowed within the last century, always to the detriment of the land.

But sometimes the intelligence of man is victorious, turning the destructive force of the ocean to the advantage of the inhabitants. The river delta creates special problems for them, because the slight shifting of the tides aids its formation. The fertile land that it creates may be useful or dangerous according to the industry and genius of the men who take it over. In these spots (always to one side of the delta) great harbors have been difficult and costly to build—ports like Alexandria, Marseille, and Salonika; only in such natural bays as those of Toulon and La Spezia is it easy.

In France a classic alluvial territory has formed in a southerly direction from the mouth of the Rhone. Islands turned mainland, river mouths from the foot of the Pyrenees to the Alps form the support of eight arches connecting one set of foothills with the next, like man-made structures. The bottom goes down with such gradual regularity there that fishermen judge the distance from their boats to shore by the slowly increasing depth of the ocean.

And yet, because of its increasing changes, this gracefully curving shore has been abandoned in the course of the last six or seven centuries. Narbonne, which some people would assign to Homeric times, has been pushed back in each century, and even in the Middle Ages it was connected with the sea by an artificial inlet. Aigues-mortes, a seaport as late as the thirteenth century, is now a mile from the coast, and the land of Agde has changed in a hundred years from ocean floor to vineyards. Fréjus, Montpellier, Arles, Sète have become inland towns. Opposite, on the western coast of Italy, La Spezia keeps moving back, the gulf of Portofino grows ever narrower, the mouth of the Tiber extends, and part of the coast is silting up at Carrara.

All these cities are like amphibians that develop wholly into land animals in order to survive under the pressure of a new environment.

VI

WHILE THE UPPER WORLD has changed, not only through the struggles of nations but through the battle of the elements, so that even the best ancient map is not like a modern one, the hidden world below the sea has remained the same. If a diver of Homer's day had gone down with modern equipment, he would have seen the same creatures as we do.

The ancients feared the depths of the Mediterranean and tried to appease the sea by temples to Poseidon and the many demi-gods of the deep. Modern science has explained the life there. Here as in many other cases science sides with antiquity, rationally confirming by its instruments what the ancients guessed from their feeling for nature and adorned with pantheistic names. In the long interval, wavering between belief and knowledge, people thought that no creatures unless they were divine could live in the depths. A single starfish that a captain pulled up clutching his sounding line from a depth of 9,000 feet first proved in 1818 that there was another realm of life far below. The creature was like the messengers summoned from the nether world by Dante and by Goethe.

But only when engineers' cables instead of ships' hawsers began to plunge into the water did this new, sea-borne idea stir the world of the deep sea. An old, worn-out English gunboat on a short voyage in 1870 accomplished in the water what the great archaeologists were doing ashore. By uncovering hidden life it proved what had formerly been disputed. Carpenter, the man who then cast the first light into the deep sea (and into the Mediterranean at that), later showed by long voyages and explorations that organic life knows no bounds anywhere.

Down to its uttermost depths the Mediterranean is habitable and inhabited. Only the Black Sea, where the fresh water travels in great streams on top of the heavy salt water, with circulation hampered by the narrowness of the Dardanelles, is in its lower depths almost a realm of death, where only a few bacteria can live. Enormous pressure then does not destroy all life, as was formerly supposed, for the Mediterranean goes as deep as 17,000 feet. The astonishment, nay horror, of a man who has been pampered by life, when he touches upon the slums of the metropolis and sees people living and even drinking and laughing despite terrific need, is paralleled by the amazement of the diver who, bearing enormous pressure himself the while, peers dimly into the eerie eyes of unknown fish and dragons who seem oblivious of the water's weight. And just as a few men climb from the lowest levels to wealth and power, so inhabitants of the deep sea have reached the sun alive. In both cases these have been exceptions—a handful of powerful individuals.

The fish life of the Mediterranean is aristocratic by comparison with that of the north. The fish are fewer but better, for the swarms of herring and codfish caught even by the barbarians in the north have no counterpart to southward. The only one that appears by the million, the tunny, is an outsider, coming in each spring from the Atlantic to spawn in the Black Sea, then swimming back. All the fishermen attest to this, while many scholars dispute it. Its strange course, first along the Asiatic coast, then back to the European side, was fantastically explained by Pliny on the ground that its right eye was the stronger—just as elderly men sometimes used to make excuses for a roving eye at the ballet. The Byzantine emperors had the passing tunny caught in swarms, much as they did other foreign interlopers. Aristotle, who could not live without a system, systematized even the fish. He was considered the greatest student of them.

The Mediterraneans, unlike the English and the Northmen, have never been great fish eaters. The consumption of fish in Homer is as restricted as it is in the popular cooking of Rome or Istanbul today. Because the Greek Church allowed only the lower orders of sea creatures to be eaten on fast days, the dried cod was introduced from the north, and great shipments are imported even today, while the Mediterranean sends little of indigenous origin to the north except sardines and anchovies. The fact that Italians use the cruel method of fishing with dynamite shows that their fishing is on a low level as an art and a sport. The fisheries on the Mediterranean have been exploited—rather than cultivated—so long that the number of varieties has declined and many fish that can live in the Mediterranean must now be introduced from the Atlantic.

But by tradition and by cultivation the Mediterranean is richer in small sea creatures, which are heaped on the plate of the poorest peasant in Minorca or Lipari, in San Lazzaro, Leukas, or Paros.

There is a host of green or gray mussels, round or hexagonal, with silvery pink flesh, which the peasant has removed shell and all from the rocks. There are blue domed oysters and gray flat ones, black sea urchins, red inside, five-pointed starfish with little nubbins, yellowish pink crabs, blue crawfish, bigger than lobsters but without claws, and brown lobsters, too, pink shrimps, sole, plaice, and mackerel, and the many-armed cuttlefish, the ideal of the *rostizzerias*. The Mediterranean would be unthinkable without this microcosm peopling seashore, bay, and rocks.

There are also three great fish that populate our ocean without imperiling it. For even the shark seldom appears, with his four hundred teeth, in a size dangerous to man. When he did, he used to terrify the ancients. Once when a shark strayed into the harbor of Ostia, Emperor Claudius and his Praetorian Guard set out in battle array to kill it for a great popular holiday.

But the dolphin, above all, so often shaped by the ancients in stone and bronze, has delighted the Mediterranean voyager in all ages. It has always been spared; the dolphin is not hunted at sea any more than the stork on land. It has been held sacred by singers ever since it carried Arion on its back; so it ought to be idolized by horsemen, for none but a master rider or a mad poet could keep his seat on one of these leaping fish. He who watches this gayest of all Mediterranean creatures from the vantage point of a steamer deck as it leaps up in the stillness of a summer noon, flinging its back, sometimes its whole body, into the air, has seen with his own eyes one of the marvels of the Mediterranean.

VII

THE TWO UNEQUAL PARTS of the Mediterranean differ in more than one respect. The eastern portion, ending at the western tip of Sicily, near Marsala, abounds in islands more than any sea on earth; aside from the two great islands of Sardinia and Corsica, the western part has almost none but the Balearic group.

And the character of the peoples that ruled in the one part and in the other developed accordingly. The archipelago made the Greeks into a nation of seafarers, and consequently of traders; the Romans, entirely a land nation and a land power, were educated to sea power only by the Carthaginians and fought their decisive battles on land. The Greeks built the finest vessels and harbors, the Romans the best wagons and roads. The Greeks, grown up as adventurers betwixt imagination and guile, established the laws of beauty and wisdom; the Romans, of justice and the state. The disunity symbolized by a thousand islands destroyed the Greeks politically; solidity helped the Romans to world power. Athens and Rome are placed in the world of the Mediterranean like the two focuses of an ellipse, to catch and reflect all its radiation. This interplay of east and west is matched by the other interplay of north and south. The northern coasts with all their bays and islands are abundantly broken up, while the south is monotonously uniform. As the southeastern Mediterranean is almost without islands, it forms the geographically uninteresting part. This half desert, half rocky corner saw the rise of monotheism, a faith without images, great but colorless. The one and only God arose from the desert.

As the Adriatic, a spur of the eastern basin, reaches to the Alps, the greatest expanse in width is from Fiume to the Gulf of Sidra (Syrtis Major). The two clumsy peninsulas of the Balkans and Asia Minor become interesting on the map only at the point where the Balkan Peninsula frays out and ends, dissolving toward the Asiatic coast across the way into a hundred gulfs, promontories, peninsulas, and islands. This utterly fantastic geography gave birth to the most colorful of all divine communities, that of the Greek gods.

Italy has the loveliest shape. Likening it to a boot is a slur—unless it were one of those elegant riding boots that the duchesses wear in Van Dyck's paintings. We have only to show the map of Europe to a child and he will immediately point to Italy and try to trace the lines with his chubby finger. The two isthmuses that once ran between Tunis, Sicily, and Italy are proved by the bones of animals, and also by the shallowness of the water, only 1,000 feet deep at Pantelleria, and only 325 at Messina. From the peak of Etna the naked eye can distinguish the coast of Africa; no one who has seen the spectacle can ever during the rest of his life be quite unhappy.

The eye that looks upon the map naturally replaces the two bridges to Africa, thus closing the eastern basin. This makes it easier to understand why so many centuries passed before curiosity and trade combined to bring about a true conquest of the west by the east. The beautifully outlined gulfs, rhythmically repeated along almost all the Mediterranean shores, have built up the later hollows at the mouths of valleys. Along with the rich brown of the mountains that cut and usually delimit the surrounding mainland, they give the eye studying the map a suggestion of all the varied events that have taken place in a scene so richly divided and articulated.

Then the spectacle and the thought of the two Mediterranean basins are made more vivid by the north-and-south contrast that we see running from the Alps to the desert. The sea, joining civilizations in fruitful interchange, and being at the same time a narrow sea, indeed almost a lake, seems a stage from whose wings northern barbarians and southern sons of the desert have rushed alternately, to fight as corsairs upon the water. What a poor sea is the Black Sea by contrast, cold and confined in its solitude, what a monstrous space was the Atlantic, which in the days of slow travel used to part the inhabitants of its remote shores! With the air trip from Corsica to Tunis today taking one afternoon, the civilizations joined by science have become neighbors; the trip from Port Said to Trieste, from the desert to the Alps, is so brief that in our thoughts we almost tend to lump the places together. To understand the struggles of these civilizations in earlier days, we must completely forget the swiftness of our own time.

What grandiose contrasts! Between the Sea of Azov, in the latitude of Zurich, and Libyan Bengasi the ocean receives the icy wind of Siberia and the African khamsin. Except for their borders, Egypt and Lebanon actually belong to the desert. Here, as in Baby--

lon, lack of rain led to artificial irrigation, and thus to collective units, defending themselves jointly against the nomads, and thus to centralization, autocracy, despotism. On the other hand the natural rain of the Mediterranean led to individual establishments, independence, liberty, and so to political parties. This is one of the two differences between Orient and Mediterranean; the second is the art of seafaring.

If we look at the natural surroundings from which the chief peoples of the Mediterranean sprang, we can see what helped or hindered those people, and why they conquered or succumbed.

Here lies Mesopotamia, shut in by steppes and deserts and the Armenian highlands, open to travel from the east, from Iran and India, trading as far away as China, while the Mediterranean, upon which this country turned its back, was still in darkness. There on the other hand lies Syria, hindering travel by its great Fault, but full of life along the narrow slope to westward, whence the Phoenicians set forth upon the Mediterranean. The situation is similar in Asia Minor, cut off on three sides by mountains, and accessible only through high passes; it is free only toward the west, and thus is wholly dependent on the Mediterranean, to which Persians, Turks, and Moslems thrust forward. Through the Dardanelles and the Bosporus a connection was established with the completely unrelated tribes of the Russian steppes, and through them grain has been imported since ancient days.

The Balkans, bordering on the lowland of the lower Danube, were easily crossed by a pass, and hence became the pathway of the Scythians, of Darius, of the migrating tribes, of Russia itself until the First World War. Here Macedonia, Thrace, and Serbia were joined to central Europe, by military roads in the old days and later by railways. On the western coast of the peninsula rise the Dinaric Alps, shutting in Albania, which is approximately ancient Illyria, the wildest mountain country in Europe—the breeding place of men, proud, haughty, racked by wars of liberation, sending its insignificant trade toward the Adriatic. Southward, in the direction of Greece, the Balkans feather out into a mountain chain, shattered in a thousand pieces, along the Ionian Sea, where high mountains plunge into gulfs, and snow and green meadows are but a few hours apart. The limestone rock of the Greek mountains, the lack of level plains, the breaking up into inlets and islands—all are circumstances that seem at first to be unfavorable, and yet they created the highest civilization of Europe. We shall be exploring the reasons for this.

The Ionian Sea has one famous bay, the Adriatic, with few harbors, but with a single one that has more history than all the other ports of the Mediterranean: Venice. Lying between two mountain ranges, the Adriatic has developed little cross traffic, but all the products of the south in all ages have been taken northward by way of Venice and her sister cities. Then the same vessels carried back the amber to the women of the south, insatiable for adornment.

It was not amber alone that they brought. Since the end of the Adriatic is the northernmost point of the whole Mediterranean—the Black Sea is an adjunct, not an integral part—it became, in times when every mile counted, the great artery connecting north and south, carrying civilization from Scotland to Palestine, and even to India. Venice, after Athens, Rome, and Byzantium the fourth focal point of the Mediterranean world, was better located than any other port for traffic in goods and ideas.

As a whole, too, Italy is uniquely shaped, placed by nature in an incomparable situation. Where else can we find such a templelike portico as the Alps form to northward? Stretching in an arch from one sea to the other, they enclose the most fertile plain in Europe, Lombardy. This rounded shape of the mountain range admits all the radiating passes to the interior, to Turin, Milan, Verona, Venice. A situation like this even in ancient times was so tempting an invitation to northern trade that Italy, isolated as it seems by the wall of the Alps, still attracted the earliest and liveliest traffic—and the barbarians too, it must be granted.

Similarly the Apennines, stretching in a narrow chain through the narrow country, are easily crossed in both directions by many passes, and they slope off to fertile plains and productive volcanic hills. If an architect were to design a bridge that would connect

Europe with the two great continents flanking it, he would build
it just about in the place and shape of Italy, for the end of the
Adriatic is much more favorably situated than Cape Bon in Tunis,
which looks like the shortest way. Until airplanes can carry the
cargo of steamers, Venice or Genoa and not Marseille will remain
the natural gateway from north to southeast.

Italy was created to dominate the Mediterranean, and it is not
by chance that Rome is in the center of this middle country. But it
has seen its day, and an old nation can no more rise up to youthful
deeds after an abundant life than an aging hero can. The peoples
of the Mediterranean, combating and replacing one another, have
not got the most interesting of all histories behind them with
impunity. Of the six or seven nations that have lived on the shores
of the Mediterranean and dominated the ocean, Phoenicians, Carthaginians, and Berbers have perished. And the survivors are all
in the situation of a public figure who hopes to enjoy what he has
won and to retain in memoirs what he has experienced.

Neither Greeks nor Italians, neither Spaniards nor Frenchmen
nor Turks nor Egyptians now display the warlike fire, the passion
for conquest that inspired them all in their youth. The peoples of
the Mediterranean, differing in so many ways, are perhaps—if we
except the Spanish—alike today in one thing: they are all conservative, and any revolutions among them are volcanic outbursts, coming from below. The social disturbances of our age are vertical, like
earthquakes, not horizontal struggles for provinces and cities.

Southern France has also always been favored by her fortunate
situation between the two high ranges, and this in two natural
ways. Even in antiquity there was a road from the Mediterranean
to the Atlantic through the narrow hollows of Languedoc, over
a low watershed from Narbonne to Bordeaux and into the Garonne
valley. Still more important is the valley of the Rhone, one of the
most beautifully curving rivers on earth, connecting Marseille with
Lyon, and thus with the north. Without these two valleys the history of France would have been provincial. If either of the two gods,
Vulcan and Pluto, who quarrel over the building of mountains
had shut off at the coast the two river valleys that connect the Alps

with the Pyrenees, France would have remained as isolated from civilization as Germany. For the only way to reach Germany was in the saddle, on the mules that crossed the Alps. Vienna alone had a sort of trade route in early times, and even today Vienna is more civilized than all Germany.

Spain is in worse case with its lumpish form, its two difficult ranges, its enclosed plateaus and narrow strips of coast. The Pyrenees and the Sierras enclose two triangular plateaus, largely shutting them off with steep barriers from the sea, so that the Iberian Peninsula appears like a somberly armored sea fortress, holding everyone at a distance. Here the northern mountain wall makes the country into a complete island, because the passes run parallel, instead of seeking and creating a center as they do in Lombardy. In addition, the real seafarers of the peninsula, the Portuguese and Catalans, were oppressed from within, whereas in Italy the people along the coast were the rulers.

Thus in two thousand years only three nations have passed up and down through Spain to Europe. There has never been any world route like that along the Rhone and the Po to connect Europe with the Mediterranean, or even with west Africa.

The countries of the Atlas Mountains, dominated by the longest and highest range of our zone, enjoy the advantage, as compared to Spain, of long, wide troughs between the mountain chains. The fact that on the south they fall off into desert does not affect the indigenous civilization. Broad valleys and plains have always brought people and goods to the seashore, particularly in Morocco. On the other hand the eastern part of this coast is lacking in bays, and toward the Syrtes its history, like the landscape, becomes arid and monotonous. One glance at the map and we see why even Egypt never entered decisively upon the Mediterranean, and why the wars and trade, intellect and arts of the Mediterranean have developed on the mountainous coasts of the islands and peninsulas.

Thus the conflict between sea and land comes more plainly before our eyes, for mountains are the strongest form of land, and stand in direct contrast to the flat ocean. On almost every Mediterranean shore, where the two collide, tensions grow up between the two elements as they would between two fundamentally opposite characters.

VIII

AFTER SEA AND LAND, the third element is rain; it decides what shall grow and provide mankind with nourishment. Here too the Mediterranean maintains a truly golden mean. Between the rainy north and the parched south its territory is gifted with successive droughts in summer and rainy spells in winter, which determine the lives of animals and plants. Thus to southward the ever running rivers and brooks decline; the amount of shipping is small, and even bridges, which would be too short in the fall and much too long in summer, are few. Masses of rubbish are swept down the dry river beds at the beginning of the rainy season. The rivers bar their own way, then swiftly shrink again. The wells too run dry, although they are driven far deeper than in the north. Natural springs are held sacred, for they alone seem to be everlasting.

In ancient times the landscape was more beautiful but colder. There were still great forests around the Mediterranean then, which had to be thinned out; consequently there was more underbrush, and more hunting. Ancient authors from Aristotle to Ovid complain of the snow and cold; Vergil even has the rocks bursting with the frost. The weather has never been warm enough for thinkers of any age. Greenhouses of a sort with windows were actually put up in the fashionable gardens around Rome, and the Roman ladies, enthusiastically imitating Isis, took a plunge in the Tiber, "covered with ice in the morning." Here as everywhere, the disappearance of the primeval forests was the result of civilization. Asia Minor was forested as late as the Crusades; the nomads finally destroyed the woods. Tremendous oil presses have been found in the present Syrian desert, indicating a change that can be explained only partly by the decrease in rainfall and the retreat of the snow line, as in California, which is similarly located.

Human greed and indifference have been the worst culprits

through the centuries, here just as in America. Fire, ax, and goats have done more harm in the Mediterranean than in the north, because the dry spell prevents fresh growth and the ground does not hold up during the rainy season. The growing river deltas have silted up and turned to marsh, the barrier walls and terraces are crumbling, and the inhabitants, impelled by no passion for cultivation, lay waste the woods they despise. When this is reinforced by a cycle of erosion, increasing with the lack of trees, the mountains grow barer and barer. Today we see the color of their yellow cliffs, like a geological map, for the delicate covering of plants is gone. And yet here nature has changed less than men. Sicily, which has blossomed out again during the past century, shows what is possible in the Mediterranean climate.

Weeds, bushes, grass, everything nonligneous adapts itself to the rainfall, sprouting in autumn, growing slowly in winter and again faster in the spring, while in summer the ground lies bare, covered with stubborn thistles or parched weeds, going through a sort of summer narcosis instead of a winter sleep. On the other hand the ligneous plants need both seasons, and it is the evergreens that determine the aspect of the landscape. They shield themselves from scorching with a hard, dark green or gray outer skin, usually shiny, and also are armed with aromatic oils and sometimes thorns, which perform the function of leaves, as on the steppes.

The leaves of these evergreen oaks and olive trees, dry, leathery, and thus safe from evaporation, are all small; the laurel leaf is among the larger ones. Thus, protected by shade, habit, and color, and by matted growths of hair, these evergreen trees may go up as high as 5,000 feet. Just as on the steppes, they stand far apart, so that the shade-loving undergrowth finds it difficult to get a foothold. Even the deciduous trees tend to stand apart, particularly the oaks and chestnuts.

But what the Mediterranean alone possesses in such abundance as to be a basic element of its life is the slopes covered with herbs, whose odor, taste, and chemistry determine the customs, cooking, and pharmacology of all the surrounding countries.

Seamen approaching Corsica or the southern Spanish coast

after a long voyage can tell their homeland by the scent; even strangers sometimes recognize it—a mixed aroma, half sweet, half bitter, now strong, now delicate, but always spicy and good, with a touch of salt. You might call this mixture the smell of the Mediterranean.

Most of these plants are low-growing. They cover the stony slopes with cushions, soft or matted, in a symbiosis so close that we find its like only in the primeval forest. Thyme, growing up from the stones and among the cracks in gray-green bushes, has a stronger scent when trodden on; thus it offers itself especially to the more arrogant passer-by, as certain human characters do. It is not the lilac-colored blossom but the lancet-shaped leaf that gives off the aroma. Rosemary, "dew of the sea," is harder and more unyielding than the silvery-blue sage, which doctors and wizards, witches and pharmaceutists—who of course are all originally related—have used since ancient times. Marjoram, with its bluish-pink elongated umbels, is equally indispensable to the fish cookery of the Italians and the *origan* perfume of the Parisian ladies that were. Earthy and strong, delicately lavish in scent, this herb is like the love of the Mediterraneans.

Amongst all these sway the sweet shrubs of fennel and basil, with which the Genoese spice their *pasta* and the Spaniards their sausage; and then again there is spearmint, which the French turn into a green liqueur regarded as a stimulant to love and which has made its way to England, where it is familiar especially in a sauce, and to America, where it is familiar especially in chewing gum. Wild parsley grows on the slopes next to hemlock, its wicked stepbrother, which Socrates's name has enshrined forever. And the lavender bush, somewhat taller, and stronger in scent, thrusts out sharp, spearlike blossoms from its fragile silver-gray stems to search for any drop of moisture. Taller yet, and sharper, we find hanging over it needles of the juniper, which, turned into gin, has driven many a woman mad, and close beside it grows the myrtle, a tall shrub supposed to evoke the power of love.

Rising strong and solemn above them all, and casting a kingly shade, is a tree whose gray, slightly spotted branches put forth the loveliest of all leaves and bear blue berries among their dark green foliage. As a humble bay leaf it went to the kitchen and as a wreath it crowned the poets even in Apollo's day. It is the laurel. Once Daphne, the nymph, was changed into a laurel, a symbol of the Mediterranean, combining glad life, the pleasures of the table and of love, with thoughts of fame and immortality. It is this double affirmation of soul and senses that has developed the healthy human beings around our sea.

Along all the coasts the scent pours from aromatic shrubs and plants, making possible the art of perfumery for Arabia and Paris. And all these herbs and shrubs, as well as grasses and papyrus, which ranged from Egypt as far as Sicily, are almost independent of moisture. Throughout the year they take the place of northern meadows, which flourish here only in damp hollows.

There are still tall forests on the Mediterranean, and since the height of the strongest trees increases to southward, the forests of evergreen oaks in the Atlas Mountains, at 5,800 feet, reach an elevation that only conifers can endure in the Alps. Mostly the trees do not stand in masses, as they do in the north, but rather, like statues, they are found singly down by the sea. Thus the cedar, portrayed by a hundred painters, bright green and somewhat storm-tossed, standing aslant and just above the blue sea, impresses itself on the eye; so too does the stone pine, which flourishes chiefly in Provence, and the cypress, commoner at the eastern end.

From Alexander until after Columbus, much has been brought to the Mediterranean from similar climates; the scene today is different from what the ancients saw. There was no rice here before the Greeks, no cherries before Lucullus, no mulberry before Justinian, neither sugar cane nor lemons before the Arabs. The Portuguese were late in bringing the orange from China; without it the shores of the modern Mediterranean would be unthinkable. It was left to the discoverers of the Western Hemisphere to bring from America Indian corn, potatoes, and tobacco, as well as the agave, whose aspect in Palestine is now so biblical that painters love to show Saint John with it. Since nearly all of these imported cultivated plants must be watered, irrigation has been developed to a fine point in Lombardy and parts of Spain, as it was in Egypt.

In the orchards of Sicily people actually live as close together as they do along the Nile. In Tunis land irrigated for cultivation commands high prices, and the slopes of the Atlas Mountains were once so rich that the invading Arabs, gracefully exaggerating, wrote that one could walk from Tripoli to Tangier in the shade of the fruit trees.

But the three characteristic plants of the Mediterranean have always flourished without water, probably since long before the time of Homer and Moses. They are grain, the vine, and the olive tree.

Even the Bible distinguishes between unwatered and watered grain. Greek bread is still made as it was in Homer's time: sown in the autumn rain, harvested at the first of the dry spell, threshed outdoors by horses and oxen on a trodden clay threshing floor, and then carried home on donkeyback. All this is easier, and safer too, than in the north, where the ground must first be painfully cleared of stones and where a heavy rain after the harvest may spoil everything.

It is only where the drought begins too early that man's daily bread must be earned, as in Egypt, by watering the grain—for instance at Palermo (where water is sold by bulk, rivers are dammed, and canals and well wheels used), or in parts of Spain and Syria. Indian corn, which ripens from Mexico to Canada under summer sun and summer rain alike, flourishes only in upper Italy and Hungary, not in the south, where heat and drought coincide. Sown as a summer crop in May, it can be harvested in August on the Po plain and in parts of the Balkans, and in those districts it even displaces wheat, in the shape of polenta and corn bread.

Wheat, on the other hand, is at home around the Mediterranean; in these latitudes it needs only the winter rains and can be harvested in 170 days, whereas in the north it requires 300. Consequently wheat bread, expensive in the north and unobtainable in time of war, is the food of the humblest in the Mediterranean region; the poor man eats it with his cheese and olives, and asks no more than a glass of light wine to go with it. Everything—grain and wine, sex

and wisdom—ripens more quickly there than it does north of the
Alps. Here, where life is simpler, man more easily contented, sea
and sky bluer than in the north, the happiness of the individual has
remained untouched by questions of power and continues to flower
even in the face of national decline. This is because these dry regions
have seen so few catastrophes of nature. Earthquakes are the only
ones, corresponding in their suddenness to the abrupt passions such
as cause a modern Italian to smash everything in a fit of jealousy.

Social upheavals rather than natural obstacles caused the decline of grain in Italy. If Egypt had not been discovered and subjugated so as to become the granary of Rome, the Romans would by
no means have starved. Then as now the will to power had to be
backed up with a suggestion that without conquest the people
would starve. In the Roman Empire at the time of Caesar grain
production had declined because the emperors needed soldiers and
the returned warriors did not like to go back to farming.

For around the Mediterranean everything depends on terracing,
and has for centuries, and under bad management the terraces
crumble away. Famines like those in Russia are possible here amid
the wealth of plant life only if ambitious kings hatch wars or corrupt governments bestow unjust privileges that start bread riots.
No country on the Mediterranean today needs colonies in order to
live, for everything can be bought and easily transported across
the sea that borders them all. Where man works with nature, he
and his soil flourish. If the productive land in Italy (before the
First World War) amounted to 85 per cent, and in Greece to only
41 per cent, the causes were but half geographic, and the other half
were social.

Like grain, the grape is cultivated today as it was in Odysseus'
time. The Mediterranean countries still offer the world's best wine-
growing soil. The best wine may be produced in the interior of
France, but these vines were once exported thither, and even today
Mediterranean grapes are used for blending. Quality is not what
proves the point here, although a volcanic Falerno, a Marsala of
the salt breezes, or a Spanish sherry need fear no comparisons. But

the genius of the country is shown rather in the carefree planting
and harvesting, the readiness to accept any lack of moisture, and
above all in the general standards of the most ordinary types. Here
we find revealed the strength and sunniness of a soil, a people, a
man. A Greek shepherd who cannot read but can still sing is like a
little king beside a Russian peasant on the same social level; just
so a random cask of Terracina from the neighborhood of Rome,
or a Xeres from Andalusia, uncut and unstored, just as it dripped

from the grape, awakens the vital spirits that would retreat shivering to their shells if faced with a thin Moselle.

Along the Mediterranean no vine hills are needed; indeed they are avoided because they shed the water. Spring rain is carefully captured around the foot of the vine. Nor are pillars of wood or granite necessary. In the neighborhood of Vicenza and Pisa the vine is looped from elm to elm, garlanded, so to speak. In Andalusia and Corinth the vine is allowed to grow at large, often among grain and olives and often near the fig tree, which Holy Writ mentions in the same breath with the vine, and which ancient authors called the sister of the vine.

In the south, where the vine requires less work than the potato, which must be sprinkled if rain is lacking, people are less inclined to be fat and are freer in spirit than farther north. The Italians devote a fifteenth, the Greeks a tenth of their entire cultivated land to wine, showing that it is as much a part of their life as bread. On the Mediterranean there are fewer drunkards than in the north. There wine makes a feast day to break the dull monotony of life; here it preserves man's balance, for it is a native element like bread and love.

IX

ALL THE PEOPLES of the Mediterranean hold the olive tree sacred. It happens but seldom that a symbol is as useful as it is beautiful, and perhaps no other ever survived the centuries as a source of life. Oak and beech, linden and birch do not determine the lives of their native lands; they might conceivably die out. But take away the olive tree and there would be no life on the Mediterranean. The date palm is as rich, for it houses, clothes, and feeds whole tribes in northern Africa. But the olive trees are infinitely more numerous, and the olives more abundant, so that they support more human beings than any other tree in the world. They demand almost nothing, neither rain nor sun nor hard work, and yet they give more than any other tree can produce. This much the Bible knew, for in the Book of Judges the trees choose the olive as their king.

In Spain 300,000,000 olive trees flourish, and in Italy more than 100,000,000. In some parts of Asia Minor a daughter's dowry is reckoned in olive trees, and the Tunisian who has 1,000 trees is rich. In Tunis as many as 1,800 people may live on a square mile of olive land, while close by, on a bare spot, there will be but 15. In Spain only dividing walls prove the whole expanse to comprise separate plantations, rather than one wild forest. When olives are allowed to grow wild, they have been known to reach 30 feet in height, and there are trunks in Corsica that three men cannot span.

The history of the olive is almost the history of the Mediterranean. Here, where the Bible and the *Odyssey* grew up side by side, the oldest olive trees have survived as if to prove the truth of the legends. For when the Arabs took Jerusalem, they gave orders that a medino must be paid to the sultan for each olive tree, and there were trees centuries old even then. Eight of them were in the Garden of Gethsemane, spared by the crusaders, and up to the Great War the sultan received eight medinos for them every year; there they stand to this day. Under one of these eight trees Jesus may have sat in his darkest hour.

The observer who knows the vitality of the olive, and recognizes the intimations of immortality by the new leaves at the outermost tip of a single branch, can see today, north of the Acropolis in Athens, olive trees under which Plato may have taught his pupils, and whose oil Socrates bought at one cent a quart. In those days anyone who cut down more than two olive trees a year, even on his own land, was fined 200 drachmas, half of which unfortunately went to the informer. Since olive oil took the place of all other fats in many countries, an enemy could be destroyed by cutting down his olive trees.

Both of the Mediterranean religions, Greek and Jewish, forbade this wicked method of annihilating a foe, because they regarded the olive as the tree of life. Sophocles said:

> 'Tis the gray-leaved olive that feeds our boys;
> Nor youth nor withering age destroys
> The plant that the Olive Planter tends
> And the gray-eyed Goddess herself defends.

What is forbidden here for fear of the vengeful gods is prohibited in the Bible on purely moral grounds, thus showing us the contrast between the two ethical teachings. Both codes halted the barbarians short of a weapon that, after all, like poison gas today, merely represented another form of killing; yet every other form they allowed. Despite this prohibition the olive trees fell before the ax of the conqueror as men do today before his chemistry, because the very idea of "humane warfare" is nonsense.

The oil too was sacred in both religions, for it stood upon the altar of Athena and also filled the horn of Samuel when he anointed Saul king. One of the earliest bishops poured it upon the first king of the Franks, and to this day it sprinkles the brow of the dying. In the Bible the heathen are compared to the wild olive tree, which must be made fruitful by grafting. Conversely, too, the Palestinians would rejuvenate an aged olive tree by grafting in a wild shoot, much as some elderly gentlemen try to do today; the Apostle Paul found the full savor of the parable.

Everywhere the olive tree shades the pages of ancient history, and everywhere its leaf is a sign of peace and happiness. Is this for its grace or for its abundance? At the same moment—for all mythology is timeless—Noah's dove brought back the olive branch and Athena, vying with Neptune, caused the olive tree, her finest gift, to sprout upon the Acropolis. When it afterward perished in the burning of Athens by the Persians, she caused it to send out a tall new shoot in two days. The same olive tree that is said to have given Hercules his first wreath at Olympia decked the brows of Olympic victors through the centuries; to this day a withered wreath of olive rests upon the brow of a mummified king of Egypt.

As far back as legend goes, the olive tree has served both gods and mortals. Bits of an oil press which had crumbled long before the building of the Pyramids have been found on the island of Santorin. There are olive stones in the royal graves of Mycenae. In the *Iliad* cloth was smoothed with olive wood, and Odysseus built his marriage bed on the root of a wild olive tree. At the same time King Solomon paid 20,000 quarts of olive oil to the carpenters of Lebanon who hewed the cedars into beams for his temple.

The Greek savant Thales showed how much a professor may gain by his learning, for once when his knowledge of the winds led him to foresee a good harvest, he leased all the oil presses of Miletus, just as a good coffee agent in Brazil might speculate today, and reaped the profits. The olive branch honored Platonic academician and triumphant victor, the birth and the grave of mortals; and on coins the owl of Athena perches in an olive tree.

In the name of both religions the olive next conquered Italy and Provence, reaching Lombardy under the Roman emperors; meanwhile olives were carried in great vessels from Tripoli to Rome. Democritus and Pliny said their health depended on oil, and when Augustus asked the aged philosopher Pollio Romilius how he managed to stay so healthy, the graybeard said, "By wine with honey within, by oil without."

That the oldest olive trees should keep their youthful vigor through tens of centuries is probably no less than the common courtesy they owe to the legends about them. More surprising is the frequency with which young trees often look old, for even on young trunks the bark is cracked and gnarled, like the spirits of certain young persons unwilling to think of bearing sweet fruit. As the trees, particularly in France, are pruned back to six or eight feet, they grow broader and broader, and thus the strips between them, on which grapes and grain were originally planted, grow perforce ever narrower. Wherever the olive tree adorns the landscape of the Mediterranean coast, the effect is recumbent, idyllic, inviting one to rest, not to wander, as the northern forest does. Its domed shape gives to the whole the aspect of Romanesque buildings, while in spots where the cypress or the stone pine dominates we tend more to a Gothic, soaring feeling.

The olive tree lives in, nay feeds on, drought, and so it is altogether the tree of the Mediterranean man, whose thoughts and emotions are serene, clear, simple—not somber, yearning, and damp like those of the northerner. The nostalgia of the Gothic cathedrals is alien to him, and indeed his Christianity has always remained half pagan. A fat or moist soil produces poor oil; in fact at Lake Garda the olive ripens best on morainal slopes. Thus the south dumps itself, so to speak, upon the north. Even a level plain is too heavy for the olive tree; it prefers airy, sunny hills and porous lime-stone soil. If in addition to this it can have seven hot, waterless months, its fruit will ripen in such profusion that even long rains will do no harm.

As it is older, and likewise richer, than other trees, we accept any seeming paradox, as we would from a gray-bearded genius. Who, for example, would expect the wild, uncultivated olive tree, a native probably of the Atlas Mountains, to put forth thornless, almost round branches such as we see to this day in the groves of Majorca or Algiers? Instead it is the cultivated variety that has a thorny bark and usually squarish twigs. Here we have a graceful tree being refined by grafting on a thorny one. Certain Kabyle tribes in north Africa have received this art as a heritage from the pagan priests, who are supposed to have learned it long ago from African merchants.

This refinement takes effect slowly, like everything done or undergone by the olive tree, scaled as it is to immense periods of time. A wild olive tree brought under cultivation at the age of eight or ten years takes as long again to come to full bearing. Though in France they prune a tree every two years to make picking easier, in Algiers they wait as much as twenty years, laugh when questioned, and reply that their father pruned it once when they were children. On the other hand, in Tunisia especially, people making a business of pruning would often cut the trees down to the stump, for they received the wood instead of day wages. Now they get money, which is a gain to the owner and to the tree, but a loss to the worker. But thanks to its sound constitution the olive tree survives everything—excessive pruning, storms (which almost never uproot it), and dangerous injuries. Even against old age the olive tree has discovered a specific that no human sage can boast of: as its live wood walls grow thinner and thinner, it divides into two or three trees, the bark growing around from inside at the split point, so that the crack is soon healed.

Like Mediterranean man, the Mediterranean olive tree is pros-perous and fruitful when but half cultivated. The highly civilized

Greek, as statesman and gardener, asked of his peasants and his olive trees no more than was actually necessary, in other words, next to nothing. Solon merely decreed that the trees must not be planted less than ten feet apart, and this is the rule still largely followed in Provence. But at Sfax, in southern Tunisia, where the best olives grow, the trees are seventy-five feet apart. They are slightly watered at the necessary intervals, and frequently manured. Elsewhere they are generally manured at five-year intervals. In the Atlas Mountains and southern Spain the olive tree thrives at elevations up to 5,000 feet; on Lake Como, its northern limit, only up to 1,300 feet. In years of frost whole groves freeze inland, but along the sea almost nothing can happen to them. The mild winter there is a sign of the tree's true home.

Not only has the fruit of this most venerable of trees and the way of gathering it remained unchanged through the millenniums, but in parts of Syria even the oil press is the same as in the time of the Phoenicians. To this day the women stand below with great cloths while the men pound and shake—a deeply symbolic scene. Soon the cloth is full of fruit, varying in size from the bigness of cherries to that of apricots, according to tree and variety. The same trees may bear green, red, and black olives, and in Syria even white ones. The olives turning from red to black are the finest. Only trees that bear too heavily, like women of similar fecundity, seldom produce very rich fruits. On a hard-packed circle of bare ground the press is turned, as in the time of Homer, by farm animals, like a wine press, and the black juice flows out into a masonry basin below. Since the press often consists of a massive old olive trunk, the mother seems to be bringing up, or perhaps throttling, her children in hard-handed fashion.

The value of orchards has varied from age to age; today it runs as high as 4,000 gold francs for an acre of good olive-growing land; from a single fine tree the grower expects as much as 28 pounds of oil. In France twelve departments live on their olives, as do almost all Corsica and Corfu. But the great days of export are past; and one man, an American, alone made it unnecessary. With Edison the oil lamp disappeared forever, even where gas had not yet come in. Until the time of our grandparents, the world would have been pitch-dark at night if the Mediterranean olive trees had withered. In the Middle Ages Italy shipped her fuel oil as far as Flanders and even China.

Today oil no longer gives light; in fact it hardly supports the people who produce it. For centuries every house along the Mediterranean had great vases full of burning oil like those outside the Merchant's Shop at Pompeii. Today almost no one lives on oil any more, and pampered Americans gnaw on olives between courses at dinner. The products of the Mediterranean olive groves that are exported now go in casks to factories that use fine oil for cooking, to make soaps, perfume, and medicaments. Yet even today the Mediterranean peasant sits in the shade of his olive tree, living on the olives, the wine, and the grain that his fathers planted; and if the tranquillity of his features does not speak false, he is at rest.

For amid all the storms of the sea and the battles of nations, down through a bloody history filled with lust for power and revenge, amid earthquakes, seaquakes, and shipwrecks, still the man of the Mediterranean keeps his steady serenity. But we must not measure time by battles, nor peoples by Caesars. Healthy and carefree, living in the country upon what will grow for him or what falls to his lot, he suits the climate as the climate suits him.

But even in cities he lives an outdoor life, consuming very little meat or distilled liquor, for the factory is an exception even today, and in time of peace it gives him two free days a week. The house with its open verandas, the open brazier in winter, the loggia on the town square where he lounges, smokes, reads the paper, or sits over his coffee—his forefathers too exchanged their gossip in the time of Pericles on the Agora—all this gives him a life in the sun and wind, such as neither the north nor the tropics can enjoy.

Hence the suppleness of the Mediterranean type, the slenderness of figure, the swiftness of foot and understanding, the courteousness, abundant gesture, eloquence. Hence too the vanity and demagogy, the treating of public life as a game, the partisanship, the disintegration of national purpose into a hundred petty aims, the resistance to authority, and the limitation of individual dominion to the length of time that one man can amuse the crowd. The Mediterraneans are all alike, for the Frenchman from Marseille is more like the Italian from Messina or the Greek from Patras than any of them is like his fellow countryman at Le Havre, Milan, or Larissa. They are all united more by the water they live beside than by the land they live on.

X

AMONG ALL THE IMMIGRANTS and emigrants that the Mediterranean has attracted and sent forth, the most naïve are the animals; they prove that the sea is sometimes a barrier, sometimes a bridge. Within historic times lions and hyenas have wandered through the Balkans, but only the jackal remains. Instead the North African monkey has reached Gibraltar, and the porcupine, Italy. Ruminants and rodents in many forms have divided up the continents, and the mountain goats have remained in Greece, the gazelles in Africa. The camel, familiar to the Phoenician, seems only to have reached the west about the time of Caesar. Morocco in those days was not a camel but an elephant country, where the Carthaginians captured their war elephants, and King Juba amused himself with his rhinos and crocodiles.

The donkey was tamed earlier than the horse, and even among the Egyptians and Cretans it bore its master with a patience that men can never appreciate until finally the brute turns ugly. The little Egyptian horses, used at first with war chariots, and only later under saddle, spread terror as part of the dazzling barbarian marauding expeditions—thus for instance when the Garamantes thundered four abreast across the Spanish plain. At the same time the horses on some of the Greek islands shrank to dwarf ponies, and these are still running at large there.

Without the mule, on the other hand, life in large areas of the Mediterranean country would be at a standstill even now, for no motor can scale those slopes and cliffs.

Like the small donkeys and half-horses, the smaller farm creatures have been more vigorously bred by Mediterranean food and climate than have cattle, whose breeding has declined. At a few places in Asia Minor the ox until recently was still pulling narrow-gauge cars from the coal mines, and in Sardinia men are still found capable of riding him. But as the meadows are so few, and stall feeding impossible, the calves have grown smaller and poorer. While Germany in 1900 had 4,000,000 cattle, Spain had but 500,000; on the other hand Greece has ten times as many sheep and goats as Switzerland.

Around the Mediterranean the goat is almost as useful to man as the olive tree, for this animal furnishes milk, cheese, cloak, blanket, and leather jacket. Depending on the countryside, goats or sheep may predominate, but the Greek shepherds mix the milk of both to make cheese. The damage done forestation since the arrival of the nomads, those enemies of the woods, followed by the Turks, is incalculable. When the goats and sheep come down in autumn from the upland pastures, they do not go into the barns as they do in Switzerland, but go on grazing outside, devouring the landscape in the process.

Since there has been no chance here to build up a close connection between agriculture and animal husbandry, the herdsmen live in their own way, spending their lives almost entirely under the open sky just as their animals do. Albania, Thessaly, parts of southern France and Spain where fields were filled in ancient times, all are peopled today by a sort of nomad and his animals. These tribes spread around the Mediterranean in the Middle Ages.

The question of whether the sea is a barrier or a bridge has really been solved by just one creature, on the wing: the bird of passage, traveling from Siberia and Greenland across the Black Sea to the Nile, or from the Rhone valley to Algiers, must obviously have the best maps, for it uses every projection of the land, crossing the sea at its narrowest point. But ibis, flamingo, and pelican also come up from the south. Thus the bird migrations are repeated through thousands of years, for their instinct was tested long before that of man. Long before the first carrier pigeons of antiquity flew toward their goals, the birds of passage had hastened to the shores their ancestors knew. Long before the first love letter traveled in a pigeon's feathers, the pigeon flew to its own love across the sea.

Yet countless birds did not return to the north but were killed in nets upon coasts and islands by the Greeks and Romans. And so too prophets and thinkers have arisen again and again from the Mediterranean to carry their thoughts to distant shores. They were harried and killed in the nets of the priests, on the limed twigs of the authorities, by the stonings of the petty bourgeoisie, so that they should not reach their distant goals. But always there was some messenger surviving, some pupil or missionary who arrived. Thus wisdom went out after all from the schools of the Mediterranean into the world—the doctrines of God, of truth, of beauty, to the peoples who still cherish them today.

XI

OUT OF THE DESERT came the first ship, only a river vessel at the outset. Egypt, the land without wood, could not conquer the ocean, but the Nile flung a challenge to man, for it was at once the father and the god of the land. The yew was rare, the acacia too heavy, and since there were no other trunks and no bark, people bound together papyrus in fat bunches, coming to a point fore and aft, slightly reinforced by a flat board. This craft, without rudder or oars, propelled by paddles, would hold one man, perhaps at most a cow as well. Even later, when wood was made available, people clung to this shape, and they spoke not of building but of "tying" a ship. Sycamore and acacia by their special nature shaped the construction.

When the Egyptians ventured upon the sea, in about the year 2800 B.C., forty ships laden with cedar wood came back from Syria. According to the pictures the rowers stood up, working sweeps put together of three steering oars. Soon afterward they invented the fixed rudder, hanging by a loop over the side, so that the water, not the man, now depressed the decks. Then there were sails on the Nile, and probably in the coast waters of the ocean as well, and there were pilots on the perpetually changing river. By the year 1500 there were even regular owners of fleets.

We have told in *The Nile* what the ancient Egyptians did and left undone in their battle against the Assyrians, and also against the pirates. Here, where the destiny of the Mediterranean is our subject, we shall recall only the first men who tried to free it of its fateful locked gates. Why should not the Pharaohs, who had built pyramids and obelisks without cranes, deal successfully with the Isthmus of Suez as well? What did they do?

They cheated the Mediterranean. Wanting to carry the treasures of India northward without transshipping them on their primitive vessels, they did not pierce the isthmus: they could circumvent it. Ramses the Great, three thousand years before de Lesseps, carried out a plan as simple as the egg of Columbus. He designed a canal system joining the Nile delta to the north end of the Red Sea, so that a cargo vessel took only four days to get from one sea to the other, while the present Suez Canal requires from one to two days.

But because the Egyptians had no feeling for the sea, because they thought only of their own sacred river, the canal fell into disrepair; and when Necho restored it seven hundred years later, 120,000 slaves perished in the process.

This was not what troubled Pharaoh. Indeed he was the first to conceive a sort of passion for a navy, and his propaganda even went so far that the court ladies about 700 B.C. wore little ships as brooches at their bosoms. What was it, then, that prevented him from going on? Not the perpetually trickling sands, not the death of his slaves. Nothing but an oracle, which said to him: "You are building for the barbarians." Thus the wily priests caused the god to speak when the work was half finished. Just so today a tunnel between Dover and Calais is prevented only by the two nations' fear of reciprocal invasion. A connection was feasible then too; a system of canals already joined the eastern arm of the Nile delta with the region of modern Ismailia.

The oracle came true: a century later Darius the Persian appeared and had the work on the canal resumed in order to conquer Egypt. But he was interrupted by the fantastic supposition of his engineers that it would flood all Egypt.

To the Egyptians, large-scale seafaring remained no more than an episode. The ocean did not lure but merely protected them, and the river god seems to have fascinated them in their narrow, fertile strip, instead of enticing them out upon the larger waters. Bounded by desert and sea, they felt safe. As they could build no sea dominion, they lost their power in an age when another people discovered seafaring and commerce. When the Phoenicians made their appearance by 1200, with the might of Egypt slowly fading, they seem to have succeeded to the Egyptians' trade, and by peaceable means.

For what the Egyptians lacked the Phoenicians had growing in abundance, namely, the timber of Lebanon; and on the other hand they had no Nile to cast a spell on them. Harassed by other nations that had pushed them from the east, and living on a very narrow strip from five to twenty-five miles wide, this little nation was thrust out upon the sea by a bare and infertile homeland. Thus they became the first great colonizers. Probably they came from the race of Ham, whom the Bible had cursed with perpetual servitude. And yet this very tribe brought forth the most powerful states—Egypt, Babylon, Phoenicia, and Carthage. They called their land Canaan, that is, the lowland, and so did the Bible. Only later did the Greeks speak of Phoenicia, the Land of the Purple; the Italian tribes called them Poeni, and then Carthaginians.

We might call them the first amphibians, for Tyre and Sidon were the first ports of the western world from which a land nation put forth to sea for trade and conquest. Isaiah and Herodotus speak their praises, and since they flourished until after the time of Alexander, we may allow them a thousand years' life. If nevertheless the world hears the name of the Phoenicians less often than that of the Egyptians and the Greeks, it proves that in the long run only religion, art, and wisdom assure immortality. The Phoenicians lacked all three.

If conquest and trade were enough for glory, the Phoenicians would lead all the rest. No one before them had ever founded a real

colony such as Tripoli or Carthage, and no one before them had an
armed navy. Independently of the Egyptians they discovered navigation, astronomy, and arithmetic; they invented glass, fine linen
fabrics, purple dye, and even a better form of the alphabet. They
gathered wares from all the world, the silver of Tarshish, the gold
of Thasos, the incense of Arabia, and ivory from India.

A native mercantile spirit must have been inborn in these non-
Semites (for this the best scholars today consider them to be), or
neighboring and superior civilizations with an equally favorable
situation between the rivers, such as the Hebrews, would have taken
over their mission. The Phoenicians were the first and for long centuries the wiliest race to shape the economic life of foreign nations
as do the great banking houses in our own day, first as peddlers and
swindlers, then as merchant princes and grandees. A lack of national
sentiment helped them, as it does the banks. Everywhere, Herodotus
tells us, they accepted the best they could find. They exploited
Lebanon, and sold the timber across the sea, as Hiram writes to
Solomon: "My servants shall bring (timber of cedar and timber
of fir) down from Lebanon unto the sea: and I will convey them by
sea in floats unto the place thou shalt appoint me, and cause them
to be discharged there, and thou shalt receive them."

Judging by Egyptian pictures, their vessels about 1200 B.C. carried a ram as a prolongation of the keel, and shields were hung
along the upper rail of the ship, which later centuries imitated
down to Alexander, and even down to the Vikings. Such a message
as this from the old chronicles, such a handing down of customs
through years and to such remote nations, gives us a sense of serenity.
These serried shields that passed from the Phoenicians to the Vikings are like the family trees whose study consoles a belated grandson amid the hurly-burly of the general destiny.

The Phoenicians had built their boats broad in the beam, so
that they should not be too long and yet should be able to carry a
big cargo; they also began placing two or three rowers one above
another. Aboard these vessels they carried across the Red Sea and
from the mouth of the Nile the gold from the land of Cush, the
ebony of Nubia, or they fetched silver, then as precious as gold.

All these were objects of luxury for kings, priests, and courtesans. For since ships then, like airplanes today, were too small to carry grain across the sea, the earliest merchants dealt only in luxury goods. Whatever they found in the way of gold and jewels they paid for with some shining trumpery, like the glass beads that were later to fascinate the African Negroes. Their skill in convincing the savages of new wants almost entitles them to be called the first Englishmen.

We see them before us as Herodotus tells the tale: Somewhere on the Libyan coast they discharged their goods and returned to their ships, whence they sent up a pillar of smoke as a sign to the natives. These in turn came, deposited their produce, and withdrew. The traders came back and called to them, demanding more, again and again. The neutral ground was considered inviolable; it was protected by the gods, though each party called them by different names. This first historic form of trade represents greater confidence and a higher morality as between completely strange peoples than would be possible between foreigners today, three thousand years later. There is more suspicion these days not only on Fifth Avenue but even when an airplane lands in Greenland.

Where they would settle down to exploit the precious raw materials, and even to make manufactured goods of them, was, like all seafaring, a matter now of plan, now of accident. When they had landed in Malta and Sicily to trade for local products, they made a settlement, planted olives, grapes, and grain, connected the new bases with the others, and pushed as far north as Elba. Indeed they were the first to reach the Atlantic, for they founded Cadiz, "the fortress," beyond Gibraltar, because gold and silver, tin, copper, and the purple fish were there, and they seem to have reached the tin islands, Britain. On the Moroccan coast they bartered their salt tunny fish for ostrich plumes and pelts that were brought to the shore from inland. All of this, too, while Italy still lay in twilight, and the Greeks were only just awaking from sleep.

Enter the Greeks—to trade and found colonies, but also to create beauty, to think for thought's own sake, to glory in being human and in being free.

XII

THE GRECIAN WORLD first arose in Crete. This largest island of the eastern Mediterranean flourished in the days of the early Phoenicians, but only a few adventurers seem to have risked the voyage across the sea to Syria, which requires a mere four hours by air today. This is astonishing, for on Crete the abundance of wood soon led to the building of rigid ships, and its insularity made necessary the early development of defense techniques. The excavations that have here uncovered the first civilization of the Mediterranean show us circumstances rather than history, which remains shrouded in darkness. It is not even certain whether the Cretans were really established before the true Greeks, who are supposed to have settled Greece in the second millennium before Christ, coming as nomads from the northeast with the so-called Indo-Germanic migration.

If it is true that Crete flourished even before Homer, the palaces and temples of Cnossus and its sewers and baths, are absolutely astounding. We also admire the vase decorations, the bronze daggers, and the celebrated golden goblets.

But in beauty the Cretans never attained to what Egypt had done before them or what the real Greeks, limning and singing, created immediately after them. We are too easily tempted to confuse the early date of a civilization, and the skill of the excavation, with the beauty of the objects, just as we may admire a child for his precocity rather than for his actual talent. No doubt standards of beauty do change, and the paeans of praise to classical art have wearied many a young listener to the point of contradiction. But in the remains of Cretan art the human form, particularly of the women in the famous sacrificial scenes, is half repulsive and half comical. The warriors on vases, the youths modeled in lead, let alone the female idols from Cnossus, are things to be admired only by the snob who would prize the carvings of the Congo Negroes equally with paintings by Titian or Renoir.

If we compare Crete with Mycenae, which it influenced, we are ready to believe in miracles, as if the Goddess of Beauty had taken a capricious fancy to little Greece. For the Peloponnesus, in the north of which Mycenae is situated, is so close to Crete that today a long-range gun could drop a shell upon one cape from the other. There the vaults are rougher and a fortress of almost unfaced stones with no windows (Homer calls it "shadowy") takes the place of the airy royal palace at Crete. And yet the eye need only light upon the two lions, the ear simply catch a song from the *Iliad*, which must surely have been composed on Greek soil—and Greek art has begun.

The Cretans, who also sailed the seas, to bring home precious metals, seem to have established no colonies; they were conquered about the year 1400 B.C. by the Achaeans, that is, the Greeks, soon after the Indo-Germanic migration.

About this migration almost as much ink has been put upon paper as there was blood shed in the actual event—both in vain, for the one has left no traces, and the other no proof. Thousands of years of barbarism not only preceded these migrations, but followed them. Those Germanic and Slavic tribes, if they really did come from India, vegetated as primitive forest dwellers for another thousand years or two after the laws of morality and beauty were first mirrored in the sunny waters of the Mediterranean.

Anyone who has ever broken his way through the twilight of the jungle, or had it broken for him by Negroes in the muddy, stifling thickets, and has suddenly found a single great orchid blossoming before him, has experienced the emotions that possess us at first sight of Homer in the midst of the pathless anthropological jungle. Here everything is truthfully observed, cleanly shaped; the story is solid and pithy, the locale so plain that later readers have sought and found it. Here is a report so convincing that Homer's rhythmic lay appears like history, and by comparison the prosaic ethnographers of today seem like dreamers and poets.

Aegean seafaring, a stunning legend, is better established. What these earliest Greek voyagers accomplished and endured, their adventures and perils from the Black Sea to the Sahara, from Smyrna to Gibraltar, is greater than the conquest of India and America, when we consider the radius of the unknown seas and the mere planks called ships in those days. Yet the heroes of the time are all forgotten; who has heard of Autolicus, a man of Miletus, who founded Sinope? They had no Homer, or they did not interest him, although they were no less heroic than Odysseus. We can understand better then why emperors and generals from Alexander down have surrounded themselves with artists and journalists, upon whose talents and whose favor all fame depends.

Neither as artists nor as colonizers did the Greeks spring suddenly into the world. At first they voyaged from one island to another within their narrow circle, learning the seaman's craft gradually, until by the sixth century they had settled all the shores of the Black Sea, the islands of Crete, Cyprus, and Sicily, and then the coast of Provence. And they were urged to more daring deeds than the Phoenicians by the goad of curiosity, in which philosophy and enterprise meet. They seem to have been less greedy than the Phoenicians, less sensual than the Cretans. The Aegean schooled them first, but then they were fired by an innate desire for knowledge—hence their mastery in geography. All in all, the native genius that elevates the Greeks above any nation in history allowed them to excel in everything they touched. Even in political life, constantly disrupted by their never-ending disputes, they were more prolific of ideas than other people.

Why else did they prevail against all comers as seamen, and even tower above them? Why did they discover and subjugate the Mediterranean, and subdue all the other dwellers there without a single great battle? Homer recounts no naval battles, and utters no panegyrics to the ocean, though the *Odyssey* is a sea poem. The pictures on the later vases, although they show many sea fights, always give an impression of war games. In the hands and heads of the Greeks everything became graceful, elegant—language, art, government. With their mixture of courage and guile, of emotion and hard-headedness—a bit of Odysseus and a bit of Achilles seemed to be combined in every Greek—they were born to be seamen, that is, initially, pirates. Thucydides mentions this profession by name, and expressly adds "that no stigma attached to the business."

But joined in their minds with this system of trade and plunder, this urge to surprise, to brawl and cheat (accounts of which we find in Homer and the vase paintings), was a constant formative drive that turned yesterday's adventures into tomorrow's gods and heroes. The feeling that a deed is nothing unless depicted develops earlier and more strongly in the Greeks than in any other nation. If the keys to wisdom and beauty lie in Greek history even today, and the western world makes common nouns of royal names that actually belonged to a few petty pirates, the credit belongs entirely to the Greek poets, sculptors, and wise men. What the modern state propagates in its own interest on rotary presses, the people formerly put in the hands of a few geniuses, even though it afterward treated them ill.

Troy, an old fortress of no interest at all, was not merely made immortal by lays in which the seafarers, like modern huntsmen or discoverers, exaggerated their adventures and allowed their sons to go on imaginatively improvising until the whole was collected (probably on the island of Chios) by the clan of the Homeridæ. The Hellenes, a small Thessalian tribe scarcely named at all in Homer, did not merely give a name for all time to everything that is beautiful. No, something much more amazing happened. It was not merely that poetry arose from legend; out of poetry came history. Names and images, figures and myths, in which the poets united all the Greek tribes, actually did produce the union of all the Greek tribes. It was Homer who fused the Greeks into one body. Without Homer they could not later have conquered the Persians.

The development of the Greeks into the greatest seafarers was also due partly to their skill at lying, that is, at romancing. Odysseus and the Argonautic singers merrily stretched their real deeds into marvelous lies, a fact which all their listeners fully realized. They were so avid of glory that the audience would be spurred on to new adventures, trying to outdo the heroes—for hero and singer were blended into one. Being accused of some crime, a politician who was at the same time a bard and soldier started to declaim his latest version of an old myth, and the delighted jurymen acquitted him. His exaggeration proved his genius to the judges, although it seemed to disprove the very truth of his testimony. Even the Greek heroes' remotest descendants always listened sharply to see whether a singer gave due praise to their forefathers in the Catalogue of Ships, Homer's most tedious lay.

Such was the power of the poets in Greece. Greek mastery of the Mediterranean was not due to the tyrants and presidents of the little republics; in all seriousness it was due to Homer and Hesiod, Herodotus and Thucydides, Plato, Aeschylus, and Phidias. Mind and art have created a world power but once in history. Out of a few dozen loafers and pirates who called themselves kings the hero epics made models for the glory-loving men and women of modern times. And indeed in the imagination of the Greeks even the gods, whom they finally relieved of their awful animal heads in favor of human ones, found shapes that recur in the frescoes of Michelangelo with his one God the Father.

All this could be gained only by sea, for it took sea and islands, bays and coasts, to give the practical imagination of the Greeks space and opportunity to prove itself. In prehistoric times the timber of their countryside led them to build skeletons of keel and ribs. The gifted hands of the Greeks were the first to produce a light, mobile boat, which compared to the heavy Nile ships as their statues do to Egyptian sculpture. Low in the bow, towering in the poop, with forecastle and quarter-deck raised, ram projecting, a half deck that gave the commander an outlook—such were the vessels of the Mediterranean throughout antiquity. Athena sat down with Telemachus on the afterdeck, the preferred spot even today. The commander did not move up amidships until iron made vessels so long that a shout could not be heard along their full length. Almost everywhere there were sails and oars, but the whole part amidships remained open; thus we find Odysseus dragging his shackled companions under the benches. The rudder, hanging overside near the deck, was used on both sides. Usually the Homeric vessel had fifty oarsmen.

After Odysseus and the other adventurers who disported themselves at sea came the merchants and colonists, pushing forward in every direction, just as the English and Spanish did afterward. Very early, even before 700 B.C., they seem to have reached Sicily and

Naples to westward, and to northward the Sea of Marmara and the Black Sea, which the Argonauts had sailed. At the Syrtes they encountered the Egyptians, among whom one prince made himself king with the aid of the Greek sailors. He gave them the city of Naucratis on the western arm of the Nile. Thus the first connection between the two most important nations, a precious cultural bridge, was made by sea rovers.

Here and everywhere, even with all its tragic entanglements, the history of the Greeks shows those strokes of good fortune that also befall the individual genius—sunny moments for which we must thank the kindness of the gods. Economists, who like to attribute the destinies of nations to physical statistics, do not stop to consider that the physical surroundings in which a people or a man grows up depend on the favor or displeasure of the gods. The export figures for olives or coal cannot determine the character of a community unless suitable human beings have established themselves on a soil offering coal mines or olive trees. No matter whether chance or good management brought them there, brought there they were. A Turkish proverb—that is, a saying of the Mediterranean—declares that only the able man is lucky in the long run. But this is only half the truth; the other half is that only the lucky man is able in the long run.

The Greeks, who were both, found the most favorable conditions for shipping awaiting them wherever travel and trade led them to make new settlements—whether foothills, or a group of harbors facing different points of the compass. In Crete they found a cape thrusting out far to westward, and likewise in Rhodes, Miletus, and Corinth, where the crossing of the roads from east and west demanded a center, was ideally situated, and is so even today, for the peninsula blocks traffic, which goes from the harbors through the city; warships were carried across the isthmus. An entirely feasible canal, planned as early as the fifth century, was prevented only by the jealousy of the city of Corinth, which defended itself with a navy. Thus early a single powerful community opposed the establishment of an institution that might, like the modern League of Nations, have been equally advantageous to all.

But the more they quarreled, the more skillful the Greeks grew.
On the island of Delos, in the middle point of the whole archipelago,
they built in the eighth century not only the shrine but the first pier
in the western world, 25 by 250 feet long, as the bottom step of the
temple. Gravel and irregular chunks of rock served as fill; ships
tied up here instead of being beached as they had been. To protect
them at the same time from the stormy north wind, a stone mole
900 feet by 15 was built of gigantic blocks, starting from the point
where the bluff changes to sandy beach.

The beloved of Zeus had brought Apollo and Artemis into the
world at Delos because, according to legend, the little island swam
hither and thither, escaping the curse of Hera. And precisely upon
this shiftiest of all islands people built the first harbor for eternity;
it is still there to be seen. The later Greeks regarded the tremendous
moles, the work of the first engineers, as a creation of the gods.
Today people are trying to unmask the works of the gods as human
engineering.

By the sixth century moles of this sort were built even through
city gates, harbor basins were dredged out, enclosed within the city
walls as at Samos, provided with boathouses; and all this was continued up to the Renaissance, in the fashion devised by the early
Greeks. Thus their fame as seamen spread throughout the Mediterranean—from the Bosporus, which the Argonauts had discovered,
and the Archipelago, which they called the Ruling Sea, to the
mouth of the Rhone, where they founded Marseille, and on out
beyond Gibraltar.

From trade they progressed to industry, for most of the metals
were to be found in the mountains round about: iron ore particularly in Syria and on the Greek mainland, copper in Cyprus and
Asia Minor, tin in southern Italy and Spain, gold in the Aegean
islands, and also lead ores containing silver, and quicksilver, all to
be had by a flourishing mining industry that did not decline until
the Middle Ages. In Miletus the Greeks made linen, in Chalkis
metalwork, in Athens and Corinth pottery. At the same time they
bought so many slaves that as early as 500 B.C. attempts were made

to restrict the slave trade by law, attempts just as futile as those made in modern Ethiopia.

As trade increased they began to coin money, and immediately after the coinage came debts, and with debts came interest, which the money lenders of the time raised as high as 30 per cent owing to the perils of the sea. Even in those days merchants and usurers enjoyed a comfortable life in the seaports, while the peasant enslaved himself and his family. As early as in Solon's laws there was an ingenious decree outlawing all public and private debts. Stone pillars set up in the middle of the field proclaimed the peasant's debts to all comers. Possibly we ought to set up such inscriptions again today at the marble entrances of banks, to show him who enters the truth hidden behind the splendor.

XIII

ON THE MEDITERRANEAN the Greeks found two adversaries, the Phoenicians and the Etruscans. All three came into conflict far away from their original homes; their struggles were colonial wars in which the most gifted nation was finally victorious.

A great migration before 1000 B.C. is supposed to have sent the Etruscans, the third seafaring nation of the Mediterranean, to Italy. According to his own taste every scholar has the privilege of connecting the invasion of the Etruscans from the north with the journey of the Argonauts, the first heroic voyage. Some believe them descended from the Tuscans who sailed from Asia Minor as corsairs, a masterful stock but few in number, landing in Italy about 1000 B.C. as the Normans landed there in A.D. 1000. Here an impartial mind prefers to follow the legend: it was Aeneas who went from Troy to Italy and became the progenitor of the Italian Romans, which indicates the connection of both myth cycles.

In any case the earnest and gifted Etruscan nation ruled for several centuries between the Po and the Gulf of Salerno, pushing out the Greeks and Phoenicians between the eighth and the sixth century. But at the same time they themselves were attacked by the first Celts, pushing in from the north, and by the slowly and tenaciously spreading Latins from the south.

During those centuries in the great oven of Italy new layers were constantly being piled up, which people are now cutting apart again like a mound of pancakes; but we must not be surprised to find the layers unrecognizable after three thousand years. What was actually possible for the student in the small space of Troy becomes a mere plaything of the imagination in so large a country. Who can say when and to what extent the aboriginal race of Italy, that is, the Ligurians and Tyrrheni, and also the aboriginal Sardinians and Corsicans, mingled with the immigrants, the Etruscans and Phoenicians?

Around 600 B.C. Rome seems to have been an Etruscan city, and Ruma means "the exalted." The Etruscans, not the Greeks, seem to have been the teachers of Rome. By the time the tribe of Romans, crude city builders and herdsmen, pushed out or absorbed the Etruscans in the middle of Italy they had already learned much from them, including seafaring, which did not come naturally to the Romans. A century of Etruscan kings had filled little Rome with foreign customs, probably Lydian. Augury by birds and livers, the toga, the curule chair, the fasces (a bundle of wands, from which Fascism took its name), even the round arch afterward called Romanesque after Rome, all are Etruscan. The Roman triumphs, winding up with the killing of the prisoners, and other bloody performances, are evidently Asiatic. They serve to distinguish the religion and customs of early Rome from those of the Greeks.

This explains the contradictions in Etruscan nature shown by the discoveries in the graves. A bloodthirsty intoxication induced by victory, as shown in various sinister performances, confronted the practical bent of a people efficiently but painfully working their way up—the Romans, who resembled the Prussians in the dryness of their soil and character. On top of this came the influence of the Greeks, indisputable in face of certain statuettes. It proves the conquests of genius where all race study fails. The Etruscans left behind them such masterpieces as little bronzes of warriors whose slender grace might almost make us think they represent maidens disguised in the borrowed helmet and arms of their brothers; a woman's head in an Etruscan mural at Tarquinia; and the "Mars of Togi," who looks savage and stupid, as is fitting for Mars. They are all Etruscan works in the Greek spirit.

The struggle of the Greeks against Etruscans and Phoenicians, their two rivals in the Mediterranean, led to long-continued alliances between Etruscans and Carthaginians. Carthage had already been enlarged and fortified under the pressure of the seafaring Greeks. Just between the two basins of the Mediterranean, where they had once camped for Spanish silver and African products, the Phoenicians built their mightiest city. Here for the first time they gained historic power, and here they perished. Carthage was founded nearly one hundred years before Rome, about 850 B.C. At the spot in the Gulf of Tunis where a spit of land narrows down to half a mile wide there was space sheltered by the gulf and the reefs for two harbors, an elongated commercial port with wide quays, and a circular naval port, which could be shut off between the two town walls. When we look at the remains today, we cannot but be touched by the tiny scale upon which we must imagine world power, just as in Troy.

Symbolically, each of these nations had always owed its power to its pursuers. The Phoenicians had first been pushed from central Asia out to their flat seacoast, and thus led to the sea; the Greeks had been driven to their peninsula and the archipelago. Now these same Greeks continued to push the Phoenicians in the Mediterranean, and the Phoenicians in turn the Romans. Thus a constant movement forced the three most gifted nations of the era to grow partly from merchants into warriors, partly from farmers to seamen. Only the fourth nation, the Hebrews, remained almost total strangers to the sea.

None of them was born with the urge for conquest. They took the first steps toward world empire under compulsion, defending themselves. The two greatest conquerors of the old world, Alexander and Caesar, came from nations impelled neither by warlike instincts nor by the urge to expand but interested at first only in self-defense, in being allowed to live. And yet their empires over-topped in extent, and in the case of Rome even in duration, the dominions founded on the Mediterranean by subsequent nomadic tribes of barbarians whose instincts were all for war and expansion.

When the young Greeks traveled westward, reaching Sicily about 700 and north Africa about 600, they already felt themselves the heirs of the old Phoenicians. An oracle said, as if speaking in our own day, "He who arrives in Libya too late for the distribution of lands will regret it." The Greeks were determined to be in time; they established themselves along the Syrtes, and founded Cyrene and Barca. The Phocaeans, who were considered the best seamen among the Greeks, plundered and traded around the mouth of the Rhone, founded or enlarged Massilia (Marseille), sailed across from the Balearics to Spain, and landed in Corsica—not, Herodotus tells us, in round-bellied merchant vessels, but in long, slender, fifty-oared ships. The mythical king of Tarshish, apparently supreme for eighty years on the Atlantic coast beyond Gibraltar, helped the Phocaeans, who in turn alternately waged wars and made alliances with the Etruscans and Latins.

Now Carthage rose to strike back. As the leader of many Phoenician cities, and Italian tribes as well, she attacked the Greeks. She was half beaten in the first real naval battle of the west, but drove the remaining ships away, and then allied herself with the Etruscans. Carthage next made two important treaties. In one of them she reserved all rights to Gibraltar. The rock, separated from them by the whole western end of the Mediterranean, attracted the Carthaginians, evidently because they were dreaming of the unknown ocean that began there. The Carthaginians forbade their own citizens under pain of death to occupy a certain island outside in the Atlantic, "a dwelling more for gods than for men," because a settlement might have drawn the attention of the Etruscans to the place. The excuse seems rather that of a miser than of a productive mind.

Their second treaty was with young Rome (whether in 450 or 350 is uncertain), which had assumed the leadership of the Latins. It was agreed that the Cathaginians might trade in Roman territory but must build no fortifications, nor stay overnight in certain spots. In return, westerly limits to navigation were imposed on the Romans.

Soon enough all these seafarers of the west were harassed by a far more powerful enemy from the east. He was Darius the Persian, who sent threatening envoys to Carthage, demanding auxiliary troops. With his terrible scythe-chariots the Asiatic conqueror imposed on the Carthaginians three new prohibitions—on human sacrifices, the eating of dogs, and the burying of bodies (instead of cremation). These humanitarian flourishes make him seem like certain modern dictators.

The shadow of a Persian across the Mediterranean remained only a fantastic interlude; two hundred years later the shadow of a Greek fell across Persia, and the great king's descendant, another Darius, was overthrown by Alexander.

The decision between the two rivals in the Mediterranean was bound to come at the middle. Sicily, which divides the two basins, was the obvious battleground. The Carthaginians won the battle of Himera in 408, only to lose it again through treachery.

This is the first time we hear one of the names which are all that remains of Carthage: Hamilcar, a name with an earnest, manly sound, fitting for the nation whose own name was so hard, almost threatening. Where no art nor any significant portrait remains, the sound must make up to posterity what the eye lacks; we hear these names like distant surf—Hamilcar, Hasdrubal, Hannibal.

The Carthaginians paid for their defeat with thousands of subjects enslaved and delivered up to the enemy, and these slaves began to erect the temples of Selinunte and Girgenti, which to this day tower above anything that later conquerors left behind them in Sicily. But the Carthaginians were still too powerful for the Greeks to attack in their own city.

For perhaps the first time in the history of Europe a woman played a part in this first Sicilian decision. To Damarete, the wife of the Syracusan whose plotting and treachery had brought about the defeat and murder of Hamilcar, the vanquished Carthaginians gave—in addition to paying the victors the enormous indemnity of 2,000 talents, half a million dollars—a personal reward of 100 talents, "because she helped them to obtain peace." Further, a silver coin bearing her portrait, and called a *damareteion,* was minted. Thus through the centuries this woman's name has remained in the mouths of the people because after a terrible war she did what no woman of our day has succeeded in doing.

XIV

IN GREECE ITSELF the seventh century world of the Homeric aristocracy had developed into a half communistic system. Homer speaks of the kings, usually hereditary, and how they lived in their palaces—somber, cyclopean castles in one of which Priam and all his children occupied sixty-two rooms. Wealth consisted mostly of cattle, but tillage had also been carried on since the time of the heroes, and the barbarians were despised because they knew nothing of it.

But in the post-Homeric Greek states there were many communistic usages, of which the common village pasture has survived to this day, for example, among the Swiss and the Russians. The immigrants to the Lipari Islands introduced the custom of working and eating together, a Grecian contrast to their enemies the Etruscans, who lived like a master caste. Part of the people fought the pirates, another part tilled the fields: thus some protected the rest and received a living in return. Later the fields were redistributed every twenty years, to prevent any idleness due to inherited wealth. At a still later period the Lipari peasants grew gentler, or we might say shrewder, for by annual tribute they bought from the pirates undisturbed enjoyment of their fields.

Although the Athenians did not invent money and coinage (these are attributed to the Lydians), when the money economy was introduced, in the seventh century, the Athenian commercial spirit early showed its superiority to that of the other Greeks. The nobility developed from a land tenure that had become hereditary, and indeed constituted nothing more than landholding plus robbery and piracy. This new nobility of Athens, Corinth, Samos, and other cities began even then to take part in seagoing trade, which previously had been considered degrading. Thus between the time of Homer and of Solon there was a development from nobleman to merchant, as there has been from the older to the modern English lords. As the Greeks were constantly crossing the sea and colonizing the Italian and African coasts for the purpose of plunder, barter, and trade, they could try out and replace political systems more quickly there.

Everywhere the many Greek tribes in the Mediterranean, and soon also farther to westward, stumbled upon old Phoenician establishments, which they crowded out, peaceably or otherwise. In Egypt and Libya they captured East African goods, in Cyprus the wares of Syria, in the Pontus grain and slaves from the Russian plains. Some Greek colonists got along peaceably with the Carthaginians, and worked with them, as they did in Cyrene; elsewhere, as in Corsica, they were beaten by both the Carthaginians and the Etruscans.

Everywhere individual cities and tribes came sailing across the sea on their own account. This absolute individualism was born of the Archipelago, and expressed itself in a hundred petty wars between Greek and Greek on their voyages, and later also in the multiplicity of philosophies and political doctrines.

Since the country had no central lowland, and no broad valleys, each valley wished to remain or at least to become autonomous, to isolate itself in the depths of the mountains. But of course these valley people met time after time on the high seas. If you were to cut out of the map the rent and torn coast of Greece, as children do, the silhouette when held against the light would look like a dry maple leaf in autumn. And for several centuries its history was equally rent and torn.

Yet with all their dissension the Greeks were different from the other colonizers because from the very beginning they brought with them, besides their goods and their avarice, the things of the mind in many forms. It was as if a Greek hem had come into being on the barbarian garment around the Mediterranean. What was it that held together these few men so far away from home? Homer and the Panhellenic adventure of Troy. There were also the political shrines of Delos and Delphi, the "common hearth," as Plutarch later called it, which assured the priests of influence for centuries, as Rome later did the Popes. For Delphi was by no means merely an oracle that made prophecies; it was also a moral and political power that gave directions. Indeed about 600 B.C., by uniting with another shrine, it indirectly laid the foundation for the first Greek union, the Amphictyonic League.

In this religious league the Mediterranean gave birth to the first historic league of nations; with it as a model another league was to develop later. Twelve little independent cantons of peasants and fishermen united for mutual protection, about 1,800 years before the Swiss confederation and 2,500 before the Geneva League of Nations. They decided all boundary and water questions and not only imposed sanctions but compelled the punishment and overthrow of the aggressor by joint attacks from the members. The basic ideas of international law come not from the lawgiving nation of Romans but from those philosophical sailors the Greeks, and certainly, like all good things, from the Mediterranean. In fact apparently this offensive and defensive alliance was made before any civil laws had been written down. The first lawgivers were worshiped as gods of light, and only afterward were called by human names. It was characteristically Greek to humanize the ruler, instead of deifying him, as the Romans did. Alexander, the only Greek who ever deified himself, was but half a Greek.

About this time a single state, Athens, rose above the quarreling multitude.

The destinies of extraordinary men do not follow any single plan. Even if their education has been shrewdly directed according to their special gifts, cracks or flaws develop. There is no predicting who will be the chosen one in a group of gifted young people, how fast he will develop, or perhaps retrogress, or what forces he will succumb to in the end. If there were, history would be logical, and hence tedious. A backward look at the youth of great men easily leads us to the mistaken conclusion that everything was determined from the start. And so it is hard for us to imagine a time when people spoke of Athens as of one among thirty little towns fighting each other for power and glory.

Yet a glance at the map of Greece, and another at a photograph of Athens, will show that the situation and nature of the ground were bound to favor this particular settlement, as the endowments of a young man together with the happy environment of his birth prepare him for a great life. Among the states of the Mediterranean only Byzantium was as happily situated. Perhaps we may compare Athens, in its situation, to a guardian allowing a lot of children to bathe in the sea, watching them from his point of vantage and keeping them in check while they bring shells or boats for him to see. For if the islands fixed the destiny of Greece, they could do it only in view of a mainland whose hundred arms received their boats, or whose hundred mountains hid it from them.

The civilization of Europe was begun wholly on the little scrap of land we call Greece, indeed wholly on the eastern side of this scrap, whose natural center is Athens. As there is always some slight favor bestowed on genius, though it must develop for itself, so Athens was chosen to be lord and center, whereas Rome had to develop with slow tenacity despite unfavorable circumstances. Hence Athens was able to rise gloriously in a hundred years, while Rome required five hundred—though she also survived much longer.

In the Archipelago, generally described as the Aegean, there are innumerable islands. In the west a broad, deep basin, the Ionian Sea, separates the islands from southern Italy. The only narrow point is at Corfu. In the east, on the other hand, the islands, remnants of an isthmus, still form an easy road to the mainland of Asia Minor. The masses of the Cyclades and Aegean Islands at this point run all the way from Andros to Rhodes, and a giant could easily go leaping from one continent to the other, as if on stones across a brook. Besides, the ships are helped by the winds, which connect the two mainlands with each other and with Crete, and

with Macedonia and the Dardanelles to northward. Athens owed
half her power to the islands and the winds.

Her land location earned the other half. The tiny territory
originally occupied by Athens, whose name has rendered immortal
the concepts of Attic beauty and of Attic salt, lies on the mountainous northern side of the Gulf of Aegina, which alone contains 62
islands. This Attica is sheltered to northward by mountains and
to westward by the Isthmus of Corinth, which can be approached
only by a difficult mountain road and rocky paths. On the other
hand, to southward Attica lies quite open and therefore tends to be
sunny and dry, suited less to grain than to olives, wine, and figs.
Thus it could not but turn seaward—to the east. Right here the two
basic forms of its culture are fixed. Commercially too Athens was
superior by location to Corinth, which developed into a transshipment port between the two gulfs.

We have only to compare Attica with its neighbor to the north,
Boeotia—shut off from the sea, with lakes, a moist climate, a cool
winter, a fertile soil. These factors have produced a people countri-
fied, phlegmatic, reserved.

Or look at the mountainous herdsman's country beyond
Corinth, Arcadia, whose antiquated-seeming peasants even today,
together with the lovely name of their country, constitute a symbol,
an idyll of inertia. Between the two lies Attica, whose southern
gulf attracts all the elements from across the sea and from the
islands, all the people in search of a port, of mercantile spirit, or of
diversion. Thus Athens has shone on the Archipelago for three
thousand years, a beacon constantly revolving, casting its rays upon
ships and shores, and sending abroad the report of its brilliance
in the mouths of seamen even before its thoughts and creations
reached the distant coasts.

Yet though this city became the capital of a confederation, it
had no natural harbor. From the beginning, however, it was much
closer to the sea than Rome was, and the marshy spot that was to
become a great seaport was not built up by engineering until quite
late, under Themistocles. It was filled in by dumping stones and

rubble in the water, and the entrance was narrowed from 1,300 feet down to 160 feet, not to be rewidened until modern times.

On the other hand nature had given Athens something more necessary to her development than a harbor. There towered from the plain to a height of 500 feet an isolated slab of rock, surrounded by precipices from 100 to 150 feet high, and leveled off on top. The legendary Pelasgians were supposed to have flattened it still more. It was 1,800 feet long by 430 feet wide. This natural fortress was the truly ideal location of the first settlement, rather like a robber baron's castle—except that this hill was to have a greater career than any other castle on earth. For from the fifth century B.C. on it bore the Parthenon.

XV

THE HISTORY OF ATHENS proved that a nation may understand and cultivate wealth and the mind, commerce and beauty, at one and the same time. The pure will to power is the one thing that makes any people barbarous in the long run. The fact that almost all the springs of our intellectual culture rose in Greece, very few in Rome —and indeed that the Romans as political conquerors of the Greeks merely became their pupils and heirs, taking over from them and coarsening literature, wisdom, and sculpture, without adding any brilliant innovations—proves the superiority of intellect to force, and allows us to draw hopeful conclusions in a time when barbarians are pushing forward anew.

Without their commercial sense the Athenians' genius would have had no solid basis, and without the Mediterranean there would have been no gold to be carried off to a natively poor Greece, for subsequent transformation into ageless works of art. We cannot form an estimate of the nature of the Athenians simply from their art, but must also base our judgment on the critical works that their detached irony naturally created. We can grasp the emotionalism, the love of beauty felt by the Mediterranean man today through the statues and tragic choruses of classical times, but we need satire and genre picture to understand his guile and his mirth, his love of money and slander, his ingratitude and spite—all of which go together to make the seafaring trader. These qualities are immortalized in Aristophanes and the Greek vases.

It was the Athenians who invented the phrase "make money," for they used to whistle and sing the words, "Money, ah, money makes the man!" Thucydides wrote of his countrymen: "The Athenians are always bestirring themselves, always voyaging to multiply their money. They seldom stop for quiet enjoyment, because they are always scheming for new profit."

Thucydides and Herodotus, immortalized together on a double herm—a column surmounted by a head of Hermes—look alike. But the former seems fresher, more the observer, while the latter makes a more somber, perhaps more cynical, impression. These first metropolitans of Europe had little fertile soil about them, but their ships carried them all around the ancient world. Their money sense kept them company through all the political transformations, even when the oligarchy, the successor of the kings, turned to democracy. Aristotle forthrightly defined the two systems as the one for the rich and the other for the poor, and for this reason Plato rejected both.

If, then, Athens in all ages was dominated by the commercial spirit and money sense of her citizens, which paired remarkably well with their love of beauty and wisdom, all these elements depended on an indomitable will to freedom. That is why they are like the modern French, and indeed a *déjeuner* in ancient Athens was very like one in Paris today—or at least yesterday. And they had in common a neighbor and enemy who occasionally defeated them, for the Spartans were the Prussians of their time.

How indeed could somber, mountainous Sparta, cut off from the sea, have developed a domestic political morality more successful than what the world ever since has called Spartan? Two snow-capped mountains rose before their eyes into the same sky that reflected hills and bays from the heights of Athens. A stony, niggard inland countryside produced an earnest people and a frugal life. A necessary consequence of their constricted native land was the determination to subjugate their neighbors, and this determination in turn was bound to increase the power of the state over the individual. Half communism and half dictatorship joined to transform dull slaves of duty into soldiers, soldiers into conquerors, and conquerors eventually into nothing.

The distance between these barbarians and Athens can today be spanned by airplane in one hour. So tiny is the space in which our childhood heroes battled and in which took place the only part of world history that has become legend, the very flesh and blood of every nation on earth. Nothing could be more touching than the sight of diminutive, dainty Olympia.

In the Greek sense the Spartans were not barbarians, simply because they spoke Greek; but in our sense even the Athenians were barbarians, because they kept slaves. That idea has changed, like the concept of the tyrant. The thirty-three-year rule of the tyrant Pisistratus was afterward called the golden age of Athens, proving that the autocrat as such is not necessarily bad, that a wise and just dictator was preferable to party quarrels and intrigues, at least in ancient times. Altogether the Greek democratic spirit, like any democracy that functions with slaves, must be accepted with great caution. "The Greeks," said Goethe, "were lovers of freedom, yes. But each one only of his own. Therefore there was in every Greek a tyrant who merely lacked the opportunity to develop."

What actually prevailed in Sparta was a sort of aristocratic government of estates, whose masters were the generals and officers. The modern doctrine of the subordination of private good to the good of the state was softened in Sparta, however, by common food and eating places for all citizens; by the right to share in the use of horses, dogs, the produce of the fields, and slaves under certain circumstances; and by equal distribution to all soldiers of newly conquered territory. Once when Lycurgus, the leader and lawgiver, was walking through the freshly mown fields, he is said to have remarked, "Why, this looks like the property of brothers who have just divided up their inheritance." The poor man was not enriched but at least he was kept from starvation by the state. If he was very sick or very old, he might be killed according to eugenic rules.

This view of the protection of the strong against the rise of the weak began to take shape in the form of money and property, as we can see from the terrible statement of Isocrates, made in criticism of the Athenians: "The people fear their enemies less than their own fellow-citizens. The rich would rather throw their property into the sea than give it to the poor, and the poor desire nothing more fiercely than to rob the rich."

If social stratification in Sparta was by no means more equable than in Athens, in Sparta the mind of a whole people was directed toward the craft of warfare, and all ambition was turned in that direction, quite in the spirit of modern Fascism. The mingling of sport and war in Sparta even went so far that the boys had their allowances restricted in order to train them as clever thieves, and the girls and women did gymnastics along with the men, although they might not eat with them. This was as much of a break with tradition as if our grandmothers, clad in shorts, had done gymnastics with our grandfathers.

A nation in arms, no education except that of the warrior, disdain for the intellect, regulations providing when the citizen must marry and when the state should take him away from the family again, restricted liberty of movement, autarchy even to the point of iron money—Sparta presents a perfect model for the ideals lived by and preached today in the totalitarian states.

Since dictatorship, then called tyranny, was known also to Athens, and social inequality also to Sparta, the difference lay primarily in the idea of the state, which permitted the Spartan leader unlimited interference in its favor, by contrast with the mercantile state of Athens, which rarely wanted to conquer but only to defend herself, to live at peace with everyone, to criticize and philosophize. Consequently Athens allowed almost complete freedom to her citizens. And so freedom, beauty, and enjoyment of life perished in the inland military state of Sparta, and eventually there was nothing left. In the sea state of Athens everything derived from liberty, immortalizing the concept of Greece. The fact that one day Sparta was victorious merely caused a very brief interlude in the everlasting glory of Athens.

XVI

THE ORACLE OF DELPHI is said to have advised Themistocles: "Build wooden walls!" He understood and created the Athenian navy, strengthened the fortifications of the Piraeus, made use of the naval harbor of Phaleron Bay, and thus prepared for his victory over Xerxes at Salamis and the liberation of Greece from the Persians (480 B.C.). It was when the Asiatic world power was putting down the revolts of the Greeks in Asia Minor, and all Greece was paying tribute to the Persians, that the concepts of Panhellenic interests, Greece, and the idea of high treason as applied to Greeks who refused to make war upon the Persians, first came into being. For a time Sparta joined the Hellenic League and the great Greek army. But the navy was what proved decisive.

The thinker today feels ashamed on behalf of his ideas when he sees a victory of liberty and justice, even of health and life, threatened by the superior construction of a bomber or a tank. When we consider that Pericles is said to have taken part in the decisive battle of Salamis, we get cold shivers two thousand years later at the thought that the entire Periclean age was dependent on the construction of the vessels, the seamanship, and the strategy that brought the decision at Salamis between the barbarians and the most highly cultivated nation in the world. When in addition we think of the ingratitude with which Pericles, the savior of a whole civilization, or of his own nation at the very least, was treated in the end, we who come after are filled with resignation and inclined to forswear all faith and all ambition in the life of the body politic.

As we read about earlier naval battles we can understand better how Themistocles at Salamis saved the spirit of the Mediterranean. A series of vessels would move straight at the enemy's ships. Each one tried to drive its ram into an adversary's flank, a feat which was possible at high speed. That was how Corinth fought Corcyra (Corfu) in an early Greek naval battle, about 660, and that was how an Austrian ship sank an Italian in two minutes at Leszno, in the

last naval battle of the kind, as late as 1866. The torpedo traveling
under water today is fundamentally a modern development of this
technique. As late as 500 B.C. Athens had to borrow twenty ships
from Corinth to fight Aegina, and was beaten even so.

But Themistocles knew that the Persian barbarians were, or
considered themselves, great seamen, and could be defeated only
by a new departure. And so he decided to stop the usual distribution of the profits of silver mines to the citizens, choosing to make
himself unpopular by using the money to build more than 100
triremes in three years.

The idea of these rows of oarsmen one above another came from
the Phoenicians, but the manner in which Themistocles constructed
them before the great naval conflict was Greek: everything planned
for speed and grace of maneuvering. The so-called Attic triremes
were the first to have an overhanging deck that projected by the
width of a man's shoulders. This led to the outrigger, an oarlock
projecting outboard, which is still used on rowing shells. Naval
battles then were more like land battles, in that people tried to jump
from one vessel to another, man after man, and therefore the number and skill of the oarsmen were all-important.

Thus such an improvement as a flat battle deck might be a deciding factor. The elongation of the vessel, up to more than 130
feet, was not outdone even by the Vikings a thousand years later,

nor by anyone else until iron and steam power arrived, in the nineteenth century. As there was no closed hold, cloth and leather
screens on top protected the oarsmen from waves, sun, and the
enemy. Mast and sail were usually left ashore. When Mark Antony
took them aboard his vessel at Actium, people concluded that he
meant to flee.

Themistocles also invented the rich sponsor, who got his advertising from being called the triarch of a ship, but for safety's sake
had a representative serve as captain. The stroke for the rowers was
set by a flutist playing a sharp, rhythmic melody. Boats reached a
speed of five knots under human power, and the modern achievement of thirty with the most powerful oil motors is so slight an
advance that we must award the blue ribbon to Themistocles. At
Salamis, incidentally, he had but fourteen armed men and four
archers to every fifty oarsmen. Since it was usual to eat and sleep
ashore, and a stay of several days on board was seldom necessary,
there was no place in the crowded boat for cooking. There was
usually drinking water; wine was rare.

Shipbuilding went faster than training. Hiero built two hundred vessels in forty-five days, and Caesar maintained that he could
launch a whole squadron within thirty days of felling the trees.
On the other hand the boats wore out as fast as automobiles do in
America. (What would Themistocles say if he were to learn in the

afterworld that the ship in which Cook first circumnavigated the globe was in use from 1764 to 1874 and would be afloat today if it had not gone down in a collision?) Themistocles' regimen for training the oarsmen, however, was long and drastic. The men practiced on special stagings ashore, rhythmically shouting the word *rypapai* until they were called by that name themselves. Aristophanes parodied all this in an immortal scene in which Dionysus is learning from Charon how to row, with the croaking and the singing of frogs striking the beat.

The great enemy was not the Persian, however, but the weather. In ancient times far more vessels went down in storms than in battle. With a draught of only about three feet and a deck six or seven feet above the water line, even though the keel was ballasted with as much as twenty tons of rock, nobody would have dared risk a battle on the high seas; they stuck close to shore.

In order to train his countrymen as good sailors, Themistocles introduced conscription. Far from making him odious to the common people, this merely redoubled his popularity. The only annoyance was felt by the three classes that had hitherto been privileged to do military service; they were displeased because now they had to share the rower's bench with proletarians. Aristides seems to have been opposed to the crucial battle, but as a good citizen he fought too, on the land side.

The Persian strength was tremendous. They had six hundred vessels against three hundred for the Greeks; why were they nevertheless defeated? We are told that it was because the gulf at Salamis is so narrow they could not maneuver, and anyone who looks down on the spot from above can see that no nine hundred vessels could fight there. Besides, the Greek ships were sharper, slenderer, and swifter.

Xerxes, from his throne watching the whole scene like a play, was a sign of the overweening Persian pride. He could scarcely have known that yonder amid the thousands there fought a forty-five-year-old Greek who, though but an unknown soldier in the ranks, had a better right to the throne than he. Aeschylus was the man who saw the king of the Persians enthroned afar. The Greek

poet prevailing over the king of the barbarians at Salamis was a
great symbol. For Greece, now liberated, began a century's development of art, which cannot breathe under pressure. The Greeks
must have hoped to reconcile Mars through the Muses. Aeschylus
at Salamis cleared the path for himself and his successors, while
the king of the Persians fled from his ocean throne, to be murdered
at home and then consigned to oblivion.

The Attic sea alliance was a result of the victory at Salamis,
just as the union of Germany was a result of Sedan. The league
stretched out as far as the Propontis, incorporating pieces of Asia
Minor because of the general fear of the new sea power, Athens.
But it was the wisdom of Aristides and his men that now induced
most of the Greek peoples to acknowledge the league council, the
league treasury, and the navy, and to support them, even in time
of peace, whereas Sparta planned to do this only in war. It was the
first time in history that a federation of states quickly turned into
a state confederation.

Athens assumed the moral leadership of Greece, while Sparta
retired, grumbling, to wait half a century until she dared deliver
the great blow. Democracy in Athens was shaky, the party system
corrupt and disunited. Themistocles, a problematical character at
best, was banished six years after his victory, and condemned to
death. He had to flee to the king of the Persians, the son of Xerxes,
who gave him a princely reception and bestowed a princedom upon
him. His life came to an end there long afterward, probably by
violence.

XVII

ONLY AUGUSTUS in all of antiquity is comparable to Pericles as undisputed master of a great age, and in length of reign and personal
beauty. But the Greek is superior to the Roman at every point. His
face expressed the manliness and restraint that imagination demands of a Greek statesman. Even if no statue had survived, we
could reconstruct the head of Pericles from the verses of Sophocles,
Socrates's thumbnail sketches, and a statue of Hermes. He was not

an heir, nor a youth like Augustus when he came into power, but a settled and self-developed character. He was not a libertine like Augustus, but a physically mature man with enduring passions.

His skill as an orator lifted him above Augustus beyond any cavil. He spoke only on great occasions, first secretly imploring the gods to preserve him from incautious words. When someone asked a political adversary whether he was not at least a better wrestler than Pericles, he replied: "I am, but what good will that do me? If I threw him, he would make a speech denying that he had fallen. He would convince everyone, and even the very onlookers at the match would end by believing him."

Though the realm of Pericles was much smaller than that of Augustus, his victories were no less. The navy that he found awaiting him, and developed, won new victories. For the second time a sea battle brought to Athens the leadership of almost all the peoples. But the Long Walls with which Pericles connected and protected capital and port seemed threatening to the Greeks, just as the new navy once had. They all gathered under his authority with the exception of Sparta. By 440 the power of Athens extended to the Pontus and southern Italy; in the course of twenty years Athens had become a metropolis, with Syracuse her only rival among all the cities of the Mediterranean. The new Piraeus became a great seaport, with a monopoly on grain from the Black Sea, Sicily, and Egypt. The rich temples founded the banking system, but large holdings of land were not tolerated. Slave labor, which renders impossible any economic comparisons between antiquity and our own day, increased through importation. There was almost no private luxury in housing or dress, no direct taxes in time of peace, but there were festivals for everyone.

For Pericles heard the call of the age. And though he belonged to a rich and distinguished family, he got himself elected by the enemies of his class, the laborers of the Piraeus. While he governed on behalf of capital, he fought the conservatives and established the first and certainly one of the best democracies in history. Perhaps it is fairer to say that as an unavowed dictator he led the citizens to believe they were doing the governing. He was strong enough as a soldier and strategist to desire peace, and he tried to preserve it for thirty years. It was only in his last days, when the ungrateful Athenians had preferred charges against him, that his peace with Sparta collapsed, and he saw the beginning of the war he had long avoided. A psychologist and rabble rouser of the first rank, he was more than two thousand years ahead of Count Mirabeau in realizing that the old economic structure could be preserved for the privileged classes only by making great concessions and great innovations.

His acumen as a statesman consisted in cheating the people for the people's good. When he paid the admission of the poor to the theaters out of the state treasury, when he gave salaries to judges so that even the proletarians could hold these offices, he was simply buying votes, for he had to be reelected each year, as in fact he was for the fifteen years of his dictatorship. Of course he loved power, as any artist loves his instrument, but at the same time he felt that his bribery was keeping the best man at the head of the state. When the people's assembly shouted that he was spending too much money for the new temples, he replied that from now on he would pay for them himself, and would in return have his name inscribed under the statues. Thus with a few words he won over thousands, and they shouted to him to go right on building with state funds. He increased his popularity by allowing the poets and the couplet singers to speak as vilely as they pleased about his mistress Aspasia.

Pericles is the only Greek whose life was guided by a woman and not by a male favorite. Everyone knew that Aspasia kept young hetaerae in her house, perhaps even offering them to Pericles. Socrates too went to hear her, and although he was never interested in the love of women, under her influence he gave up his first wife and presented her, with her consent, to another husband. No public affront to his beloved could ruffle Pericles.

To show the Athenians his incorruptibility he had all the purchases for his household made in the market; but on the other hand he sold the produce of his own estate as dear as possible, like any other farmer. He allowed free play to caricatures making fun

of his abnormally long skull, but he never uncovered it, almost invariably wearing a helmet. While he deceived the people about
the length of the peace with Sparta, he was constantly arming, and
he bribed the Spartan government year by year in order to gain
time. Pretending perfect equality of all the states for the benefit of
the allied Greeks, he took tribute from them like a conqueror, and
few people realized that he used this very money to adorn the
Acropolis, which was to mean his own glory.

Fighting for Miletus, where his beloved Aspasia was born, in
the conflict between Miletus and Samos, he endured the censure of
his fellow citizens, but in the end he came home with a great
victory that brought money and prestige to the nation. Thus he
regained and redoubled the respect he had staked on the woman's
account. He never spared himself in battle, and at Samos, Pericles
and Sophocles fought side by side. Interest and honor alike urged
both men to risk their bodily lives in order to gain the spiritual, for
wisdom never quite forsook these two. A true Athenian was like
a snow-capped volcano; the best of them were veritable Etnas.

Pericles seemed Olympian to his fellow citizens, and Plutarch
said the epithet, hackneyed even then, was altogether appropriate
for him. From the start of his virtual dictatorship he appeared in
public but seldom and spoke only on great occasions. And why
should he not have the Olympian fire hidden within? What was
to prevent this man of great dignity from amusing himself in
Phidias's studio with the young models, who had no more need to
realize in their lives the attitude of chaste Athena than he had to
play the anxious father of his country? Why should he not adopt
his gifted natural son, and fight his good-for-nothing legitimate
son through the courts? Nobody has heard of Pericles's wife, but
Aspasia came to symbolize an idea. At the point where private
lives were suddenly lit up by Athenian gossip, Pericles displayed
a poise evidently calculated for posterity.

He embodied the Greek ideal stated by Thucydides. "In our
manner of living we show an elegance tempered with frugality, and
we cultivate philosophy without enervating the mind." For with
all his shrewdness and clarity of thought, he had his imaginative

side. He loved glory and saw that it was to be found in statues and buildings. Probably Pericles was not a character with aesthetic tendencies but merely a dictator who wanted by means of statues and festivals to occupy his unemployed and keep his capricious subjects in a good humor. The fact that he knew music and sometimes staged a Panathenaea himself shows that the general level of education then compared favorably with that of French statesmen in a later period. But the sure touch with which he discovered the greatest masters of his time, held them, and had them write, paint, and carve, the freedom with which he chose a brilliant woman of ill repute for his mistress, and defended her against all accusations, while she held a seminar for the study of love, all give him a kingly aspect and in a sense place him above the men whose patron he was, just as a brilliant director fuses together all his actors. The works of the age named for him take the place of letters and documents; indeed we understand him the better because we have no memoirs, scarce half a dozen speeches and replies. At any rate this is better for his fame. If anyone objects that Pericles was fortunate in finding such great masters in evidence, we can only reply that he was unlucky enough to govern the most ungrateful people.

Why are Pericles's defeats forgotten and his victories preserved? Why does history not reproach him for building too much on too narrow a foundation, on a substructure only twenty years old, and for apparently not realizing that Persians and Spartans together were too strong for young Athens? Why does no one hold against him his bribery of the masses with state funds? Why does his jealous banishment of Thucydides not weigh him down as similar acts do Napoleon? Why does no one deny his glory, when the glory of Alexander and of Caesar is disputed? Why did he, who lost the game in the end, take no shadow with him to the nether world?

Because as a philosopher he knew the difference between glory and ambition; because he never misused his people for the quick sparkle of a triumph, but now cherished them, now seduced them for the advantage of a great era. Because this dictator was perhaps the only one who could say, dying after all his battles, that no

Athenian had put on mourning because of him. Because he combined self-assurance with acumen, power with the will to beauty—this made Pericles the perfect Greek.

XVIII

TRAVELERS APPROACHING the bay of Athens by steamer at dawn, not knowing where they are, awake with the same sensations that Odysseus felt when, between sleep and reality, he found himself again on the beach of Ithaca after his long voyages. This, you feel, is the home of dreams that were guided half by romantic premonitions and half by pictures to plant temples yonder on the sunny hills.

For it is that hill, that low, isolated, precipitous hill, flat on top, which brought safety to Athens at the dawn of her history and still preserves her beauty today, long after her grandeur is gone. The Acropolis of Athens, set down in a plain, would be no more than the Temple of Theseus at its foot, which looks like a model and leaves us cold despite its perfection. It is the hill and the patina of landscape, situation, and age that make the spectacle unique. How startled we should be if we were suddenly to see it all in the blue, yellow, and red that Phidias ordered and Pericles looked upon! Yet even five hundred years later it looked as if it were new, for Plutarch describes it so. Today everything is changed; the beauty of a torso is never that of the original, but another, a new beauty, just as the marvelously wrinkled countenance of an old woman is but dimly connected with the portraits of her blooming youth.

Its imperfection makes the Acropolis a living legend—a Homeric legend, because it all stays close to mortals, not reaching into the clouds. From below we first come face to face with the well-preserved west façade of the Parthenon, and so cannot see the other, shattered parts to begin with. We do not even realize that the building lacks a roof, for the eight gigantic western pillars of the Parthenon with their architraves dominate the whole Acropolis.

As we go up, the impression grows stronger and stronger. Here no one thinks of the people he may meet, as he would in the cele-

brated squares of Venice, Rome, or Paris; actually one thinks only
of the gods he is approaching. For everything is tremendous, yet
nothing is beyond reach. It is just like the gods in Homer, with
whom every reader feels a bond.

Suddenly, at the Propylaea, one is in the midst of ruin, so to
speak among headless statues. As in Beethoven, this chaotic expression is interrupted by an amusing scherzo: on the right appears the
little temple of Athena Nike, all dainty, the columns excellently
preserved with capitals and feet, only the goddesses headless. The
most beautiful of them, one with her right foot uplifted, seems sheltered by the great wings. When one has known her a long time her
head slowly fades in, and one can see it in his mind forever after,
as a lover learns to hold converse with his dead beloved as if she
were still alive.

It is all given vivid life by the presence of the gods. Hard by to
the northeast, at the Erechtheum, another portico recalls the memory of Erechtheus. For there it was that Ares tried to violate Athena.
But the Eternal Maiden, resisting, cast the seed of Ares on the
ground, and Erechtheus rose up from it. In memory of this, and in
retribution, Athena's handmaidens now have to carry his temple,
though they turn their backs upon it with a remnant of pettishness.
Indeed when we look at the Erechtheum from behind they seem
more like petrified columns, half shadows who have not yet decided
to become mortals. These are the caryatids, maidens bearing the
roof upon the stone cushions on their heads. This was very daring
of the sculptor, for no man likes to see a woman carrying a roof
when he would relieve her of a basket. Yet the thing is so airily
built that we might believe them to be dancers carrying a light
canopy over their queen in a procession.

They are all healthy young women with long, thick hair, but
the differences among them would be sufficient in themselves to disprove the theory of "typical" beauty in Greek figures. Of those
before us, two are sharp and unfriendly, two charming, one is
simply a dark serving girl, the sixth knowing and discreet. What
homage to a god who was not born of woman!

In the Parthenon, however, thirty paces away, everything seems more gigantic than even the temples of Egypt. These Doric columns seem to have sprouted straight from the ground. But the one thing that no copy can show us is the golden-yellow honey color that seems to be dripping down the cracked and broken flutings of the marble. This color gives the pillars of the Parthenon almost a living skin.

Only by craning our necks, as in the Sistine Chapel, can we see the part of the long, festive relief, the so-called Panathenaea, that has not been carried away. Knowing the details as we do from the British Museum or from copies, we greet the shadowy originals on high like old friends. These horsemen, breaking the long rhythm of the columns with a horizontal rhythm of their own, are all young gods or princes, and all seem to be inspirited by the wind blowing through their cloaks. Their horses are racing, leaping, tossing their heads, often raising both forefeet together, and so they seem like living figures.

There is no woman here, nothing but lively naked youths, occasionally followed by an older man. Thus this marble procession gives an erotic effect, the more so since they are all here to celebrate a single maiden, the goddess Athena, who once shone splendidly in gold and marble at the rear of the temple.

But the other gods who flourished here are almost all gone too, and are standing in museums. What we see, and still more what we have seen elsewhere, seems cooler and calmer than the mounted host of mortals. Indeed these gods are here only as visitors; they are critically disposed, as most mortal artists are when asked to sing the praises of another. Poseidon and Apollo especially feel like guests, and would rather dwell in their own temples; Artemis is busy with her gown, Aphrodite summons Ares to her knee.

If we turn about, the Greek landscape is at our feet. Among the double columns, perfectly preserved on the entrance side of the Parthenon, is one at whose foot the stranger sits in order to survey with a single glance the platonic ideas of the Greeks. It is the southwestern corner pillar whose broad, yellowish-brown grooving he leans against, with his legs dangling. For these giant steps were made for gods alone, and mortals cannot reach them. We can tell

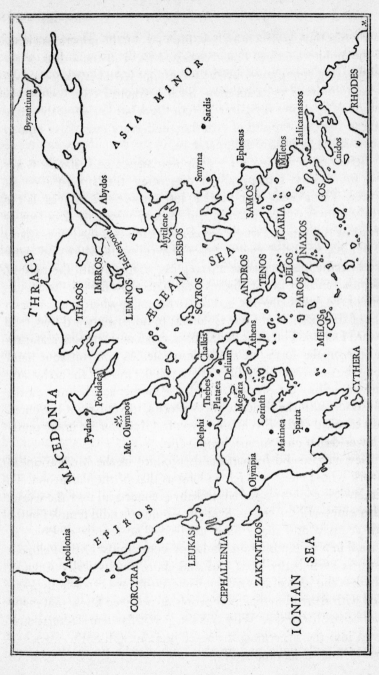

THE GREEK WORLD ABOUT 450 B.C.

how white those pillars must have been (when the imperious glance
of the architect Ictinus first recognized them in the ledges of the
neighboring mountains) by the pieces that have been knocked off
broken columns in restoration. Such a fragment lies before the
author as he writes these lines. From the white inside of the stone
we can tell that the sun of two thousand years must have tanned
the marble as if it were a human face.

Before our eyes spreads a symphony of sea and islands, water
and mountains, symbolically representing the structure of all
Greece. The closest, over yonder, just outside the Piraeus, is the
gently hilly island of Salamis, and the bay where the freedom of
Greece was saved in a single day. Farther south is the larger island
of Aegina, with the shadows of a few columns. More and more
islands come into view, one intercepting another, until the coast of
Corinth vanishes in the distant heat haze. Southward the mountains of the Athenian coast go back to the point where one catches a
hint of the foothills of Cape Colonna; to northwestward they fade
toward Delphi. Thus islands and bays, capes and temples, seafaring
and the oracles form one symbolic whole. As you run your hand
along the grooves of the pillars, above you the mass of the architrave,
the remnant of the procession of the Panathenaea, below you the
balustrade with the dance of the Victories, to your right the outermost caryatid of the Erechtheum, you feel that you are in the center
of a world that once meant the universe.

Never again did human hands produce in the Mediterranean
a work whose effect was felt so long as that of the Parthenon. To
this day it is copied on a small scale by architects all over the world.
Other cities—Elis, Acragas, Syracuse—built splendid temples in the
fifth century, and many have survived. The temple of Phigalia,
situated in a wild mountain landscape in the midst of the Peloponnesus, is even better preserved and more romantically situated.
Why has the idea of the Acropolis nevertheless been wholly iden-
tified with Athens, so that most people do not even know that many
other acropolises exist? Why was this particular temple-fortress received into the innermost shrine of humanity, like the names of
three or four of its prophets?

Because a thousand years of civilization culminate here, and each drum-shaped marble block that was piled on the next in building the gigantic, tapering columns is a monument to the spirit which created that civilization and held it together. Because here the power of the state and a sense of beauty have merged, as they do in the Doges' Palace in Venice and the Palazzo Farnese in Rome, or in the old Seraglio in Istanbul. Here, however, it is deepened by a third force, the religion of the gods. A Persian king burned down the old temples that once stood here. Then the victor over the Persians built the Long Walls that joined and sheltered Athens and her harbor. Now the time had come to cap the useful with the beautiful, and the necessary with abundance.

Only then (about 450 B.C.), neither before nor after, could the Acropolis be built anew; only Pericles could venture to spend three million dollars in building there—a sum worth perhaps three hundred million today. Even his pace was modern, for without the aid of our modern cranes and machinery the Propylaea was built in five years, the Parthenon in nine, whereas the building of the great pyramids near Cairo is supposed to have taken between fifty and a hundred years. The reconstruction that modern Athens is carrying out with the help of Rockefeller's money and modern machinery has already taken more than twenty years and is not finished yet. Further, all this was done in a completely new style, quite unknown as little as thirty years before.

Five hundred years after the completion of the Acropolis, Plutarch wrote these fine words: "Judging by its beauty, each one of these works of Pericles might have been considered old then. Judging by its perfection, each one is still new and fresh to look upon today. An ageless soul seems to live in them." Thus a genius seventeen centuries ago foresaw what we confirm today.

The amazing thing is that whereas Greek tragedy was fundamentally the product of three brains, and even the Homeric poems could have come from but a small group of poets, the buildings, sculptures, and vases of the Greeks sprang from countless hands and the four or five celebrated names represent thousands of unknowns to whom the monument is due. as to an Unknown Soldier. It was the common cultivation, the general level, that lifted the Greek people above all others. Democritus, the universal genius, could state as an axiom: "Cultivation is an adornment in good fortune, a refuge in misfortune."

But at the same time they were all filled with a craving for glory. "You see," said Diotima to Socrates, "how people strive to become immortal. They are all willing to sacrifice property, children, every kind of happiness, willing to die for it. Or do you seriously believe that Alcestis died on account of Admetus, or Achilles on account of Patroclus? They well knew that the memory of their virtues would live forever."

It is all the more astounding, then, that thousands labored together in Athens for beauty's sake, although the glory gathered around only a few names. Obviously Phidias did not carve the statue of Athena all by himself, far less the marble frieze of the Panathenaea, several hundred yards long. If he planned and supervised the whole, he certainly was not much closer to the details than Pericles, who in turn worked with Phidias in designing the frieze.

Far more survives from the master hands of Michelangelo in Florence and Rome than could ever be proved the handiwork of Myron, Phidias, or Praxiteles.

Throughout the ages the genius of the people builds temples and cathedrals with the aid of unknown architects, from Egyptian Thebes and Athens to Strasbourg. The very anonymity of the Acropolis shows the rich endowment of the Athenians as much as the art and artisanship that emerged and the criticism and public opinion that influenced the progress. All of this was crowded into the short intervals between continual wars. Pericles, who knew the malice and ingratitude of his people, tried in vain to safeguard his friend Phidias by having him weigh out every ounce of gold that he was going to apply to the garment of the goddess Athena. But in the end the master was prosecuted for theft after all, and perished in prison. Ictinus, the architect, had to flee, and Pericles himself almost lost his life at the very end in a scandalous trial.

It is typical of the Athenian mind that the trials of Phidias and

Aspasia, Pericles's friend and his mistress, were begun almost together, for in both of them he, the head of the state, was really the
accused. Aristophanes went so far as to blame the start of the
Peloponnesian War, which Pericles had so long delayed, upon the
dictator's wrath at the trials. The Athenians accused Pericles of
ordering Phidias to portray him on the shield of Athena as a bald
old man. This was certainly unlikely, considering that Pericles hid
his long skull with hair and helmet throughout his life. And Pericles's accusers wanted to know where the money had gone that he
and Phidias had embezzled in making the statue—where except to
the wench Aspasia?

Yet the marvelous interpenetration of state and culture, which
is the secret of Greek history, was never more forcefully shown
than during those years. It was all concentrated here, for fundamentally the flowering of Athens lasted but forty years, just as did
the Renaissance in Italy two thousand years later.

Salamis was won, and Pericles was the victor in a practical sense,
simply because the Greek wise men all started with matter—one
with water, one with fire, a third with earth, a fourth with air.
They it was, two thousand years before Kant, who cleared the path
to transcendental reasoning. From the multiplicity of phenomena
the Greeks derived unity of idea. This was how they could safely
keep so many gods.

XIX

A MAN CLIMBING the Acropolis in the year 440 and sitting down on
the steps of the Parthenon, then almost completed, amid the pound-
ing and shouting of the thousand workmen, could easily have seen
in one glorious hour half a dozen men who meant Athens then
and the world's glory thereafter. Such congruence of immediate
and after fame in one group is unique in history. Invariably either
genius is unrecognized in its own time or the successful man is forgotten by posterity. The Athenians recognized genius and after-

ward avenged themselves by rejecting it; but then came history to pick it up again with a smile.

Slowly three men are mounting the high steps of the Propylaea. One of the two bearded ones, who seem to be about fifty years old, is showing a third, younger man what is finished and what still planned. Pericles, walking in the middle, seems to be the master in every sense, the more so as he tries not to be brilliant. More of a king than a god, still he has the Olympian calm that is chiefly expressed in eye and intonation. And he knows very well why he is giving his time to the stranger at his left, who often stops at Athens on his great voyages. This man has an inquisitive way of looking around and swiftly combining remote elements. He sees and hears everything, instantly filing it away in his infallible memory. This is Herodotus, and Pericles is very much concerned to cut a good figure in his books, which the author sometimes reads aloud to the people. Every cultivated Athenian tries to get hold of a manuscript copy.

Silent and rather apart the third man climbs, a figure with a hero's face, whom one would take for a general sooner than Pericles if a deeply wrinkled brow did not betray the thinker. Long-headedness he has in common with Pericles, though not to so abnormal a degree, and also the short beard, but his hair is curlier, his grave mouth less indicative of earthly enjoyment. His name is Sophocles. Even as a boy he was so handsome that he led the chorus at the victory festival. In their harmonious development he and his verses are akin to Pericles. And the two have also been working together on the new constitution, for art and the state go hand in hand at Athens. For the success of his *Antigone* Sophocles is said to have received a high command in war. This poet is just as much a man of action as the statesman is a thinker, and the building of the temple is an event that will fix the later careers of both. For the thought of glory is ever present in the poet's mind, too, and perhaps this very morning he is pondering his Ode to Herodotus, which he has yet to write down.

At the top, Phidias comes out of the noisy crowd to meet them,

and with him the most interesting woman in Athens. He has been showing Aspasia sketches for the carving of the Caryatids. Pericles, Plutarch tells us, used to kiss her on the brow at each meeting. This woman of no name or family, who called herself simply Aspasia, the beloved, had found Pericles at his prime, twenty years her senior. Following Athenian custom he thought little of leaving his wife, since only the hetaerae counted for anything in society. Obviously a man born to rule alone could never endure a second great mind around him if it were a man.

Up here Herodotus is very much the man of the world as he speaks to Aspasia, but at the same time, being analytically gifted, he watches every muscle in Pericles's face. All of them, these four great men and the wisest of women, know that they are now standing before the people, and that their encounter will be discussed this evening in the town.

Phidias's manner is that of a host, and he is far too conscious of his prodigious capacities to dance attendance on the head of the state. On the contrary, the way he singles out Aspasia in talk is a matter of careful calculation. In the eyes of the people it is advantageous to him, to her, and to Pericles.

Undoubtedly he has noticed at some distance, talking to an unknown youth, the man with the musician's head whom all Athens calls the rising star in the theater of Dionysus. He is Euripides, who recently won the prize by daring to put a woman on the stage for the first time. Now he has come over from Salamis and is watching the progress of the building with a critical eye. The young man next to him is casting no less searching glances at Herodotus, the Greek guest from abroad. He is devoured with ambition to become a great historian himself, or better yet a great statesman—Miltiades and Herodotus in one. His name is Thucydides. Since both he and Euripides are some twenty years younger than their rivals yonder, they stay apart from the other group in a mood compounded of arrogance and respect. Both artists find their confrères too classical; both are more concerned than their elders with the weaknesses and passions of mortals, and probably the group of four is too robust for their taste.

At a distance from them a man of thirty is sitting among the laborers on the north side. Beneath his monstrous cranium are a pug nose and a mouth that smiles often, shaded by a short brown beard. All the workmen are sitting on the scattered blocks of marble, dangling their legs, gazing down into the valley. They turn to look at the man in the middle only when he asks one of his queer questions. Then one man will laugh suddenly and another will

look at him mistrustfully, for the man with the nose always steers
a course halfway between mockery and benevolence. This is Socrates, who both embarrasses and amuses everyone with his com-
monplace yet damnably penetrating questions.

Perhaps with all his sharpness he has not noticed the young student who has crept in among the men to watch him from close at
hand. His eye is much keener, his malice much more tart; young
though he is, he will allow no great man near him. So he discovers
weaknesses everywhere and seems to record them in his head. This
is no lover of mankind like Socrates, no worshiper like Herodotus,
no rhapsodist like Sophocles, no sculptor like Phidias. This is the
great caricaturist without whom Athens would not be Athens; this
is the Aristophanes to be, who will soon put them all on the stage
in farce and thus immortalize them better than the poets and historians round about.

Suddenly a group of youngsters comes bounding across the
hilltop, playing catch, tumbling over the stone slabs, whooping,
screeching, and laughing. They are led by a boy who leaps the
most wildly of them all and is so beautiful with his flying curls
that all the grave men turn to look at him. For a matter of seconds
the boy holds the eyes of the two poets, of the two historians, of
Aspasia and Phidias, even of Pericles; then he is gone, and they
all return a trifle absently to their conversation.

And that was the ten-year-old Alcibiades.

XX

AT THIS TIME, and indeed throughout the two great centuries of
Athens, Sparta scarcely produced a single intellect of consequence
—not an idea, not a work of art. Physicians and philosophers,
rhapsodists and orators went out from Athens to all the colonies
of the Mediterranean, and some of the great names came from
the Greek coast of Asia Minor and Sicily. Athens was the seat
of the ancient book trade, and Plato soon founded his Academy
there. Meanwhile the military state of Sparta was in darkness.
While Pericles was exploring natural philosophy with Anaxagoras

and arguing ethics with Protagoras, Sparta literally closed her frontiers to wisdom, the drama, and music. Near the very center of world civilization as it was, the soldier nation punished anyone who dared talk philosophy instead of practicing gymnastics and marksmanship. Meanwhile the Athenian youths were also learning gymnastics and marksmanship, rowing and fighting like their heroic forefathers.

Perhaps Pericles could have altogether avoided the war with Sparta that he so long put off if the Athenians, impatient of his thirty-year reign, jealous and fond of innovation, had not stirred up revolts and lawsuits, in the hope of getting rid of their outworn leader. Then as in our own day parties united to overthrow the man who stood above parties. Radicals and aristocrats prosecuted first the philosopher, then the architect, then the beloved of Pericles; they banished the first, allowed the second to die in prison, and would have seized even Aspasia if the lord of the state had not barely managed to save her by a superhuman effort—even, it is said, by his tears. Apparently Pericles, menaced himself in the end, took refuge in war, like other dictators when harassed from within.

Relying on the naval superiority of Athens and her impregnable walls, which would be compared today with the Maginot Line, he believed he could still avoid war. But he found himself blockaded by the Spartans, who advanced under various pretexts. He had to give up parts of Attica to their invading hordes; after their withdrawal he was already regarding himself as saved when the plague laid low a quarter of all the people who had fled to Athens. Confusion. Charges of embezzlement were laid against the head of the state, whereas actually he had accumulated the greatest hoard of any treasury in ancient history, nearly ten million dollars. Deposition, suffering, sadness, melancholy. Upon the next invasion of the enemy, recall—and then death by the plague.

The Peloponnesian War went on with varying success for twenty-seven years, and brought Alcibiades, then a man in his middle thirties, briefly into power fourteen years after the death of Pericles.

In Alcibiades, whose character we lack space to consider here,

Athens once more showed the Mediterranean world a genius that became immortal, like those of his greater predecessors. He was both fascinating and hated for his beauty and grace, his wit, his cynicism, and his extravagance. His character and talents remind us of Lord Byron or d'Annunzio in modern times. Needing a victory to satisfy the war-weary Athenians, he organized a campaign against Sicily, or in other words a new fratricidal war between Greeks. He undertook this venture with the amazing number of 134 vessels. When he was recalled by the judges of Athens, more scheming than just, who always had a puritanical accusation in readiness, much as the English felled Byron and Wilde, he ran away to the Spartan enemy. The madness of a colonial war in a remote quarter was repeated, while Sparta threatened close at hand on shore. Athens was beaten, and Alcibiades enthusiastically restored—and deposed once more after his first defeat. He fled northward, entered into intrigues with the Persians, and was murdered.

If Pericles was immortalized by buildings through whose colonnades his name still echoes like the pedal note in a fugue, Alcibiades also owes his fame to art, for Plato introduced him in his *Dialogues*. But he and Plato alike circle about Socrates, the fixed star of their era, who was even supposed to have saved Alcibiades's life in battle. For Socrates loved this pupil, twenty years his junior, although the youth jeered at the virtues the wise man preached. Nothing shows more movingly the paradoxical nature of the Athenian world and the way its weaknesses grew from its talents, eventually bringing ruin, than this friendship, which ended with the violent death of both men, but in very different surroundings.

The long war ended with Alcibiades.

Now the Spartans, under the iron discipline that was the sole idea of their state, marched into the Piraeus. Then they camped on the Acropolis and tore down the Long Walls. Taking the navy away from the defeated enemy, they demanded the surrender of all colonies, forced the Athenians to enter the confederation under Spartan leadership, and overthrew democracy in Athens by appointing a few men to control the government.

Then as now the barbarian fell upon the vanquished without

bringing him a single new idea. And the reasons for the downfall of a weary people likewise resembled those characteristic of our own day. Democracy, having ruled Athens for fifty years, had long since grown rotten inside. The proletarians, that is, the majority, had received concessions from Pericles; his juries (which were at the same time judgeships) were thrown open to the poor, then predominantly the uneducated as well, while the rich kept to themselves. A separate class of sycophants, shyster lawyers, arose to represent the people. As a matter of fact Athens came to glory not through but in spite of her democracy, which however finally caused her downfall. Pericles really toyed with the common people who thought they were governing through him. For that form of constitution the fifth century B.C. was much too early. How, indeed, could a true democracy develop in an ancient state that had citizens, foreigners, and slaves—three classes of inhabitants with completely differing rights? Because Athens was not a true democracy she fell a victim to autocratic Sparta.

The only man to live through the whole war and see its end was Socrates, friend of the people and enemy of democracy. The fact that he won the greatest fame of ancient times, even greater than Alexander's, is due entirely to his death. Among the men of the Mediterranean, who philosophized so much upon death and life, Socrates was alone in going voluntarily to his death, simply for the sake of truth, or, we might say, as a gentleman.

The suicides of Brutus, Antony, and others were merely the acts of gamblers who, having lost, saw nothing but slavery ahead. Even Seneca wanted to escape the collapse of his happiness, and Empedocles, the philosopher, who is said to have hurled himself into the crater of Etna, was settling his account as a pessimist. Caesar fell fighting against cowardly murderers. Jesus called upon God at last to save Him. Of them all, Socrates alone freely forwent escape, in spite of his natural bent for living. He was, we must remember, twice as old as Jesus. The jurors indicated to him that he had only to flee, like the others. He was not painfully ill, and he did not need Athens, for all men were equally suited to his investigations, which he hoped still to pursue in Hades. He anticipated the moral foundation of Jesus' teaching, and lived it straight through to the end.

If Greek history had bequeathed to us no document of beauty and wisdom but Plato's *Apology of Socrates the Athenian,* that alone would be enough to lift Athens above all the later civilizations of the Mediterranean. But at the same time the malice and bitterness of the Athenians become a symbol in Socrates's glorious end.

For how did all these great men perish? Not one fell in battle. None died young. In fact they almost all lived to be much older than their energies and accomplishments would lead one to suppose. The dramatists: Aeschylus, sixty-nine; Euripides, seventy-seven; Aristophanes, about sixty-three; Sophocles, ninety. The statesmen: Pericles, seventy; Aristides, about eighty. The philosophers: Socrates, seventy-one; Anaxagoras, seventy-two; Herodotus, seventy-six; Pythagoras, about seventy-six; Plato, eighty; Isocrates, ninety-nine. Nor is it true that the Greeks preferred death in youth. From Homer on, the wish is always for a gentle death in old age.

Yet if we pick out the greatest Greeks, representing the flower of a hundred and fifty years, chiefly in Athens, just one among seventeen—Sophocles and perhaps Aeschylus—was allowed to develop his talents unhindered. The fate of the other sixteen shows the revolt of the community against genius. These Greeks died between 456 and 322 B.C., all between their fifty-fifth and seventy-fifth year, and all under persecution:

Aristides was banished for five years in his old age, and then pardoned. Themistocles, banished, died in a hostile land. Pericles was accused and deposed. Phidias died in prison. Ictinus fled and died among the enemy. Anaxagoras, condemned to death, died in exile. Pythagoras, banished, probably starved to death. Herodotus died in exile. Euripides, who was virtually expelled, died abroad. Thucydides went into voluntary exile. Alcibiades—the only young one—was banished and murdered. Socrates was condemned to death. Plato was first sold into slavery and later freed. Aristotle, accused, fled and died far from home. Demosthenes, persecuted, took poison.

The last two were driven out more by events than by their fellow citizens. Right in the midst of the democracy under which the others rose and fell, we see the spite and impatience, the jealousy and ingratitude of the Greeks. It seems as if Faust and Mephistopheles were in league to make the nation of thinkers and artists demoniacally destroy what had created them. It is a blessing for the world that the Greeks' sense of beauty prevented them from finally destroying the works along with the artists.

XXI

Music is of all arts the most sensuous; it has accompanied the love stories of all ages, from the Egyptians' to the films of our own day. But it remains intangible, floating in air, and is wafted away more utterly even than poetry, whose ideas can be retained and even scrutinized. Nor can a picture be handled, nor can more than a tiny fraction of a building. Statues alone can be felt.

The Hermes of Praxiteles tempts men and women alike to stroke his foot. He stands at Olympia, where he was discovered only sixty-five years ago, but he is in a dull museum, and it can hardly be the surroundings that fascinate us. Still he is the one Greek marble statue that has unquestionably come down to us from classical times. Some decorative and later works are original, and probably some bronzes. But all the statues we see on the pedestals in the museums of the world, adorned with a great name and studied by scholars and collectors in the past four centuries, are copies. Even the decorative friezes, such as that of the Parthenon or of Phigalia, are studio works executed by unknown hands, scarcely by a Phidias or a Myron. The invoices for the Acropolis tell us that these unknown artists received the equivalent of fifteen dollars per statue, whether of man or horse. But Hermes as he stands at Olympia, without his right arm (which some professor afterward restored, affronting the statue), is the one piece of Pentelic marble embodied in a work of art that we can actually touch, something chiseled by a master's hand in the fourth century. When it was dug up, the resurrection of

Greek beauty after its long sleep occurred. Hermes arose like a sort of Messiah, long heralded. No doubt there are male statues of equal physical beauty, for instance, the Delphian Charioteer, or the so-called Hermes Psychopompus, but the former is cast in bronze, and the latter is a late Roman copy.

Each expert calls a different work genuine, but no other work has the sensuous delicacy of this Hermes. Its suggestive power is so strong that we feel we have touched a foot of flesh, not stone. If we must try to capture physical beauty in words rather than in music, we may perhaps describe the masculine ideal of the Greeks as *natural grace*. For despite all differences of expression this quality remains dominant, from the Athens of Pericles to Pompeii, from Polycletus to the artists of Pergamum. Aristotle, who considered every possible shape of nose or mouth beautiful, taught that there was no typical Greek beauty. And indeed why attempt a definition? If we see a young man approaching along the beach and someone calls him a Greek god, everyone knows what is meant.

This natural grace was possessed by the Romans only when they were copying the Greeks. They are separated from anonymous beauty by the fact that they excelled in portraiture. Even Alexander was too pronounced a personality to be a Greek ideal.

Perhaps the secret is that the Greeks, and the Greeks alone, created their gods altogether in their own image, and never idealized them. "If lions could paint," Xenophanes wrote, "they would paint their gods as lions." For this reason a Greek statue of a god never was more beautiful than one of a mortal. We say of a beautiful girl, "Doesn't she look like Diana?" A Greek, seeing a statue of Diana, would say to himself, "She is really as lovely as my Phryne."

If anyone in Athens had ever dared to represent so horrid a being as the Egyptian deities with their animal heads or the Indian goddesses with their twenty breasts or the Nordic gods, of whom one is one-eyed and another one-handed, he would have been lynched. The gods in Greece were neither super- nor sub-human; they did everything just like mortals, only better, more easily. They too had their faults and made their mistakes. They did not always foresee the future, and they were subject to Fate. According to Homer,

Zeus once feared that Achilles might capture Troy sooner than his calendar called for. The Greek was never grateful to the gods for making him happy; instead the gods thanked him for being happy. They could not endure an unhappy man.

And what was happiness? If we inquire into the teachings of all the Greek philosophers through five centuries on the subject of happiness, we find a reiteration of health, slumber, glory, beauty, cultivation, friendship, a painless death at an advanced age. The Greek gods were so human that they even envied and persecuted happy mortals. Only Dionysus, who is considered Asiatic, was more savage and dangerous than the rest; hence his Mysteries.

If a people invents remote and vengeful gods—no matter whether there be several, as among the Egyptians, one, as among the Jews, or two, as among the Christians—fear or veneration will fix the image of those deities. The Greeks too tried to bribe their gods. Indeed they were more superstitious than most other peoples. But the abundance of their myths, their animating of all the elements, plants, and animals, brought their deities closer to them and prevented the erection of the great barrier that divides other votaries from their gods. The perpetual interest of the Greek gods in their mortals, without whom they would have been bored to death, determined the mystic as well as the idyllic aspect of their religion. It made all these gods much more real and present, through their hundred everyday images, than any single invisible god can ever be when rendered omnipresent by an abstract idea alone.

For this reason the Greek religion is the only one possessing neither a theology nor any written documents, not even at Delphi. Protagoras, the first Sophist, who was only a little older than Socrates, dared to write: "About the gods I can say nothing, neither that they exist nor that they do not exist, nor what their nature is. Many things prevent us from knowing this—the obscurity of the subject and the brevity of human life." No greater scope has ever been allowed to imagination. Everyone could invent his own gods, and did.

The fact that the images were mostly masculine is partly explained and partly caused by pederasty. Since all the artists—even the actors—were men, they naturally chose to portray the naked male body. The number of nude female statues is very small. Almost all of them conceal their charms, whereas the youths display them; even the Amazons wear clothes. The first exceptions, like the Venus of Milo and the recently discovered torso of the Aphrodite of Cyrene, are from a late period. The celebrated nude Niobid in the Thermae museum at Rome, the only piece from the classical period, is merely an isolated case proving that the Greeks could do everything. But their passion was the portrayal of the male body. They carried it so far that the legendary Phaeacians had living boys as gilt torchbearers in the palace of Alcinous. Plato says there would have been no Greek philosophy without such beautiful boys in Athens; it was only the sight of them that produced a sort of intoxication in the soul of the wise man.

In women too beauty was everywhere preferred to morality. Even such perpetual virgins as Atalanta, the huntresses, and the Amazons usually wound up in a love affair after all. The fidelity of Penelope, even if credible, found no counterpart in her consort Odysseus, who amused himself for years with nymphs and kings' daughters and was obviously glad he did not have to go home right away. No such thing as unhappy love existed among the Greeks. How could a people who devised so varied a love life for its gods demand renunciation from its own women? Love, beauty, and glory—this was the trinity of Greek virtues.

The Greeks embodied their political and cultural ideas in temples, statues, and tragedies. Daily life is portrayed in comedy, and especially on the vases, which might be called the photographs of the Greeks. For a gifted people with so much time and so much gaiety it was easy to paint everyday scenes on the vases. Cheap and plentiful, often valueless, sometimes costly, hundreds of them have been preserved whole, and hundreds of thousands have survived in fragments. If we were to put them all together, photograph them, and bind them into a book, we should have a regular Baedeker of later Greece; the earlier is perfectly reflected in Homer.

Here girls are bathing in honor of Dionysus, others are just completing their toilet with salves, others are gossiping at the lion-headed fountain. We see their wine jugs and bowls, textile patterns and fabrics, couches and chairs; if a woman holds a drunken man's head at dinner while he vomits, of course someone is there to sketch it. Here are the departure for the hunt, the putting on of armor, training in posture and dancing, and a hundred scenes of seafaring and seaports. None of it is rigid, nothing classical, and above all nothing godlike, although often great gods' names are written below these little girls and pretty boys. There are a hundred caricatures of old age, of suffering, of avarice, of sloth, of drunkenness; all Aristophanes is on the vases, plus an anticipated Rabelais, Molière, and Frans Hals.

Yet these were the Greeks who built a shrine to their arch enemy Philip after the battle at Segeste, simply because he was so handsome. These were the Greeks who had Adonis, because of his beauty, dividing up his life to spend half the year with Aphrodite, half with Persephone. These were the Greeks who did not set fire to captured Rhodes for fear of bringing harm to a painting by Protogenes located in the endangered quarter of the city. These were the Greeks who acquitted the aged Sophocles simply because at his trial he recited to them a new song glorifying his homeland.

XXII

IF WE CONSIDER the year 400 B.C., we find three symbolic events grouped closely about it: the Spartan invasion of Athens, a new Carthaginian invasion of Sicily, the Celtic invasion of Italy. Culture was assaulted from all three quarters. In east, west, and north various forms of force or barbarism, military science and wealth were victorious over civilization.

The invasion from the north remained without influence, and that of the Carthaginians left scarcely a trace. Even Sparta, conquering the greatest stronghold of civilization in the ancient world, remained with all her victories still outside the gates of the vanquished. The walls of Athens, which the victor destroyed, were rebuilt a decade later. Within twenty-eight years Sparta was being beaten at sea by a resurrected Athens. While Sparta even during the first years of victory was brooding in her dull, vacant, rigidly military world, Plato in Athens was founding his Academy, and soon afterward Praxiteles began carving immortal sculpture.

No warlike nation has ever been able in the long run to subjugate an intellectually superior people. The brilliance of Athens, the summit of all ancient Mediterranean civilization, outshone victorious Rome through centuries, while Roman arms could only overshadow Athens. At this point, about 400 B.C., the two old peoples, Carthaginians and Greeks, were struggling for power. But their fight to a finish was confused and finally nullified by the appearance and slow growth in strength of a third Mediterranean power—the Romans.

The wars between Greeks and Carthaginians were bound to break out over the great islands that halve the Mediterranean. When the two civilizations collided in Sicily, the Carthaginians were fighting for the colony closest to home, the Greeks for a very remote one. In the nature of things the Carthaginians were much more deeply interested in Sicily, only three days away. As seafarers these merchants had a sort of historical right to the island; the Greeks had only the aspirations of a nation grown into a universal power and accustomed to preempting all important harbors and coasts. The shifting fortunes of these two masters of the Mediterranean as they fought for Sicily prove that neither Greek nor Carthaginian commercial spirit was predominant. The deciding factor was rather the type of vessel, for against the originally Corinthian trireme the Carthaginians sent the quadrireme—the four-banked galley against the three-banked.

The deeper cause of the struggle lay in the nationalist pride that had possessed the Athenian younger generation. As always, the idle young heirs were more arrogant than their worthier forefathers. Pericles had never striven for world dominion, but even Themistocles had already been on the way to nationalist megalomania and had named one of his daughters Italia. The young hotspurs under Alcibiades seized upon the outcry of the Sicilians, hard pressed by the Carthaginians, as a pretext, and even began to talk of con-

quering Carthage. In such a frame of mind, in the very midst of
the Peloponnesian War, threatened by Sparta, inadequately prepared, between an inwardly shattered homeland and a frightened
and divided colony that really belonged to no one, the Athenians
were bound to fail utterly in their expedition to Sicily, about 413 B.C.

But the Sicilians, divided into a multitude of city-states, did not
want to be Carthaginians either. They were like the Alsatians,
dragged to and fro for centuries between Germany and France,
and resentful of both in the end. Incessant wars, particularly between Carthage and Syracuse, and new Greek thrusts about 350,
brought on conspiracies, murders, and the victory of scattered
tyrants. The central figure of the era was Dionysius, tyrant of Syracuse, who about 400 established a Sicilian empire as powerful as
Athens, taking in Corsica and half of Italy, to the mouth of the Po.
By his passion for culture we can recognize him as a true Greek,
and he would have had a great place in history if there had been
poets and artists around him as there were around Pericles. Even
today the mutilated lion heads on the mighty walls of his fortress
castle of Euryalus look out over the plains of Sicily.

And yet the first Dionysius, with all his great victories and successes, is remembered only for Plato's attempt to govern jointly with
him. Plato's letters from Syracuse show for all time that statesman
and philosopher may perhaps some day be united in a single soul
but that they cannot work together in two persons. Dionysius had
more intellectuality, respect, hospitality, and craving for glory than
the emperors and popes of later centuries offered to their artistic
companions. Besides this, Plato was more determined to carry
through his idea. Never was a philosopher less platonic than Plato.
He alone, during the first half of his life, was not satisfied with the
contemplation of platonic ideas. He wanted to accomplish; he
wanted to achieve a new state, a new idea; he wanted truly to govern
on behalf of culture.

His letters and his final departure show how completely he
failed. He could not achieve even remotely what he himself called
the second-best state. The vanity of his ruler, who kept wanting to
be praised for his veneration of the philosopher, and the distraction

of rulers in general, were things that Plato described in words still striking to any thinking man who hopes to influence the mighty:

"There is a way to find out whether anyone is inspired by the holy flame of philosophical living and thinking, particularly in the case of powerful men who have a few random scraps in their heads, as I discovered on arrival at Syracuse. One must show these gentlemen what it means to study something solid. In this way one may test personages who can endure no exertion or sustained effort, so that they may not afterward put the blame on their guides, but on themselves and their sloth."

When we see this greatest mind of his age shut into the palace garden, which he was not allowed to leave without orders from the tyrant, when we learn that he was in danger of being murdered, while all the time he kept receiving proofs of royal favor, we can understand better Corneille's position under Richelieu, Michelangelo's under Julius II, or Voltaire's under Frederick the Great.

But this was not merely the morality of Plato, or even of the Greeks. True, intellect and art were exclusively on the Greek side then, and when we do find a noble Carthaginian grave monument it is a copy of an Athenian model. But there are signs of a chivalrous moral code everywhere. This was what distinguished the ancient Mediterranean world from the barbarians who pushed in from east and north, from Persia and Gaul. When all the sieges of Selinunte and Sybaris are forgotten, and no one remembers Hanno, the greatest general of his time, one gesture survives. Hanno's son, recalled from banishment to power in Carthage, renounced vengeance. He did not have his unlucky enemies killed; he publicly set his foot on the necks of the men, lying prone before him, and then released them.

We cannot distinguish the three ancient Mediterranean rivals by race, any more than we can ascribe a high moral code to any of them. The ludicrous present-day attempts to purify the blood of nations mingled from a hundred races would have been futile as early as 400 B.C. Greeks, Carthaginians, and Romans were as much a mixture of aborigines and immigrant tribes as the Mexicans today. What counted was not race but soil.

Where blood has been indiscriminately mixed through thousands of years of history, the nature of the soil remains the only constant. Just as the build of imported cattle along the Nile will always adapt itself to climate and fodder, so the peoples of the Mediterranean have always been conditioned far more by the elements than by races, which are confused and indecipherable. The elements are eternal. The bay, the harbor, the sail, the desert, the wind, the olive tree, grain, fish, change the human beings that live along a coast far more than the human beings change the coast.

This is why the assaults of the barbarians have left so little trace. Anyone who cares to amuse himself with the name Indo-German must imagine uninhabited deserts that were eventually discovered and occupied by aliens. In reality there are neither Indians nor Germans around the Mediterranean; those who live there are the aboriginal Mediterraneans, mingled with many hundreds of alien peoples. Rome has as much to do with the Germans as the animal drawings of the ice age have with Raphael: both were within the territory of the Roman Empire. All the studies of word roots, linguistic elements, potsherds, and vase paintings are as nothing compared with the power of the eye. The sight of a face in Sicily and Provence, Florence and Barcelona, Salonika and Smyrna, Haifa and Cairo, is enough to show the impartial layman that almost all these men and women have dark eyes and dark hair, resembling one another far more than any one of them does the occasional blue-eyed blonds found in Venice or in Armenia.

XXIII

ACCORDING TO LEGEND, Rome was founded on the same day as Carthage. Why did Rome win the hundred and forty year struggle?

Perhaps because it was not a coast town. Rome, less than a hundred miles from the sea, was built on a navigable river that would take the largest vessels then built up from the sea, but kept the pirates at a distance. Even today Rome enjoys the advantages of a coast city without the dangers. Since she also dominated the only military road between mountains and sea, she was able to stand off the invading Etruscans and Latins to north and south. The location forced energy and unity upon this little inland nation, educating its people as soldiers and citizens. The Athenians in the young days of their state were scattered among bays and islands, but the Roman plain could grow only bit by bit.

The earliest Romans had as much in common with the Prussians as they both had with the Spartans. But the legendary first kings of Rome were after all only presidents of a republic that was governed originally by the landholding nobility or patricians, and then by all classes together. The two consuls, who were probably elected even under the kings, corresponded with the two kings by whose jealous vigilance the Spartans tried to forestall tyranny. On the other hand, the Senate, a sort of hereditary upper house, afforded the only continuity. But at a very early date the poor rose up against oppression of any sort; with their popular assembly they built up a sort of state within the state, which very swiftly grew in power.

The Roman constitution, enduring through a thousand years on a basis of liberty and order, can be compared only with the English product, but it differs in point of form. The English based their political and business life entirely on tradition and honor, with as few written laws, injunctions, and prohibitions as possible. The Romans early recorded everything on tablets and developed legal concepts that passed from the Mediterranean to the whole western world. Even today a man in Patagonia marries his wife or inherits from his father according to the principles formulated in young Rome more than two thousand years ago. But law and justice can never flourish on a grand scale without liberty. It is evident, then, why Sparta and Prussia, with their equally stringent laws, could not conquer the world. In military discipline, frugality, and seriousness the early Romans were far more like the Spartans than the Athenians. The Romans too sacrificed culture to the state.

But not liberty. Roman loyalty to the state was not founded on compulsion from above, not on cold brutality; obedience was not an ideal, as in Sparta, but a freely granted necessity. To achieve this the Roman patricians hit upon the trick of a state religion, which until then had been effective only under the Pharaohs. The Greek imagination had peopled the world with gods. The unimaginative Roman, who could think of none for himself, took over the Greek gods, gave them different names, and set them up as symbols of his own law and justice. Probably no nation ever had so many gods and so little religion as the Romans. They established a sort of double-entry bookkeeping system with the gods, who owed them so and so much for so and so many sacrifices. How could such a people have produced statues and vases, songs and dramas such as the Greeks did?

In compensation the Romans developed their military state far beyond that of Sparta, and managed by a new device to reconcile the military and the civil authority. For cases of emergency they created an office combining both powers: dictatorship. This concept, as well as that of the imperator, likewise created by the Republic—for instance, Cicero was an imperator—represented a form of power since known through all nations and all centuries. Just as the words senator and consul have survived in many countries to this day, the dictator has descended from the fifth century B.C. But in Rome his appointment hinged on the double stipulation that the country must be in danger and that he himself must invariably hand back his power after six months to the legally constituted authorities.

The Roman people clung to and watched jealously over these rulers until the time of Sulla and Caesar; this applies to the common people even more than to the nobility, for the first plebeian was elected as early as the fourth century B.C. At the same time, small and insignificant as the Romans were, they managed by reliance on law and the structure of state to found a sort of confederation with the surrounding cities. Our modern federal states still follow its organization.

The Roman sense of statehood, built on liberty and order, became the basis for a growing world empire. For this the Romans needed no greater commercial spirit, but much stronger discipline, than the Greeks, less inventiveness but more perseverance, far fewer ideas, but much greater unity. Whereas the Greeks had only driven off the invading Persians after severe defeats, the Romans, far weaker at the time, threw back the very first assault of the barbaric Celts close outside the city. The foundations of their character, determined by situation, combined all the qualities needed to make them capable of world dominion. They lacked only one thing: seamanship.

This they learned from their rivals, the Carthaginians. Being entirely a land and military nation, still on a small scale with their army of three thousand men and three hundred horsemen, they gave way to the marauding Greeks along the coast line of their city federation as late as the fourth century. The earliest Roman document that has been preserved is an agreement to stay off the sea. A treaty with Carthage about 350 B.C. prohibited them from sailing the ocean south of Sicily. There is a second treaty, with Tarentum, which forbade them the eastern Mediterranean. Roman history, like that of so many great men and nations, begins with two defeats.

It must be remembered that these treaties were concluded just after the first barbarian invasion, that is to say, under pressure of heavy armament expenditures for land defense. The Etruscans had been broken by the invading Celts, and the Latin League was shattered. Perhaps these Italic peoples were astonished when Brennus, the barbarian leader, suddenly withdrew, marauding, instead of settling. Like Alaric and Genseric afterward, this first northerner to break in on the Mediterranean intended only to plunder, not to settle or build. What we call raw materials today were golden treasures in the temples then; and the vanquished used to be carried off as slaves.

But pagan morality when Rome made her treaty with Carthage stood far higher than it does today. The pirates were under laws that would make modern submarine captains laugh. Merchants taken at sea could not be sold as slaves in countries friendly to Rome and Carthage. An ancient Roman legal principle forbade the selling of any person into slavery in a state where he had been born or had lived as a free man.

Meanwhile, however, these and all the other struggles of the three Mediterranean peoples were outshone by a meteoric star that rose over the Mediterranean and quickly sank far to eastward.

XXIV

ALEXANDER THE GREAT was born not in the splendor of the Acropolis but in the shadow of the primeval Macedonian forests. In his childhood he saw not the owl, the bird of wisdom, but the lion. Instead of Athenian choruses and brilliant popular orators he knew wild hunting songs and masses of subject people. He saw kings and nobility ruling as in the days of Homer. His father was the first to try to bring light to this wild country, which was much like the Germany of Caesar's time. Brought up amid sinister family strife and barbaric manners, young Alexander saw his mother cast aside and remembered being assaulted by his drunken father. It even seems probable that Philip was not Alexander's father at all, which would explain why hatred and suspicion arose between father and son and why the one helped murder the other in the end. All this left its barbaric aura around Alexander's life and work, and he might easily have been no greater than Genghis Khan or Genseric, whose world empires were equally short-lived.

Instead he became one of the deathless figures of history, owing primarily to his father's unusual notion of bringing to his court one of the great thinkers of his time to tutor Alexander from the age of fourteen to seventeen. Aristotle was an envoy from the supreme civilization of the ancient world, dispatched to the home of the most abysmal barbarism. He was like a sea breeze whirling a few seeds across valleys and mountains to start a more noble growth in the depths of the primeval forest. Greek ideas prepared this son of the wilderness for deeds of reverence, magnanimity, and intellect that meant more to his imitators than the conquest of India. A leonine barbarian who had seen and done fearful things, who personally fought in all his battles and carved out decisive victories literally with his own sword, Alexander also scattered the blossoms of Greek civilization upon all the countries he conquered.

If Alexander, like his father Philip, had merely had stronger soldiers, or, like the modern barbarians, had put superior engines of war in the field, he would have been no more interesting than Genghis Khan. But by absorbing the ideas of the great nation that was his neighbor before he subjugated it, he put himself in the rare position of a conqueror combining force and reflection. Caesar and Napoleon, both of whom likened themselves to him, could copy him only in part, because both sometimes had to fight against advanced civilizations. The cultural superiority of Greece, lying so close to the primeval forests of the Balkans, had dawned even upon Philip the Macedonian, who first beat the Thebans, then offered a mild peace to the Athenians whom he had menaced. Indeed he founded a league of nations by uniting all the peoples except Sparta at the Congress of Corinth. Alien king though he was, he became president of a Greek league.

As crown prince Alexander saw all this at first hand. Indeed he decided the victory of Chaeronea by his personal daring. He saw his father, the half barbarian, summoning the Greeks to make war on the king of the Persians, who was more civilized than the Macedonian. Philip's thirst for power kept growing; his and his daughter's marriages of state ended with murder, dethronement, and more murder.

Never did a king assume power under more sinister circumstances than the dazzling Alexander. Nor did he set out to liberate the Greeks from the Persians; his purpose was to subjugate the Persians to himself. Indeed Athens and Thebes were in the act of leaguing themselves with the king of the Persians against the Macedonians. Alexander's inherited position as lord of the Greeks was so uncertain that even after a fresh victory he had to take a conciliatory attitude toward the Athenians.

Instinct and statecraft told him to spare Athens but destroy Thebes. At the downfall of that celebrated and overripe city a contemporary wrote that the moon in the firmament seemed to have been put out.

One reason for Alexander's fame was the fact that destiny allowed him so brief a time to conquer the known world; another was his physical beauty. With a less magnificent head the world would never have taken him for a Greek. He knew this, and took care to spread his propaganda through sculptors, journalists, and historians, who caught and recorded moods and anecdotes for posterity. Alexander loved fame perhaps even more than power, and his finest deeds were due less to morality than to his craving for glory. The speed and the extent of his achievements, which so astonished the world, have the pace of a man hounded by premonitions of early death and, like Napoleon, squeezing into thirteen years what Caesar distributed over twenty and Charles V over thirty.

Since Alexander set out with a plan not to conquer the world but merely to defeat the Persians, his road led him eastward. Hitherto the conquering nations, Greeks, Carthaginians, and Persians, had always turned toward the Mediterranean. Hence he no more than half belonged there. He was only in the eastern Mediterranean, and even here he did not really overstep the longitude of the Peloponnesus. But if his mission as a bearer of Greek civilization ever occurred to him during his military campaigns, it was logical to carry it eastward; in the west it had reached Massilia and Gibraltar centuries before. Alexander found the Greeks with their gods and their arts even along the shores of western Asia, and it was often doubtful whether they preferred the Macedonian armies to the Persians. They were often compelled, too, to fight as Greeks against Greeks, and what is now known as liberation from the Persian yoke was after all only a struggle between two mighty kings for dominion over peoples tossed from one iron fist to another.

The Carthaginians, at that time the only competitors of the Greeks, encountered Alexander on one of his first campaigns at Tyre, north of modern Haifa—in the mother country of Phoenicia, whence thousands fled before him to Carthage. When a Tyrian dreamed that their tutelary deity, Apollo, was about to forsake the city, his fellow citizens chained the statue to its column.

In this easternmost quarter of the Mediterranean (where Alexander spread out from the Hellespont to the Nile) he performed simultaneously the shrewdest and the most permanent of his acts.

By his mere appearance he forced the priests of Ammon to declare him the son of that god, and he founded Alexandria at the exact point where the greatest Mediterranean seaport ought to be and where for two thousand years it has remained. We may talk about engineers' advising him, but the brilliant accuracy with which this young soldier, a stranger on a desolate shore, foresaw the future and laid out a modern city, still remains to astonish us.

Alexander recognized in the uninhabited western promontory of the Nile delta what no master of Egypt before him had seen—a spot where a sheltered harbor could join Egypt to the Mediterranean. The Nile mud did not come this far down. He seemed to see before his very eyes merchants loading the grain of Egypt. He was the first to lay out straight streets, crossing at right angles, as an American would do today. He called the streets by the letters of the alphabet, as in the city of Washington, and marked sites for temples to Isis and Zeus, the competing local gods. It was only then that Egypt became a Mediterranean country. Legend reports that when Alexander sketched all this for his architects on an outdoor table covered with a layer of meal, birds came and pecked up the meal, which was considered a propitious omen.

The only part of Alexander's expedition to India by way of Persia that belongs in Mediterranean history is the story of how he brought the Greek spirit to Asia, for his world empire as an expression of power was fragmentary and impermanent. Here Alexander's dual nature is evident; no one can say whether the leonine barbarian from the forests of Macedonia conquered or yielded to the pupil of Aristotle.

Brought up to be a soldier, living a daily life that was almost one unbroken military campaign, he could not act otherwise than as Sophocles had done in battle. He always fought with his sword and usually on horseback in the front rank; so he had a moral right to kill equal to the danger he constantly defied. Killing and winning were his profession. Thus we see him on the magnificent sarcophagus that is preserved in Istanbul today. Thus he is portrayed in the mosaic of the battle of Issus, bareheaded, with flying locks, spurring his horse against the Persian king.

Alexander proved his genius in the way he managed to avert danger by alternate fighting and talking. When a conspiracy arose in the army, he shouted to the troops: "What I have won, after all, belongs to you! Syria, Egypt, Mesopotamia—all yours, comrades! *You* are the satraps, the strategoi. What have I kept for myself? I wake only that you may sleep! Show me your wounds, and I will show you mine! If you want to go, go—depart, all of you! I will let my conquered barbarians stand guard over me!" After this address he shut himself up and negotiated with the Persians. Two days later the troops sent to ask a reconciliation. There was no punishment. This was one of the moments that earned Alexander the cognomen of the Great.

Then again he would offend against the Greek moral and philosophic code to the point of megalomania. He senselessly burned down the enemy capital, Persepolis, but sent the body of Darius there so that it might be buried with royal honors. He personally caused a mutinous general to be condemned by the assembled army, but immediately afterward he had the man's innocent father, his friend, murdered. As a man of superior intellect he was fond of talking philosophy over the wine with his companions. But when his bosom friend once teased him about his divine descent, madness rose up in Alexander, whose mind was roaming beyond all bounds, and he struck his friend down. Probably both were drunk, but the scene is still etched in memory thousands of years after.

Alexander's Greek education did not protect him from this madness, which so few omnipotent men escape. Finally it reached the point where he himself actually believed in his boasted descent from Hercules, Achilles, Dionysus, and Ammon, which at first had been merely a matter of shrewd calculation. As a result he provoked his old guard into grumbling and revolt when he forced them to prostrate themselves before him in the Persian manner. His determination to combine Greek and Asiatic ways by marrying several Persian princesses himself, and at the same time having his higher officers marry women of the Persian nobility, simply confused both parties instead of reconciling them. Alexander's life should have given Napoleon a premonition of disappointments ahead.

More and more conspiracies followed. The nephew of his teacher Aristotle, invited by the king to record his deeds, spoke out too boldly about the ceremonial prostration and was killed. At that moment the barbarian from the woods of Epirus, the horse tamer, burst his glorious Greek shell. Then, and again when he introduced worship of the king into the Greek state religion, Alexander was no better than any Persian conqueror.

The importance that posterity attaches to these so-called small traits, which in reality are large traits, proves once more the transitory nature of invasion and territorial conquest. Only character portraits and the conquest of human hearts can endure. All his crossings of rivers and mountains, even his expedition to India, the pieces of eastern soil he captured, are mere signs of a dictator driven on by a tragic law, not by the mission of civilization. In the end, after a year of luxurious repose, we see him preparing to subjugate Arabia simply to close the gap in his power between Egypt and Babylon. For there is always a gap left for a world ruler to close, though it cost him his life.

Alexander ruled at last on a scale and with an imagination known to no man before or after him in human history. At a time when all means of communication, even most roads, were lacking, envoys from the southern Russian steppes met men from the sources of the Blue Nile in the antechamber of the world ruler, and along with them were Iberians, Celts, Etruscans, Romans, Carthaginians —petitioners all. At the same time his engineers were preparing plans for the circumnavigation of Arabia, the irrigation of the Euphrates country, the settlement of the islands in the Persian Gulf. In the same royal city there were architects commissioned to adorn Delos and Delphi, ancient even then, with new temples; there too were seen tragedians and actors from Greece.

Alexander died suddenly at thirty-three, after enormous but fragmentary achievements with no underlying plan.

And yet the results were immeasurable. The richest civilization and language of the era had been scattered across half of Asia and Egypt. It continued dominant among the cultivated, and to some extent also among the sailors, long after the political power of this half Greek was broken. In parts of Arabia it survived some six hundred years, in Syria and on the Nile a thousand, till the Arabian conquest. When the Romans came on the scene as world conquerors soon after Alexander's death, they found Persians and Indians existing as races, no doubt, but spread over them, like a priceless carpet, was a covering of Greek culture. Alexander had not been alone in bringing it to them, but he was the first to establish its authority in the grand manner.

And also, before the intoxication of world power seized him, he was capable of immortal gestures that proved his Greek training. In Thebes he caused the house of Pindar the poet to be spared. In Persia he treated the mother, wife, and daughter of the fugitive king as a medieval knight would have treated the women of his enemies. In Tyre he allowed the Carthaginian embassy to sail home unharmed. And at the games in Olympia he issued a proclamation ordering all the Greek cities to take back their exiles. Athens was very much put out, for the estates of political exiles there had been appropriated by others decades before. The émigrés, however, poured into Olympia to hear with their own ears the wonderful tidings of a just ruler.

And so it remains memorable for all time that a non-Greek and non-Christian was the man who broke down the frontiers between Greeks and barbarians, and suffused the intellectual heritage of Greece with the fire of a wild young tribe to protect that heritage and make it victorious over its own dissensions, its incessant civil wars.

XXV

ALEXANDRIA IS THE ONE CREATION of Alexander that has survived to the present day. Three or four other new cities, likewise adorned with his name, perished in Asia, as the sons of his body did; his wives and his mother were all killed too. Gone is the boundary stone he set up on the Hydaspes in India to show posterity how far the first king of the Mediterranean had advanced. But Alexandria was not just another port on a Mediterranean abounding in harbors.

It was a stroke of genius, a new form, the first modern city of the Old World, and at the same time a model of what harbors were to become.

It was this harbor that made Alexandria the intellectual capital of the world for the last three centuries before Christ, although Rome was much the more powerful city. It linked the three continents as no other port did. Above the harbor was the most celebrated library in history, excelling any modern institution in completeness. When it burned after three centuries, an irreplaceable monument of antiquity was destroyed, just as in the later explosion on the Acropolis. The founders were so jealous of their collection that one of them forbade the export of papyrus when Pergamum started a library.

These richest potentates of antiquity lured the great scholars with gold. Now for the first time knowledge without a purpose was cultivated and royally rewarded. Those in power did not prescribe what anyone must think or write. Alexandria rivaled and in some ways eclipsed Athens as a center of Greek thought and learning. Later Egyptians and Jews were able to expand their ideas, which were to some extent subversive, in the Library. All this went back to Alexander. The spirit and the harbor of Alexandria, two great symbols of the Mediterranean, remained his greatest creations.

Seagoing vessels and ocean trade had been modernized before the time of Alexander, and he did not really change them. As a matter of fact, he kept pulling away from the ocean, and that was why he could not establish a lasting world dominion. Centuries before his time silks from China, jewels from India, gold from the Sudan, amber from the North Sea, had been carried into the rich ports of the Mediterranean. Salt, wax and honey, grain, gold, and slaves had come to the Aegean from the northeast through the Black Sea. And Miletus, the richest of the ancient ports, vied with Tyre and other Phoenician harbors, but scarcely with the Nile delta, which was and is irregular and difficult to navigate. The Nile, greatest and most adventure-laden of rivers, had nothing to do with the Mediterranean beyond being buried there after a long life, like a great explorer dying on a journey abroad in his old age.

The best index of the popularity of the sea and everything to
do with the sea among the Greeks, even when they no longer ruled
it undisputed, comes from their coins. For coins always follow the
taste of the time. Thus on coins from Ephesus, Syracuse, Aegina,
Apollonia, Poseidonia, and many other places, we see depicted the
dolphin, the anchor, cuttlefish, sea serpents, water birds, crabs. A
celebrated Greek bowl shows Dionysus sailing a ship on whose
masts vines are growing and grapes ripening, while many dolphins
play about the boat.

The sea was and remained the real home of the Greeks, and the
famous cry that Xenophon records was a true outburst of the Greek
soul. About 400 B.C. he led his ten thousand men back to the Black
Sea, and when they caught sight of the ocean after years of adventure, they burst out shouting: "Thalatta! Thalatta! The sea at
last!" Out of the whole of Xenophon's *Anabasis,* which is inflicted
on boys at school, the one word *sea* is all that has really survived.

Since the great harbors of antiquity were at the same time the
industrial centers, the ships plied back and forth in their own little
part of the Mediterranean, somewhat as do the steamers that connect the shores of the alpine lakes. Up to about 400 B.C. all the
harbors were also naval harbors, to the extent that they were armed.
For in antiquity piracy was not merely permissible; in the early
days it was considered more manly than trading by sea. It was not
until later that the Greek gentlemen discovered the things trade
could bring them, just as the English lords were late in beginning
personally to operate mines and factories. In the days of their commercial prime the Greeks jeered at cities that did not trade by sea,
and said the inhabitants of Cyme had discovered three hundred
years too late that they were situated on the ocean.

Meanwhile they built well-contrived quays and dug their harbor
basins deeper, for ships had grown rapidly. While Herodotus in
the fifth century mentions Nile boats up to 130 tons, half a century
later there were warships of 262 tons, and at least one, a floating
fortress with superstructure and towers, like our armored cruisers.
The vessel in which Columbus made his voyages weighed but 150
tons, whereas the greatest vessel of antiquity, the third century

"Alexandria," can be estimated according to her cargo at 1,050 tons.

Along with this size went a speed that amazes us even in the Diesel age. There were Phoenician pirates who took but three days to get from Rhodes to Tyre, which means six knots an hour. The voyage around Sicily, all under sail, took a week. These vessels used oars only for turning and docking. Aristotle compares a cargo vessel under oars to an insect whose wings are too weak to carry its body. To hold these great vessels in the harbor, the captains used anchor hawsers, which were customary until almost yesterday. But there were iron anchor chains too at a very early date; apparently Alexander was the first to use them. For when he besieged the harbor of Tyre with ships moored by hawsers, the divers of the beleaguered city went under water and cut the enemy's hawsers, whereupon he put down chains. Long afterward Caesar remarked upon the anchor chains of the northern Gauls as a peculiarity.

Geography in the Mediterranean did not really begin until about 500 B.C. The Hebrews and the Argonauts about 1200 B.C., and later King Solomon and Homer, believed the earth to be a flat disk, surrounded by ocean, with Olympus as its center. This conception suddenly ceased to exist when the first maps were drawn from nature. Astonishingly enough, these were made, not *by* a barbarian, but *for* one, King Darius, by Greek scholars. About this time Himilco the Carthaginian sailed around the west coast of Europe, discovering the British Isles, but the Carthaginian government, as hidebound as any modern one could be, reproved its Columbus. Whether from jealousy or guile, it declared the Atlantic unnavigable.

Sixty years later Herodotus, with superb storytelling art, gave his people a new picture of the distant world. He arranged by significant ideas a hundred details seen or heard. In the ancient world one had to be physicist, historian, and poet all in one. Today it is rare for the same man to combine literary and scientific talent, which is why the most important works of scholarship make heavy going. Herodotus, Thucydides, Plutarch were great scholars because they discovered much, and true creative writers although they imagined nothing.

The art of map making developed with marvelous speed because the Greeks had already perfected the science of mathematics. When we think of Galileo and Kepler and the insults and the suffering they had to endure for their discovery of the solar system, we feel that mankind must have gone backward. Pythagoras and Plato alike taught the spherical shape of the earth, and Aristotle actually proved it, yet no priest lifted a hand against them. Alexander the Great, interested, like all conquerors, only in his own territories, had western Asia and India described, but not mapped.

It was only after his time, in the third century before Christ, that methodical surveying was added—the actual calculation of a given location. The high state of Greek geography is evident from a single example: Eratosthenes calculated the location of Gibraltar as 36°21′25″. We put Gibraltar at 36°0′6″.30.

Lacking the magnetic needle, ancient sailors could not set their course by points of the compass, but they recorded the foothills, peaks, reefs, and trees that indicated good or bad landings and the lofty temples that offered drinking water or shelter from the wind. The constellations, first recorded in the Mediterranean by the Phoenicians—particularly the Little Bear, much used in laying courses—could hardly be distinguished except in summer. Consequently seafaring in winter was almost at a standstill. The Greeks recognized these fundamentals of navigation so surely that the first naval school, established about A.D. 1500 in Salamanca, went back to the teachings of Euclid and Ptolemy, who had written respectively eighteen and fourteen centuries before.

If we compare the ancient with the modern market place, the difference between Athens and Paris by day is not too great. But when night fell, the ancient world became shabby and insubstantial. And indeed no modern sailor could find his way if he saw, instead of the familiar coast lit up for miles, only the black line that dully awaited the ancient dawn. Even in the biggest ports an open fire, glowing darkly red, took the place of the marvelous revolving lamp we know. The first beacon seems to have been kindled on the Piraeus about 400 B.C., atop a Corinthian column. Somewhat lower down, on a round altar, glowed the sacrificial fire to Athena. Thus the deity that protected the fire also sent her own light toward the approaching sailor, significantly symbolizing the double source of humane ideas.

But the most celebrated lighthouse of antiquity, indeed the most wonderful in the history of any sea, is the lighthouse of Alexandria—and equally astonishing is the whole port. The harbor walls ran parallel to the streets in a fashion then new. An artfully built, solid mole almost a mile long formed a double harbor, with arched entrances at the two ends. Although the eastern one did not join the waters of the Nile, it became the chief harbor because it was more easily defended. The smaller one was separate, and was defended by itself as early as the time of Antony. The big harbor had room for even the largest vessels to tie up at the dock.

The lighthouse towered at the eastern end of the long mole, and the island of Pharos, joined to shore by the mole, gave its name to the lighthouses of the world in many tongues, just as the Kaisers were all named after Caesar. This early skyscraper was 350 feet high and so built that the entrance, 50 feet above the water level, could be reached on horseback by a ramp. The noble shape of the tower, its second story octagonal, its third cylindrical, was an innovation in architecture. Being roofed over, the beacon was partly protected from rain and storm. But an open wood or pitch fire would have shone only seven miles, and so a concave mirror was constructed to carry the light twenty miles out to sea—an invention as great as the electric light.

Through sixteen centuries Alexander's tower was considered a wonder of the world. It saved the lives of countless sailors and survived all the earthquakes. About A.D. 1300 it suddenly collapsed, just as the other heritages from Greece collapsed.

XXVI

ALEXANDER HAD REMAINED A MERE EPISODE. For thirteen years the nations of the Mediterranean had trembled at his decrees and implored their gods to send him on and on to eastward, not to the west. When he was dead and his empire fell, Rome and Carthage resumed their struggles, but with far greater resources.

The inland peasant state of Rome became a sea state only under duress from Carthage, just as England became a maritime power when confronted by the Normans. Both grew by having to defend themselves, and both finally vanquished their stronger adversaries. The school of necessity teaches nations as well as individuals, and just as the greatest inventions are born not of luxury but of necessity, so too great characters grow strong in danger. It is seldom indeed that peoples or geniuses grow up, as did the Egyptians and such individuals as Sophocles and Goethe, in harmonious balance—and even in such cases the struggles are only less evident because they are internal.

When the fight for world dominion between Carthage and Rome began, to continue until Rome was victorious a hundred and forty years later, Rome possessed three advantages: she had her base in the middle of the Mediterranean, she applied her military methods to naval warfare, and above all her people were poorer. They were therefore ambitious, warlike, and self-sacrificing, whereas the rich Carthaginian merchant princes wanted to enjoy their blessings in peace and imagined themselves sufficiently protected by mercenary soldiers. Like the rich men of Manchester, who in 1900 were still trying to compete with antiquated machinery against young Germany, the third century Carthaginians clung to their crude weights from the fifth century, for they regarded tradition and monopoly as everlasting. But the time came when their Spanish customers realized that the Sicilians made better tools and more beautiful vases.

With her vast gold resources, however, Carthage, with 400,000 citizens, kept under arms enough soldiers (about 60,000) to hold the 4,000,000 natives of her African and Spanish colonies in check.

About 300 B.C., after the death of Alexander, Carthage and Rome were the only remaining world powers. The Greeks had lost in sea power as much as they had gained in cultural influence under Alexander. Such Greek adventurers as the Sicilian Agathocles had tried their luck against Carthage, invading Tunis and Utica, where no enemy had landed since time immemorial; but in the end the Greeks were beaten back here and for the most part in Sicily as well.

The reputation of Carthage grew, and many a Greek colony was glad of her protection. At that time the Carthaginian empire included the Balearic Islands, Malta, Corsica, large pieces of Sicily and Sardinia, and also Libya, half of Morocco and half of Spain—all using the Punic, that is, Carthaginian, official language. They were all subject peoples bearing the flattering title of "allies."

The Carthaginians drew their navy from all these alien races, Spaniards and Celts, Corsicans and Numidians, but the citizens went to war only when the enemy invaded their country—in other words, practically never. A "sacred host" of young dandies affected a warlike spirit, parading with gilt shields and costly armor, and showing off to the young ladies the ivory sheaths of daggers they probably never used. This army inspired terror everywhere by the use of elephants, which the Carthaginians probably got from Alexander, who was said to have brought them from the Indus. When the first war elephants appeared in Italy they won the initial Carthaginian victories by their mere appearance. At the same time they kept their own masters constantly uneasy. They were like modern allies: the general can never be sure that tomorrow morning they will not be attacking him.

The Carthaginians were feared as sailors, however, for here the century-old tradition of the Phoenicians was behind them. Their merchant ships had been transformed into the best warships, the quadriremes and quinqueremes that they were the first to build on a large scale. Aboard them even the citizens were at home, for the Carthaginian, like the Englishman, was more familiar with the oar than the lance, more devoted to any boat than to the war chariot. Their navy was so strong that in one of the wars against Rome they could lose five hundred vessels and still escape defeat. When the Romans built their first navy they used as a model a Carthaginian quinquereme that had run aground near Messina.

In these world-shaking struggles nature played a decisive part. The forests, then abundant in central Italy, gave the Romans stouter wood for shipbuilding than the Sicilian trees offered to their adversaries. Carthage was also at a disadvantage because its harbors were silting up, and therefore were more difficult to defend. How tiny and confined it all was! The traveler looking at these pitiful remains today cannot imagine how any world power could ever have centered here. The history of Carthage would have been different without its two promontories and that of Rome without the hard wood of the Campagna.

Just before the first war the two rivals, Rome and Carthage, were still fighting side by side against the Greeks in Sicily, who had summoned the Balkan king Pyrrhus to their aid. He thought himself inspired by the spirit of Alexander as he pushed swiftly forward out of the northeast, from victory to victory. But Pyrrhus, whose busts show genuinely Slavic features, was after all nothing but an adventurer without land or faith, and he quickly lost what he had won. Sicily, the loveliest pawn and center of the Mediterranean, remained in the hands of the allies. It was bound to lead to a decisive struggle eventually.

We can appreciate the fierceness of these first two Punic Wars, which covered sixty-three years, forty of them occupied with military action, from the huge figures—150,000 Romans and 400 warships. Both duration and man power overtop our modern war statistics at least tenfold when we remember the short distances and small populations of ancient times.

Why did the two nations sacrifice whole generations?

Because a younger and more vigorous national community wished to dominate the sea and shouted out the name "Mare Nostrum" for the Mediterranean after their first naval victory, at Mylae in 260 B.C. The boarding bridges that suddenly dropped from the Roman quinqueremes upon the decks of the enemy brought victory to the Romans, who had been consistently defeated for years.

Sicily became the first overseas province of young Rome, and at the same time the first granary. Syracuse, far larger and lovelier than Rome, became a Roman colony. The very Rome that hitherto had not been allowed to sail across a certain line could now compel great Carthage to reduce her colonial territory, while Rome herself established in the western Mediterranean a swiftly growing sea dominion that endured for six hundred years. With the enormous war indemnity that their rich rival had to pay, the Romans built

a new navy. The other nations along the Mediterranean did not
stir a finger while this went on. The free-for-all wars that continued
long after Alexander's successors were dead distracted energies and
attention from the rising military power. Besides, the corruption
on one hand and the prosperity on the other outweighed any common interest in keeping down the new and strong contender. Prosperity kept Egypt, in particular, perfectly tranquil; there a successor
of Alexander, the general Ptolemy, and his children after him,
reigned over the richest Mediterranean state of the third century
B.C.

But Rome, rising toward the top with every earmark of a
healthy, violent nation bent on world power, also struck eastward,
though for the moment without fighting the Greeks. Instead she
joined them against the Macedonians. When the first Roman embassy appeared in Athens and Corinth, the Greeks made Rome a
sort of junior partner: they allowed her to join in the Isthmian
games. The first Roman competitor to be received into the old
tradition of the Greeks, about the year 230, and to win a laurel
wreath, amazing the decadent onlookers, was a man who perhaps
spoke nothing but Latin. Possibly he threw the discus a little farther,
and he certainly broke the record for running, but he was in reality
the threatening messenger of the young west—the first Roman
come to herald a new age to the Greeks.

At the same time the fresh Roman strength radiated not only
westward and eastward but northward as well. To protect themselves from the attacks of the Celtic Gauls in that quarter, the Romans even made a treaty with the Carthaginians, dividing up Spain
and its silver mines and thus stirring up a second war, which produced one of the immortal figures in Mediterranean history.

Great families whose sons and grandsons have greater power
or capacities than their fathers are not so common as those whose
heirs lose their heritage. Among sculptors and musicians these upward steps from one generation to another are marvelous to see,
for works of art cannot be squandered. But in royal and commercial
houses, where it is a matter of power or money, the accumulation
is soon used up. In antiquity such families were to be found but

rarely among kings, and never among self-made men, for Augustus was not Caesar's son, and the second Pompey was scarcely a great man.

But Hamilcar, Hasdrubal, and Hannibal have entered into the storehouse of mortal memories, although other sons of the family did their part but ill. The lion's brood, as their father called them, had about them an aura like Alexander's, but more somber—typical heroes of tragedy, ennobled by the failure of a magnificent design. Evidently Hamilcar, the general and party leader of the middle class in Carthage, planned the war against Rome and taught his son what the son accomplished. He must have had some premonition of departure, for he made nine-year-old Hannibal swear to carry out his plans.

The fierce wars that the Carthaginians had to fight against rebellious tribes in Libya and Morocco, and the victories Hamilcar won there, at last taught him the perils of Roman expansion. He had brawled with the Romans at sea for decades, from one island to another, along the coast and in harbors. Now he hit upon the idea that the oldest seafaring power should attack the youngest by an immensely roundabout way—by land. He spent years in Spain building up his base of operations, and when he was killed in combat there the leadership shortly fell to Hannibal, his twenty-five-year-old son.

Just a century after Alexander's first victories, Hannibal might well compare himself with the Macedonian so far as youth went. He too was an heir, though not a crown prince. Whether he was as handsome is uncertain, for the Naples bust bearing his name certainly is not a likeness of him. Slightly built, a daring horseman and swordsman, this young half barbarian, like Alexander, grew up in army camps and like him had enjoyed Greek education, from a Spartan. In faithlessness Hannibal seems to have outdone any Greek tyrant, but at the same time he is portrayed as more humane than his Roman antagonists, and he seems to have abolished human sacrifices. Perhaps the Spartan taught him the art of handling men, at which he was so conspicuously successful. In single combat and strategy he could have had no better teacher than his father. Both

father and son must have had a historical sense for the mortal combat of two great nations, and must have felt themselves chosen for
victory in it. Both were filled with thoughts of honor and revenge
because Rome had taken away their authority in Africa and furthermore had snatched the island of Sardinia by demands and threats
in time of peace.

Anyone who would dream in 218 B.C. of taking a great army
across the Alps and the Apennines to push from Spain through
Gaul to Italy, must have been no less daring than Alexander in the
Caucasus. The surprise of the Italians was great, particularly because
the Alpine slopes did not yet belong to the Italic League but were
in the hands of Celtic tribes. Apparently Hannibal crossed over the
same Saint Bernard pass that Napoleon used two thousand years
later. But the snow of the passes then was trodden by elephants, even
less accustomed to winter than the half-Spanish mercenary soldiers,
who were familiar with the Sierra Nevada.

The shadow of these elephants as they crossed the Rhone on
rafts and then swayed through the Alpine pass has etched itself on
the memory of mankind. They are shown on an ancient platter,
carrying towers from which two armed men peer out, as if from
modern tanks. This crossing stirred even Livy and other enemy
historians to enthusiasm, for what hazards the fantastic African
had to fear! How many of these beasts that he dared to lead like
demons from a strange continent succumbed to the climate or
plunged into the abyss from paths that only a mule could follow!
In twenty-six days Hannibal led some forty thousand men from
the Rhone to the vicinity of Turin, and he lost more than half of
them in battle against natives at first horrified, then venomous. This
Alpine-crossing, which makes the dangers of Bonaparte's expedition
pale in comparison, finds its match in Bolivar's crossing of the
Andes in 1815.

The second picture that remains to us from this war is Archimedes at Syracuse, destroying Roman vessels from shore with his
burning-mirrors and his catapults, and then asking the Roman
soldier who would kill him for a few minutes' grace to solve a
mathematical problem. The third picture is the pincers that Hanni-

bal invented, the new battle array with which he surrounded and
annihilated at Cannae a Roman force of twice the strength of his
own.

What a galaxy of dramatic scenes! That war needs a volume
of its own. The finest scene of all is the world combat focusing in
the single combat of two youths. For Scipio the Roman was eighteen
when he first saw Hannibal, his great enemy, victorious at the
Ticinus. Scipio too was his father's pupil, and afterward had to
avenge him when he fell in a Spanish war. This darling of women,
with his romantic features and long curls, behaving and being
treated like a matinee idol, radiated as much brilliance as Hannibal.
And each praised the other as if they had been troubadours.

The other events of the seventeen years' war that raged through
Italy—victorious Hannibal halted at the last moment before Rome,
then wearied, delayed, and left in the lurch by his bungling brothers,
finally going home gray-haired, urging his people to make peace,
and leaving his country, a disappointed exile—this is a tragedy of
a great general that Shakespeare forgot to write. What history has
preserved is the tenacity, the self-sacrifice of the Romans and their
skill at learning from the enemy. Once they had copied the Carthaginian warships; now they learned Carthaginian tactics, and with
them beat the enemy in Spain and Africa until the deposed leader
and hero, Hannibal, had to flee to Crete, and then to Asia Minor,
forever stirring up new enemies against Rome. An almost forgotten
man, thirty-five years after he first began the world war they
trapped him at last. He saw Roman murderers before his house,
and took poison.

But Scipio, the victor, who definitely brought Rome through the
war to world power, also died—probably in the same year as Hannibal—in voluntary exile, like so many ancient heroes. His last wish
was that he might not rest in Roman soil.

XXVII

THE RESULTS WERE WORLD-SHAKING. After the Second Punic War
the Mediterranean, or, in other words, nearly the known world,

belonged to the Romans. It remained in their hands for five centuries. Carthage managed to go on living, and indeed lived quite handsomely, for a few decades as a commercial state without colonies. But since she had produced nothing but her commerce, and no civilization like Athens, since she had sent forth no songs or tragedies, no temples or statues, no philosophy or natural sciences, her name soon faded, whereas defenseless Greece went on to exert a stronger and stronger influence.

For now victorious Rome began to send her quinqueremes and her legions, her rams and eagles to Greece. About the year 200 B.C. Rome, previously on the defensive against Carthage and, properly speaking, under attack, began to seek conquest on her own account. Protection against Gauls and other Celts was still the necessary cause when an almost entirely united Italy pushed northward to the Alps, acquiring Lombardy and then Liguria. In the east, on the other hand, the campaigns of the young King Philip of Macedon were really a mere pretext for the Romans. Actually it was simply an urge for world dominion that impelled the most efficient Mediterranean nation to keep fighting new wars on sea and land. In this fashion they built up between 200 B.C. and A.D. 100 the greatest empire of antiquity, and one of the greatest in history.

The law of inertia applying to bodies in motion created this first empire. These were no barbarians like the Persians, no traders like the Carthaginians. But neither were they geniuses at improvisation like the Greeks, who advanced from island to island as the mood or the whim took them, without plan, and above all with no center, constantly fighting one another. This was no sudden thought of a Pharaoh, sending out gigantic armies and then letting them perish in deserts or sea. Nor was this the fantastic expedition of an individual like Alexander, chasing a dream to the ends of the earth. The Romans continued during those three centuries, with methodical determination, to build up slowly province after province, in a manner that only the English have since been able to imitate.

Far-sighted planning in British policy has been doubted, and many observers have decided it was all a matter of successive separate instances. And we need not assume a pragmatic system in the mind of Scipio or Caesar. Usually it is the separate visions of individuals that are later recorded in legend, poetry, and philosophy. The fact that the descent of the Romans from the Trojan heroes was not devised until the year 300 B.C. is symbolic, as is the imitation of Alexander by Roman generals when they sailed into the eastern Mediterranean. Their strength was irresistible, but it was interesting only because conquest followed conquest in magnificent succession, leading finally to the peaceable world sway of the Pax Romana. The Roman Empire, whose construction could not begin until Carthage was beaten, soon rested on a foundation of arms and authority, just as the British Empire was to do many centuries later.

The interplay of forces in the Aegean and Asia Minor shifted bewilderingly. A later Philip and an important Antiochus combated the advancing Romans in Macedonia and Syria, holding them off Egypt. Hannibal, beaten, sought help for Carthage in Phoenicia, whence his forefathers had come. As if in some poetic recollection he looked to the east for what he needed and could not find in the west. But losing the aid of a faithless Asiatic king, he lost his life as well. Not only the Roman thrust but the Roman navy was victorious everywhere, and when in 191 B.C. they gained their first victory in the Aegean Sea, the fate of the whole Mediterranean was sealed for centuries.

The trick of appearing as the liberator of nations that have no desire to be liberated is as old as the Romans. But the Greeks, or at least their shrewdest leaders, were wily enough to dissemble, celebrating their new freedom with the victors at the Isthmian games as if they did not feel the marching tread of the Roman legions trampling on liberty. The new Roman system of protecting the little states against the big ones, occupation of key points instead of conquest, weakening the adversary from within, has become a model for the most recent conquerors. We have only to look at the face of Antiochus the Great in the Louvre to recognize the lonely, reflective bitterness of one of these first vassals. Philip V, who was called the last Greek, must also have felt this form of defeat deeply.

But by now the fascination of Rome was so great that the rulers

of two eastern Mediterranean states willed their countries to the
Romans, thus establishing the province of Asia. This was before
the Romans carried through their campaign against the pirates
and before they established their law everywhere. They simply
advanced relentlessly; they gave the impression of invincibility.
Rome, inheriting or adopting everything from the Greeks—gods,
philosophy, statues—held the culturally superior Greeks as well as
the other eastern Mediterranean nations in check simply by soldiery
and a sense of order. The secret of three hundred years' dominion by
a power at first culturally inferior lies in the fact that it fully accepted the civilization of the conquered.

It was also part of the Roman plan to venture upon the sea. When
the first Roman sold his land to buy a vessel, the rhythm and tempo
of Mediterranean history changed. The fact that the Roman world
dominion, established in the third and second centuries, became a
sea dominion, exercised by a land power, is a paradox to be explained only by the technological and social organization of Rome.

The methodical-minded Romans needed no such imagination as
the Greeks were inspired by; indeed they shunned it. Accustomed
to combat on shore, they did not rest until they had devised the
boarding bridge, a twenty-five-foot movable beam on the forecastle.
Hannibal in his first battle simply went at the enemy ship, as was
his custom. He was startled to find himself immediately facing his
adversary, and escaped capture by a hair. This sea victory of a land
power over the Carthaginians signifies the defeat of experience and
mobility by mechanics and tenacity. At the same time the Romans
kept their readiness for self-sacrifice, building two new navies at
heavy expense after their first defeat.

Another source of Roman success was the thrift so often found
in unimaginative persons and nations. The riches Rome drew from
the conquered countries for the first one or two hundred years were
productively saved by the state as a whole and by her merchants
individually, thus increasing many times over the power these riches
sprang from. While oil and wheat came over in huge quantities
from Sicily, while gold, silver, and metals poured in from Spain and
Asia Minor, the ambitiously rising generation did not content itself

with landed property. It launched new vessels and founded new commercial houses in the distant provinces, while the government built roads and warships.

Beauty, expressed among the Romans entirely in roads, machinery, and buildings, was not expended upon vases and marble, as in Greece; it remained consistently utilitarian. Even the gods had to make themselves useful in the temples. Organization and practical sense, the virtues of the prosaic temperament, were capable of conquering the world faster, and above all more permanently, than intellect and imagination. Instead of making busts or tragedies, the Romans methodically improved tillage and learned to fatten poultry. Geese were fattened in the shadow of the Acropolis too, but the man who did it was less admired there.

In the rising days of Rome mere money was not worshiped as it had been at Carthage—only active money, transformed into productive values. Credit coins—sealed leather packages, contents unknown—could have been invented only in Carthage, though others later adopted them. Anyone curious enough to open the package destroyed the value of his money, because he could not seal it up again. As the state would take it back at the same value at which it had been issued, nobody bothered about the real value—a perfect symbol for deification of the unknown and for the gulling of the layman by the priests.

During those two centuries Rome set humanity an example of how energy and devotion and a deep-running sense of statehood can lift one nation above other nations even without the help of genius. The bright noonday that lit the Roman heavens, outshining any comets or meteors, has often inspired astonishment in posterity, seldom admiration, perhaps never love. For despite all their virtues and accomplishments the Romans left behind them nothing but a model of resolute citizenship—an intangible that one cannot lay hands on, and that can be seen only in their buildings. Any radiance in the Roman world was Greek.

The finest thing about this is the undisguised cult that mighty Rome built up around powerless Greece, her mother. The formulas of liberation for the Greek cities were written quite in the ancestral dramatic spirit. The Roman artists felt that they were imitators, and adopted all the proportions of classical Athens. It was a sign of good breeding to speak Greek in Roman society. Highly paid Greek slaves taught their language to the sons of the nobles. Thinkers and philosophers imitated Greek models in their way of life, including the vices—even suicide. Cicero coined the word *humanitas* as a symbol of this fusion, and it was Vergil's supreme ambition to write a new *Odyssey*. But ironically enough it turned out that he was not only no Homer but no sailor, for his great epic of ships remained in fact a land epic.

The great Asiatic wars at the beginning of the second century, in which Rome vanquished one after another of Alexander's succession kingdoms, and made provinces of them, closed the circle of a Mediterranean empire whose like has never existed. It went on growing only up to the time of Trajan. But the empire was not at any period created by an individual's ordinary desire for conquest. The Romans did not need overseas possessions everywhere; indeed often they were the ones attacked—for example, by Hannibal, Antiochus, and Philip. The great battle of Pydna, in which Perseus the Macedonian met defeat, was forced upon the Romans. They wanted client states, vassals who would be neither subjects nor too independent. There were Roman colonies and allies just as there are in the British Empire today: Spain was a colony as Bermuda is, while Africa and Greece were weakened states ostensibly on an equal footing, like Canada.

Yet with all their power the Romans had become masters of the Mediterranean coasts, but not masters of the Mediterranean. Cicero praised Rome for the very reason that it was not on the sea, and Horace, who (like his patron Augustus) always got seasick, wrote a special poem putting a curse on the inventor of seafaring. Out yonder on the broad expanse, yonder on the blue or green waves, there was in the second century before Christ only one real power— the corsairs, with their stronghold usually in the no man's land of Crete. These pirates were the business allies of the seafaring merchants, who bought their best slaves from them. There was even a slave king of Cilicia, near the present Alexandretta, and he under-

stood the pirates as well as our dictators understand their spies. Fear
of the freebooters disturbed sea trade all over the Mediterranean,
and it is almost funny to read how the merchants chose to send their
ships to sea in winter because then the pirates were usually taking
their ease.

Despite all this unfolding of Roman power, conquered Carthage
began to flourish again, offering a threat to Rome after all. There
was one man, old Cato, who really hated Carthage more than he
feared her. He was by no means the greatest, but he was perhaps the
most Roman, of Romans.

That healthy, spare, sinewy figure, the tanned skin covered with
scars, the sharp blue eyes probably cold as ice, the reddish hair and
metallic voice, embodied all the old Roman ideals. For here was evidently a man who sought neither pleasure nor wealth but devoted
himself, or thought he was devoting himself, to others, to his family
or the community. What he wanted was less a sense of power than
a sense of his own virtue. When he efficiently supervised his great
estates, ate porridge and millet along with his men, and slept on a
hard bed in his fine house, he would quote Pythagoras, who recom-
mended moderation, not pleasure. In general he seems to have done
what he did less for the gods than as a model for his fellows; he announced his unpretentiousness to the world by accusing others in
well-turned orations and proclaiming in epigrams what a splendid
man Cato was.

The first true puritan of history, he displayed to his fellow citizens neither money nor knowledge nor culture, but only his virtue.
With all his simplicity Cato would not have cared to live by himself
as a philosopher, like Diogenes. In one way or another he let his fellow citizens know that he had sold a carpet, a valuable heirloom;
that he wore no garments worth more than a hundred drachmas,
bought no young, tender slaves, but only stablemen, and never had
his house whitewashed. All Rome talked of how Cato, while consul
in Spain, left his horse behind in order to save the state the shipping
charges, and how he went on his official rounds in Sardinia without
a carriage, on horseback with one servant. His very bravery he en-

joyed only because it allowed him to say that anyone who had seen him in the thick of battle must certainly believe the people owed Cato more than Cato owed the people. Even when he reproached himself there was no dissatisfaction in it: "I regret," he said, "only three things: having entrusted a secret to my wife, having spent a day of idleness, and having gone by sea to a place I could have reached by land."

He was happy only when he could play the censor, supervising the morals of his fellow citizens, prosecuting immoral colleagues, setting the limits of luxury in carriages and jewelry, in food and clothing—in short, when he could avenge upon others his own incapacity for enjoyment. He had a senator excluded from the assembly because he had kissed his wife in broad daylight before the eyes of his daughter; and in his denunciation Cato added that his own wife had never embraced him except in a violent thunderstorm. When, as an old widower, he took a young wife, he excused himself to his astonished son: "I want to leave more such sons to my country."

At the same time he had a splendid head for business, and while he deprived the rich of the water for their gardens, he himself grew ever richer. Surreptitiously he profiteered in sea trade by gathering his debtors into a shipping company. At the same time he fostered disharmony among his slaves so that they should not join to cheat him, but he never had one killed unless all the other slaves concurred in finding him guilty. He called Socrates a chatterbox but quoted Greek sayings in his writings, wrote and spoke an exalted Latin style, and warned the Romans, as the first nationalist among authors, that they would lose their power if they aped the Greek love of the sciences. Thus Cato, who for ninety years always insisted on the last word, was the most virtuous and insufferable of Romans. His great achievement was the destruction of Carthage; the question remains whether it was an achievement.

In Africa the great and unfortunate Hannibal had been succeeded by a wild, healthy barbarian, a benevolent dictator and true educator of his people, who ruled for sixty years and left a one-year-old son behind when he died at the age of ninety. His name was

Masinissa, and he was considered the most fortunate man of his time. He wanted to make his capital at Carthage, adjoining his nomad kingdom, and this gave the Romans an excuse to intervene. The frightened Carthaginian democrats preferred to throw open their city to the hereditary enemy rather than to be governed by the able barbarian. Cato came over himself to pay the enemy a farewell visit before destroying him. That sort of thing was part of his puritan etiquette.

Only at the last moment did a sinking Carthage save her honor: the city council liberated all the slaves, showing that established authority seldom makes moral gestures except in supreme distress. They took arms down to the last peddler, and all went to their deaths against the huge Roman army. The Carthaginians, like their forebears fighting at Tyre against Alexander, perished as true heroes in one of the most awful sieges of antiquity. Those who did not fall were sold into slavery, and the Romans literally destroyed the last house. A curse for all time, pronounced by the Senate, was said to have horrified even Scipio, the victorious general. Where one of the mightiest cities had flourished for five centuries they left a meadowland instead of a Roman province. Implacable Cato's dream was fulfilled, but the world's sympathy was now with Carthage.

The Romans pronounced the same imprecation and inflicted the same destruction a few months later in a distant part of the Mediterranean, at Corinth. In that year, 146 B.C., they reverted to the savage ways of primitive times. Quite unnecessarily, through sheer jealousy and hatred, they burned down two of the oldest cities, sold the sons of old families into slavery, and left behind ruins that Caesar vainly tried to restore a century later, whereas they might have fostered and ruled a metropolis. Corinth, the city of Aphrodite, once leader of the Hellenic league, magnificently situated between the oceans like no other Mediterranean city except Byzantium, venerable and almost as lovely as Athens, perished with Carthage.

Alexander had treated Thebes thus, but no Greek ever used a vanquished enemy so ill, and centuries of Greek philosophy and tolerance had passed since Alexander's time. The Romans showed the world that they had remained barbarians in spite of all.

XXVIII

BUT WHAT THE ROMANS BUILT WAS GREAT—roads and harbors above all. Though they had learned navigation, their real genius was confined to land, particularly to land where it dissolves into sea, in harbor engineering: moles, breakwaters, artificial islands. If we survey their faces in the first century B.C., as we see them on a tour of the Capitol, the Romans seem much more modern than the Greeks. Good looks among men were as little admired then as they are now. Brains were valued more, and energy most of all. These were men who did not want to understand or enjoy life as the Greeks did, but to dominate it. Those who looked different, for instance the handsome Agrippa or the decadent Augustus, were exceptions. The immortal head of Caesar looks as if he were the son of action and intellect, while Alexander looks like the son of action and beauty.

It was thought marvelous when they first built the mole at Puteoli near Rome out of arches, transferring their own invention, the round arch, from land to sea. Initial mistakes were natural enough; the new harbors at Ephesus and Seleucia were destroyed by masses of silt. When we read the outbursts of modern hydrographers, who are arguing these matters yet, we are not surprised that the laws of alluviation and delta formation were then unknown.

Only when the Romans began to separate their harbors from the cities did they profess and assume the mastery of the other element. This was as great an event as the first airport in the desert. The center of Roman Miletus, said the witty Greeks, is on its outskirts. Splendid façades were built out into the ocean, public squares were laid out along moles sometimes as much as twenty feet high, and halls and monuments rose along the sea. Misenum was the first harbor founded without a city; the town later followed the port. So it was with the port of Ravenna, established at the same time. The channels cut through the lagoons here and at Arles, which were forever being protected against silting up, were proofs of a new skill at engineering, as impressive as the great dams of our own day.

The Roman masterpiece was Ostia, built by Nero's father. In early times great ships are supposed to have sailed up to Rome; but later on silting up blocked navigation, and everything arriving for the capital had to be transshipped in small boats. Neither the Gracchi nor Caesar succeeded in conquering the element that washed Rome's feet, though they wanted to land conveniently the grain, wine, and oil which the swiftly growing city was importing from abroad. Finally the Emperor Claudius managed to open a port and canal to the north of the Tiber mouth, to build a splendid semicircular mole, and actually to sink there a huge vessel that had brought an obelisk across the sea. Gigantic piles were sunk with the ship, and when it collapsed an island with a lighthouse was built upon it. Later it all silted up again; Trajan tried to clear it, but Mussolini was the first to succeed.

Caesar too applied his generalship to the ocean in a truly Roman way; he made troop shipments possible by constructing vessels of a new design. The sole reason why he won the decisive battle of

Pharsalus was that he succeeded in getting forty thousand men across the sea from Brundisium. He defeated the Veneti on the west coast of Gaul by a new dodge. To oppose their tall sailing ships he built light rowing vessels in the mouth of the Loire. These were swift, heavily manned, and outfitted with long curved knives on poles. With them the Romans, rowing past, slashed the enemy's sails and rigging, and took him captive.

But even Caesar could not handle the pirates; they outlived all the Mediterranean civilizations. A single strain runs from the king of Cyprus who complained to the Pharaoh Amenophis, in 1370 B.C., down through the pirates in Homer, the thefts of the Phoenicians, the marauding of the Philistines, to the very latest books on navigation, which warn the seafarer against false beacons on the north coast of Africa, where pirates lie in wait behind reefs. The slave trade among the coral islands of the Red Sea, which the present emperor of Abyssinia has never seriously combated, is merely a fragment of it, moved slightly southward. Like the modern parachutist the corsairs in the time of Caesar used to land somewhere to find bread and water, at the same time hastily occupying a gate or tower. Thus they plundered the warehouses at the seaports and the island temples. The heavy indebtedness of most Greek communities has been laid to this. A Roman poet wrote: "Apollo is so impoverished by the corsairs that when the swallow comes to visit him he cannot show her one grain of gold."

The new morality that developed among the pirates was significant. The corsair state that arose about the year 100 B.C., made up of fugitives, slaves, and discharged soldiers, insisted on comradeship, secrecy, and valor after the fashion of Robin Hood. All were agreed in their resolution to take revenge on the society that had cast them out. They justified the killing of their prisoners by pointing out that any pirate who was taken at a port would be killed by the city dwellers. Their realm was simply the Mediterranean, and a map of that realm would be like our ocean charts, where the water bristles with a thousand little symbols, while the land seems bare. A system of stations and signals told each pirate of safe hiding places for food, treasure, women, and children.

How could they help stirring the imagination of the young people? Then as now the younger generation was intellectually sated, bored with good order and monotony, avid for danger, daring, and glory. The pirates plundered the island of Delos before the eyes of Lucullus and his fleet. They levied an annual tribute on Lipara in return for leaving the island alone. They would suddenly sweep into great harbors like Syracuse. A praetor who had brought along the chains to shackle them found himself bound by those very chains to the mast of a captured Roman vessel. Rich members of society at Baiae no longer dared go bathing. The rule of the seas had passed to a nation that was no nation and had no country: a sort of state afloat.

Pompey was the man who finally divided the Mediterranean, with Roman thoroughness, into thirteen watery provinces, each belonging to a land province, and devised a way to exterminate the pirates as we today would exterminate an epidemic. At the same

time the Roman set up a new morality of his own in opposition to
his enemies, and with it he won. He emphasized gentleness, did not
crucify the captives, spared the hired rowers. Indeed even the boldest
sea kings, who had taken their women and treasures to their mountain castles in the Taurus and then gone to lie in wait for Pompey
along the coast of Asia Minor, were granted land and liberty if they
offered no resistance. Within a few months the eastern Mediterranean was clear. The Roman leader is said to have destroyed thir-
'teen hundred vessels, brought back four hundred, and boasted that
he had killed no more than ten thousand corsairs.

This naval victory without a name was perhaps the greatest that
Rome ever won. It was also the only conflict that might have been
called the battle of the Mediterranean. Italy, which had gone hungry
despite all its wealth, got its cargo vessels back after this victory.
Everyone sang the praises of democracy, just reintroduced at Rome,
as the indispensable premise for the great expedition.

For during the pirate domination a secret and an open revolution had been shaking the Roman Empire. The victory of the new
world empire had brought money, the money had brought luxury,
and corruption, invading a hitherto thrifty nation, had destroyed
the old civic morality. Generals and senators were for sale to foreign
rulers; masters thoughtlessly provoked slaves, who had to stand by
in ominous silence at mad banquets: civil war between rich and poor
was close at hand.

The peasants, earlier the mainstay of the Roman power, were impoverished because anarchic conditions in the east of the empire
made the capture of human quarry easier, and slaves grew ever
cheaper. Man hunting, without which the whole of ancient civilization was really impossible, grew to such an extent that as many as
ten thousand slaves were sold in one day at the port of Delos, the
great commercial center of the east. This slave labor, which cost the
master nothing but a little bread and wheat, and the constant wars
condemned the peasants to misery. By the year 100 a Roman orator
could cry out: "At least the wild beasts of Italy have their caves and
their lairs. You peasants and soldiers who are going to your death
for Italy have only air and sun. They call you the lords of the world,

but you have not a single span of your own soil." A voice like this, just one such utterance, sets the gravely rumbling pedal note that goes on beneath the splendid melodies of antiquity

People were fond of telling anecdotes to show the friendly relation between Roman masters and slaves. These exceptions could not bring light or air to the stables and dungeons where the slaves brooded in chains through the dark half of their lives, after tilling the fields all day in chains under the threat of the lash. Yet among these figures crushed by fate one arose who was offered an opportunity—and a master—to develop his native gifts. Livius Andronicus, a Greek slave freed by his Roman owner, founded Latin literature in the third century B.C., translating the *Odyssey* and writing comedies in the Greek manner. Only fragments remain.

On top of the dungeons the Romans built their palaces. This sudden wealth, a result of constant victories and new vassal countries, was bound to destroy the austere virtues by which Rome, the poor little country town in the century of the Punic Wars, had grown to be a world power. In the course of one hundred and ten years it had acquired Sicily, Sardinia, Spain, Macedonia, Greece, Pergamum, Carthage. The eastern trade, concentrated for centuries at Miletus, Rhodes, Antioch, and, later, at Alexandria, had come to Rome, where it stayed from 150 B.C. to A.D. 150.

From these new provinces the *homines novi,* the new rich, drew their millions. Tax collectors, army contractors, bankers advanced money to the vassals so that they could pay tribute. Since they, as high officials in the provinces, were charged with the dispensing of justice, it is no wonder that they preferred to dispense injustice in order to cover the peculations of their friends. Their sons did not need to go to war, for the fathers paid. The wars the Romans had once carried through to victory as a united nation now became the big business that brought the highest returns. Even the allies in Italy threatened defection. All the signs pointed to revolution.

The men who stood up to prevent it, particularly the Gracchus brothers, wear the aura of one last battle for justice, and of martyrdom too. They were killed by their own class after a magnificent and wholly unselfish struggle. They had dared to take away from the rich their holdings above five hundred acres and to give the surplus to the poor. Even in those days senators, heirs, and bankers would tolerate nothing of that sort.

The younger Gracchus, the greatest revolutionary of antiquity, earnest and simple like his father, became tribune in 123 B.C. He began by winning over the people through a corn law and a law for the relief of the unemployed. Then, still relying on the poor, he managed also to enlist part of the newly rich class by joining them against the conservative Senate. He founded colonies of citizens overseas to relieve the overpopulation of Rome and tried to give Roman citizenship to all Latins. Through shifty party politics and under the wiliest pretenses he managed to carry out his social ideas. He represented the idealist who is at the same time an adroit politician—a type we are seeing again these days.

The collapse of the Gracchic revolts, the victory of the rich and powerful minority over the only outwardly sovereign majority, was bound to lead to military rule—to the crisis of the Roman Republic. Now more than ever before, peasants and proletarians were compelled to fight the wars of the capitalists. These wars went on far from Italy for more than fifty years, until after Caesar's death. Then came the moment that history so often records in great inner crises: foreign rulers, Mithridates and Jugurtha, stepped into the fight from the outside, seemingly as saviors of the oppressed. This was the first occasion when conscription in Rome was replaced by so-called voluntary enlistment; at this time the unemployed came to form the heart of the Roman army. Here was a fundamental shift that brought politics into warfare. The provisioning of the troops, their willingness, and even their valor now depended on the political situation at home.

Just as in our time, the social revolution produced the first Roman dictator. An aristocrat named Sulla made use of the proletarian army in his employ to break the dominion of the middle classes. This paradoxical alliance, which has been paralleled in modern history, shows how ambitious leaders overstep their own principles in order to retain power. Marius the democrat, seven times elected consul, was beaten in the streets of Rome by Sulla the reactionary. In

addition Sulla could boast that he was the savior of the country who
had put down the uprisings of the Italic peoples. But he was wise
enough to let the envoys of foreign nations speak their own languages in the Roman Senate, a concession which no great power
would make today. The new Roman colonies in the Mediterranean,
the provinces, were the only thing that saved the world power of
Rome, for in rapid succession the Germanic barbarians assaulted it
from the north, and the Greeks from the east. Marius and Sulla beat
them separately, so we can truthfully say that these bitter enemies
both saved the fatherland.

In the Black Sea and then in the Aegean, two hundred years after
Alexander, there seemed to be a repetition of the old spectacle—a
half barbarian freeing the Greeks. This time it was Mithridates,
king of Pontus, a Grecized Persian. He used the Roman civil wars
to ally himself with the pirates and the Greeks and defeat the Romans. In this year, 88, Romans and Greeks fought for dominion
over the Mediterranean for the last time. And in the end it appeared
that the Romans were trying not to be barbarians. For the Persians
put to the sword by thousands the Italians settled in Asia Minor,
while Sulla spared the inhabitants of Athens after his victory, saying
he wished to save the living for the sake of the dead. Both sides
ravaged the countryside, but then so did the Greeks, occasionally.
The well-known epigram about the Tartar in every Russian may be
generalized: Scratch a civilized man and find a barbarian.

At any rate Sulla, more of a general and nobleman than a statesman, had greater imagination than was usually given to a Roman.
Rich and fashionable as he was, strutting on his war horse, he
dragged the social problems after him. But often, too, he would lie
enthroned like a king among singers and dancing girls. He was hot
and cold by turns, always arrogant and cynical, with the proscrip-
tion list of his personal enemies always at hand, crueler than any
Roman before him. In every way he proved himself the opposite of
Cato, the opposite too of broad-headed Marius, whose death finally
made him sole ruler.

This was the first time that the Roman Republic surrendered its
laws, turning over to the stronger general the power of dictatorship,

which it tolerated for years without reelection or interruption. But tradition was powerful enough to induce Sulla's voluntary retirement a year before his death. Perhaps it was personal weariness; at any rate he set an example of a ruler surrendering power seldom emulated in history.

The social revolutions, the second of which Sulla went through as a young man, disturbed such an autocrat but little. The uprisings of the Roman slaves about 130 and 100 were as closely connected with the raids of the pirates on the law-abiding world as the revolts of workers and sailors are in modern revolutions. Here too an act of justice led to violence. Certain Sicilian judges, correctly sensing the trend of the times, had simultaneously decided eight hundred lawsuits of slaves against their masters. Then a new government upset all the decisions. Whereupon thousands of miners and other slaves rose up and took to the mountains. The government had no soldiers ready. As in the war on the pirates, they made an alliance with a robber chief who was to catch the runaways. But another group seized arms. Syrians, sold into slavery abroad, now parodied their slave king at home and elevated one of their own number to the throne.

The Mediterranean then saw not the first, but the most momentous, rise of a proletarian to power. And it was significant that the first slave in history to become a ruler was born a free man in Thrace and only later enslaved, through capture. Spartacus, who, about 70 B.C., had terrorized the Roman Empire for three years, had only one predecessor in antiquity—the slave Drimacus, who led a successful slave uprising in Chios about 300 B.C., extorting a just peace. But the citizens broke the treaty and put a price on his head when the slave had disbanded his army. He evaded pursuit for a long time, but finally got his favorite to kill him in his old age so that the favorite might collect the price set on his head—a truly tragicomic epilogue.

Spartacus, on the other hand, had escaped his tormentors, taking seventy men with him, who soon swelled into an army of seventy thousand. He was thus the ancestor of all the revolutionists who have since risen from the lower depths to convulse the Mediterranean, the last of whom is named Mussolini.

XXIX

THE GREAT MEN OF HISTORY can be explained individually as extraordinary characters or by the surroundings into which they were born. A double analysis shows the whole man, but we incline more to the one method or the other according to the point we have reached in our story. Seeing these marble heads of the first century B.C. while wandering through a gallery on the Capitol, we find the Romans much more appealing to modern man than the Greeks. Male beauty alone was of no greater value then than it is today. Only intellect counted, and energy even more. They did not want to experience or to understand life as the Greeks had done before them. They wanted to rule. And the few softer looking faces, as for instance beautiful Agrippa or decadent Augustus, were but exceptions.

Caesar's immortal head makes him appear the son of Spirit and Action, while Alexander seems to be Action and Beauty's heir. If Caesar was not the most powerful ruler of the Mediterranean, he was at any rate the most mature. He can therefore be sketched here only in the light of the Mediterranean situation in the middle of the first century. Furthermore, he was not the sole pretender, and it remained uncertain for decades whether he would be victorious.

The Romans were more strongly dominated by the thought of money in Caesar's youth than in earlier times, when they were frugal, or later, when a new faith made them thoughtful. Rome housed 2,000,000 inhabitants, twice as many as today, and more than any other city of antiquity. At times she is said to have counted 900,000 voters. The elections were decided by money. Money also decided to whom, what class and what individual, the armies belonged. An inborn trading spirit had once established Greek power; now the same spirit was reducing the Roman strength, which had derived from moderation and soldierhood. In rather the same way history led Prussia and the new Germany from soldier state to trade. Both Romans and Prussians turned from warrior nations into commercial nations, and for that reason had to grow toward the sea.

But only the Romans, awaking to life on the Mediterranean, were sent to sea by their position. The island nation of Greeks was at home on it from the first. The Romans had none of the playful spirit of the Greeks, none of their imagination, and therefore produced very little great art, but as a political power they were happier and more powerful in the long run. As traders they were equally great in the end, though very different. By the time of Caesar they were more merchants than warriors. The patricians, whose sons had won battles in the old days, were now deeply involved in credit transactions. Everyone speculated in shipping ventures, held shares in clay pits for the production of bricks, built or bought tenements in Rome or Alexandria, chartered vessels, and became a millionaire or went bankrupt because a grain vessel did or did not escape the pirates. When Lucullus dared to abolish the exorbitant rates of interest in Asia Minor, the Roman capitalists deprived him of his supreme command.

The produce of the Mediterranean, wine and oil—why leave it in Greek hands? What was the use in having thousands of slaves (dearly bought from the pirates) who had once made their living as experts in vine growing? At Rhodes, the world's market, where oil and wine were warehoused, people kept paid employees to learn the art of growing, storing, and selling, so as to improve the wine at home in the Romagna and raise its price. Horses, sheep, and donkeys, which had always run wild in Italian pastures, were now scientifically bred after the Greek fashion. Selling at higher prices, they became the means of supplying Romans with villas and rose gardens, slaves and hunts, banquets at which the host opened the crust of a great pie to let a couple of living doves fly out. The whole Greek world, including architects, orators, and physicians, was bought up by its rich Roman conquerors.

Thereupon the Roman philosophers, statesmen, and orators wanted a better life too. What did Lucullus do after living modestly and with distinction for fifty years as a soldier and general? Laden down with the gold of the Persian he had vanquished, he built a lovely palace on the Monte Pincio; he lavished statues and loggias and brilliant society on his Villa Tusculum in the Campagna. Few people today realize that he had conquered half of Asia before he began to give the banquets that have made his name a household word. And what of Cicero? Looking like a British cabinet minister who has studied Plato in the original at Oxford, and incorruptible as prosecutor of the two enemies of the Republic, Catilina and Verres, he was the first modern mind of antiquity. Austere, self-assured, resolute, and yet narrow-eyed and nervous, he suppressed his cravings all too long. Even he, a philosophical statesman, was seized by the craze of his time. Although gray-haired, he ran up huge debts with Crassus in order to forget his simple paternal home for a palace on the Palatine.

And they were all generals, even Cicero the orator and Crassus the banker; indeed you were nothing in Rome unless you were constantly returning to the battlefield. What did Pompey, with his broad top sergeant's face, all nose and no forehead, do to reward himself for his onerous campaigns? He had carried before him at his triumph not only the arms and ship's prows of the defeated pirates, but the treasures, crowns, and idols of the vanquished kings. A train of mules carried the sacks of captured silver for the state treasury. After them came princes and hostages, the seven sons of the Persian king, captured Arabs and Jews, slaves and freemen, the bust of Pompey, and finally the man himself in the tunic of Alexander the Great.

Young Caesar saw all this and much else of the same kind; and he saw that he was poor. Born of a distinguished, decadent family, and knowing his own talent, he decided, in spite of his philosophical leanings, not to be wise or devout or a great author. He was determined to be rich and powerful. He ran up many debts and was the lover of many fashionable young women; his reputation as a man about town merely made him more interesting. At smart gatherings he saw King Mithridates' perfumer, a slave who had bought freedom by his skill and was now engaged in perfuming ladies on the Tiber instead of in Pontus. He saw Greek cooks, magicians, goldsmiths, painters, all exiles, making their fortune faster in wealthy Rome than in their old, impoverished homeland.

Caesar missed by a hair becoming a slave himself. When he went as a student to fashionable Rhodes, his ship was captured by pirates. Fifty days passed before he was released for a high ransom. His ironical letters boasted of having lived like a prince among the pirates, arranging games, reading his verses aloud, and always threatening his captors with eventual hanging. As Marius's nephew he found Rome closed to him for a long time. He refused to go back when he was offered the chance on condition of leaving his young wife. He did not return until after the death of Sulla.

Caesar was thirty when, with the worst of reputations, he entered politics. He took the conservative and nationalist side in order to get ahead. But suddenly he turned to the popular party and started stressing his relationship to Marius. He even became an early riser in order to act as advocate for every petitioner in the Forum. While he seemed to be listening attentively to what his slave wrote down, he was thinking of the charms of Servilia or some other lady whom he had left an hour before. As the people's friend he worked with public criers, flower sellers, coachmen, barbers, flute players. He was determined to become pontifex and recapture this office for the people, from whom Sulla had taken it away. Thus he would become sacrosanct, a sham which was doubly amusing to him as an atheist.

Not until he was almost forty did Caesar's great rise begin; it was to carry him beyond all the other stormy petrels—above the clouds. Yet even then he was long regarded as but one of three; Pompey, and at first also Crassus (who, with him, made up the Triumvirate), resided in Rome. Caesar, meanwhile, was in Gaul; his sense of superiority and swiftly rising ambition emboldened him to leave Rome, which reveals him as predominantly the soldier, for Gaul had still to be won by force of arms. He developed the four legions that he secured, along with his five-year proconsulate, into a private army of his own; since Pompey had already preempted the east, he went to seek conquest and glory in the west. He accepted his authority not from the Senate but from the popular assembly, which in itself was a sort of *coup d'état*. Practically speaking, Caesar was depriving the Senate of power, for the first time in centuries. At the same time, quite in the spirit of Gracchus, he offered new farms to the people and aid to veterans and plebeians. Like Sulla he, an aristocrat, wanted to govern with the people and against the nobility.

Caesar's stay in Gaul, where he spent almost all of his best decade, meant a great sacrifice for a worldly man of his particular nature and habits. In fact Caesar's remedy for weakness and headaches was simple food, tremendous marches, and life entirely out of doors. This offset the excesses of his youth in the city. There, among foreign barbarians and simple soldiers, with neither women nor luxury nor culture, he ate plain porridge along with his men, a few friendly officers, and many more jealous ones. And there he became a great man. His victories over Gauls and Germans were the more splendid since he had not spent his youth in camp, like Napoleon, but in boudoirs, academies, and the Forum. He had done little fighting before he went to Spain. He was a dilettante on the peaks of Greek culture until he began to feel a universal ambition. He was very late in beginning his great venture, which lasted but fifteen years. Improvisation was one secret of his greatness.

The other secret was his peerless ability to adapt circumstances to himself. He could alter decisions swiftly, come to a military and intellectual halt in the midst of the fiercest assault. And always he remained a gentleman, though he was not particular in choosing the means to serve his purpose. Long after he had been the lover of Pompey's wife, and after her death, he married his daughter to Pompey—a piece of broad farce, unless it was a stroke of genius. In any event his daughter died too soon to keep the two men from falling out. After her death and that of Crassus, who fell as a general in Asia, the rivalry between the two remaining men had to be settled. The constitution and regular consular elections had long since gone overboard. When Caesar marched his private armies against Rome in the year 48 B.C., thus bestowing immortality on the insignificant river Rubicon, he was risking more than had Marius and Sulla. And no doubt his plans were bigger. He beat Pompey at Pharsalus; Pompey fled, and was murdered on landing in Egypt.

Caesar was dictator of the Roman world empire for the next

four years. Whether he pushed the crown away three times is uncertain; all we know is that he did not assume it, because he wanted first to earn it in the grand manner. The life of the aging Caesar has determined the figure he presents in history, whereas Alexander always appears as a very young man. Each garnered his deeds and fame within the span of fifteen years.

And while Alexander's early start and swift pace, like those of Raphael and Mozart, foreshadowed his early end (nature having exhausted him in his mid-thirties), Caesar by that time was only beginning to stir from a life of contemplation and enjoyment. Army, command, and throne fell to Alexander by inheritance; Caesar had to serve the people for long years, consolidating his power against his rivals by incessant combinations. Alexander inherited power, carried it to the ends of the earth, and left behind him an empire that was bound to fall apart forthwith. Caesar fought for power, carried it to the ends of his ocean, and founded an empire that survived for three hundred years. Alexander's path was steeper, Caesar's was longer. Alexander's figure was handsomer, Caesar's richer.

Alexander accomplished all that was in him. Caesar locked his plans in his bosom and fell before his world enterprises could begin, stabbed in the back by the cowardly hand of a murderer. This is why he has been the more attractive in history and on the stage. Brutus, who engaged in usurious trade, Brutus, glorified by revolutionists of all ages, was a small mind crushed not by the unfreedom of his country, but by the sheer greatness of his master.

Caesar's life was much more bound up with the Mediterranean than Alexander's; he almost never left it, performing his deeds in the four great realms along its shore. He was a son of the Mediterranean, and his empire was the Mediterranean empire. Even if he had followed Alexander to Persia, as he intended, the true significance of his work would have remained where he was born. On the other hand Alexander was away almost all his life from his native land, to which nothing bound him at last.

Alexander carried Greek civilization farther than anyone who followed; this was not Caesar's task, for that civilization was known

before his time to the Spaniards and the Egyptians. To Gauls and
Germans it meant nothing. Yet Alexander remained a half barbarian, which Caesar never was. He was far more of a Greek than
Alexander; indeed he was in the advance guard of the platonic
world, and scarcely even a pagan at all. He practiced a morality
previously unknown to antiquity. If we take the man of action and
not the philosopher as our standard, ancient morals end with Caesar.

He was the first ruler of the Mediterranean to be sustained by a
new emotion. Caesar turned into reality the finest virtue of a ruler:
he forgot the names of his enemies.

BOOK TWO

THE ASSAULT

OF THE BARBARIANS

Ah servile Italy! grief's hostelry,
Ship without helmsman in a mighty storm!
No Dame of provinces, but house of shame!
That courteous spirit, at the mere sweet sound,
His country's name, was then immediate
With welcome warm to one of his own land;
Not without warfare do thy living now
Inhabit thee, and one the other gnaws
Of those a single wall and moat enclose,
Thou wretched one! Search thy seacoasts all around,
E'en from their shores; then on thy bosom gaze
And see if peace be anywhere enjoyed.

DANTE

AT THE LIGHTHOUSE

WITH A SLOW GESTURE *the keeper closed the book. His left hand still lay flat on the cover; he stared ahead of him, drew a deep breath, and exhaled noisily, as if with effort. The story had occupied him two nights, for much of it had been new or hard to understand. Finding the night still dark, with the revolving, thrice-broken motion of the beacon still flashing across the sky above him, he took time to ponder for a while.*

. . . So really, he thought, they used to do the same thing on our sea as they are doing now. A few nations wrangling for leadership; goodness knows why they didn't want peace! Did it make so much difference whether the Carthaginians or the Greeks gave orders in Sicily? What did it really matter whether Hannibal or Scipio ruled this coast of ours? Anyway, they conquered our forefathers, and made themselves at home on our islands. Or maybe I'm descended from the conquerors. Let's take a look and see when these Gauls finally discovered the ocean and turned into Frenchmen. There may be a good many surprises left in a thick book like this.

The vessel that carried the obelisk, it says, could hold as much as twelve hundred tons. The obelisk must have been as big as ours in the Place de la Concorde. Oh, those pirates! These days they come from below; that's the only difference. No one's ever able to deal with them, and they can't deal with each other. Things may start up again tomorrow. Who knows how soon my beacon may be put out? We may be the modern Carthaginians, but that man in Rome is certainly no Caesar. He doesn't know anything about the sea, loud as he talks. If he starts anything, he'll find out what the Gauls are like!

Alexandria! That's where fat Johnny used to work. How he did love the bottle! Afterward he'd be perfectly steady on his feet, on duty bright and early. He knew the whole history of his light by heart, and when he started to tell it he acted as if he had per-

sonally demonstrated the radio to Alexander the Great. One thing that isn't in there I'd like to know—how much a lighthouse keeper made in ancient Roman times. . . .

Slowly the keeper mounted the steps, eighty-four of them—how often had he counted! Looking east from the upper gallery, toward Saint-Raphaël, he espied the first greenish-blue tinge of dawn. There was not much yet, but the victory of morning comes quickly in August. He waited a patient half hour while the narrow strip spread like an opening fan across the vault, brightening the world long before the first true red appeared. He saw the stars dying away, and gazed after them for a few moments with the religious feeling that always moves the mariner.

His colleague arrived to take over the instruments. The keeper, having already changed his coat and shoes, picked up his cap. He spoke a monosyllabic greeting, then strode toward his white cottage. The most wakeful of the birds were raising their voices, first by fits and starts, bashfully, trilling softly, like the instruments of an orchestra tuning up but trying not to be heard; then a more alert reply, and then louder and louder. By the time he reached the house the joyous tumult was in full swing. But the people still slept, and his wife was only awakened by the familiar creak of the door, which he kept forgetting to oil.

He stood for a moment beside the cribs; in one a sleeping body stirred with a brief, faint moan, feeling another presence near. The keeper thought for a second how lucky it was that the boy was still small, and that the war might be over before his turn came. Quickly dismissing the thought, in a few moments he was close to sleep himself.

. . . A new emotion? This was his last thought. Had not that been the author's ending? Why, of course, Jesus comes right after Caesar. Well, tonight we'll see. . . .

S TONY, HARD, AND BARREN, full of caves and gaps, the land that gave birth to Jesus rises on low hills. It lies cold, hostile, treeless, and austere, remote from fertile valleys to east or west, which the eye cannot reach. Amid a somber landscape stands a defiant city of gray and yellow stone. Not far to northward, however, a green land of mountains stretches softly out, abounding in springs and trees. This is Galilee. An observer of the two landscapes, which are only a few hours apart today, realizes at once the difference between the two creeds that began here: yonder the strong, masculine dogma of Judaism, avid for life and battle; here the more feminine Christian doctrine, turning its back on life, leaning toward humility and idyllic peace. The difference between the landscapes, Mediterranean both, emerges from the original visions of Moses and Jesus, not from what fate and history later made of their teachings.

The Hebrews, a cattle-breeding nomadic tribe that once lived as the Bedouins do on the middle Nile today, learned to raise grain in Canaan. They found ahead of them traders who had used a caravan route there long before Homer. Before and in common with the Phoenicians they had imported from Arabia Felix, and even from India, spices and incense with which to tempt the kings on the Euphrates and the Nile. These Semitic tribes had cattle also, and they grew grapes and olives. But the poor soil of Palestine, never a land of milk and honey—it could only have been called so by contrast to the desert—forced the inhabitants to become traders. Like the neighboring Phoenicians, they grew rich in this fashion; the Book of Judges says that even the camels wore golden collars. Later, after the first exile, their sons were forced into commerce all the more; and when that sort of thing goes on for a dozen generations, certain capacities recede in favor of others.

Ancient revolutions took the form of migration. This is why we see so many peoples migrating between 1000 B.C. and A.D. 600, and so few revolutions at home. In countries where rich river valleys bordered on steppes and deserts, the nomads in the poor pastures were sure to start advancing upon those in the lush ones. The Hyksos, probably Bedouins from Canaan, moved into Egypt, whereupon the Egyptians made a counterthrust at Palestine. The Hittites drove out the Egyptians, the Assyrians the Hittites. The Hebrews, another group of wandering Bedouins, invaded Palestine, pushing out the Philistines who barred them from the Mediterranean. Samson and David were robber chieftains who defeated the Philistines. Then David took the inaccessible town of Jerusalem and thus gained control of the Egyptian trade. But his most active commerce, the period of which was later known as King David's golden age, could be carried on only in concert with the Phoenicians, because the Hebrews knew nothing of seafaring. Neither they nor their Jewish descendants have become a maritime nation in the three thousand years since.

This odd unfamiliarity of the Hebrews with the sea and to some extent even with the land partly explains the amazing degree to which, in compensation, they cultivated the intellect, the logical faculty. It prepares us for events to come, even for the thrice-repeated loss of their territory. The strength of a people is closely connected with its weaknesses; a lack of imagination means lack of the artistic gift, but it also leads to clear thinking.

At the same time the sharp contrast between rich and poor, which prevented the rise of any middle class, had weakened the peasants in Palestine so severely that Isaiah predicted the downfall of the nation, and the prophet Amos, like a socialist leader, summoned the people to rise against their ruler. Soon the event that had not been very hard to prophesy actually occurred. The Assyrians, who had been harassing Palestine for centuries, and who depicted Israelites paying tribute as early as 800 B.C., finally took away the leaders, then carried off the flower of the people from Samaria and other districts and showed their skill at statecraft by distributing the Israelites among the Assyrian rebels at home. Thus an end was put to these Ten Tribes of Israel; only Judah was left, with its capital, Jerusalem. When the struggles in that zone ended, with the victory of Babylon, Nebuchadnezzar broke into Solomon's Temple, destroyed the golden vessels, burned down everything, and led the men and women of Judah into captivity. This took place about 600 B.C.—six centuries before Titus and the Roman conquest.

The Jews, as they were henceforth called, drew their greatest prophet from the Babylonian captivity. Memories of the homeland had long since faded in the people from Samaria, as in the Americans today. But the Jews, released by Cyrus, the conqueror of Babylon, were fortunate enough to go home within fifty years in a mood that kept old desires and memories alive. During that time the metropolis had pushed them more than ever into commerce, since army, state, and landholding were closed to them then as in Europe many centuries later. But at the same time Babylon had taught them higher forms of commerce. After they returned, to be subject for centuries to Persians and Greeks, they found the ocean no longer free. The Greeks had already occupied their seaports at the mouths of the Nile. But the Egyptians and the early Romans needed traders, and many Jews went abroad again centuries before they were compelled to.

Culturally too the Babylonian civilization had advanced them. The priesthood, which had assumed leadership as the one central power in exile, adopted from the Babylonian legends the creation, Paradise, the fall of man, the Tower of Babel, the Deluge, even the strict observance of the Sabbath, which had never been customary before.

But the one thing that singled out and finally brought world fame to this obscure little people, namely its relation to God, had been established long before. We now place Moses, who was for a long time believed to be of mythical origin, a thousand years before the Exile.

Moses is supposed to have been the first to preach a single God, Jesus the first to teach love of one's neighbor. Both statements are erroneous.

The Egyptian priests as long ago as the Old Kingdom taught (though only as an occult doctrine) that there was one and only one God. Amenophis IV struggled with the priests to proclaim even to the common people that the sun-god was the only one. Moses must have been aware of these ideas in Egypt, even if he lived before Amenophis, which is uncertain. At about the same time the similarly concealed monotheism of the Babylonians was familiar in Palestine along with the Babylonian language: Marduk, the sun-god, was worshiped as the sole deity.

On the other hand Yahweh was not for some centuries the one and undisputed God of the Hebrews. Baal and Astarte, whose feasts were mingled with those of the one God in Canaan, did not remain without rivals, as is shown by the dance around the Golden Calf. Sacred stones, caves where gods lived, and the teraphim fetishes that Jacob stole from his father-in-law, also bore witness to the fact. It was not until 600 B.C., under Josiah, that the strange gods were solemnly burned. Especially after the return from the Exile the priests tried to emphasize the one God by way of contrast with their neighbors and other enemies.

For among the Hebrews belief in one God had come not through philosophy, as with Plato, but through consolidation, through the reduction of all gods but the one God. His origins were more worldly and patriotic than mystical. The God of the Hebrews was often a war god and a national god, a symbol of the tribes united in war. The sword of Yahweh led in the battles of Gideon and David.

The magnificent conception of one single God was darkened by nationalist feelings, of which Moses was not free. And when the people returned from Babylon they felt it a passionate duty to rebuild Yahweh's Temple in Jerusalem and nowhere else; the feeling was so strong that the priests tied Yahweh to the spot, telling the people it was the race chosen to proclaim His gospel. As Isaiah said, "But thou, Israel, art my servant, Jacob whom I have chosen, the seed of Abraham my friend."

Oppression is likely to bring exaggerated self-esteem in its wake, and the Jews at this time conceived the idea that they were the one people chosen of God. This was something new to the ancient world. Such pretension to the exclusive possession of truth was bound to exasperate other peoples, with other gods—the more so if the peoples were more powerful and well aware of a little people's inability to impose its God on the rest of mankind. Here we have the source of all the anti-Semitism in history.

And yet the assertion connoted no real presumption or inner uncertainty. It was the policy of the priests, who were trying to reconcile the worldly wisdom of a large cultural area with the feelings of a small tribe of herdsmen and traders, to elevate Yahweh to sole godhead after the fact, so that they might explain the Exile as an expression of his wrath. For deliverance from such sins a Messiah was needed, not merely the old, unreal one, but a mortal sent by God, a king to establish a thoroughly earthly kingdom.

When the scriptures made the Jews famous, a century before Plato, the prophetic tone was rather disconcerting. The Greeks especially had a feeling that the strange nation on the far coast was setting up laws where they themselves would have put ideas or images. The Messianic idea, the whole tone of the Prophets, had a new sound as far as ancient ears could interpret it. While all the Greeks lived day in and day out with their gods, among the Jews there were a few chosen spirits who communed with the one God now and then, in moments of rapture. The philosophers were interested to learn from travelers that the Jews had begun to adopt a religious way of talking and thinking, in place of Greek logic. But nothing astonished people so much as the fact that this peculiar Yahweh had no image. How was a Greek, a creature of eyes and senses, to imagine a deity that not only was invisible but forbade portrayal? Had not Egyptians and Greeks rendered the fetish, the god or demon tied to a certain spot, omnipresent precisely by making an image? And yet nomadic tribes had often contented themselves with a symbol, because in their wanderings they could neither make nor transport statues. The Hebrews even after they became sedentary were no draftsmen, and if we cannot exactly call them unpractical, still as traders they were nomads of a sort, and they were artistically untalented in any case. In building his temple Solomon had got not only the wood but the carpenters and masons as well from a foreign king, at a heavy cost in grain and oil.

Later, however, the priests began to be obstinately proud for the very reason that all alien gods had images. An abstraction was elevated into a virtue, a custom into a principle; the lack of idols made it easier to imagine a single God and deepened the mystery among one's own people, as well as the amazement of strangers. What an abstractly moral people, which did not give its one god a wife!

And yet they were not without imagination. Here as in all religions, with the possible exception of Calvinism, religious services were a piece of theatrical display; but they were celebrated in honor of an abstraction. This solitude of the masculine God distinguished the religion of the Jews from all those before it and most of those after it. The freshly bubbling spirit of the Greeks had invented a fantastic, bustling world over, on, and under the earth, and had found its destiny fixed between gods and demons; the begetting of gods was the most natural of functions, and a joy besides. The idea of the immaculate conception, which recurs in various civilizations, was a surprising exception in Greece and connoted no special holiness. Demons rose from the seed of a god scattered upon the earth, and a goddess sprang from her father's head. But love was the primal current from which everything came in the legends of the Egyptians, Asiatics, and Greeks. Love carried Greeks to Elysium, whereas the Biblical legend begins with the expulsion. Achilles, Odysseus, all of Homer would have been impossible without the love affairs of the gods enthroned among their clouds and serving as models for mortal loves.

Yahweh was the first god to lead an ascetic life. He was not, however, a seraphic angel, nor a spirit, ghost, or star. He was a thunderer and warrior, whom we can imagine as Michelangelo did, absolutely masculine—far more so than Jesus or Buddha, both of whom were surrounded by women. This God without women is doubly surprising in the Jewish people, so strong in its affirmation of life and its advocacy of the virtue of fertility. What is behind this contradiction?

An ethical requirement. Yahweh, demanding no asceticism, urging priests and laymen to increase and multiply, could not impose his moral laws upon his votaries as supreme lord and judge unless he himself lived without fleshly desires. He demanded less of his believers than of himself, whereas the Olympian gods had done the opposite.

To what extent Moses invented this will always be uncertain, for a thousand years lie between him and the Five Books of Moses, the Pentateuch. But certain it is that these prophets, a hundred years before Plato, proclaimed a moral law. In the face of an ancient world which gave free rein to the passions, they taught that one must not slay his enemy, but feed him and give him drink. He who hates is on the side of them that shed blood. They allowed the stranger to share in their laws and customs, remembering their own days of exile. Most astonishing of all, to the Greeks, they said that labor was a blessing and not a humiliation. Aristotle had taught that slavery could not be abolished until the self-moving tools of Hephaestus—machines—became universal. Here was a poor and downtrodden people that gave almost equal rights to the slave. He was given the Sabbath for a day of rest; he was invited to table and to the festivals. If anyone knocked out a free man's tooth, the law was, a tooth for a tooth; but if he knocked out a slave's tooth, it was freedom for a tooth, for he had to give the slave his liberty. The culmination came in Ten Commandments such as no predecessor had formulated with such ominous earnestness, such boldness, or such resolute logic. An insignificant little tribe of nomads, herdsmen, and traders produced a canon that was wholly new to the ancients. This page, given to the world by Jews, will remain forever spread upon the knees of history.

II

JESUS ADDED ANOTHER PAGE, equally precious and equally momentous: he offered the Jewish moral law to the world.

Why was he a phenomenon unique in the Mediterranean? Why would he have drawn the eyes of all posterity even though no one had come to propagate his doctrine? Why was it left for this particular Jewish prophet to carry the ideas of his forefathers to the ancient world, and thus finally to the modern world?

Because the Greeks lay between Moses and Jesus. He came four hundred years after Plato but fourteen hundred years after Moses, and meanwhile the austere, rigid, warlike Mosaic law had been transformed, as bronze seems to be made more delicate by the patina that time bestows. It was a history rich in struggle but poor in victories, full of manly defiance but without increase of power. At the same time the Jews on their coast had watched the rise and fall of many Mediterranean nations. They themselves did not enter into the contest. They strove for expansion as little as the island of Cyprus, which was so close to them, or Antioch, or Rhodes; their material goal was trade, their spiritual goal the godly state. The relaxing of the rigid ideals of this state had to come from within. Having been twice exiled and enslaved, as they were by the Romans in the time of Jesus, the Jews were bound for this reason alone to turn their minds inward, especially since they had no recourse to art or to science.

Moreover, the Mediterranean air was full of a philosophy that had accepted the moral standard of the Jews and anticipated the Christian doctrine of the hereafter. Since Plato and Pythagoras had first taught that the life of the soul was the real life, a belief in the immortal destiny of man had permeated Greek theology more and more, retreating from an Elysium of wine and dancing girls toward a realm of the spirit. With slight variations they, Empedocles, and his pupils, all taught that as a reward for its earthly wandering the soul would altogether cease to exist after death or else would return to the Deity. Plato described the wanderings of a dead soldier's soul between heaven and the nether world four centuries before Matthew's vision of everlasting fire, and before the Revelation of Saint John.

Later, under the Romans, such feelings as these gave rise to a strangely mixed emotion—a longing for death and a fear of it. Both had been strange to the Homeric world. Hence the wish for a doctrine of the hereafter, which would make earthly life a mere preparation; hence the wish for salvation. Seneca, who wrote between the death of Jesus and the writing of the Gospels, brought his doctrine of death close to the Christian teaching: "The body is the burden and punishment of the spirit, weighing it down and holding it in thrall. The soul struggles against the burdensome flesh, striving to return whence it was sent forth: it awaits everlasting rest in the place whence it first beheld truth and clarity." At about the same time Philo Judaeus wrote: "The soul is buried in the body as if in a grave-mound. Only when we are dead does it come to life, freed of all evil." How close the two philosophers—pagan and Jew, in Rome and Alexandria—were to the prophet of Nazareth!

In the preceding century the Homeric gods had been hard pressed from every quarter. It was long ago that Achilles in Hades had been allowed to grumble that a living peasant was happier than a dead prince. It was long ago that the gods had accompanied mortals as daily companions in work and warfare. Later they had become rare and miraculous figures, exalted from the flowering earth to a more and more abstract world—exalted, but also crowded out. Instead of fellow warriors they had become onlookers and judges.

How easily we find the transitions! When Paul went to Antioch he could attend the great spring festival of Adonis, in which the image of the dead god was buried and wailed over by the women, to rise again on the second or third day amid the cheers of the people who resurrected him. If a predecessor or disciple of Jesus, studying or traveling, chanced to encounter Egyptian votaries, he must have heard them tell of Osiris, who was born of a virgin, as Apis, the bull sacred to him, was born of a virgin cow. Both were impregnated by a sunbeam, or, according to others, by a moonbeam.

Throughout the Roman Empire the Persian cult of Mithras was studied by philosophers and professed by soldiers, who delighted in its magic arts without practicing its renunciation and penance. Among the sacraments of Mithras we even find communion—consecrated bread and a goblet of water or wine. And all this not in contradiction to but in harmony with the ethics of the Greek world. Thus Plato's mother was said to have received Apollo; Pythagoras discovered former human souls in the animals, conversed with a she-bear, and stroked an eagle.

Jesus had not to seek all this afar; it was growing close around him. The moral law under which he was born, first the hewn stone of the Ten Commandments, then the hundredfold elaboration of the Torah, gave him all the dogmatic and legendary forms necessary to present his visionary raptures to his own people. He was never in opposition to Judaism, never in sympathy with any hostile doctrine. He did not, for example, set up a new humanitarian ideal in opposition to the old prophets; instead he continued them. Jeremiah and Isaiah returned after five hundred years as John and Jesus. Jesus did combat certain empty ceremonies—the very thing Isaiah had denounced in the same words—and the new prophet's prophecy that the Temple would be destroyed earned him the same priestly hatred that his predecessor had aroused. Both were persecuted as enemies of the fatherland.

It was not only that Jesus found already in existence all the things now regarded as the basis of his dogma—creation, Providence, the Last Judgment, obedience to God, love of the weak. The Psalms of Solomon, written seventy years before Christ, and the Gospels, written seventy years after his birth, display the same Messianic hopes. He even found the actual phrases for the morality he taught. Hillel the Elder, about 30 B.C., addressing a doubter, expressed the quintessence of Jewish ethics in the words, "Therefore all things whatsoever ye would that men should do to you, do ye even so to them."

If Jews and pagans had already anticipated legends and epics, history and commandments, and had written down everything that makes the essence of the Gospels, what then was the special merit of Jesus?

A step of incalculable consequences. He broke down the gates of the Jewish fortress and opened his arms to the world. Jesus made a world religion out of the jealously guarded faith of a little people that had fled from oppression to a belief in itself as the chosen. He overcame the cleavage between nationality and faith that had troubled the hearts of the old prophets, because he was far more deeply concerned for the salvation of mankind than for the order of precedence among peoples. One of the greatest of Jews, Maimonides, later said that Jesus and the Arabs had prepared the way for the Messiah.

Out of the jealously guarded dogmas of an outworn and obstinate priesthood Jesus saved the precious elements of a moral code that had failed for a thousand years to conquer the world because it was burdened with national pretension. His appeal went beyond the boundaries of his people, and so he established a community without nationality, a new sense above that of statehood. In summoning everyone to found a catholic league of humanity instead of a league of nations, excluding neither slaves nor barbarians, he went beyond the shores of the Mediterranean. Although he never left the confines of his little country during his brief life, he became a conqueror greater than Alexander.

By taking mercy and justice, salvation and the Messiah from the stone walls of Jerusalem to the gardens of Galilee, Jesus transformed the austere Yahweh, god of war, punishment, and revenge, into a gentle and magnanimous deity, even into a lamb, which was himself. Not in ecstasy but in humility he called himself the Son of God and the Brother of Men. He did not offer up his life voluntarily for the sake of its truth, but his death was so cruel and so unjust that it seemed to be a sacrifice confirming and crowning his mission. Two human factors, his death and the figure of his mother (the first goddess among the Jews), lent him a splendor beyond that of any Jew before him. When the Jews forsook him, he gained the world. Mortals believed he was bringing them peace.

III

IT WAS NOT HIS FAULT that he brought a sword. Prophets and philosophers would not be what they are unless they were misunderstood and misused by greedy or jealous creatures. This seeker after God appeared at a time and place that necessarily falsified his noble purposes. He, Jesus, whose soul was constantly aloft with his great Father, and who strove to rise above the state, passed for a revolutionist within the state. He was not the first whom a doctrine of a better hereafter made into an unwilling tribune of the people. Any man who declares that health and strength, productive labor, enjoyment, and happiness are evil, or who at any rate does not strive after them, will naturally attract those who are deficient in these attributes. The dispossessed have always been submissive to fate, and anything that promises them a better world they call fatalism; the others, the flourishing and dominating natures, the creative ones, would rather have themselves to thank for their success, and accordingly they resent fate.

The idealistic teachings of Jesus made him a communist in the life of society, and brought him close to a sect that had been leading a quiet existence in Palestine for more than a hundred and fifty years. The Essenes were not revolutionists but serene idealists. At that time they formed an order of four thousand members, living in villages in common households without property of their own, sharing food and clothing, prohibiting arms and trade among themselves, leading a life of cleanliness, gentleness, and prayer, and turning over all money to an elected administrative group for distribution. These were no ascetics fleeing from the world and allowing others to support them, like the hermits or Diogenes. They worked as peasants and artisans, and did not forbid marriage but mistrusted it. They declared it permissible to beget children, but not to enjoy the act. This one puritan principle aside, everything about them was kindly.

It has never been conclusively shown that Jesus belonged to this order, but the spirit was the same. And no one questions the dependence of the Apostles on the Essenes. Their history bears frequent witness to their communism, and their indictment of the rich recurs in the church fathers of the fourth century, who forbade all private property within the congregation. John Chrysostom even preached that everyone would be well off if only all things were still held in common, as among the primitive Christians. Jesus himself says in Luke: "Whosoever he be of you that forsaketh not all that he hath, he cannot be my disciple. . . . Sell that ye have, and give alms. . . . Sell all that thou hast, and distribute unto the poor, and thou shalt have treasure in heaven."

The strange attempt that is being renewed these days to part Jesus from communism occupied even Matthew, as well as many subsequent theologians, down to Luther, whose truly German fear of the authorities made him try to hush such things up. But actually the communism of the primitive Christians had nothing to do with modern political communism; it was always confined to joint use. Neither in the agriculture nor in the small-scale industry of those days could production be effectively combined, let alone turned over to the State.

And yet Jesus was far more revolutionary (and not simply in his contempt for money) than he seems from a distance and at first glance. The present author has tried to show from the Gospels (*The Son of Man,* 1929) the development of Jesus' character from tenderness and kindness to ominous commandment, the dramatic turning point at Caesarea Philippi. In this later part of his ministry he sometimes has all the ponderous force of the Jewish prophets. Here is the prototype of the Byzantine Christ we see in the mosaics, enthroned as Lord of the World.

In his own time, however, this later Jesus was not recognized, but only mocked or pitied.

The three most powerful men of the ancient world were friends of the Jews. Alexander attracted them in great numbers to his new city, where they occupied two out of five city quarters. Caesar protected them against Greek and Roman cults. Augustus exempted them from certain imperial laws, and when the Jews could not attend public banquets because of the Sabbath, he had his gifts distributed afterward in their district beyond the Tiber.

These statesmen's reasons were founded on the conservatism, the wealth, and the fecundity of the Jews. Since the Roman law divided inheritances among the whole family, the peasant nations restricted the number of their children. This and the exploitation of slaves and tenants brought about the depopulation of Italy, while the Jews, who were everywhere traders and not peasants, could distribute their money among many children. But they also aroused the curiosity of the mighty because of their one God. A world weary of its old gods was pursuing Persian and Jewish customs from sheer exhaustion. Indeed there were historians at the time of Christ who expected a sort of world revolution from the Jews. As the spirit of scientific investigation around the Mediterranean declined, love of marvels and credulity grew, clutching at anything that deviated from the old gods.

During and shortly after the time of Christ it became fashionable in Roman society to embrace Judaism; two oriental kings even had themselves circumcised in order to marry the sisters of the Jewish king Agrippa. Both woman afterward deceived their husbands, Berenice with the Emperor Titus. Nero's wife and many distinguished Roman ladies were Jewesses, or protected the Jews. The intellectual leaders began to be ashamed of their many gods, their sacrifices and ceremonial fights with animals, and Greek authors adopted the one God and morality of the Pentateuch. They merely left out the disagreeable things, the Sabbath and circumcision or the dietary laws, and became first century Jews in the spirit of nineteenth century enlightenment. In Antioch all Jewry was said to consist of converts.

At the same time the Jews aroused hatred by their wealth and worldly wisdom. They did not acknowledge, as the Greeks and Romans did, any other possible religion; they wanted to bring their invisible God to the rest of the world. The whole Mediterranean was the field of Jewish missionaries then.

The Roman letters SPQR appeared, according to legend, beneath the cross of Christ, and in countless places afterward, and so the world's interest has focused on the political background of that Good Friday, probably in the year 30. Herod, whose forty years' rule provides the key to the era, drew his power from Caesar. Few Jews of the time knew how truly they lived after that great man's nature. While Pompey had defeated the constantly rebelling little Jewish state after long struggles, and made it into a Roman protectorate, so that its theocracy was like that of the Vatican after 1870, Caesar soon summoned the new protégé to aid him in Egypt at his time of greatest distress. The half-Jewish freedman Antipater, who helped save Caesar, learned to know the rarest of all qualities in a dictator—per-

sonal gratitude. To him and afterward to his son Herod, Caesar gave
the best position that any Roman protectorate ever enjoyed: freedom
from tribute and conscription, restoration of the fortress of Jerusalem. Augustus, continuing Caesar's tradition, even added the royal
title.

Herod, more Roman than Jewish, was very much the fashionable flatterer of his powerful patron. The very archetype of a rich
ruler aggrandizing his country abroad, and corrupting it at home,
he satisfied the Romans with temples, theaters, and games but at
the same time angered the Jews and was eventually regarded as a
traitor by both. This is an interesting symptom of decadence that
usually precedes intellectual revolutions. His every note was false,
but cynicism made him alluring. He maintained Egyptian satellites,
Arab legionaries, Germanic bodyguards, and eunuchs and soothsayers, catamites and spies. He married ten times and regarded himself, with his many children, as the father of the fatherland.

Yet his marble Temple did not serve to tempt the Jews, who
could never see anything but the gate surmounted by the golden
Roman eagle with which he outraged it. For a long time neither
rust nor rain could obliterate the shadow of the eagle, even after it
was torn down.

Nevertheless the Roman potentates must have continued to feel
a deep respect for this defiant little nation. When Augustus finally
made Judea into a province after the death of Herod, he did not have
his head stamped on the coins, lest the province be affronted. And
no Roman soldier was allowed to enter the Temple on pain of death.

When the Emperor Caligula tried to set up his statue in the
Temple, the godly state arose to dramatic grandeur. A sort of
national strike began. No one tilled his fields; the whole nation
declared it would rather perish than see the Emperor's statue in its
Temple. Soon everything was one unceasing revolt, and since
spiritual matters were in question, many illuminati appeared, both
sincere and fraudulent, each professing to be the Messiah who
would save Judea. Nobody knows how many thousands were killed
by the Romans. On one other occasion, immediately after the time

of Jesus' martyrdom, a Roman Prefect, Quintilius Varus, seems to have had two thousand rebels crucified.

An embassy to Rome, finally catching the emperor in a bibulous mood, induced him to withdraw the order. The desperate courage with which the Jews defended their passionate hatred of idols—it was more the idol than the pagan that outraged them—this civil war for the sake of a statue, showed the Romans that they could ultimately preserve their authority in that corner of the Mediterranean only by force, against what they were bound to regard as a handful of madmen.

But another twenty years of revolts, a four years' war, and a long siege of the overcrowded metropolis were still to come before the city and its Temple perished. This conclusion of the Jewish tragedy compelled admiration even among contemporaries. It was the climax of their history; isolated sects perhaps, but surely no other nation as a whole had ever defended its faith with such sacrifices. This was no class struggle like that of the Jacobins; it was not a struggle for liberty at all, for liberty could never be won. It was one of the heroic moments of history, when peddlers and artisans fought for the spirit alone, for an idea, for a God.

To this day on the triumphal arch of Titus in the Roman Forum a Roman soldier holds aloft the seven-branched candlestick he has snatched from the burning Temple. Yet the Jews went on trying for a long time, even down to the time of Hadrian, to recover Jerusalem from the Roman power by uprisings which they carried abroad to Cyprus and Alexandria. But the double garrison held a mute and desolate city. No Jew might enter it, and not until long afterward did the descendants of those who had been driven out return to mourn by an old wall of the Temple of King Solomon.

IV

AUGUSTUS WAS AN INHERITOR. Despite all idealization, the disagreeable head that we reconstruct from the many statutes and coins is that of a slow, shrewd, and crafty man, his features all pointed—the mouth, the chin, the long, sniffing nose. He seemed to shrivel while yet a youth, without ever becoming a man. Yet sexually he was always normal, even lascivious, and he lived to be seventy-six. We can gain further understanding of his nature from the sculptured head of his wife, the marvelously cold and passionate Livia—one of the loveliest women's portraits in history. This choice alone would be enough to prove Augustus' knowledge of love.

He had also a great knowledge of men. With superb art he hood-winked the Senate, constantly playing the man of the people, constantly retiring and being urged back into power. He silently endured attack, merely leaving the chamber when things grew too fierce. He concealed his wealth, waiting until his old age to build a palace. Thirteen times consul, and perpetually imperator and ponti-fex, he allowed the office of emperor to creep into history without a *coup d'état*. Suddenly it was simply there. What caution, what circumspection, what consideration for the people he meant to rule! What an abundance of wise acts without a single great deed! Augustus is one of the best examples in the history of fame showing how an adroit politician may substitute duration of power for genius and still seem a great man to posterity.

He not only got all his power from Caesar's genius, but used him as a warning: but for the ides of March he would never have been Augustus. His portrait and his character prove that he had not a drop of his stepfather's blood. But the blood Caesar shed under the daggers of assassins at the Capitol was made a sort of fetish by his successor, who guarded against a similar death by keeping this constantly before his mind's eye. Caesar's end befitted his great nature; the senators could endure his power but not his spirit. The soft-spoken acumen of Augustus provoked nobody, and his ostenta-tious professional courtesy made him look like the supreme govern-ment functionary, whereas in reality he was the first emperor. This technique suited his gifts: although he knew very little about war-fare, he relied entirely on his army, and no general with the excep-tion of Varus ever disappointed him. While the generalship of Alex-ander and Caesar overtopped that of all their contemporaries, their successor Augustus had all his battles fought by others. The man who founded the standing army, invented the Praetorian Guard, and by it assured his own long life, was neither born nor trained to be a soldier.

But he knew how to find the right men. Agrippa was Augustus' friend and later his son-in-law. His was one of the finest Roman heads, gazing out into the distance from deep-set eyes, like the best type of modern flier or explorer. If we compare the busts of the two, we find the bold man of action distinguished from his reflective imperial partner. We see a matter-of-fact, productive nature contrasted with a self-seeking, calculating one. Agrippa seems the born king, Augustus but his chancellor.

The splendor of his reign, which earned him the name of Augustus—the Majestic—makes it easy to forget that he spent his youth, from nineteen to thirty-two, struggling with political rivals. He had to pay a high price for his heritage. Finally Agrippa won the naval battle of Actium, on the east coast of the Adriatic, for the absent Augustus.

Actually it was a woman whose defeat brought world dominion to Augustus; it was typical of him that he gained it not by love but by hate.

Cleopatra is the most beautiful female figure the Mediterranean has produced. She came after the prime of her line but before its decadence, just as the finest Mediterranean grapes ripen immediately before the end of the vintage. From the Greeks she got the intellect and freedom of Aspasia, from the Romans a share of statesmanship. She should really have lived in the Renaissance, but it was fortunate after all that she did not come seventeen centuries later. She would have met only a Borgia then, not a Caesar. If she, in her mid-twenties, had accomplished nothing beyond winning the love of Caesar, thirty years her senior, Cleopatra would have been one of the fairest legends of history.

Plutarch tells how she met him. Caesar had taken Alexandria from the sea side and landed at the palace of the Ptolemies. Now he walked in. The Queen of the Egyptians had hidden—what else could she do? During the preceding hour she may have considered what was to be done, and she could think of no recourse except to

function as a woman where she could not function as a queen. What then? She had a slave wrap her up in a costly rug and carry it as a gift of submission, so to speak, before the conqueror. Caesar, who was sitting at dinner, obviously bored, glanced up indifferently as the present was brought in on the slave's shoulder. The slave unrolled it as if to display the beauty of the gift. Suddenly his gesture revealed a woman, who coquettishly hesitated for a moment before standing up.

Thus Cleopatra conquered the conqueror.

After Caesar she loved no one but Antony; and here they were, posted with their ships in the bay near which the three greatest naval battles of the Mediterranean took place.

The Ambracian Gulf, known today as the Gulf of Arta, is a bay some thirty miles long, with an entrance little more than half a mile wide. It is priceless to those who seek shelter but perilous in war, for it can be blockaded even more easily than the Dardanelles. Here, near the promontory of Actium, in the very middle of the Roman Empire, the Roman armies of Antony and Octavian, later to be Augustus, met to decide the course of history. No doubt Antony suffered just such inner uncertainties as Shakespeare's soldier forcibly presented to him:

> O noble emperor, do not fight by sea;
> Trust not to rotten planks; do you misdoubt
> This sword and these my wounds? Let the Egyptians
> And the Phoenicians go a-ducking: we
> Have used to conquer standing on the earth
> And fighting foot to foot.

Octavian drew up his army north of the inlet. He stood guard like a watchdog, never taking his eyes off the gate.

Antony's whole fleet lay in the bay, keeping touch with the greater part of his army, which reached far inland. Antony's galleys blocked the narrow entrance, but only defensively; outside, stretching farther than the eye could reach, lay Octavian's ships, ready to pounce on the emerging fleet. On the advice of Cleopatra, who was aboard his ship, Antony (feeling that luck was deserting him before the cautious advance of Octavian) decided to fight a naval battle. This meant neglecting his land troops, which were much better prepared.

Like crouching leopards the armies lay face to face at close quarters. Cleopatra reclined in the gaily colored tent on the deck of her ship inside the bay. Bored, worn out, facing the threat of disaster, yet still hoping for victory, she toyed with her jewels, scolded the slave girls, and hummed softly to ease the awful suspense. She could feel plainly the rising anger of Antony's officers, who wanted to fight on land and concentrate the thirty thousand men at his disposal. They had no confidence in the ships as against the enemy's excellent fleet. One or two generals had already gone over to Octavian, who was within easy reach, only a mile away.

Antony laughed off the bad news, but when his friend Aheno- barbus deserted, he grew angry. In savage mood he entered the Queen's tent to pour out his wrath on her. There in the perfumed silken tent, the lovers had a scene of blind anger, hatred, passion, and scorn. Antony's friends were beginning to give him up.

Cleopatra had already resolved to take her own vessels out of their prison in the bay and leave Antony to fight his own battle. She did not propose to share the fate of her sister, to appear in a chariot as part of a Roman conqueror's triumph amid the howls of the Roman mob.

So she gave her orders, and next morning her sixty vessels fol- lowed the flagship "Antonias" out to sea. The gateway was open, and the battle began; Agrippa's light, graceful vessels swooped down on Antony's heavy ones in the bay. But by Octavian's order not a single Egyptian vessel was touched. The queen's glistening triremes passed out among the fighting Romans like magic swans and took to the sea, leaving blood and fire and the din of battle behind them. Antony recognized the sign. Cleopatra's fatal fascination led him to forsake the men fighting in his behalf. He set out at once in a boat, rowing after the queen's vessel. Enemy ships soon pursued him, but he fought them off and continued southward.

For three days Antony sat in the bow of the queen's vessel, mute, his head buried in his hands for hours on end. His career as a soldier ended when he abandoned ships and army, leaving them leaderless. They were destroyed. Octavian was master of the Medi- terranean. He pursued Cleopatra and her lover to Egypt, drove them to suicide, and killed Caesarion, the son of Caesar and Cleo- patra, the only rival Caesar had left behind.

Again in the battle of Actium the decisive naval factor was a new type of vessel, the *liburna,* a mobile one-banked galley, designed by

Agrippa to accompany his high-walled, turreted ships (also a novelty), as destroyers accompany cruisers.

When the defeated Antony fled with Cleopatra's sixty vessels, there was more than a love story involved. It meant that a worn-out, voluptuary Roman surrendered the Roman tradition to an ambitious younger man who lived entirely in that tradition. The battle did not decide between the world dominion of two nations; it was simply the end of a civil war to decide which of two Romans should rule.

Nothing about it is more amazing than Cleopatra's mistake in backing Antony. She really had nothing in common with the Egyptians, for she came from a Macedonian family, thought in Greek, and remained all her life devoted to the Mediterranean, not the Nile. She and the house of the Ptolemies might have created a new Carthage, rivaling Rome. But they did not. The family, who became kings by the intervention of a general after the death of Alexander, could not match the Romans in either strength or sea power. They spent in comparative idleness the three centuries during which Rome fought her way up. Actium, therefore, did not measure two civilizations, but merely decided the possession of Egypt. With magnificent swiftness Augustus followed the fleeing pair, and Alexandria fell into his hands as if of its own accord. Thus he was able to bring grain for seven years from Egypt, the seven fat years, to feed the people of Rome. Through him a quarter million souls received their bread gratis.

The Romans did not love him for it, but then, whom did the Romans love? At any rate they endured him for a long time without revolting, because he was so shrewd in what he did. The crowd, wearied by long civil wars, were glad enough to see a single steady hand at the helm. They hoped for the continuity of a limited monarchy, which might have been kept alive by abler successors. Surely this was better, the people told themselves, than perpetually venal senators. Did they deserve anything better than the right to mint copper coins, while Caesar kept gold and silver for himself? No previous government had ever offered them war games in which three thousand Athenians and Persians presented the battle of

Salamis on thirty vessels in an artificial lake. No one had ever given them the same sweet thrill in the circus, where criminals were used to demonstrate the various deaths of celebrated Romans.

Now Rome, the old brick town, became a splendid marble city, at least in the spots where the people assembled. One fine day the Pantheon, loveliest of all Roman buildings, even when unfinished, made its appearance at the heart of Rome, whose seven gods were to be worshiped there. Sons and grandsons of slaves, and later even manumitted slaves, could become Roman citizens. The arrogance of the provinces increased, and if there were scandals in the imperial family, the mockery of Roman gossip merely made them the more popular.

But, most astonishing of all, the gates of the temple of Janus were closed. Fifteen years after the assassination of Caesar his heir had made a Roman province out of the last independent Mediterranean country. Warned by Caesar's Persian plans, he resolved to keep the peace from then on. When the great bronze gates closed one solemn day in the year 29, an era was at an end: two hundred years of war were finished. A young man of thirty-three proclaimed peace to the world: and at least within his world empire he actually preserved it for forty-three years. The ambition of Augustus was fulfilled. The Pax Romana had come true.

First Augustus had considerably enlarged the Empire, more by threats than by war. He acquired the territories approximating the modern Tirol, western Switzerland, Styria, and northern Spain. Now peace and security under a single power, seldom interrupted, scarcely disputed, extended from Britain to the Nile, from the Atlas Mountains to the Syrian Desert. The only danger came from the north and the east, where the barbarians were at work. The Mediterranean, a peaceful lake, was united as never before or afterward, and so it remained for three hundred years. "Ubique Pax," Augustus inscribed on his coins. The golden age seemed to have dawned.

Peace actually did come with the monarchy. The monarchy inherited the power the Republic had won in fierce battles, and it followed like blessed summer upon the stormy spring, but still the seed had been sown in spring. If we allow three hundred years for each of the two forms of government in Rome, we find on comparison that the Republic was more creative by far. Yet with all its excesses and weaknesses the Roman Empire did set mankind an example of how a slowly established democratic world power can be preserved under absolute rulers, giving protection and security to the millions. But the first Empire did not create a civilization of its own. Everything that made the Romans great in history developed under the Republic—roads, buildings, law, great men.

The emperor's propaganda created the Augustan age of art. He wanted to play Pericles, but he had no Sophocles or Euripides, no Phidias or Ictinus, no Socrates or Herodotus, and above all he was no Pericles. Scarcely a name remains from what the fine arts and the stage produced. Livy, Pollio, Strabo, and Capito represented science, and then there were four poets.

Augustus took some pains with Vergil; wanting a Roman national poem to match the Homeric poems, he put Vergil to work on the *Aeneid* and sometimes inquired about progress. But the poem always remained the work of a lesser descendant. It never had any life outside of Italy, and found no really productive reader except Dante. Vergil's loyalty to Augustus, who made him rich, was very useful to both. It was touching to see the poet finally leaving a quarter of his fortune to the emperor. The farewell of the poet, dying on his way home, to his patron is perhaps the most beautiful scene in the cold life of Augustus.

The three other great Roman poets, Ovid, Horace, and Catullus, were rather against than in sympathy with the government. Ovid's eroticism was much too graceful for a newly consolidated state. There was a scandal at court in which he fell under suspicion of pandering, but probably it was only his magical verses that sent the emperor's granddaughter off her head. In this highly literary sense Ovid was indeed a pander, like every poet. Augustus prohibited his books, first reading them with great relish. Ovid was banished to the Black Sea, where he finally ended a long, gloomy life of exile.

Catullus, more of a lyric bard of the sea and of country life, died at thirty-three on his place at Lacus Benaeus (Lake Garda), leaving behind some of the greatest love poems in the Latin language.

Horace, the son of a freedman, probably of Oriental blood, fought against Augustus as a young officer in the Republic, left the country with Brutus after the battle of Philippi, and so lost the small estate he had inherited. This venture into politics might easily have cost him his life and did for the time being exclude his talents from the reigning society. He seems never afterward to have overcome a fear of public life. For many years he lived in and around Rome, associating only with actors, usurers, and barbers, and he was timid and ill at ease when he had to make an appearance. Although he had a native gift for satirizing society, he kept up a light note, in order to hurt nobody's feelings.

Perhaps the world owes the delicately serene tone of Horace's poetry, never recaptured by any other poet, to his initial failure in the political arena. Repulsed by events, he sank wholly into a pastoral idyl, and only an occasional flash of malicious irony sparkles like dew in the flowery carpet of his song. Hence the timidity of his attitude. When attacked for the impropriety of his verses, he hastily veered back to morality. How fortunate that Brutus did not win at Philippi! Otherwise Horace would have become his minister and made a career of setting the duty on imported perfumes from Antioch or limiting the prices at the brothels on the left bank of the Tiber. Even if he had conquered a new province, indeed if he had been emperor and conquered Persia, the world would still have lost the music of his verses, which have outlived all the generals of his age, even great Agrippa. Never has the beauty of the Latin tongue, and seldom the tenderness of a lover, found voice so perfectly as in the lines:

> The snows have fled, the fields are green again,
> The trees their young leaves show—
> The world is changing and their banks restrain
> The rivers running low.
> The sister Graces and the Nymphs at play
> May dance in Nature's dress—
> The changing year, and time that steals each day
> Unmeasured hopes repress. . . .

Whether Tomorrow's dawn succeeds today
　　Lies with the Gods alone—
Your greedy heir his hands can never lay
　　On what you've made your own!

But as he remained a poet, Horace was discovered by Vergil, who introduced him to Maecenas. The latter gave him a little estate with eight slaves and thus won with ridiculous ease an immortality greater even than that of the poet, for everyone has heard of Maecenas. Horace remained grateful to him in sweet verses and died immediately after him. At the house of Maecenas, too, Horace met the emperor.

Augustus, recognizing the genius in him, tried to turn him also into a eulogist, offering him the post of a secretary, which could be built into power and money. But Horace declined and merely wrote a hymn on the battle of Actium, which after all was but the last round between Caesar's heirs. Later Horace sang the victories of the imperial sons and devoted an ode to the whole age, but we can truthfully say he did it at the command of Augustus. And these compositions are no more indispensable to his complete work than the two triumphal marches are to Beethoven and Wagner. When he was finally set to work on an ode annihilating the emperor's great enemy, Cleopatra, the result was a secret paean. The poet vacillated between his admiration and his instructions to such an extent that even Augustus must have smiled, if smile he could.

For despite huge successes, which he gathered in greater abundance than any predecessor on the Mediterranean, the emperor's own character cheated him of happiness. This was the price he paid for the double meaning of his existence. He would play the moralist and yet have his creatures examine into the beauty and health of women who attracted him. The man who exiled the unseemly Ovid was probably a libertine himself. And so it was natural that he should discover in his family the vices he was concealing. He had to repudiate his daughter, who led the life of a harlot. Enmities, adoptions, and tragedies resulted from the series of sons, stepsons, and nephews who were successively chosen for the throne. While the emperor tried to assure his dynasty, the hearts of his nearest and dearest were destroyed, as they were with Napoleon. Fear and uneasiness harried him before he died, in his middle seventies.

The reason was not merely the succession. Augustus' last look went northward, toward the Alps. The peril came from the Germans. At the time of Christ the Mediterranean was threatened from the north for the third time.

V

MOST OF THE PEOPLES the Mediterranean attracted were not seafarers. The Gauls, it is true, are supposed to have sailed to the coast of Britain under leather sails before the Romans came; they did not venture out upon the great ocean. The Germans were complete landlubbers. What attracted peoples to the Mediterranean, then, was not seafaring but the coast. Because they never grew accustomed to the sea until the time of the Normans, the victorious Nordic tribes could not remain long in the south. What drew them thither? They had land enough, even if they were harassed in their turn by eastern tribes.

What they sought was better land. The legend of brighter shores, of fertile slopes, of warmth and blue sky had reached the somber oak forests and barren thickets of Germany. In their native territory between the Baltic, Hungary, the Vistula, and the Elbe, there was neither grain nor fruit nor wine. Posidonius, who traveled there about 90 B.C., adds to his description the comment that Homer must have voyaged here to find the model for his realm of the dead. By that time the Mediterranean sun had already painted three hundred years' golden tint on the marble of the Athenian temples.

The same three centuries had passed between the assault of Brennus on little Rome and the German invasion in 113 B.C. And the same terror took possession of Rome, risen meanwhile to a great metropolis, when word came from the north that an immeasurable host of barbarians had scaled the Alps, the natural barrier—no, not a host, a nation, whole peoples, bringing wives and children and household goods and tents with them in their carts. The Roman called them men with old men's hair, for such was the impression their blond manes gave. The impact was like an earthquake or the plague.

The fighting of the strangers was as rude and raw as the flesh they ate, as the howls of their women in the stockade of carts, urging the men on to fight. With shields as tall as a man, clubs, and long swords, they advanced in a battle line formed by roping themselves together. They pushed on through country after country and battle after battle, winning and winning year upon year. They killed their prisoners and sacrificed the youngest to their gods. The old women caught the blood and prophesied from the entrails. All this was new to the Romans, though they had fought with plenty of barbarians in the east and practiced all sorts of cruelties themselves.

These Germanic peoples, the Cimbri and Teutons (the *furor Teutonicus* now once more so fashionable originated then), failed to advance upon Rome in the course of a ten years' invasion. But in Gaul, along the Rhone and the Seine, and even as far down as the Ebro, people watched them with astonishment. They would seize the vineyards and fence them with the bones of their captives. After each victory they sent messengers of triumph to the Consul, asking pitifully for a little land, and then suddenly fell upon their enemies as negotiations began. Strabo and other chroniclers tell of this Germanic guile and treachery. When Marius finally defeated them after eight years, he saw many of the women hurling their children under the carts and then killing themselves to escape captivity.

The memory of this "Cimbric terror," which became an awful legend in Rome, had been one of Caesar's reasons for going to Gaul. Today we would say that Italy conquered France to protect herself from Germany. For France was harassed by the Germans in the first century B.C. for the same reason as two thousand years later: because France was richer and more fertile. The Gauls had received wine and oil from the Greek settlements on the Riviera centuries before, and then had learned to raise grain and sheep from the Romans in what is now Belgium. Caesar went across the Rhine three times, but on each occasion only for a few weeks. The Celtic tribes formerly located between Romans and Germans had meanwhile disappeared. The Limes, an ancient Maginot Line along the Rhine, was not built between the two nations until a century later.

When Augustus came to power, he at first mistook the nature of the Germans, treating them with kindness—which even thus early they thought was weakness. He gave lands and privileges to certain tribes and received some of the dukes' sons as officers at his court, where the blond, blue-eyed savages with their youthful vigor had swift success as lovers of pampered women. Teuton blondness became the fashion in the city, and the ladies developed a growing demand for imported curls from Germany. The poetic eye of Horace saw further then than the emperor's world-spanning gaze. He wished Augustus a victory over the Germanic tribes as the greatest triumph of his life.

Yes, Augustus had a weakness for the Germans, and he was fond of employing them among his Praetorians. But once, while they were holding their shields over the sleeping emperor during a stormy night on Mount Etna and suddenly heard the mountain grumbling from within, these sons of the north are said to have been utterly terrified. There they stand, guarding the slumber of an alien emperor, on an island in the Mediterranean. Suddenly the elements burst forth. The young bears, undaunted by any storm in their forests, fall back before that which is strange to them, yet which they are striving to possess. Perhaps their number that night included Marbod and Arminius, the sons of German dukes, who were trying to learn all they could in the emperor's bodyguard, that they might the more easily annihilate his legions later in the primeval German forests.

For it was this that darkened the last years of Augustus. Being inclined to finish every work of Caesar, or at least to copy the man from whom he had inherited name, power, and glory, he undertook a conquest of Germany in his old age. He meant to establish the Roman frontier along the Elbe and the Danube. He would fortify the whole district from the Black Sea to Lake Geneva. He

landed his troops from a fleet in the Baltic, and had 150,000 men
winter for the first time in the wild forest. Arminius, as a former
eques, playing the Roman in the camp of Varus, spied out all the
details of the Roman army. The accounts of the German victory
in the Teutoburger Wald (A.D. 9) are few, for the victors could not
write, and the vanquished would not. Besides, few Romans ever got
home. The great army was led into swamps and jungles by an
ancient "Fifth Column." The head of Varus, who killed himself,
went on a strange journey by way of Bohemia to Rome, just as
similar trophies afterward made their way from Byzantium to
Paris.

Augustus was a broken man. He did not live to see his revenge.

Nobody, neither emperor nor pope, ever ruled Rome so long
as Augustus; and yet, trying to establish the first dynasty, he was
led by shortcomings of character into a poor choice, and not a lasting one, among his successors. The four emperors who followed
him in the next 55 years squandered their great heritage, without
being able to destroy it. These decadent or dissolute personalities—
three of whom perished by murder or suicide, and the most interesting, Tiberius, of melancholia, in retirement—are interesting
chiefly because of their wives. One, Messalina, has lived through
the centuries. How rotten the Republic must long have been, if it
did not dare govern itself within a mere half century of Caesar's
death! When Caligula died the Senate haggled until the Praetorian
Guard dragged a trembling old scholar out of hiding, and proclaimed him Emperor Claudius.

Nero, a man of many gifts, is more attractive, with all his assassinations, than Seneca, his chancellor, whose pretensions should have
carried with them an obligation. The philosopher who denounced
avarice and left an estate worth twenty million dollars is more contemptible than his master, who had spells of constructive activity
and began the Corinth canal. There is a burlesque side to Nero, a
sort of cynical innocence, from which his crimes arise.

Nero's end makes clear two qualities of the Roman national
character—one in the upper classes, one in the lower. The conservative Senate forgave him assassination and arson. But for an

emperor to appear as a singer and actor at the festivals was too much for Roman dignity; the Senate rose against him because he was talented. Phryne had shown her beauty to the judges and been set free. The Roman authorities, however, punished just what the Greeks praised—art, talent, beauty. The Roman people, at first clinging to its benefactor in the crisis, finally abandoned him when the expected grain ship from Egypt turned out to be full of sand that was wanted for the athletic arena.

Even the Flavii, who followed, counted but one achievement for the Empire among them, and that a tragic one, the fall of Jerusalem. There is nothing interesting about them except the fact that a crown sat on a plebeian head for the first time in history. Vespasian, a fat banker, though he distinguished himself as an officer, was greatly amused himself to think that he would one day be worshiped as a god. Sly like a peasant, heavy and thickset, he was perhaps almost the Stalin of his day; he was the latter's inferior only in education. He immediately forbade all philosophy because the leader of the opposition in the Senate was a Stoic. But he also had his say in a gesture of kindness to the people. An inventor once showed him a machine designed to move loads for building. He rewarded the man but dropped the invention, saying he did not want to take the people's bread. Titus, a chip off the old block, was scarcely better. Domitian, the brother of Titus, can lay claim to the important step of restricting Italian viticulture in favor of grain. The law remained in force for two hundred years.

When we read of the passionate revolts against the Romans that the Jews kept up for twenty years, the failures of Vespasian and Titus in fighting them are understandable. A fierce flame turned the little theocracy into an army that shook the authority of the Empire. When a colonial power tries to confiscate the holy of holies, the temple treasure, for taxes, it need not be surprised if the defeated nation unites to drive out the victors. There were more Jews in Palestine then than ever—three million. Revolts alternated with pogroms there and in Alexandria, until finally a great Roman effort was necessary. Forty thousand Jews are said to have fallen, and only two were captured in the siege. These amazing figures are credible because they come from one of the two, Josephus, the Jewish governor, who was himself a friend of the Roman emperors and afterward wrote a history of the war.

About this time there dawned on the Mediterranean a day as important as almost any battle day. The destruction and downfall it brought were of immeasurable benefit. On the twenty-fourth of August, A.D. 79, Vesuvius buried the cities of Pompeii and Herculaneum. The people who perished then did not fall by human hands to make a state or a king more powerful; they fell victim to the elements, or, we might say, by the hand of God. With them there perished Pliny, the naturalist, who had gone near the volcano to study its eruption. They died within minutes, like the inhabitants of London under enemy bombs. But when the curiosity of science dug them up centuries afterward, it revealed an ancient city petrified, with houses and furnishings, statues and frescoes; a dog was even caught in the act of turning to scratch.

When we consider how many millions have since been killed deliberately but to no purpose, the people of Pompeii seem like victims who aimlessly served a real end. Anything of antiquity that our time has brought to light has been resurrected only in fragments. At Pompeii alone the sudden rain of volcanic ash preserved a whole segment of life so complete that it seems to be smiling at us mysteriously.

VI

THE STARS SHONE DOWN on Athens as the wise old men gathered on the Hill of Ares, next to the Acropolis. They were met to hold a sort of spiritual trial of a stranger who had been unsettling the crowd in the market place for some time. According to legend the Areopagus had formed since time immemorial a sort of intellectual nobility, and now, under the Romans, it also had state approval. This was A.D. 51. Socrates had been tried and condemned in the same city, though not by the same court, four hundred years before.

But the man whom they were questioning now was not accused

of crime. What the Greeks demanded of the stranger took the cautious form of a trial lecture, that they might judge whether to allow him to speak in public. He could not, he knew, be condemned to the poisoned goblet. But he had already come close to being stoned, he had prisons and chains behind him, and probably some premonition told him that more awaited him. For he preached the teaching of the Nazarene, only a few years his senior. Two decades after the Crucifixion there was no market place on earth where that doctrine would have been received with enthusiasm—there was nothing but uproar and heckling. The first believers were converted one by one in poor little cottages.

Here was this man of fifty, probably with a gray beard, who stood there swathed in his toga, in a true Roman oratorical pose, with right arm outstretched. Who dared to speak, here in the heart of Athens, about this new God of the soul? This was the home of mocking and pride, the dwelling of the hostile schools of Stoics and Epicureans, who held themselves far superior to anyone that dared to doubt them. The man who would introduce a new doctrine to the Areopagus must have a combination of knowledge and boldness, faith and resolution. He needed to be a Jew for devoutness, a Greek for civilization, a Roman for cosmopolitanism.

It was the Apostle Paul who confronted the skeptical Athenians that day. He actually possessed all three qualities in greater degree than almost anyone else of his time. The effect he produced, the heritage he received and handed on, gave his life an upward sweep, and he now became one of the most influential minds of antiquity. His footprints were as everlasting as those of Pericles, Alexander, and Caesar. He was the man who began to transform the new Christianity from a Jewish sect into a world religion. It was only because his origin and career focused the strongest impulses of Jew, Greek, and Roman in an aggressive movement that he was able to prepare for the organization which has dominated most of the Mediterranean shores for the past two thousand years.

Only a man of action could have benefited from the convulsions he had gone through. This brilliant aggressiveness distinguished the character of Paul from that of the other Apostles. If he had been born at the same time and place, but the son of a pagan, this worldly-wise Roman might have become a senator, the proconsul of a province, perhaps emperor in the end. Since he was a Jew, there was a greater calling before him.

He was born at Tarsus in Asia Minor, which, along with Alexandria and Athens, was then a great center of Hellenism. There and at Jerusalem he was trained in Greek and Jewish learning; he was a tent maker and the son of a tent maker. Later, as a man of thirty, he went back to Jerusalem. There he fought with all the passion of a Pharisee against the small new sect of Jewish Christians who regarded a crazy prophet as the Messiah and dared to question the iron rigor of the law. One of them, Stephen, was seized and dragged off by the crowd for preaching such doctrines. Paul was the only scribe who followed, and he gave the waiting throng the signal to stone Stephen.

And so the history of Jesus' two great apostles began with their denying him: Peter had betrayed the Lord, Paul had killed His disciple. Afterward they met and each confessed his darkest hour to the other; there was nothing left for them to do but fall upon their swords in despair or else to devote their lives to the teachings of him whom they had wronged. This they did for more than thirty years, atoning in the end for their unbelief. How much greater a man is Paul! Peter, who first denied his Master, again proved the weaker in the celebrated dispute with Paul; he yielded, allowing pagans to eat at the same table with Jews. It is only because of Jesus' one famous utterance that he has taken his place in history with his keys of heaven. Certainly Jesus trusted him all too far. His denial of Christ just before His death was terrible, whereas Paul, the fanatic, who never saw Jesus, is quite easy to understand. Peter had none of that knowledge of the world to which Paul owed almost everything. Little is known of Peter's accomplishments in the Roman Empire; the great theologians doubt that he was ever in Rome or was crucified there. Actually, St. Peter's ought to be called St. Paul's, and the statue whose bronze foot people kiss should be carrying not the keys of Peter but a book and sword.

For these were the attributes of Paul, the scholar and warrior.

The style and cultivation of his letters, to which he owes his fame, show that he was a highly educated Greek. As a child in Tarsus he saw old Athenodorus, the teacher and friend of Augustus. He may have heard him in one of the shady avenues of trees at Cydnus, expounding to his pupils his famous doctrine, "Live with men as if God saw you, and talk to God as if men were listening."

But he was also a Roman citizen born, and this rescued him from the two most precarious situations of his life. It gave him the manly bearing, the natural dignity, that were later to astonish the highest officials. And above all, it brought to his church thousands of Romans who would have paid no attention to any such religious innovation if it had been presented by a non-Roman, the son of an inferior stock. If Luke the Evangelist had introduced him by his full name of Caius Julius Paulus or Saulus, posterity might have understood him better. Especially because he was a Roman, Rome attracted him all his life. When finally he got there after ten years of effort, he found the world capital the broadest field for his endeavors. He is the founder of the Roman Church—not because he was finally beheaded there but because he had labored there for years; not because of his martyr death but because of his active life. Only a man of the world could have established the Roman Church.

The manner of his conversion, too, was thoroughly in character for a Roman. Shortly after the stoning of Stephen, Paul rode on horseback to Damascus in order to have other adherents of Jesus stoned there. On his way, Christ appeared to him in the famous vision, and the vision was Roman in form. Paul and his companions were on horseback. His story and the many paintings of the scene show a knight falling noisily from his plunging horse. An arc of flame threw him to the ground, as when, in the ancient legend, Zeus appeared to mortals. He was cast down not by a spirit but by superior strength. As he could not vanquish it by force of arms, he suddenly surrendered.

This dramatic scene was unlike any other in the Gospels. It ended with true Roman vigor. For instead of tearing his hair in remorse and regret and imploring mercy, Paul immediately replied to the overpowering apparition with the manly question, "What

am I to do?" Only weaklings could describe Paul as a dreamer,
only doctors as an epileptic. He was a manly Roman who put all
moments of depression behind him and became a warrior for Christ
the very moment he became a Christian. Again, although Paul's
masculine nature, as well as the rabbinical tradition, urged him
toward marriage, he always remained single. (Peter married.) He
was always surrounded by friends but usually quarreled with them.
If he did not disown his three best friends, he at least sent them
away. His friendships, his fanatical hatred as a young man, his
universally dreaded will, all were evidently outlets of a strong character that was determined to dominate. For that reason, too, he was
always as remote from nature as Jesus was close to it. Paul was a
real city dweller; born in Tarsus, busy and happy in Antioch,
Ephesus, and Corinth, and finally in the capital of the world.

His adventures, too, were not with the stormy elements or wild
animals, but on castle walls, between which he descended in a
basket, in temple yards, in gatherings whose sticks and stones he
dodged like an agile warrior. Throughout his active career he lived
by the work of his hands whenever it was necessary. Even late in
life he earned his bread as tent maker and rug maker. He never
displayed the intellectual arrogance that demands free support from
less intellectual mortals.

At the same time Paul was a politician and, increasingly, a
diplomat. In this he was very much the Greek. That night when
he saw the searching faces of the Athenian judges, he proved his
mastery by opening with a reference to their Greek world: "You
charge me," Paul began, "with being a messenger of strange gods,
and trying to introduce them among you. Do you know what I
most admired on my stroll through your city? An altar with the
inscription 'To the Unknown God.' Then you worship something
you do not know? What is this? Must I prove to the people of a
town which produced great Plato the existence of this one supreme
God, far superior to the poor Olympians? You lock your idols in
the cells of your temples. There is no image of the true God. And
He is not the God of a single people, like Zeus and Athena, who
despise all except the Greeks as barbarians. All nations are of one

blood. In all of them God has put a spark of light so that they may become seekers after God. And it was your great seers, your Homer, Pythagoras, and Pindar, who sought God through myths, and your great artists who searched for Him in works of beauty."

But all his adroitness did not avail this Christian on Greek soil. Finally passion ran away with him. He charged the wise men with ignorance, haste, and error and threatened them with the approaching Day of Judgment. "And I who stand before you saw with my own eyes this man appointed of God. His people persecuted Him and condemned Him to death, just as your forefathers did with noble Socrates. But God confirmed Him and His mission by resurrection from the dead."

This was going too far. The judges burst out laughing, and left their seats. The stranger was glad enough to escape to his poor lodging in the potters' quarter that evening, and to Corinth the following night, without legal difficulties. There remained one of the great Mediterranean legends; the apostle of Christ before the thinkers of Athens.

But it was not the Greeks who persecuted this Jew in the Roman cities—Athens, Corinth. It was the Jews, combating a dangerous sect as he himself had once combated it. The first two consultations at Jerusalem, whose purpose was to reduce the anarchy of the new church, set an example of endless formalistic dispute for later councils. It was only after jealous wrangles that Paul managed to get a sort of authorization to carry his mission to the shores of the Mediterranean. He became an ambassador of a nonexistent government, in a fashion familiar again these days. He spent the last fifteen years of his life more than ever as an ambassador at large.

He was imprisoned at Jerusalem, and as an old man he spent two years in chains; the Jews delivered him up to the Romans just as they had done with Jesus Himself. The similarity of his position seems actually to have strengthened the resolution of this fanatical disciple. It is even asserted that Caiaphas, the high priest who had presided when Jesus was condemned, appeared in court again as an old man in order to put Paul in the Roman prison at Caesarea.

On two occasions Paul the Roman showed how strong was the

attraction drawing him to Rome despite his premonition of dying there. When he justified himself to the cultivated Jew Agrippa, the latter observed ironically, "We could have released the man if he had not appealed to Caesar at Rome." And after Paul's first acquittal some demon or angel drew him again to Rome, where a judge weary of all these dissensions condemned him, as a Roman citizen, to death by the sword.

Paul has been called an expert sailor, and indeed the celebrated chapter about the mariners in the Acts of the Apostles shows him as a savior in a dreadful storm that finally carried the vessel to Malta. This vessel, aboard which he and other prisoners were being taken to Rome, and the way in which the manacled man was honored and called on for advice are symbols; they show Greek and Christian faiths in mid-Mediterranean trying to agree in order jointly to soothe the enraged elements. When the invisible God became all too visible in the lightning and storm at sea, all hands knelt in haste and prayed for their lives.

VII

THE ADVANTAGES OF the monarchical system have always been best appreciated in democracies, its disadvantages in monarchies. One is inclined to condemn the form of government one lives under and to overestimate the system of one's neighbor, whose faults fade with distance. From the Pharaohs to the Hapsburgs every dynasty has given its people the advantages of continuity and the disadvantage of incompetent monarchs alternating with competent ones. The best solution lies in a ruler's choosing his own successor; if the successor is adopted and called son, that is a great forward step. But of course it requires a strong man to prefer an able stranger to his own incompetent son.

Augustus' choice was vitiated by deaths and intrigues, and the succession was thrown upon the mercy of a few dozen officers, who would proclaim a new emperor in some army camp and sometimes three emperors in three camps. Old Senator Nerva, proclaimed

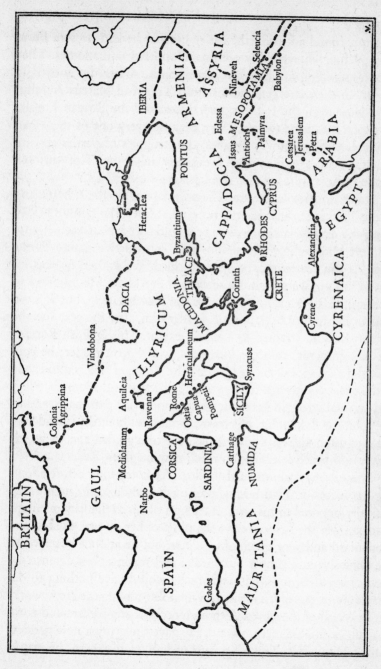

THE ROMAN EMPIRE AT ITS GREATEST EXTENT, ABOUT A.D. 100.

emperor, found adoption the easier because he had no son. From then on four emperors by adoption followed one another. They were outstanding in unbroken succession as no hereditary dynasty ever is. In the three generations from Trajan to Marcus Aurelius (A.D. 98 to 180), the four emperors governed the Roman Empire best, each for about twenty years, because every one of them had slowly earned his power. Besides, the struggles of parties and individual armies, which had previously made years of turmoil, stopped; there were neither revolts nor assassinations.

Trajan understood the sea. The ports he built in the Adriatic and on the Tiber, the canal he had restored at Suez, the famous bridge across the Tagus—a masterpiece resting on six arches, each eighty-five feet wide—show the serious and constructive nature of the man. At the same time, being very much the soldier, he was involved in long wars with the rebellious Parthians. He followed in the footsteps of Alexander as far as the Indian Ocean, but was too realistic not to turn back in time. Under him, after the year 100, the Roman Empire attained its greatest extent. This Spanish Roman, the first emperor from the provinces, was a great reader; he conducted a correspondence with Pliny the Younger that reminds one of the great eighteenth century rulers. Tacitus and Plutarch, Pliny and Juvenal wrote in his time, mostly under his patronage, and so did John the Evangelist. His reign, though without the splendor of the Augustan age, was nevertheless the true golden age, in which power and peace combined to reach new heights.

This earnest and mistrustful soldier hesitated long before adopting his successor, Hadrian, whose quick and dazzling nature was basically opposed to his own. As a sign of his Hellenistic feelings, Hadrian was the first to revive the philosopher's beard. He too was a Spaniard and very much of a soldier, but he at once retreated to the defensive and simply built walls and fortifications against the Germans and Britons, with whom he would have nothing to do. He was universal in his ideas, a cosmopolite among the races, working in behalf of the slaves. Although occasionally bizarre and paradoxical, he upheld order always. He gave the army a new goddess named Disciplina. Traveling during half of his reign, he stayed by preference in Athens, where the remains of his temple at the foot of the Acropolis give a very un-Greek effect today. On one side of the gate to his new city quarter he inscribed: "This is Athens, the old city of Theseus," and on the other side, "This is the city of Hadrian, not of Theseus." He extended the system of adoption by stipulating that his successor must in turn adopt a highly gifted nephew.

This was the delightful, delicate, and reflectively ambitious youth of seventeen, Marcus Aurelius. Antoninus Pius, the uncle, thus had his young pupil beside him, and we find a collaboration between an emperor and his heir such as scarcely ever occurs in hereditary dynasties, with their family intrigues. For twenty-three years there was not a shadow upon this remarkable relationship, not even when the boy married the old man's daughter. These two noble characters preserved the outward peace that united them inwardly; a Greek orator said: "The Empire is but a single city." When Antoninus at the age of seventy-five caught a fever just outside Rome, and was on his deathbed, it is said the watch making his nocturnal rounds did not recognize the emperor and asked for the password.

The emperor's last word was: "Aequanimitas."

Marcus Aurelius was forty when he became emperor, but for eight years he had as coadjutor a degenerate adoptive brother, whom he endured patiently. A sophist by education, a philosopher by inclination, doctrine, and association, and active by temperament, Marcus Aurelius was better prepared than most princes of antiquity for an active life, and especially for the throne. True, the doctrine of equanimity had here taken hold of a spirit equable by nature. His religion, Renan says, springs from no race and no dogma; it was simply one great system of morality. The question was: could he reconcile wisdom and reality?

Perhaps the long-continued school for princes, in which he had to keep proving himself to the older man, taught him while young always to strike a true balance. Governing was not new to him, but only responsibility. Marcus Aurelius had long actively studied characters and institutions, Rome and her provinces, the vassals of the

Empire and its enemies, the demands of the masses and the well-to-do, the state and mankind in general. He could boast of mastery from the start. There is no other explanation for the balance of thought and action, resolution and reflection shown by the two decades of his reign.

We must remember that all these emperors were pure dictators, ancient tyrants with a mere stage setting of consuls and Senate. Actually they listened entirely to the moods of the people and the army. How much greater, then, the temptation to surrender to the pleasures of autocracy—whims, women, arrogance, revenge! The bust of Marcus Aurelius as a youth is not that of an ascetic or a wise man but rather of a visionary. Thirty years later the bearded statue at the Capitol shows a thoughtful, resolute man. His conception of duty, taught him by the grandson of Plutarch himself, in addition to equanimity, firm purpose, economy of time, but never haste— principles that often recur in his notes—directly guided him both as general and as statesman, always with a consciousness of his philosophical situation.

In order to understand the fusion of thought and action in Marcus Aurelius, we have only to think of other philosophical princes. Frederick the Great, for instance, separated the two worlds and devoted a leisure hour to wisdom, as he did to music, without permitting it to enter the study of the king. The Roman, on the other hand, was, so to speak, a Protestant, anxious to earn the favor of heaven each day anew, to deserve his office by care for every detail; he was never tired or impatient, perhaps never even angry. Fate seemed determined to put him to the test, for his reign began with fire, pestilence, flood, earthquakes, and murders, and soon went on into long wars. Once more Germanic tribes pushed in from the sources of the Danube, and the emperor spent several years of war in Carinthia, the Tirol, Serbia. He also had to fight revolts of the Jews and Egyptians, the Parthians, and finally the Gauls. In most cases he was victorious.

But he made everything a source of reflection. Loving nothing so jealously as time, he would have somebody read softly in his ear when he had to waste time in the imperial box at the games; or he would make notes. How he got along with the younger Faustina, his wife, is uncertain, and it is hard to distinguish court gossip from the actual accounts. With her proud, piquant, and extremely modern face she seems the very opposite of her husband, to whom she bore eleven children. Perhaps her love affairs were malicious inventions; he is not known to have had any.

He was averse to Christianity for various reasons, notably because he felt himself altogether a Roman, and was perhaps the most Roman of all the emperors after Caesar. To him as to Caesar revenge was unknown. After the death of a rebellious general who had established himself as an opposition emperor, he asked the Senate to spare the man's wife and children. When the general's letters were brought to him, he flung them into the fire unread.

But Marcus Aurelius, dying at the age of fifty-eight in the middle of a war, probably at Vienna, showed one odd weakness. He had twice seen the purpose of free adoption; yet he, the philosopher and man of duty, returned to dynastic principles, completely mistaking the character of his son Commodus. For with him the carefully forged chain of great emperors breaks off.

Commodus, a little Nero who had himself sculptured in marble as Hercules (which made him look like a masquerading shopkeeper), fought as a gladiator, killed hippopotamuses at the games, and was finally strangled in the bath by his trainer. The Senate afterward cursed the son of the man it had deified, whose bust the citizens of Rome used to set beside their penates. Once more the meaningless struggle began among the candidates of various legions and parties. The emperors of the third and fourth centuries were subalterns and assassins, megalomaniacs who put up gigantic buildings or introduced the cults of strange gods with sexual orgies, and had one another murdered. Not one of these soldier emperors died in his bed. There was no more adoption, still less any attempt of the Senate to rebel. Instead, the dynastic craze had grown so in the course of two hundred years that nephews and children by previous marriages of the later empresses were preferred to men of ability. The decline of the emperors was merely a symbol of events in general. When we look at the Mediterranean of that era,

or in other words the Roman Empire, displaying so many signs
of a life too rich and therefore decaying, we are surprised not at the
tyrants whose mad Caesarism the Empire endured but rather at
the model careers of the four second century emperors chosen for
their talents. We admire Marcus Aurelius' strength of character
doubly when we know the temptations that Roman society offered.

VIII

FOR THE ROMAN EMPIRE was like one of those baroque cathedrals
whose cold splendor and supreme magnificence tempt the visitor
rather to worship the human spirit than to become absorbed in God.
This tremendous structure, built by great architects of state, by
engineers of human society, formed a brilliant center under whose
dome, as in St. Peter's, thousands could assemble to enjoy the protection afforded by a famous plan. The people who were to live
there found everything—quiet, order, security, dignity—everything but God, who, here as in the cathedrals, had been turned into
a lust for power. He had fled from the emotions of the heart, from
the quiet landscape of the soul; he had stiffened into gold and marble, and nothing was left but imperiousness and a certain justice.

Yet faith, beauty, and wisdom were still alive in the Roman
Empire. Out of the infinitely long evening of the Greek age gentle
yet glowing colors still shone beside the bright, cold noonday light
of the Roman world. Everything that gave color to the united world
empire around the Mediterranean still emanated, after six or eight
centuries, from the contentious little island nation that had discovered or formulated art and ethics and had bequeathed them to
the new masters of the world. For the Romans and the Christians,
to whom our debt in ways and ideas is so great, were both heirs of
the Greeks. Just as surely as everything good and beautiful that we
possess comes from the blue Mediterranean, not from the gray
north, the Mediterranean in turn received it from Greece.

The Roman Empire was a cold, massive structure. Sixty, or according to other estimates ninety, million people lived within its

imposingly ordered area, where everyone could feel that he was
a Roman colonist, and later a Roman citizen. The Roman city had
its counterparts everywhere—on the Rhine, on the Danube, at the
Dardanelles. Ephesus, Smyrna, Pergamum numbered more than
a hundred thousand, Alexandria a million, Rome two million inhabitants. The area most densely populated was a coast that has
declined today, north Africa, embracing twenty million Romans
between Turkey and the Atlantic.

It was all thought out and planned in a Roman national spirit,
for Augustus had abandoned the world schemes of his predecessor
and set up a national policy in the place of the universal visions of
Alexander and Caesar. Roman architects immortalized the genius
of their people in the magnificent arches of their aqueducts, which
carried water from distant mountain wells to the cities. In Nîmes,
Marseille, Segovia, and many other places along the Mediterranean
coast we stand in admiration before these imposing arches running
for miles across the countryside. Roads such as the ancient world
had never seen now linked Rome with the Alps, Rome with Byzantium, Rome with Athens; though they were planned for military purposes, they also opened up trade, which went out to India
and China. All were uniformly marked with the little gray Roman
milestones we find all over Europe today. Along the roads inns
sprang up, though dirty ones—for the rich man in his carriage carried a tent for the night, like our week-end excursionists. And since
the poor man could not travel if he was an honest citizen, the inns
were, according to the descriptions, full of swindlers, pimps, magicians, lion tamers, an assortment far more interesting than our
modern hotels offer.

The Roman mail, copied from Persian models, soon became a
work of art. With the Greeks, as with the modern French, everything was quick but nothing was orderly, and Herodotus speaks
of the fastest messengers, but no one mentions regular communication. Caesar was the first to introduce relays and remounts at fixed
intervals. Soon there were four-wheeled wagons running on regular
days, with a change every twenty miles. Of course the peasants had
to hand over their horses during harvest time so that Emperor Dio-

cletian's express and parcel post should run regularly through the Roman territories. Slaves ran forty miles a day—sometimes, as a punishment, sixty—until they fell dead, and the letters did not arrive. Secret messages would be hidden in the belly of a drawn hare. On occasion someone would shave a slave's head, write on the scalp, let the hair grow back, and then have the recipient shave the messenger again. Slow but sure.

The impression made upon an observer by the perpetual bustle of the Empire is expressed by the church father Tertullian in words that might have been written not in A.D. 200 but in 1939: "The world grows richer and more cultivated every day. Roads are thrown open to trade, the deserts grow fertile. Seed is now sown where forests used to be, the marshes are being drained, the herds no longer fear the wild beasts. No island and no cliff inspires terror now. Everywhere houses, cities, nations; life everywhere."

The order praised here was made possible only by a bureaucracy that became the model for all later bureaucracies and keeps recurring as Roman law does. Everything was regulated, numbered, systematized. Even the Porch of the Stoics was transformed, from a Greek philosophy into a Roman system. Coinage, weights and measures, money became uniform. Grain and raw materials were on the whole efficiently distributed. The Mediterranean then meant the Roman Empire, and this in turn practically the western world, so for once we find realized the Europe of which we dream today.

The power of the provinces was bound to grow as a result. The emperors made it easy for them to feel at home in the great Pax Romana. After Trajan, the first provincial to make his entrance as emperor into an astonished Rome, many others followed, even foreigners and former enemies. Since the emperors did not care under what title they were obeyed, they sacrificed Roman pride to their own security, and also to their treasury. Thus when Caligula bestowed Roman citizenship on every subject, he did so in order to collect a special imperial tax. The cry, "All men are brothers," then, was first uttered for the purpose of balancing a budget. The emperors needed a great deal for their soldiers; now that the army

and not the people made the choice, the rulers' love turned from
the proletarians to the mercenaries.

Augustus had extended the Empire to twenty-two provinces, so
that it and its client states reached from Scotland to the Atlas Mountains, from Caucasus to Aswan; still it could not furnish everything
that pampered Rome required. Pliny reckons the millions in national
wealth lost by the importation of Chinese silk, Indian jewels, Arabian
spices. Most of it remained in the Empire, however, particularly
after Augustus conquered Egypt, then perhaps the richest Mediterranean country. The Romans brought thence not only grain but
glass and linen, granite, alabaster, basalt in great cargo vessels, and
even bronzes and musical instruments. Besides this the province of
Asia, more or less equivalent to Asia Minor, furnished grain, wool,
and industrial products. That great commercial country was still
peopled by the bustling successors of Phoenicians and Greeks. A
manufacturer from inland Phrygia had inscribed on his tombstone
the statement that he had sailed around Matapan to Italy seventy-
two times, just as European traders on the transatlantic liners used
to lay bets as to which of them had made the crossing oftenest.

Antioch, the great luxury city of the Empire, sent all kinds of
precious things to the metropolis from its well-situated corner in
the neighborhood of Alexandretta. It grew ever richer, even attract-
ing the mint, and for a time was the most brilliant city in the Roman
domain. Colonnades ran for three miles along the main street to
protect the stroller from sun and rain. Marble baths with hot-water
heat promised every sort of piquancy, the fountains played in the
public parks as if in Versailles, and by night the main streets were
lit—something not even the Romans had. Farces, ballets, Syrian
cocottes, called harpists in those days, made the city with its easily
gained wealth a sort of ancient Bucharest. At last its own frivolity
destroyed it. For in the sixth century the citizens on the walls jeered
at a Persian king who was approaching for a parley. Flying into a
rage, he ordered a sudden storming of the city, and sold off the inhabitants into slavery. The city had declined in any case, having a
poor harbor and better actors than engineers.

Across the southeastern corner of the Mediterranean, Alexandria was flourishing at the same time, but in a quite different way. It too was a commercial center; it too served insatiable Rome; it too was all money, irony, and intrigue. But here was the focal point of Greek civilization, supplanting an Athens now grown provincial. The academy, the library, and the museum, which made up the fame of Alexandria, had been founded by the first Ptolemies, half-barbarian generals of Alexander. Here history and geography rose to new heights. The great physicians came from here, for dissection was allowed. Here Euclid taught, Eratosthenes calculated the size of the globe almost exactly as we do today, and Hero built the first steam engine. Separate papyrus rolls were made into whole volumes. The texts of Homer were critically arranged for the first time; and here, on an island near the great city, the legendary seventy-two scholars in seventy-two days translated the Bible into the language of Homer, which was at the same time the language of half the Roman Empire.

Learning was no novelty to the merchants. The city paid its academicians well, knowing that the astronomers passed on their discoveries to the world-famous Alexandrian steersmen; that Archimedes, trained here, turned his mathematics to new military machines and weapons; and that the mechanicians could re-regulate the arms of the Nile. The technical experiments of the academy produced new types of vessel. The greatest ship of antiquity, the three-master "Isis," was 182 feet long by 39 in the beam. In no other great city, except perhaps the Paris of the nineteenth century, have culture and wealth, art and science, existed as they did in Alexandria.

This was because the city was more Greek than the other towns, and remained so longer. True, the first successors of Alexander played Egyptian Pharaoh, but the language and constitution of the state were neither Egyptian nor, later, Latin; they were Greek. Since Ptolemy himself promptly founded this cultural center, he was obviously carrying on the tradition Aristotle had established for Alexander at the Macedonian court.

Of all the provinces Greece was the one whose favor was most sought. Every class of the Roman power in every period worshiped the great mother. The emperors vied with one another in appeasing

the wrath of the Greeks over the destruction of Corinth, a deed that was never forgotten. Caesar tried by every means in his power to wipe out the enormity of his forefathers, and just before his death he established a new Corinth as a capital. Augustus, taking over Greece at her lowest point, after sixty years of war, transformed her into the province of Achaia. He began the road that was later to carry the Roman armies to Byzantium. The Roman roads were the only good highways Greece was to have in two thousand years; they

represented the abject gratitude of Rome for the incalculable benefits and teachings of Athens. Rome could think only in terms of
roads and laws.

But when Nero, who felt himself a poet and therefore a spiritual
descendant of the Greeks, tried to outdo Augustus and liberate the
province, the Greeks had forgotten how to be free. Vespasian had
to reestablish the provincial status. Hadrian later united all the
Hellenes, thus creating the unity they had never attained even in
their great days. It was like a gentleman of seventy marrying his
early love, who after all can hardly do him much good by then.
With all her honor, Athens remained impoverished. It is symbolic
that the only income of the Greeks stemmed from the export of
marble and purple dye. There was more begging in the Piraeus
than there is today. The country was retrogressing in every way,
even in population. Plutarch's grandfather told how Antony had
forced him and his fellow citizens, for lack of horses and slaves, to
carry the last grain down to the harbor on their own shoulders for
the troop ships. Caesar, on the contrary, distributed grain to the
starving Greeks in these same wars.

In the third century wild Germanic hordes invaded Greece, and
the awful year of 269 remained in memory as the year 1941 will
remain for ages to come. Even in those days many of the barbarians
bore the swastika on their shields. The Academy of Athens shone
forth once more in the fourth century, but the city remained unfree.
Dominated from 300 B.C. to A.D. 300 by Rome, and then for fifteen
hundred years by Constantinople, the most brilliant people of the
West served inferior powers and men for two thousand years. But
of all the aliens that appeared on Greek soil, only two were fruitful:
the orange, arriving from Asia in the eleventh century, and the
currant, in the sixteenth.

IX

CAPITAL AND SOLDIERS were the two powers on which the Roman
Empire stood. We might also add seafaring, but that depended
entirely on capital. After the great days of the pirates were over,

people scarcely put to sea at all between November and March. In summer, however, they sailed swiftly, making Corinth from Naples with a favoring wind in five days, a voyage that takes two even today; from Rhodes to Alexandria took three days, from Messina to Alexandria six. Diodorus has travelers in the time of Christ going from the Sea of Azov to Egypt, from the coldest to the hottest zone, in twenty-four days. It was not steam power but the electric spark that changed the whole pace of the world. As there were no passenger vessels, and few cargo vessels were suitable for travelers, the boats were often overcrowded. The Apostle Paul tells of having set sail for Alexandria with 276 people.

But what things these vessels brought to the great warehouses at Rome! Whole herds from Gaul and Britain, not to mention cheese; there was even Swiss Alpine cheese in Rome. Tunny fish came from Chalcedon, oysters from Tarentum, strange fish from the Rhine, the Moselle, and the Danube. Sturgeon came from Pontus in clay jars: artichokes came from Carthage, lentils from Egypt, plums from Syria, apricots from Armenia, peaches from Persia (hence their name). In addition there were wines from all the coasts, and as early as the third century there was a special section of the harbor for the wine from Bordeaux. Oil for use in the public baths was distributed gratis to the people by Caesar. There were also salt from the mines and springs, wool from Spain, pelts and skins from the north, and from Phoenicia, as a thousand years before, purple garments and golden sandals.

The buying power of money was so great that a lamb cost half a dollar, and a gallon of wine a cent. A philosopher could live on four cents a day, said Seneca, the millionaire philosopher. These prices show us how enormous were the wages of the soldiers, who received about a hundred dollars a year and an imperial gift of roughly a thousand dollars on their discharge. So it happened that in the days of the decline a legion sometimes carried more cooks and actors than soldiers. Slaves too could buy their liberty after long military service, and then grow so rich that the impoverished nobility courted them while it despised them. Many of them married daughters of distinguished families. A freedman named Pallas had a family tree of Greek kings drawn up and endorsed by willing professors.

Among the Romans, as everywhere, the degree of decadence was manifested in two vital forms: corruption and slavery.

Perhaps old Cato was right when he cried out: "What will become of Rome when there is no other state left for her to fear?" Usury, or in other words the ancient form of banking, had begun even in his day. A man who collected 48 per cent interest for a few years could well afford to buy a Roman knighthood. Under Sulla there was a joint-stock company that lent the Roman Republic 30 million dollars and demanded 150 million back ten years later. The noble Brutus lent money to the city of Salamis at 48 per cent. Under the emperors this practice extended to the expropriation of farmers who were in debt, the plundering of the colonies, commercial warfare, and slave trading, just as in modern days. But since surpluses in those days were not reinvested but squandered on luxury, the chief necessity for a dazzling life was political corruption.

As early as the time of Caesar, the richest man bought the Republic. The triumvirs confiscated the estates of their opponents, and Crassus, as an outstanding usurer, was the deciding factor. Caesar gave the plebeians twenty-five dollars each in addition to grain and oil; the modern equivalent would be a gift of roughly a thousand dollars from the government to each citizen. The emperors coined nothing but silver for the people, and gold for the troops. The provincial delegates who negotiated the amount of tribute at Rome bribed the senators; when Scipio turned over one such gift to the war treasury, he was considered a queer fish. Consuls at their posts who behaved in strict conformity to law were recalled in several instances, for during a consul's second year in a province it was customary for him to recover the costs of his election to the unpaid honorary post of consul. He would let out the taxes of the province to a profiteer, who collected twice the amount for himself in his own country.

Slavery, on which all the ancient states were founded, grew under the Empire at a higher rate than the population. Morally it contrasted with the lax, overrich Roman society in a way classical

Athens had never known. Since millions of Roman slaves were
recruited from among the citizens of subject states, their average
education increased while their price declined. In the grand houses
of the newly rich Romans, where there were often several hundred
slaves, there would be not only servants, cooks, and grooms but
tutors, physicians, and musicians. How often a smile must have
come to the lips of a captive Greek witnessing with his own eyes
the triviality of the society that paid him—perhaps a young philosopher standing behind the chair of some Roman banker, listening
to his talk and thinking of his own father, whose only purpose in
keeping the few slaves he owned was to be able to philosophize
undisturbed.

In earlier days only household and garden work had been necessary, but eventually underpaid workers began to be used in the great
Roman establishments, competing with the slaves. For these workers could be turned out of doors in the winter, while the slaves had
to be fed, and kept busy with woolen work and the making of pottery. Capitalists took an interest in unending new wars, which extended the opportunities for investment, but also cheapened the
value of slaves. After a successful conquest a slave cost not twenty-
five or a hundred dollars, but a mere four or eight, whereas a fine
saddle horse might cost three hundred. With the price, however, the
standing and human dignity of slaves declined also; they were
called "talking tools." The only ones to be courted despite their servitude were beautiful Orientals who understood love, slaves who knew
the fabrication of poisons, and others who were good at painting
pornographic frescoes on the walls of the rich man's dining hall.

As today, only the wisest realized that things could not go on
in this fashion. While Pollio had a man thrown to the morays in
his fishpond for having broken a crystal vessel, Hadrian tried to
improve the condition of the slaves, and Pliny spoke approvingly
of them because their leader Spartacus forbade them to carry gold
and silver to camp.

The last slave rebellion was put down, but the Romans put in
two years fighting it. The best of the rich men were in the nihilistic
mood that prefers new dogmas even if prejudicial to their own

wealth. In eras of intellectual change such signs are familiar; the most recent instance is the communistic leanings of some rich people.

Thus Christianity came to this twilight of the gods not as a surprise but as the fulfillment of a premonition that had long been stirring keen minds and eager hearts.

The astonishing thing is that it by no means acted against the state—certainly not in a revolutionary way—and yet it profited largely from opposition to the state. For although the Christians in the first two hundred years had to endure no large-scale persecutions, still the individual martyrs attracted attention. While the catacombs and the pursuits by wild beasts aroused popular curiosity and pity, the churches increased under the eyes of governments and emperors during those two centuries, so that in Rome alone there were soon more than forty. And yet the church—*ecclesia,* meaning popular assembly—immediately asserted a claim to power in a way that did not indeed oppose the state but tried to win away its power over men's souls. The first Apostles, men of action who knew how to transmute a longing for heaven into a united congregation, a melody into a symphony, set to work with their organizing talent and the strong determination of revolutionary leaders. Though they meant no revolution at all, the will to power was as strong in the first bishops as in the priests of Thebes or Delphi.

It was simply a younger force breaking in upon a weary world with an idea that was, if not new, at any rate presented in a new form. It showed the amazed onlookers how an old philosophy can be transformed into a new religion. Of the two powers, church and state, the younger strove for an alliance with the elder. But the state long remained passive, apparently waiting to see what should be done. And indeed what was there to alarm the emperors? Instead of being apprehensive about a possible international body— a fear which has so often made statesmen antiecclesiastical since— they actually welcomed the tendency. There was but one Empire, and the intellectual union of its many peoples had become the task of Rome.

For that reason the Christians were at first more welcome than the Jews, whose religion was nationalistic and furthermore proud enough to proclaim itself the one true faith and its people the chosen. Only the innate Jewish adaptability, along with the gratitude of Caesar and his tradition, and finally the acumen of the worldly Jews (who did not proclaim their dogma of the chosen people indiscriminately), mollified the Roman emperors. In fact the Jews had an odd influence: their wide disperson made possible the rapid spread of the first Christians. An important statement of the church father Tertullian, which has a new timbre now after seventeen hundred years, bears witness to this: "Christianity grew up under the protection of the Jewish religion."

The philosophical foundations, which reminded the world of Plato more then than they do now, also made it easier for the Christians to enter into the Roman world. In a carving of the fourth century (at Berlin) the Apostle sitting next to Christ looks like Socrates. And in the mosaics of Ravenna there is a beardless Christ resembling a young Roman noble. The four great emperors, all of them philosophically trained, found nothing to object to in this quarter. If Marcus Aurelius rejected the Christians, he did so simply as a Roman statesman, and his attitude remained vague in any event. Imperial passivity and the cult of Mithras, particularly prevalent in the army, made Christian soldiers possible.

The first bishops shrewdly established themselves in the great cities, at Antioch, Carthage, and Corinth, so as to make use of the existing organizations. In Ephesus there was indeed a persecution, originating (as if in some comedy) with the goldsmiths, who were anti-Christian because fewer statues and emblems of the old gods were being ordered.

But along with these motives of loyalty, philosophy, and worldly acumen there was a fourth—at first the chief—reason for Christian success. Christianity was the faith of the dispossessed, the hope of the oppressed, the consolation of the poor, and of these there were more legions in the Roman Empire than there were legionaries. For this reason it was not only the first disciples and friends of Jesus at Galilee but the first thousands of Christians in the Roman Empire who consisted of beggars, artisans, peasants, old

women, the poor and uneducated. The music of the Gospels came
to them as sermons. At first the settled and substantial citizens made
mock of this strange pauper sect, and because the paupers were
proletarians and not students the reports of the first two centuries
are scanty. These people could sometimes speak but never write.
For a hundred years, only a scattered few of the rich and aristocratic
turned Christian.

Imagine a wine-growing peasant from the Campagna, a potter
from Pergamum, a porter from Alexandria, a shepherd from
Rhodes, a few dyers, cooks, and barbers from the quarters beyond
the Forum: would they not be bound to agree solemnly, or at least
to rumble sarcastically, when they heard that Luke sent the poor
Lazarus to heaven and his rich neighbor to hell, not because the
rich man had been wicked but only because he had enjoyed his
goods in this world? Were they not bound to apply it to themselves
when they heard the new prophets say, "Woe unto you that are
rich! for ye have received your consolation. Woe unto you that are
full! for ye shall hunger."

But if the rich read and remonstrated, the shrewd bishops had
Matthew at hand to make all seem decent and respectable. The rich,
who were inclined to hedge even in those days, sometimes let their
decisions depend on queer signs. When a Roman pagan started
his horse against one belonging to the Christian Marnas in a great
horse race, and Marnas's horse won, many of the crowd accepted
baptism. This old story, which could not have been better if Voltaire
had made it up, shows the multitude deciding between two gods
just as it does between two party leaders. When the quarrels of
theologians or Talmudists weary us, we should remember the Roman horse race that secured a number of converts to Christianity.

The pagan world had grown so superstitious that the idea of the
hereafter, presented with such fire, fascinated many. The first Christians could have come at no more favorable moment, not only for
themselves but for the ancient world. Their universalizing tendency
actually did save community life around the Mediterranean at a
time when it was threatening to collapse. If the Germans, invading
again in the fourth century, had found a pagan Rome, they would

have met with no resistance: ancient civilization would have gone to pieces.

Great, powerful Rome had grown old. While the chaplet of coast countries had formerly extended further inland with every century, the breadth of the colonies now began to shrink. There is no more moving parallel to the decline of the Roman world power than the fact that beginning with the fourth century the desert advanced along the coasts of Asia Minor and north Africa. Here was a threat to the world.

But the historical situation was repeated with magnificent logic. The rise of young, aggressive Rome had shielded Greek civilization half a millennium before. Now Greece was lifted from the tired hands of Rome by young, rising Christianity. In the ancient world of the Mediterranean neither Romans nor Christians did anything greater than to save Greek civilization.

X

THE COASTS OF THE MEDITERRANEAN now began to be deforested. Of course this process, a thousand years long, had many causes, of which Christianity was but one. The ancients had protected the sacred groves, and solicitude for public health was partly responsible for this order of the priests. In primitive days wisdom and art were more naïve, more directly connected with gods and elements. The people knew that forests maintain themselves in the mountains, moistening the air by evaporation and increasing rainfall. The Jews and Christians, whose feeling for nature was lost in the invisible God, no longer spared the woods.

In Syria it was for centuries forbidden to trespass upon a cedar forest, let alone to cut one down. Italy, less green under the Romans than under the Etruscans, still had richly forested areas at the time of Christ. Of Sicily Diodorus wrote: "The carpet of flowers in the forest there was so thick that hunting dogs lost the scent in all the perfume." But a sense of nature remained alive deep down in the people, and sacred trees were cared for into the Middle Ages. Even today a cypress is pointed out on Mount Athos that was planted by Byzantine monks in A.D. 859. Another ancient cypress, near Soma in Lombardy, was spared by Napoleon's running the Simplon road around it—probably because his forerunner Caesar had looked upon the tree.

The grandest destiny was reserved for the cypress that Zarathustra planted at Khurasan probably in the sixth century B.C., at a period when they still had broad-branching crowns, before they had grown taller and adapted themselves to the glaring light. When the Arabs conquered Persia in the year 1000, a caliph had the sacred tree felled, and brought the trunk, cut into pieces, to Bagdad on rollers, while thirteen hundred camels carried the branches. At this the people were horrified and killed the caliph. Among all the murders and assassinations that have befallen powerful Mediterranean rulers in two thousand years, no fanatical deed was ever so darkly and splendidly avenged as this felling of a tree after fifteen centuries because it had been planted by the founder of an alien religion. The three religions that arose in the desert were not kindly disposed toward trees, whereas the barbarians of the north worshiped them. Only the Greeks worshiped nature without being barbarians.

But it was a love of trade and adventure, the attraction of the sea, that caused them and other seafarers later to denude their shores. The struggle between land and sea, this contest of the elements in the hands of man, now fruitful, now tragic, took away from the land what it gave to the sea: timber for ships. It could not be brought to the coast from very far inland, for the rivers, those intermediaries between land and sea, frequently dried up. By a vicious circle the dryness increased as the wood grew scarcer. The Carthaginians began the practice of sacrificing the shade and moisture along their coasts to the building of a navy. Always seeking new profits afar, they exchanged the near for the remote, the sure for the fantastic.

In Athens too, as later in America, no one thought of the future when the forests were devastated. There is a parable in the fact that the Athenians denuded their islands to build a navy against Syracuse, for at that point national pride was leading them to their downfall. In fact the desire of the Greeks for world power at the end of the fifth century may have been balked by this deforestation. The forest of Sila in Calabria is an exception today, and likewise a symbol, for there in the neighborhood of Cosenza, hundreds of miles away from the bustling cities, the old forests that nobody could clear are still standing, preserving one another, and enriching the soil. The Italians later had to fetch their wood from the Danube valley, from Macedonia and Pontus.

The entire water supply of the Mediterranean countries, much as they differ, is bound up with the forestation. There is no wood available, but a great deal of stone. Hence villages even today are built where stone is quarried, always by preference on a slope rather than on the plain, because many millions of people must depend on the rain water in the cisterns or on the roofs. The art of building reservoirs, which originated in Spain, the distribution of the water pressure and the terracing of the ground, spread along many Mediterranean shores; and indeed nothing else could have saved the life of dry and rocky Italy when its population grew dense. The artificially watered soil near Murcia brings a thirty-seven-fold return; an acre of irrigated orange groves at Valencia brings in as much as four thousand dollars. When we travel through the rice country of Lombardy, planted under Caesar, we can understand more easily how people will develop new arts and skills out of a naturally poor soil, further impoverished by their own fault.

Whole nations have here brought hydraulics to perfection in battle with the elements and their own passions. So too we find contradictory individual characters who have built new safeguards out of their weaknesses, developing them to a degree that might serve as a model for better-endowed natures. Since the hydraulics of the Mediterranean are basically different from the older Nile systems, everything that went to make the art of irrigation is due to the growing deforestation around the Mediterranean.

XI

THE NEXT EPOCH-MAKING EVENT, the invasion of the Mediterranean coasts by the barbarians, represents a three hundred years' development and can no more be pinned down to a few battles or dates than the so-called fall of the Roman Empire. In reality empires perish but seldom, nations never; instead they merge into others. Neither the Romans nor the Jews, not even the American Indians were destroyed. Victorious peoples mingled with the vanquished, absorbing human beings and traditions and going through a gradual transition where the historian marks an epoch with a horizontal line. In cultural life a new idea has occasionally produced a sudden creative effect, the brain of a single scholar or poet causing the downfall of one age and the rise of another. But no conqueror could do it, nor even the migration of a whole people.

Anything that the Goths, Vandals, Franks, Alamanni, Huns, and Lombards as conquerors of the Mediterranean tried successively or sometimes in rivalry to create crumbled swiftly away. The nations they conquered did not perish in any instance. Since the invaders brought almost nothing with them, but adopted everything, their civilization and their blood too merged in antiquity and early Christianity. The fall of the Roman Empire, a hundred times cited, was really no more than the slow aging of a political structure about to break up into younger parts. From the third to the sixth century the Empire was like a rich king of legend, who married his ten daughters to ten strange, warlike, and menacing princes, and bequeathed portions of his kingdom to the insistent heirs but held the whole together for a long time by his own vitality.

The first suitor was at the same time the most dangerous—the tribe of Goths, who came from Scandinavia (as the Normans did later), and were fundamentally seafarers. They traveled along the rivers to south Russia and became sailors again on the Black Sea. Their division into West (Visigoths) and East (Ostrogoths) nations, which recurs later in Italy and Spain, goes back to the Russian period. The Dnieper is said to have divided the nomadic tribes. When they pushed to the mouth of the Danube about 250, thus becoming neighbors of the Romans, the man who happened to be called emperor of Rome at the moment was the first of Arabic descent, Philippus Arabus. The great invasions of the two races that were to disturb the Mediterranean alternately for almost a

thousand years began with a symbolic conflict. Arabus was defeated
by the sons of the north, who left him on the field of battle with
his skull cleft open.

Once, shortly before his time, there were six Roman emperors
in a single year. During the third century more than fifty men, most
of them soldiers, pretended to rule the Roman Empire; all but two
died violent deaths.

From two reliefs carved about this time we can see how the
empire rocked under the thrust of the invading barbarians. An
ancient sarcophagus shows the barbarians bearded, unarmored,
in blouses, some of them wearing a sort of Jacobin cap. By contrast
the amazed, daintily groomed young Romans in fine uniforms and
helmets seem like gentlemen of the modern foreign office straying
among workmen. The other relief is hewn in a Persian cliff and
depicts a Roman emperor as the slave and captive of the Persian
king. The confusion resulting from the election of emperors by
remote legions increased to a point where the soldiers, in sheer
indecision, on one occasion turned over the new choice to the old
Senate in Rome, which had been leading a shadow existence for
three hundred years.

Two strong personalities, Illyrian officers of humble birth, successively occupied the throne at the end of the third century. One
of them, Aurelian, played the part of Roi Soleil, proclaiming the
sun as the imperial god and calling himself "god and master by
birth" on the coins. He did to Rome something that no Roman had
done for a thousand years—he made the city into a fortress. This
is the wall we still see at the Porta San Paolo under the cypresses,
looking like an old engraving. As general, besides displaying this
foresight, he put down various provincial revolts. As emperor he
forced an innovation: wishing to cut as much of a figure as the
Pharaohs and the kings of the Persians, he was the first to wear an
Oriental diadem and a gold-embroidered gown.

His successor, Diocletian, put the finishing touch to the Oriental
cult by riding through the city in a triumphal car drawn by four
elephants. He had risen to be emperor from a commission in the
imperial bodyguard. His rival for the throne was originally a rower

but rose to be an admiral of the Roman navy at Boulogne, then became defender of the Channel coast and had himself proclaimed emperor in Britain. His portrait as emperor was stamped on coins for seven years before he was killed. Otherwise, however, Diocletian held undisputed sway for twenty years. He was a tyrant in the good ancient sense but with one new feature. He abolished Augustus' three-hundred-year-old half republican constitution, and chose a joint emperor ("Augustus") to rule with him. Each man had a sort of sub-emperor ("Caesar"). He called the whole group a divine family, sons of Jupiter, Hercules, and others, and at the same time introduced a carefully divided administration of four prefectures, thus restoring the system of adoptions that had produced the four best emperors a century before.

Diocletian was the first state socialist, and since he was the son of a slave and also a dictator he doubly reminds us of some of the masters of our own day: like them he deprived his subjects of liberty in return for a sort of state guarantee of food and shelter. In the indispensable occupations, the army, transportation, and foodstuffs, sons had to continue in the trades of their fathers. Every landholder was responsible for the taxes of his people; the middle class and all ecclesiastical education ceased to exist. The first maximum-price list in history, fragments of which we possess, regulated wages and the price of goods; it runs from gold and purple dye to hens' eggs. It distinguishes between Marseille ham, Belgian ham, and the udder of the sow, and sets the scales of pay from day laborer to lawyer, from sheep shearer to sewer cleaner. Any violation was punishable by death. The police and penitentiary state, with its capital at Rome, was an accomplished fact as early as A.D. 300.

No wonder Diocletian also regulated the religions in his empire, destroying churches, threatening public assemblies, and confiscating church property! He went on to take government posts away from all those who called themselves Christians and to put them quite outside the law, as is being done with the Jews today. Gibbon, who estimated the number of those killed at two thousand, wrote that there were, however, far more Christians murdered in the sixteenth century by Christians. There were martyrs who grew famous. One Christian who had reviled and destroyed the public edicts of the emperor was slowly roasted. He was the Unknown Martyr of Nicodemia. In contrast there was a viceroy who suddenly on his deathbed issued an edict "allowing these unfortunate people to profess their religion and to assemble, so long as they hold the law in honor. But we hope that this our clemency may induce the Christians to send their prayers to the Deity for our salvation as well as for their own and that of the State."

Diocletian was neither murderer, libertine, nor spendthrift; he was an excellent ruler and obviously a just one. Moreover, he did the rarest thing in history: he voluntarily surrendered his power, as only Charles V and Edward VIII (both under hostile pressure) have done since. Diocletian, who conceived of government in the earnest spirit of Marcus Aurelius, retired in his mid-fifties and compelled his weaker coemperor to follow his example, thus making room for the sub-emperors, long since trained to their tasks. None of the four was related to any of the others. As a French *rentier* will at last buy a little mill and a vineyard, where he can go fishing and spend the evenings bowling with his neighbors, Diocletian built a palace in his Dalmatian homeland, where he, the son of a slave, lived the carefree life of a great nobleman. Today half of the town of Spalato covers the ruins of Diocletian's palace.

His colleague, who could not stand this, soon interfered in a struggle for the throne. He found no peace, quarreled with his son, endured new struggles and defeats, and died mysteriously. He had tried in vain to lure Diocletian from his idyllic retreat, but there the latter remained, demonstrating to the world that even a ruler worshiped as a god may in his old age prefer serenity of soul to all the temptations of power.

XII

HE WHO IS FORTUNATE ENOUGH to look down on Istanbul, not from a speeding plane but from a gently swaying captive balloon, will see a city whose situation has no peer in the world. It lies on and above two seas, connected by the twisting ribbon of a broad stream. Khartoum and Lyon, lying at the meeting places of the forked Nile and Rhone rivers, may remind us of it; but neither possesses this monumental yet romantic domination of two seas. As we float above the city, our eye can see northward and southward for an immense distance, which makes doubly impressive the moderate scale of the connecting ribbon. As we stand on the Asiatic shore in the afternoon, with the midnight-blue surface of the Black Sea rising somberly to our right, and then turn to that gentle, glassy white mirror, the Sea of Marmara, on our left, we seem to behold the symbols of the wild element and the pure, and between them the winding road, like a bridge between good and evil.

There on the Bosporus, within strict confines of length and breadth, life goes on between the two dæmonic elements. Sails belly out, vessels move, the fortunate ones toward the white sea, the venturesome ones toward the dark; bright spots stand out against somber hills, bays spring from the cliffs at turns. Then domes and towers appear yonder in the evening glow, cypresses and palaces rise from the shuffle of white houses, the minarets shoot abruptly upward, and the muezzin's call to evening prayer sounds from afar. In former times an old caliph lived in his marble castle by the beach, and finally the new ruler of young Turkey died there. This is Istanbul between its two seas, resting like an empress; the white sea lies at the feet of the reclining Oriental lady, as quiet, ingratiating, and dangerous as a Persian cat.

The man who founded this city could no more enjoy it than the forester can enjoy what he has planted. But he left his name, as Alexander did, and thus he is more familiar to posterity than most of the Roman emperors.

The advent of Constantine marks the beginning of a new type of leader. Like Augustus, he had to earn his long, productive reign by years of factional strife. He was the illegitimate son of an officer and an innkeeper's daughter, born in Serbia. He was carefully brought up, and as an emperor's son-in-law he became, like Augustus, a sort of heir apparent. He too devoted himself wholly to improvements at home. His wars were simply to protect the frontiers against the invading barbarians.

Constantine had in common with Augustus a long head, a grave, watchful expression; but he had not the secretiveness, the false democracy, or indeed any of the false notes of Augustus. Augustus played the censor of morals while leading a highly dubious private life with a dissolute family. Constantine, coming immediately after the Christian persecutions, made Christianity a pillar of the Empire frankly as a matter of expediency. He did not pretend to any conviction, and was not baptized until shortly before his death. Even then it was merely to set an example. There was more strength and more solitude about him than about the perpetually spying Augustus. Of the two most powerful rulers the two great cities produced, Constantine was obviously the more courageous.

Even in that great life there were dark moments of revenge and slander. But when Constantine's coemperor (later his brother-in-law), turned against him, and was defeated and captured by the emperor's son, he found mercy at the victor's hands. Such forgiveness is almost unexampled, and in any case it was unknown in classical antiquity. But the son was afterward persecuted and poisoned by his stepmother. When her false accusations and guilt came out, she was herself the victim. The empress was slowly boiled to death in her bath. Her brothers and nephews fell with her in a veritable blood purge. Here again the dynastic idea, revived by Constantine as it had been by Augustus, disintegrated in the reciprocal struggles of sons and heirs.

Nothing about all these men is more amazing than the energy with which they kept starting new enterprises after and even during such catastrophes. Constantine was probably fifty years old when he founded the new residence, and he had completed the third decade of his reign when he died. Milan, Lyon, and Durazzo had already profited by the fact that the emperors kept leaving Rome or did not reside there at all. But for one of them to move east, transferring thither the center of the Roman Empire, and this on a huge scale, was an entirely new idea. We are led to wonder whether the emperor was not thereby emulating Alexander rather than Augustus.

Certain romantic tendencies drew him toward Troy, and he actually began to build his capital in that northwestern corner of

Asia Minor. Other factors pulled him toward his native Naissus (modern Nish), others again to Sardica (Sofia), to Salonika, and back again to Troy. It was only in fighting his rival, who retreated to the site of Byzantium, that he discovered the unique situation between the seas and saw how easily the master of that city could close the passage to Asia. "He who has Constantinople has the world," said Napoleon.

According to legend the emperor had begun to lay his foundations in Scutari, on the far shore. But eagles snatched the surveying lines, carrying them across the Sea of Marmara and dropping them in Europe. Here the deliberating nature of Constantine is apparent, for no legend attaches itself to a man by chance. The hint of the birds brought decision to the doubter. Alexander did indeed see birds at the founding of his city. But he had attracted the birds by scattering meal; the birds did not lead him. And Constantine interrogated the Delphic oracle and his astrologers before making his decision. He did not lay the cornerstone for the great city wall until the sun stood in the sign of Sagittarius.

When, five years later, he consecrated the city that bore his name, amid endless festivals, keeping closely to the Roman pattern, he opened great games and surprised the Roman senators who had been transferred here with the loveliest villas on the Bosporus. With the skill of a hotel manager he flattered the old guests by remembering their special tastes. There was much for these conservative gentlemen to see and criticize: the new Church of the Apostles, the mausoleum for the emperor, extravagant gifts of wine and oil for the people, and above all a host of stolen Greek statues.

For since young Christianity had as yet no art of its own, it took over that of the Greeks, as young America later took over the art of Europe. Tyche and the Dioscuri had new temples in this first Christian state. The first time the senators mounted the steps to their new council chamber, they found the Pallas of Lindos and the Zeus of Dodona set outside the door, and the serpent column of Delphi as well. In Constantine's gigantic new forum the protector of the Christians, the emperor himself, stood portrayed as Apollo on a tall porphyry column.

This whole pagan structure was neither a hidden foundation under nor a protective arch over the young Christian church. It stood alongside, almost entirely separate. Constantine had begun his reign with an edict of toleration, a purely political step. Though he later wrote upon his triumphal arch at Rome that he had won the victory "by inspiration of the Deity," the word Deity was left vague in many official documents of the time. Incidentally, in his first civil war Constantine protected the pagan senators and aristocratic Romans and not the Christians. He had the acute ear of a true politician for the whispers of the crowd. Christianity within the Empire had gained as much inner strength through the severe persecutions by his own master and predecessor Diocletian as it is gaining today under German persecution. Recognizing that this powerful community must be authenticated, he had Christian symbols painted on shields and banners; but he himself was shown as Apollo.

Constantine, who passes for the first Christian emperor, was evidently a complete infidel, as we may learn from the best sources —his character and his councils. A thoroughgoing despot, he developed and completed the police state of his two predecessors. The peasants were even degraded into serfs and forbidden to leave their land, because slaves began to be scarce. When he held the celebrated Council of Nicaea, which promulgated the Nicene Creed, he sat above the bishops like a deity.

Then and at the three following councils arranged in rapid succession he was the first to strike the autocratic note which the Popes later adopted. As emperor on a golden throne, directing these first princes of the church, he was at the same time a Pope, the first to combine both capacities in one person.

No one then could guess what this fusion of spiritual and temporal power was later to mean, what battles it was to cause. When Constantine saw the quarreling bishops below him at Nicaea in 325 and guessed, largely from gesture and intonation, what they were saying, he regarded the gathering merely as a new Senate, in which the emperor would do well to make a number of friends.

This complete autocrat, who fed his self-assurance on Oriental customs and garments and the new fortifications of his capital, waited till the last moment before bowing down to the cross emblazoned on his banners. Falling ill at the start of an expedition against the Persians, he hastily had himself baptized. The Christians made him a saint, the pagans a Roman god.

Constantine has been called the Great because he recognized the mission of Christianity. Certainly it owed more to him than to anyone since Paul. But the question remains whether the emperor was carrying out a great idea or merely helping to put an energetic priesthood into power. At any rate the bishop of Rome proposed to exercise this power like an emperor himself. The "spiritual company of favored believers," as Augustine soon afterward beautifully described his City of God, actually became a league of power states with the church as leader. The struggle for world dominion that convulsed the next thousand years might perhaps have been won by the church if it had not split.

The invading barbarians utterly confused this new problem. Here was a peril that the otherwise far-sighted Constantine misunderstood. He was the first to put Germanic officers and court officials in important positions; he even invited Germanic tribes to cross the Rhine and chastise the Gauls. The Franks, breaking in from the lower Rhine, the Alamanni, coming from west and south across the upper Rhine, and the Vandals, who crossed the Danube into Hungary, were tolerated and even encouraged by him. Still, the devastating inundation, which lasted five centuries, could not have been held back even by determination. It was elemental.

A successor quickly arose to combat Constantine's Christian decisions. When the emperor, after the murder of his son, had half his family killed, a five-year-old boy whom nobody paid any attention to was spared. A bishop and a eunuch brought him up to be a priest, and when two of Constantine's relatives began to rule together after his death, the lonely lad was studying rhetoric at Constantinople. But then he met a Greek philosopher in the provinces and through him learned to know the wisdom of Neoplatonism. He had seen many Christian atrocities at court and had heard a great deal about the bloodshed in the family, with its Christian pretenses. He was skeptical of what he was supposed to believe and receptive to the ancient ideas he learned at their very sources, in Ephesus and then at Athens itself.

In the midst of his happiest months he found himself, at twenty-four, snatched from his studies at the Platonic Academy by a lonely emperor. The very opposite of a soldier, he was sent off to fight the barbarians. He became a brother-in-law and coemperor and a military commander on the Rhine, which the Alamanni had crossed to invade Gaul, burning and murdering as they went. But not for nothing was the prince a Roman and a member of a soldier family, and probably also a genius. He was victorious. Now Strasbourg and Paris rose for the first time from the dim mists of the barbarian jungle. At Strasbourg he won his great battle, in Paris (like almost all generals and thinkers after him), he made his headquarters.

He, obviously, was both; his name was Julian. In a sense he was the first Parisian, for his name became prominent in the early days of the city. Since he was a general and a governor, and very young besides, there is something attractive in imagining a Roman soldier and secret revolutionist, a Byzantine coemperor, in fourth century Paris.

Julian built a castle at Lutetia (as the Romans called the town of the Parisii). The old city on the Seine, known to Caesar, had been almost ignored by later emperors. Julian was so popular with the troops that the jealous emperor ordered him off to Persia, whither it had always been customary to send unwanted rivals. Julian was about to obey, but at the farewell banquet the legions, who wanted none of this change, started an uprising. They broke in upon their general at night and offered him the choice of death or becoming emperor at once. This comic-opera scene, confirmed by all the sources, ended as it was bound to do. A few officers, very likely drunk, thus made a turning point in intellectual history. But it was the first time that Roman soldiers lifted up their new master on their shields in the manner of the barbarians. The shield and its symbolic use are the first bit of civilization that the warrior nation of the Germans gave to the Mediterranean. The emperor in Constantinople equipped an army against the rebel, who marched down with his legions. But the emperor's sudden death rendered a new civil war unnecessary.

Julian's likeness on the coins has the naïve expression of an early Greek bust, with wide-open eyes, a big nose, a small mouth, and a matted beard. He does not look fanatical, nor was he so in fact; but the striving for tolerance that he rightfully derived from his Platonic ideals was constantly upset by his anger at the intolerant Christians. He had seen them at work as a child. History shows that the fury of this Greek was induced only by the fury of his anti-Greek predecessors and that his determination to undo the decisions of Constantine was the only thing which made him intolerant in turn. Otherwise his nature was close to that of Marcus Aurelius, who was an enemy of the Christians and yet a great character. Julian, however, lacked clarity and proportion; he was nervous, and violent in speech.

He neither prohibited nor destroyed the Christian faith. He simply excluded Christians from preferment and forbade public instruction. At the same time, as a man of political skill, he outlined for the pagan priests an organization derived from the highly efficient Christian clergy. He appointed leading thinkers to high state positions. But he was only half a Greek, for he was enthusiastically studying the sun-god Mithras; to a certain degree he fell between the two religions. What he lacked above all was time to grow. He fell in Persia after three years, perhaps by the hand of a Christian soldier—that is, from motives of revenge.

Of his brief, thrilling attempt to revive antiquity, as of that made by the Egyptian Amenophis, nothing remains but the model of an intellectual revolutionist and the resonant epithet that has been given to many religious rebels since his time: *apostata,* the Apostate.

XIII

THE GERMANS FIRST LAID WASTE the Mediterranean on a large scale about the year 400. The migration of the peoples, which had actually begun two hundred years earlier, in the reign of Marcus Aurelius, now grew into an avalanche that destroyed everything in its path. When Mongolian peoples began riding from the east through Asia, driving the tribes that had come in from the north ahead of them in south Russia, the latter were pushed to the Mediterranean by necessity and curiosity alike. By contrast with the ancient nations, who had brought everything with them and built the land up, the Germanic tribes brought nothing with them, destroyed almost everything, and after a few centuries vanished nearly without a trace. The scraps of a Gothic Bible discovered on the Nile are as great a treasure as is to be found in the grave of these peoples, who possessed neither knowledge nor faith to enrich those they conquered.

The Visigoths, advancing southward, had gone humbly to the Byzantine emperor, asking for land along the lower Danube. Valens had scarcely given them parts of almost uninhabited Thrace before quarrels with the officials began. They laid waste the country they were supposed to cultivate, and, born warriors that they were, defeated the emperor at the great battle of Adrianople (A.D. 378). Wounded by an arrow, he was carried into a house. The victorious hordes knew nothing of this and deliriously set fire to that house along with all the others, thus destroying their most precious booty. What else could the weak emperors do but receive their savage new neighbors into their army? Even Theodosius, who was not one of the weak emperors, accepted Germanic tribes as allies. He was the last emperor to reunite the Roman Empire from Scotland to the Euphrates, for a short time; dying, he entrusted his young sons to a half barbarian. The splitting of the Empire into two parts, accomplished by the grandsons, had thus been prepared by his own doing.

The half barbarian was Stilicho, the son of an unknown Vandal, and himself a private soldier who had earned his promotion. He was to lead the two halves of the Empire against each other in protracted conflict, carrying the war from Rome to Constantinople. The Roman nobles constantly suspected him of being some sort of Germanic spy, and so he lived out the tragedy common among those energetic natures born of mixed blood that we find so often among Jews today. No matter what they do, both races abuse them.

And yet Stilicho's efforts were directed against another German, Alaric, who had brought his Visigoths to Constantinople about 400. The Vandal was spoken of as the savior of Italy, having delivered it from Alaric the Goth.

These two Teutons were the real masters of the shadow monarchies centering in Constantinople and in Rome (the latter had its headquarters at Ravenna). Soon the two adventurers joined to make war on a third German robber tribe, the Ostrogoths. When Alaric demanded a million dollars in gold from the Roman Senate, which still officially existed, Stilicho gave orders that the extortion should be approved. For the first time resistance was stirred. The burning of the Sibylline Books, sacred old Roman relics, the senators had submitted to. But now that they had to pay, even the old gentlemen who had been asleep for two hundred years awoke, and the petty Honorius, Theodosius' heir, ordered the execution of his Germanic general and chancellor, Stilicho, who had made him great. A terrible massacre followed. Once again the Roman spirit stirred against the Germans. Three thousand Teutons are said to have fled to Alaric.

Alaric, whose portrait on a seal is barely recognizable, had wide, childish eyes, a naïve expression, and a small mouth that makes him look not unlike Julian. But intellect is lacking in his features, and indeed where was it to come from? In youth the Greek had drunk of wisdom at Athens. Alaric, a barbarian who could perhaps not write his own name, had chosen Greece for the victim of his ravages. With the excuse of pleasing the God of the Christians by destroying pagan works, he laid waste Olympia and Eleusis, then Corinth and Arcadia, all systematically and thoroughly, smashing hundreds of ancient statues on the way.

What he left standing, fanatical monks destroyed in his name; the temple of Ephesus was laid in ruins at that time. He did not find the Athena of Phidias on the Acropolis, for the Byzantines had carried it off a few years before. Under the hands of this Teuton, Greece ceased to be. Only Athens was saved, as if by chance, and when it had a brief cultural revival half a century afterward, it was the doing of Eudocia, an Athenian professor's daughter whom an eventful career had made the wife of an emperor.

In the summer of 410, Alaric's hordes went looting through captured Rome—the first sack of Rome, to be followed about A.D. 1500 by new German hordes, no whit reformed after a thousand years. Where the great Carthaginian had failed, the petty German adventurer succeeded. But he died suddenly as he was about to sail for Africa. He was still a young man, and his death was like that of many other aimless and indiscriminate robber chieftains. But he had the honor of being romantically buried by his army in the dried bed of a river, so that he would rest afterward in fresh water, and perhaps also so that his body would be hidden from the vengeance of his enemies. Brutal and mystic impulses are close together in the German soul. His successor Ataulphus (Adolph) married into the Roman imperial house but immediately betrayed it to the rival emperor, and became famous as one of the great destroyers of his time. He was assassinated in the midst of his successful marauding.

The Vandals, who began just after the Visigoths, earned a sort of immortality. After they plundered Rome, the fiercest forms of destruction were named for them. But the name of Andalusia, once Vandalusia, has remained too, and it is fortunate that we see no traces of the robber tribe in traveling through one of the loveliest countries on the Mediterranean.

They went from the Baltic by way of the Rhine through Gaul to the Pyrenees, dodged southward to evade the Goths, and thus reached Africa. There was no national idea behind them; they shared nothing with the defeated Romans or the native Berbers, and earned the hatred of the Mediterranean world by the crimes that their very name indicates. And yet they remained long triumphant, because they had learned seafaring in their northern home.

Genseric was the first and really the last king of the Vandals. He reigned almost half a century, and was probably the only barbarian who grew old in power. A contemporary describes him: "Of middle height, limping (after a fall from a horse), taciturn, quick-tempered, avaricious, despising all debauchery, a gifted instigator of rebellion, skilled at sowing the seeds of hatred and dissension." He called himself King of Land and Sea and terrorized the whole Mediterranean with his fleet. The Vandals went plun-

dering as far as Egypt and Greece. They were the first northern
pirates in the south. North Africa, the three big islands, and the
Balearics belonged to their realm; all the rest was their adventure.

The Vandals were summoned to the aid of Rome by an emperor's widow. Genseric, the first alien, landed at Ostia; he found
two competing powers. The emperors usually resided in Ravenna,
but this time there was a second court as well. Pope Leo I received
the Vandal at the city gate and handled him so deftly that he forbade the burning of Rome. Instead the hordes confined themselves
to the gilt tiles of the Temple of Jupiter and the golden vessels of
the Jews, which Titus had stolen from the Temple of Solomon
four centuries before. This was half a century after the sack under
Alaric. The candlesticks and treasure went by way of Rome to
Carthage, whence a later conqueror took them to Constantinople.
Then they are supposed to have returned to Jerusalem, there being
a curse upon any unlawful possessor.

At this time, about A.D. 450, four great northern peoples were
moving toward conquest. The Czechs, a Slavic people, advanced
into Bohemia and Moravia. The Angles, Saxons, and Jutes went
over to Britain, and the Celtic Britons fled before them to Brittany.
The Vandals and Alans founded kingdoms in Sicily and Africa.
The Huns advanced.

Of all these barbarians the Huns were the most interesting because their invasion was more naïve, without sham Christianity.
A wild nomadic tribe of horsemen, Turkish-Mongolian by race
(insofar as such things can be determined at all), slit-eyed, small,
and quick as the wind, by the time of Christ they had subjugated
some of the Chinese. Through centuries they remained what they
were by nature, what the race mongers hope to breed again by
artificial eugenics. They left the weak behind on the endless steppes,
while the strong rode on and on, decade after decade, constantly
grazing territory bare rather than conquering new. They were veritable centaurs. "We warriors and horsemen," their celebrated leader
said, "are a nation that brings terror to all the barbarians. No matter
if we die, our glory will live, and our children's children will be the
leaders of many nations." At that time (the fifth century) they

governed a loose-jointed nomad empire from Siberia to Denmark.

The wind had carried their fame from the steppes to the Mediterranean. In the endless civil wars between Constantinople and Rome, among Christian sects and also among Germanic tribes, the name of the Huns had become a sort of synonym for success. A priest wrote from Marseille: "Our countrymen, even the nobles, are going over to the enemy. They are seeking humanity among the barbarians, since they can no longer endure the barbarism of the Romans." And a Greek in the camp of the Hunnish king said: "This is a fine life here. But in the Roman Empire only the poor man is punished."

Attila, "Little Father," had a wooden palace near the Danube, but he slept on a hard bed and ate simply. He was always with his horsemen and always outdoors, even when he held council. The Byzantine emperor had reason to tremble before this fierce neighbor; he appointed him a marshal and paid him tribute. While the people in the marble palace on the Bosporus took him for some sort of wild beast that had to be appeased, Attila seems to have been a more responsible ruler than the emperors of his period. The report of an embassy shows him sitting by a wooden table at the banquet, while the bards sang of his heroic deeds, as in Homer. After the first, fiercely emotional song, they recited a sort of farce, which drunkenness made wilder and wilder. "Only Attila remained as grave as was his invariable wont."

After a plan of the Byzantine ambassadors to murder him had been discovered, he let them go scot free and gave them gifts and horses as well. But he sent a letter to Emperor Theodosius, from whom the plot seemed to emanate, pointing out to him how shamefully he had behaved—a magnificent document, with the simplicity of a folk poem, that Marcus Aurelius himself could not have drawn up and composed more perfectly. That alone would raise Attila, with all his barbarous deeds, above the civilized kings of his time.

Romantic love stories too surrounded him. The Byzantine emperor once betrothed an unwilling sister to a courtier because of a forbidden love affair. The girl turned in her bewilderment to Attila, a friend and dignitary of the Empire, and sent him a ring so that

he might marry her. The reputation of the noble marauder may
have driven her to this astonishing step. The Hunnish king, who
had many wives, immediately realized the honor and advantage.
He sent ambassadors to the emperor requesting her hand, and asking also for half the Empire as her dowry. Refusal provoked war;
Attila left the Balkans with his hordes, rode to Gaul, and was defeated at the great battle of the Catalaunian Fields in Champagne.
This did not, as is usually claimed, represent the salvation of European civilization from the Mongols, the way it did twelve centuries later outside Vienna. In Champagne there were Franks,
Saxons, and Visigoths fighting with the Romans against the Huns,
who in turn had Ostrogoths in their ranks. If there was not a complete Roman victory, at least it was the first failure of the hitherto
invincible Huns.

Attila, whose self-assurance suffered a staggering blow, was still
strong enough to make Rome tremble from Lombardy in the following year. The same Pope Leo appeared in the camp of the Huns
and managed to turn aside this barbarian, as he did Genseric about
the same period. Attila died suddenly just afterward, during one of
his many wedding nights. Possibly he was murdered by the German
woman who later made her appearance in the Nibelungenlied. But
up to the last he spoke of the princess who had sent the ring as his
betrothed.

This fierce horseman must have combined traits of cruelty and
vengeance with honor and nobility in an amazing fashion, and
apparently he must have been quite free of Caesarism. His empire,
reaching from the Rhine to the Caucasus, disintegrated at once. His
heirs were killed.

XIV

AROUND A.D. 500 the western and southern Mediterranean was a
Teutonic, Christian lake. A chance Germanic chieftain by the name
of Odoacer, commanding a motley army, liquidated the Roman
world empire by violence as early as 476. The troops, having a right
to one-third of the territory they had ostensibly freed, now wanted

a third of Italy, which was considered to be a mere province. An adventurer by the Greek name of Orestes had proclaimed his infant son emperor. When he maintained his claims against the Germans, the soldiers killed him; the Teuton seized the territory that he already possessed in any case, and was about to kill the last heir of the crown as well. The heir, Romulus Augustulus, symbolized by his names the first Roman and the most powerful one. His childish grace touched the barbarian, who spared his life.

This strange figure ends the line of Roman emperors. Italy had become a German colony.

Yet not this conqueror but the adversary he overpowered at Ravenna, Theodoric the Ostrogoth, founded the Germanic Mediterranean state that all the invading barbarians dreamed of—Genseric in Africa, Alaric in Italy, Attila in France. For a little while Theodoric, and Theodoric alone, managed to make the other Germans recognize his kingship; at the same time he awed Constantinople with his navy. For more than thirty years he actually maintained a loose sovereignty over Italy, Spain, southern France, Rhaetia, and Dalmatia.

That he succeeded in doing what his predecessors in the fourth and fifth centuries had failed to accomplish was due to his Roman culture. For this Germanic warrior had learned much as a hostage at Constantinople. He collected Latin monuments, was a patron of Latin literature, and his churches and tomb at Ravenna are in the style of a northerner who had become a complete Roman. He formally recognized the emperor at Constantinople as his liege lord, and had his business managed by a real Roman.

The man who followed him, not as king of the Goths but as the most powerful Mediterranean ruler, was a Byzantine who rose once more against the Germans, relieving the Germanic pressure during a magnificent reign of almost forty years. A true son of the Mediterranean, he intervened vigorously between the immigrants from the Ostrogothic and the Lombard kingdoms. Yet he was neither a Latin nor a Greek, but a sort of Thracian Illyrian—what we would call an Albanian.

Justinian (reigned 527-565) was chosen by Dante as a symbol of

Roman world dominion, instead of Caesar or Augustus, perhaps because he combined Empire and church, perhaps because he called
the law "an infallible power," and placed it above himself, or perhaps simply because he was the last one who held all together. Two
hundred years after Constantine he was more easily able to unite the
Mediterranean in the Christian faith, which meanwhile had grown
stronger. Like his predecessor, however, he wanted power, not faith.
If he regarded himself as imperial pope, as a missionary who had the
princes of the Huns and other pagan peoples baptized at Constantinople, he was always the old-style Roman autocrat, not a deeply
convinced Christian. What he wanted to rule was not the hearts of
his subjects but the coasts of the Mediterranean. The army and navy
were his aim, the Gospel his means. Between the two was a third
power, the law, in which he tried to combine his two missions.

The son of Illyrian peasants, but the nephew of a high officer at
Constantinople, he grew up in the army, and all his life he cultivated both soldier and peasant qualities. He wanted to do everything
himself: he designed a new tower, and he rubbed the new fabrics
in his hands, comparing their quality with Chinese silk; he tested
the light warship, the dromond, and tried a new kind of saddle. The
Greeks called him "the ruler who never sleeps." At the same time
he was so much of a born autocrat that he issued orders for everything, not merely for baptism but for true repentance. Without
these, he threatened his subjects, everyone should lose his rights and
his money. Though he restored and Orientally exaggerated the
splendor of the Caesars, he was simple to the point of asceticism,
indulgent, and kind; at the same time he was vain of these qualities.
He was absolutely determined to be the best of men, the Just.

Justinian's passion for justice was perhaps only an expedient of
nature to calm an intellectually active despot. Napoleon as First
Consul immediately created his legal code, and so did Justinian as
the first expression of his own power. The only permanent survival
of his long reign is his code of law. It was ready within two years
and was merely extended afterward. Since he had no need to establish his autocracy by laws, some deep impulse must have caused him
to form a committee and draw up the Corpus Juris Civilis. This

first collection of laws was finished even more swiftly than the Code Napoléon, in fourteen months—the length of time needed by a modern student to memorize its fundamentals, if he works hard. For it was also planned as a textbook, and has been the foundation of all Occidental law down to our own day.

Of course Justinian began with a magnificent heritage, one that we may say was a thousand years old. The main outlines of Roman law come down from the Twelve Tables of the first kingdom. Everything here was logical and at the same time practical, whereas the later German law was kinder to personal feelings and to individuals and therefore also more difficult for foreign nations to adopt. Latin clarity and German mysticism are reflected in these two systems of law. Tribonian, the celebrated head of Justinian's commission, was a philosopher; he was also a man of the world with a keen eye to his own advantage. His organizing skill is evident from his announcement of the "Digest" or "Pandects," soon to be completed, in which he calculates like an American advertising man that they condense two thousand books into fifty, three million lines into a hundred and fifty thousand. If we look in these codices for the character of the emperor who approved them, we may find indications for instance in the complete equality of rich and poor, who had always before been sharply distinguished, in an un-Roman consideration of human frailties, and in a marked diminution of paternal rights, in conscious opposition to Jewish legal principles.

But even as a lawgiver the statesman was always vigilant. There were disturbances in Constantinople between the two parties, the so-called Blues and Greens of the Racetrack, and when he punished the culprits of both parties, he had more motives, evidently, than justice alone. He wanted to keep them from uniting against him. This they actually did during the very first year, and Justinian gave himself up for lost. The combined parties swept forward in one huge popular wave against his palace, which they destroyed, constantly shouting, "Nika!"—"Conquer!" A splendid watchword for revolutionists, and one that was never again to be shouted at a ruler from the streets! This was not the middle of a war; the shouting indicated the same scorn and derision with which Roman soldiers had once called to Jesus on the cross, urging the Son of God to save himself.

Justinian was saved that day by his wife. Theodora, whom he did not meet until he was about forty, the woman whom we see enthroned as queen of heaven in the Ravenna mosaics, was a child of the circus. The daughter of a bear keeper and a prostitute, she entered the ballet chorus as a child, later attracted the emperor's attention in the circus somewhere, and finally after but a few years' interval marched into that arena wearing a golden diadem, as empress of the world dominion. Girls from the common people had had similar careers in Constantinople before her time, as many others did afterward. But Theodora, in contrast to the type represented by Messalina, made something of her eminence. In this moment of panic she made her husband pull himself together, saving the day and the throne for them both by ordering her general to assist the Blues against the Greens. More important than the list of her lovers is the fact that the great Justinian loved and honored her until her death, through twenty years, and afterward mourned her until his own demise.

The abortive revolution put an end to all popular rights. As a result the hot-blooded Byzantines, worthy successors of the Athenians in their incorrigible opposition, rebelled again and again in the next few centuries. Justinian had no other revolt to put down in his time. It was only now, on the basis of a solid autocracy, that he began his twenty years of war to unite the Empire. His means was the navy. Like Augustus he was no general or admiral himself, and he turned over the navy to strong hands. His general, Belisarius, as swift-moving as Agrippa six hundred years before, defeated the African king. To keep the fleet together he had all the sails painted red. When he sailed into Carthage a hundred years of Germanic empire in the Mediterranean went down with the last Vandal king. This time it was a true deliverance.

He found it much harder to subdue the Goths in Italy and Spain, and even after twenty years he succeeded only because the Goths were no sailors. Rome itself became the battleground of Goths and Byzantines during these long wars. It was besieged, liberated, taken again: finally Narses, the general from the new capital, marched into the old one, which he had always been taught to reverence.

The Romans, their nobility, their senators—so fond of tracing their ancestry back to Romulus—suffered a monstrous calamity: Italy was declared a Byzantine province. Rome was a provincial capital. Rome was ruled from Greece. This was the great revenge of the Greek world upon the Latins, five centuries after Augustus degraded Greece into a province.

Soon the last Germanic Mediterranean power was broken. At the moment when the old capital of the Roman Empire was conquered, the Roman Empire rose again. But its symbol, hitherto a disk with Rome as its center, was different now—an ellipse with two centers. The Mediterranean, once divided into western and eastern halves, and then united for five centuries, seemed again to be streaming in two directions. The Dardanelles and Gibraltar, the two straits that free it from the restraints of an inland sea, belong from now on to two different nations and civilizations.

What Justinian finally managed to do in the west was almost impossible in the east. While fighting the Germanic kings who occupied the western Mediterranean, he was too greatly weakened in the east; he had to give ground and pay for the conquest of one barbarian group by tolerating the other—quite literally, for he paid tribute to the Persians. These perils advanced upon Constantinople, while he had to move his own troops farther and farther away. Around A.D. 550 too, the Huns and Slavs were approaching his capital, while the young nation of Bulgarians pushed toward Corinth. The Serbs and Croatians entered the light of history for the first time along the northern frontier of the Empire. The cost of these twenty years of war was great in human life and money; the Emperor spent all his inherited millions in gold.

But during this time he had also built roads and sewers, baths, monasteries, and libraries everywhere. One gets the impression that he did this with more knowledge and true passion than he waged war. The accounts tell us how he became absorbed in silkworm culture, with which at last he made Byzantine splendor independent of the Chinese. This guardian of justice thought it perfectly natural for two monks to steal the silkworm eggs in China and carry them home in hollow staves—in other words, for one priest to cheat another on behalf of wealth and power.

"I have outdone Solomon!" cried Justinian when he saw Saint Sophia and his palace completed. The fact that the old buildings had been burned in the revolution redoubled his zeal, and five years later the church was larger and more beautiful than ever, built of fireproof material that he commandeered everywhere. He even made the columns of the Artemis of Ephesus carry the dome for the glory of Christ. By his order the great marble ball that had been sacred to Aphrodite at Pergamum now became a font for holy water. This passion for building, common to so many autocrats before and after him, is obviously a sort of insurance of fame, due to a premonition that states crumble more easily than palaces.

Justinian always took pleasure in details, and at Ravenna and Jerusalem we see him personally sketching or changing the proportions of the new churches. But the same hand that traced the floating dome of Saint Sophia in the drawings signed a decree which darkens his memory more than any death warrant. Justinian closed the Academy at Athens. Of course this was a Christian measure, for he forbade the instruction of those "who believe in the madness of the Hellenes." But at the same time it was the revenge of a Byzantine whose city had been disdainfully treated during the two centuries of its existence by Athenian scholars. Eight hundred years after Plato, the Neoplatonic philosophers had to flee to the grandsons of the barbarians in Persia, whereas their forefathers had sat in the shadow of the plane trees that had shaded Plato himself.

This act, seen in perspective, looks like the sack of Rome by the Goths. It is the harder to justify since the church by this time was already leaning on Aristotle, who was to become the patron saint of Christian theology in the Middle Ages. Augustine put it gracefully by saying that we should do as the Hebrews did in their departure from Egypt: they left the idols there but carried the gold and silver with them. So we too should take unto ourselves the treasures from the pagan writings. The Christians said of his famous *Confessions* that they would have been very similar if Socrates had written them.

The bishops and popes, with their slow modification, were frequently wiser than such an emperor as Justinian, who never could—and never can—stabilize a state religion by edict. In the Roman Empire it was impracticable. There were entire pagan countries in north Africa in the fifth century, as there were in Spain and Laconia down to the ninth. Thus the interpretation of the two worlds could come only by assimilation. No doubt there were violence and cruelty, and one bishop in Africa is said to have forced baptism upon seventy thousand people in a few months. But on the other hand there were also customs and institutions for the Christians to take over, such as the right of asylum, tonsure, relics, canonization. Had not Caesar been elevated to the gods by Vergil and called Soter, that is, the Savior? Had not Hadrian managed in the course of a very few years to make Antinoüs, who was drowned in the Nile, a god throughout the Empire simply because he was handsome and Hadrian's favorite? Thus Constantine had become a saint, and Justinian had great hopes of similar promotion.

The factor continually disturbing young Christianity after the fourth century was not the old gods, whom no one but the visionary Julian had tried for a moment to recall. It was the quarreling of the sects and their combined jealousy of the emperor.

The sects had arisen over a single letter, an *i*. Was Christ equivalent to God, or similar to God? The difference, expressed in the Greek word by an *o* as against an *oi*, was of course more than a letter. Anastasius of Alexandria, a church father, had proved the unity of Father and Son, which was understood by every believer with the clarity of the Occident. The Orient, however, was more inclined to give ear to the doctrine of Arius, after whom they were called Arians. According to him Christ was merely a creature of God, and therefore could not be one with Him. When the Council of Nicaea decided against the Arians and in favor of the Anastasians (Catholics) the problem was by no means solved; it was more acute than ever and was argued for several centuries.

As time passed, the quarrel grew more and more vivid in the popular mind, more and more passionate. It typifies the spiritual life of the era that people flew at each other's throats over a mystical question, not an economic one. Neither money nor power had anything to do with this popular struggle. In the palaces, however, patriarchs and popes, popes and kings wrestled for precedence. It was as yet by no means sure that the bishop of Rome was to be the most powerful down through the centuries. The celebrated passage in Matthew: "Thou art Peter," and its Roman interpretation roused the bishops of Antioch, Alexandria, and other great cities to a frenzy.

As the councils contradicted each other, the relation of Christ to God sometimes depended on the question of which princess or which eunuch happened to be dominating the emperor at Constantinople. The disputed letter, at first a symbol of deep emotional meaning, became the battle cry of parties, which in turn defended their divine right with the letter. Cleavages went through the church, which was still in its youth; the Syrian and Egyptian Christians broke away from the accepted dogma, and the Copts and Oriental Christians have remained separate to this day. The emperors could choose only whether they preferred to be considered heretics in Egypt or in Rome. At the same time they had themselves depicted with golden haloes, while the archbishops stood humbly in the background. The Popes took their revenge by showing themselves on the throne in the act of bestowing the crown on a tiny emperor. God had long since disappeared from both pictures.

The episcopal throne was a symbol to show that the bishops of Rome followed upon Caèsar and derived their power from him as well as from the Apostles. Such marble seats as the one still standing in Saint Gregory's represent a temporal throne, dispensing justice and power, not humility and love.

Justinian took part actively in all these problems. When he died at the age of eighty-two, having reigned for half his life, a contemporary might easily have compared him with Genseric, the Vandal king, who had ruled as long just before his day. Yet what was left of the Germans in Africa? Chaos and cruelty, more suitable to the wild forests of Germany. History remembers Genseric now only because the idea of vandalism arose under his rule.

Justinian had also sacrificed masses of human beings in his wars and in the revolution; he even tried in vain to destroy the Athenian heritage of Plato. As we have seen, he closed the Academy of Athens, so that the last Greek scholars had to flee to the king of the Persians. For a long time after this the name Hellene indicated only the heritage of the hated Neoplatonic idea. The Parthenon became a Christian cathedral, the temple of Theseus a Church of Saint George. And yet this was a splendid effort toward unity, restoration of the Roman power, service to a church along with the wish to curb the Pope, and a lifelong urge to produce buildings, art, craftsmanship, inventions. Just before his death Justinian consecrated the third Saint Sophia, an earthquake having destroyed the second.

But above all this, the law he set up for the future endured. The strange human weakness for bestowing more glory on generals than on philanthropists is found in all activities except those of the law-giver. A sense of law seems to be deeper rooted in men than culture and faith, perhaps because there are many philosophies and theologies but only one justice, on whose principles almost all nations agree. Justinian established these principles more firmly and developed them more elaborately than Solon, Lycurgus, or Napoleon. His book of laws has brought more peace and happiness to the inhabitants of every zone during fifteen centuries than any religion, because up to 1933 no one ever combated it. In this sense he is among the greatest leaders of mankind.

XV

WHEN JUSTINIAN LOOKED OUT at the Golden Horn from the windows of his new palace, a white, gleaming dome floated before his eyes. He had built the church and dedicated it to the supreme wisdom, Sophia. Probably even in those days a mass of surrounding buildings detracted from the impressiveness of the spectacle, for Saint Sophia, like Cologne Cathedral, is not on an open or elevated site. High outside walls and a crowd of low domes clustering outside like parasites half hide the picture. The four graceful minarets of today were also absent. The beauty of the cathedral is inside.

Within, the gigantic unsupported dome overpowers anyone

who has been irked by the subdivisions of even the greatest cathedrals. We shall look in vain for another space so high, so vast, and so lightly roofed in. The absence of all pictures (which held good to some extent under the Christians), strengthens the impression of a single vaulted unit. The tremendous oval nave, 100 feet wide by 240 long, is 180 feet high to the top of the dome. Even Saint Peter's, wider and almost twice as high, has not a nave of this extent, and there as in all other churches the eye is halted by two or three rows of half walls. It is not the hundreds of green and porphyry col-

umns, not the wealth of marble arches and capitals, not the portal
with its nine gates, the double arcades or the enchanting gallery for
women, not alabaster, mother-of-pearl, and gold mosaics that make
Saint Sophia unique. All these exist in the Occident as well.

The free dome alone gave to this church the name Supreme
Wisdom. The light pours in through forty windows. When the
eye travels upward to the light from this spot of immeasurable
measured space, it finds a sun in its midst. A hundred doves go flying through; probably Justinian himself first released their ancestors
here. They pursue each other under the sun, cooing, nesting in
secret nooks, dying, and multiplying, and no one feeds or attends
them. The beat of their wings makes the music of this noiselessly
floating vault.

Justinian was the first to make Constantinople the capital of the
Mediterranean, or in other words of the Western world. For the
few centuries before and immediately after Christ the city remained
provincial. After its second founding it grew up, but it was still
overtopped by Rome, Alexandria, and Antioch. Then Theodosius II
built the great circular wall with its hundred towers. We recline
beneath cypresses among the ruins today, as if in a neglected park.
Until the time of the Crusaders no enemy was able to take these
towers, which stand in a single row toward the sea, a triple row to
landward. Persians, Huns, and Bulgarians vainly stormed the walls.
And so Constantinople survived eleven centuries, from 300 to 1453,
when the Turks came—longer than any other Mediterranean empire, if we except the inland Egyptians.

Constantinople, ruling Italy, Spain, north Africa, Palestine, Asia
Minor, and the Balkans as far as the Danube, was more reminiscent
of Alexander's empire than of Caesar's. The Byzantine Empire was
actually a Greek empire, and no doubt some of its scholars saw
themselves foreshadowed in the well-known prophecy of Herodotus. Yet of the two great Greek rulers, Constantine could speak no
Greek and Justinian had a bad accent. This is a failing in which we
sometimes surprise conquerors confronted with their dreams; it
has a faintly comical effect, like the bad French of Napoleon.

But the innermost nature of the Byzantine Empire is like neither

Alexander's empire nor that of the Caesars. Indeed it has remained unique ever since: Constantinople was the very embodiment of form at its greatest. The history of the Byzantine rulers is really the history of ceremonial, in the sense of deeply felt parables symbolizing power and faith. No one else ever deified ceremony to such an extent except possibly the Pharaohs, but they were more naïve; they proclaimed themselves gods, and possibly in an unguarded moment some of them may have laughed at the credulity of the common people. But the Byzantine emperors always felt that they were mediators with Christ.

Since power and belief reinforced one another, there was no conflict between Pope and Emperor. Spiritual and temporal powers actually coincided, as they did with the caliphs. Yet at the same time they were parted by inviolable ceremony, which described them as the two halves of God. The patriarch was appointed by the emperor; the emperor was crowned by the patriarch. Both acts were felt to be ecclesiastical, and both received worldly solemnization. When the investiture in the golden hall of the palace was finished, amid hallelujah choruses, the emperor barely lifted the cross with his right hand. Before the door a magnificent horse awaited the prince of the church, and the senators accompanied him home on horseback. The functionaries of the Empire, in a graduated pyramid, each and all, down to the last doorkeeper, received a share of the sacred significance of the whole. There were no temporal offices, and everything together symbolized the form of the second life, the life of Paradise. No other sect or era of Christianity ever developed a power so completely imbued with theology.

In order to consolidate this foundation of the state, emperor and court had to set the example. They could do nothing on the spur of the moment, but had to practice even the posture of a finger for hours at a time. Hence the influence of the masters of ceremonies, who managed politics at the same time. Mostly they were eunuchs—not, however, of the emasculated kind but merely sterilized in the way that has now come into use again. Among them were some of the greatest figures; Narses, considered the finest general of the Middle Ages, defeated the Goths in his mid-seventies. But no eunuch ever became emperor. As the centuries passed, bringing greater proficiency, it became the chief aim of domestic politics to maintain the equilibrium of power and devotion. Finally form altogether took the place of intent.

"One might have supposed," wrote an eyewitness of the Council of Nicaea, "that one was viewing a picture of the heavenly kingdom of Christ. It did not seem real, but a radiant dream." Hence the complete muffling of the body in Byzantine art. In many of the mosaics the very feet of the brocade-decked emperors and empresses are invisible; instead of open crowns, great hoods hide their heads; even of the rigid faces only a small part appears. They are so close to the Christ enthroned above them that his feet touch their chests. Nakedness, motion, and profile are unknown to Byzantine art. There are miniatures showing chancellors sitting on a sort of throne, wearing magnificent brocades adorned with lions' heads and looking haughtily at the missal held out to them by the choirboy. At the same period in the north, the other emperor, Henry II, was having himself and his wife portrayed on a golden altarpiece at Basel with bowed backs and so small that each of the two heads was half as big as one of Christ's feet, but with crowns on the heads.

The pretension to being the world's first Christian empire found expression in a dignity made possible only by the tradition of centuries. As the motionless emperor performed his evening devotions, his mind would be full of the thousands of troops on Danube, Nile, and Euphrates, all mounting candles on their spearheads before the battle, lighting them, and singing the same monotonous chant that was heard now from the choirboys' gallery above him. The worship of form grew with the cultivation of it. The Book of Ceremonies provided that anyone who dropped a plate at a court banquet was to be killed, and anyone who had watched this happen was to be blinded.

Thence there developed quite naturally the great school of diplomats from which the masterly political skill of the Venetians and Arabs later took its rise. The young officials were given courses in the psychology of foreign nations, particularly the barbarians.

The manners they had to learn in the process became world-famous. The dignity, deliberation, and courtesy that we like to ascribe to the Orient were actually perfected here, on the frontier of Europe. The ideal was the gentleman who always kept to the background, seemed to admire everything foreign, and expressed his self-assurance more in glance and bearing than in words; it was also to be found in a pretended tolerance. Arab mosques were built in Constantinople for captives, and the defeated prince of Crete got back his land and his palace, though not without first having been humiliated.

Armed tourneys, in which the emperor himself had to excel, were part of a court education; so too were literary correspondences with foreign philosophers. The daughter of the first Comnenus recorded her father's reign in splendid style. The Christians of Alexandria butchered one of the wisest women of the Academy, but at Constantinople thinkers and poets were rewarded so long as they obeyed the great *Codex*.

Such a spectacle of sovereign grandeur demanded spectators. Coronations and triumphal marches afforded the best opportunities; they lasted for many weeks, and emissaries from other lands, quite carried away, sent home amazed reports. It was not the splendor and wealth alone; it was a formal dignity such as no nation had ever seen on such a scale. The deifications in ancient Thebes, where the Pharaohs marched through the streets as gods of the Nile or the sun, and the delirious extravagances of the Caesars, reeling between lust and revenge, were followed by the imperial presence of Constantinople, never approached in the West except possibly by the Spanish court and the Venetian ducal coronations.

Amid solemn trumpet blasts, constantly interrupted by the chants of the priests, a splendid cavalcade of a thousand horsemen passes down the great shore road in the midday sun; the horses are decked with long brocade covers, with pearl hangings, brow and breast pendants. The spearheads of the bodyguard, the shoes of the knights glitter with stones. There are golden breastplates and old Persian daggers. The ladies watch from gorgeous sedan chairs, while arched boats, trailing brocades behind them, bring senators and governors to the bank. They all sweep forward with measured tread, just as in the gold mosaics, men and women with jeweled crowns on their heads and long, winglike sleeves that almost hide their hands. Then comes the patriarch, with incense and organ music, and behind him hundreds of the clergy, carrying burning candles despite the sun.

The emperor, assisted by the patriarch, exchanges the tiara for the crown, the cross for the sword. The trembling captives huddled into a mass are white with terror. Captured tents are displayed on slow-paced camels. Then follow two prefects, bearing garlands of victory; the emperor thrusts his arms through. At the same time the most distinguished of the captives are seized and dragged to the foot of the cross that has been set up beside the emperor. There the highest in rank flings himself flat on the ground and puts his shaven skull under the purple shoe of his conqueror. At that moment the conqueror gazes heavenward, so that the connection between victory and God becomes visible, from neck to shoe to eye. The master of the horse holds the spear to the neck of the captive. The prisoners fall upon their knees and the captured weapons are hurled to the ground, all to the accompaniment of pious chants. The crowd shade their faces with their sleeves, as if before God. The patriarch prays. The emperor draws back his foot. The captives arise and retreat, walking backward. The following day the emperor rides in his four-horse triumphal chariot to the hippodrome, with the Madonna, represented by a picture, going before him in a chariot. A thousand loaves of bread are scattered among the multitude; baked in each is a freshly minted gold piece, which must not be spent even in dire need. Wine fountains splash around the palace. The captives, released yesterday, are already sitting with the crowd on the benches, betting on the riders and race horses. All the garments of the aristocracy, all the gifts of the emperor, must be of fine gold; Justinian once spent the yearly income of Egypt for this alone.

Is it possible for human rulers to keep their sanity in the midst of such immoderation? Constantinople struck the necessary balance by establishing a second sphere beside the sphere of ceremonies—

the world of the circus, where the people had their passions and their games, their party politics and parodies, just as in the Athenian agora and the Roman Circus Maximus. At the endless festivals and races the crowd make their wishes known to the emperor by shouts and songs. He listens, learning whether his ministers have deceived him. He may increase the quantity of water in the public baths or attend to the removal of mud from the streets. Actors and dancers, wenches and magicians appear, casting a second spell upon the crowd. Many races are mingled, for thousands of captives have become traders here, and languages, customs, and wares are tumultuously exchanged. The crowd is allowed to sing couplets about the empress and her old love affairs.

How people laughed when the patriarch once hastily rattled off his litanies at the circus in order to hurry to the stable, where his favorite mare had just had a foal! He kept the finest race horses, which he fed on grapes and currants in their marble stalls, until finally he broke his neck steeplechasing. Racing, gambling, and the struggle of the Blues against the Greens were the passions of the common people. The emperors knew it, and even with all their power, all their armies of warriors and priests, they listened to the voice of the mocking throng. While they appeared before the people as saints, they also gave them the illusion of living with them as one great family. When the empress brought a child into the world, all the warriors in the palace had to drink the same gruel she did, and they felt honored into the bargain.

There were sixty-five revolutions in the Byzantine Empire during eleven centuries, from about 300 to 1400. Of 107 emperors, two-thirds were murdered, and most of the patriarchs ruled for less than a year. Yet the people never revolted against the system, but only against individuals. Only in Egypt and Germany has there been any such millennial kingdom without change of system. Even the iconoclasts of the eighth and ninth centuries, with all their fanaticism, brought no overthrow of the state.

The secret of this stability lies in the unchanging trinity of ceremony, people, and soldiers. Except for the last few of the line, the emperors never neglected their army and navy, as Persians,

Greeks, Carthaginians, and Romans did in the wealth and indolence that followed their great days. Decadence was late to arrive. The Byzantine emperors built and maintained at Aleppo, Ephesus, and Smyrna the best ports in the Mediterranean. Great fairs held there and at Salonika were frequented by Egyptians, Indians, Chinese, and also by Scandinavians and Russians.

At the same time the Byzantines served as naval police regulating the pirates. For a hundred years it was regarded as their greatest task to take Crete from the freebooters. In the ninth and tenth centuries the pirates put out under black sails from their Cretan castles, ports, and hideouts. Each vessel was rowed by two hundred gigantic African captives. It was not until A.D. 960 that two thousand vessels were at last ready to sail out of the Golden Horn, laden with an expeditionary force, military engines, and the newly invented Greek fire. On board were Normans and Russians, Armenians and Danes; the heavy rainbow-hued sails of the admiral's vessel bellied in the wind, and the silken flags with pictures of the saints fluttered abaft the gilt prow.

Then came victory, and Constantinople succeeded where others had failed: Crete, the stronghold of the pirates, fell before her arms, and the black sails vanished from the blue Mediterranean.

XVI

A NEW SAIL HAD APPEARED LONG SINCE. It came from Arabia, the peninsula that does not touch the Mediterranean, and could not then reach it through the canal, which was silted up at the time. Nomadic tribes, sailing at most along the coasts of the Indian Ocean and the Red Sea, came almost abruptly out of darkness into the arena of history. Unlike the Phoenicians, their neighbors, who were nothing but sailors from the start, or the Jews, who never became seamen, the Arabs reached the Mediterranean by land conquest. They conquered great parts of it with incredible speed. There is but a few years' interval between their first appearance in Syria and their capture of Alexandria.

Yet the new alien invasion, whose effects were to last almost a thousand years, began with quite different means and purposes from that of the Germans. We hesitate to call the Arabs barbarians, for what they brought to the Mediterranean was productive. The name infidel applied to them is as unjust as the same epithet applied by them to the Christians. The two nations and races, from north and south, were a world apart.

Nomads both, scarcely endowed with the written word, both were strangers to the high Mediterranean civilizations that attracted them. But the Arabs had been poets and singers before they could write down their poetry. And so the Arabs came to find intellect and cultivation, to conquer and settle, to found kingdoms, carry their language and their faith to unknown lands. Where they mixed with the native population, a productive new element appeared in history. The Germans, however, could propagate only their rough-ness, not their language. Their kingdoms vanished as swiftly as they had risen, because they neither brought any intellectual capaci-ties nor accepted anything noteworthy. This is how it happens that the eastern, southern, and western Mediterranean preserves to this day countless memorials of the Arabian character and scarcely one of the German.

Mohammed, born just after the death of Justinian, resembled him more than either Alaric or Genseric had done. Like Justinian he was a thinker and a soldier, a philosopher and a statesman; and with all his worldly wisdom, his was a deeply emotional nature. He resembles Justinian, too, in that he combined rather than invented his ethical principles. His teaching, which remains an unfinished torso, adds little that is new to what he took from the Christians and the Jews. He traced his own relation to Abraham, Moses, and Jesus, and declared that he was continuing their work. He had fewer new ideas than Jesus had. There is nothing essentially new in Mohammed's sermons. They were not really a doctrine—merely a fund of shrewd rules for practical living.

If we discard the forms and simply compare the ethical systems, we are increasingly surprised to find two moral structures almost exactly alike. We find it harder than ever to understand the zeal of the Crusaders, the imprecations of caliphs and popes, constantly increasing in vehemence as they were led into a life-and-death struggle by their analogous concepts of God. The struggle was senseless because the principles—there is but one God; love thy neighbor; help the weak; despise riches; beware of retribution in the hereafter—all are the same in both doctrines. Even love of one's enemy was known to the warlike prophet as to the gentle one. Mohammed says: "It is the highest virtue to seek out him who has repulsed you, to forgive him who has offended you. Every Moslem is the brother of every other Moslem. In Paradise the slave and the caliph are equal." There is even an almost complete paternoster in the Islamic tradition.

Mohammed came from the desert. Moses and Jesus knew the desert also, for it was but two paces from the valleys of the Nile and the Jordan. Even if Moses did not wander in the desert forty years, still he must have been there long enough. But Mohammed was the only one of them who never left the desert and never saw the sea. He lived in Mecca for fifty years, then twelve years in or between Mecca and Medina, in the glaring noonday light of the desert. The clearness of the red-and-yellow evenings, the dryness of this air without salt made him more logical and colder than the other three prophets.

Hence the lack of feeling for nature in Moses and Mohammed. Hence the wealth of imagery in Plato and Jesus, whom the sea inspired. As nomadic chieftains, too, Moses and Mohammed were similar in temperament—practical, truculent, complete dictators, captains and prophets impelled by anger and vengeance. Plato and Jesus admonished and persuaded; full of devotion, they were first philosophers, then prophets.

These are symbols of national character. For the Jews and Mohammedans have always given an affirmative answer to life, vigorously and positively rejecting asceticism, praising fertility. Their two prophets lived with women—Moses even with a gentile, the elder Mohammed with as many women as he pleased. On the other hand the early Christians and later Greeks taught asceticism, and their prophets lived accordingly. Here seeking the world, there fleeing it, the faithful found awaiting them on one hand a paradise of laughing women, on the other a heaven with solemn choirs.

The dogmatism and sophistry of the rabbis and the Arabian scholars, constantly wrangling over interpretation, also served to distinguish the Jews and Mohammedans from the early Christians and later Greeks, who were far too remote from the world to bicker. Later, as they began to mingle in hatred and love, the Christians and Arabs influenced each other increasingly.

The Koran constantly refers to the Torah and the Gospels as earlier revelations of God. It was not contrary to Moslem dogma to learn from others. The thousands of Jews and Christians who became Mohammedans in the early Middle Ages through habit, conviction, or self-interest and the thousands of Arabs who became Jews or Christians were merely repeating what the Romans and Greeks had done in their productive exchange and combination. It was precisely these converts among the Mohammedans who adapted the isolated desert religion to the Mediterranean civilizations. At the very moment when the Occidental and Oriental Middle Ages finally represented one single civilization, the closely related creeds flew at each other in murderous wars, killing millions of men for the sake of a symbol.

A tragicomic occurrence such as has been often repeated in history made the pupil hate and persecute his teacher. As a young herdsman Mohammed was familiar with Arabian soothsayers and singers, magic stones, tree and fire cults. He derived his later significant insights from Jewish traditions, which obviously were stronger in western Arabia than the Christian and Zoroastrian traditions. There was a united Jewish community at Medina. The ancient Jewish idea of the judgment day inspired the happily married merchant of Mecca, rich at the age of forty. The Jew's Judge of the World was the one God who took the place of nomadic talismans. How easy for such an inspiration to change into a prophetic sense that one was personally appointed to carry the new message!

This vision of the God-seeker, surrounded by a very small circle of listeners, brought him into even closer contact with the Jews. Indeed the Hegira, which was not a flight at all but an emigration two years in preparation and only hastened at the end by threats, took Mohammed to the Jews of Medina. They asked him to decide their quarrel with some heretics. His assertion that he was the successor of Moses evidently caused the Jews to deride and rebel against the stranger.

If the Jews of Medina had accepted as their political leader this obscure man whom they themselves had summoned, Mohammed might have been known in history simply as a seventh century organizer who converted the pagan Arabs to the Jewish faith. But because they laughed at him and drove him out, this great disciple of the Jewish faith became the greatest anti-Semite in history. Quite in the fashion of our modern party leaders he fouled the spring from which he drank. The part of Judaism that he no longer liked he now proclaimed a forgery. At first he drew on both Testaments because they pointed to himself. Then as his lust for power grew, he took offense at the self-assurance of the Jews, who refused to recognize him, and the resignation of the Christians. To satisfy one of Mohammed's temperament a prophet must above all be successful; accordingly he declared the crucifixion of Christ a Jewish invention.

During his last decisive decade the prophet became a conqueror, the missionary of the one God a politician among parties. Like our party leaders, he altered his formulas. While Islam had at first meant "submission to the will of God," Mohammed himself later defined it as "submission to the will of God and his emissary." In expeditions against Bedouins and Jews, at assemblies of his growing organizations, in negotiations for a ten-year peace, during the years of his swiftly increasing success, Mohammed became a general, governor, diplomat, and party leader, and rich and sensual besides.

Entirely a creature of the senses, he thought much about eating, drinking, and sleeping. He enunciated wise laws and prohibitions that parallel our own eugenics and hygiene. For the Koran is also a colorful book of life, regulating the practical details of the day from hair curl to toothpick. His family and inheritance laws occasionally reveal the natural, jealous equity of the nomad. In his double character of prophet and warrior he concerned himself particularly with women; but he did not solve the problem any more than Christianity did.

As a true son of the desert Mohammed loved kindred, the tribe, the family. "The breath of a son is like the breath of Paradise. Two prayers of a married man are worth more than seventy of an unmarried one." Primitive Christianity had preached asceticism, later merely compromising on the asceticism of the priests. Mohammed showed doubt of his own strict commandment of fidelity in marriage by various skeptical utterances: "Women are the firewood of Hell. Pious women are as rare as ravens with white or red legs and red beaks." Then again he yields tolerantly to womankind in a charming parable: "Woman was created out of a rib, a crooked bone. If you try to bend it straight, it will break. Therefore, ye faithful, have patience with women." And while allowing an unfaithful wife to be beaten with thongs, he hastily adds, "But not too fiercely. And ye may take her unto you again afterward."

This mundane pliancy, and even more the Arab character, which (like that of most nomads) combined freedom, passion, and generosity, resulted in a tolerance that was only afterward impaired by Christian excesses. Of all three religions Islam was the most tolerant. It alone, through long ages and in many countries, allowed those of other faiths to keep their churches, gave humane treatment to the conquered, and scarcely permitted the conquerors anything more than leadership and freedom from taxation. The desire for booty or revenge was seldom carried to the point of general persecutions. The cry "Death or Islam" was heard only at the beginning of their conquests and in Arabia alone. Later, temporal dominion and nothing else was wanted. Tribute and obedience, not a new religion, were imposed on the conquered. The Koran, after all, recognized other faiths. Christian festivals and funeral processions were always allowed in Bagdad and Cairo; until the time of the Crusades there were high Christian officials everywhere. The reason for this superiority seems to lie in the inner assurance with which these monotheists professed complete faith in human nature, just as the Greek polytheists had done.

XVII

ALONG THE SHORES OF THE MEDITERRANEAN a new kind of tower made its appearance in the seventh century.

The temples of the Greeks had been destroyed or transformed or had crumbled. The Parthenon had been turned into a church in the fifth century. Where the statues of Zeus and Athena had once risen against marble columns and sky, where the naked body celebrated its own beauty, and the mysteries of the old gods became symbols in marble or in sacrificial processions of worshipers, heavily shrouded priests now knelt before a crucifix. The corner of the huge structure where they were hidden away lay in candle-lit twilight. Not Greek sun and Pentelic marble but the chapel and the rigid mosaic icon served as symbols of a suffering and renunciatory faith. The marble procession of the Panathenaea with its horses and youths was shamefacedly shrouded by those who would deny sex; but they must have wanted to shroud themselves and their spirit too, for all this was perfectly alien to them.

After the columns came the domes. The sailor approaching shore at Constantinople, where the new cathedral stood by the beach, could see the domes reflected in the Mediterranean. The cedarwood Temple of Solomon, the marble colonnade of the Parthenon, and the masonry dome at Constantinople had successively represented the austerity, the beauty, and the devoutness characteristic of the three religions. All the faithful who had prayed there were one in their desire to vanquish death in another life. This was the universal source of kindness and mercy; tablets in Hebrew, Greek, and Latin beg the one God or one among the gods to be merciful to the giver in the hereafter.

Then came the minarets. This fourth road to God was distinguished from its predecessors by a new elegance. Temples and churches hitherto had sat heavily upon the earth. The slim towers

of the Arabs shot upward, standing in the sky like frozen fire-
works. The tall, slender structures seemed, as it were, to have been
tossed into the air from a narrow base, separate from the mosque.
Close to the top one of the faithful in a white cloak, with a cloth
wound about his head, would appear on a pierced gallery. Turning
his face upward, he would cry out three times to the skies the
praises of Allah and Mohammed his prophet. This tower it was
that held the faithful together while they spread, more swiftly than
the followers of any previous religion, around the Mediterranean.

The Greeks had lost their unity early and often because philosophy offers no watchword to the crowd. The Romans survived
longer with their common law and their firmly organized state.
The dogma of Islam, suddenly imposed by decree like a new party,
fused many races and nations—longer and more firmly than the
Christian did. Finally it split, as Christianity had. Here too the seed
of a world empire was planted by a thinker, at once as idea and
conquest. Mohammed left only the beginnings of a united Arabia
behind him: his kingdom could not easily disintegrate. And when
his generals, like Alexander's, divided Persia, Egypt, and other
countries after quick new conquests, they felt themselves united by
a fresh new religion. It was neither mystical nor ambiguous like
that of the Greeks, but rather a program for the conduct of life, a
moral and hygienic legal code. While Christianity held together the
old Roman Empire for another three hundred years, Islam did not
develop fully until the building of the Arab kingdoms, which were
united by faith and a common speech only. The extension of
Christianity was slower and more peaceful, that of Islam swifter
and more warlike. Each of the two religions today counts its adherents by the hundred million.

The conquests of the Arabs, which were not triumphs in religious wars but the victories of a vigorous warrior nation, differed
fundamentally from the Germanic Mediterranean conquests in
their intellectual basis—their watchword, so to speak. The fact that
they turned anti-Christian is a political result, not a cause. Thus we
have the paradox that the Germanic tribes overrunning the Mediterranean from the fifth to the ninth century (their Christian

coloration in most cases already complete) were coreligionists of the peoples they attacked, but behaved and were regarded altogether as barbarians. On the other hand the Arabs, with their capacity for assimilation—in which too they resembled the Jews and Phoenicians—carried on the high civilizations they found.

When Omar, Mohammed's second successor, captured Jerusalem five years after the prophet's death, no atrocities were practiced on the Christians. Those he drove out were Persians. The Christian patriarch who surrendered the city was a Byzantine subject, or at least his predecessor had been. Jerusalem had been Roman almost uninterruptedly for six centuries, from Jesus to Mohammed. Now it was Mohammedan, to remain so with one brief Christian interlude from 637 to 1918.

No Moslem harmed the tomb of Christ; after all, he was one of their prophets. Not until later did bigotry bring wars and crusades. It was left for the keenest of all Mediterraneans, Frederick II, to regulate the various religious services at Jerusalem tolerantly by one chat with the Sultan. The same thing was later done with the Turks.

Omitting any account of the Persian and Egyptian wars of Islam, which do not directly concern the life of the Mediterranean, we find the Arabs from the seventh to the ninth century struggling with two groups of powers: Byzantine and Germanic. The rapid maritime development of the sons of the desert was amazing. "One fortunate battle by sea is worth ten victories on land," Mohammed says. And sure enough, the Arabs repeatedly beat the Byzantine navy, pushed forward to Rhodes and Cyprus, and found the way to Constantinople clear. There at last the walls of Theodosius and the new Greek fire halted them. This seven years' siege of Constantinople by the Arabs was the longest known to the Mediterranean since Achilles had camped before Troy—longer than the sieges of Tyre, Corinth, Carthage, and Syracuse. And still Constantinople held firm. As we are in the habit of saying, she saved Europe.

The cultural influence of Islam was altogether a productive one. When the Persians and Egyptians learned Arabic, when the Arabs studied Greek mathematics and medicine, when Alexandria, Basra, Cairo, and Córdoba became Arabic universities, spreading their teachings through Christian students to Paris, Oxford, and Padua, the Mediterranean found itself caught up in a new intellectual movement. Within two hundred years the old nations were learning from the Arabs about algebra, the decimal system, the pendulum, astronomical instruments, and narcotics. They learned about dyeing and tanning, glass, clay, embroidery, carpets, paper, gardens, irrigation, new fruits, a new architectural principle (the horseshoe arch), the arabesque order of decoration, stylized animals and plants, inlays; and water flowing everywhere, in houses, courtyards, gardens.

There was one individual who formed a plan to make peace between the two related faiths. Emperor Leo, an Anatolian and a Hellenist, encouraged by the movement of the iconoclasts, tried to find in the oneness of God and the rejection of all images the reconciliation that would have been feasible and fruitful. But the monks were against it. The Pope resisted, using the political interests of Italy for his own purpose. And when the Byzantine navy was shipwrecked, either Christ or Allah or perhaps both were present in the storm to prevent the reconciliation.

The two invading bodies of strangers first collided in Spain. There, apparently, the splendid mixture of races began which improved the breed, as it always does among human beings, thus emphasizing one of the greatest differences between man and beast. Later the most marvelous crossbreeds were produced, notably in Sicily.

As late as the sixth century Justinian had annihilated the Ostrogoths and Vandals; and the Lombards, later invading northern Italy, were shut off from the Arabs by the Byzantine navy. But the Visigoths, still settled near Gibraltar, were within easy reach of the Arabs who conquered north Africa about 700. In north Africa Berbers and Byzantines, in other words Africans and Greeks, had long been struggling for power. When the first Arab prince crossed the Strait of Gibraltar in 711, he was perhaps the first Asiatic in fifteen centuries, since the Phoenicians, to come as a conqueror to the western Mediterranean. His armies were composed largely of warlike Berbers from the Atlas Mountains, who had been converted to Islam. The offspring of their union with the Arabs and the Roman and German remnants in Spain were called Moros, Moors.

This stock, interchangeably called Moors and Berbers, and supposedly numbering twelve millions even today, is distinguished by physical beauty. Blue-eyed blonds were reported among them by their forefathers three hundred years before Christ; no Germanic strain has anything to do with it. But it is remarkable how closely they resemble the Arabs by nature. They too were warlike and imaginative, proud, crafty, and fanatical; they were known as remarkably good conjurers, but also as decidedly honorable. In national analysis they have an odd tinge. By this time they were farmers and orchardists, skilled at irrigation, at turning wild slopes into olive and fig groves. They taught the nomads from the steppes the skill in gardening that later became their specialty and filled their poetry.

For twenty years Arabs and Berbers together, sometimes fighting among themselves, pushed forward through Spain. Crossing the Pyrenees, they reached the Loire in France by constant fighting with rebellious Christians. There, in 732, they met the Germans in the battle of Tours and Poitiers, and were beaten by them. That famous day may be considered decisive between Christians and Mohammedans. It set a limit to the Arab advance, just as the Germans had done to Attila three hundred years before in near-by Champagne.

Though beaten back and driven out of Gaul, and soon defeated on the Tigris as well, the Arabs, or rather one of their leaders with his hosts, plunged westward again. He established himself as Emir of Córdoba, building an island of Arab civilization. Fortunately Charlemagne, whom the Christians summoned to their aid, was forced by revolts among the Saxons to turn back, and the Arab garden continued to flower. But the great power and civilization of the Arabs were not in Europe now. They moved to Bagdad. The stories of the caliphs that have filled the imaginations of men in song and opera were wellsprings for the romances of Western poets, just as their rugs and jewels, their medicaments and perfumes are universally copied to this day.

A torrent of beauty and ideas poured out into the Mediterranean after this invasion. It mingled so strongly with the other waters that at certain points the current seems to swerve. Just so the influx from the Black Sea increases the salt content at the Dardanelles.

Of course the Arabs were pupils of the Byzantine Empire in a hundred ways, too. For instance, in their art of shipbuilding. Also, they made the Suez Canal navigable again for a century, and they certainly did not learn how on the camel trails of Arabia. Their quickly acquired trading ability, in which they recall the Phoenicians, seems to have been doubled by the Mediterranean; they took over all trade with the Far East and soon reached Russia and the Baltic. But the greatest achievements that the Arabs brought to the Mediterranean were intellectual—cultivation and taste. Pope Sylvester, whose celebrated learning was attributed to magic, had in reality studied the Moorish wisdom of Seville and Córdoba.

The court of Charlemagne stared in astonishment at the embassy that Caliph Haroun-al-Raschid sent to the Christian king about A.D. 800. Singers and historians told the tale to the world. Never had anything like it been seen in the Occident, not even from the hands of the Persians, who had preceded the Arabs in some civiliza-

tions. The story merchants and scholars told—especially later, around A.D. 1000—of the magnificence of the Fatimids at the newly founded city of Cairo, or at the courts of the Muses maintained by the kings of Aleppo and Damascus, had a fabulous aura because the Arabs and their successors alone among all the newly rising nations seemed to combine wisdom and valor, dignity and beauty.

Now began the fame of the schools and art of Córdoba, where the fugitive emir established a princely house that reigned for three hundred years. The only possible comparison was Alexandria. The

Christian Occident was amazed at the culture and tolerance of the infidels. Mohammedans and Jews of the same rank worked together. Both were fugitives from Asia and opposed to the Christians. From 800 to 1000 southern Spain was the intellectual center of the world.

A new system of irrigation made Andalusia the most fertile country on the Mediterranean. A historian using Isaiah's words wrote: "Under the Caliphs of Córdoba swords and spears were beaten into spades and plowshares"—the finest thing one can say of any government. In that little realm were seventeen schools and seventy libraries, used by great Christian scholars from all over the world. About A.D. 1000 Córdoba, with its million inhabitants the most populous city of the West, had more than six hundred mosques, nine hundred baths, and half a million books. Here, as in other Spanish towns, Jewish spirit was producing philosophers, poets, and physicians—some of them even then well known throughout the medieval world, as Jehuda ben Halevi, Ibn Gabirol, and Al Harisi.

Although it was at odds with the caliphs of the East, still Arabic Spain relied on an Islamic power that united north Africa and half of Asia, and reached as far as the south of France. This intellectual empire stretched from the Persian Gulf to the Atlantic. On the old maps it looks much bigger than the united Byzantine state, which included the Balkans, Asia Minor, southern Italy, and Sicily.

The Mediterranean was never to know an invasion by alien peoples so fruitful as that of the Arabs.

XVIII

ABOUT THE YEAR 1000 the German king Conrad II ordered an imperial crown made at Mainz. It was tripartite. The middle and largest of the three bows had an almost square cross. There were huge pearls and jewels, not quite regularly distributed; the cross was adorned in the same way, and placed only a little higher. For centuries this crown kept passing from the kings' hands into those of the popes and back again. The size and costliness of its jewels showed that the diadem was no greater, yet certainly no less, than the cross. The whole struggle between emperor and pope that filled the Middle Ages is expressed in these proportions; surely the jeweler at Mainz did not adopt them without royal instructions.

The alliance and conflict of kings with priests, running through history in all ages and times, assumed a complicated form on the medieval Mediterranean. Power was constantly divided and fought over, whereas religion was a single force, of whose two sects only one, the Roman, carried weight. But the Pope was in Rome, while the emperors had been in Germany and the land of the Franks since the end of the Roman Empire. The result was a geographical monstrosity with two heads, one of which wore a miter, the other a crown. The man with the miter could crown or refuse to crown the other, whereas the emperor had no symbol to bestow on the Pope. The illusion that the crown came from God, and God was represented by the Pope, was such an acute invention of the priests that the powerful kings were more dependent on them than they on the kings.

The Germans chose their kings from warlike stock, and the Franks, the Saxons, the Lorrainers, and other peoples took the leadership by turns. The man whom the Pope at Rome had to endow with title and blessing, crown and the so-called anointing, represented a new group almost every time. As an international spiritual power, spreading out over the nations, the Catholic Church exercised a dominion that divided Europe vertically, as socialism afterward did, and thus cut through the horizontal lines and frontiers on the map, as degrees of latitude and longitude intersect.

There were no more oracles whose priests could be considered infallible, as they long had been at Thebes or Delphi. So the Pope, who presumed to divine wisdom, found himself and his party interests constantly at odds not only with the kings but with the nations. In the Middle Ages the struggle for power lost the church millions of devout believers. For doubt and criticism, once begun, destroy all faith in infallibility. The Popes' claim to temporal power was a stumbling block to their purely spiritual dominion over souls between A.D. 500 and 1870. Even the little Vatican City they possess since 1929 is rather calculated to weaken their spiritual power.

The struggles between emperors and popes that troubled the Mediterranean for five centuries cannot be studied in detail here. We shall inquire only into the philosophical foundations; on these rested the heritage of the Roman Empire, which was not wiped out by the invasion of the barbarians but preserved as a sort of shadow realm.

Christianity had taken possession of the Germans in a very special way. When Clovis, king of the Franks, the first constructive figure in the north, united Germans and Romans on the soil of France, about A.D. 500, and got himself baptized along with three thousand Franks amid fierce uproar, he had carefully calculated the effect. He recognized that the basic instinct of his Germans was love of battle, bloodthirstiness, and vengeance. How could he impose overnight upon this fierce nation, not prepared, like the Mediterraneans, through wisdom and art, a God who demanded a soul instead of a strong body, justice instead of war, and humility instead of pride? Whether he foresaw the fact or the future merely proved it true, it is certain that only a complete contrast could surprise and win over these passionate tribes.

The abrupt and extravagant nature of the Teuton, and later of the German, his natural ponderousness, the nebulous, ecstatic side of his being, his rapt submission to the whim of fate, all required some counterweight to balance arms and doughty deeds. Here, suddenly, was a God who forgave instead of taking vengeance, who blessed instead of punishing, a court of judgment that called forth emotions instead of commanding revenge and atonement. A tremendous spiritual struggle began to rack these millions when they were asked to submit to the new God. It was seven hundred years from the time of the first mass baptism until the last Frisian accepted Christ.

We cannot understand the passion stirred in these converted barbarians by the conflict between state and church except as the result of some profound shock. The struggle of greedy kings and princes to snatch a few more bishoprics and monasteries or provinces would have been impossible except for a genuine popular feeling which divided the pious and the cynics in the north.

The emperors simply acted as the expression of an always restive national character and an urge to expand southward. Dreams of warmth and fertility kept pushing them toward the Mediterranean. To this, Rome was the traditional key. There lay the tomb of the Roman Empire, as it were. German knights and Crusaders alike considered themselves pilgrims. For in Rome the symbols of Caesar and Christ stood side by side; the Pope sat on the ancient throne of the Caesars, and over him was the sacred dove of the Jordan. Thus the misty Nordic imagination of the Teutons was doubly stirred.

In the eyes of a German king, Rome combined world dominion and Christianity. He saw at the Capitol the spot where the first Caesar had been assassinated, and half an hour away the place where the first Apostle was killed. To no national character was the mingling of temporal power and Christianity better suited than to that of the Germans. And so there arose the preposterous idea of the Holy Roman Empire of the German Nation, which realistically speaking was complete nonsense, yet which had profoundly emotional effects.

The Franks, later as inhabitants of Gaul called French, one of the most gifted Mediterranean nations and at the same time the earliest stabilized, took the fateful first step about 750. The usurper Pepin, a Christian, offered help to the Pope but demanded coronation by him in return. The moment when a king first led a Pope's horse by the bridle, and the moment immediately after when he knelt before the Pope to receive the crown (then still a simple gold hoop) and the holy oil on his brow—these led to the insoluble conflict.

In return the king had to promise the priest the city of Rome with the so-called ecclesiastical state. His successors increased and confirmed the gift. This nebulous legal status, always mingled with a little incense and sword jingling, was balanced by another according to which a German king, being elected, was not a real "emperor" until crowned by the very Pope who was actually his vassal. In this way the German was exalted to the successorship of Caesar, making him ostensibly the ruler of the Roman world empire. He had even less historical right to it than the Pope had to Rome. Thus two powers or two persons confirmed each other's pretensions with a mixture of pretended devoutness and real guile—all at the expense of the Italians, who wanted neither pope nor emperor, but simply a united Italy. The very first German to become emperor on the Mediterranean gave a hint of this development.

XIX

CHARLEMAGNE, ONE OF THE three important German emperors, belongs only to the fringes of our story. As depicted in the Paris statuette he has the features of a born ruler, round head, short neck, sharply curved nose, and round upper lip. The imperial orb in his left hand seems to have been dropped there by nature. At the same time his active life shows a typically German urge for world dominion, which derived, then as now, only half from a craving for power and half from mystical impulses. He was the first of a long series of emperors who were seeking not unity and consolidation, nor even their natural eastward expansion, but the Mediterranean.

He was always learning; he was not proud of his rank or race, and a hundred traits show that he was trying to get beyond his barbarism. He imposed Christianity on foreign peoples by violence, and then suddenly he would show broad tolerance in intellectual matters and questions of the heart. Severe to the nobility, he appointed freedmen to high offices. When he learned to read, as a gray-haired man, he was soon trying to teach the art to his children. He allowed his many children the emancipation of his own ample love life. In many ways he was centuries beyond the crudity and dullness of his people.

The most surprising event in his long reign happened to him on the Mediterranean, at Rome—a scene unexampled in history.

He had been on excellent terms with the Pope, who had sought refuge with him in Germany; no kneeling and no holding of stirrups had lessened the dignity of this Frankish king. When he went to Italy to establish a Pax Romana after the fashion of Augustus, he intended no Mediterranean conquests beyond the Lombards in the north. On Christmas Day, 800, the Christian king, his knights, and his court attended Mass in St. Peter's. The Pope was celebrating Mass, and he pretended to be deep in prayer when the king knelt before the altar. Whether the king was thinking of his Saviour or of his business nobody knows; the only thing sure is that he had no idea of the surprise the Pope had prepared for him.

For suddenly the Pope picked up a crown, secretly held in readiness, and set it on the head of the kneeling king. At the same moment a group of Roman knights stepped forward, crying out: "Hail and victory to Charles Augustus, Emperor of the Romans crowned by God, hail and victory!" The music joined in, and the excited throng shouted and cheered; evidently a great event had taken place before their eyes. Charles, past sixty at the time, was surprised and distressed. Refusal was impossible. In fact the shrewd priest added an irresistible gesture; he knelt to the emperor he had just crowned. Charles rode silently back to his castle. The following day he learned from a solemn manifesto that the Pope had "transferred the Roman imperial authority from the Greeks to the Franks, and exalted King Charles to be the seventy-third Emperor of the Fourth Empire."

Charles was, as his contemporary biographer tells us, bewildered and angry. As a boy he had watched his father Pepin leading the Pope's horse by the bridle, in order to be anointed king by him. Now, being quite without any Caesarist ambition, he saw himself suddenly crowned Caesar. His plan of marrying a Byzantine princess was spoiled by the enforced coronation. For the symbolic designation of Rome as the permanent center of the world confirmed the very thing Constantinople had been disputing for centuries. In the Middle Ages a title was a gesture, often more important than an act. But since he was not a real conqueror, and wanted no war with the Byzantine Empire, Charles's wishes in the direction of the Mediterranean were more hampered than forwarded by the coronation.

After more than three centuries the coronation resurrected the Roman Empire, which had ended in A.D. 476; it survived for another thousand years as an empty symbol. But Charlemagne's remained the only undesired coronation. All the succeeding German kings pursued the crown, sacrificing thousands of lives, the interests of Germany, and of course their own convictions to the honor of being called Caesar's successor. Indeed Caesar's fame would never have reached its present height without these extravagances; the Germans created it.

From now on they rode and plodded in endless procession across the Alps, entangling themselves in decades of war to conquer Lombardy before the coronation or southern Italy afterward. But they never went to the Tiber to gain Rome, where no German emperor ever ruled more than a few months. They went simply to be crowned at St. Peter's, like Charlemagne. The suggestive power of the idea was so compelling that even Napoleon, who made fun of every noble gesture, still used the so-called Lombard crown to give his Paris emperorhood the authority of Caesar.

As a sign of their legal status, Pope and Emperor applied the feudal relation of the era to their own power. If the mightier man at home or the conqueror abroad invested his inferior with a piece of ground—that is, lent it to him—the other might possess it and devise it to his heirs. But he had always to safeguard the interests of his liege lord. In the land of the Franks, as earlier in Macedonia, the young people in old families thus gained land, castles, posts as officers—maintenance and protection that is—but had to defend their lord when revolts or party dissension threatened him.

Starting from the solid, neatly divided soil, the kings took a sort of leap into the dark by proclaiming that they in turn received their kingdoms in fee from God. The crown with which Pope Leo surprised Charlemagne was a selfish gift; it created a precedent that made Rome supreme and the contest with the temporal power necessary and unending.

This struggle, which ended inconclusively after five centuries, brought neither happiness nor religion nor civilization to mankind; at best, one work of art, Dante's poem, can be ascribed to it. What

mad plans were made to solve this problem! There was the plan of
Otto I to establish the Pope jointly with himself as emperor of the
world; the emperor would supervise the election, and in return
would protect the ecclesiastical state. Against him were the Roman
nobility, who deposed several Popes because they wanted to appoint
one themselves. One Pope, deposed by Otto II, fled to his great rival
at Constantinople, only to be killed in Rome after all. There were
alliances between Constantinople and the Arabs to defeat the Christian emperor. In the intervals the bishops of Constantinople and
Rome fought each other, excommunicated each other, and had
their bulls of excommunication solemnly deposited on the steps of
St. Peter's and Saint Sophia.

The century after the Ottos, a strong Pope snatched the idea of
the Roman Empire from the German kings, leaguing himself with
German princes against the democrats of Milan and the Normans
of Naples. This was Gregory VII, the ugly little son of an artisan,
who tried in vain to subdue the handsome and distinguished Henry
IV.

When that emperor, as a penitent, stood shivering for three days
in the snow-covered courtyard of Canossa, a Lombardic castle,
where the Pope was lodged in 1077, the church seemed to be enjoying a triumph. Centuries late the barbarian invasion seemed
avenged, the Germans humbled, the powers of Rome resurrected
beneath the tiara. Gregory was like one of those Byzantine despots
who set their foot on the neck of the vanquished king. Actually
this episode ended with the flight of Gregory, his deposition and
lonely death, while Henry was crowned by another.

How strong the bishop of Rome considered himself to be at the
time we can see from a sheet which Gregory dictated as a memo-
randum for his own use. He did not publish it, but he followed it
out on a grand scale. The original may be read in the Vatican today,
twenty-seven numbered paragraphs written down in superb Latin
script. No Egyptian priest could have had a greater sense of power
than this Christian of low birth who said of himself: "All princes
must kiss the foot of the Pope. His name only shall be spoken in
the churches. That name is alone in the world. He alone may bear

imperial insignia. He may depose emperors. He may absolve subjects from their oath of fealty. No one may repudiate his decree. He alone may repudiate the decrees of others."

We must not imagine these priests, with their insatiable lust for power, as living amid pleasures and palaces. Gregory, for example, was a puritan, a product of the reforming ideas of Cluny Monastery. Following that exalted school of intellect and purity, he desired only the emancipation of the church from temporal powers. But he reversed the religious purpose, making of it ecclesiastical supremacy over the temporal kingdoms.

The fiction of "bestowing the temporal sword upon the kings" survived. But when the great quarrel immortalized by Dante in his *Divine Comedy* seemed to end after three hundred years, with a peace between emperor and pope signed at Worms in 1122, neither was victorious. The German church and its property had not become independent of Rome. But neither had the election of the Pope become independent of the emperor. Many powerful Popes were yet to fight against, curse, banish, or depose their emperors, and many emperors their Popes. In reality the question of power never subsided.

Even in those days there were two sorts of Christian faith and life on the Mediterranean. Pope Innocent III and St. Francis lived at the same time, about A.D. 1200, and near each other, at Rome and Assisi. It was not only the mighty who did battle with the Pope. The monastic orders too turned from him to a true Christianity such as the first monasteries on the edge of the desert had produced centuries before, monasteries that were now fortresses with arms, books, and wine.

Francis of Assisi, suddenly converted in the midst of a gay youth, became a seeker after God who cared for the sick and wretched. His primitive Christian preachings reached across the Mediterranean. Hundreds flocked to him and believed in him. The proud Innocent listened keenly to see what sort of echo this strange ecstatic would evoke. The Pope was a member of the powerful Roman Conti family, rather Slavic-looking if we are to believe the mosaics. He represented the masterful sort of man, contrasting with Francis, whose only remaining portrait shows him as a visionary. Innocent shrewdly recognized the new order of the monk who had grown so quickly popular, but at the same time he vitiated it by imposing discipline and obedience. Francis resigned his leadership. By the time of his death, in complete poverty, the order already had large properties.

The same thing happened to Francis that happened to Jesus and all the other prophets and philosophers who meddled, even unintentionally, with the march of history. Twisted, distorted, misinterpreted, they were horrified at the results of their teachings, which they had meant quite differently—had composed in a vacuum, so to speak, not for the world. These teachings came to resemble an idyllic bark venturing upon the Mediterranean between Matapan and Crete, where the great storms roar.

XX

AT THE PIRAEUS, the port of Athens, stood an ancient lion, untouched for fifteen centuries. If a seaman carved his name upon it, he used Greek or Latin letters.

One day about A.D. 1040 the lion was found covered with a strange script that no one could decipher. The characters were Nordic runes, in which blond and blue-eyed people a thousand miles from the Mediterranean wrote down their myths. When these people first appeared in the south, they were stared at by men and particularly by women. The sexual attraction of strange races has perhaps never been stronger than it was when the Northmen, called Normans, appeared on the Mediterranean. They had the very sort of elegance and good looks that the men of the Mediterranean lacked—tall, sinewy figures, slim hips, golden blond manes, light, rather piercing eyes.

Just at this time, the eleventh century, the Arab too had arrived as an interesting newcomer. He represented the physique of Greeks and Spaniards in an Oriental way, for his eyes were fiery and dark like his hair. Though slender, he was usually shorter than the men from the north. At the same time he was skilled at arms and in the hunt, interested in horses and clothes, an orator, a flatterer, a master of law and formality—in short, the very opposite of the rude, dull Teuton who had previously reached the Mediterranean.

The Normans were the first northerners with any power of assimilation who appeared here. The Germans hitherto had remained barbarians, and the Arabs did not want to become Christians. Going to Normandy from Scandinavia in the tenth century, the Normans had accepted the language and religion of the country, and within a century after they went over to England they had become English. But while they found there a nation to which they could adapt themselves rapidly, in Sicily, where they now landed, they were slow to be assimilated and dissolved.

In the eleventh century Sicily became the crossroad of two civilizations again, as it had been in the time of Pericles and Pyrrhus. Here, where the Arabs had been ruling for two centuries, the sons of the desert and the sons of the North Sea now stood dramatically face to face. Songs and legends tell of this collision between two races perfectly certain to attract each other with every physical sense. The beauty of the Creole may give us some idea of what came into being then, a thousand times more from the simple sex instinct than from marriages. The bastard as Shakespeare sings of him has never been more charmingly begotten from the crossing of two alien races than he was there and then. We have few pictures, but many poems, fables, and tales. The gold-mosaic banquet hall of Roger the Norman in his palace at Palermo shows us today the beauty of his Arabic-Norman combination, as do the Moslem domes we still see peeping out of Sicilian orange groves next to the severe outlines of the primitive basilicas.

Who could have been a better subject for the romantic dreams of dark, lovely, languorous harem women than these blond knights and robbers who appeared on the Mediterranean in small troops, not in great hostile armies, like the Arabs? Had not the most famous of them, Robert Guiscard, of the house of Hauteville, wandered through Italy in pilgrim garb, hiding a sword under his smock?

Indeed the Arabs had summoned him and his knights to their assistance from Apulia. These men had gone on daring voyages to
Epirus, and, like the Arabs, had cast their eyes upon Constantinople.
They could not take it, but they could take Sicily from the Arabs,
which Constantinople had never managed to do. As the Eastern
Empire was too much for him, Guiscard led his hosts to Rome.
There he repeated the farce of the emperors by having the Pope
invest him with his duchy. Roger, one of his successors, even had
the Pope crown him king of Naples and Sicily.

Only a seafaring people could have conquered all this so quickly.
All the Northmen in north Germany and Scandinavia, whom the
Roman Empire had never reached, were sailors on the North Sea

and the Baltic. Anglo-Saxons and Jutes, and later Danes as well, had crossed over to Britain. Later the Vikings had gone from Russia to Constantinople and had there become famous soldiers and captains. By the ninth and tenth centuries the Normans were appearing in the Mediterranean as soldiers or pilgrims, and in any case as pirates. In that business they were very much akin to the Saracens, in other words, the Mediterranean Arabs. There were often Arab rowers aboard a Norman vessel; thus north and south were united on the same decks.

The romantic age of freebooting had long since passed. Piracy was not considered heroic on the Mediterranean. One learned piracy as one learned seafaring, and this too the earlier traders had first learned here. The desert nation of Arabs learned seafaring so well that they reached the Atlantic by the eighth century, and were supposed to have landed in Brazil by 1150. In the ninth century they were the terror of the Mediterranean, plundering Marseille, Nice, and Ostia. The Vandals too had first acquired the art of seamanship here. The Berbers seem to have been the only nation who were sailors and horsemen simultaneously, because they bordered on the sea and the desert.

Only the Normans were real sailors from the start. They seem to have brought to the Mediterranean a new type of vessel, the galley, which remained dominant for centuries. This was a covered rowing vessel built entirely of wood, up to 180 feet long. It carried as many as four hundred men, with the rowers ranged side by side, not on different levels. The sweeps, up to 40 feet long and often manned by as many as nine oarsmen, were swung to the commands of a man with a resounding voice, in three beats: stand up, stretch arms, pull and drop back on the bench. There were from twenty-two to twenty-six strokes a minute, each one carrying up to 30 feet; the vessels made a speed of eight knots on short stretches and during attacks; at other times, the rate was as low as five, or sometimes two, knots. The vessels, square-rigged, sometimes traveled under sail, often without sail. The sail hung from a long yard; it was used only before the wind, since the draught of the vessels was slight and the art of tacking unknown.

In their galleys, which were soon adopted by other nations, the
Normans and Saracens made the sea unsafe—now together, now
fighting each other, like great banking houses. And as banks use
their nations, so they used cross and crescent as pretexts when they
chose to destroy each other. For a long time the Popes paid tribute
for being left in peace by the Saracen pirates. No wonder the mercantile cities banded together, built fleets for defense, and thus grew
more powerful in their turn. This is one reason for the later power
of the Italian merchants. The first joint offensive we know of was
undertaken by Pisa and Genoa in 1015, when they took Sardinia
from the pirates.

The concept of freedom of the seas was established about this
time. The cities of Gaeta, Amalfi, Salerno, Naples, Brindisi, Otranto,
Bari in the south, Pisa and Genoa in the north, and Venice,
soon overtopping them all, began more and more to take the
place of Constantinople at the time of the Normans and the first
Crusades. Their defense began to swell into a great sea power,
but there was originally no plan of world dominion behind it. Very
gradually their galleys began to cover a larger radius, trading with
Tunis, with Tripoli, with Alexandria—with Christians and Mohammedans quite independently of religious prejudices. This was
the time when the school at Amalfi developed the first maritime
law, when the medical school of Salerno attracted all nations. The
marble cathedral of Pisa was supported down the middle by sixty-
eight ancient columns, Greek and Roman, which the Pisans had
carried off or bartered for. Thus trade and culture cut across nations
and denominations, flourishing with complete freedom in the very
Middle Ages that we think of as intolerant. What quarrels there
were took place among Christians or among Italians—Amalfi was
broken by Pisa, Pisa by Genoa. When two cities were at odds, one
of them would call in the Arabs against its Christian compatriots.

No one can truthfully say whether law or anarchy dominated
the medieval Mediterranean, safety or robbery, negotiation or force.
All of these held sway at the same time on various coasts. If
we look at the history of Genoa, we find the city ravaged by
Teutons in the seventh century; in the eighth century a Frankish

count who ruled there fell in battle against Arab pirates; one hundred years later the city was plundered by African Saracens. At that time they also took the ports on the Tiber and looted the left bank and St. Peter's. Apulia was plundered of wine and olive oil by Dalmatian pirates. Then the Normans pushed the Saracens out of Sicily. Subsequently there was such brisk free trade on the coast of Provence that the bishop of Fréjus arranged trade fairs of the modern kind at St. Raphael in order to attract foreign traders.

At the same time Venice appeased the pirates from the neighboring rocky coast by a treaty and paid heavy tribute to the freebooters. In return for this the latter captured the slaves the Venetians wanted to sell. Genoa and the Knights Templars banded together against the united Berber and Saracen corsairs. Soon no Christian prince thought of waging war on a Moor without first making an alliance with some other Moor.

The endless stream of outlanders kept flooding the coasts. Each new group displaced and plundered its predecessors; at the same time the groups mingled in endless new racial combinations. More traders than pirates, the Phoenicians with their first wretched boats had sailed from Syria to the Syrtes and then to Gibraltar. Fifteen hundred years later the Saracens from the south and the Normans from the north sailed into the old Phoenician and Greek ports. Nothing was changed except that the standard of morality among these Christians and Mohammedans had declined, for by now they were more pirates than traders.

XXI

AGITATION OF THE MASSES for an idealistic purpose has been attempted very rarely in history. The defense of a nation, a natural instinct without special merit, is described in high-flown words as heroism, and the war of conquest is ascribed to false motives. Actually, of course, one group wants to gain money and property, the other to avenge itself on or measure itself against its neighbor. The gambling instinct, greed, and a desire for admiration unite to stir up the so-called enthusiasm for a war of conquest.

The first crusade is perhaps unique in history because it aroused a religiously inspired multitude to defend a relic. In such waves of emotion as this the common man feels himself lifted above his destiny, gaining new strength. The layman may bear arms that otherwise are fitting only for knights. If in the past he has noticed and rather envied the gay insignia worn by passing soldiers, now he is actually urged to accomplish an idealistic end, for no gain save honor, and his excitement rises to the point of ecstasy. In the crusades he was ordered to kill all day, and to kneel down at night, thanking God and praying for the morrow. The cobbler was made a hero.

When Urban II cried out at the end of a fire-eating speech to the Council of Clermont in 1095, "It is God's will!" the crowd went wild, wanting to start for Jerusalem at once, and protect the Holy Sepulcher. Imaginary visions and messianic hopes stirred the masses. Most of them were French; so were the Pope who went to France to deliver this speech and the hermits who undertook the propaganda. "A new road to heaven and forgiveness for our sins!" was the Latin war cry. But in addition to these truly religious motives, the instincts of the knightly world were stirred—adventure, courage, devotion. For in the long run it was the healthy and largely the young men who set off, armed and helmeted, with a cross sewed to their tunics.

What was there to defend? Were Jerusalem and the Holy Sepulcher in flames? Had the infidels killed the true believers?

For more than three centuries, after the conquest by Omar in 637, the Arabian masters of Palestine had been gentler and more tolerant than most conquerors. Haroun-al-Raschid had turned over to Charlemagne the keys of the city and the office of protector of Jerusalem, along with the right of proprietorship in the Church of the Holy Sepulcher. The German and English kings had maintained constant friendly intercourse with the Arabs through buildings and charitable establishments.

Not until the Seljuk Turks captured the city in 1076 did matters take a turn for the worse. A hundred frictions were bound to arise when parts of the Mohammedan world in Sicily and Spain were reconquered by Christian powers, lost again, and conquered once more. Finally almost all of Asia Minor was taken by the Turks. Both parties felt themselves menaced, while each was menacing the other—a typical frame of mind for the unchaining of a war that tolerance and statesmanship had avoided for centuries.

On top of religious passion, racial ambition, and the desire to be a hero there was the attraction of the little-traveled Orient, which in tale and romance had constantly occupied the imagination of the Occident. There was also the desire to earn gold and treasure along with fame and the reward of God. A great pestilence, too, raging from Flanders to Bohemia, drove out thousands who dreamed of Syria as a paradise of golden apples and perpetual blue sky. Other thousands hoped to escape persecution, or their monastic vows, or their wives. All the human weaknesses and a few human virtues were worked on to make thousands surrender their security, their livelihood, their families, and sail across the Mediterranean into the unknown. Complaining voices were heard, even from bishops residing at the Rhine, about outrages and persecutions of Jews, committed by "scum" at the start of these pious crusades.

The Pope seems to have created a great conception when he gave the world the word "crusade." A universal church needed the Holy Land, and though he certainly did not mean to move from Rome to Jerusalem, he certainly wanted to rule Jerusalem from Rome. At the same time this idea enabled him to pose as a power above all states, to appeal to doughty and warlike men over the heads of their kings, to bring the patriarchs of the East under his sway, and to put princes and other great lords under obligation to him by finding glory, wealth, and posts of honor for their younger sons.

And what fervor took possession of the bankers who had financed it! What a gigantic volume of transportation, exports, and imports fell to the rising cities of Italy! While the Occident echoed with the cowled agitators' shouts that the Holy Sepulcher must be protected, while prayers and choral chants wound up public gatherings that were almost crazed with emotion, thousands of traders, pen in hand, were adding columns of figures. In the vaulted chambers at the port of Genoa and the brighter and more colorful

ones of Venice the merchants of the Occident sat in endless conference, calculating how to make the most of this unexampled rush
of business. Of course a few thousand crusaders were seeking the
salvation of their souls, but a hundred thousand were seeking their
fortunes. Here was perhaps the first war waged not by soldiers but
by everyone.

The four or five crusades that fill the twelfth century, which cannot be detailed here, varied in style, duration, and success. Their fabric was like the Oriental rugs that every crusader brought home in order to explain the colorful world of the Orient. The rugs showed marvelous beasts and plants, richly caparisoned knights and ladies, ships, horses and camels, all combined into one great phantasmagoria. If the crusaders had taken nothing but Oriental legends, these alone would have been worth the trouble. Truly the treasures of art and poetry, the hero lays and legends of the adventurers were all that Christendom gained. No one ever checked the power of Islam.

There were noble robbers and fanatical monks, young counts seeking a princedom, natural sons of pious kings, uncertain whether they dared boast of their blood, brilliant strolling orators and avaricious ministers of state, bishops who took over the harems from the Arabs, and usurers who sank ships for the insurance, players, students, and vagabonds who sang and wrote poetry in crabbed Latin, troubadours beneath the windows of veiled Turkish ladies, and parodists of them who made everyone laugh, inventors of new ships, and dealers in counterfeit relics. There were rich Genoese who sent their sons in aristocratic legions to do battle in golden harness against the infidel and forthwith sold him wood and metals.

After the first flush of enthusiasm there was the same mutual suspicion among the allied leaders as we have seen in our own day. We have only to read of the horror that seized the Byzantine emperor Alexius and his cultivated daughter when the expected crusaders, finally reaching port, trampled on the nerves, usages, and formalities of the Byzantines, and not of the court alone. Their lost provinces in Palestine were supposed to be recovered for them, but the whole affair went against the grain because it had originated with their great rival, the Pope of Rome. Only through painful negotiations that almost led to fighting could the leaders, who hated each other, be got to Asia with their armies by separate routes. When the Byzantine emperor exacted an oath by which the leaders promised to receive in fee from his empire alone any territories recaptured from the Turks, one of the princes refused to take the oath, another swore a false one, and a third broke his.

Close to so many homes of miracle echoing with the old Biblical names, the leaders used every resource of superstition and suggestion to urge on their soldiers. Antioch withstood a siege of
months. When a relieving Turkish army threatened, a Provençal
peasant saved the desperate situation. Lifting up a lance, he shouted
that this lance had pierced Christ on the cross. Under that sign
the crusaders vanquished the besieged. Only the Christian legate
smirked and wrote home that he had very grave doubts.

Jerusalem finally fell in 1099. The conquerors' passion for revenge grew. When we read in an old account, "The Crusaders filled
the courtyard of the Temple of Solomon with blood up to the knees
of the horsemen and the bridles of the horses," we are chilled to
the marrow by this first entry of a pious host of champions into the
Holy Place they had liberated. And yet the prophet in this sepulcher
was a prophet of the hostile religion as well, and the unbelievers
also believed in him. Both doctrines, furthermore, enjoined tolerance, slaying one another as they did so. Once more we see the power
of symbols and signs, overshadowing all reason and justice.

The Latin kingdom of Jerusalem, begun amid endless intrigues
and rivalries, lasted formally for three hundred years, actually for
one hundred. The first knight who was chosen king, Godefroy de
Bouillon, declined the title with a noble gesture because he wanted
a religious state. He even proclaimed himself the vassal of the new
patriarch and "steward of the Holy Sepulcher." But his brother,
who succeeded him after one year's rule, called himself Baldwin I.
Instead of a unique religious state there was simply one more vest-
pocket princedom. What ought to have been a model for kings and
priests merely provoked endless struggles between the kings and
priests of Jerusalem, between Normans and French, between Lorrainers and Italians—struggles based on sheer questions of power
without the slightest interest to posterity or influence on the minds
and hearts of contemporaries.

The crusade of Christendom against the infidels had turned
into a free-for-all fight among five or six princes and nations. The
Normans fought against the Byzantines, Pope against rival Pope,
the new orders of Templars and Knights of St. John against

the kings of Jerusalem, the German and Byzantine emperors against the French and Norman kings. Basically all the Christians were fighting one another. The only ones who concluded state treaties, thus reducing the fundamental religious idea to absurdity, were the Franks and Arabs. Later, about 1220, the sultan of Egypt offered the Christian princes the most sensible solution—the entire Holy Land, on condition that the crusaders should leave Egypt. But Cardinal Pelagius was more interested in exploiting rich Egypt than in possessing the impoverished Holy City; he declined, and got neither.

XXII

THE CONTRAST BETWEEN Christian and Arab kings during the century of the crusades is most clearly demonstrated by two men who fought each other without victory, finally reached an agreement, and came down to posterity with equal glory. They were Richard Coeur de Lion and Sultan Saladin.

A continent and an ocean divided their birthplaces, their races, and their religions. Yet these two born soldiers and champions who met in brief conflict were similar in education, rank, and capacities. They differed in character even more than in race or faith.

The son of the English king had become a duke in France at the age of fifteen. He was trained to power, led into arrogance by his knightly prowess, and early impelled, as a prince more or less in a strange country, to conspire against the French king. He was humbled, pardoned, and established in power again. At the age of eighteen he saved his liege lord from the rebellion of another count. Wars against his elder brother (who watched him jealously from England), were followed by the death of the brother, which made him, in his middle twenties, heir apparent to the throne of England and Normandy. His fire, his talents, his hopes drove him forward, an onrushing, insatiable warrior forever seeking new excitements. Being also a troubadour, a poet and singer, he looked ahead to double glory, and hastened in pursuit.

At a corresponding time of life the son of an Armenian Kurd, a general and governor of humble origin, had set out with a

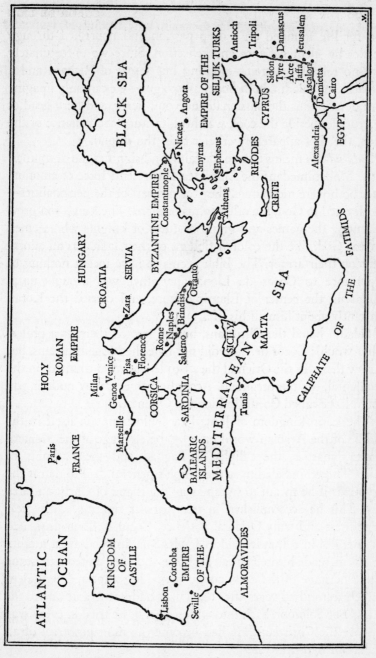

THE MEDITERRANEAN REGION ABOUT A.D. 1100.

plan for life founded on a deep passion and nourished through decades by silent patience and reflection. Since we unfortunately have no reliable portraits—nothing but a seal of Richard and a miniature of Saladin, both hopelessly vague—we can only imagine from descriptions the passionate, nervous, fierce, and fiery head of the crusader beside the cool, watchful, taciturn countenance of the Turk, the first apparently crueler than the second.

Sula-ud-din means true to the faith, and signifies the devoutness of the Mohammedan; the Lion Heart represents force of emotion. Since both were nicknames, they form a part of the personalities— one devoted to God, the other to his passions. The king's son grew up among the games and grand gestures of knights who seemed to wear God, like the colored ribbons of their ladies, as an adornment on their armor. The Bible seems to have meant nothing of importance to Coeur de Lion. The other was brought up at Damascus, the center of Islamic culture, and carried the Koran constantly about him all his life.

Saladin hated the Christians, but he treated them as a philosopher would; Coeur de Lion did not hate the Mohammedans, but he slew them. In the Oriental the attitude was what counted; in the Occidental, the temperament. According to everyday notions you would have called Coeur de Lion the Oriental.

The Latin kingdom of Jerusalem could maintain itself in the middle of the Arabian world only by the cleavage of the Mohammedan dynasties, the caliphs of Bagdad and the Fatimids of Cairo. Therefore Saladin, as the caliph's general, had to defeat the Egyptians if he meant to sweep away the island of Christian territory. This he accomplished in ten years of fighting, with great earnestness and truly Oriental patience. Coeur de Lion dissipated his energies in a hundred local feuds. Saladin subdued a mighty kingdom, made himself sultan at thirty, and soon united almost the whole heritage of the early conquerors. He recaptured Jerusalem scarcely a hundred years after the Turks had lost it, and turned the Temple of Solomon back into a mosque, but he tried in every way to spare the Christians. He had become the most powerful of all Mohammedan princes.

But he was two decades older than the Englishman. He was in his middle fifties and at the height of his power when the other, at thirty-two, became king and hearkened to the call of a new crusade. Saladin's conquests had stirred Europe to a new campaign: who would regain what was lost? Such a mission could not but quicken the imaginative unrest, ambition, and adventurousness of Coeur de Lion. He went to Sicily.

Wherever he went there was quarreling. In Sicily, where he found his sister, the king's widow, he began his crusade by storming and looting the Christian city of Messina in a dispute over some small question. Being altogether a French knight, who cursed the English whenever he could, he was extravagant and fond of display, at once generous and avaricious, chivalrous and passionate-tempered, spoiled and moody, and always attractive—hence a diffuse, contradictory character, given to sudden inertia and melancholy, followed by fresh bursts of activity. Coeur de Lion was the man who, wanting desperately to free the Holy Sepulcher, would nevertheless forget the appointed day for his appearance before a fortress. He conquered the island of Cyprus in passing, married a king's daughter there, and finally arrived six months late before Acre, to be welcomed as a deliverer and the child of good fortune.

But he was also the man who twice appeared before Jerusalem without making an assault because he feared a lack of water for the troops, a consequent failure, and the loss of his name in history. Yet when Saladin, trying to gain time, promised but did not pay tribute, Richard caused two thousand hostages to be killed for the sake of two hundred gold pieces. Saladin's leniency to captured Christians was world-famous; indeed it once cost him the fortress of Acre, which was relieved at a moment of crisis.

The swift, erratic life that carried Coeur de Lion from one country to another kept him away from his kingdom so long that a brother tried to usurp his place in London. On receipt of this news he had to leave Syria in order to save his crown. Whether in confusion or in weariness, he made a premature peace, which cost him and Christendom almost everything he had won in his first assault. Only a piece of the coast and a corridor to Jerusalem became Latin.

The Holy Sepulcher remained in the hands of the infidels, and pilgrims had to go unarmed. Coeur de Lion left like a beaten man and reached home without an army.

But his self-will had made half of Europe his enemies, and he could not venture across the sea. Nor could he travel through France, whose king he had affronted. And when he dared to beat his way through Germany he fell into the hands of spies acting for an Austrian duke whom he had insulted when in an ill humor before Acre. The trouvère Blondel found the captive in a fortress. In violation of every right of the crusaders he was delivered over to the German emperor, who held him prisoner. He was released only on receipt of a great sum in gold, for which the citizens of England had to pay their first personal-property tax. Coming home, he quickly retrieved his power. He forgave his unfaithful brother and returned to his beloved France. There he found his wife, whom he had abandoned in flight. A new castle, a new quarrel, and Coeur de Lion fell before an arrow in some senseless private feud with an insignificant petty nobleman. Apparently he slighted the wound, did not wash it, and thus it proved fatal.

When he made peace with Saladin, he sent him kingly gifts. Hospitality, love of children, protection of women, a kindly eye and manner later brought him the reputation of a saint. Coeur de Lion was no saint, but he did become the center of a cycle of legends such as he had dreamed of. Saladin was the great bulwark of Islam and Asia against Christian Europe; Coeur de Lion was the ideal, the tender dream of the Middle Ages. Both have left the realms of history. No one cares about their wars, which were soon concluded by the death of Saladin. But they enriched the higher realms of legend, Saladin as a fairy tale, Coeur de Lion as a song, both as champions of the Middle Ages.

XXIII

CONSTANTINOPLE WAS RIPE FOR DOWNFALL. If ever a Mediterranean Empire lost its power by the decay of its navy it was the Byzantine Empire, whose life was too extravagant and too self-assured.

As late as the twelfth century the house of Comnenus had maintained a lavish court, forgetting security for the sake of splendor and formality. While knights and princes, poets and wizards thronged endless festivals in this most beautiful city of its time, to make their fortunes or to show them off, the sea wind was gathering new perils from every point of the compass. Armies and navies threatened the imperial city. From the south Robert Guiscard, the Norman adventurer, was driving his soldiers and pirates on to defeat the emperor's troops. From the east the Turkish sultans were threatening the Aegean. From the north the Bulgarians, just converted to Christianity, were pushing swiftly forward to the Adriatic, with their flank against the straits. And in the west the young power of Venice was spreading her navy abroad.

Ever since the Arabs had parted Europe from the grain vessels of Asia and Africa, thus forcing European peoples to till their own fields, everything had changed. Only the resolution to build a new and tremendous fleet such as Rome had sent against Carthage might possibly have saved the Byzantine Empire.

But Rome in those days had been a strong, rising republic; Constantinople now was the seat of an empire of pomp and splendor whose festive, brocade-bedecked vessels landed with flags and music at the Golden Horn. The spirit of the republic seemed to be reborn at Venice, where it was further strengthened by an unexampled commercial genius. Thus the richest man in the world, the Byzantine emperor, whose daughters were sought in marriage by German emperors, became tributary to Venice and the Bulgarians, more and more with each generation. When the thousands of crusaders overran Constantinople, and hastily went on without paying their score, the people rose up. There were conspiracies and murders. The Byzantine emperor Isaac II, who made treaties with his Christian colleague Barbarossa, had no choice but to sign simultaneous secret agreements with Saladin, the sultan of the infidels, against whom the two emperors were going out to fight.

In the west, in Rome, a German emperor, the son of Barbarossa, united Italy for the first time. He married a Sicilian princess, and thus began to realize the old German dream of world dominion.

The Norman crown treasure was carried northward on the backs of hundreds of mules, over the Alps in winter—a great symbol to show that the heir of the German castle of Hohenstaufen had extended his power from the Baltic to the shores of north Africa. Indeed Germanic domination of the Mediterranean had become a reality, and only an expedition like Alexander's was needed to complete the imagined picture. The Pope, great Innocent III, was encircled by the Germans. He must have felt it was the judgment of God when the emperor suddenly died while arming for his world war.

But between them, in Venice, stood an eighty-year-old-man of iron, Doge Enrico Dandolo, whose inflexible will had for a lifetime been preparing the fate of Constantinople. Now at last he struck. When the army of crusaders had no money left to cross the sea, he told them that the voyage could be paid for by the booty in store. The booty, as his old head and his perpetually young heart knew, was to be found not in Palestine but in Constantinople. In this fashion he meant to checkmate both the great rivals at once, the German emperor and the patriarch of Constantinople, uniting all Christendom anew under the bishop of Rome, and thus himself becoming both king-maker and banker of the Mediterranean.

And he succeeded. Constantinople—which Huns and Magyars, Goths and Arabs had vainly tried through the centuries to conquer —Constantinople, with her invincible walls and her Greek fire, fell at last, not by the hand of a pagan barbarian army but before crusaders under the leadership of Venice. And this crusade ended before it had begun. After scarcely a year's siege in 1204 all was over; the capital of the world literally went down in flames, blood, and murder.

Strife and treason within the city had aided the besiegers. The joint emperor Alexius was imprisoned and murdered by a Greek usurper, whom the victors afterward killed by throwing from the top of the column of Theodosius. The pious conquerors destroyed all the ancient beauty that Constantinople had collected during seven centuries. Almost nothing was saved but the four bronze Attic horses, which stand today on the roof of St. Mark's, furnishing the great paradox of the world's only horseless city.

But the Doge, afire with hatred, could demand more than four horses. He increased the three-eighths of the booty that he had stipulated for himself to three-quarters of the Byzantine Empire. He took for Venice all the precious ports and islands of the Aegean, then Crete and Euboea. For the Franks, as the Germanic peoples were jointly called, he left nothing but the crumbs from this royal banquet. The shadow of an imperial title was invoked for the tiny remnant, and the Byzantines led a sham existence under it for another two hundred years.

The crusades were at an end; they had failed. The east had not been conquered by the Christians, but the west by the Mohammedans, for the Ottoman Turks invaded the Danube. Neither the religion nor the power of Europe had been victorious in Asia. But commerce had discovered splendid colonies and correspondences. Sciences, the art of warfare, and navigation had made advances such as had not been known since the Greeks. France and the Pope rose as leaders of culture and commerce. The poetry and art of the east that came to the west, and particularly to the north, were incalculable.

But during and after the crusades a fantastic power rose from the Mediterranean, literally out of the sea, like Aphrodite. Its name was Venice.

BOOK THREE

THE DECLINE OF POWER

Your mind is tossing on the ocean;
There, where your argosies with portly sail,—
Like signiors and rich burghers of the flood,
Or, as it were, the pageants of the sea,—
Do overpeer the petty traffickers,
That curtsy to them, do them reverence,
As they fly by them with their woven wings.

SHAKESPEARE

AT THE LIGHTHOUSE

THE KEEPER *did not return to his book until nearly morning. Fog had troubled the night, and the man's deeply ingrained sense of responsibility had kept him from his reading. He no longer seemed to hear the foghorn, which resounded atop the tower for hours on end —a long note, more plaintive than warning, every five seconds; nobody on the island ever heard it. It was familiar and natural to the keepers' families and to the people who slept in the little vineyard huts. They noticed it as little as they noticed the sun by day.*

The keeper on duty knew every rock and every shoal for fifty miles around, northeast of the islands of Hyères toward Saint-Raphaël, southeast toward Corsica. How long ago was it, he wondered, that the Sardinian cutter had run aground and been wrecked there? His eyes kept returning to the radio, as if he expected from it a cry for help. Then he went up the iron spiral stairs to test the effect of his horn rather than his lamp. The latter, useless today, revolved in its triple rhythm with the immutable persistency of an enslaved soul.

The foggy air of the summer night blew warm and damp about the keeper's face, barely touched by a sluggish, treacherous wind. The red and green glasses, alternating with the white, stained the gray fog ghostly colors, suddenly causing an irregular bit of the mass to flash magically, like a man of genius walking among the crowd and animating them with a word.

Tonight the keeper was all ears, not eyes. In the uncanny silence he strove to distinguish the note of a distant foghorn, perhaps trying to warn other vessels of its own course and thus reporting to the lighthouse as well, if it was close enough. His beacon, the keeper knew, would send its light out thirteen miles from the 100-foot tower; but the effectiveness of the horn remained uncertain, for it depended on the density of the fog. With his great sense of duty the man had sometimes asked himself of late whether his hearing was failing. He had even sent his boy across the garden to the cliff, ostensibly in search of something but really to shout to him and listen for the answer. As a matter of fact he heard perfectly and had simply become doubtful through living alone, which makes one either hypersensitive or sluggish.

All remained still. At daybreak the fog retreated in great squadrons to the south and southeast. With the feelings of a devout man who has fortified his soul by fervent prayer in a gloomy church, the keeper returned to his workroom, which was almost nothing but a waiting room. As an old seaman he had learned always to fear danger, indeed to reverence it. Never for a single night on duty had he surrendered to any habit of negligence. During these previous nights he had read steadily on, and so he was able to finish a second part of his book during the morning hours. When his relief arrived, he called to his comrade to wait a minute—only two pages more to the end of the chapter.

Between sleep and dinner the keeper was fond of spending some time in his garden. With a seaman's heavy tread he walked silently behind his wife, who was pulling the weeds out of the beans and gathering them up in a basket. He emptied it on the rubbish heap, trod it down with his feet, brought back the basket, and went over to his dahlias. The buds were large, and the first of them promised to bloom today. The tranquillity of age lay upon his face as he looked at the yellow glow of the buds. Seamen wait through twenty years of fog and storm for such moments as this in a quiet garden. Scarcely one of them would rather grow old as a captain, with money and authority.

He sat down on the shady bench under the big stone pine between the house and the dahlia beds. His wife had gone inside with the beans, and he could hear her bustling about the kitchen. The keeper had a quiet half hour to himself, and his mind returned to the book:

. . . So there used to be markets at Fréjus in those days, he thought, and San Raphael was there too. Too bad the man has nothing to say of our islands. When you read about foreign shores, it's funny how pleased you are to see your own mentioned. He really ought to talk more about the sea than the coast. But of course, that *isn't very different from the Atlantic. The sea really has no history; it's always the same. I wonder if the man knows everything that's on its bottom. That story of the cypress that the king ordered cut down: it served him right. Those kings are just as savage to people as they are to trees; they were then, and they are now. The walls of Constantinople—what a wild night we had there! That blond François lugged a girl into one of those towers, and the floor crashed, and he was fooled. How we laughed at him! And the woman was furious and tried to hit him! I wonder if that shaky lighthouse is still standing there, north-northwest of the Seraglio point. Sometimes you feel like getting a shaky floor under your feet again. . . .*

But now the children came bicycling home from school, and their mother announced supper. Only when darkness fell again, beginning another clear night, only in his quiet cell among switches, tables, and instruments did the keeper turn back to the Venice that had been promised him the day before.

I

THE TRAVELER who glides into the broad roadstead of Venice between four and five of a July morning, through the soft, greenish-blue glare from the east, feels as if he were approaching a dream mirage, not an orderly provincial capital. He has crossed the Mediterranean from Alexandria in three days aboard a modern cabin steamer. The stewards repairing the nocturnal devastation of the bar, clearing out tables littered with ash and glasses, the cabin boys sluicing down the promenade deck with buckets, the mountain of trunks built yesterday to be wrecked today tell even a romantically inclined traveler that all is as it should be near the middle of the twentieth century; that the time of the bucentaur is past, possibly never more than a legend.

And yet, as one approaches by sea, this unique city is bathed in the bright, unreal light of dream. Indeed, the impression grows, instead of fading, with each return. Even through centuries it will surely remain the same, for no city on earth can be the equal of a city built in the sea. Flat islands, distinguishable only by tall campaniles and the shoulders of the palaces, seem to be floating in an ocean as yet barely tinged with pink, and one would not be surprised to see them swim away.

The towers rise from the morning haze, first the tallest, then a group. Much lower down, two domes, then five bob up from the mist. Swiftly sights and sounds multiply about the almost noiselessly gliding steamer. Along the broad quays the new day with its colorful bustle has awakened. Everywhere narrow, black streaks of water give upon the great, bright basin, as if it were still dressed in night while morning reigns outside. The house fronts grow richer and grander; then the façade of a marble palace rises to a modest height. It stands above the splendid sea, a simple but not quite regular structure. Turning a sharp corner, the building reaches out to face upon a square of moderate size.

The whole is put together of pink marble slabs; halfway up

310

we see slender white balconies; below them, a double row of columns like strong arms supporting a pink-silk ballerina. This Palazzo Ducale on the wide quay is flat; nothing juts or shoots upward. The gondolas stop by long, flat stairs, and the countless piles
to which they are made fast guard the shore like a host of lances.
On two pillars that set off the open square, a knight and a lion keep
watch over the incoming seafarers, and on the other side the palaces
continue, over arcades. The whole represents authority, power, the
Republic.

At the side, however, beyond the massive marble gate to the
Palace, the style abruptly changes. Close against the half-Gothic
front rises the completely oriental façade of Saint Mark's. The
piazza, a sort of huge, open ballroom, evidently intended for the
dancing of a thousand couples, opens out to westward. It is surrounded by other long buildings, carried on columns, always somewhat irregular and thus safe from any tedious magnificence; its
worldly wantonness is anything but shamed by the many-domed
façade of the cathedral along one end.

At just one point in the flat, horizontal world of the Piazza
San Marco a sign seems to point upward: opposite a corner of the
cathedral the campanile indicates the skies. You ascend the tower
in a lift now. In days past you could ride on horseback up a spiral
incline inside the great structure. No other town can offer such a
view from the top of its highest tower, because this city alone, built
in the ocean, lies facing the slope of the Alps, yet far enough away
to enclose the whole as one picture in a vast frame.

The thousand house chimneys rise like little towers guarding
the citizens. A multitude of black lines like strings seems to run
through a labyrinth. These are the narrow canals, and over them
little stone bridges keep rising and dipping, arched to let through
the heavily laden boats. This necessity saves them from the monotony of straight lines. And now, out beyond the great center,
the islands lie in broad daylight, and the student will know their
lovely names and their secret purposes, for these, too, have the ring
of ancient legend.

Yet this is no museum, no mere exhibit. Everything is astir with

a modern life that runs more slowly than our own and rejects at
this one spot on earth the futile haste that takes the soul out of our
century. It all derives from the piles on which the houses are built
in the water, the piles clutched yet seldom eaten by greenish water
weeds. They stand both below and above the water line, by fours
and tens, outside the great palaces, functioning like caryatids.

II

THIS WONDER CITY was born from the battle of the elements, but
also from man's victories over the elements. The rivers form deltas
on many Mediterranean coasts, and the whole northwestern shore
of the Adriatic has been outlined by the alluvial deposits of rivers,
whose lower course has constantly changed, enlarging the main
land even now. The Po, Ticino, Adda, Brenta, Piave, and half
a dozen smaller intervening streams have so shifted the coast
line between Fiume and Rimini by bringing down masses of
earth from the north that the map has changed since Roman
times, indeed even within the last few centuries. At some points
the east coast of Lombardy grows four miles every hundred years.

The fertility of the district is partly explained by the likelihood
that in prehistoric times a deep Adriatic reaching far to the west
divided the Alps and the Apennines in place of Lombardy. The Po,
winding magnificently through this plain from the Piedmontese
Alps to Ravenna, has never quite given up its kingly prerogative.
The natives call it "beloved and dreaded river." The fifty million
cubic yards of sand that it washes down every year are built into
artful dikes and dams. Though it brings fertility with it, everyone
thinks, Woe to us if it breaks through! The river is like one of those
dangerous dictators under whose dominion the people quake in
the very midst of their successes in war.

But there is a second force working against this first one, like
the natural resistance of the masses among nations—the inundation
of the coast by the sea. In the northern Adriatic the prevailing strong
east winds increase this counterforce. Nevertheless, calculations

show the possibility that the growing northwest coast of the Adriatic may reach the farther shore of Istria in 120 centuries, so that the Gulf of Venice will become an inland lake after the fashion of Lago Maggiore. There or on Lake Como we can assume only that this inundation took place in prehistoric times. In Asia Minor we have actually seen the advance of the Maeander transform into a lake the gulf on which ancient Miletus lay.

The elements have taught guile to the men of these coast countries, who cheat the rivers of their courses. Perhaps the most celebrated school of diplomats came from Venetian territory, because their wits had been sharpened by the whims of the mighty river Po.

The history of marshes and lagoons is bound up with that of Mediterranean man, and has, along with the whole aquatic system, made weather prophets of peasants and physical scientists of city dwellers—men able to interpret and enlarge upon the irregularities and excesses of nature. As late as a century ago the French lost huge fortunes every year by the silting up of the Rhone delta. The Italians have been trying since antiquity, with increasing success, to narrow the inhospitable belt of bays and marshes that keeps the interior country sometimes as much as twenty miles from the sea.

The battle has wavered to and fro, with shifting fortunes. The marshland around Ferrara and Ravenna has been turned into fertile fields, and at infinite pains the Venetians have succeeded in diverting the Brenta southward so that it would not silt up the city. But the inhabitants of the northern bay have fought the Isonzo in vain to save the old cities of Grado and Aquileia, northwest of modern Trieste. At the mouth of the Piave, river and sea by turns have devoured the land and, finally, the ancient city of Heracleia with it. As late as the Middle Ages, Treviso and Padua were on the sea; today they are accessible only to small vessels by canal.

The life of these districts has been fateful indeed, now victorious, now vanquished, sometimes assaulted by two foes and saved by that very fact. What a tragic spectacle is Ravenna; what a happy one Padua—as if they were accepting their similar fates quite differently, according to their separate characters! Indeed, every single lagoon of the hundreds that lie along this coast differs in structure

from every other. The phrases *laguna viva* and *laguna morta* show
that one sort, facing on the ocean, is kept in health by the tide,
whereas the other, turning it back, and thus tideless, is a prey to
insects and consequent fevers, and presents such gloomy scenes as
the bit of territory between Mestre and Venice.

The Po, a creative force comparable in a limited sense to the
deltaic Nile, made the great bay country and has triumphed over
the originally alluvial coast formed by the ocean. To tame this
victorious stream in turn, the natives have kept building new dikes
and dams against its inundating forces. Since the early Middle Ages
they have pushed their restraints farther and farther upstream,
reaching 250 miles today. The mud and soil thus poured into the
ocean have been further increased by the growing deforestation.

Comparing old and new maps, we are amazed at the labor devoted by whole generations to winning narrow strips of land, while
broad expanses that might be tilled lie fallow. A person of normal
judgment feels here as he does about tales of war in which whole
armies fight and die for a fortress instead of marching around it
In both cases human effort is demanded by circumstance, but in
both cases, too, there is an element of ambition to outdo the enemy,
whether army or ocean. The general who has set his heart on a
capture of this sort is moved by feelings like those of the engineer
who keeps building dam after dam. The community whose fathers
lived on those islands and rowed and fished in those canals would
rather conquer nature at home than emigrate.

Almost the whole outthrust delta of the Po, which finally splits
into seven arms, with a triangle more than thirty miles wide, represents human labor. But as such it remains fragmentary, fixing
neither the course of the seven arms nor the speed of the masses
of mud. Here we have one of the rare cases in which we can trace
the creation of a delta on maps and documents from about A.D. 1200
and can even calculate by the sidewise shifts in the advancing delta
the counterforce of the sea invading from outside.

The perfection of human craft and beauty shown in the history of Venice depended upon the structure of this delta. The brief
flowering of the neighboring duchies and city republics is due to

the uncertainty of their situation. New towns keep being founded to seaward, and inland cities and peoples quietly disappear, just as classes decline in the social history of great nations. On this coast there lay in pre-Roman times the rich city of Spina and about the time of Christ the bustling town of Adria. When that little city chances to hear the roar of the storm-tossed ocean fifteen miles away today, perhaps some burgess may recall with a smile that the ocean is named for his town.

Of all the lagoons, the worst situated were those where the Veneti built their city. He who settled there had neither meadow nor pasture, no water except rain to drink, nothing but fish to eat. The rivers emptying into the sea constantly imperiled the flat islands, the more so since their flow was irregular. What later became the Grand Canal was obviously a river reaching the ocean near Mestre, and the present canal at the Giudecca was the river Brenta. The deserted islands outside were covered with tall grass, peopled with game and even wolves.

Fishermen seem to have settled there from the earliest times, and strange conjectures have been made about their origin. Strabo believed that the first inhabitants of the district came from Brittany. Another Roman says that they came from the Baltic; a majority favor Paphlagonia, while others suppose that the first inhabitants were Illyrians. At any rate they came before the seventh century, when the fugitives fled Huns, Goths, and Lombards in the region of Aquileia. The making of bricks from the local mud seems to have begun about this time, when a first church was built. The priests apparently enjoyed great influence.

A commonwealth of liberty and church rule developed here in a special way and went on through a thousand years. The segregation of these islands, which the water rendered almost impregnable to primitive armaments; the poverty; the grimness of their isolated existence; the lack of predecessors or traditions—all bred in these fishermen and fugitives, particularly at the beginning, a sense of freedom impossible in the mainland communities of Italy, where continual assaults by neighbors and inroads by barbarian hordes prevailed. Such islanders naturally grew independent, sober, money-loving. Venice is perhaps the only power in the world that never sought to produce heroes. Made of islands, yet not an island realm in the sense that the Aegean is, even as a state Venice led an amphibian life. She was half a land and half a water city; with her cool blood she escaped dangers that hindered the rise of the passionate little countries on the mainland.

Keeping their eyes on the sea, the thrifty merchants of Venice bestowed their only extravagance upon the navy and upon buildings meant to impress the incoming stranger. Their three thousand vessels were impeccably manned by citizens with centuries of skill behind them, whereas their mercenary soldiers ashore were easily beaten. A *laguna viva,* Venice was great so long as she sought no hinterland. In her expansion toward distant shores, starting from a little island, she is comparable not with Athens, only slightly with Carthage, but most of all with colonizing England. And just as the English merchant nation produced poets and thinkers, this other bold race of island traders put forth marvelous painters and architects.

Like the English and the Phoenicians, the Venetians had sea power forced upon them by their location and their fear of pirates; and the close quarters at home sent them abroad. But their first great successes transformed this necessity into a passion and en-

couraged them to make treaties with everyone, to accept any enemy
of civilization and religion so long as the circle of distant shores
continued to be planted with their warehouses. Like the Phoenicians, they were not impelled by an urge for beautiful things, the
dream of the Orient, or desire for world dominion. Great entrepreneurs as they were, producing both merchants and statesmen, they
found their greatest successes under the outward form of an oligarchy to which they willingly submitted. The Greeks alone had
preceded them, but their genius was so much greater than that of
either Venetians or Englishmen that they have remained peerless
even in trade.

III

SOMBER, STEEP, AND ROCKY, another great port rises from the sea
toward the mountains that stretch menacingly skyward close to city
and bay. Genoa, perhaps the most masculine of all Mediterranean
cities, the very opposite of the feminine and reclining Venice, seems
to spring from a people ready to appear strong rather than beautiful,
hostile rather than inviting, a seafaring nation, yet one depending
upon solid ground, where fortresses can be built and riches gathered;
already Dante had recognized and attacked their power in his
Divina Commedia.

Along the harbor rise the stunning masses of the castlelike banks and mercantile houses. But the main streets offer so little room for expansion that the leading men and women, or at any rate their servants, could have talked to each other from their palace windows. What is now called the Via Garibaldi scarcely has an equal even in Italy for beauty of façades. But the streets and buildings do not spread out before the beholder; they rise ominously from their inescapable confinement like the mountains behind them.

A natural harbor of the first importance attracted Etruscans and Greeks as early as the fifth and sixth century B.C. Carthaginians and Romans had to sail past this coast, whose name is said to come from its knee shape (*genou*). Between the foothills of the Maritime Alps and the Apennines, lying at a narrow point below the mountains, a people was bound to arise that could act either as traders uniting the nations of France and Italy or as gatekeepers parting them. The situation of the town developed a vigorous fighting spirit in the Genoese. But he never attained the adroitness of the Venetian as a colonizer. Venice was sheltered by her lagoons and canals from the quarrels of her neighbors; Genoa had to defend herself against French kings and German emperors.

As seafarers, these two most powerful republics dominated the Mediterranean for centuries. How, we wonder, could a small country win such great colonies—and not colonies of colored, uncivilized races but the oldest shores and ports and islands of a Mediterranean that had once been Greek, the oldest strongholds of Persian and Arab civilization? Why did the slim city-states of Venice and Genoa succeed in the Orient where the great Western powers failed?

The first of several reasons is that the small powers, united, usually agreeing among themselves, set sail persistently for a definite goal. The great powers consumed themselves in dynastic struggles before progressing to union in national states. Furthermore, the two sea states had but a single front, the Mediterranean, whereas France, Spain, and the German Empire were bounded by other seas also. And above all, these cities had a tradition demanding not the symbols of power but the rights of commerce. There were no kings and emperors desiring to hold court on the islands of the Aegean or to marry their sons to princess heiresses and invest their great noblemen with lands.

These traders, who have been quite mistakenly called merchant kings, felt no ambition to run up their flags above the battlements of foreign castles, to hold down subject citizens on foreign shores by force of arms or to throw them into prison because they would not salute the conqueror's statue. They found their happiness elsewhere, in the balance they struck at the end of the year, that of their bank and their city. They handed down to their sons what they had inherited from their fathers—not guns and crowns but monopolies, cargo vessels, and sacks of golden ducats. It was no dream of world dominion or of subduing the Pope, no ideal of imposing the true faith on the infidel that sent them venturing across the stormy Mediterranean. What impelled them was a desire to test with their own eyes, noses, and fingers the wares and markets of Tangier and Tripoli, Rhodes and Chios, Sinope and Trebizond —the satins, damask and muslin, silver pendants and dagger sheaths, embroidered carpets, pepper, and incense with which agents filled the holds of the great vessels, to trade them later for gold or other goods in the West.

It was only at home that these "merchant princes" wanted to rule in the sight of the world, to be honored and feared; for at home, offices and dignities and the golden chains and costly velvet garments that doges and senators bestowed upon themselves and their friends as privileges in the provinces were worth thousands of ducats. The natural jealousy of the oligarchies in medieval Venice and Genoa at their prime prevented the rise of single individuals. Lack of conquering instinct prevented *coups d'état* by the sort of *condottieri* who arose in other small Italian towns. This was the sole reason for their republican sentiments; they despised the multitude, no less than the dukes, margraves, and Popes of the neighboring countries did.

Genoa in her key position was constantly courted and threatened. She thrust her domestic rivalries, particularly the rivalry of the Spinola and Doria clans, upon foreign powers, whose help one side tried to procure against the other. Frankish counts and Milanese dukes, kings of France and kings of Naples succeeded to each other's influence, sometimes even to complete sway over Genoa. She was thus ensnared in the hands of Guelphs and Ghibellines in the struggle between Popes and emperors. Only two things remained through the centuries: the Bank of San Giorgio, which financed and cheated crusaders and Mohammedan princes alternately, and the navy, which was feared throughout the Mediterranean. In these adventures the people of Genoa kept capturing new rights from the nobility, and they never entirely lost them.

At Venice, too, the Bank of San Marco and sea power were constants; but there was a third element here that strengthened both the others and finally decided the long rivalry between the two cities: a sense of independence, more easily implanted and consolidated by Venice in her isolated and inconvenient location. When Constantinople (now Istanbul) at her height in the sixth century demanded sovereignty, the defenseless young city in the marshes sent an embassy refusing her in these fine words: "No emperor and no prince can touch us here. We have raised this city ourselves from the lagoons." Lombards and Franks threatening Venice from the land side later had to pocket similar replies.

Even thus early these born fishermen and oarsmen were so famous for their skill as navigators that Narses, the greatest general of his time, summoned the unarmed people from the lagoons as pilots to transport his army from Grado. Similarly, Emperor Frederick II later hired Genoese by preference to steer his vessels. With these ships and from this location the Venetians defended themselves against Attila on shore and Pepin on the sea. And yet it was not until about A.D. 1000, fighting the pirates from Dalmatia, that they began to arm their vessels. Then their fame as navigators spread until the Byzantine landlubbers granted them monopolies if only their vessels would help against the Norman peril. Their merchant fleet later reached the then unheard-of and still amazing figure of 3,300 vessels.

From the time of the crusades on, the treasures of the Orient came to Europe aboard the sailing ships belonging to banks or companies in Venice and Genoa. Since periods of war increased

the general anarchy and there were islands that belonged to no
one, the era was a favorable one for some bold doge to make himself
master with the help of his bankers. But the spirit of independence
in the people of Venice rose against this. As a counterweight to the
three ambitious dynasties whose members tried to bequeath the
office of doge to one another, a council and a sort of two-headed
consulate were established. The merchant princes, who really ruled,
succeeded in decreasing alike the autocracy of the doge and of the
elective council. At its prime, after the fall of Constantinople and
then throughout the thirteenth century, Venice was dominated by

a money aristocracy, the caste of patricians, proud of their blood and their family trees, a sort of senate that, in turn, served the doge and was itself simply appointed by the supreme court. And yet it would not tolerate dictatorship, and when the doge Falier tried to make himself "Prince of Venice" by a *coup d'état* in 1355, they had him publicly decapitated on the steps of the "Scala dei Giganti." Some of the conspirators were strangled between the two columns of the piazzetta in view of the sea. Two previous revolts of the people around 1300 had also quickly collapsed.

Hostility to Genoa was then reaching its height, for in Genoa, too, colonial power had grown to such an extent that for a while she hoped after her western successes to conquer the markets of the eastern Mediterranean, where Venice, as successor to Constantinople, commercially dominated the Greek and Asiatic coasts. Genoa had now finally vanquished Pisa, the third great trading power in Italy, after centuries of struggle.

Thanks to excellent descriptions, we have in the decisive battle of Meloria, off Pisa harbor, in 1284, an example of what a naval battle looked like on the medieval Mediterranean. The long warrior tradition of the Genoese, the sense of honor that was perhaps deeper in them than in the Venetians, led a Doria, the captain of the city, not only to take the lead in person but to bring his whole family aboard the vessels with him, to conquer or sink with the ships—a gesture of personal sacrifice such as the leaders of our time no longer make.

In the sun of an August morning we watch the navy of the Pisans advance at sight of the Genoese, anchoring in the mouth of the Arno. During prayers all the men are horrified when the statue of a saint falls overboard and vanishes in the river. The awful silence is suddenly broken by a cry: "Do not despair! If Christ is leagued with Genoa, the wind is with us!" In the afternoon, when the Pisans have sailed out in proud array, comes the battle for which generations have been preparing—the blast of horns and trumpets, the ports of the quarter-decks barricaded, a hail of arrows, metal scraps, and stones, the ships' prows turned always toward the enemy to prevent him from ramming the flank. Since the ram of the galley is the strongest weapon for those who lie before the wind, one well-situated squadron may ram or at least stand off half a fleet.

Now the vessels lie alongside for hand-to-hand combat. The missiles cease. Each tries to board the other, to storm the quarterdeck and towers. At close quarters the fighters go down not only under the blows of their adversaries but on the grease and soap splashed over their decks by enemy catapults. The admirals' vessels are fighting each other with molten lead and hot water; the commanders recognize each other from ship to ship. The podesta of Pisa is dragged off with a grave head wound. The flag of Pisa is hauled down and torn up. But still the staff rises on high, rallying the desperate Pisans. When it falls, all is lost. Thirty-six Pisan galleys and two transport ships have been taken or rammed and sunk. Five thousand men are dead, eight thousand taken captive. A remnant retreats to the home port and puts up the great chain. Night ends the battle. The flag of the Pisans, previously torn and spat upon, is solemnly consecrated in the cathedral at Genoa the following Sunday.

Thus in a single day Genoa destroyed the competition of Pisa.

A hundred years later Venice defeated Genoa, her last rival. Once again the stronger navy told the tale.

In those days merchant was not distinguished from naval fleet, or sailing from rowing vessel. The largest transport vessel might be a cargo boat, in which case she would be painted gray-blue. As a warship she would display colors, perhaps a bright yellow or white with red crosses. In those days people had not yet learned to conceal their arms; instead of disguising, they defiantly emphasized them. These great boxes could hold as many as a thousand men or even stow twelve marble columns from the palace of Judas Maccabaeus (columns that never arrived and now rest at the bottom of the sea).

The most common type of vessel was still the galley, as it had been for centuries and was to be until the eighteenth century. Their sides inscribed with the beautiful names that we find in the old ships' registers, "Stelleth," "Gazella," "Falco," "Dulcis," "Paradisus," these rowing vessels, fitted with sails for pleasant weather only, put out of port with their steps overside, like our gangplanks, and with anchors on ropes instead of the anchor chains of antiquity. When the merchants came home with rich cargoes from the Orient, this half navy guarded trade in the fashion of modern convoys. Often one of the great vessels would belong to several owners, one of whom would be aboard.

It certainly was no pleasure jaunt to sail the Mediterranean in the Middle Ages. The crusaders were loaded on board like cattle and had to be grateful if they were as well cared for. An old chronicle tells of a French king who ordered the Genoese to lay in horse fodder for eight months and wine for four. When a rich merchant carried live poultry with him, the chroniclers recorded the luxury as newspapers do today when a film star takes his saddle horses with him on shipboard.

The battle galley developed into two great types. The galleon was purely a sailing vessel, taller and fatter than the galley, with several decks. It was ninety feet long by thirty in the beam, heavy and clumsy, but strong enough to carry two guns. The galleass, up to 180 feet long, drawing as much as 13 feet of water, was slower but was more suited for bombardment. Its mortars, firing projectiles up to 36 pounds at close range, could kill masses of people on an enemy vessel. This type appeared in naval battles as late as 1800.

In war the Genoese sent out their consuls, sometimes under the title of admiral—an Arabic word that began during the crusades to displace the Latin name *capitanus, dux, rector*. In Venice only a noble might command a large ship of war, and he was required to swear beforehand that he would fight even alone against twenty-five galleys, as actually happened at Lepanto.

What these vessels found awaiting them on peaceful voyages abroad was not colonies but markets and commercial houses. If there was a winged lion carved in stone above the gate, that was doubly odious to the Genoese, for it was the Venetian lion of Saint Mark. Both powers extended their trade as far as the Euphrates and the Black Sea, where, indeed, half the Venetian navy once perished because of disagreements over the export of Russian furs.

This fur war of 1353 was perhaps the first truly commercial war in modern history.

The struggle for power between the bankers of Genoa and Venice, which in the course of a hundred years cost far more blood than money, at first involved Constantinople. There Michael Paleologus, a Greek, had risen to the imperial throne and allied himself with the Genoese against the Venetians. After the victory of the Genoese, he turned over to them the quarters and monopolies of the Venetians. Reverses and defeat followed, and this might have gone on indefinitely if the Turks had not appeared, long before their conquest of Constantinople, and taken Syria, automatically ending the monopolies of the western ocean cities. Venice, which had just financed a crusade, immediately joined with the Turks; Genoa replied by closing the Dardanelles; Constantinople turned over to the Venetians the island of Tenedos, which commands the entrance to the Dardanelles. Surely all this sounds as if we had read it yesterday in the paper.

After all the sham truces a fight to the finish was inevitable. For two centuries Venice had seemed to the world too fortunate, too rich; she was envied and hated. Everyone united—the Hapsburgs, who were then approaching Trieste; the Hungarians, who had been fused into a Balkan kingdom by an Anjou; the Genoese, who invaded the lagoons of Venice from the sea and blockaded her until, without access or supplies from land, she seemed ready to starve. The Venetians had thrown Pisani, their defeated admiral, into prison. At the last moment they fetched him out, and he succeeded at one blow in turning the beleaguerers on the outlying island of Chioggia into the beleaguered. In a short time he forced Doria's thirty-two galleys and five thousand men to surrender. This was one of those brilliant strokes by which an intrepid officer sometimes transmutes despair into desperate courage and downs a victorious enemy by his own methods.

At the critical moment, when everything depended perhaps on the more powerful rowing of three hundred men or the brilliant, aggressive spirit of five hundred or the suicidal daring of ten captains, Venice proved itself superior. A chronicler long before had written: "The Venetians, dwelling in the midst of the water, are superior in battle at sea to every other people."

It was only the mortal fright of the blockade that taught the Venetians that they could not go on living on their floating base without bread and meat, could not dispense with a broad hinterland. With splendid energy the merchants became warriors. The amphibians went ashore and proved that swimming was not all they could do. True, the bankers preferred to buy silver bullets, hiring mercenaries and letting the Swiss do their fighting; but they armed their own sons as well.

The peaceable sea power that had sent three thousand cargo vessels from its fantastic lagoons to trade with all the world now transformed itself into a conquering nation on land. In a series of successful wars, particularly against the duchy of Milan, Venice created in northern Italy a hinterland extending as far westward as Bergamo and Brescia and deep into Dalmatia, beyond the Adriatic, a territory it had once occupied in its earliest days, seven hundred years before. Venice was now approaching her perilous apogee.

The power of Genoa, however, was at an end after the battle of Chioggia in 1380. In the west she still retained large markets and influence, taking up arms once against the French and later against the Turks. But the great trade of the Orient was now reserved for Venice alone, which survived the Genoese power by one hundred and thirty years.

Cutting straight through the enmities of the nation came what people in the Middle Ages called "the scourge of God." Perhaps they were quite right to see divine punishment in the plague that befell them. Around A.D. 1350, some twenty-five million people are said to have perished during two years of this pestilence, probably what we know as the bubonic plague, perhaps half of the victims being on the Mediterranean.

One result was the spread of the flagellants, who tried to win forgiveness for their sins by scourging their own bodies. Their number swelled to such an extent that during the Black Death the Pope forbade the journeys of flagellants, mostly Germans, to the Mediterranean.

IV

DANTE AND SAINT THOMAS AQUINAS seem to be the most profound thinkers of the Mediterranean and of the Middle Ages. They came in quick succession; the poet was nine when the saint died. Both were visionaries, both scholars, and both theologians and philosophers. In their day the influence of the Dominican was greater than that of the poet; in later times the reverse has been true. Which was the greater, no man dares say.

But it is symbolic that Thomas Aquinas, who looked upon half of Europe during his brief life, remained fundamentally nonpolitical, whereas Dante, who may never have left Italy except perhaps for a trip to Paris and who lived to be twenty years the older, received at least a great part of his political impetus from the banishment that took him scarcely a hundred miles away, depriving him of neither language nor nation nor religion nor scholarship, indeed not even of friends. Without the political passions of hatred and revenge, without his judgeship, he would perhaps never have gone beyond the fashionable poems that scarcely distinguished him from the companions of his youth. Thomas, on the other hand, would have been just the same without his travels, his connections with royal houses, and his polemics. Amid uncontrolled Popes, pleasure-loving prelates, and crusading adventurers, this religious figure is an inspiring image, even to posterity.

Like Saint Francis, Thomas retreated from worldly society. He came of an old family, the counts of Aquinas, near Naples. He was born in a mountain castle, not upon the plains, like Francis and Augustine. So it was easier for him to forgo worldliness. In doing so, he retained all advantages; he could advise the king of France, travel from Cologne to Paris with Albertus Magnus, and transact important business for his order. Thomas, who refused to become an archbishop and thus, possibly, Pope in the end, appears to have been the only *grand seigneur* among the saints.

When we hear that his contemporaries called him Doctor Angelicus Universalis, we may be reminded of Erasmus, who earned the same title 300 years later but who smilingly declined the "angelicus." Thomas showed that he had risen above his century by his effort to introduce Plato's ideas and Aristotle's methods into theology, or at least to reconcile them with it. Of both inspiration and reason, he taught, we can understand only the lower levels. But as both spring from the one God, the *summa theologia* is at the same time the *summa philosophia*—a revolutionary dogma that might in other times have made a cleric into a heretic instead of a saint. How completely he lived between religious ecstasy and cold logic, and perhaps suffered between them, too, we can see from the tradition that he had a vision eight or nine months before his death and never wrote anything afterward. This magnificent self-surrender alone would be enough to mark him as a genius.

Dante as a poet had the gift of form that Thomas lacked. Though they may resemble each other in certain of their writings, these are not the central part of their works. Dante wrote his book on the vernacular language in Latin, and no doubt Thomas could have written Italian sonnets. The two are close to each other in their ideas about the Platonic state—indeed, Dante always regarded himself as a pupil of Saint Thomas.

Dante was in the prime of his life, thirty-seven years old, a high official of the city of Florence, by no means inclined to surrender worldly power like Thomas, when he and fourteen others were exiled for ordinary party reasons. As we look at this list of unknown politicians, and number eleven suddenly springs to our eyes as Dante Alighieri, we recognize anew how the temporal power fades and that of intellect alone outshines the ages.

It was not until then that Dante's destiny became significant, his character plain; only then did his genius emerge. While Thomas, in his mid-thirties, was achieving ever greater harmony, Dante was snatched into the great passion of his life. For that reason he required verse form and vernacular, which he had to create for himself, in order to unfold a picture of the world in his titanic triptych. That he portrayed God and Jesus much as Thomas the scholastic did is not surprising. But in the political world, down to his own time, he displayed not universal but truly national tendencies:

Dante wanted a united Italy, not an ecclesiastical state. Exile made him a poet of the world, but not until he was nearly fifty.

What distinguishes him from others who have summed up their knowledge of human and divine things in poetry is the partisan passion with which he consigns his friends and enemies to heaven and hell. Because the Pope has banished him, he hates the man as a prince of darkness. He transposes his age and his most intimate destinies to the hereafter, making himself at once narrator and hero of his poem. He thus lifts himself above the assumed impartiality that so ill becomes a historian because it makes him cold and tedious and permits him to hide his lack of vision behind the moralizing attitude of a universal judge. This so-called scholastic, whose opinion of long-forgotten princes interests no one now, has within him a heart so deeply stirred by human emotions, so humane a confession of his own strengths and weaknesses, that his marvelous upward gaze toward God moves us deeply.

After fourteen years of exile Dante heard from Florence that he might return if he would openly acknowledge his sins in church, wearing the garb of a penitent. His courageous reply showed all the pride of the poet. Only with honor would he go home; otherwise the world was full of sun and stars that he could watch, of deep thoughts that he could pursue. Five years later still he died at Ravenna. The one link between his house and Florence was a gift of gold that the city later sent to his daughter, who remained in Ravenna. Her name was Beatrice, the name of Dante's ideal beloved, and the man who brought the gift was named Boccaccio.

The two Mediterranean philosophers are little read in the outside world—Saint Thomas by theologians chiefly, Dante no more than Vergil and much less than Homer. In mortal memory Thomas has left his white cloak and his saintly halo, Dante a deathless profile and an encounter with a beautiful girl on a bridge. And yet as symbols of the Middle Ages both survived all the kings, all the battles and treaties of peace, because they embodied ideas and not power.

One king alone embodied both. Frederick II, a German em-

peror and King of Sicily, may truthfully be called a genius among
the potentates of the Middle Ages and also one of the three great
German emperors. Four hundred years before him Charlemagne,
and three hundred years after him Charles V, stand out from the list
of some fifty German overlords. None of the three was really German; the first was a Frank, the second, half Norman; the third, half
Spanish.

When Frederick II (1194-1250) was born at Ancona on the
Mediterranean, he received two names, Frederick and Roger, to
remind him throughout life of his two grandfathers, the German
Barbarossa and the Norman Roger II. The German dream of world
dominion, always tending toward Italy, had been close to fulfillment in Frederick's father, if only for a moment. The father, a
Hohenstaufen, had married Roger's daughter in order to unite
her heritage of lower Italy and Sicily with that of his German father
and thus encircle the sole independent remnant of Italy, the little
church state, in such fashion as to make it his slave. But his early
death set all at naught.

His Sicilian wife survived him only two years, and four-year-
old Frederick was left to be brought up by a mighty Pope instead
of a mighty emperor. Pope Innocent was determined to break the
encirclement. He meant to restrict the Hohenstaufen to the heritage
of Sicily and make another man ruler of Germany.

Here again the mixture of races produced an amazing individual.
Even as a boy, Frederick caught the attention of those around him.
It was in no circle of courtiers that he grew up. The lad, alternately courted and threatened, was involved in turmoil, even in
distress, by the civil war that occupied Sicily. For a time the heir
of the empire received his food each week from a different family
in Palermo. Held captive now by the Germans, now by the Normans, he was the victim of whichever party happened to be in
power. As usual the German warriors and adventurers wanted to
make their fortune in the south, and they needed the precious pawn
for their own ends. The natives hated the German "interlopers,"
quite forgetting that they themselves were descended from "stran-

gers," a mixture of Normans and Saracens, and held Sicily by right of conquest alone.

On ill-stamped coins we find the head of Frederick II, a young genius, intense like a southerner, reflective like a northerner, avid for life, eager to learn, as receptive to knowledge as he was intent on power. We reconstruct it as more interesting than handsome. Reddish-blond and shortsighted, he was a subject for caricature by his enemies. "In the slave market," a contemporary wrote, "Emperor Frederick would not be worth two hundred drachmas." But he was not created for that market, not even as a buyer.

The husband of an Aragonese princess at fifteen, father of a son at sixteen, at eighteen he hurried, masked like a criminal, across sea and Alps to recapture his heritage from a rival in the north. In a few years he was lord of Germany. Without an army, with no help from the Pope, at twenty-six he was Roman emperor, and his little son had been chosen German king for good measure. Determined to hold both kingdoms and favored by the death of the great Pope, Frederick promised the Pope's successor, before he was crowned, a crusade if in return he himself might have the kingdom of Jerusalem. When he postponed this crusade under odd circumstances, the Pope made it an excuse to excommunicate him. Every Pope in those days had to struggle against the house of Hohenstaufen, which possessed both north and south Italy and reached from Denmark to Sicily; and this young Hohenstaufen would not yield a step.

The surprising part is that by inclination, temperament, taste, and education he was completely a southerner, living most unhappily at Worms and Frankfurt. He was happy only in Palermo and Apulia and therefore went to Germany only once more, for two years. If he had been nothing but a voluptuary or a philosopher, he would have returned to his mother's kingdom and lived there to please himself.

Frederick was enough of a philosopher and master of the art of living and had sufficient restraint in whatever he did to enjoy a southern life, free from constant struggle. Was it an heir's sense of honor or a ruler's ambition that drove him on? Was it defiance and the contest of history that kept him at his constant wars and quarrels to the end of his life? The nature of Emperor Frederick II is very different from that of Pericles, Marcus Aurelius, or Justinian. He was a thinker, an explorer, and an artist, but not merely in leisure time and secondarily. He played the part every day, in every action. He had the playful passion of a superior intellect, contemplating everything he did and trying to turn everything he contemplated into action. He was the first man of the Renaissance, two centuries before it arrived. He was equal to destiny.

Tolerance and cynicism in Frederick were blended into a spiritual harmony that preserved him from folly in good fortune and despair in misfortune. He owed this inner security to a fatalism taught him by Islam and combined in him with a splendid sense of humor. Although the Christian faith was totally alien to him, as a crowned Christian emperor he showed reverence for the church as long as it did for him. But when it excommunicated him, he made game of it. First he sent a letter to all the princes, disproving the Pope's existence with a whimsical humor worthy of Voltaire. And what did he do next? With a very small army he went to Jerusalem, met the sultan there, and reached an agreement with him in a single hour, so to speak, on a basis of mutual tolerance that gave each religion its just due. Then he had a crown prepared for himself at the Church of the Holy Sepulchre, went in with a handful of officers, and set the crown on his head with his own hands—this emperor crushed by the dread excommunication of the church and attended by no cleric. No crusader had ever yet triumphed thus in the presence of peaceable Moslems.

Now, in the prime of his life, he spoke seven languages, but Arabic by preference, amazing the sultan and his court. The Oriental, seeing a tolerant Christian for once, ordered the Moslems not to shout out their prayers from the minarets as long as the emperor was in Jerusalem. When one old man kept on according to his habit, and the emperor heard him cry out the old polemic formula that God had no son, the sultan's deputies came to apologize.

"Let him be," said Frederick. "Someday I will tell you what the

Mohammedans in my country are allowed to do. If I were not in danger of losing my reputation among the Franks completely I would make much easier terms for the Sultan."

When the news of this peacefully successful crusade traveled through the world, the emperor captivated a thousand hearts, whereas the Pope, who was having Sicily conquered for his own advantage at the time, lost many followers. Frederick, hurrying back with a few companions, was so overpowering in his surprise landing at Brindisi that the Pope gave back all he had taken, lifted the ban of excommunication, and was glad to be received by the emperor at a splendid festival.

For every inch an emperor he was. He went on through the creative middle years of his life to build up his southern state on a basis of authority and justice. He was very much the humane dictator. Germany, which he governed through his son, was somewhere off in the gray fog, torn by the unending quarrels of its countless princes. In the kingdom of Sicily, which formally began northeast of Rome but actually extended as far as the Alps, this ruler ceased his roaming at last and established the first modern state.

Here again his mixed blood was productive. The two sides of his character required two very different advisers, whom he found for many years in Hermann von Salza, a Knight of the Teutonic Order, and the Apulian chancellor Pietro de Vigna—lion and serpent. He often submitted to the full force of the dramatic conflict between the two, sometimes repelled by the thoroughness of the one or the suppleness of the other. Here we see his agile spirit attaining truly classical heights and anticipating everything that afterward made splendid the men of the Renaissance.

In his administration the German half of his heritage took shape in organization and orderliness, the southern half in intellectual activity and imagination. Both together produced a superb body of legislation seven centuries after Justinian and six before Beccaria and Napoleon.

To indicate the progressive spirit of this prince in the middle of the Middle Ages, we shall take a few random samples from various departments of this legislation. Women and young people were protected. A husband might no longer kill an unfaithful wife. Public women were protected from violence. On the other hand, a woman might not bring a charge of assault unless she had thrice attempted forcibly to repel her assailant. Maximum prices for student lodgings at the universities were established. Anyone who continued to practice medicine without examination was punished. Five years' study was required, and even then the student might at first practice only as assistant to a skilled physician. A human cadaver might be dissected once every five years, something hitherto entirely forbidden by the church. A physician had to swear to treat the poor free of charge and to visit every seriously ailing patient at least twice daily. Christians might charge no interest; Jews not more than ten per cent.

Almost everything that Frederick put into practice from his studies, notably mathematics and natural science, was of Arabic origin. To find the solution of scientific problems, he gave some Arab scholars a ship of their own. When he threw the famous golden goblet into the sea, he did it not for vainglory but as an inducement to his diver and as a prize that would urge him to tell about the ocean floor. Once the sultan of Damascus sent him a special embassy with a golden reproduction of the planetary system in which the heavenly bodies moved. The emperor said that next to his son there was nothing dearer to him on earth than this gift. He corresponded with a learned Jew at Toledo to suggest the compiling of an Arabic encyclopedia. He had a book by Maimonides translated into Latin and one by Ptolemy into Hebrew. He founded a Sicilian school for poets, where the writing was done in Italian. Seeking to investigate the effect of digestion, he gave two men each a great supper and sent one hunting, the other to bed; he then found out that the man who slept digested the better.

Like many great characters, Frederick was fond of animals, particularly of birds. *The Art of Falconry* is one of the few surviving books by his hand. The observation is thorough. The detail is Aristotelian; there is even a chapter on the position in which birds sleep. The foreword contains a sentence unique in the history of books:

"The author is a thorough man, devoted to the sciences, Roman Emperor and King of Jerusalem and Sicily."

Frederick's recreations were falconry and castle building. But the half-Gothic palaces in which he waited, like a Byzantine emperor, for the visitor's prostration were not where he was happiest. What he loved was a lonely castle in Apulia. There the builder and master could sit in a beautifully carved embrasure among tremendous octagonal towers with windows and doors of unwonted size, looking out over rich terraces, gardens, and forests, cities and castles to the sea and the mountains that did not bound his realm.

At Lucera, near one of the castles, the emperor settled 40,000 Saracens, an Arab colony in the midst of Christian Italy. Where he wanted to build a mosque for them he tore down a church on the pretext that it was unsafe. He was accused of having an Arab harem, but Frederick knew far too much about love to locate it in a living museum, and he separated the many women of his choice. Everywhere he lavished pagan splendor upon them and furnished himself with the beauties of life through constant new taxes upon his subjects.

Was it any more than natural that the Pope, feeling himself encircled and condemned to impotence by this heir of the Hohenstaufen power, should proclaim him as Antichrist? Instead of fighting the infidels with fire and sword, this Christian emperor built them a mosque and dared to deride the bones of the saints. Instead of snatching his treasures from the Orient, he brought Arab goldsmiths, astrologers, and alchemists, poets and lute players to his court at Palermo. And yet this heretic insisted he believed in immortality!

Thus it happened that Frederick was excommunicated, actually for altogether political reasons, by a new Pope ten years after his reconciliation with the old one and at the same time was deposed in Germany by a rival at papal instigation. The news reached him on a trip through Italy, while he was amusing himself with his elephants and leopards. For once his calm is said to have left him. But he soon sent for the baskets containing his treasures, and gave orders to open them, crying, "Let's see if my crowns are still there!"

Inner passion broke down his philosophical reserve, too, when disappointments accumulated and the Vatican tried to destroy its greatest enemy by assassination. He replied with gallows and faggot. During his last years Frederick suffered the fate of the half-breed: the German princes hounded the alien Norman in him; the Italian cities, the German Hohenstaufen. At the insurgent city of Viterbo the emperor hurled the curse: "Even in death I shall not find peace!

Though I had one foot in paradise, still would I draw it back if I could take vengeance on Viterbo!" He proposed to the princes of Europe that they confiscate all church property. This proposal was very acceptable indeed to the princes and might actually have been carried through if Frederick had lived longer and gained further victories.

During this gravest crisis of his life, his diary records among the momentous decrees notes on such things as illegal woodcutting in the forests, wages for the falconer, horses and leopards, training of black slaves as musicians, a date plantation for the Jews of Palermo, money to teach his chamberlain Abdulla to write Arabic, a dovecote at the palace of Palermo, the cut of the garments for the animal keepers, the ingredients of his favorite dishes. When we consider how much Emperor Frederick attempted and how little has survived, we might compare him to Leonardo da Vinci, who finished so little, with all his genius. Such minds as these, especially when imbued with ideas their age is not ready for, leave behind them less of an imprint on the solid earth than able men without imagination. When Frederick came to the end after a forty-year reign full of outward turmoil and inward illumination, his dual empire was not assured. Most of his natural and his legitimate children met with tragic fates, and in a short time the reign of the Hohenstaufens ended. The last of the Hohenstaufens was executed at Naples by their enemy the Duke of Anjou. Frederick II was not an enlarger of the realm in history; his battles ended with the downfall of his house.

And yet in all its history the Mediterranean never knew a ruler who combined such knowledge and intuition with such power or set the crown of wisdom on so many other capacities. Of the three great thirteenth century minds, the two Italian figures Dante and Thomas Aquinas represent the Middle Ages, which professed and permitted but one faith. The man of action, the emperor, bred from a crossing of north and south, was far ahead of saint and poet.

V

THE DREAM OF IMPERIAL SPLENDOR, of German world dominion, was over. The solitary genius in the line of German rulers had made one more effort, through a long reign, to fuse Germanic vigor and Latin imagination. The energy and ambition of the German princes had worn itself out in vain struggles. Because it was not on the Mediterranean the German Empire could never become the successor of the Roman Empire; it merely prevented Italy from uniting.

In the Middle Ages and afterward, Italy alone seemed chosen by nature and history to dominate the Mediterranean. Spain and France fronted upon other oceans. Greece was long since exhausted; Constantinople, Egypt, north Africa were much too remote from the center of the sea. The first glance at the map is immediately drawn to Italy, which points into the Mediterranean like an index finger. But this union could be brought about only by a feeling of national Italian unity. The jealousy of petty princes and republics, however, divided the successors of the Hohenstaufens to such an extent that two centuries later Italy between Milan and Rome fell into fourteen states as against the united "Kingdom of Both Sicilies" in the southern half. Why did Italy, the true successor of the Roman Empire, why did Rome herself neither unite nor become mistress of the Mediterranean? The great nations in the fourteenth century united through language to form France, Spain, and England; Italy still had five centuries to wait. If so productive a people, whose genius had changed no more since antiquity than its favorable situation, failed so long in achieving union, there must have been weighty reasons.

One we find in the constant wars and aspirations of the German emperors; another in the papacy, whose position was too weak to prevent national wars but strong enough to preserve the rivalries at home by political intrigue. And finally, a people cannot with impunity be the most civilized on earth; and this was what Italy became during the next two or three centuries. The glorious unfolding of her poetical and fine arts in an age when the country was torn asunder by foreign armies and conquerors reminds us of the apex of German civilization, in a prostrate nation. Perhaps Michelangelo was the price of Italian unity.

As the crusades drew to their close, in the time of Frederick and Dante, Italy was not yet the leader of Europe. Civilization still spread over the whole Mediterranean. The songs of the troubadours came from Provence down the Rhone to Marseille, then sailed before favoring winds across the western Mediterranean. The court etiquette from the county of Toulouse and the duchy of Gascony spread to the rich houses of the burgesses in Italian republics. For a time the arts and customs of the Mediterranean, at least the western part, were wholly Frenchified.

Even then, two hundred years before the Renaissance, there was evidence in all the sciences of an impatient will to break loose from the Catholic dogma—to learn the astronomy of Ptolemy, the medical science of Hippocrates. The legal faculties of Bologna and Pavia analyzed the principles of Justinian; the Paris university transmitted its revolutionary discoveries to Oxford by way of students whom the king ordered home. At Montpellier and Salerno, generations of scholars rose above the foundations of the theological sciences. As the head of the Platonic school at Chartres said: "We stand like dwarfs on the shoulders of the giants of Antiquity. Our worship of the ancient gods need by no means lead us astray from the road to Paradise."

To this day there sits at the royal portal of Chartres, carved in gray stone, the patron saint of all Christian scholasticism. Aristotle the Greek, with a beard and stylized mane, holds a big writing tablet on his knees, as if he were Tolstoy or some Eastern wizard, not a Mediterranean sage. But the most astonishing thing about this revival of ancient science is that the Arabs in Spanish and southern Italian schools were the ones who led the Christians back to the greatest sources of their civilization.

The buildings erected in those days for the greater glory of God, however, were quite the opposite of the antique. Chartres Cathedral, with Aristotle standing guard outside, is the loveliest of all purely Gothic structures. The slender supporters seem to rise airily to pointed arches, and the central nave is held harmoniously aloft. The magnificent portals, the tremendous center rosette, appear to dissolve the whole into filigree. Yet the massive towers give it a battlemented solidity, as if the true faith dwelt here alone. The cathedrals of Chartres and Notre Dame were built about 1200; a century later came those of Reims and Amiens.

For what was later called Gothic, or, in other words, barbaric, is French in origin, though mixed with Germanic elements; with but one exception it reached perfection only north of the Alps. The so-called Gothic lettering also came from the north; it seemed to apply the form of crystals to the familiar curves of Latin script, with the effect of letters suddenly frozen. Pointed arches, built in stone and written in ink, came into being as a perfect counterpart to the chiseled figures of the kings at Chartres and the first Gothic music.

It was natural that the loveliest cathedrals were built in France, for France in those days constituted the culmination of Christian civilization. During eighteen centuries the bishops of Rome reigned outside Italy for only one century, the fourteenth. Their flight from Rome to Provence and their rule at Avignon (1309-1408) resulted from a combination of fear, lust for power, and calculation. From it the Popes gained far more sense of power and enjoyment than they lost. They were protected by a powerful state, remote from the endless onslaughts of German emperors and Roman knights, and free from all the inner crises of Italy. They lived in a lovely countryside, shaded by vineyards, among the songs of the troubadours. More regal than any king, they even secretly dominated the power whose guests they were. The story of the Popes at Avignon is a long romance wherein love and jealousy, intrigues and secret struggles keep the heroes constantly astir.

For while the great national states took shape under absolute rulers in the fourteenth century, the fugitive Pope, the guest of France, was becoming the first absolute ruler in modern history. Synods and councils, the democratic foundations of the church, ceased to be; the Pope became a dictator. Parishes, dioceses, cathedral chapters that had previously appointed their own priests

and administered themselves were now deprived of their rights. Their lord and master in his romantic exile appointed the officials of his universal state, from cardinals down to village priests, from heads of orders to professors, from court dignitaries down to the washerwomen who scrubbed his shirts in the swift-flowing Rhone below the towering castle.

It was only in the so-called exile of Avignon (which was every bit as voluntary as Mohammed's flight) that the papacy as a modern administrative machine, and particularly as a state bank, rose to be a power that could regulate the finance capital of all the Christian nations. The flood of dependents and petitioners, of litigious, ambitious, and greedy men and women that poured into the broad halls and estates around the palace on the hill, hoping to snatch some of the fabulous golden treasure of the Popes, recalls the darkest ages of the Roman Empire. But here, however, everything was falsified by the moral power of an institution that could bless or curse and force the devout to pay money by threatening their eternal life. When the idea of selling indulgences was invented, the noblest thoughts of Saint Paul and the deepest emotions of Jesus were betrayed. But the indulgence was not invented in Italy; it originated in France a century and a half before Luther.

Lying like a mighty fortress above the battlemented old town and the beautiful Rhone, the castle of the Popes has been called a huge prison. These cyclopean towers and aimlessly rambling, gigantic, almost austere walls, the work of several generations, would seem from the outside to justify the expression, "Babylonian captivity of the church," coined by priestly demagogues of the time. But on entering, one found a court whose wealth and splendor outshone all others. The so-called Peter's pence, taken from poor believers the world over, or the tithe for the crusades, which alone brought in fifteen million gold dollars, was received in these splendidly bedecked halls and poured into banquets, receptions, tourneys, and concerts. Pope Clement VI spent $120,000 in gold on his coronation festival alone. The celibacy of the prelates merely enhanced the blitheness of their love life. The only shame is that from all this not a single work of art emerged in an entire century.

John XXII, the greatest banking brain among the Popes, perfected the system of taxes in all the chancelleries. He is reputed to have possessed an eye especially adapted for detecting papers that bore no stamp. The usury practiced by him and his successors amazed the world. And when voices were raised to point out the poverty of the apostles, the Holy See damned this doctrine as heretical. Since almost half of all the apostolic income now went to the cardinals, there was less jealousy among the prelates. The odium of embezzlement was evaded by shrewd manipulation: the accumulated money was turned into bank loans and the favor of the banking houses secured by heavy percentages. The king of France, patron and protector of this ecclesiastical idyl, also profited. He got the Pope to dissolve the Order of Knights Templars (which had moved from Rhodes to France), ostensibly for devil worship and perversion but actually to secure its huge treasures.

This cynical drama went on before a backdrop of utter political turmoil. The days were past when the German emperor had led the Pope's white horse around the Piazza San Marco and kissed the foot of the Holy Father. But the Pope was still powerful enough to assure France of great advantages. When he was appealed to as umpire in the Hundred Years' War with England, he decided the history of Europe in favor of France (though, of course, he was not the sole factor). After their struggles with the Hohenstaufen the Popes determined to maneuver the imperial crown from German into French hands; but this was impossible, because any kind of world dominion had become impossible. The nations kept closing more tightly around their natural centers, and the spirit of the age set at naught any universal power, even the church. No king was willing now to receive his land in fee from the bishop of Rome: he had it, whether from God or by his own sword.

As always when nationalism reaches a climax, it now took up a position on moral grounds, demanding that the spiritual power lead a life above that of nations and at the same time snatching away its temporal foundations. The men who hurled their threats and jibes at Avignon, saying that the church must not allow itself to be governed by one great nation, quite forgot that even in the old days they had been governed not in Jerusalem but in Italian Rome; the Pope had almost always spoken Italian. The voices of Avignon's enemies were full of jarring notes. The German princes were indignant simply because they envied France her growing power.

Only the poets and the saints still spoke the truth. Petrarch, homeless like the Pope, glorified Italy from Avignon. He followed Dante, who had spoken to the whole world, in capturing the mood of exile that rendered the best talents productive, even in those days. Although both men were banished to only a few hours' distance from little Florence, their national sentiment reached the point of poetic ecstasy. Petrarch declined the poet's crown at Paris so as to receive it in Rome.

How great must the political stresses of the era have been for its two greatest lyric poets to squander half their passion on parties and polemics! Petrarch, who kept fleeing to the bosom of nature, continued even in the wilderness to think of men. His celebrated first ascent of a mountain produced almost nothing.

In contrast to the intellectualized, eaglelike features of Dante, Petrarch's head reveals the characteristics of an aging woman, at least in the cassocked profile drawing left to us by his friend. These poets lived as clerics on church benefices, as Horace and Vergil had lived on Augustus and Maecenas. But they, too, were snatched into the hurly-burly of events, a fact that may offer some consolation to artists who fare no better in our day.

Boccaccio, a contemporary of Dante and Petrarch, born, like them, of Florentine parents, but in Paris, solved the problem of his time by his dazzling skill in living. Unlike Dante and Petrarch, he did not live and die abroad. Nor did he embitter his life by prophetic meddling in an age shaped by the sword and not by ideas. When he wrote the *Decameron* in his mid-thirties, he twined a hundred tales with a light touch into one garland—tales that he and others before him had told. Since everything moved him and nothing staggered him, he could drift along in the carnival procession of humanity as an observer. Like Balzac, he created a great comedy that still amuses the world and gives hints to a thousand loving couples of how they should manage their affairs.

In the same Florence and at the same time, there labored a holy virgin, Catherine of Siena (1347-1380). Of the six Saint Catherines, she had the most interesting childhood; she was one of twin sisters, the youngest of twenty-five children born to an artisan and his wife, a great exception in the biography of outstanding individuals. The exhaustion of the mother and probably of the daughter, too, the poverty and distress of the family seem to have intensified her early visions into yearnings for a convent life. When illness struck at the family and her father died, she suddenly became active after the fashion of a modern feminist. She discovered a great talent for speaking and particularly for persuasion. From her convent she tried to settle social and political conflicts. She was soon enlisted to bring Pisa into the league against the Pope.

Here the two aspects of her mission were blended. Though she was politically active, she had not ceased to feel her ecstasies, and one day in church she was surprised by the stigmata of Christ on her hands, feet, and heart. The Dominicans were very much incensed, for only Saint Francis was entitled to these signs, which therefore ostensibly could recur only among Franciscans. This ludicrous jealousy between orders excited the world to such an extent that a Pope who had been a Franciscan allowed that order a monopoly on similar miracles.

The double mission of this pacifist saint culminated at Avignon. The twenty-eight-year-old maiden was expected to induce the Pope to come back to Rome. Like the Maid of Orleans soon afterwards, she was immediately cheated by the diplomats. And still she succeeded. Gregory XI, the seventh French Pope at Avignon, decided to end the exile at last. He took ship at Marseille, with feelings in his heart such as a ruler has seldom carried across the Mediterranean. Catherine traveled not with him but by land; we can see her importance, however, from the fact that at Genoa she had an interview with the hesitant Pope. He gave her a castle, which she bestowed on the convent. From Rome he sent her to Florence with a message. After his death a revolt broke out. Catherine was nearly killed, and she bewailed the fact that martyrdom had escaped her. In the midst of her activity on behalf of the new Pope, mediating with the Roman people, she fell ill and quickly died. Perhaps under her leadership the schism that immediately followed would have been avoided.

A number of motives besides the influence of this genius combined to bring about the return from Avignon. Rienzi, a tribune of the people, had a hand in the game. He was like modern dictators in his mixture of nationalist enthusiasm and play acting. The son of a Roman innkeeper, he filled himself full of Latin orators and ancient heroes. When a nobleman killed his brother, he felt himself the incarnation of Brutus. By ambition and intrigue, the two weapons of dictators, he carved himself a niche at the court of Pope Clement in Avignon. In turn the Pope employed him to gain a foothold in a Rome that had now grown stronger. Returning to the anarchical city, Rienzi one day suddenly announced an assembly at the Capitol for the next day. He in person, richly armed and romantic to look upon, but without an army, surrounded only by flags, musicians, and papal substitutes, headed a procession of the curious and discontented. At the Capitol he delivered a heady speech upon the natural rights of the Roman people and the return of the Golden Age; and then he assumed unlimited powers by popular acclaim. He called himself the Liberator and held a pompous reception at Saint Peter's, all very theatrical but completely popular. His intention was to rule justly.

There was only one thing that Rienzi failed to do, namely, to work. He lived upon symbols and propaganda, at which he was a master. In great splendor he was crowned tribune of the people, with laurel and flowers. Always close to the edge of caricature, he lived in fact upon the fears of the Roman nobility, who had abandoned the city without a struggle. He maintained himself in power for a time without troops and without money. Halfway between pathos and comedy, he enjoyed a quick success when two houses struggling over Naples appealed to him for a decision. But when he invited Pope and emperor to found a new empire under the sovereign will of the Roman people, or in other words his own, he became ridiculous. Suddenly the gambler saw that all was lost. After seven months' rule he abdicated, fled to the German emperor at Prague, and was turned over to Avignon and condemned to death. Actually he was merely kept prisoner and was liberated on the death of the Pope.

The new Pope was planning a blow at the nobility that had returned to Rome; he released Rienzi and sent a legate with him. Once more Rienzi's eloquence won him power. But meanwhile seven years had passed; disappointment had taught him nothing except how to be brutal and partisan. After a few weeks he was deposed and killed in flight, when he was not yet forty-two years old. In his full life Rienzi had one great prophet, Petrarch. The archaizing rhapsodist praised him as the new Romulus and Camillus. Then he was quickly forgotten, to be glorified only much later by Byron and Wagner. The statue of him in Rome is a small one, not on the Capitol but on the slope a little way below the bronze figure of Marcus Aurelius.

After these failures there appeared a Spanish cardinal who could manage the sword and the horse as well as the host and the exegetics of the church fathers. In ten years' fighting he broke the power of the Roman barons, who had made Rome a mass of turreted castles: fortresses fighting one another, built from the stones of the ancient imperial palaces. Next he prepared the way for some future Pope to return. Political interests led to a double choice. This had happened before, but now the two Popes had space and time to rule simultaneously. The nationalist cleavage of the great powers became evident in the two groups that rendered the idea of a universal dominion impossible. And, of course, no Pope would be satisfied now with purely spiritual power. The schism lasted forty years.

The world watched, between annoyance and derision: two Popes were a ludicrous affront. A series of weak personalities followed. Whenever one died, people hoped the other would retire. On being elected, each man promised he would retire if his adversary would retire also; and so they all clung to power until death. The oldest faculties and cardinals offered their mediation—in vain. Once when an agreement was near, one Pope was annoyed by the manner of the other, and the Frenchman was happy to return in haste to his beloved Provence.

At length a council was agreed on at which Christ invisible should preside; an empty throne was set up for Him. The council elected a new Pope, the two old ones refused to retire, and the farce produced a trio of Popes.

Another council, at Constance, finally elected a Roman Pope in 1418, after long negotiations. Meanwhile the magnificent buildings at Rome had decayed; two years were needed to restore them.

VI

A CATHEDRAL AND A FORTRESS close together, one a little above the other, at the top of a slightly rising square—this is the impression the stranger gets as he approaches Saint Peter's and the Vatican. We are at the northwest end of Rome, to the right of the Tiber; the greater part of the city lies on the far side of the river. Hills and fields, roofs, towers, and domes rise on both sides; but all are lower down. From the very first glance Saint Peter's and the Vatican seem dominant, thanks to their height, size, and situation and the multiplicity of their styles, which hint at their antiquity. By no means the most beautiful, Saint Peter's is nevertheless from the outset the dominant church. The Vatican, by no means the most beautiful, is, however, the most interesting palace of any ruling power, if only because the power has governed longer than any other—more than eighteen centuries.

Along the edge of the metropolis, where the gardens still spread out as of old, the first Christians dwelt. Thinkers and solitaries, they fled the turmoil and lived a tranquil life with God or nature. In one of these gardens about A.D. 67, Peter was supposedly crucified. But Roman law left the dead bodies to the survivors, and so Peter's friends built a tomb. His successors put up a church, where they in turn were buried. Much later Emperor Constantine gave the Christians full scope, the original group of visionaries having meanwhile become a power. He himself is supposed to have built a great church at the same spot, A.D. 334, over the tomb that still survives.

The golden cross he set up to mark the grave might more probably have betrayed it. But the first bishops of Rome managed to protect the tomb with sheets of bronze in such fashion that even the barbarians could not find and destroy it. The grave of Peter has triumphed over the thieving hands of all the barbarian troops, over Alaric and Genseric, then over the Saracens. As late as the sixteenth century it escaped the depredations of Charles V's Protestant troops—perhaps because of the walls built around it by a Pope, perhaps because of its mystic power.

Even more surprising is the way the dead Peter has escaped the artists. Bramante wanted to give the new Saint Peter's a different ground plan and therefore to shift Peter's sarcophagus, or what tradition takes to be his sarcophagus. The Pope stopped him on grounds of reverence. Later even Bernini, who was allowed to ruin the fairest ancient buildings, proved weaker than the spirit of Peter. He merely succeeded in outraging by gold and the baroque splendor of spiral columns the simple wooden chair from which the Apostle had preached.

It was a coincidence that the old Saint Peter's began to sway at the very time of sharpest ecclesiastical struggle during the schism. According to the testimony of the experts the south wall had sunk out of plumb by almost six feet. Thereupon a Pope decided to demolish the church, some 1,200 years after its foundation. What we see today no longer includes a single stone from the old church, whose poor remains are preserved in a small museum.

But even the new Saint Peter's, virtually unchanged since 1626, had a dramatic history of 120 years of construction. The building embodied the ambition of the Popes, the rivalries of the artists, changes in taste, and above all else the power of money. The greatest artists of the Renaissance, Raphael, Bramante, the brothers Sangallo quarreled for forty years over the shape of the building and accomplished almost nothing. Finally Michelangelo was summoned. He contributed two brilliant ideas, one complementing the other: the dome and the Greek-cross form. In his mind's eye was a temple of harmonious proportions, equally long and wide, in whose center, over the tomb of Peter, a dome of unrivaled loftiness and expanse would seem to float on air. He made drawings, but a hundred intrigues blocked their execution. Even in his extreme old age his mind was occupied with the symbol of this dome. When he died, nothing had been done.

Half a century after his drawings and a quarter century after his death, Paul V at last had Michelangelo's great bequest, the dome, built almost exactly according to the drawings. It took less than two years. Still some evil spirit seems to have watched over this Pope's plans. Already a century removed from the Renaissance, he was afraid of the classical form; so he decided upon a long nave, the so-called Latin cross. He had the eastern arm extended, creating a church whose shape was that of a hundred others, and the gigantic dome no longer suited it. Today the structure lacks the mysticism of the Gothic portals from outside, the mysticism of the colored windows from inside. It is more of an official chamber, where 40,000 fashionable Roman gentlemen and ladies meet on holidays. Saint Peter's Cathedral, like Pauline Christianity, expresses power rather than reverence. It is only when one approaches the metropolis from a great distance that one sees the dome rise alone as a deathless symbol.

A more varied and picturesque impression is created by the Vatican, from which the Pope enters the cathedral through a sort of corridor. With a few interruptions the Popes have resided there fourteen centuries. As we might gather from its varied shapes, tangled and overlapping, the Vatican is 1,000 years older than Saint Peter's. It contains many walls and castles, fortified battlements, underground passages, and armed yards. The visitor today, allowed in this area only on foot, has a real chance to study this strangest fortress in the world. Since there was no underlying plan, the warlike spirit of certain Popes, the idyllic spirit of others, and the humanistic spirit of a third school had free play. Turreted palaces grew up beside dainty gardens and profoundly scholarly libraries.

Now that the Pope is no longer a temporal prince—despite his latest "Vatican City"—these structures seem like the magic arts of old fairytales. As in the old razed fortifications of Europe—among them the pleasant promenades along one of the outer edges of Paris —everything here has stood still. We shake our heads as we reflect that all this dark armament seems to exist in order to protect a single, solitary priest.

This is also the paradoxical impression gathered by the onlooker in the audience chambers as he waits to be received by the Pope. Below, at the great stairs, he has been met by the corps of gigantic Swiss in their yellow-and-black *Landsknecht* doublets. For 400 years these guards have held in their hands their big spears, which they have not wielded for at least 200. They are monosyllabic, firm, with the extreme taciturnity that distinguishes the Swiss.

Upstairs the five or six equally high, equally large, equally empty chambers are all decorated in silk. A hundred great armchairs stand stolidly on the edges of the costly carpet, like page boys. There is no table; the broad double doors, thrown back, join the whole into a single suite. All the curtains are drawn, and the noonday light of the Mediterranean is replaced by softly shaded lamps. Everyone speaks in low tones. We feel that we are in some Arabian legend, inside an enchanted powder box. Noiselessly the officers of the papal bodyguard, gleaming in gold and silk, every one a son of the old Roman nobility, pace back and forth, while clerics in purple, lilac, or black appear and vanish with noiseless deliberation.

All the Pope's antechambers are open, and when we are invited into the last one, we can sometimes hear him speaking softly to his guests in the next room. The elegance of most of the prelates limits to a second the ceremony of prostration and kissing the ring. The Pope usually does not sit but stands alone. After the fairytale preamble, the reception itself is not more solemn but rather simpler than it was at the old imperial courts. And as one listens to the Holy Father's words, one hears behind him the faint tinkle of the never-unsheathed silver swords and golden spurs that lend a touch of legend to our worldly era. They make the visitor forget that he is in a fortress that once bristled with shotted cannon.

But in compensation the art of Italy has remained alive all over the palace. No museum can rival that which has been created here, especially between 1450 and 1650. For this is not a museum but a living expression of the devoutness and joyful vitality that by turns, and sometimes together, have animated the palace according to the changing spirit of the times. There are richer museums than the marble gallery and the Vatican picture gallery; both are excelled in Madrid and Florence. But there is no other palace of equal artistic wealth; even the Palazzo Ducale at Venice takes second place. We cannot mention one name, or we should have to mention all.

The most astonishing part is the tolerance of the church whose power is focused here. No other Mediterranean religious center would have risked what these artists were allowed and sometimes told to do. The beauty of the nude body was displayed in Greek temples; golden haloes gleamed around the heads of emperors at Byzantium. But those were expressions of dogmas, religion. If signs and symbols expressed an invisible god in synagogue and mosque, the invisibility was the strict commandment and the pride of those philosophies.

In the Vatican nymphs and satyrs could take their pleasure, Dianas display their charms; the pagan representations of Greece, as painted by Raphael, carry on their disputations. Beside them Christ stands forth, a naked ruler in the kingdom of the dead, in the work of Michelangelo. Youths of Grecian beauty uphold the framework of Old Testament friezes; the most beautiful of all women reign in paradise. A few galleries away the mistress of the Borgia Pope smiles down from a wall as a Madonna, and his daughter is located near by. And yet these things are gathered under a single sign, the cross on which Jesus and Peter died. As the boys' choir strikes up in the high dome of Saint Peter's, all worldly thoughts fade away, and we can see into a heaven where Saint Peter sits beside his Saviour.

VII

ONE IS SOMETIMES TEMPTED to call the Mediterranean a sea of commerce. But are not all oceans that? Has not the infinite expanse of water everywhere seen fewer battles than trading voyages, fewer warships than cargo boats? On land the restriction of space, the clashes of interests, the millions of human beings constantly breed quarrels. All the things that make a tenement dweller annoyed with the noisy neighbor he hears through the wall, the things that set the peasant against the man across the fence or one nation against another across a river disappear in the shapeless expanse of the sea. Except by accident or in battle, two vessels never disturb or destroy each other. The idea of the freedom of the seas, which developed before the Middle Ages, was possible only because the sea belonged to everybody and nobody.

For that reason the seaman has more self-assurance and a stronger religious sense than the peasant. Freedom is not a thing he must fight for; no one denies it to him. It is one of the benefits of life that he greets anew every morning as the iron ladder brings him from his bunk to the deck into the light and the open sweep that belong to him. On shore a man must flee into forests or deserts to be alone with himself. If he seeks God, a hundred strange faces will look at him in church. But at sea he must search with a spyglass for any trace of another soul. No king or dictator has ever been so free as the captain on his bridge.

In the hold below lie the bales and casks for which the voyage is being taken. Until modern times it was unknown to dispatch vessels for travelers alone, and even now the freight of a liner brings in more money than the passengers. Even these passengers are pure traders; for among a hundred crossing the sea there is seldom more than one who means to study a nation, enjoy a landscape, or win a woman instead of money.

The Mediterranean, the smallest sea of them all, shows its nature as an inland sea by the way it has sent vessels great and small from coast to coast since earliest antiquity, bringing the countries close and bartering civilizations along with goods.

Which are the colonies no man can say, for Alexandria and Carthage developed earlier than Venice and Byzantium. The smallness, the continuity of the Mediterranean give to shipping there a mission withheld from the commerce on the great oceans. Long before the discovery of America, before any real knowledge of China and India, the Mediterranean had splendidly developed a modern form of trade and civilization.

Italy took the lead. When the crusaders made a new system necessary, Italians became the first great European bankers. They invented double-entry bookkeeping. The bank was at first a *banco,* that is, a long bench on which you put down your money for exchange, to receive less in return. The great bankers, who still think they rule the world, ought sometimes to remember the vulgar origin of their trade. Interest, too, was first largely introduced in Italy. The Popes, needing money as they did, had to abolish the canonical prohibition of interest. They pawned the various contributions and tithes to Italian banks in return for loans of millions.

For since credit is nothing but faith in shrewd or strong persons, it is most easily attached to Popes and kings. With the rise of the great royal houses, petty usurers became great bankers who would take a few per cent less for the sake of a patent of nobility. The deeper they were drawn into the shady deals of the great lords, the more political influence they wielded. In order to give a refined name to the exploitation of whole nations through taxes and excises, it was called "necessity of state" from the time of Machiavelli. Later the term became "reasons of state" and *"Realpolitik."* Actually the exploitation meant the end of all Christian morality. Princes and dictators, even in their bitterest struggles, despise each other less than any one of them despises the crowd that is killed on his behalf. Similarly the money men became messengers among powerful enemies, and they felt no inner reluctance to betray their country. So the sons of small local traders often became the famous bankers of their nations, and the grandsons international financiers.

The skill of the Italian merchant far outgrew the Mediterranean. German and English kings pledged their expected revenues, monopolies, and licenses in Milan and Florence. When there was a great bankruptcy at Venice in 1345, King Edward, in London, owed huge sums to the estate. The English were much slower to become good traders than the Italians, since they were also much later in becoming sailors. As early as Frederick II it was customary in Palermo to make state loans at Florence upon the Sicilian grain export.

Just as the credit structure developed out of banks, the first joint-stock companies came from the colonial trade. Here, too, Venetians and Genoese displaced their Greek and Arab competitors in the southern and eastern Mediterranean. They ventured to send shipments from the Black Sea and Tripoli as far as England. These were not colonies in the real sense, however, except when so-called unoccupied coasts were preempted. But the "factories" established by the foreign masters were so fortified that Venetian quarters sprang up in the ports of Asia Minor, with their own courts, consuls, and national administration. The forms of veiled subjugation introduced by Venice served afterward as a model for Spain and fostered imitation by Dutch and English colonizers as late as the eighteenth century. This era was first called the beginning of the Renaissance; later, the beginning of imperialism.

The fact that tremendous fortunes poured swiftly into a few hands after the crusades is due primarily to stupendous profits such as have become impossible now, with the end of private monopolies. The risk of wars, seafaring, and uncertainty of jurisdiction was great, no doubt, but the traders abused the idea of risk. When the Florentines sold their stuffs at Nicaea or Acre, they increased the prices by as much as 300 per cent. They also continued the slave trade as blithely as if they had still been Greeks and pagans and no prophet had ever risen in the Mediterranean to call all men brothers and leave a vicegerent preaching the Gospel in Saint Peter's.

Among the Italian cities none was more adroit than Florence, and it is no accident that the best traders and diplomats came from there and from Venice. The Cardis, Baldis, and Peruzzis became great men of whom the whole Mediterranean spoke with awe.

The first to progress from finance to statecraft were the Medicis, who ruled Florence for three hundred years. For one century they showed high gifts and had no title, and for two centuries afterward they had titles and showed no talent.

The greatest of them, Cosmo de' Medici (1389-1464), himself the grandson of influential merchants and city councilors, made his great fortune chiefly at the council of Constance, as a Pope's companion. Others, Italians and Germans, also grew rich in these political deals. But why, in the end, was no Albizzi, no Fugger, but only Cosmo de' Medici alone called *pater patriae?*

Because he loved liberty, protected the nation, helped the poor, lifted up the oppressed, his was a life still outside the gates of the Roman Renaissance, successful, high-hearted, almost innocent. Among the millionaires of our century none is like him, no matter how they may try to ease their consciences by charitable foundations.

This Medici left almost nothing to his fellow citizens and yet endowed his name with a celebrity that shone afar because he had not gained his wealth by oppression and by the sacrifice of other people's livelihoods.

Cosmo, for forty years the real master of Florence, caused the entire real property within the state to be recorded. On the basis of this general land register, he taxed the nobility heavily, the people more lightly. He deprived the corrupt tax collectors of their power and lent or gave money to his fellow citizens—all with the restraint of a man who meant to appear less than he was. He endured quietly a year of the customary Florentine banishment, and sought no revenge when he came back. Shown as an old man in Verrocchio's relief, he is dressed very simply with a big cap. Everything about him is heavy—the long, pointed, curved nose, the big ear lobes; but every trait shows earnestness, caution, harmony. In old age he began the study of Plato. He recognized true artists and gave work to Donatello and Gozzoli. Though he loved to walk back and forth in the charming hall of his villa at Carreggi, philosophizing with poets and sages, he was always the businessman. He could have told exactly the profit he had made that summer.

Lorenzo the Magnificent, the grandson, was much more of a dictator and tyrant. The fresco by Ghirlandaio shows him with defiantly outthrust chin, the nose broad and flattened, the hair wild and thick, the eye not tranquil but searching, the mouth always ready for speech. And he was, in fact, no merchant. He was an artist who was fond of playing king; yet he had too much sense of irony to make himself ridiculous in both roles. Charming *canzoni* (written by him, not by the court poets), music and literature, parody, thirst for knowledge, enjoyment of a vigorous intellectual life, love, friendship, romance—all these together animated the sickly heir and drove him at a pace that was perhaps too swift. His death mask is amazingly like the mask of Beethoven.

The fusion of the two religions that had shaped the spirit of the Mediterranean was the Florentine ideal of the time; it was rather coyly called "the theology of Plato and the philosophy of Paul." Botticelli painted Venus like a saint and portrayed bloodless ladies as ancient goddesses. At court he was allowed to work on illustrations for Dante and Boccaccio at the same time. There was a strange atmosphere, something between sensibility and sensuality, extending over these pre-Raphaelite years. They represented a mood of decline rather than the true mood of the Renaissance.

Then came Savonarola, in the white cassock of a Dominican, proclaiming to the mob the phantasms of his nights and prophesying the death of Lorenzo. But though he fulminated against the turbulent masked processions of the Medici, he was no less theatrical himself when he had a great troop of garlanded boys and girls burn trinkets, singing, "Long live Christ our King!" But Lorenzo, the apostle of beauty, did not in any way submit to the fanatic. Afterward Savonarola ruled Florence for five years, until an unsuccessful attempt at martyrdom deprived him of all credit. After awful tortures he was hanged and his body burned over a pile of faggots such as he had just raised for the burning of all worldly vanities. He had sacrificed Petrarch to his frenzy, along with mirrors, veils, harps, and chessboards.

The Medicis produced two Popes, one of them Leo X. But the high morality and generous kindness of Cosmo, the tender and brilliant spirit of Lorenzo did not reappear. A series of weak successors tried in vain to transform the money and talents of their fathers into grand-ducal titles and coronets.

VIII

While more and more Italian republics and principalities fell to fighting, the two Mediterranean countries of the future were becoming united nations. In the fourteenth and fifteenth centuries France and Spain became national states, England having preceded them. The Roman universal idea, embodied alternately in Pope and emperor, was dead; the universal Latin speech was silenced outside the monasteries; and vernacular tongues made their way even at the universities. Troubled Italy herself found common ground through her language.

France above all, under a few strong rulers, gave shape to her state concept. The older Capets had been weak and inferior to the German kings, but the German idea declined after the last of the Hohenstaufen. It seems significant that King Louis IX of France outlived the German emperor, Frederick II, by twenty years.

Louis, oddly enough called a saint, was manly, proud, handsome, self-assured. He was on such good terms with his rival Frederick that, on being deposed, the latter invoked the Frenchman's mediation. Louis, as serious about his crusades as Frederick had been ironical about his, was less fortunate. On a first crusade he was taken captive, and on a later crusade he died of the plague.

His successors emphasized the national idea. Philip the Fair deserved his name. Masterful, sly, faithless, and at the same time forceful, a sort of anticipated sun king, he had one ideal—France. He fought the feudal nobility in order to strengthen the state through its functionaries. Hence came his mistrust of the Pope, on whom he levied taxes. The Pope, the same priest who had canonized his grandfather Louis, now warred against the grandson. This turmoil culminated in physical maltreatment of the Pope, which had probably never befallen any of his colleagues in office. At length the Roman people liberated the old man of eighty-five. This was the parable of the new powers of the age. The next Pope, a Frenchman, stayed in Avignon, beginning the so-called captivity of the church.

We can see what one of these fourteenth century absolute monarchs thought of himself from pictures that we might suppose were painted not then in Paris but rather about A.D. 800 in Constantinople. A diet is assembled as if for the Ascension. At the bottom are two groups quarreling across a bench; above them, a group of eight seated men, who look like parliamentary stenographers. Over these, in separate groups, are nobility and clergy, the latter with high bishops' miters, each with his coat of arms above him. At the very top the king is enthroned like the Lord of Hosts.

The Hundred Years' War with England diverted only a part of these French forces from the Mediterranean. Earlier it had been the crusades, then it was the turmoil in Italy that pulled the navy of newborn France to the south. When the mouth of the Rhone passed into the hands of France about 1480, she gained the great coast stronghold of Marseille; and the raw silks that had long since begun flowing to Lyon now remained in French hands. A banker from Montpellier was so powerful that Venice and Genoa had to unite in overthrowing this French Medici.

The great rival to a growing France was Spain. She required two centuries to unite her very divergent stocks. A glance at the map will show how the clumsy shape of her peninsula made conflicts between the inland mountaineers and the coast dwellers. At the narrowest points of gracefully shaped Italy, for instance, from a mountaintop near Nicastro in the south, on a clear day you can see both oceans at once. This geographical slenderness gives every inhabitant of the interior a sense of living always close to the sea. In Spain most people feel cut off, indeed sheltered from the sea by high mountains and great distances; they are unkindly disposed toward the coast. This explains the long struggles of the two most powerful peoples of the country.

For in the Middle Ages the elevated kingdoms of Castile and León, which formed the center and northwest of Spain and which were divided from the Atlantic by high mountains, fought as inlanders against the low-lying kingdom of Aragon, which reached from the Pyrenees about to the Guadalquivir, corresponding fairly closely to modern Catalonia. At their northern limit both were divided by the little kingdom of Navarre, which bordered on the French territory of Gascony. Here flourished all the fine names that became immortal in the songs of the troubadours—the counts of Roncesvalles, of Roussillon, the lords of Pamplona, of Perpignan, of Tarragon.

The whole south, almost half the peninsula, belonged as late as 1200 to the Moors, whom the Spanish tried for three centuries to expel. Hence the religious intolerance, the Inquisition, the persecution of the Jews, who occupied important positions among the Moors. Only when we keep in mind that the national enemy in Spain was at the same time the religious enemy can we understand why such gloomy shadows rested on all the things that passed off so easily in Italy despite alien invasions. In Italy intellectual life could expand into a half-pagan Renaissance, for a widespread and undisputed faith need not go very deep. Spain, however, having to defend herself, became fanatical.

For this reason chivalry and the religious impulse had a pure and long-continued influence as genuine motives among the knights. The Cid, with his emotional aura, is as truly an ideal literary figure as Don Quixote later was in his irony. Yet neither one is the Spanish national hero. That honor is Don Juan's; among all the miscreants of history he has had the greatest career; now that he is in hell, Masses for his soul are said throughout Spain on a certain November day of each year. For salvation, then, it seems safer to conquer many women than many men.

History made a gift to the Spaniards in the shape of foreign aggression. For they, unlike the Italians, united against attacks.

As early as 1236 the hostile Castilians and Aragonese joined to re-
take Córdoba from the Moors. The sources are in partisan disagree-
ment as to whether the church or the Moors did more burning and
murdering. In the history of war hundreds of thousands always
remain anonymous in death. A single cold mathematical figure
represents destiny; we read in the history book as we do in the papers a figure with many zeros, without forming any conception of
what it means.

But the things that perish in the process remain in men's memory as, for example, when we hear that the whole Byzantine nation mourned the loss of a marble Helen, or when we see a picture
of the lost Athene Promachos or the copy of a burned Rembrandt;
or hear of vanished songs by Ariosto and Milton; or remember the
Alexandrian Library, the Parthenon, Reims Cathedral, all of them
burned or blasted. The anguish of posterity for some special lost
treasure glows through a thousand years. Paradoxically, immortal
works are more deeply mourned than mortal men.

The library of Córdoba, too, was mourned for. Here the wisdom
of the Mediterranean was assembled in the twelfth century. The
Jews had a considerable share in this intellectual center but were
soon persecuted—even Maimonides, the greatest of them all, who
had to flee to Fez and afterward to Cairo. It has been said of him
that in Córdoba he learned humanism, in Africa, humanity. Later
the bankruptcy of a brother compelled the philosopher to earn
money, and so at the age of more than forty he became a physician.
He forthwith became so great a practitioner that the sultan appointed him his personal physician. He wrote a commentary on the
Talmud, and compared the teachings of Aristotle with Jewish doctrine, much as Saint Thomas used Aristotle in illuminating Christian doctrine. Maimonides' emphasis upon reason and tolerance in
religion put him some three to five centuries ahead of his time.

The tolerance was one-sided: in the Inquisition Spain established a tool of the fiercest fanaticism known to history. Persecution
of an alien religion was unheard of among the Greeks. As a principle it cannot be traced back further than the fourth century, and
then its only expression was in excommunication, followed by the

surrender of the victim to the temporal authorities. Constantine caused the books of the Arians to be burned. Justinian only set fire to the Talmud and later to Aristotle. Heretics were punished with enforced pilgrimage, fasting, confiscation of property. Thus early the egoistic practices begin, for half of such property fell to the church and the other half to the judge.

The reversion to barbarism finally began with torture, introduced by the Inquisition. It was in the year 1252 that a Pope first permitted torture of the accused, which had previously been forbidden. Torture of witnesses soon followed, far more dangerous because in this fashion anything could be proved. The people rose up and slew an inquisitor. King Alfonso forbade torture, showed his tolerance, and thus earned the noble cognomen "the Wise."

The Popes were angry; one of them goaded the king against the Moors; another, against the Jews. At a council in Vienna complaints were made that the Mohammedans were allowed to cry out their God from the tower. The councils of the fourteenth century gave rise to the first massacres, heretofore unknown and repugnant to the people. The Spanish clergy opposed the tolerant king, first holding autos da fé of books, then burning houses of worship, finally killing non-Christians.

But nothing was so disgraceful to humanity as the compulsion put upon people to accept a faith they had neither inherited nor arrived at of their own accord. About 1390, in Salamanca alone, the Spanish clergy forced 11,000 people to accept baptism. The butcheries of the Jews who refused baptism or recanted between 1450 and 1470 have been taken as models for our own dark days. It was a time of great bewilderment for the "converted" Jews, who were afterward called *marranos*. Once they were baptized, their opportunities actually improved, and they could hold any office; accordingly hatred of them as competitors grew instead of disappearing. Purity of blood was preached, but after the multitude of baptisms it was more and more impossible in practice.

The Inquisition, which at first had been used only against wavering Christians, flung itself upon the Jews after the conquest of Granada. It had become purely Spanish, for King Ferdinand no

longer wanted to share the confiscated property with the Pope. The persecutions in Spain were now quite independent; books prohibited there were allowed in Rome. The Roman ecclesiastical state sold remission of punishment. Its Spanish counterpart declared the prices were too low and charged double. The marranos, the secret Jewry of the forcibly converted, haunted the public conscience. In vain popular instinct rebelled in many cities. The head of the Inquisition was murdered before the altar at Saragossa, by a nobleman, at that. But the whole machinery was built on a tremendous scale and was operated by countless agents; the individual citizen was without rights, for the state protected no one from the hidden hand. There was no appeal from its sentences, from its lootings and abductions. The agents of Torquemada, the Great Inquisitor, marched under arms through the countryside, killing people and confiscating property without being accountable to a soul.

The reasons were racial feelings and envy of success. The methods were secret police, a private army, spies, secret courts, murder. The results were destruction of liberty, a crushing verdict in history.

IX

THE SPANISH INTELLIGENCE did its work along the Mediterranean coast. To this day one is shown the stock exchange, the *lonjas,* in Barcelona and other cities—Gothic palaces embodying the civic pride of Spain's merchants and sailors. The markets they captured and the civilizations they assembled are far more interesting than the struggles and inheritances of the royal houses of Anjou and Aragon, which Sicily and Sardinia kept passing from hand to hand.

We are inclined to regard the Castilian as the most typical of Spaniards. On the high plateau in the center of the peninsula, in their castles or along the three beautiful rivers, the hidalgos—the feudal lords—lived and rode abroad. They were chivalrous, proud, and lazy. But along with them the Cortes of Burgos were functioning as early as the twelfth century, before England had a Magna Charta. The struggle with the infidel seems to have preempted all the instincts of overlordship; the knights allowed their burgesses liberties that no private citizen on the Mediterranean then possessed. This was not love of the common people—how could a born lord in those days have dreamed of such a thing? It was the sheer necessity of arming even the commoners against the Moors. All this was an inland affair, turning its back on the sea.

Things were otherwise with life in the east, where the twelfth century Catalans (Gothalans) along the coast had united to form one kingdom with the Aragonese living up the Ebro. Everything here was Mediterranean, that is, mercantile. The more they were pushed back politically from southern France the more tremendous their warehouses at Marseille became. The nobility were called *ricos hombres,* for they did business instead of lounging at ease in their castles. They, too, were feudal lords, but the ocean animated them, and the consciousness of having friends on distant shores made them more independent of king and church. For instance, their Great Catalan Company was allied with Constantinople about 1300 and ruled Attica for seventy years.

The fortunate dominion of the Arabs brought these people under the influence of a civilization whose exponents they did not drive out until they had taken over from them, in the course of centuries, all the productive elements. Here in the east even the kings were educated. If Alfonso the Wise, chosen German king during the interregnum, had gone north and actually assumed his crown, the Germans would have had at least one lawgiver and poet, astronomer, and historian among their half barbarians. An old miniature shows him enthroned like King Solomon.

A successor to Alfonso proclaimed toleration for the Moors and abolished torture. Around 1300 the crown was supervised by the estates as closely as it was in Oxford by the "Mad Parliament." In those days the Cortes of Aragon could grandly say, "The King of Castile rules over subjects, he of Aragon over free citizens." As a result Castile was for France and Aragon for England in the Hundred Years' War.

All three western national states resembled each other in having strong state power, in central administration, and in economic policies; a state of functionaries with bourgeois sympathies took care of all classes, eliminating many privileges. It stood out new and fresh against the spirit of the Middle Ages.

In the west, the seafaring Portuguese nation, with its back to the Mediterranean, occupied roughly its present position. By 1450 the Portuguese were shipping wine, oil, raisins, sugar, and silk to England. Directed by Prince Henry the Navigator and then by King Emanuel the Fortunate—a unique epithet for royalty—they explored to the west and south, to the Azores and Canaries and down the African coast and by 1500 they had rounded the Cape, reached India, captured the spice trade, and begun what was soon to grow into one of the greatest colonial empires. The other half of this empire fell to Spain.

Ferdinand and Isabella, called the "kings," ruled together for thirty-five years, and when Isabella died she was only fifty-three. The marriage was without parallel in history. Here was no heiress to a throne seeking a husband in order to have children, no king marrying an heiress in order to gain land. To unite two hostile countries, Castile and Aragon, its two heirs married. All their lives they ruled jointly, and sometimes disjointedly, with equal rights and responsibilities. They also had time to beget children, perhaps to carry on love affairs as well, without losing each other. This was possible only through continuity and a very early marriage, at the ages of seventeen and eighteen. There is a great fascination about the couple, even though the husband had no fascination at all.

Scarcely ever has a queen had such an opportunity to prove herself. Elizabeth and Catherine, Maria Theresa and Victoria ruled alone as responsible heirs, and in their cases the counsel of a husband or lover was merely weakness. But Isabella, the daughter of Castile (the prouder family), was not to be put off by her wily husband. He tried to deceive her after the death of her father but found this woman with whom he had just begotten a daughter standing rugged and manly on the threshold of her paternal castle. On that account she was called "king," and though the change of sex is by no means a promotion, still this title has remained a singular distinction for a woman.

She was superior to her husband in every way—talent, vision, and color. She must have suffered moods of deep depression on lonely nights because of her husband's cold shrewdness, the mercantile calculations of the Aragonese. She could endure living so long with him only as two engineers or actors might do, continuing year after year with their joint inventions or dramas because they shared an enthusiasm for the same cause.

Theirs was the same ambition: hope of a united Spain made the young people marry and then kept them together. For at that time it was by no means decided that powerful Castile should go toward the Mediterranean rather than unite with Portugal. Even as a child in a convent the young heiress had been politically betrothed half a dozen times. Indeed, the long-planned union of Castile with

Portugal would have distributed colonies differently during the following century and thus have changed the world.

Along with ambition, they had in common their religion. And though fundamentally Ferdinand did business with God exactly as he did with people, he, like her, was afterward called "the Catholic." She seems to have deserved the name better.

Like most women when they are on fire for a man or a cause, Isabella was fanatical, and she passionately supported the godly crimes of the Inquisition. Ferdinand, by contrast, was more interested in the money the persecutions brought in. He was a cynic and is said to have cried out when told of a complaint by the King of France that Ferdinand had twice cheated him, "He lies! I have hoodwinked him more than ten times!"

Among the long struggles by which the kings enlarged united Spain, the struggle for the winning of Naples is uninteresting, because Naples simply passed from hand to hand by marriage and conspiracy. But this and the conquest of small border territories beyond the Pyrenees kindled the Franco-Spanish conflict that later brought on such fierce wars. Completely insignificant in purpose and result, these dynastic jealousies fall into oblivion and are good for nothing but to burden the memory of school children. Only the conquest of Granada was fateful and momentous.

The remnants of Arab civilization had been pushed down to this southern tip of the peninsula; most of the Moors had returned to north Africa, whence their fathers had come. The Spanish royal pair had both national and religious reasons for their action. A new Spain must be both united and Christian; the world accepted the expulsion of the infidels from Europe as a symbol.

They could have used the Moors, who, after all, had built up the Spanish territory, as a bridge to the African Berbers. In vain an eager cardinal tried to urge the king forward, and advanced with his troops to Gerba and Oran. But Ferdinand was mistrustful of warring orders, and his thoughts were always on Italy, on alliances and marriages.

Thus the advance against Islam halted. It was a famous moment when the cardinal declared, "Today there is not one unbaptized Moor left in the Kingdom of Granada." But there were thousands of unbaptized hearts all over Spain; six centuries of Arabic civilization could not be rubbed out. Even today the south looks half Moorish. The Alhambra is the most famous example of Moorish architecture, but the loveliest are in Seville and Córdoba.

Of the two kings, evidently only the woman was beloved. But in his own way Ferdinand was the strongest head of a state in his time, a model for Machiavelli, who was Spanish in his preferences. "These are people," an Italian ambassador wrote of the Spanish court, "seemingly humble and grave, men of endless ceremony, with wonderful titles and hand-kissing, every one a lord. They are ready to serve everyone, but they must be kept at arm's length, and trusted but little."

After Isabella's death Ferdinand's character was even more plainly revealed. His passion for gaining advantages by the marriages of his children and brothers and sisters took its toll in a dreadful hatred of his son-in-law, the son of Maximilian of Hapsburg. Johanna, the strange daughter of the two kings, was or became insane. Finally nothing was left of this highly gifted couple except a mad daughter and the memory of a scene in which an alien, a Genoese citizen, handed over to the two Spanish kings the treasures of an unknown continent.

X

THROUGH ONE GATE of the Mediterranean, Gibraltar, Islam had been driven out of Europe; through the other gate, the Dardanelles, it had entered victoriously not long before. In 1452 (the very year when Ferdinand, conqueror of the Moors, was born in Spain), twenty-one-year-old Sultan Mohammed was at the gates of Constantinople. He was supervising the building of the fortifications from which he would capture the metropolis the following year. Mohammed II was lucky enough to perform his most amazing deeds at an early age, but Turk and Spaniard alike became important rulers by similar traits of character. Mohammed was evidently the greater general, but both were acute students of human nature and therefore successful statesmen.

Both made use of the true faith to plunder their enemies and to explain their lust for conquest to themselves and the world as good works. Certainly Mohammed prayed to Allah with the same easy conscience as Ferdinand did to Mary, having that morning read through the latest list of infidels killed the day before. The Turk, like Alexander (whom he resembles also in his youth and upbringing), had ascended the throne by means of murder. The Catholic rose to power by marriages and inheritances. As dictators both were completely unmoral, constantly ascribing their actions to the will of God. And both were vouchsafed a long period—thirty and forty-seven years, respectively—to impress their personalities on the West and the East. Seldom, perhaps never, has the Mediterranean seen two conquerors of such stature in simultaneous action for a dozen years. At the extreme ends of the Mediterranean, the two showed Renaissance characters and capacities even before the concept of the Renaissance man had crystallized in the center.

The Turks, steered toward Europe by Mohammed, had arrived and pushed to the fore between two great nomadic invasions. First Genghis Khan, coming from China about 1200 and setting the peoples of central Asia in motion, had driven them ahead of him along with many other nations. And Timur, the other Mongolian world conqueror, advancing from Samarkand about 1400, smashed the Turks so completely that no one believed they could revive.

Why did nothing but empty names remain of these two rulers, who amassed more land than Alexander? Why, on the other hand, did the Turks, called Osmanli, after their leader, remain for four centuries one of the great Mediterranean powers?

Because they were held together by a great faith, which Timur and Genghis Khan lacked. Because Arabian Islam bequeathed both fire and fanaticism to them, a single god with the sword as his instrument. They were born warriors and taught others to be warriors; they offered the world the paradox of the Janizaries, who were their best troops and who were also the sons of subject Christian peoples. Every year they installed a thousand of these as an elite to be trained as a religious order for Allah and the crooked saber. All reports agree that Spaniards and Turks were the best soldiers in the fifteenth century.

It cannot have been a matter of race. For when Osman established his state in Anatolia, he found ahead of him all the elements that had passed through in twenty centuries—Italians, Greeks, Mongols, Germans, Semites, a mixture that goes far in itself toward explaining their energy. But even in those days the illusion of pure blood gave such an impetus to the active peoples that the Turks proclaimed themselves a purely Turanian race and therefore superior to the Christians across the Bosporus.

The thing that favored the Turks in their advance upon Constantinople was the same decadence that the Spaniards found among their antagonists. After the Venetian victory, Constantinople and the Greek empire were as thoroughly weakened as the remnants of the Arabs in Spain were worn out. Both Byzantines and Moors fell before younger nations after an amazingly long flowering. Strong young organisms, active for only a century, overcame wise old ones with eight and eleven centuries behind them. In national struggles, as in boxing, it is not race but youthful vigor that decides the victory.

We have only to look at the heads of the last emperors of Constantinople and compare them with those of the first Turks or Serbs, who were then establishing great realms around Constantinople. We have only to read of the coronation festival of the last Paleologus, in which the dining went on with unbroken solemnity during the ancient ceremonies (but on earthen plates, for there was no silver left), while Dusha, king of the Serbs, had himself crowned in barbaric pomp amid crashing uproar, or glance at the Croatian heads that were carved about then on the cathedral façade of Sebenico; they look like the Bolshevik leaders of our day.

The Osmanli Turks, whose capital had been in Europe since 1365, had long lived in false amity with Constantinople, encircling the ever-shrinking empire and letting it wonder and tremble, like Odysseus with his comrades at sight of Polyphemus, uncertain which would be devoured next. Half allies and half conspirators, the Turks through several generations learned much of the worldly wisdom, the court intrigues, and the murders of the Byzantines; they made marriages with them, gave them military assistance, and all the time kept waiting for the moment to knife them. This the Byzantines knew, and they simply made the best of their reprieve.

In tumultuous struggles whose ebb and flow cannot concern us here, the fortunes of war between Turks, Serbs, and Hungarians and also between Seljuks, Osmanlis, and Mongols, shifted into Asia Minor and the Balkans and as far away as the environs of Vienna. None of these wars brought a clear division between Mohammedans and Christians, but every atrocity was justified on the alleged ground of the religious struggle. The cruelty of the Mohammedans increased, in contrast to their attitude during the crusades. By the fifteenth century Islam had none of its twelfth century tolerance left. Faced with dreadful warfare, the council of Constance absolved every Christian from keeping his word to an infidel—a very natural and very dangerous measure, which was bound to shake the foundations of Christian morality.

And yet there could be no crusade; the mood for it had long since evaporated. A hard, cynical craving for the enjoyment of life and power at any price seemed to contemporaries a sign that the age later known as the Middle Ages was over.

In the shape of business acumen, this unmorality was most pronounced among the Venetians. In eighty years they concluded nine treaties of friendship with the Turks for privileges that would make their commerce independent in shipping, right of domicile, and courts of law. Once, in alliance with Constantinople and Hungary, they beat the Turks. But they immediately parted with their Christian allies to avoid provoking the Turks further. Doge Mocenigo uttered in the senate words that might have been heard as late as 1938 in the British House of Commons: "Peace is better business. If we keep quiet, we shall make good matters better and become the lords of money and of Christendom. The world will fear our wealth, and God will be with us!" These great traders were so hard-headed that they even declined Emperor Manuel's offer of Constantinople, since the city was in danger and was sure to be an unprofitable property.

The masters of Constantinople, in turn, acutely sensing their early downfall, were now even ready to unite with the competing Christian church for the sake of Catholic arms. In this twilight of the gods, Cardinal Bessarion, a Greek, actually formally united Plato, Aristotle, and the two sects with Christianity. But this was dishonest and unsound, and the ostentatious brotherhood of the Council of Florence in 1439 abounded in false notes. The monks of Mount Athos also sensed the coming hurricane and put the venerable monastery under the protection of the sultan.

Mohammed II made short work of things in the end. Having just ascended the throne at the age of twenty-one, like a new pharaoh he gathered an enormous number of workmen and had them build, supposedly in forty days, the tremendous fortifications on the Bosporus whose remains today enhance the romantic charm of the landscape. Then came the siege of Constantinople, which put up a truly heroic resistance for thirty long days. The evening before the last assault, emperor, priests, and people assembled in the church of Saint Sophia for a farewell that was like a state funeral. Here the decayed, corrupt, wretched nation rose at a blow to the death-defying splendor of ancient legend. Next day the last Byzantine emperor fell, sword in hand, a noble example for the world.

Mohammed, who had led the fight in person, marched into the metropolis so enviously desired by his fathers. In the arena he paused to display his strength to the assembled multitude by shattering with his axe one of the three bronze serpents that had supported the golden tripod of Delphi two thousand years before and had adorned this public square through a millennium. Reining in his horse at the gate of the palace, where but yesterday the emperor had lived, he recited the verses of the Persian poet Firdausi: "The spider is doorkeeper in the Emperor's hall, and the owl raises the battle cry in Alfrasiab's palace." Traditional civilization and barbarism were near neighbors in the soul of this Eastern ruler who smashed a bit of civilization to show off his strength.

Next day in that same Saint Sophia's, in the year 1453, the sultan

held a great celebration in honor of his god, whom he called Allah
and whose house he called a mosque. The barbarian in him got the
upper hand, for he galloped into the church on horseback and
stormed the altar.

XI

THE IMPRESSION ON EUROPE was catastrophic. Barbarian infidels
establishing a second world empire! Venice was no longer strong
enough to withstand Turkey; she was concerned to save her colonies only, not Western civilization. Two and a half centuries earlier
the Venetians had overthrown the world power of Constantinople.
The successors of the power Venice herself had reduced to a petty
state had now received Venetian help, though it was but feeble,
against the Turks. So the Venetians sent Mohammed a document
after his victory, humbly asking him to forgive their aid to the
enemy. And they dispatched their greatest painter to Constantinople
to portray the new tyrant. To this we owe the marvelous half-length
portrait of Mohammed from the hand of Bellini, showing him
under an Arabic arch, almost in full profile, with a long, pale nose,
little black beard, thin, dangerous mouth, and a great white turban
that may have been more exciting to a painter's eye than the new
world power.

Even so, Mohammed would probably have conquered Italy.
Swiftly he took the whole Balkan peninsula and was soon threatening Venice from her own shore. She surrendered to him parts of
Albania and even Euboea and territories near Sparta and promised
tribute and levies if only he would have the personal kindness to
tolerate Venetian trade in the Levant. Neither the Pope nor the
emperor rose up when Mohammed (the first infidel to do so)
crossed the Adriatic and landed at Otranto. Nothing but his immediate death saved Italy.

It was at this time, about 1500, that the great European hatred
of Islam began. Tales of atrocities at the fall of Constantinople and
the contemptuous treatment of Western ambassadors by later sultans started the defamation of the Turks that lasted down to the

A GREAT MIXTURE OF RACES

First World War. Yet the Occident did not exploit the Turks' predicament when they were hard-pressed by their coreligionists the Mamelukes in Asia Minor. On the contrary they remained on excellent terms. The Sheik ul Islam, a sort of Mohammedan pope, allowed the Greek patriarch to perform his offices and let the subject Balkan peoples worship the Madonna according to their custom.

But the deeper reason for discord lay in the spirit of the Renaissance. Its holy places were not at Jerusalem now but at Athens.

Even a brief sketch of Greek history between 1000 and 1500 gives a strange and colorful picture, an ironic insight into the forces that animated the later medieval Mediterranean. It seemed as if the stronghold of the old gods attracted the Christian knights who despised it. The great light of wisdom and beauty still lighted up the faces of its most distant heirs in the long afterglow.

When the Vikings came from the foggy northern seas to the blue Mediterranean about A.D. 1040, an emperor of Constantinople sent Harold, a prince in his service, to Athens. All names there had once ended in *as* and *es*. Now there were new sounds; the knights of Athens were named Snorrison, Haakon, Ospäkson, or perhaps Thord or Ivar. They now subjugated the Athenians under the pretext that the latter had had dealings with the invading Bulgarians.

These sons of the north mingled passionately with the Oriental women, who apparently had everything their own women lacked and certainly understood more of love. Fair Helen made a last appearance; Manuel Comnenus, a Greek nobleman risen to be emperor of Constantinople, married the most beautiful woman in Greece, a daughter of Princess Constanza of Antioch and Count Raimund of Poitiers. Those romantic names alone would have sufficed to indicate her mixed blood. A Count of Tripoli, whose sister Melisande was originally supposed to marry the Emperor, arrived in the Aegean with twelve warships to take his revenge by murder and rapine, as in Trojan days.

The romances abound with passions that were played out in convents or that began with abductions, while the monks of Mount Athos wrote clerical poems. Learned Jews shared in the hybrid Greek civilization of the day. Few of them were merchants; many were silk weavers and dyers; some were celebrated medical men such as the personal physicians of the above-mentioned Emperor Manuel.

The two conquests of Constantinople, in 1204 by the Franks and in 1453 by the Turks, cast light and shadow upon Greek history. Athens and Sparta were provincial towns, and the islands were provinces of the empire, almost all reluctant. They never quite outgrew the sulkiness of a subject people. Thus the Christian rule of the crusaders had effects quite different from those of the Mohammedan sway.

The Mediterranean perhaps never saw more interesting mixtures of races than about A.D. 1000 in Sicily and from the thirteenth to the fifteenth century in Greece. What adventurers, mostly from the West, thronged this tiny space! They all found a much older blend of peoples ahead of them: Armenians had settled here as early as the fourth century; gypsies (whose fathers came from the Indus), in the seventh; and then there were the oft-persecuted Jews. To this day there are abandoned Hebrew and gypsy strongholds in Greece.

Next came conquering Serbs and Rumanians from the north, Catalan soldiers from the west, and above all, French knights, fighting one another in their turn. These Western feudal lords fought both the Roman Church and a Constantinople always anxious for reconquest. They had grand titles and little power, and they fought over classic soil in a way that gives to that segment of history the glamour of romantic opera.

An emperor of Trebizond appeared on the scene; a queen of Georgia; an admiral who established his realm at Rhodes; an archon who ruled in Philadelphia; a count of Blois who made himself duke of Nicaea; a Roman general who strove for the Byzantine throne; Venetians in search of new Aegean islands and ports; Provençal grandees who fortified Thermopylae. There were even Greek philosophers joining German knights in the crusades at the period when young Dante was under arms.

Genoa was still fighting Venice, this time in a ten years' naval war over Corfu and Crete. After winning in Crete, Venice distributed several hundred "fiefs" to noblemen and burgesses. In the process some of the Venetian knights became peasants and herdsmen, some of them merchants and pirates. All alike were decked with stupendous titles.

A rich Frankish adventurer with a host of hired knights and a few galleys seized the moment of complete anarchy in the struggle between Genoese and Corsairs to conquer seventeen rich islands, among them Naxos, the queen of the Cyclades. He styled himself duke, built a fortress on the foundations of the ancient temple, ascended a most uncertain throne as Marco I, and even took Smyrna. He gave islands in fee to his knights, and suddenly the archipelago was alive with strangers. The new duke in his turn did homage to the German-Byzantine emperor Henry, who invested him with the "Duchy of the Dodecanese." War followed between emperor and duke. The duke was beaten, but his fine looks and majestic bearing made such an impression that the emperor contented himself with Smyrna and even gave the adventurer one of his nieces to wife.

The reader who skims through such tales of an evening may feel that these people went out to battle simply to supply true material for yarns of adventure; and yet their passions must have gone deep. Since this oldest of civilized territory was virtually without a master and the crusades had thrown it into turmoil, medieval Greece produced no history; it produced stories worthy of the *Decameron*. They actually were the treasure trove of a hundred armchair romancers.

The French chevalier Villehardouin, perhaps the most dazzling Mediterranean figure of his time, followed the fashion of his native Champagne in introducing baronies to the Peloponnesians. Picturesquely somber castles were built on rocks in the sea and on mountains inland; their remains still delight the traveler. Yet for the observer it all borders on comedy, on prestidigitation. A knight from Languedoc became lord of Patras. A gentleman from Charpigny used the Greek form of his name. And a third called his castle Mata Grifon, "Strike the Greeks dead!" Each baron would bestow half a dozen knightly fiefs; the new-made lords, who had perhaps left for the Holy Land with no property but their swords and who even now owned only a couple of hundred goats, would begin within a score of years to talk about augmenting the power of their houses.

They could sell anything. A Byzantine emperor or regent, hard-pressed by a rival, pledged Christ's crown of thorns to get money from the Venetians. When he could not redeem it, Louis of France bought it.

In those days the great school of the French nobility was not on the Rhone and the Seine but in the peninsula of Morea, as the Peloponnesus was now called. A certain Godfrey always kept "eighty knights with golden spurs" at his court there. This prince of Morea (more powerful than the shadow emperor at Constantinople) coined his own money; so did his brother and others. At the same time such a system of credit developed that no traveler through these robber-infested woods and mountains needed to carry silver in his pockets. He could get a check cashed by the castellan of the nearest castle, signed and sealed A.D. 1300 in the wild mountains of southern Greece.

They delighted in the ancient legends and names of the places they ruled, and they had the taste to restore Olympia. Where Hercules had won his first victories they held tourneys, which they got bards to sing of—their form of advertising—in the Occident. A certain powerful Otto de la Roche, ensconced as lord of the old fortress of Cadmus at Thebes, fought side by side with Venice against a rival from home. Then, growing old, he turned over his land and castle to some nephews and ordered all his sons to follow him. He went back to France in a galley, escorted by the members of his house, like a Swiss grown rich in America, returning to his canton to show off his wealth to the stay-at-homes.

Then there was a grotesque interlude provoked by one of the German knights, notorious for their barbarism. A certain Walter Liedekerke fell upon the powerful Greek Pothios, on his travels through Corinth, and would not let him go except for a heavy ransom. The Greek refused, and his teeth were knocked out. When he decided to pay, he was released. But he plotted revenge. He and his men lay in wait for his tormentors in a pass south of the Gulf of Corinth. A French knight voyaging through the gulf with his men in high good humor put ashore and fell to picnicking with his companions—that is, carousing. The Greek, slowly stalking his quarry, mistook him for the German Walter and struck him over the head with his sword. He learned the truth, regretted it, bemoaned it. But the following day the Frenchman was dead, and the day after that a new war between Greeks and Franks began. About five hundred years later, Goethe in the second part of *Faust* gives a symbolic interpretation of all this operatic theater.

For one moment during that war the Greeks recaptured their country. It is worth noting that a Platonic philosopher had cleared the way, though quite indirectly.

Georgius Gemistus (or Pletho), who flourished around 1420, took his doctrine of pagan idealism to Cosmo de' Medici in order to found the Neoplatonic Academy at Florence. He was thus a sort of successor to Plato, who had once carried the same ideas from the same Greece to Sicily. This passionate patriot, hoping to rescue his brutalized people from foreign domination, preached a communistic republic that drew upon Plato's theory of the state and the constitution of Lycurgus; and he did it from a point close to Sparta, Lycurgus' own city. He proposed to have all land simply leased out by a state that owned everything; there was to be no private ownership of land; barter instead of money. The princes honored him and did nothing about his proposals. But the last Palaeologus succeeded in driving out the Franks—that is, the Western foreigners. For some twenty years Greece was independent again.

But it was too late to revive the nation: like the Byzantines themselves and the Spanish Moors, it had flowered and gone by, and fallen into younger and firmer hands. Immediately after the fall of Constantinople, Greece also became Turkish, to remain so for almost four hundred years. The Greeks became taxpayers and soldiers for a foreign sultan whose religion was not their own.

But Mohammed II had an inspiration born of statesmanlike guile or old Mohammedan tolerance or perhaps both. He allowed the Greeks to be governed by their own clergy, and appointed a celebrated monk as Greek patriarch. The Greeks were the more grateful, because shortly before the conquest the last patriarch of Constantinople had fled to the Roman Pope, whom they hated. Though Mohammed reserved to his throne the right of confirming the Greek primate, he gave the church complete independence. A learned monk of Athos expressed thanks in an extravagant biography of Mohammed, which he made worthless by sending it to the subject for inspection beforehand. The Mohammedan conqueror, then, understood how to get along with the Christians, though he did not really know them at first hand.

In besieging Corinth and blasting it to pieces he seemed simply to be copying the Romans, who had laid waste that countryside thirteen centuries before. But the infidel stopped short of the Acropolis at Athens, quite surprisingly, because he was impressed by its temples.

Here again we see a half barbarian in the style of Alexander the Great—here as well as at the reduction of Constantinople. For he at once installed Turkish barracks in the temple and put a harem for the commander in the Erechtheum, so that the caryatids supporting the roof took on an ironic meaning. It was not until later that new revolts and conspiracies led him to snatch from the Athenians the Christian cult that had been cherished in the Parthenon for just ten centuries. The sultan turned it into a mosque and set up a chancel where first Athena and then Mary had been deified. At the southwest corner he built a slender minaret from which a praying Islamite shouted the name of Allah afar three times a day.

It was the same worship of a single God that Plato had preached just after Pericles had set up the immortal columns. It was the same one God whom the apostles had worshiped above the other two gods of the Trinity. Each had possessed the hearts of the Athenians for exactly a thousand years. The muezzin now saw the sun set every evening across the same bay, between Salamis and Aegina. If he looked to the right from his little round balcony, the same double line of Pentelic marble columns rose above the Mediterranean. Untouched as yet by all the conquerors of Athens, the loveliest temple that human hands ever dedicated to the Unknown God still kept watch on the hill.

XII

ABOUT THIS TIME THE GREEK SPIRIT, which had never slumbered, awoke to new and fiery life. The Renaissance dawned.

What is the secret of the Renaissance? Why, two thousand years after the Greeks, did it bring the second climax in the life of the Mediterranean? Was it the triumph of a great people? The victorious rebellion of an oppressed class? The dawn of a fruitful peace? The appearance of a new apostle? What was it that made the period around 1500 stand out from the steady stream of history? Was it liberty sweeping through Europe, faith, brotherhood?

It was none of these. Countries changed rulers no less often than ever. Classes were not shaken up by revolution. The religions fought each other as they had before and did afterward. Navigation produced no new machinery. The mechanics of everyday existence remained the same.

The new factor was an increased sense of life. The chariot of fortune stood at every door, inviting those who came out to seize the reins and drive off. Today was god of the age; activity, insight, art were the goddesses. The man of the Renaissance, who loved life and did not fear death, had the spirit to challenge fate. In discovering personality, the Renaissance found a new ethics.

By endless compromises the Christian religion of renunciation and suffering had tried to make terms with man's natural instinct for health and happiness. Ever since the last Greek statue of a god in a Mediterranean temple had been overthrown or smashed in religious frenzy, people had constantly been taught of a hereafter to which they would go from this earthly vale of tears. For a thousand years that doctrine had held men captive to a hidden future. And at the same time it had consoled millions who felt themselves discriminated against in this life. But it was only seldom, as in the first crusades, that that faith had become active, allowing normal human effort in this life.

The great personalities that kept on making headway from the decline of antiquity till the Renaissance did so with a guilty conscience. They were constantly being held back by those weaker than they with the help of a philosophy that the state preached and supported, though as a temporal power the state constantly defied the philosophy. For the devout Christian more than anyone else, the contradictions running through the Christian Middle Ages destroyed the kind of harmony the Mohammedan had; his religion deified war and strength as well as the one god, and it did not make everlasting life and paradise depend on a life of misery here. These false notes were bound to be more conspicuous in the south than in the misty north. Cold and rigor were the natural northern surroundings, whereas sun and blue sky, fruits and wine filled every Mediterranean life. Every shore and island still had the shadows of the ancient gods, whose like had never been seen beyond the Alps.

The Renaissance was not due to the mere discovery of a few dozen statues. In the earth, in rivers, or in the sea these statues had slept away the Christian Middle Ages; now they awoke to an unknown world and brought new splendor to mankind. It was like a confirmation of their vital force, which had now set men on the trail of the Greeks and led them to the statues. It was nature that the artists admired in them; they copied the Apollo Belvedere, the torso of Hercules, the Venus of the Vatican (these were among the earliest to be found) for the sake of their nakedness. For a time artists preferred bronze to living models.

French Gothic, which had never been at home in the south, was transformed in the churches with incredible speed by these men of the new spirit. The buildings began to spread out; the façades widened; the columns became elements of horizontal articulation. Many of the façades we see in the modern world, even entrances of banks in New York, come from the Renaissance, which got them from the Greeks.

But it was not the statues and the domes alone that had influ-

ence; it was the return to the wisdom of the Greeks, to their sense
of life. The saints were not suddenly displaced in favor of gods.
Nothing was cast aside at all except the glorification of pain. Plato,
whom the leading minds put in place of Christ, had, in fact, been
recognized as a monotheist himself. And Lorenzo de' Medici wrote
that the world was no mere prelude. It had been created by God's
love: He had never ceased to be its Creator, and in Him the soul
could grow into infinity.

This was the beginning of a frank desire for earthly happiness,
earthly love, earthly glory. The ancient gods, found and copied
everywhere, were not set up and worshiped; yet their spirit ruled
the Mediterranean from which they sprang—Italy above all. The
supposed humility of the crusader was no longer an ideal; pride
took its place. If the Middle Ages were like an endless autumn, the
Renaissance was a blazing summer. Neither Jesus nor Apollo was
glorified; only man was worshiped. But the fame of the ancients
became the example of the moderns. People seized upon Plutarch
in order to search out the secrets of the great characters in history.
The young Romans of 1500 wore modern arms and doublets, but
they talked like Brutus and Cicero, whom they quoted in Latin,
or like Plato, whom they cited in Greek. To fight and talk, to handle arguments and the sword with equal brilliance was the ideal
of the younger generation, and not of the nobility alone. "Riding
and reclining, this is the life I love," said Cesare Borgia.

Great talents were springing from all classes—and this in an
age that knew no popular education. The bastard, formerly despised, now had excellent opportunities, for his very origin made
him interesting to a world in ferment. The self-made man was also
favored, and even the nobility had their place. At the courts of
princes, men of vigor and intellect now vied with women of beauty
and intellect; they had given up languishing and jousting for the
dainty colors of some fair lady at ceremonious tourneys. Creative
minds of all classes met at the rural seats of ambitious countrymen.
And yet people seem not to have made themselves ridiculous in
their imitation of ancient greatness. This was not a masked procession but an attitude aimed at developing mind and body alike.

That which was expanded much later as the ideal of the English
gentleman was tried out here far more brilliantly, because women
had a share in it.

The position of women in the Renaissance was something new.
What women gained around 1500 was as much of a revolution as
the one by which they have transformed the society of the last thirty
years. Only the young girls, who led a life of tedium in convents
until marriage released them, had no share in events.

The women were riders, huntresses, students of Plato, models
of the great painters, and mistresses of the *condottieri,* then at the
height of their power and fashion. The family was safeguarded,
even if fidelity was not; but for the first time in history one could
ask a divorce without being ostracized. Women seldom bestowed
their favors according to wealth; sometimes they went by rank;
but the looks, manliness, and courage of their suitors were what
really counted—roughly, what we think of today as sporting
prowess. The great hetaera had never before occupied such a dominant position, not even in ancient Athens. The sonnets and romances linking the celebrated Imperia with one of the Popes
depicted her not ironically but admiringly.

In this mood Christian virtues were not derided, but they paled
quite naturally. Revenge—a pagan passion, not a Christian virtue—
took the place of repentance. Since inner assurance was expected
of both men and women, no one needed salvation, either through
his priest or through Christ. The forms of baptism, marriage, and
burial were maintained—but, so to speak, in the absence of the Holy
Ghost. Holy women like Catherine of Siena were highly regarded
for their social usefulness, and they went among the people like
suffragettes. The virago, the warrior maiden, was rare. Women experienced in love who had mastered manly arts were oftener seen.
Duchess Catherine Sforza inspected her soldiers daily in the public
square. Once somebody shouted at her that her lust for power would
be visited upon her children. She shouted back: "All right, then
I will bring new ones into the world!" Such words as these encouraged a whole generation of young women to live for their
passions.

This worship of the body, of skill, of records reminds us of certain modern American ideals. If there had been weekly magazines in Florence as there are in New York, many of the pictures would have looked much the same, except that the subjects would have been less smiling. Of the long series of magnificent portraits that show us Renaissance men and women, celebrities, or popular types, only one, the Mona Lisa, is smiling; and she is smiling entirely to herself.

So dazzling a vitality could not be sustained without shadows, which were darker than in the romantic age preceding. Revenge begot murder, ambition fed the never-ending wars among princes and republics, and the general admiration of adventurers mixed all classes helter-skelter. Power, falling not to the treacherous conspirator, as in Constantinople, but to the bravest and most skillful, was universally desired. Unknowns often attained it. Whatever a man had omitted to learn in his proletarian youth he quickly acquired by reading Castiglione's *Book of the Courtier,* which could teach anyone the bearing of a nobleman and therefore became the most celebrated book of its time. Women learned about etiquette and style from Firenzuola's book on the *Beauty of Women,* which restored ancient ideals and demanded for the first time since the Greeks a broad breast instead of delicately sloping shoulders.

What everyone strove for as the summit of existence was not the virtues of devotion, fidelity, gratitude; it was, above all, health and beauty. He who possessed these might dispense for a time with liberty itself. Handsome men and beautiful women could find a liberator even from prison. But there was no similarity to the dissolute pleasures, the orgies, and stupid amusements of the Roman Empire, whose three centuries had produced no art and little science. Art and science were what shaped and to some extent ruled the world about 1500 in a way that no nation had known since the Greeks.

If we hesitate to call the people of the time in Italy the equals of the ancient Greeks, that is not because the age was a fleeting one or because the level of the arts was inferior. The arts we may submit confidently to comparison. Never before or since have so many

creative personalities lived at one time as under Pericles and under
Leo X. Both eras were equally brief. Everything was compressed
into about forty years. To stretch it, we may call the fifth century
B.C. in one case and the period from 1450 to 1550 in the other the
Golden Age.

We have during the Renaissance in Italy the phenomenon of
many geniuses appearing in one generation—more than the age of
Augustus or Justinian or the Sun King or Elizabeth or Philip or
Napoleon can boast. The sound of the names alone is enough to
fill anyone's soul with a longing to have lived then.

They almost all lived at the same time: the sculptors from Verrocchio to Michelangelo; the thinkers and poets, from Tasso and
Ariosto to Mirandola and Machiavelli; the painters, from Botticelli
and Ghirlandaio to Piero della Francesca, from the Bellinis to
Giorgione and Titian, from Perugino to Raphael, from Correggio
to Leonardo and Luini; the architects, from Brunelleschi to Bramante; the three great Popes, in succession, Alexander, Julius, and
Leo; the *condottieri,* from Cesare Borgia to Colleoni; the kings,
from Ferdinand to Mohammed; the discoverers, from Vasco da
Gama to Columbus.

And a hundred minds of similar genius rose within the walls
of the Italian cities, forming an assemblage such as the Mediterranean had seen but once, when Pericles was building the Parthenon—just a thousand years before the Medicis. Resembling each
other in beauty and lavishness, both ages were full of ingratitude,
crime, partisanship, and revenge. Yet precisely because they were
nothing like paradise the sight of them enchants posterity even now.

Still there is a hidden difference between the unmoral foundations of the two eras. The Greek age before Plato, in particular,
was the more naïve; the Renaissance was the more cynical. To bring
back the gaiety of the thronging gods, people had to lay aside something the Greeks had not yet possessed. This is nowhere plainer
than in the writings of Machiavelli, whose state morality was based
on a rejection of everything he himself had been taught as a child.
His admiration of Cesare Borgia is a covert diatribe against the
moralists who would allow no sons for the Pope and no conspira-

cies for a duke brought up in the Vatican. This lack of naïveté is the very thing that makes Machiavelli such an exquisite analyst. But his unmorality is as different from that of Homer as Michelangelo's figure of Night on the Florentine tomb is different from the sleeping Medusa of the Greeks.

For the man of the Renaissance resembles in only one way the ancient whom he rediscovered; otherwise he is completely modern, more akin to our age than the men who lived between him and us. The Renaissance was individualistic to a degree, and it has no elements in common with democracy except love of liberty. Liberty in the two ages is sought through quite different channels for different groups of people. The Reformation, the other form of rebellion against the Middle Ages, brings out the double face of the Renaissance.

The statues rose from the old soil in the south on the Mediterranean, and seemed to stretch their marble and bronze limbs after long sleep. Naked or in superbly draped garments, Diana and Apollo rose again, Hera and Zeus, Poseidon and Demeter, Tritons and Nereids, fauns and nymphs; all awoke to a new sun that was recognizable as the sun of Homer. Artists and laymen, princes and collectors rushed to build them costly pedestals, forgiving them a missing arm, foot, or even a head.

But at the same time the Christian insurgent from the north kept his eyes fixed on the sins of the Popes. One Pope had his mistress painted on the wall of the Vatican and made her brother a cardinal and his son a duke, while he arranged three political marriages for his beautiful daughter Lucrezia Borgia. Luther was in Rome at the time, and it is significant that in the full splendor of the new day he saw only the vices and none of the glory.

The two world movements rose simultaneously to implacable antagonism—unmoral and moral regeneration, sensuality and spirituality, diffusion and contemplation, activity and prayer: Renaissance and Reformation.

Of course, there were men of the Renaissance in the fifteenth century north and fanatics in the south. The greatest of the former was Erasmus; of the latter, Savonarola. Both faced their adversaries,

and settled with them in their own ways. They stood exposed to
the gusty winds of their time, and occasionally the cloak would
fly open, allowing quite similar mortal bodies to be seen. For they
resembled each other in one point: they were aiming at strength
in personality. No wonder Savonarola strutted with his processions
of penitents quite as proudly as Machiavelli's heroes did in their
parades. There was an equal element of histrionics in both, and
fame was their highest ambition. With all his tolerance, Erasmus
turned his back on Luther because the man's lay fanaticism was
more repugnant to him than the naughtiness of Pope Leo, whose
life was devoted to beauty and culture. Machiavelli, with all his unmorality, was an apostle of Moses and Theseus, the great ethical
state builders. He allowed neither amusements nor leisure to the
princes he instructed.

In fact, we must not regard Machiavelli's *The Prince,* which has
filled the minds of later centuries and even of modern potentates,
as the bible of the Renaissance. Few people were familiar with it
then, and very few needed it. Machiavelli taught nothing that antiquity had not long since tried out; only the Middle Ages with
their *civitas dei* had lost it. The solitary innovation was his cynical
rejection of Christian morality. In later centuries this fed the desires
of power-seeking readers. Actually great princes, before and since
Machiavelli's time, have always lived according to his doctrines.
Only they have sedulously avoided saying so.

The Renaissance uttered truths that dwelt in every heart. The
mood of these emancipated spirits was so intense that even the high
clergy chose none but freethinkers as Popes. The two pious,
somber men who occupied the throne in intervals between the three
great Renaissance Popes died after very short pontificates. Amid
this lavish life antiquity seemed like the reappearance of some comet
that old chronicles said one's forefathers had seen; it was recognized now as the guide of bold sailors on mighty seas. After Machiavelli's death people told how saints from paradise and men of
antiquity from hell had appeared to him. Upon God's asking
whither he would go, he was said to have replied, "Better to argue

politics with great minds in Hell than to be bored in Paradise with such poor wretches!"

Among the Renaissance leaders we seldom find physically large heads; usually they are thin, with big noses and voluptuous mouths. Everything about Machiavelli was sharp and delicate; even his mouth was tight. Alexander VI, the Spaniard, had nothing Spanish about him but his son, and the head of Leo X, the Medici, is heavy in a way that rather recalls his ancestor Cosmo. Julius II, altogether the warlike prince in Raphael's portrait, shows very little of the spirit appropriate to a scholar and art collector.

These men had the good fortune to be immortalized by the greatest portraitists of all time. It was not undeserved; they and their forefathers as patrons had developed these talents and by their commissions had cleared the road for them. If Michelangelo went unpaid and Bramante was cheated, if Raphael, the son of fortune himself, had to dun the great for his money, still it did not really matter. Money did not hypnotize the artists or the princes, or even the enterprisers of the period. Why money was not worshiped in so worldly an age is one of the secrets of the Renaissance; that is the greatest difference between that period and our own day, in so far as we cherish Renaissance ideals. Yet the artists' standard of living was much more pretentious than in earlier times. The Renaissance rediscovered beauty among the Greeks, and the artist became its hidden monarch. Everybody craved honor and glory, so women were not the only ones willing to spend time and money to perpetuate their beauty.

Here, as in classical Athens, art and the intellect became dominant; feeling for them was what produced the immortal results —not because a few individual artists chanced to drop from heaven but because the world wanted them and cherished them.

The Renaissance was the only time after the Greeks when persons distinguished by talent and authority were expected to make their own lives a work of art, to present a spectacle to their contemporaries and an example to posterity. Every great action or accomplishment was done with an eye to eternity; but this eternity was not the Christian heaven. In that emotionally pagan era the build-

ing of Saint Peter's stirred the soul of the world far more deeply than the French conquest and loss of the kingdom of Naples. The one was a work of art and a symbol; the other a mere temporary accident. Evidently people even then could feel that we, five hundred years afterward, would care nothing for Anjou and Naples but everything for Saint Peter's.

And were not the artists in this their time of flowering quite right to change sides so long as somebody was there who would give their genius a chance to unfold? Almost all of them abandoned any master or patron who lost his power and ability to finance the artists' creative efforts. "Good fortune," Machiavelli wrote, "is the ability to see things as they are." Although his eye was sharper than anyone's, he was almost always unlucky. Whereas antiquity had spoken of envious gods and urged the fortunate to make thank offerings, everyone now was snatching whatever victory, wisdom, and success might bring him. Superstitious astrological interrogations of fate were rather an afterthought.

Along with the triumphant artist, the victorious general was the lord of his time—the general, but not the born prince. Not the victor in the protracted struggles of the great powers but the mercenary captain who won many short fights and was forever in the pay of some new employer. He could change masters the more easily because they all shared in a common civilization; they were not fighting for religion or principles. Again it was the artists who carried these men to greatness. Caesar without busts and even without Shakespeare would probably still be Caesar. But who outside of Italy would ever have heard the bare name of Gattamelata or Colleoni without the monuments?

None of the leaders in war fought famous battles: they were simply war contractors who hired out their troops to the highest bidder, dealers in the fortunes of war. Thanks to his splendid build Colleoni, an impoverished nobleman, became the lover of a queen. This gained him a patron, and then he was enlisted by the Visconti in Milan against Venice. He was put in prison by these same Visconti, escaped, mediated between the antagonists, and was rewarded with great estates. In his old age he lived like a prince at Venice as an instructor of young officers and a host to great lords. His will contained a bequest, which still exists, for the dowering of poor girls at Bergamo. Of all this, posterity would know nothing unless Verrocchio had erected to him the most beautiful of all equestrian monuments near the abrupt wall of a church in Venice.

The Visconti themselves, adventurers, starting with the archbishopric and seizing absolute power over the city of Milan, extended their sway through favoring fortune into a mighty duchy. Though invested with titles and rights, they are immortal only

because they began one of the world's wonders, Milan Cathedral.
The creator of such a work stands unapproached, like the founder
of a state. Though Milan Cathedral continued to develop for four
centuries, not unlike the Roman Empire, still Caesar and the Visconti were the first to dream of the two creations on a great scale.
The cathedral, like the empire, had good architecture and bad, with
many mixed styles. The pink marble structure gleaming in the sun
sometimes looks like the dream of a pastry cook getting his fill of
turrets, peaks and curlicues. Inside, however, it will remain for
all time the loveliest of temples. One seems to be entering a shadowy
forest of trees whose trunks rise at regular intervals, nobly parallel,
with the crowns spreading and touching overhead. The glowing
colors of the windows cast the same mystic aura that prevails in the
cathedral at Chartres. It makes this marble forest a place of inner
contemplation, whose equal is not to be found in Saint Peter's, not
in Seville, not in Istanbul. Whereas high walls shut off the naves
of the cathedrals of Strasbourg and Notre Dame here no structure
or ornament, no pictures or banners, bar the view anywhere in the
grove of fifty-two giant trees. After the bewildering profusion of
the exterior comes the noble simplicity of the interior. He who does
not find God in this twilight forest must be forsaken indeed.

True enough, all these adventurers, like the Visconti, had a concept of the state, and Pope Julius II spurred them on for some years
with the cry, *"Fuori i barbari!"* Italian national sentiment and the
new league with Spain and Venice, founded by the Pope, was actually victorious over the German and French kings in the end. But
the succeeding council could not establish a united Italy, and there
was another 350 years to wait.

Neither national nor religious ideals excited the men of the
Renaissance in a decisive manner. It was not important whether a
man called himself a Guelph or a Ghibelline, whether Ferrara allied
itself with Florence, whether the Swiss or the Romagnoli protected
the papal state, not even whether the sultan worked off his excess
energy in the Mediterranean. These facts, though they fill many
modern history books, are still less interesting to us. In quite another

way the era has given us deathless models for daily conduct, sign-posts to the art of living.

It was Pico della Mirandola, mystic and friend of Lorenzo de' Medici, who summed up the beliefs of the age in his discourse on the dignity of man. He had God say to Adam: "I have put you in the middle of the world so that you may more easily look about you, and see everything in it. I created you as a being neither mortal nor immortal, simply that you might shape and conquer yourself. You can rise to be a godlike being. Animals bring what they need with them from the womb; but almost from the beginning, the higher creatures are what they will remain into eternity. You alone can develop according to your own free will."

XIII

HE WHO EXPECTS to see the spirit of the Renaissance summed up in some one figure such as Pericles, Augustus, Justinian, or Frederick II will be disappointed. Lorenzo de' Medici was one luminary, but he and his court were the spring before the summer; the Renaissance began at his death. Alexander VI was a bit of a barbarian after all. Pope Leo X was a focal point and patron of the arts; so were Julius II and Ferdinand I as statesmen, Ludovico Sforza as a brilliant adventurer, Cesare Borgia as an intellectual general, Machiavelli as the philosopher of the era, Titian as the richest among the artists, Michelangelo as the most versatile.

Michelangelo, portrayed elsewhere by the present writer, was in reality nothing but a sculptor after all. Even as a painter he chiseled his statues, and as an architect he carved the dome of Saint Peter's. In the latter case the technique was advantageous; in the former, sometimes harmful, for we have to translate each figure on the ceiling of the Sistine Chapel from an imagined marble of three dimensions to the painted reality of two. Only when he wrote poetry was Michelangelo altogether a painter.

Anyone who would limit him to the theme of love through his depiction of youths cannot be acquainted with the painted Eve in the Sistine Chapel or the sculptured Night and Dusk on the grave of the Medici in Florence, whose feminine beauty is without peer. No one after the time of the Greeks ever excelled him in the perfection of his skill with marble. As he was rambling through the mountains near Carrara, he saw a certain figure in a marble block, and he had the very rock quarried into which he had dreamed his statue.

But the greatest symbol of the Renaissance was Leonardo da Vinci; for universality he had no peer. All the creative forces that the Popes gathered around them Leonardo combined in himself. The engineering skill of the artists, which Michelangelo himself developed out of painting by way of statuary into a cathedral dome, was only part of Leonardo's work. The world called him a painter; he liked to call himself an inventor. In reality he was a physicist of the stature of Galileo; a mathematician like Pythagoras; an astronomer like Copernicus; a military engineer like Archimedes; and a mechanical genius like Edison.

He constructed mortars, pontoons, and mine galleries for the duke of Milan and built the first tanks—tortoiselike machines with double decks, with horses inside and loopholes in the armor. He laid out the sewer system of Florence, invented modern fireplaces, self-closing doors, spits turned by the hot air from the fire. His sketches for canalizing the Ticino, the Arno, and the Saône were carried out three or four hundred years later on almost identical plans. He made drawings for the first diving apparatus, flying machines, parachutes, submarines, steam cannon; he compounded gunpowder, built a glass furnace and a still. He made sawing, spinning, shearing, washing, and potterymaking machines and artesian wells; he constructed scales, the concave mirror, the pendulum. He found sea shells on mountaintops and founded paleontology, the science of rock strata and fossils. Two hundred years before Newton he discovered the law of the acceleration of falling bodies, and he was ahead of Galileo in discovering their actual speed. He found the causes of whirlpools, eddies, the law of capillarity, and established the science of hydraulics. He applied the wave-movement theory to sound and light, measured sound waves, explained the echo and the sympathetic vibration of high notes. He recognized the function of the crystalline lens and the retina.

No medieval genius could ever have done all this, because it was only the Renaissance, with its belief in nature, that reverted to actual experiment. Leonardo was able to employ the experimental method long before Bacon, as the Greeks had done in their more primitive way. When the dogma of the Middle Ages melted under the light of knowledge, when experience, curiosity, and gusto became the lords of creation, the senses were reestablished in their natural dominion. An eye that understood nature could draw discoveries from its conclusions. Laws leaped like golden fish at Leonardo from the cascades of his investigations. The contact with nature that concerned him all his life would have been impossible a century before, if only for fear of heresy.

The rush of intellectual liberty that passed across the Mediterranean, with little sunlit ripples like a sprinkling wind without a storm, did not reach the north. In Germany, shortly before Leonardo's time, Dr. Faustus had to hide behind masks and formulas. Leonardo himself did not entrust his deepest intuitions to the world; he took the precaution of writing the journals containing his assembled wisdom in mirror writing. But around him he found alert minds that strove as he did and a church that allowed every liberty to the intellect. A cleric was appointed to read Kepler's book to the Pope in his garden even though the author deprived the earth of its central position and contradicted the Bible. The revolutionists of thought were eagerly received because they were expected.

So Leonardo did not pass for a wizard; he appeared in the character of a physicist and investigator. He loved beautiful boys and beautiful fabrics, and would sometimes parade through the streets of Milan accompanied by a pair of graceful pupils. This attitude accorded with the times and was not confined to the courts. That he was also a "painter and lute player" was a fact that he mentioned only at the end of a long letter of application. When he served Borgia, he was simply "Engineer in Charge of All Fortifications." For Duke Sforza of Milan he painted beautiful women; designed equestrian statues; planned grotesque surprises for a wedding procession, including bowing mechanical lions; regulated rivers; and built siege machinery. His versatility was, of course, inherent in the times, but Leonardo could do more and had more different talents than any contemporary.

Yet he was also an enemy of war, who separated his preaching from his practice with all the cynicism of the age. It was a matter of indifference to him what party he served in war. He cared nothing for either side; all he wanted was to exercise his gifts, to stir up his mind, and otherwise to live undisturbed, without wealth, simply in beauty and liberty. When the Sforza whom he had served so long was defeated and imprisoned, Leonardo promptly went over to the victor, and changed an equestrian statue that had been years in preparation for the Sforzas into a monument to their adversaries, the Visconti. Three times he went over from an employer to the victorious enemy, just as the *condottieri* did. Anyone who would damn this as perfidy is forgetting the fickleness of the masters, who dropped declining artists just as publishers do today. The self-assurance universal among people of talent in those days had grown to such a point that the artist outmatched the accustomed faithlessness of princes and rich men.

The sense of personal liberty, unknown in the Middle Ages, rose to great heights in Leonardo. Society he could not change; but when he saw caged birds in the market, he bought them and let them go. Believing that work, activity, all life was simply an experiment, he poured out his genius for himself alone, as it were, not pleasing God by pious works or serving the mighty except for money. Only once again in a thousand years did so great a genius—Goethe—work in this tentative fashion, and he saw himself as a reflection of Leonardo. The fact that less of Leonardo's work has survived is due not so much to the constant disturbances of war as to his experiments with paint chemistry, and especially to a self-sufficiency that never sought outward success but was content with diaries. This is the one point at which his character diverges from that of the age. He alone among the men of the Renaissance took no thought for fame.

Posterity has received but nine paintings by him, only five of these absolutely certain and perfect and all painted late—the four in the Louvre and the Milan mural of the Last Supper, which crumbles increasingly and had faded even in the painter's lifetime. These women and youths, all resembling one another, not wholly distinguished even as to sex, also have in common the lack of innocence in their smiling features—a trait typical of Michelangelo as well. In these beings love has indeed been refined to the utmost, but it has remained earthly. Those mouths and eyes, those cheeks and shoulders give no sign of humility but speak of subtlety.

This was possible in the Renaissance, with perfectly healthy instincts—this and even the hermaphrodite John whom Leonardo painted last and who might also be called Dionysus. Saint Anne, perhaps the loveliest of all his figures, smiling upon her daughter and her child, is what Goethe called "sensually supersensual."

Balancing her and her mysterious sister the Mona Lisa, we have another woman from the hand of Leonardo, Isabella d'Este, whom he sketched in red chalk, perhaps in a single hour. He is said to have worked for four years on the Mona Lisa. Isabella, a decade younger, and therefore more expectant, more reserved, is not smiling; her vigorous, as yet unformed features, shown in profile, are at first less attractive to the observer. But the noble throat, caught in a single line, the metallic cascade of hair that seems to helmet her, the boldness of posture, clearness of eye, the whole freedom of her figure create the great type of a fiery mistress of life in a way that shines through the centuries.

Such were the loveliest women of their age; such were the strongest personalities; such was the Renaissance.

XIV

A GOLDEN SHIP, high-sided and splendid, with brilliant figures and silken banners, glides out to sea from the south façade of the Palazzo Ducale, followed by a hundred smaller boats. This is the May morning of the Feast of the Resurrection. Greatest of Venetian festivals, it was first celebrated about the year 1000, when a doge solemnized his conquest of the Dalmatian coast; and since then the ceremonial boat has floated among the islands on the same day each year. It is rowed, but seems to glide. Leisureliness is the manner natural to Venice. Once out, the vessel heaves to, and the scarlet-silken cardinal, standing upright in plain view of all amid many vestments at the prow of the boat, lifts up his arms and prays to God "for tranquil seas for us and all those who are to sail the ocean."

Next to him, surrounded by the senators, sits the doge in his golden cloak, his white pointed cap on his head. He stands up. The priests sing, then fall silent; all necks are astretch, all hearts pound, everyone stiffens. Only the sea takes no thought of what is about to befall it and goes on slapping the ship's sides. The doge steps to the bulwark, raises his left hand on high, and then slowly takes from his finger an old, heavy gold ring set with stones. He lifts it up so that everyone can see it shining in the sun, draws back his right arm, and cries: *"Desponsamus te, mare!* Thus we espouse thee, O Sea!" Then he hurls the ring into the billows.

This is the marriage of Venice to the Adriatic, and thus it was repeated six hundred times through some six hundred years. And six hundred golden rings must still be lying at the bottom of the sea today—if no diver has succeeded in salvaging them. A Pope, Alexander III, first had this poetic notion; or perhaps some court poet or mistress whispered it to him. He wanted to thank Venice for her help against Emperor Barbarossa. The bucentaur, however (*buzino d'oro,* or golden vessel), afterward grew more and more splendid from one century to the next—the outward symbols of power always grow more beautiful as it declines. Among all the lords who sailed the Mediterranean and conquered its coasts, none ever had an inspiration to equal this gallant gesture. Xerxes the Barbarian once tried to bind the Mediterranean with chains, but the doge of Venice married it, and felt that his city was the bride in the nuptials.

While the populace rejoiced in the sunlight outside, some thousands of human beings were sitting in black vessels in stuffy corners of the ocean city, dull, mute, brooding. These were the galley slaves, who remained shackled to their benches day and night, year in, year out, a whole life long. They heard nothing but the clank of their chains, saw nothing but their neighbors and their overseer, hoped for nothing but death. These slaves, who propelled almost all the Mediterranean vessels, were like the piles, rotting and moldering in the water, on which the splendid palaces of Venice stood. They it was who paid with their happiness, their humanity, for the intoxication of the Renaissance above their heads.

Ancient civilization was based on slavery, but this did not conflict with the foundations of political morality, which did not change significantly even after Plato. In Homer and even as late as Aristophanes, Zeus and Apollo looked down placidly from heaven on the rulers consumed with hatred, the women with jealousy, and the slaves with submission. As long as men were not brothers and had no common father, slavery was quite in order. This is true of Islam, which permits slavery.

Christian civilization did outrage to the name of its founder by tolerating slavery, then by failing to protect slaves, by using them, and finally by sharing in the slave trade. A Pope, a bishop who had slaves in chains carrying his galley across the Mediterranean, a patriarch of Constantinople, an archbishop of Venice who blessed the ships as they put out to catch and sell human beings and build bankers' palaces with the money, all these were more utterly contemptible than any heretic they ever burned.

If the earth was deprived of its deities, if the loveliest of all legends was taken away, if men were robbed of the gods whom they loved and feared, and the warring multiplicity of forces making up fate was reduced to a single rigid judge of the universe, at least one thing should have been gained in return—justice for all the sons of the one and only Father.

When the Renaissance invalidated Christian morality, people were free to fight and murder. It is significant that Alexander VI, the Renaissance Pope, died of his own poison. But galley slavery, which altogether dominated Mediterranean navigation, was practiced and extended from the Christian state of Constantine in 500 until 1800. The church used to send priests on board to celebrate "galley Masses."

Of the 400 men who rowed an ordinary galley, usually 250 slaves sat almost naked on hard, narrow benches, each man chained

by the ankle. Seven men sat side by side at one forty-foot sweep,
day and night, rowing, eating, digesting, sleeping in the same
place. For the weeks of a voyage they could not stretch out; they had
no roof in storm and rain and were merely dragged into a stifling,
windowless cabin when ill. They could see their armed overseer
walking up and down the elevated runway. In winter they exchanged their bench for a prison, a bagnio, in which they lay chained
by the same shackles to the same neighbors. In storms at sea their
cries of terror echoed across the deck. Unarmed in battle, they stared
at the enemy advancing with drawn swords and awaited the moment of butchery.

No one dared unchain them, even in the most desperate conflicts; they could have taken revenge by flying first of all at their
tormentors. For a threat or a bite they were flogged by the overseers.
Since they had a cash value, they were not thrown overboard in
chains except in the worst cases. When they were exhausted a piece
of bread soaked in wine or vinegar was stuck into their mouths; if
they howled with terror, a wooden or leather gag took its place. If
a chain broke, if an attempt at escape was made, first their ears were
cut off, then a foot. Such responsible witnesses as Jean de Bergerac,
who was a galley slave for years because of his Protestant faith, recorded these scenes. People heard of a drunken overseer's biting off
a slave's ear.

Anyone who got hold of a knife and drew it for revenge upon
his tormentor was nailed to the mast with the knife through his
hand. Anyone who secretly received a communication was hanged.
Epidemics, which spread swiftly among prisoners confined so close
together, carried off the galley slaves in such numbers that even the
bankers who did the financing were horrified. In one war Venice
lost 40,000 men in this fashion.

Since strangers stole from them any sums they themselves had
managed to steal, the slaves hated every visitor to their vessel. Cervantes had them hurling Sancho Panza clear across the deck. But
if they stole from the visitor and he crippled the manacled culprit in
revenge, the visitor had to reimburse the captain to the value of a

hundred ducats. We have reports of such things as late as the seventeenth century.

All states tried to exploit their criminals in this fashion, so they restrained the judges from condemning murderers to death. Sitting on the same bench with a murderer would be a captive Knight of Malta or a scholarly victim of the Inquisition. The great lords were not in the habit of chaining their peers after capturing them, but the Genoese once took the admiral of Venice and shackled him in a galley. Unarmed, naked, shorn, branded on the brow with a red-hot iron like the rest, the admiral who had commanded thousands of slaves now sat on the rower's bench of his enemy. He could not, like Brutus and Antony, like so many captives, male and female, put an end to himself with sword or dagger. What did he do? Waiting for an unguarded moment, he charged with full force against the bulwark and smashed his skull. This heroic man's name was Dandolo, descended from the great doges of that name.

They had made part of their fortune from the slave trade. Indeed, the wealth of Venice would have been as much smaller without that trade as the wealth of Florence without the wool factories. The golden bucentaur would have had less gold to dazzle the world, the palaces of the doges less marble, the portals on the Grand Canal fewer ornate pillars if the Venetians had not paid pirate vessels to lie in wait for the seafarers of the Mediterranean and sell them at the southeastern slave markets on behalf of a Venetian banker who might be having Titian paint him at the feet of the Madonna. The Mohammedans needed eunuchs for their harems, as the Popes needed them for choir boys, and castration became a sort of side line of the slave trade. We have reports of it up to the early nineteenth century. The chief profit went to Venice, whose annual accounts about A.D. 1400 show some 50,000 ducats in export duties on slaves.

When the Pope tried to prevent the sale of Christian slaves, at least to Mohammedans, the traders took Greek Orthodox Catholics, maintaining that these were not real Christians. Otherwise, however, not only did the Corpus Juris Canonici allow slavery but the Council of Toledo had the notion of making slaves out of priests' children. Pope Gregory XI gave orders in 1376 to enslave every

Florentine citizen who might be taken in the war. When Henry
VIII founded the English church, the Pope threatened with slavery
every Englishman who was true to his king. After the Battle of
Lepanto Pius V accepted a gift of seven hundred infidel prisoners of
war as slaves. The papal galleys were rowed by slaves until 1800.

The picture of the galley bench, the naked, shorn, manacled man
whose fellows by the hundred thousand rowed upon the Mediterranean, shows what human degradation went to pay for the
splendor of the Renaissance.

XV

THE MOST CELEBRATED BOOK of the time was that of Marco Polo. For
over twenty years he had been in China, India, and Japan; and
among the few men who had gone there he was almost alone in
writing anything. The more extravagant the public considered his
story, the more they read it; and the longer the time that passed, the
less exaggerated the tale seemed. This magnificent document
sounded so extravagant that people took it for untruthful, because
few realized that a true record of nature and history is always more
fantastic than romances and fantasy. For God is a greater poet and
has more inspiration than even the most gifted of His sons.

In 1300, when the book was written, it was not yet fashionable to
describe one's travels, and even in antiquity neither Herodotus nor
Plutarch had put himself in the center of his own stage. And this
book by an unlearned man would have remained unwritten but for
two remarkable accidents, which first brought him home, then got
him to write. Today his experiences have paled, but the story of the
author has the same youthful freshness as ever; here as always, deeds
fade and personalities remain.

The Polos, two brothers from Venice, whom export ventures had
taken by way of Constantinople to the Crimea and on to Persia, had
finally gone on and on to eastward with some ambassadors of the
khan of China. This grand cham, or emperor, who had probably
never seen any white men but missionaries and a few scattered diplo-

mats, invited the Polos to return. He gave them letters to the Pope
with the naïve but fundamentally noble request that the primate
send a hundred sages who might prove to the khan that the religion
of Christ was best. When the brothers returned there was no Pope,
only Roman turmoil. So the sages were missing on the second
voyage; but there was oil from the sacred lamp in Jerusalem. And
the Polos took along the son of one of them, seventeen-year-old
Marco, whom the father had found alone at home since the mother's
death. When Marco came back he was forty.

The years during which the party crisscrossed Asia did more
than bring new information. They were so abundantly active that
territories like the plateau of Pamirs, described by Marco Polo, were
not rediscovered until six hundred years later, by English travelers.
In China, where the twenty-two-year-old youth was given the administration of cities and state offices, he seems to have been a favorite of the emperor, who would never have let the three Venetians go
at all except that his friend the khan of Persia lost his favorite wife
and wanted a Mongolian to take her place. For this purpose he sent
envoys to China. When the Persian ambassadors asked for the
"Franks" as guides across the sea to India, apparently the emperor
had no choice but to let them go. Most of the expedition died during the two-year voyage. Only one envoy, the bride, and the three
white men remained alive. Meanwhile the khan had died in Persia,
and the Mongolian lady had to content herself with his nephew.

The Polos, coming home after some twenty-four years, were not
recognized. They were turned away as impostors from their own
palace in Venice. Finally, at a great banquet, they cut open their old
Tartar garments and stood forth in magnificent silks and jewels. Is
this not a story fit for the *Arabian Nights*? But the world in those
days was full of adventurers, and not all the Marcos have died out
yet.

Soon after his return, being taken prisoner by the Genoese in a
naval battle, Marco spent almost a year in prison. A second happy
accident conjured a young romancer from Pisa into his dungeon,
and the two of them passed the time by recounting and dictating the
Chinese journey. Being released, the author returned to Venice,

where he enjoyed up to his seventieth year a peaceful life, of which we know nothing except that he was surrounded by three daughters.

The world took him for a Munchausen, a teller of tall tales; he was called Marco Milione, because his stories teemed with millions of men, and particularly of ducats. The romances that appropriated names and scenes from his book converted him altogether into a braggart. He preferred the easy way of telling a story to the hard way, and so people did not think him learned—which is said to befall certain authors today. Marco Polo's book had prepared the Mediterraneans to face the coming of a great Eastern conqueror, Timur the Great, better known as Tamerlane, who disturbed the south of Europe and Asia Minor, sweeping with his riders across the countries he coveted but holding sway in the Mediterranean for only a few years.

But the influence of this one book on coming discoveries was even more important; it originated a misapprehension whose consequences were magnificent. The Arabs had learned from Ptolemy that the earth was round. Arab and, later, Christian scholars drew maps on this principle, while the church still preached a disk surrounded by the ocean, with Jerusalem in the middle. They also believed in islands in the Atlantic, to which clerics had once fled before the Moors, and they put their trust generally in an unbounded life on that ocean; Dante, a contemporary of Marco Polo, still designated Gibraltar as the impassable boundary of the world. However, the existence of a Western Hemisphere not merely was unknown but was never suggested, even theoretically, and so everything depended on the breadth of the Atlantic, on whose western shore India and China were, of course, to be found.

Now Marco Polo had stated the distance across Asia in day's journeys. Judging by speed of travel in Europe, his readers naturally thought the distance much greater than it is. If Asia was as big as all this, the Atlantic was obviously narrow; if it was narrow, one might more easily venture to sail across it and seek India by way of the west. The breadth of the unknown ocean, which exercised the seafaring nations of the time, was the decisive factor; and this misunderstanding diminished it by half at least. His true account created a misapprehension without which Columbus would hardly have ventured forth to turn his second, world-famous mistake into reality.

As much as five centuries before his time seafarers and adventurers had set sail to search for islands in the Atlantic and treasures along the southern coasts. Who could better start such enterprises than the Portuguese, with the longest Atlantic shore line and the best Atlantic seaport in southern Europe? Their commerce turned them toward west Africa, close to their only seacoast, whereas Spain and France also abutted on the Mediterranean, which held their attention through twenty centuries. In 1444 and 1451 the Portuguese discovered the Canary Islands and the Azores. What could be more natural than for them to seek the road to India from west Africa? There were two ways, the second of which led straight across the continent. They knew more of Africa's outline than of the interior, and only their calculation of a sea route around the cape was correct.

It was Henry the Navigator, a Portuguese king, who began as early as 1430 methodical attempts to reach the East Indies by way of the west. He was the first to abandon the Mediterranean in the grand manner. He was called the Navigator, strangely enough, though he never went on voyages; but he designed, prepared, and financed the vessels at home and drew his conclusions from the reports. As Grand Master of the Christian Order, he wanted to fight the infidels. This Christian missionary motive that he attached to his discoveries has never disappeared since; we hear it repeated even today, five hundred years later. Probably the motive was genuine in him in the same way that it is in the English exporter, who is concerned above all to sell his wool but who takes a missionary along on general principle.

He fought the infidels, of course, with their own Arabic tactics, for cosmography (the splendid name for geography in those days) as an instrument of navigation had been transmitted to the Christians largely by the Arabs. This meant not only Ptolemy and the spherical shape of the earth, but the magnetic needle, which the Arabs took from the Chinese about 1200 and which alone made navigation possible in fog and at night. Other things had come from the mainland: a Nuremberg scholar had published ephemerides on the position of the constellations, and the learned Jew Levi Ben Gerson had invented an instrument for precise astronomical observations which afterward served all adventurers for the reckoning of their position.

In the eyes of the voyagers even fame and religion were less attractive than the fantastic prices paid for Oriental fabrics and stones at Paris, Amsterdam, and London, and especially for spices. For the Turks, who had now turned Byzantium into their own city of Constantinople, shut off all overland trade. When they reached Egypt in 1517, no corner of the eastern Mediterranean remained free.

What sums the rich men of the north did pay for pepper, cloves, nutmeg, cinnamon! And even in those days no Englishman could live without ginger. Around 1300, 100 pounds of pepper cost $60 in Marseille, $200 in London. When only one of Magellan's vessels got home, the entire cost of the three-year voyage was paid out of the sale of the 525 hundredweight of spices brought back from the Moluccas, and there was an additional clear profit of $3,000 in gold. All seamen dreamed of fortunes to be amassed by the new routes, and there was more and more voyaging, more and more discovery.

It was during the Renaissance that great characters discovered distant lands. Their understanding of Christianity, not as an emotion like that of Jesus but as power like that of Peter, brought these fanatically battling men far more success, for Christianity as well as themselves, than the crusaders ever had. Their murders, devastations, and enslavements, stemming more from temperament than from necessity, could be excused by the gift of the true faith that they brought to the colored heathen. And yet not one would have set sail unless the three great motives of power, gold, and glory had lured him out to sea. This is the chief difference from at least the earliest of the crusaders. Here were *condottieri* who paid for their habit of command by the greatest privations. They drank ill-smelling water or ate mice and lived without women on board. Why should they not have flung themselves savagely upon the natives at every landing?

The finest looking head of them all belonged to Vasco da Gama, a Portuguese noble, heavy and dark, but sharp-nosed, piercing-eyed, bold, collected, completely the man of action and command. Diaz had discovered the Cape of Storms in 1486, later rechristening it the Cape of Good Hope, and Vasco followed him. Eleven years later he explored the east coast of Africa as far as the equator. Then he cruised the Indian Ocean for a month in the monsoon, finally dropping anchor at Calicut. Thus Vasco da Gama was the first great enemy of the Mediterranean.

XVI

THE MAN WHO EARNED the greatest glory among the discoverers was a son of the Mediterranean and never its enemy. An Italian, he was born in Genoa, no matter if fifteen other cities do vie for his birth—otherwise, quite aside from other evidence, he would not have bequeathed the prayer book the Pope had given him, "which was my consolation in battle and dungeon, to my beloved homeland, the Republic of Genoa." That he was a Jew can be neither proved nor disproved. In favor of this origin we may cite his portrait and two characteristic traits: obstinate persistence and avidity for honor, which exceeds avidity for money in most Jews.

Columbus's glory outshines that of all discoverers in history, because he alone found not an island but a continent. Since to do so was accidental and he died in ignorance of his discovery, this achievement would not suffice to show his unique eminence. But if we consider his genius and character, his superiority to others becomes evident. His greatness is independent of the greatness of his object.

We have only to compare his portrait, the one that is obviously genuine, with those of the other discoverers of his time to see how much more he was than a mere *condottiere*. The intellectual side of him is stronger than his will power, yet his will too he proved magnificently. Beardless, with little hair, a delicate forehead that does not really rise into a thinker's abrupt brow, a small mouth that asks little enjoyment and seems mostly to be silent, a chin quite lacking any brutal forward thrust, dark eyes that look altogether within—

here we have the head of a lonely and reflective man who loved maps and books more than discovery and discovery more than conquest. As a son of his age, he weathered as many perils as other seafarers and perhaps more, yet his passion was not command, but the proof of the calculations made beforehand. He was capable of living alone, which no *condottiere* is.

Neither adventure nor the desire for gold swept him into the great movement. Nor is he among those pupils of antiquity made restless by the will to glory, like Cesare Borgia and Bolivar. Columbus, whom Humboldt called a great scholar, seems to have been impelled by the desire for honor to substantiate what he had believed and known before he ever lifted a hand to act. Without this impulse, born say as a duke instead of a commoner, he might have spent his life happily in a study, like the Florentine Toscanelli, whose maps and letters were evidently his chief stimulus.

Many factors joined to push him into his apparently mad impulse. A petty wool merchant in the port of Genoa, like his father, the bored lad hankered for the sea. Between the ages of fourteen and twenty-four he evidently saw much of the Mediterranean, for example, Sicily and Chios; then he sailed the Atlantic to west Africa, to England, perhaps to Iceland. All the time he kept drawing maps, studying cosmography, questioning men of experience, trying out instruments, and reading ancient authors. Probably entirely self-taught, he seems to have studied and pondered, sitting on a coil of rope in some corner at the foot of the mast, grasping what others only saw and taking from the fragment he was sailing the elements for understanding the structure of the world, the distribution of sea and land on the globe. No man has ever yet become a discoverer without first being a poet.

At about the age of thirty, foreigner as he was, he managed to marry an aristocratic Portuguese lady, the daughter of a governor and relative of an archbishop. This decisive stride into a higher class cannot have been the result of looks, fashion, or money on his part, for these he did not possess, but only of intellect and personality. At the same time he was certainly no Don Juan, although here, after the death of his wife, he did win an equally aristocratic Spanish lady, whom he made the mother of his second son but did not marry.

In Portugal he avidly seized upon the long-untouched charts and papers of his late father-in-law. Now that he had definitely left Italy, his external life and inward vision were turned completely westward; yet at this very moment he was borrowing all his resources from the Mediterranean, corresponding with the Florentine Toscanelli, who knew everything before he did but never went to sea. It was evident long before the time of Columbus that China and India could be reached by way of the west. Columbus had plenty of brains and energy. What he lacked was a king and a vessel.

The prospect of finding unknown islands and fantastic treasures in the Atlantic was bound to tempt a seafaring monarch. Evidently, after long waiting, Columbus the stranger succeeded only through his wife's relatives in reaching the king and fascinating him with the idea of conquering lands rich in gold. During this period everything seemed to be coming his way. He was in good health, a happy husband, the father of a son. He had risen from obscurity, been accepted in a foreign land—and all this before he had the slightest achievement to his credit. No one except himself knew of his vocation (for he had an idea and with it the two forces to carry it through: scholarship and energy, the skill of a sailor and a geographer). Nothing but the charm of his personality can have put the king in a willing mood.

The king cheated him at once, however, sending others, native Portuguese, upon the proposed voyage; but they grew afraid and returned in haste. Columbus left the country after this disappointment. He made his way secretly to Spain, like a fugitive, as was the habit of his era; the departure was made easier for him by the death of his wife. To win over the Spanish Ferdinand and Isabella was far more difficult. We cannot but admire the decade of waiting during which this outsider with no money or position kept futilely approaching court and government, only to be laughed at or suspected of fraud. The truly Spanish form was not a no but an empty excuse.

He was able to endure this period thanks to the two elements of strength that remained constant in his character. The first was his belief in God and the spherical shape of the earth. The dual dogma could by no means be taken for granted, for the Renaissance shook the first by insisting on the second. Columbus escaped from this dilemma like Copernicus and Kepler but seems to have remained even more religious. If he kept quoting the Revelation of John, the prophet Jeremiah, and other parts of the Bible again and again in his letters to the kings by way of proof that his westward path was foreordained, he can have done so only as a devout believer or as a cynic who meant to please the clerics at court.

But a cynic Columbus was not, nor did he ever become one under the bitterest disappointments. He merely insisted as a seaman on his right to interpret divine revelations in a concrete fashion. On his third voyage he even shifted paradise in such a way that it might lie within his new lands. The fragments of his *Book of Prophecies* and his last arrangements likewise indicate a religious spirit.

The second force that made Columbus able to endure first a decade of waiting, then deposition and chains, was a self-assurance of unbelievable proportions. We must remember that he was no inventor, no alchemist or magician possessing secrets by which he could raise himself above mortals and demand what he pleased of them. What he knew—that the earth was round, that Asia was vast, and that it would therefore be possible to reach India by way of the west—the best minds of the day knew and believed also. The Italian's maps were already in the hands of a learned Spanish cardinal. Many ships had put out of Lisbon and Cádiz for the west, and almost all ships alike had the necessary instruments. The legend of gold or spice islands was so widespread that when Columbus finally did bring gold back with him, everyone regarded it as merely the confirmation of a hundred tales read in Marco Polo and elsewhere.

Both Spain and Portugal had long since acquired Western colonies, whose possession a pope had confirmed them in when Columbus was barely born. Since, furthermore, no one suspected or sought a new continent, all Western plans seemed merely extensions of former enterprises. And on top of all this, our Genoese brought neither money nor a celebrated name or a great recommendation; no new sail, oar, or cable, no proof of any previous achievement. To make mighty kings give several ships to an unknown dilettante,

Columbus required the profound self-assurance that ennobled him.

This explains his decade of persistency. If he had been only a gold seeker wanting riches, only a geographer seeking proof, he could probably have found some adventurer to go with him. But he demanded straightway to be made grand admiral, governor, and viceroy of all the Utopian countries he was about to discover, and this by hereditary title. How could the cardinals, admirals, and generals around the kings help thinking him mad? What had got into this poor, unknown stranger's head, that he should demand things fitting for the heir of a noble house or a tried-and-true hero of the seas or a world-famous scholar?

Isabella alone—a woman again—recognized him. She it was who finally acceded to all his demands. His insistence on a tenth of all the treasures he might bring home with him was customary and not surprising. But only his self-assurance made Columbus irresistible when he finally received his great contract. His letters after the first discoveries reflect it again: "The Lord vouchsafed to me what has been granted to no other mortal. Much as has been written about these islands, no man before me had ever succeeded in seeing them, and therefore they had been banished to the realm of fable. . . . Let services of thanksgiving be held in the land, that God may rejoice in the earth and the spreading of His Kingdom among the nations of the heathen." Or, again, in his will: "I gave the Indies to our Queen, in the name of God I gave it to the Kings, as a thing that was my own. I abashed them by forcing them to receive. For these lands were hidden, and no man knew the way thither."

Columbus, who believed he was in the Old World when among the Antilles, always spoke most amazingly of the "New World" he had discovered, and he had no idea how right he was. Histrionics were born in him. Declaring that he owed everything to God, he had no hesitation in recognizing all the signs of his own genius. Therefore he was not in the least surprised by his triumphal procession from Seville to Barcelona amid the jubilation of the country on his first return or by the celebrated scene at Barcelona when he alone, before court and country, sat by the throne of the royal pair. He told what he had seen and displayed what he had taken—he, the foreign-born son of a petty merchant, making gifts of gold to the mightiest rulers of his time. Then he remained for weeks of constant association as a favorite of the king, setting up his son as a page, making noblemen of his brothers, assuming a title and coat of arms. In the rococo age he would have become his queen's lover.

All the more splendid was his courage when the envy and intrigues of the court and of perennial ill-wishers descended on the too greatly favored foreigner. A few years later the man who had discovered and was governing the strange land with all its treasures found himself taken prisoner in his islands, and brought home in chains by a governor sent by this very king. There came the superb moment when he refused to let an understanding captain take off his manacles; he voluntarily spent the return voyage in chains, waiting for the kings to order his release. This story, told by his son, is evidently true, for he afterward hung up the chains in his study.

Here Columbus was sublime; no Roman in Plutarch surpassed him as he set for all time an example of a man undaunted by fate. The whole tragedy of this third voyage should have fallen into Shakespeare's hands. The restitution of his honor and rank was finally but half complete or, if you please, unaccomplished; for Columbus died as deposed viceroy before the end of the great trial. In the end more than ever, he had only his self-assurance to keep him going. The one soul who understood him, Queen Isabella, died shortly before him. The will of the impoverished and powerless man reads like that of a king.

A good many people are inclined to think his heroic end sad. They would shout after him into the grave what it was that he really discovered. They do not know the secret ecstasies of the visionary who feels unconsciously what has not yet taken form as a perception. This emotion Columbus possessed; his intuition and self-assurance told him all. His celebrated mistake was only on his map, not in his soul. He wrote in his copy of Pliny these words from Seneca: "Centuries will come when the Ocean bursts the bonds with which it encloses us, when an immeasurable land will lie open, the steersmen will discover new worlds, and Thule will no longer be the uttermost end of the known universe."

XVII

THE CENTURY PROCLAIMED by Seneca and marked by Columbus had come. Distant seas were discovered. People soon knew that another ocean stretched beyond the supposed Indies. What, then, was the Mediterranean now? Where was its historic mission of carrying commerce, goods, and culture back and forth from Asia and Africa to the oldest civilized nations? If you could go by the Atlantic to India and the new, unknown continent, if you could conquer and loot endless lands with unimaginable riches, of what consequence was the little inland sea that had been the world's center from 1000 B.C. to A.D. 1500?

The Mediterranean was deserted. The power, the kings, the money, the sailors turned their eyes toward the Atlantic. So swift a change was unique in the history of the seas. It was not to be repeated for more than three hundred years, when the Suez Canal made the Mediterranean once more a great ocean.

But civilization was still at home there; and the Pope as the supreme cultural power arranged the property of the New World according to his own whims. A few months after Columbus' first return, Alexander VI issued two papal bulls. As the moral arbiter he divided the newly discovered lands between his two Catholic children, Spain and Portugal, along a specified line. The line was soon afterward shifted four hundred miles, giving the greater part of South America, as yet unknown, to Portugal. For three centuries the new seafaring nations quarreled over this judgment of Solomon. A new freedom of the seas was late in being established; where there is anything left to discover now, as in the polar zones, the right of the strong prevails, and no Pope or League of Nations has any authority.

A German professor proclaimed the Italian Amerigo Vespucci discoverer of the new mainland, bringing him by this proposal a stupendous honor that he never earned. Humboldt has decided against this credit. The only country that Amerigo did discover was named after Columbus and is still called Colombia. Both men were

Italians, but no part of the continent speaks Italian or ever has.

The merchants were the first to realize the great turning point in Mediterranean history. The achievement of Vasco da Gama frightened them far more than that of Columbus. The gentlemen of Venice realized their fate sooner than any of the others did; some, indeed, were far-seeing enough to look at once to the Isthmus of Suez. A canal might be feasible there, and one had, in fact, already twice existed, though in most rudimentary form. We know only that Venice entered into negotiations with the Egyptian sultan about 1510. But the Turkish sultan was already advancing by then; finally he bought the title of caliph and the holy banner of the prophet from the last Abbasside at Cairo. The rising Turks were far too powerful to make any concessions to the declining Venetians. All western Asia belonged to them now, and Egypt as well. Why open the road through Suez and make things still easier for the Christians?

In other ways, too, the decline of Venice symbolized the decline of the Mediterranean. Pisa and Genoa had long since lost their power. Italy was broken up into more than a dozen independent states. On the other hand, Spain and France were unified, and even Germany was or seemed to be. The Turks were the one great Mediterranean power, since the Western powers were turning more and more away from the inland sea.

When the League of Cambrai about 1510 destroyed Venetian hegemony, there was revenge involved. The Pope, the emperor, and the king of the French were infuriated at the constant alliances of Venice with the infidels. They took much land away but avoided actually humiliating her. Spaniards and Portuguese, enriched by the new discoveries, would soon begin to dominate the Mediterranean. The English and the Dutch would strengthen their power there. It was not barbarians who would descend upon harbors and shores now; but strangers they would be still.

This development coincided with the swift rise of the new Western national states. The Mediterranean, the teacher of mankind through two thousand years, was abandoned. The imagination of the world took wings toward other oceans. Culture did not disappear, but it retreated to lonely chambers. Where it did emerge, it was seldom visible beyond Mediterranean shores.

The world entered into a period in which people were occupied with trade and commerce. The new continents did not create this interest; they were discovered because men were ready and curious. For the next three hundred years intellectual struggles were not significant. From now on the history of the Mediterranean becomes a commercial and political history. The ocean that had hitherto originated everything now received all its great impulses from without. Its vessels became more important than its ideas, the goods they carried more important than the men.

And even the goods appealed less to the greed of Europe than they had. Gold came now from the distant new lands, and native products soon were carried to far countries. The sea that had been the center of the world became an inland lake, and the possession of its seaports and coasts was no longer the goal of power. The sons of the old mother were off to the New World.

BOOK FOUR

THE FORSAKEN OCEAN

And you, ye blue-sea waves!
I have seen you dyed ere now, and deeply too,
With Genoese, Saracen, and Hunnish gore,
While that of Venice flow'd too, but victorious!
BYRON

AT THE LIGHTHOUSE

ON THE SOUTH COAST *of the islands of Hyères the rocks are eaten away by the breakers. Stone and sea are almost of an age. In such periods of time a few thousand years hardly count. How, then, could the one element have helped carving itself upon the other? Are they not setting men an example of mutual destruction? Sometimes this battle is called love, but battle it remains. The caves and grottoes that the Mediterranean has chewed in a hundred islands, in Corsica, Corfu, and Capri, are named, after their various colors, light-green or blue grottoes.*

The keeper was not thinking of this drama. He had been close to the ocean all his life, born and brought up on the coast, on shipboard in youth and manhood, in gray-haired middle age a keeper of the revolving beacon that safeguarded ships at sea. He had always regarded the sea, his true element, as a mother; the rock really existed only to carry the lighthouse. Down below he had put out his lobster pots; lobsters were easy to sell on the coast, and he might also take one home with him. He went back with his boy to the pot set yesterday—a basket into which the lobsters were lured, never to escape. This time six were caught, and he decided to sell five. Making his boat fast in the bay, he took out one of the lobsters, and laid the wriggling, tail-lashing creature on his soaked knees. He went on to show his son how this red-brown creature of the Mediterranean is put together.

The first striking point about the armored animal, the first thing it puts out from its tank, are the two long feelers, twice the length of a pencil, pointed, graceful, mobile; they are reddish-brown, mottled with six or seven bright yellow spots such as one finds on butterflies' wings. On each side there are five long legs, articulated into four joints, heavily provided with bristles to keep it from slipping, and again adorned with yellow spots. The eyes are black hemispheres on marvelously mobile globes. They can be touched without the creature's wincing. No one knows whether the lobster is watching the

417

human animal, for its eyes are empty. Below them, exactly in the middle of the front, it has two bright red feelers, shorter than the shortest hind legs; these alone have small pincers at the end; otherwise the creature lacks the weapons of the crab. One may pound smartly on the brown armor, which is dull and scaly on top. The tail, rather longer, divided into twelve bands of about the same width, is darker, gleaming. At the end is a double flipper for propulsion, each part divided in three.

The keeper turned the creature over and showed the boy how from inside the tail was like a pine cone, with a great many flat, overlapping seed covers. In this position the middle of the body was sensitive and thinly protected. When the man tapped lightly with his finger, the creature drew its feet together. One saw it breathing heavily in its yellow saliva. The boy wanted to go on tapping, but the father tossed the creature back into the basket.

That evening, at his observation post in the tower, the keeper sat down in his armchair and opened the book he had shut the day before. He read the heading with annoyance:

. . . What does he mean, our ocean is forsaken? Just because the big vessels started to sail the Atlantic and go to America? Haven't the millions living on the coasts here stayed for all these centuries? Haven't our boats gone on sailing among the islands, just the way they used to, only faster, and more of them? And weren't French boats the very ones that dominated the Mediterranean then? That title is an exaggeration. Let's see what he's going to tell us next. . . .

I

LOOKING AT A MAP dated about 1600, we see two colors almost exclusively on the coast countries. Never in fifteen centuries, since the height of the Roman Empire, had this ancient world, split up into so many peoples and interests, been in so few hands. Sometimes as many as twenty independent states had bordered the Mediterranean, and as late as 1940 there were fourteen. But about 1600, aside from the two big spots of color, there were only five small ones on the shore: the French coast, about as it is today, the petty states of the Vatican and Tuscany, and the sadly shrunken Genoa and Venice.

The two colors that dominated the map for centuries were Spanish and Turkish. The Hapsburg empire at its greatest extent included all Spain, Germany, and Italy. The Turks ruled much more country for a much longer time—from Budapest to Zara, from the Dnieper to Rhodes, from the Crimea to Morocco. Never since the Roman emperors had there been so great a Mediterranean realm as that of the Turkish sultans, and though we may say that their rule in north Africa was a mere formality, there had after all been some highly independent Roman provinces too.

What Trajan held in the hollow of one hand about A.D. 200, a Roman empire with one state religion, one constitution, one law, one army, had broken by 1600 into two parts, Turkey and Spain. The two were divided by the very thing that makes nations foes in periods of intolerance—ideas and the semblance of ideas. These are better tools for arbitrary rulers to arouse the masses than catchwords like "raw materials" and "gold." Between 1500 and 1700 the idealistic war cries "religion" and "color" could be counted on to excite the nations. All the millions sacrificed to this mania in the endless wars between Mohammedans and Christians perished without reason or sense. For in actual fact, the whites were not white; an Egyptian Turk is no darker than a Christian from Seville. So far as religions are concerned, Allah is as unrivaled, as invisible, powerful, and kindly as the Christian God, and Jesus is one of the great prophets of Islam.

Religion, then, served as a pretext for struggles for power; but this was not always so. The most powerful of the Spanish kings was really full of missionary zeal. In the great battles between the eastern and western Mediterranean, in the contest for north Africa, Italy, the Archipelago, and Palestine, there were moments when the Spanish kings and sometimes even the Pope thought of crusades. But the fire was long since dead; the ideas of religions were no longer compelling. When the attempt was made to appeal to the religious side of man, only mercenaries appeared instead of knights; only hatred of the infidel, not love of the Holy Places. The millions had been roused against infidelity, but the heretic was more odious to them than the Mussulman.

It was chiefly the rulers of France, bearing the title of "Most Christian Kings," who maintained a seldom-interrupted friendship with the sultans. They preferred to sustain the Turkish world power rather than divide it up with their Christian colleagues. The last of the Middle Ages in the Mediterranean had, after all, still given religion the central place in popular feeling, but this position was surrendered during the Renaissance to a new, pagan sense of life. The two feelings, so radically different, culminated about A.D. 1200 and 1700. But when the Counter Reformation, led by the Spanish Hapsburgs, began about 1550, when inquisitions, the Jesuit order, and saint worship began once more to rule the world, especially the Mediterranean, with witch burnings, trials for heresy, and autos-da-fé rather darkening than lighting up the cities, it was impossible to rouse the fanaticism of the great masses. They had already tasted tolerance and freedom of belief.

Men had a new ideal: nationality. They wanted to unite according to language and stock, not religion. Wherever religion played a part, it was in the conflict between Catholic and Orthodox and even more the struggle against the reformed sects—not to mention the quarrels of the sects among themselves. When we consider that the Thirty Years' War was ostensibly fought over the form of communion, over good works and contemplation, and that it finally

ended without a victory, we are not inclined to believe the catchwords under which the Christians repeatedly professed to extirpate
Islam. Neither on the Mediterranean nor in the north after 1500
were there leaders or masses ready, as Christians, to fight the Turks.

The Christian rulers were infuriated because the infidels were
the better soldiers. The various tribes had behind them a thousand
years of physical and cultural cultivation, which had, as a matter
of fact, become Persian rather than Arabic. These Turks, who had
established themselves as the best soldiers and as conquerors avid
to learn, were rulers of a central Asiatic empire as early as 600. They
did not change from nomadic hordes to a disciplined warrior people, however, until seven centuries later, under their leader Osman,
from whom they took their name. The subsequent decline of their
empire, continuing through centuries, produced many European
tales and operas depicting the fat, lazy Turk. It was like seeing a
frail, wan man creeping about from the age of fifty until he is ninety,
when no one can remember him as he was in the flush of his younger
days.

And yet this youth of the nation, from about 1450 to 1550, gave
to the Turks the vitality that let them live to such an age in their
decay. Their gigantic Mediterranean empire continued to rule the
destinies of the ocean for three centuries after it was moribund.
Though the Turks had nothing left of the knowledge and skill that
the Arabs had once bestowed on the Mediterranean, still their heavy,
inert mass sufficed to receive the buffets of Christian rivalries and
often to decide them.

In the century of their true strength, guided by strong rulers
and a strong army, these Mohammedans showed more tolerance
of the Christians than they themselves had ever enjoyed save from
one exceptional figure, Frederick II. Earlier, one of their great
rulers, Murad I, had been the son of a Christian woman. When
they took Constantinople, they did not repay in kind the exploitation of their former masters, and Mohammed II spared the Greek
Christians. Bajazet received Christians and Jews into his service
but instigated the murder of anyone in his entourage who threat-

ened him. Thus the sultans proved themselves half barbarians, just like the Christian kings of their day.

Before we call the Turks cruel we must remember the time and country that fixed their customs. The crooked scimitar did cut off thousands of innocent heads at the behest of the potentates. But what did their Christian contemporaries do? When the Venetians wanted to subdue the perpetually rebellious Cretans about 1570, they dispatched a governor with instructions written in blood. He not only hanged leaders and followers; he had the abdomens of four pregnant women of distinguished family publicly opened and the embryos cut out. Our sources for this information are French.

The most remarkable thing about the Turks was the position of their slaves. The Mamelukes were slaves, and as early as the ninth century they had a stronger influence on the royal succession of the Egyptian sultans than the praetorian guards had on the Roman emperors. In the fourteenth century the training of young Christian prisoners as elite troops began, and after the capture of Constantinople they formed a sort of page or cadet corps, in which the ablest young Christians were enrolled, forced to embrace Islam, and carefully schooled for from six to eight years. These were the famous Janizaries, who soon occupied high army and state positions, even including that of grand vizier. Until 1600 they were not allowed to marry, so that they might devote themselves wholly to the state, after the fashion of a religious order. Thus we see established a fundamental rule that has remained unique in history: a state maintained and governed wholly by foreign-born slaves.

Perhaps it was through the heritage of these families that Byzantine dignity, customs, and symbols were kept alive in the newly taken city. No one could have been more august in his bearing than a sultan. But the people we are accustomed to call Oriental despots merely displayed the same grave decorum that the Spanish court apparently took over from the mosaics. But the Persian throne that had been carried to Constantinople was wide, not high like the occidental thrones, and was arranged for reclining. Old drawings show the ambassadors supported rather than led by two guards of honor each. The Spanish king was enthroned no higher than the sultan; he sat perfectly woodenly under a similar canopy.

By a symbolic turn of fate the two great rulers of the two realms ascended their thrones simultaneously and ruled simultaneously for a long time; the Turk lasted a decade the longer. Each represents the summit of his time and the genius of his dynasty. In 1520 began the reigns of Charles V and Solyman the Magnificent.

II

ALMOST ON THE SAME DAY the Turkish heir to the Osmanli throne, aged twenty-five, belted on his father's sword, and the twenty-year-old Hapsburg had himself crowned German king at Aix-la-Chapelle—the former after killing his rivals, the latter after winning over the electors with a great quantity of gold lent him by the Fuggers, sons and grandsons of a German artisan.

Solyman needed only his inheritance to attain power. Charles, on the other hand, though legitimate successor to the Spanish crown through his mother, could not bring about the first union of the two Hapsburg empires until the German princes elected him. He belonged to the Mediterranean only through his Spanish heritage and never liked it.

Both men were warriors—the Turk a conqueror, the Spaniard rather a pretender to countries over which his dynasty had long quarreled with other dynasties. But Solyman needed war and would have died of boredom in his castle and harem. Charles could have lived without conquest. Neither his ambition nor his physique fitted him properly for expansion, but he would fight fiercely anybody who tried to take anything from him. His delicate frame was schooled in the arts of chivalry, but he trembled in every limb when his armor was put on; afterward, in battle, he would be the bravest of the brave. If no one had rebelled against him he would merely have administered his inherited world empire. The Turk, on the contrary, wanted to win a world empire. Starting wars on the slightest pretext, he took Rhodes, Bagdad, and Belgrade, conquered Transylvania and Kurdistan. Charles, after deposing one Pope, picked another to perform his coronation, and this not even in Rome. He was the last emperor to be crowned by a Pope.

The Mohammedan and the Catholic both shaped themselves after the same model: as youths they thought of Alexander. The young sultan, pushing from Alexander's own Macedonia into Persia, was closer to his classical prototype than Charles, who had been fed on Christian heroes in his childhood.

Both rulers had their greatest battles and victories in the first years of their youth. Charles was obliged to fight the kings of France, at first successfully, with varying fortunes in three later campaigns. What he won in the process, Milan and Naples (for we are looking at him only from the vantage point of the Mediterranean), was, he thought, his by right of inheritance. In the same way the sultan felt entitled to parts of the Balkans, where in his younger years he took Serbia and large sections of Hungary. The Turk owed his victories indirectly to Charles. For the Frenchman made treaties with the sultan after suffering defeat at the hands of Charles.

By his victories, by the pressure of his tremendous power, by threats and attacks, all his life Solyman prevented Charles V from becoming the most powerful man of his time. This was something Charles had had every prospect of, because Cortez was then just conquering Mexico.

Charles's troops, in turn, spoiled the great dream of Solyman's life, the capture of Vienna. The moment was bound to arrive when the two would come into direct conflict. History weakened the dramatic climax by merely opposing Charles's brother to the Turk in his three advances on Vienna. The first time winter drove off the infidel; the second time he evaded battle in Styria; the third time Vienna was saved by the same sort of unexpected heroism that we have just seen save an England already given up for lost. But even so the Hapsburg had to pay tribute to the sultan under the odd form of a "pension."

During these same years (for the wars outlasted the three and four decades of the two reigns) both men fought on the Mediterranean but again had no personal encounter. The Turk's almost

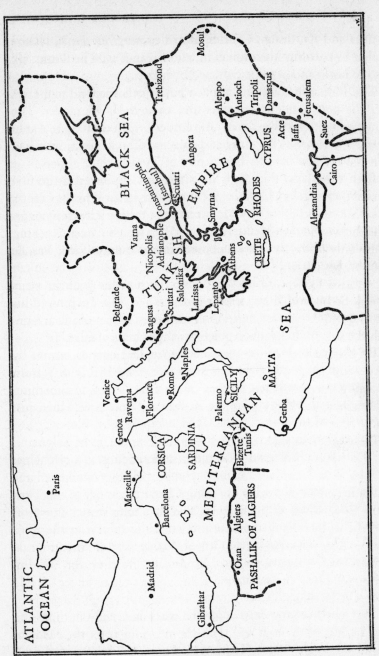

ATLANTIC
OCEAN

Paris

BLACK SEA

Mosul

Trebizond

Aleppo
Antioch
Tripoli
Damascus
Jerusalem

Angora

Acre
Jaffa
Suez

Constantinople (Istanbul)
Scutari

CYPRUS

EMPIRE

Smyrna

RHODES

Varna

Alexandria

Nicopolis

Adrianople

TURKISH

Athens

CRETE

Cairo

Belgrade

Ragusa
Scutari
Salonika
Larissa
Lepanto

SEA

Venice

Naples

Ravenna
Florence
Rome

Genoa

SICILY

MALTA

CORSICA

Palermo

Gerba

SARDINIA

MEDITERRANEAN

Bizerte
Tunis

Marseille

Barcelona

Algiers

PASHALIK OF ALGIERS

Madrid

Oran

Gibraltar

THE TURKISH EMPIRE ABOUT A.D. 1550

invariable superiority to the Spaniard at sea was not his doing; apparently neither man knew much of seafaring. The Turks, like every nation of nomad riders, were always uncomfortable on the ocean. They said: "Allah has given power over the land to the sons of Mohammed, but he has given the sea to the Giaour."

The Hapsburgs were no true sailors either. In ten days at Algiers Charles V lost half his army and came within an ace of losing his whole navy and his life. His victory at Tunis was brief and of no lasting advantage. Although he afterward appointed as admiral the Genoese Andrea Doria, reputed the best sailor of his day, he did not succeed in taking any Mediterranean territory away from the Turks. The Spanish Mediterranean power in the sixteenth century steadily declined; the Turkish power and its usual ally, the French, increased accordingly.

This changed situation was due to the superiority of the pirate powers, with which we shall shortly make acquaintance. These north African states belonged to the sultan in little more than name and were considered invincible—as, indeed, they were. In order to dominate the Mediterranean, Solyman had only to employ as his admiral the most celebrated pirate, Khair-ed Din Barbarossa.

The great corsair not only devastated Sicily but, to the Pope's horror, helped the sultan land at Reggio and take Nice. Barbarossa once defeated the united armadas of Spain, Genoa, Florence, and the papal state in a great historic sea battle near Djerba (1560).

In his youth Solyman took the unconquered island of Rhodes from the Knights of Saint John. But when as an old man he ordered his navy to seize the island of Malta from the knights, who had moved thither, his fleet had to retire after a long siege. He was so furious that he forbade the returning vessels to enter Contantinople harbor. The celebrated defender of Malta, Grand Master de la Valette, has the superbly typical head of an old chevalier, with no trace of brutality or fanaticism.

All these struggles for power, whose shifting outcomes have lost any claim to our interest, were garnished with the ideas of religion, but every now and then the religious pretense was suddenly torn roughly aside. There were Popes, too, who traded with

the sultan by way of Ancona. Ragusa used to be called the city of
the seven flags because it followed any man who happened to be
in power—a cognomen that might be bestowed on many a city
today.

Occasionally a strong Pope, like Paul IV, would venture to
prohibit trade with the infidels lest the salvation of the Christian
merchant be imperiled. But when another Pope called King Francis
I to account for his alliance with Solyman, the Frenchman sent him
the classic reply: "Even the infidels belong to human society. Nature teaches that this world's goods belong to all men in common.
Alienation is not founded in nature." It is odd that this simple truth
did not occur to the "most Christian king" until he needed infidel
guns. Charles V himself, with all his genuine piety, was capable of
an alliance with Henry VIII, whom he had himself asked the Pope
to excommunicate.

In comparing the two men, we cannot but call Solyman the
freer and more independent, though Charles, too, was a complete
autocrat and consulted no man's opinion. The sultan was caliph—
that is, his own pope; the emperor had to fight and depose Popes
and even take Rome before one of them would crown him. The
sultan might at worst have to put down the uprising of some conquered state such as Syria. But the Spanish cities and half of Germany kept rebelling against Charles for thirty years. The intellectual revolution known as the Reformation, which rose only for brief
moments to the point of political rebellion, cast the old fratricidal
struggle of the German princes in a form that engaged the devout
emperor more actively than an artillery battle for some inherited
territory. When the Protestant defection from the Pope became a
defection from the emperor, with Germany in the midst of civil
war between two armies, Emperor Charles found himself deprived
of the strength and freedom to develop according to his nature
within this world empire. Thus he eventually lost a good part of the
prize to which he had devoted his life. Without the Reformation,
indeed, the sultan's empire in its rise would probably have been
crushed by a united Christendom. But the sects fought one another
more bitterly and passionately than they did the common enemy,

just as the socialist sects of Europe have done before our own eyes, thus allowing their enemy, capital, to remain dominant up to the present moment. Luther, then, was the man to whom Solyman the Turk should have put up a monument.

These two rulers make nonsense of the old prejudice that would have the Asiatics more barbarous than the Europeans, even in modern times. Neither the Christian nor the Mohammedan soldier was effectually prevented by his religion from practicing such atrocities as his descendants still continue today, four hundred years after. When Emperor Charles's army, made up of German Protestant and Spanish Catholic soldiers, took Rome by storm in 1527, they ravaged it just as their forebears the Vandals had done ten centuries before. The emperor, it must be admitted, was so horrified by the reports that he called off all celebration of his first son's birth. The sultan would certainly have done no such thing.

Both seem to have possessed equally strong senses of responsibility. To prove this we have the popular administration of Solyman; and Charles V, emperor at twenty-five, wrote a sort of diary in which we find the following: "How hard it is to decide everything, though I wear myself to the bone! While I see and feel time passing, and us passing with it, I should not wish to die without leaving some honorable remembrance behind. Yet hitherto I have accomplished nothing for my personal glory."

It is deeply moving to see the two rulers in their old age, sick and half broken, going into battle once more with the old valor. The gouty emperor, driving or reclining most of the time, once more took the field before the fortress of Metz; but in vain. Then he made the great decision that only Diocletian before him had ventured, voluntarily surrendering his power. Although basically his life had miscarried, the speech he delivered to his followers at Brussels would be enough in itself to prove him the last great emperor, a true successor to Charlemagne and Frederick II.

The sultan, too, once the best horseman in the whole equestrian Turkish nation, finally followed his army to Hungary in a carriage. A fortress defended by the Hungarian hero Zrinyi held out stubbornly. Just before its capitulation the seventy-one-year-old sultan suddenly died; the fortress fell three days later. Emperor Charles had rehearsed his own funeral just before his death and then had died with full Spanish ceremonial. The sultan rode back to his capital a corpse, in a Bulgarian cart drawn by bony horses.

Probably no one mourned these two. Charles's son Philip had come into his inheritance during his lifetime and had never loved his father. History bestowed the title of "the Drunkard" on Soly-man's son Selim. But as always, the harem had long since destroyed family life. The celebrated Roxolana, a bought slave of the same rank as Emperor Constantine's wife ten centuries before, instigated the assassination of Solyman's favorite son, which was followed by a whole series of family murders.

Charles, in turn, who spent with his beautiful Portuguese wife fourteen years of perfect harmony that ended only with her death, only had illicit affairs before and afterward. From them sprang his two brilliant children, Margaret and John of Austria. How Philip wished he might have killed his bastard brother in the Turkish fashion! With his son Don Carlos he even succeeded in a strictly legal way.

If we compare the cultural accomplishments of the two rulers, we are amazed to see how much greater the Turk proved himself. The Catholic emperor's taste is attested by festivals, clothing, and deportment, and he succeeded in steering exactly midway between arrogance and humility. He lived in opposition to the Renaissance spirit; the acknowledgment of his natural children was really his only concession to the behavior of a Renaissance prince.

He began a magnificent circular building next to the Alhambra but did not finish it. From this great king we have no lasting law, scarcely one act of patronage of the arts. If it were not for a few anecdotes, some private letters, and his portraits by Titian, we should not know what to think of him.

To the sultan, on the other hand, the Turks gave the name of "the Lawgiver." When we see the consequences of his legal code in the East through three hundred years, we are ready to set him beside Justinian and Napoleon. The secret of his government seems to have been a financial orderliness unusual among orientals. The private seraglio funds were kept separate from the public treasury, which was located in the Seven Towers. Since he ruled thirty kingdoms, with eight thousand miles of seacoast, he could not have succeeded so long without this exceptional measure. His establishment of common schools, universities, and hospitals in Asia was not surpassed even by Europe in the sixteenth century. Three things, a contemporary chronicler wrote, were close to his heart: the capture of Vienna, the building of a tremendous mosque, and a water supply for Constantinople.

And so he built the Solymanjé mosque in Constantinople at the very time when Julius II was building Saint Peter's in Rome. Both domes still arch heavenward today. Sinan, the Michelangelo of Constantinople, was a Christian renegade. He finished his dome more happily than the Florentine, who was cheated of his plans. Like the great Italian masters, Sinan also built modern bridges. One of his colleagues actually installed the conduits from the Black Sea to Constantinople on great aqueducts and built running fountains everywhere in the metropolis. The poets sat and sang on the streets and in the palace, and people dared to call one of them the new Hafiz.

As long as seventy years after Solyman's death his name was shouted to the heavens, a chronicler calculated, from some 2,060 mosques. Emperor Charles, whose armies kept the sultan from Vienna, left behind neither laws nor monuments with the exception of the Carolina, the torture codex. The Spanish monarchy broke up thirty years after his death; the German monarchy had long since been shattered. Solyman's empire, on the other hand, endured for three hundred years with a few slight losses.

Once again, as in the life of Frederick II, we see how a ruler may lose everything and yet live on more grandly in the end than many a rival whose successes were innumerable. And so the great personality of Charles V, reflected above all through his adversary Luther, has enjoyed the same splendid remembrance in Europe that the Asiatic world has preserved for his more fortunate antagonist Solyman. In Asia, Emperor Charles is as little known as Solyman in Europe. Nothing could show more plainly than their completely separate celebrity that these two greatest rulers of the century belonged to two separate civilizations on the Mediterranean, for which both worlds were fighting.

III

THE OLDEST MEDITERRANEAN COMMERCIAL HOUSE, the Republic of Venice, tacked for a century between the struggling powers. It was not lost as Pisa had been, nor was it yet so dependent as Genoa. It still had its branches along the Adriatic and in the Archipelago, and when it defended the island of Cyprus, with the support of powerful states, the Turks were twenty-four years in taking the island. The sultan no longer distributed monopolies, and Venice, which had once conquered Constantinople and inherited what was hers, now passed on her heritage to the new masters, without being actually conquered herself. The Venetian nobility withdrew their money from shipping, preferring instead to invest in terra firma.

Turkey and France might be described as the successors of Venice, but only in the sixteenth century. Their association increased their commercial power, because for a time the sultan allowed only the French to sail under their own flag in his waters; other great powers had to use the French flag. The French merchant, being now a sort of ally to the Turks, was the only one who enjoyed protection. About 1600 France received the privilege of protecting the Holy Places in Palestine, greatly to the advantage of her Levantine trade. Simultaneously, however, the French king planned a crusade, or at least gave the appearance of doing so. His minister even based his plans for peace everlasting on the annihilation of Turkey. Every man with any proper pride became enthusiastic about crusades in those days—Père Joseph, Wallenstein, Gustavus Adolphus. But their plans gathered dust in the chancelleries of Europe, for the phrase "reasons of state" had become fashionable to excuse nationalist extravagances.

Venice went on tacking. With the Portuguese in India, goods no longer went by land from Asia to the Mediterranean. People

looked toward Suez again, and once more the canal was declared
to be impossible. But Venice, like Constantinople in an earlier day,
had made adroit diplomats of adroit traders. While these men
amused themselves at royal courts, they brought home the newest
customs and clothes to their rich, fashionable, ocean city. The young
and bustling Hapsburgs threatened Venetian trade from Trieste,
which they were then building up. If Venetian patrol boats captured German merchantmen in the Adriatic, the noble gentlemen
from Venice and Vienna would hold conferences in their beautiful
palaces, with gorgeous festivities. They would sign and seal a smooth
parchment sheet, while the sailors of the two vessels lay rotting on
the bottom of the sea. Modern diplomacy began in Venice, not Paris.

Now that they were no longer sailing north at all, and less often
eastward, the Venetians substituted their own wares for the foreign
goods they no longer dealt in. And what could this precious and
fabulous city have made but precious and fabulous things? Glass
and lace became its industries, graceful leather and textile products,
and along with these went an art of living that brought new forms
of refinement.

There was even a king in the Republic of Venice; and like the
kings of fable he lived to be a hundred. Actually everything about
him was fabulous. Anyone whose idea of perfection is steadily
growing creative power, an abundant and harmonious life, manly
fulfillment of everything God can plan for a human being, will
surely credit Titian with the most perfect destiny that any artist ever
knew.

In this sense he was the most powerful king on the Mediterranean. He served no one but the elements and the sea; he loved
no landscapes, no women, no colors but those he was born to, looking down on islands and sea from the mountains that encircle
Venice. He was descended from a captain, Tiziano Vecellio, the
son of the mountains, of arms, and of love. The portraits of him in
old age are all we have to tell us how handsome he was in his youth.
But we might guess it, too, from the favor of the women he won
from youth through old age. It was they who kept him vigorous

for this superhuman span, in gratitude for the paintings that immortalized them.

Though he lived into the Counter Reformation, Titian is more completely representative of the Renaissance than any other artist. A contemporary of Michelangelo for ninety years, Titian outlived him and all the others whose fame had filled the sixteenth century. He did not become famous himself until he was forty. The fact that nature granted him a century was typical; indeed, his old age may be said to illustrate his own artistry in living and painting. He is second to Bramante, Michelangelo, and Leonardo only in that he was exclusively a painter, scarcely touching other arts. But he outdoes them all in abundance of life; in this and in the richness of his work no later figure except possibly Rubens compares with him.

He surrounded himself with less mystery than the Florence and Milan masters; that very fact made him a brother to the Renaissance blades who became *condottieri,* dukes, or Popes. Titian could have been one of these men of action far more easily than Michelangelo or Leonardo could, though they were the ones who knew how to build fortifications. His pantheism, too, was more resolute; no one else dared paint such pictures as the "Festival of Venus" and the "Bacchanal." In reality, Titian, more than all the other artists of the Renaissance, belongs to the age of Pericles.

Venice, whose gondolas and canals are seen in so many paintings of his epoch, encouraged his pagan exuberance, whereas in Rome and Florence monitors and viewers-with-alarm kept raising their heads. It was Venice the Republic that gave his nature a far more princely quality than the princedoms did. His city and his studio were on the sea, opening up to him a vista that no inland city had. All the other great painters saw the world ride past on horseback; Titian saw it arriving on shipboard from the miraculous Orient.

But the scenes he chose to depict were very different from those of the Dutchmen, who never wearied of painting sea and ships. Titian almost never painted the ocean. He painted the ancient mythical figures of the Mediterranean and the contemporary princes and kings. This greatest portraitist of the south (Holbein came from the north) painted Charles V three times, and there were literally two emperors face to face. The legend of the brush that the model picked up for the painter has meaning, for no one ever heard any such tale of Raphael or Bellini. The imperial patent of nobility that the emperor bestowed on him was but a small symbol. While the other great artists of the age were royal guests, Titian invited the princes to his table, where they might perhaps meet Aretino, the Voltaire of the Renaissance. The emperor, who surely would rather have singled out a Spaniard or German, invited the seventy-year-old Venetian to come to Germany as his court painter. He sensed a kindred spirit.

The superb pride, the kingly gesture found in all Titian's portrait subjects irradiated his life and work to the full. His models turned into kings, his women into goddesses. Giorgione may sometimes seem deeper, the elder Palma sweeter, Veronese more splendid, but Titian embraces them all within himself—if only through the accident of his age. He was past thirty when he fled the plague that carried off his young teacher Giorgione; and decades after Tintoretto began the silent struggle against him in Venice Titian was still painting.

Titian's vast output is like Shakespeare's or Rembrandt's: no one work overtops and combines the others, as "The Concert" does with Giorgione or "Saint Anne" with Leonardo. All the men and particularly the women he painted form a sort of order whose members wear his badge. No one in the Renaissance except perhaps Michelangelo established any such assemblage of figures. But Michelangelo left many fragments, and his life swelled and faded, constantly vacillating like Faust. Titian, like the Mediterranean, knew scarcely any tides. Like the Mediterranean, he loved the blue and golden day, but he knew the storms; he lived and painted them.

A Venetian in everything, even in his greed for money and his business acumen, he rediscovered the beauty of women in this city of love and passion. He always preferred the amorous creatures of the people to any sophisticated princess. His portraits of women are not numerous, though the picture of Empress Isabella is perhaps the most perfect female portrait ever painted. But a thousand times he painted nameless women. It becomes evident to anyone who looks at the celebrated narrow picture called "Sacred and Profane Love," which ought to be entitled "Persuasion to Love," that Titian looked at women, as he did at the whole world, with the masterful eyes of a king. Thus he created a series of Queens, whom he abandoned each in turn.

We can see why nature was patient with him for a century when we examine his last pictures. He could never have done them in his earlier days. The iron courage with which the old man finally broke through his own forms was possessed by Michelangelo alone among his contemporaries. But such courage is more becoming to Titian, because it was much harder for him to cast a shadow on the last of a vigorous life than for Michelangelo, with his broken career. Yet in his very old age Titian gave up the beauty of pure colors, which he more than anyone else had perfected; eventually he painted three or four Rembrandtesque pictures, sixty years before Rembrandt. This voluntary abdication of his power might be compared with the retirement of Emperor Charles, whom he had painted so marvelously not long before. Only the emperor acted from renunciation and disappointment, the painter from wisdom and prescience.

Titian died of the plague probably in his hundredth year, and the occasion was unexampled in Venice. Fear of contagion led people to bury the dead in haste; no one dared go near them. But when Titian died, the whole city joined in solemn obsequies at the Frari church. The people of the Republic realized that they had lost their king.

IV

For THREE CENTURIES the Mediterranean was partly ruled and partly terrorized by pirates; it was seldom free of them, and then only in certain districts. They menaced or paralyzed commerce, and this had a strong influence on travel and civilization. That influence was possible only through the power of the sultans, who welcomed the activity of their piratical subject kingdoms, particularly in

Morocco, Algiers, and Tunis. When the tolerance of the Turks ceased and the clashes of the seventeenth century became acute, the Turks appeared outside Vienna by land and dominated the Mediterranean sea. The Mohammedan pirates of north Africa, defying the highly civilized company of Sun King, Spanish Hapsburgs, and Roman Popes, made the western Mediterranean unsafe.

A great principality supplied territory and backing. He who holds northwest Africa (then including the Straits of Gibraltar) can mount guard over southern Italy, Marseille, Genoa, and the entrance to the eastern Mediterranean. Furthermore anyone in that position then was almost beyond attack. The sea is usually stormy along those coasts. They were still without harbors, and the land behind had no water.

Because of their location the pirates, also called corsairs, were courted by successive Christian rivals. The mutual hatreds of the kings led them to support the infidels in secret against their adversaries. Francis I, the "Most Christian King," was not the only one who sold them powder for use against the Spaniards. Some of the Popes even sold licenses for this trade, which brought in a revenue up to 10,000 ducats a year.

Two brothers were the first to raise the old north African trade of piracy to such prosperity. Their sons and the sons' successors lasted longer than most dynasties of princely origin. Horuk and Khair-ed Din are supposed to have been sons of a converted Christian, who brought them up with all the pride of the corsairs, training them in a certain sort of chivalry, teaching them to keep their blood pure—all as much a matter of course as robbing and murdering Christian sailors. It is not certain that they also looted Mohammedan vessels, any more than we are certain of the murders that may be taking place among the elite troops of our modern dictators. It is certain that Horuk, summoned to help the sultan of Algiers, throttled his coreligionist in the bath with his own hands. This was admired as a heroic deed because the pirate, having lost an arm, had for some years used a silver one artfully contrived with springs by an Arab metal worker. Still, the action was a breach of hospitality, and an uprising followed.

After his brother's violent death Khair-ed Din (called Barbarossa because of his reddish beard) ruled, or perhaps we might say governed (and at any rate plundered), for another forty years. He lived to be more than ninety. He was very slow to approach the all-powerful caliph at Constantinople. A long time passed before the alliance of these two, joining forces because they were afraid of each other, led to the pirate's appointment as grand admiral of the Turkish navy. This relationship reminds us of the legitimizing of mistresses by the kings who could not live without them. Khair-ed Din, nearing seventy, kissed the sultan's golden slipper in the seraglio at Constantinople; he was not humbling his pride any more than the sultan was in bestowing the sword and golden staff of the law upon this potter's son.

Perhaps the pirates' strength lay in the fact that they regarded themselves as pirates. Actually they were only doing methodically, with an easy conscience, what other sailors tried to justify to themselves by false motives. Not gold alone but a deep social grudge and religious pride seem to have been what made these men expose themselves to a lifetime of personal danger. Since there were piracy and slavery among the Christians as well, the pirates intensified their own concept of honor still further; they considered themselves definitely superior to the Christians as human beings. Khair-ed Din refused to believe the prisoners who told him that Emperor Charles (whom he as a commoner hated for being an imperial heir) was taking command personally in the trenches at Tunis. The emperor, in turn, hated the revolutionary and undertook his second campaign against Khair-ed Din, the disastrous Algiers expedition, on the advice of his noble grandees and against the warning of the upstart Cortez. Charles suffered the greatest defeat of his life as a result.

Lord Byron and other poets have celebrated these rival codes of honor, which alter the ordinary conception of a pirate. Andrea Doria was considered the greatest sailor hero in Christendom, although he lived practically entirely on horseback until he was forty. He grew rich, just as Khair-ed Din did, by piracy. Then the emperor employed him to destroy the invincible foe. But on the day of the decisive battle, when the Genoese was expected to fight near Preveza on behalf of the emperor's ally Venice, he and his ships vanished. It was whispered that Doria and Khair-ed Din had reached a secret agreement to save their own reputations as warriors.

The pirates would usually surrender their prisoners for a large sum of money, and in general they were no crueler than any ship-owner with hundreds of slaves shackled to his galley benches. Accordingly, we must not look at the mighty institution of piracy, which shaped Mediterranean life for two or three centuries, in a moral light. The pirates' social grudge made itself felt everywhere; we see their attitude as a sort of constant revolution against the established powers. During a siege of Algiers Khair-ed Din had the notables and sailors of a captured galley paraded before him. First he savored their terror; then he said, "Instead of killing you I shall be merciful. The sailors I will release; the grandees shall be slaves."

These men who ruled the Mediterranean, as the *condottieri* did the mainland, were men of the Renaissance but were illegitimately descended. The energies of both were expected to be for sale, as, indeed, they were; but they were strong and redoubtable enough that all parties tried to buy them. Their unmorality was independent of any religion they might have inherited or accepted. The captains of Queen Elizabeth of England seized Spanish vessels and sold Spanish noblemen at Dover on certain market days for £100 a head. Around 1670, a seafarer was glad to fall into the hands of Mohammedan pirates, from whom he might buy his liberty, rather than of the English, who captured any ship not belonging to a friendly power, killed the crew, took the cargo, and sank the vessel.

As late as the eighteenth century the English tried to secure the African pirates to themselves in order to keep African grain away from the French. The dey of Algiers, then the pirate overlord, scented something similar when the French Revolution broke out. In 1790, he lent five million francs to young France without interest. The admiration of the corsairs was as strong as this. The story also shows what wealth Algiers had amassed through piracy.

Since robbery and murder were common on both sides, and the chivalrous gesture as well, each world erred in feeling superior to the other. When Emperor Charles captured Tunis, he embraced and kissed the first white slaves he released. A courtier warned him of the stench, and he cried out, "The fire of love cleanses the air!" Khair-ed Din, on the other hand, paid half his fortune to Doria for the freedom of a captive friend and lieutenant. During their occasional alliances the established powers hastened to do honor to their bastard colleagues. The Duke of Bourbon held a celebration for Khair-ed Din in Marseille such as the Pope himself would not have received; the ladies flocked in to see the famous old pirate, and the maidens had erotic dreams.

Piracy must have been a healthful trade; its greatest potentates all lived to an advanced age. Perhaps their simple life was what did it, for aside from women these rich and powerful men needed almost nothing. They taught abstemiousness in their schools, where young men were trained as sailor-pirates. There was nothing on shipboard but water, rusk, and rice; when they once found a live sheep aboard a captured Maltese vessel, it was regarded as a disgrace to the captain.

Their dangerous business taught the pirates a knowledge of humanity, for they had to be able to distinguish the valuable prisoners. The accounts sound like Gestapo reports. If a man had smooth hands, they concluded he must be wearing his rags to deceive; in those days, if he had not done physical labor and yet was at sea, one could safely conclude that he was rich. They scrutinized hair, gait, habit of speech. The traders who bought the captives in the market place had people who but yesterday had believed themselves lords of creation put on display naked in the burning sun. They would make them jump, do gymnastics, and sometimes have them flogged. The dey, who had first choice of one-eighth of all the slaves, was addressed as His Royal Highness by European ambassadors as late as 1820.

The vitality of the pirates was fantastic. When we see Khair-ed Din living to be ninety odd, Doria ninety-eight, after their strenuous lives, we think of the hundred-year-old Titian's mighty figure. Khair-ed Din at seventy-eight married Donna Maria, a young Christian beauty from Reggio. He made her adopt Islam

and showered her parents with splendid gifts just stolen by his men
on another coast. Reggio he spared, taking nothing and even paying for water and provisions in order to honor the beauty's native
city. In his last days he lived with her in his palace on the Bosporus. Like Colleoni, he founded a home for the sailors' children
and designed his own tomb. Even a hundred years afterward every
passing vessel fired a salute to him. It was a life of happy fulfillment.

His successor, whom he had ransomed, was a captive at the age
of forty in the hands of a Doria half his age. He suffered fearful
maltreatment and then was chained in a galley for four years. A
celebrated Maltese knight, who had been shackled in a Turkish
vessel himself and then released, now saw his enemy in his place.
"The uses of war?" he asked mockingly. "The *fortunes* of war,"
replied the other. This dialogue shows the brotherhood that infidel
pirates and devout knights felt. These same Maltese knights, the
vows of whose order sanctified any robbery of Mohammedans,
later, in 1644, boasted of breaking the world record when they took
a vessel bearing a cadi of Mecca, who had fallen into disfavor and
was therefore emigrating. He and his treasures and wives were
worth nine million dollars in gold.

In this trade also the destinies of the renegades were the more
interesting. Endi-Ali, a later figure who was considered the greatest seaman of his time, was born to a distinguished Christian family
in Calabria and captured as a child. He is said to have sat pale and
mute on the rowers' bench, refusing to accept Islam. A blow in the
face from a Turkish soldier supposedly aroused him, and he vowed
vengeance, but not upon his oppressors. Like Faust flinging himself frantically into dissipation, he swore to be avenged on those
who had given him birth. Becoming a Mohammedan he won royal
honors by strength and guile, captured and killed thousands of
Christians as the decades passed, and was dreaded as the most brutal
of all the pirates. In his old age he became suddenly gloomy, for
years dressed entirely in black, and could not endure the sound of
human voices. The Janizaries suspected him of being secretly a
Christian, for which a French bishop praised him. Finally, having

equaled his predecessors' age of ninety, he is supposed to have died, like Attila, in the arms of his last beloved.

His successor as pirate leader was the equally famous Ciccala, the son of a noblewoman from Messina. He too was captured as a boy and later was so consumed with longing for his mother that he asked the viceroy of Sicily for a meeting. Being refused, he ravaged the shores of the island for four years. When he finally had too many hostages in his hands, his mother was allowed to see him. He stayed on board his vessel with her for a few hours, then sent her back, and never touched the island again.

There were also pirates who retired to a life of quiet after some lucky capture, like simple people who have won a sweepstakes. They became Christians again, took new names, went to confession; old acquaintances or documents might reveal their hidden career long afterward. In their old age, like wicked old monkeys, these men would hold orgies of hatred, those of love being over. One aged dey of Tunis used to have an ear cut off his enemies and force them to eat it. Or he would have a man killed and skinned and then would have the skin stuffed with straw and set up as a puppet. These cruelties remind us of the late Roman emperors or of modern dictators.

Very few Christian slaves could tell their story to the world; most of them were too much broken after their escape to write anything. Many were known about, yet they could not be ransomed because nobody stumbled upon them. One great Hellenistic scholar, sent in search of old manuscripts by Francis I, perished on the benches of a galley. John Knox, the Scottish reformer, spent two years in a French galley but said little about it afterward. A British clergyman, Spragg, refused to leave his galley companions and consoled them for years. Finally he escaped with them in a folding boat that they built of canvas. They got across the sea from Tunis to Majorca.

Cervantes, four years after the Battle of Lepanto, where he had received a chest wound and lost one arm, was captured by pirates and spent five years in slavery. He could not be ransomed, because important letters of introduction increased his price. Every

seafarer then knew that the first thing to do in case of attack was
to throw one's papers overboard; only the future novelist forgot
to do this. Being useless as a rower, he was cast into the bagnio. He
had to keep waiting and waiting because the ransom for his brother,
captured at the same time, arrived first. We can feel how a great
achievement exalts a man, for everyone who reads these lines would
naturally have preferred to see the writer released rather than his
brother. Finally his mother succeeded in saving him for the world,
him and the yet unwritten *Don Quixote* as well.

The strangest of all Mediterranean slave stories can be read on
a tombstone in Corsica. It is nearly unique in the history of mankind, for here someone uses his own epitaph to give information for
the rescue of one still alive:

"Seafarer from the north, whoever you be, tell Wilhelm Loewen-
stern in Stralsund that you have seen the grave of his wife, who was
sold into slavery in Tunis, then released, and who died here in June,
1698. My son is still in slavery there. Let his father come to deliver
him. If he passes by this place, he will find the remains of his Euphrasia if he lifts up the stone that covers the ashes. If the winds
come to scatter them, his tears will moisten them. Hear my plea
to you, a stranger, or you are no being of flesh and blood!"

Later excavation revealed another document: "Whoever you be
that look within this grave, know that G. Wachtendonk brought
me the news of my Euphrasia. I sought my son in Africa, and found
him dead. I have buried his remains here beside those of his beloved
mother."

V

THE TURKISH SULTAN sat enthroned at the easternmost point of the
Mediterranean; he governed the empire through viziers from his
gorgeous palace on the Bosporus with its thousandfold decoration.
The ocean he ruled with the aid of pirates who were half kings.
At that time, too, the Spanish kings were carrying on the same
business at the extreme west; only their servants were called dukes
and grandees, and their navy an armada. In contrast with the

warmth of the colorful seraglio at Constantinople, with its rugs
and lamps, curtains and divans, fountains and parrots, there stood
near Madrid the gray, somber prison of the Escorial, which pale
King Philip had built as a castle. One was made for love, for the
pleasures of life; the other seemed built for arrogance and humility,
which Philip displayed alternately to man and God with the same
complete coldness.

These sons of the great rulers Solyman and Charles were typical
sons and heirs. They lost much of the power their fathers had
gained; the Turk ruled only eight years, the Spaniard almost forty.
But although Philip seems an earnest king by comparison with the
carefree drunkard, he left a ruined Spain behind him, whereas the
sultans were able to go on amusing themselves in almost undimin-
ished affluence for another three hundred years.

Philip II is surely the coldest figure the sunny Mediterranean
ever produced, except possibly Augustus. The pale, blond head with
the opaque bright blue eyes might have belonged to the kind of
Saxon tailor we find in old German comedies. But his bearing, his
garb, his formality plainly betrayed his Spanish heritage; and so,
more than anything else, did his fanaticism. A few people saw
him smile, and he even had a mistress now and then. But the black
leadenness of his nature deprived him of all happiness, and even
the cruelest report from his Inquisition can scarcely have filled
him with true joy.

He combined in a sort of mystical synthesis the ideas of authority and religion. Although he was undoubtedly a religious man,
he exploited dogma, church, and Pope for his political purposes,
which were concerned exclusively with the Catholic greatness of
Spain. Whereas his father, Charles V, was a king born, Philip was
one by dint of supreme exertion; hence the gloom of his life and
his court. It has been said that the sun never set on Philip's empire;
it would have been better to say that in his empire it never rose.
The strongest assault upon the spirit of the Renaissance took its
rise here in Castile—for the volatile Aragonese always rejected
Philip—and the age that goes under the name of Counter Reformation might better have been called the Counter Renaissance.

We have only to compare the pictures of the conquistadors about 1570 with the *condottieri* of 1500, both alike in courage and cruelty, to see that they are related as el Greco's portraits are to those of Titian. The fanatical belief of these Spanish conquerors in a divine mission, the chivalrous passion ironically immortalized in *Don Quixote,* together took the place of the radiant, vital spirit of the Renaissance. The Renaissance loved life, happiness, and power and therefore strove for them. All the gold and silver that the Spaniards stole from their new subjects while subduing America by the sword had to be stamped with the sign of the cross in order to seem moral. They kept repeating these false notes, and the notes rang true. The exaggeration that characterizes such great figures as Saint Theresa and Loyola brought first the triumph and then the downfall of Spain.

Neither the king of Spain nor the sultan perpetrated his deeds of violence through overflowing vitality and the sheer right of the strong. Each consulted his religion and from it received absolution, ostensibly for higher ends. Philip got his assassinations, his persecutions of Moors, Jews, and Protestants legalized; the sultan's no one recorded. Being his own Pope, the sultan may have laughed at the law over his wine or in the harem; the Spanish king took it with deadly seriousness. His bedroom, opening on the altar side of the palace chapel, had a window through which he could see the crucifix from his bed; here was the complete humility of the lord of half the world. But in the council of state his seat was elevated, and his ministers sat so far below him that they had to talk loud to be heard.

The king listened to them, and he listened also to the representatives of the people, but they were allowed only to put forward wishes. By 1600 the Spaniards were much less free than they had been two or three centuries before. This lack of freedom, which paralyzed the whole nation, is the deepest reason why Spain lost world colonial predominance to England. In England a sense of independence had awakened early, been constantly cultivated, and has never died out. In the long run no people can rule over others unless it controls itself, as the Greeks, Romans, and English did in

their best days. They were the greatest colonists in history. If Columbus had sailed under the English flag, as he intended for a time,
Spain might never have had colonies.

The strength of the Spanish body politic was not equal to its
colonies, and economically speaking the colonization came too soon.
While the gold ships and silver fleets from America kept arriving
at Cádiz and Portugal (briefly conquered by Philip), Spanish finances steadily declined for lack of responsibility and budgeting.
The largest loan in history up to that time, granted by German and
Italian banks, together with all the fabulous treasure of a newly
discovered land, was not enough to sustain the finances of the great
empire. In the course of twenty years the state was bankrupt three
times.

Nevertheless, the Spaniards gained one decisive victory over
the Turks. An October day of the year 1571 saw near Lepanto a
Mediterranean naval battle of dimensions greater than any since
the Battle of Actium, sixteen centuries before. Some five hundred
vessels were involved. It was also the last battle of galleys in which
fighting success depended on boarding gangplanks, in fearful hand-
to-hand combat on the overcrowded vessels themselves.

The battle was decided by the genius and courage of a single
leader, fighting against an inexperienced adversary. Don John of
Austria, the natural son of Charles V, had inherited some of his
genius, perhaps partly because he was a bastard, whereas the weak
Philip was merely born of the marriage bed. Being jealous of his
half brother, whom he was obliged by their father's will to recognize as a Spanish grandee, the king had already sought to check
the young man's heroic career. The Turks were commanded by a
still younger man, who had gained leadership merely as a favorite
of the sultan. Anchored in the Gulf of Corinth, in a splendid position but late in the season, the Turks need not have stirred. For
the Spaniards, then leagued with Venice, Florence, and the Pope,
had their combined navies at the opening, southeast of Corfu; but
they could not have stayed there.

Ali Pasha, however, filled with the vague urgency of a young

favorite, wanted to win glory, and he opened battle despite more experienced advice. The Turks in those days were considered invincible: people had vainly tried through sixteen battles to defeat the Turkish navy. This reputation, established by Khair-ed Din the pirate, was the more surprising because they were not and never have been sailors by nature. The superior Turkish fleet was spread out over a three-mile front; that of the Spaniards took up but half the space, so that it could push through the Turkish center. In those days a naval battle was still punctiliously announced by firing a cannon into the air, and the enemy would discharge an answering shot.

In Don John's report we read: "The fighting on the royal galley had been going on for a full hour. Twice the mainmast of the Turkish vessel had been reached, but each time the onrushing masses of Mussulmans had thrown our party back to the forepart of the Christian flagship. The Count of Pliego fought with Don John in the runway between the rowers' benches. After an hour and a half God granted victory to the royal galley; the Bassa with more than five hundred Turks was beaten, his flags and standards were

taken, and in their stead the cross was made fast to the mainmast. Don John caused the cry of victory to be raised, and all the vessels joined in. Now the victory inclined to the side of the Christian armada. Don John was wounded in the leg, but only slightly."

During the decisive six hours both sides unchained the slaves from the benches. What dreadful moments of sudden ecstasy for men exchanging chains and oars for arms and freedom! A quarter of a million slaves are said to have fought like madmen in a tiny space. The Turks lost 25,000 men, the Christians 8,000. The Pope received 800, the Spaniards 17,000 slaves. King Philip received the news of victory with unmoved countenance, and heard his usual Mass. All he did was to order a Te Deum sung afterward.

The moral effect upon the world was tremendous, but the jealousy of the Christian powers and that of King Philip of his own brother were too great for the league to exploit its victory. The Turks on their part built 250 new vessels within a few years. The consciousness of their wealth, land power, and self-assurance was as strong as the Spaniards' sense of insecurity. Both peoples were unfree, but the Turks were still the younger after all. And by threats they gained a peace as favorable as if the great naval battle had never been fought at all.

Three years later Venice, whose vessels had taken an important part in the victory, had to surrender to the Turks Cyprus, her last great Mediterranean possession except Crete.

Cyprus, the biggest island in the eastern Mediterranean, wild and mountainous in the interior, soft and enervating along its richly indented shores, is perhaps the most romantic of all the islands except possibly Corsica; its history is so, at any rate. Its location, equidistant from Asia Minor in the north and Syria in the east, in the big bay between Alexandretta and Beyrouth, made the island a resort for all fugitives and at the same time a base for every kind of pirate and seafarer. The best timber and wine rendered it attractive, and so, above all, did copper, mined here even in antiquity, and actually called *cyprium* in Latin. Copper is sacred to Aphrodite, who lived in Cyprus. For the sake of these treasures the island was taken by Phoenicians and Greeks, Ptolemies and Arabs. Saint Paul and Saint Mark stopped here in their travels; here Jews and Christians brawled in fearful massacres. The Byzantine emperors held the island longest—for some seven centuries, with a few interruptions.

The fate of Cyprus has been like that of a beautiful but defenseless woman, exposed to a constant series of new adventures and hardly finding them pleasant. When Richard Coeur de Lion passed by on his crusade in 1191, instead of fighting the infidel sultan he sent his knights ashore on a storming party, took the island from the Christian emperor of Constantinople, and sold it to the Templars, who immediately sold it to a French chevalier who happened to be looking for a small kingdom. Thus Guy de Lusignan, who bore the title of King of Jerusalem, finally found a piece of territory to match his crown. He established a dynasty, and his house actually ruled for three centuries as kings of Cyprus. They were surrounded by a tiny feudal state with all the insignia of rank, ceremony, swords, and costly garments, in a pompous operatic style. But the underlying basis was a grotesquely impoverished population.

One of these kings died, leaving a legitimate daughter and a

natural son. As usual the bastard was the more able and determined; he took the throne with scant ceremony. The daughter and her husband, eager to inherit the money and power, rebelled, enlisting the Pope and Genoa against the usurper. A family war threatened. The only stake that the illegitimate Lusignan could offer except his own person was his friendship with a nobleman from a powerful Venetian house, with whom he had spent his wild youth. This nobleman, Andrea Cornaro, wielded great influence and was able to show the doge and the council how precious Cyprus might be, provided that they would take the side of the bastard against Genoa and the Pope.

As in some comedy, the friends realized that only a great marriage could authenticate the false heir. A fourteen-year-old niece, still in care of the nuns, was chosen and betrothed to the pretender Lusignan. After long intrigues the details of the marriage were arranged. There was a great session of the senate. Catherine Cornaro, who was, of course, very beautiful, was solemnly adopted by the doge as the "daughter of the Republic." When these great traders scented anything like copper mines, they were imaginative and ingenious.

Catherine sailed down the Adriatic and through the Ionian Sea to Cyprus in a merchant vessel, thinking perhaps of Aphrodite. At the harbor her unknown, interesting husband awaited her, and she was crowned "Queen of Cyprus, Jerusalem, and Armenia" in the presence of a few thousand soldiers, pirates, herdsmen, and smugglers. A year later her husband died of the fever, and after his death she brought a son into the world. But soon there was hatched a new plot of the Mediterranean powers against Venice. Revolts and battles by land and sea followed, and Catherine was taken prisoner.

The honor of Venice had been impugned now; the desired pretext was at hand. Landing, the Venetians seized power for the daughter of their Republic. The child died, but Catherine had learned to enjoy authority, and she began to think of marrying the king of Naples. Endless intrigues of power, love, and jealousy, of pride and rapacity followed, all at a sunny little court in the middle of the Mediterranean. Finally an energetic Venetian government ordered Catherine to abdicate. A thirty-five-year-old beauty, she came home now to a castle given her by the Republic. She spent twenty years there, as the center of a court of love and the Muses, leading a life compounded of pleasure, renunciation, and imagination. That was the time at which Titian painted her.

When Cyprus became Turkish half a century later, another romantic story lay behind it. Among the Jews who fled the Spanish Inquisition, there were, just as today, great doctors and scholars, musicians and actors, who made careers for themselves among the Turkish grandees and the sultan's entourage. José Miquez, a wine merchant, had Catholicism forced upon him in Portugal and then escaped to Constantinople, where he reverted to Judaism. The Turks called him Nassi, and he rose to greater rank and fortune than any of his race. With his quickly amassed millions he managed to amuse the crown prince and to prove to him that Mohammed had never forbidden wine in certain forms. If the bibulous Selim, on his accession to power, were to remove the prohibition of wine, the sultan and the Jew could profit at the same time. It was necessary merely to take Cyprus from the hated Venetians and thus gain the best wine of the Mediterranean, along with a new naval base.

The sultan took as much of a liking to the clever Jew as the emperor in *Faust* did to Mephistopheles' plans. For a high rent Selim leased him Naxos and some others of the Cyclades, which did not belong to the sultan at all. Their expelled overlord tried in vain to stir up the Pope. Miquez-Nassi now began calling himself duke of the Archipelago. "Josephus Naci Dei Gratia Dux Pelagi 1577," reads a coin on which he looks like the sun king. But he was too shrewd to play the new Dionysus at Naxos, delivering Ariadne; instead he sent out a governor, remaining in Constantinople himself and marrying a beautiful Jewess who suited him much better than any imitation Greek heroine.

At court, with his mouth always close to the ears of the great and his ear always near their lips, the shrewd Jew succeeded in rousing the government's cupidity for the copper, the Hellenists' for Ariadne, and the sultan's for the sweet wine of Cyprus. Venice, weakened in any case, had to submit to the loss of Cyprus soon after her victory at Lepanto.

Thus a Portuguese Jew made Cyprus Turkish, and so it remained for three hundred years, until the English took it in charge by treaty in 1878.

VI

THE ISLAND OF CRETE fell into Turkish hands a century after Cyprus. This was the last great Venetian possession, the last important eastern Mediterranean base belonging to Christians. Since Crete had always been inhabited by Greeks, as it still is, the conquest is also a sample of the struggles between Greeks and Turks, which followed a curiously wavy line for three hundred years and finally ended with Greek liberation.

The Cretans, particularly in the south of the long, slender island, are wild mountaineers and warlike herdsmen like some of the biblical tribes. They are handsome and passionate, elementally violent like their steep-gorged mountains; they maintain a certain orthodox religion that is actually more of a superstition. They are of the Mediterranean type that refuses to be cowed by anything or anybody and has gradually, in the course of millenniums, brought forth civilization. We may liken the Cretans to their fellow Mediterraneans the Corsicans and Albanians, with whom they share a deep sense of honor and revenge and an unruly love of freedom. The Cretan is not, as has sometimes been asserted, a thief; no islander is ever a thief by nature.

Pirates they frequently were, and even oftener hosts to pirates, who hid away in the Cretan bays. But they seem to have been happier in the mountains than on ships. With long hair and beard, in wide jacket, a short Greek dagger always at their sides, even today they look like huntsmen from some romantic opera. Apparently they never take off their gigantic boots all their lives; they even wear them hooked to their belts with thongs.

How could such men, with such spirits and such weapons, ever have submitted to any conqueror? First they hated the Franks, then the Venetians, then the Turks; today they despise their Greek brethren of the mainland. Venice, as mistress of the island, vainly tried guile, then force. When a Sphakiote, a member of the wildest and most distinguished tribe, asked for the daughter of a Venetian aristocrat in marriage and finally got her, after long opposition, the authorities seized all the men and women present at the wedding banquet and hanged some five hundred people, most of them drunk, along with the bridegroom. In Crete a hundred years is not enough to wipe out such treachery.

Venice did worse than this: she offered a pardon to any Cretan sentenced for rebellion if he would bring the head of his father, brother or nephew to Canea, the capital. Only the murder of a man's own son was not required. It was impossible to keep a people permanently in subjection by such acts of violence. Under this pressure the proud tribes cultivated their arrogance more than ever, kept themselves entirely apart, and never mingled with the Turks, even in later times; not even a Cretan from the lowlands of the northern coast might defile the purity of the mountain maidens' blood. In consequence the people of the south coast even today are a special type, with blond hair, blue eyes, and a light complexion; no one knows whence it came.

So it would have been easy enough for the Turks to take the island from the Venetians if the Cretans had not put up a resistance to every kind of stranger. The Turkish conquest of Crete was a twenty-four years' war, and when the island finally did fall to the Turks in 1669, this conflict, twice as long as the Trojan war, with as many heroes and adventures, lacked nothing but a Homer.

The Greeks were able to remain pretty much a unit under Turkish rule and even to expand, through the expulsion of all the Franks and other foreigners whom the crusades had brought to Greece. Oppressed though it was, the Greek nation still remained united. The Christians were tolerated, and, in fact, there were estimated to be a quarter of a million Christians in seventeenth century Greece. But they were exploited by the Pasha. The tithe they had to pay was increased to a third, and the most vigorous Christian boys were conscripted in the old Turkish fashion for the Janizary corps.

The clergy were resplendent. From the patriarch at Constantinople, who, as "Pasha of the Three Horse-tails," was one of the highest dignitaries, down to abbot and monk, the men of the cowl lived in abundance. The people had to pay for this theocracy, which continued its Byzantine customs. Since the sultan appointed a new patriarch every few years, the profitable offices changed hands as they do at presidential elections in certain modern countries. This connection, shrewdly maintained by the sultans through the clergy and their independent Christians, restrained the church from any attempt at liberation. No one was more devoted to the infidel caliph than the devout patriarch at Constantinople.

The cleverest Greeks went into business, and as early as 1600 there were above 100,000 Greeks at Constantinople—the fathers of the Greeks who dominated Turkey economically during the nineteenth century and who were therefore so savagely exterminated in the First World War. An alien stock, no matter whether Greek, Armenian, or Jewish, must never venture to display too much talent and intelligence. Its hosts will make use of it for a long time, calling it assimilated, bestowing positions of dignity and trust upon it, and through it growing richer and more powerful. But some day, upon some reverse of the state, they will discover that those whose advice they have so long followed are obviously the culprits; they find a long-overgrown difference in races and avenge their quite irrelevant misfortune by the persecution of those whom they have so long professed to think their equals.

In Turkey particularly the Greeks suffered from the whims of chance that lead every despotism astray. Church, language, and opposition to the infidels did, no doubt, unite the Greeks within the Turkish empire; but their position varied greatly according to period and rank. In this they were like the Jews, whose oppressed and hated masses, as, for instance, in Poland, saw favored outstanding individuals growing rich and powerful.

Like all long and stubborn defenses, the struggle for Crete had renewed the world's sympathy for beleaguered Venice. Great political interests were also involved, and so at last it was possible, for the first time in the two hundred years since the establishment of the Turkish power, to organize the Christian "Holy League" against the Turks. This took place in the time of the Roi Soleil, in 1684. Pope, emperor, Venice, and king of Poland chose the hero of Crete, Morosini, now grown old, to be grand admiral of the Mediterranean. The German princes, as was their custom, sold their subjects at a stiff price to the united army, just as the pirate princes did their slaves.

The history of this war, practically without result as it was, would be no more worth mentioning than the other inane struggles fought on the Mediterranean at the time, except that one of mankind's irreplaceable treasures was knocked to pieces then. So this war, in which thousands of human beings perished, has become part of the history of culture, with which it has otherwise nothing whatever to do, all because of a single shot.

It was in the third year of the war, when the Christian powers, having gained a foothold in Morea, were besieging Athens. After their first losses the Turks barricaded themselves on the Acropolis, demolished the temple of Nike, and stored powder under the inner sanctuary of the little temple, just a short way below the Parthenon. The citizens of Athens sent their archbishop to Morosini's camp to promise him help if he would spare them. Matters would have gone off without an assault, for Athens was no fortress, and a peaceable solution was freely offered by the strongest of the parties.

But it happened that they were German detachments outside Athens. Count Koenigsmark, in command of the Venetian cannon, did not like a bombardment to slip through his fingers; he blazed away for two days, but in vain. A deserter reported that the powder had been moved into the Parthenon because the Turks thought no Westerner would hurt that famous temple. Thus the German count was both warned and tempted and certainly was well informed. Nor was he in the predicament of a man besieged or even bombarded. He began the battle wantonly, simply to destroy. He gave orders for the eastern battery to start firing.

It was a lieutenant of artillery from Lueneburg who aimed the gun at the Parthenon about seven o'clock on the evening of September 26, 1687, and discharged the shell. The desired crash followed; three hundred soldiers in the fortress were dead and are forgotten.

But Pericles' building, which had stood almost untouched for more than two thousand years, was blown up, its east and north sides destroyed. A miracle preserved the main western façade as it stands today.

Yet the old gods were avenged after all. Probably it was Poseidon who rolled down the chunks of marble upon the German destroyers at the moment of the explosion. The Venetians next tried to remove his statue and the horses hitched to Athena's chariot from the western pediment, and everything fell to pieces. All they got was the three ancient lions now standing before the arsenal in Venice. The only pleasure that even the Germans had after the explosion was transforming the Turkish mosque on the Acropolis, previously a church of Our Lady, into a Lutheran church.

The vengeance of the Greek gods took violent forms. Apparently a council must have been summoned on high to organize retribution. The plague broke out in Athens, killing thousands of the conquerors. Morosini's victories were over. In discouragement he dismissed his army and sent home the remnants of the Germans, who had sat idle for some months in Athens. After their departure anarchy broke out in Greece. A party in Constantinople used the swiftly growing revolt to start a revolution and overthrow the sultan—all because of the fall of Athens, because of the violence— all, we may say, because of that one shot.

The lieutenant who aimed the gun seems to have gone down in history without a name. But the German Count Koenigsmark, who gave orders to destroy the Parthenon, died shortly afterward of the plague.

VII

ABOUT 1600 two alien northern peoples made themselves at home in the Mediterranean, and if they did not seize all shipping, still they were strong enough to control the trade northward. The English and Dutch were the first outsiders to gain power here in the eight centuries since the Normans. Ways of doing things had changed, for what they wanted was not to found kingdoms but to buy or transport goods. And in order to be strong, not only against the pirates but still more against the commercial nations in the Mediterranean, they needed bases. That idea became fashionable at the time, and its importance was the same then as now, although there were no steamers or planes.

Holland has since vanished from the Mediterranean; England has dug herself in. All that England acquired there in three centuries was bases, which still remain. The two seafaring northern peoples came to the Mediterranean neither as barbarians, like the Teutons, Vandals, Goths, and Huns, nor as bringers of civilization, like the Arabs. They carried neither destruction nor light with them. They did not come as conquerors, ravaging the coasts, destroying Rome, and snatching treasures; but neither did they transplant scholarship, culture and learning, as the Moors had done to Spain. They improved the mechanics of navigation by their example and otherwise merely bought and sold, preferring to consume or invest their gains at home. In the good and the bad sense they always remained strangers to the Mediterranean.

It is surprising not that they came but that they came so late.

During the crusades the English had been neither merchants nor capitalists. By the time they became so, the commercial, seafaring, and all-round energy of the Mediterranean peoples had begun to decline. It was the familiar shift from old to young peoples that told the tale here; and since there were no more young nations on the Mediterranean, the strangers came to take over the dominion. The only difference was that they did it less noisily than previous invasions, with no struggles for countries, almost without battles, by the simple occupation of a few islands.

The last two great attempts at world power, the Spanish and the Turkish, had failed of their purpose by 1600. While the two giant realms lived on, neither was strong enough to dominate commerce and the sea. Philip's rule ended after the annihilation of his armada in the English Channel in 1588. The larger and heavier Spanish vessels—the biggest of them 1,300 tons—were outnumbered by the British, who brought into the battle 197 ships against Spain's 132. There is reason to believe that the English shipbuilding material (oak) was stronger and better resisting. Even the weather gave them an advantage against the tactics of the Spaniards. The Spanish waited in vain for auxiliary vessels expected from the Dutch coast ... some of their ships had to flee in the direction of Scotland, where they perished, and some of them went down in the Irish sea. Such was the end of Philip's proud sea power, of which Britain became the lucky heir.

The successors of the strong sultan were the fat, easygoing harem heroes who represented the world's caricatured idea of a Turk. They survived so long only through the jealousy of their Christian opponents. If the Turks had been real sailors, the English would never have conquered the Mediterranean. But they were not even traders, and their nomadic, equestrian origin clung to them for centuries. Unlike the Romans and the English, they did not learn navigation from their enemies.

England matured more slowly than Rome. For a thousand years she lived almost without colonies or distant ocean ventures; instead, she endured the invasion of foreign peoples, the Romans and the Danes, and as late as the Middle Ages she sought no more than a small kingdom on both sides of the Channel. Her kings gave monopolies to foreigners, and for two hundred years the German Hanseatic League was more powerful in London than the English merchants. Their fleet was small, their islands fronted upon two oceans, and their favorably situated river mouths did not inspire them.

The Tudors took the decisive step in connection with the new explorations. Here again the originator was not the man who gained the reward. Spanish and Portuguese discoveries in the south gave the great impulse to the island nation far to the north. Henry VIII, who represented the Renaissance in England, was the first to speak of "his empire." He built the first great navy of his time, and his daughter Elizabeth made it bigger still.

Of course, these were not the first English to visit the Mediterranean, but they were the first merchants with the power of a sovereign state behind them. When London weavers found the Genoese looting the goods they sent southward in 1412, all reprisals were ineffectual. It was not until the end of the century that Richard III ventured to appoint a Florentine as English consul. As late as 1497 English goods were still sailing to Genoa under foreign flags and in foreign bottoms. The ships that Shakespeare mentions seem to have belonged to the Ragusans. Fifty years later English vessels began to appear off Sicily, Cyprus, Chios, but still not under their own flag.

The others had a head start, all except Portugal being washed by the Mediterranean. How did it happen, then, that the English, the last comers, managed in a short time to become the greatest commercial power on the sea? How could they overtop the Turks and the Spaniards and possess themselves of not only the trade but the territories around the great oceans? The conventional answer is mercantilism, the balance of trade, the necessity of importing the most vital goods, home defense. They needed colonies in order to be independent of Portuguese and Dutch profits and also for the sake of the gold, which was commoner in America, according to the legends of the time, than copper in England.

But these reasons are only sufficient to explain a need. The actual success sprang from two sources opened up by the state, not by economics. The first was the unity of the kingdom: England did not found a colonial empire until Scotland could no longer league herself with England's enemies—until she was Great Britain. The second reason was the guaranty of liberty for all citizens. Spanish oppression and English independence decided the fate of the two great colonial enterprises. Although America slipped from the hands of both at about the same time, only England preserved and extended her other possessions. The Englishman conquered the world as the Roman had done, because both were free within certain broad limits and both could feel the support of a strong state power behind them. With all its gold, Philip's absolute state plunged from one bankruptcy into another, while the finances of Elizabeth steadily improved.

When Henry VIII gave to his seafaring traders the title and privileges of "merchant adventurers," the British Empire took its stand on three foundations: king, merchant, adventurer. The first guaranteed power and protection to the mariner; the second assured the motive of gain, commerce, money; the third, the courage to exchange a snug island for strange lands. The Portuguese too had courage, the Spaniards also understood trade, and their kings were no less powerful. But no man could tell, coming home richly laden, whether some enemy in the Inquisition or at court might not rob him of everything before he could reach a friendly judge. Along with the legal state, and often above it, there was a ruling party, just as there is in the dictatorships today. And despite all reverses, the English Magna Charta remained a mighty guaranty of justice and liberty.

Obviously this civil liberty awakened the spirit of enterprise or, at all events, made it possible. Oppression makes human beings dull and shiftless because they see no upward path before them. The Spanish people, no less gifted by nature than the English, declined in this fashion, and never started to come back until our own time. There are some telltale figures. A census of the year 1787 showed that among ten million inhabitants only two million worked for a living. Such figures as these mean defeat in the rivalry of nations, and autocracy must accept some share of the blame.

In England the kings understood the merchant, esteemed him, gave him titles. If their first colonists in America remained subjects all too long, still the kings were shrewd enough to withdraw their governing council and put the directors of a commercial company in its stead. This change led to the first voyages undertaken by the crown in the fifteenth century after Cabot's Canadian adventure. It did so again about 1600 after the distribution of crown lands in Virginia. The Spaniards, on the contrary, ruled their colonies with fire and sword in both eras. We have only to compare the heads of Pizarro and Cortez with those of Hawkins and Raleigh, and the two systems are made plain to us through their leaders. When Cecil demanded trade with India for the British in 1604 and the Spaniards no longer dared refuse, Spanish commerce lost a battle as decisive as that in which the Armada had been destroyed in the Channel sixteen years before.

It was the Spanish Crown and the British people that founded the colonies. In Spain, king, church, and court were the imperialists; in England it was the merchant. This was amply evident from the fact that Cromwell, the revolutionist who had his king beheaded, made the largest and most successful demands overseas. His political genius is shown by his inviting the Jews of Amsterdam to come to England and to reopen trade. The Pope, together with Tuscany, had for decades allowed the sale of English goods taken by the pirates, and by this receiving of stolen goods had passed them on to apparently rightful owners. Cromwell sent a squadron into the Mediterranean and so extorted reparations. He even got satisfaction from the pasha of Tunis, an archpirate, by sending his vessels directly into the harbor.

At the same time his aggressive domestic policies assured England a monopoly of her foreign trade. He prohibited the importation of non-English goods and allowed coastwise trading, fishing, and importing only under the British flag. Cromwell, who got these aims confirmed by the Treaty of Westminster, is the strongest symbol of the rising British world power. A farmer from the rural gentry, not a king, carved out that power. And this is the only reason why the English, sentimentally pitying the poor king, nevertheless are reconciled to Cromwell; indeed they put up a monument to him. Jamaica makes up for King Charles' head.

The Dutch did not become colonizers either until they were free, after 1609. They soon forced the Turks to let them fly their own flag. We can see from the annals of the time how these two northern peoples conquered the south and east as merchants. When we read the political dates from 1500 to 1600, there is almost nothing but such tedious figures as these:

1512.	French expelled from Italy.
1515.	Victory of the French, capture of Milan.
1525.	French defeat at Pavia, loss of Milan.
1527-1529.	Second War of the Two Kings, peace.
1536-1538.	Third War of the Two Kings, Francis I and Charles V.
1542-1544.	Fourth War of Two Kings.
1587.	English naval attack on Cádiz.

Comparing these with the colonial dates, we can feel the true pulse of the age:

1504.	First importation of Indian spices to the north by sea.
1517.	First coffee to Europe, first Negro slave trade in America.
1519-1522.	Mexico conquered, circumnavigation of the globe by Magellan.
1523.	Expulsion of the Europeans from China.
1528.	Cocoa bean brought from Mexico.
1553.	British Muscovite and British African companies founded.
1558.	Tobacco brought to Spain from South America.
1568.	London Exchange founded.
1569.	Map of the globe by Mercator.
1580.	Venetians bring coffee to Italy.
1581.	British Levantine Company.
1583.	Raleigh in Virginia.
1584.	Potatoes.
1595.	Dutch in East Indies.
1600.	Bank of Amsterdam.
1602.	Dutch East India Company.
1603.	French to Canada.
1608.	Jesuit state of Paraguay.
1610.	Invention of joint stock; tea to Holland.

The Mediterranean, as a secondary area in world economy, remained almost cut off from this expansion. But still the new spirit of world trade inspired the young colonial nations to assure themselves of the old trade routes around the mother sea. A sinister conspiracy of Spanish grandees, in 1618, leading to the revolt of Venetian officers against Spain, was decided by a foreign commercial power for the first time since the battle of the emperors. The Dutch intervened as allies of Venice, and when their naval hero, de Ruyter, sank sixteen pirate vessels on the Moroccan coast in 1655, the Dutch became really popular in the Mediterranean. They appointed consuls everywhere to safeguard their trade. The sultan did not finally allow the English to fly their own flag until 1597. About this time the English proved two of their greatest qualities—patience and voluntary renunciation. At first they tried to develop the land route from Aleppo to India as reinsurance in their struggle for the sea route. Failing in this effort, they sensibly gave it up, and then, but not until then, founded the East India Company. In the nature of things, a struggle between England and Holland for world trade leadership was bound to come, just as it had once come between Venice and Genoa.

In the seventeenth and eighteenth centuries there were two systems of protection against pirates: convoys and tribute. A combination of both was safest. Accompanying merchant vessels by men-of-war was customary in the Mediterranean for a hundred and fifty years. It did not stop until the decline of the pirates (and nowadays it is needed again, with a new sort of piracy making the seas unsafe).

The pirate galleys anticipated the submarines by two centuries in stopping and searching vessels on the high seas. And like submarines, they popped up everywhere, out of their haunts in obscure coves. They would mysteriously appear before Bruges, in Cornwall, at the Azores, robbing cargo vessels. A sort of unwritten agreement was made with them to let through certain privileged vessels that could identify themselves properly as having paid tribute. Two men would go over in a boat from the pirate to inspect passes and cargo.

But being unable to read, the pirates were often gulled by false papers. And so they took the precaution of carrying with them the half of a sea pass, torn irregularly in two; they would fit the ragged edges together. If a mistake happened after all and the enemy vessel slipped through, the pirate captain was beheaded at home if the story leaked out. But the thing most dreaded by the merchantmen was not robbery but the plague, which the pirates often brought on board. At one time every vessel that had been searched was held in harbor for two weeks.

All the great powers paid tribute to escape plundering; indeed the tribute sometimes consisted of war materials furnished by Dutchmen or Danes to the African pirate chieftains. Such gifts, as they were called, survived till 1817. The smaller states could not afford it, which led the American consul Shaler to write in one of his reports that these robbers in Algiers had been placated and encouraged by the first two sea powers of the world. Since they boldly despised international law, they had become the necessary instrument to injure the trade of the small powers. As late as 1825 all consuls had to doff their hats as they passed the royal palace in Algiers, and at audiences they could not wear swords. None of them was allowed to ride through the palace yard; they had to dismount, but their servants, being natives, were permitted to ride on beside them.

In the seventeenth and eighteenth centuries the English were less interested in north than in west Africa, where they carried on a lucrative slave trade, taking British iron, brass, cheap cloth, bad liquor, and trinkets to Guinea, exchanging them for Negroes, selling the "black ivory" in the New World, bringing home American products, and making a large profit on each leg of the voyage. Slavery was not abolished in the British colonies until 1834. When the slave trade was outlawed in England, in 1807, Lord Aldon objected: "The slave trade was sanctioned by a Parliament in which the greatest jurists, theologians, and statesmen sat."

While the Turks alternately advanced and retreated, being pushed out of Hungary and the Balkans, while Austrian emperors and Russian czars fought them with varying success, the Mediterranean remained always passive, with the Turkish Empire as a heavy, inert block, which people tried to hollow out slowly from within. Two more centuries were to pass before it finally exploded, in 1918. The economic dominance of the Christian nations in the

Mediterranean began about 1600 and political dominance about 1700.

This lag resulted from the lack of any truly universal concept. The church could no longer supply it, the Roman Empire of the German emperors had vanished, and the "European balance of power," which was invented about this time, held good only for the mainland. Nor was the Sun King's concept of the world capable of maintaining itself, because it did not start with the sea. France, even at the time of her supreme development, remained a land power; despite all her alliances and feuds with the sultans, she very seldom outmatched England and Holland, the sea powers.

Leadership in the western Mediterranean passed from Spain to France, from Holland to England. Louis XIV's minister Colbert built up the navy and ports of France, making her superior for a time. No doubt; but what does the record of these events amount to so long as we cannot also follow the great struggles for power whose scene was the Continent, not the sea? They belong to the history of Europe. The Mediterranean had become a robbers' den that no one cared to conquer and permanently clean up, because it was not worth the price. When France under Mazarin tried to take Naples and Sicily, England intervened to prevent her, just as Holland had done when Venice was about to be sacrificed. When the Turks about that time seized Crete, France even fought side by side with Venice against them.

None of this determined the course of history; that was settled on the German and French battlefields. Neither great ideas nor great men were fighting on the Mediterranean then—merely interests. At the very moment when France, exhausted by the forty years' ambition of the Roi Soleil, had to give up her world schemes, as Spain had done a century before, the aging king finally reached out for Spain, which he hoped to possess now that the Hapsburgs had died out. England interfered, and a great European war (1701-1713) began by land and sea. This was to be the end of French sea power for a hundred years. Both powers were looking for bases; the Balearics and Malta were surrounded or besieged. And above all, Gibraltar.

VIII

THE TRAVELER APPROACHING the Rock of Gibraltar from the land side, along the great mole, sees before him a huge buffalo's or lion's head, fat and rounded on the left; on the right there is a mountain slope, slowly leveling out like an animal's back. It is a jumbled view. Seen from the sea, on the other hand, the rock rises with a magnificent abruptness worthy of the Dolomites. As one stands below the signal station, it all seems piled up by some Cyclops, like the somber castle of the gods in Wagner's opera. The abruptness is on the Mediterranean side. From there the rock is inaccessible or could at best be scaled by some record-breaking alpinist. Whether it can be shot to pieces is something on which the experts still differ. It cannot be taken by assault.

It is a pale-gray, crystalline limestone, lying mostly in flat strata. In the course of millions of years, wind and water have dug many caves. One of them, 1,100 feet above the sea and 400 feet deep, is supported on columns like a hall; others have stalactites. Still another, called the Victoria Cave, contains lovely figures and statuettes of natural dripstone, which are said to excel even those of the American Mammoth Cave. The whole rock is not so very high—1,400 feet at the highest point—but because of its isolation and narrowness it seems much higher; it is only from a mile to three-quarters of a mile wide. As we are conducted through the fortifications built on top, entirely in tunnels, we see daylight and sky from both sides simultaneously at several points. The rock is less than three miles long, and it would not interest a soul except that it mounts guard over the entrance to the Mediterranean in an utterly fantastic fashion.

People are fond of saying that the mouth of hell is narrow; but the entrance to this sea of paradise is narrower still. As mentioned early in this volume, bones and horns of African animals found in France and the Balkans bear witness to an isthmus connecting the two continents in prehistoric times. Scholars continue to argue about how many thousand years before the dawn of history this bridge was broken, but the question is unimportant as well as insoluble. In any case the coasts come very near together; at the narrowest point the distance is only eleven miles. From the southernmost spot, the so-called Europa Point, anyone can make out the hilly coast of Africa with the naked eye. The little town lies inland, giving the effect of a smugglers' nest, which it has supposedly ceased to be. There is also a fishing village on the Mediterranean itself, to be reached only by a circuitous land road or a tunnel through the rock; a couple of old towers stand almost on top. The whole impression is simply that of a bustling group of little people gathered around one great and dangerous being, the rock.

In summer the rock looks as if the top had been burned bare; the governor's garden, carefully watered, represents the green oasis that aristocratic Englishmen the world over raise to simulate their home gardens even in the midst of deserts and crags. In the dining hall of the governor's old-fashioned official residence he has two huge old keys brought to him on a piece of red velvet at every meal. These keys formerly opened the gate of the fortress that his English predecessors captured, and so they have been set up at table for two hundred years, not simply on the anniversary but daily.

Outside on the rock, along with pigeons and partridges, there are still a few wild monkeys, the last in Europe. About 1900, the officers say, there were only five females; they banded together to kill and eat the last male monkey. After this tragicomic romance, however, the officers sent over to north Africa and got a young male for the rock. Since then there have been monkeys again, though not many. Where elephants and lions once strolled at ease across the isthmus to Europe, a single monkey now has to be brought over in a cage and released on the rocks, so that this African species may be restored to the outermost corner of Europe.

Opposite is the rock fortress of Ceuta. Hercules, who is supposed to have set up these two pillars, recognized the straits; and the earliest name, Abila, probably given by the Phoenicians, means "Stop!" The makers of legend could interpret the rock only from the east. But at the same time they were bound to feel drawn through the narrow opening into an unknown world, out upon new, distant seas, where Atlantis perhaps lay in the south, Thule perhaps in the north.

The first warrior to recognize the significance of this great sea was an Arab, Tarik. He began to build there, and so the rock was called the Mountain of Tarik, *Yebel al Tarik,* which developed into *Gibraltar.* He is the same man who led 1,200 Arabs and Persians from Morocco into Andalusia in 711 and beat the Goths at Jerez. At the same time he began to build a fortress on the rock, but he was thirty-one years in finishing it. A huge tower, standing today, is called Moorish Castle.

Six hundred years afterward, when the Spaniards drove out the Moors, a Spanish king started the first of the fifteen sieges of Gibraltar that convulsed the rock between 1300 and 1800. But after a great program of fortification in the sixteenth century, most of the assaults were in vain. In order to populate the hot and infertile city at the foot of the rock, the first kings invited thieves and murderers to live there and promised to collect no taxes. Moors and Spaniards by turns laid siege after siege; pirates and other Mohammedans, Spanish kings and dukes, fought for the rock—all in vain.

Not until the great French and English war in which Marlborough battled the Sun King did the English succeed in acquiring Gibraltar for a base. In 1704 a British admiral realized his opportunity and the value of the prize. He sailed into the Straits of Gibraltar before the rock that had been impregnable for centuries. He laid the twelfth siege for a mere three days and took the fortress. Actually, he was acting for a Hapsburg archduke allied with England, and it was his duty to run up the Hapsburg flag on any captured fortress. But the seaman, recognizing the greatness of the moment, hoisted the British colors and took formal possession for Queen Anne, whose government promptly ratified his *coup de main.*

This glory belongs to Sir George Rooke, then a man in his middle fifties, who had behind him an honorable but not conspicuous career. The speed with which he first attacked, then conquered, and finally appropriated the rock for his queen without instructions and without any other neighboring base, shows a grasp of the situation such as only Cromwell before him had possessed.

Cromwell had called Gibraltar and Cádiz "the most important aims of British policy."

French and Spaniards recognized their loss and began the thirteenth siege the same year; in its course a corps of the best volunteers was beaten off. Here was something to strike terror: the stranger on the rock could in a sense cut off all Spain if he would, and twenty years passed amid constant negotiations, wars, and surprise attacks. Finally, in the seventeen-eighties, came the greatest and longest of all the sieges, lasting almost four years, while England was occupied and weakened by American affairs. The Spaniards tried starvation, bold naval raids, used adventurers and spies of every sort; but always the English relief came in time, and after sharp naval battles in the narrow straits there would be pauses, as there are now in the bombing of England. There were sorties from the rock, victories over Spanish vessels, more new and better guns; but the only Spanish success was the recapture of the English base, the island of Minorca, still Spanish today.

Between battles there were chivalrous exchanges of letters such as those between Elliot, the commander, and the besieging Duke de Crillon. The latter wrote to his antagonist in 1782: "Your Excellency will permit me to offer you a few trifles for your table, which you no doubt need, as I know that you live entirely on vegetables. I would be glad to learn what kind you prefer: I would also add a few partridges for the gentlemen of your entourage, and some ice."

The reply read: "A thousand thanks to Your Excellency for the handsome present of fruit and poultry. I must confess that it led me to violate a resolution formed at the beginning of the war, namely to eat nothing different from my comrades. Everything is publicly sold here. Anyone may have it who can afford it. Therefore I take the liberty of asking you no longer to load me with favors whose benefits I cannot enjoy. We have quite enough vegetables. The Englishman is accustomed to agriculture, with which he passes his spare time even here."

Bets were laid in Paris and London as to whether Gibraltar would hold out. Finally the besieger gave up the siege and visited his adversary in the fortress after the armistice. At last he could see with his own eyes what he had tried for four years to puzzle out through a spyglass. He was like a man who had laid siege to a woman for years without captivating her but who had finally, after her victorious resistance, found her so amiable that as her slave he still attained his purpose in another form. The fortress of Gibraltar has been at peace almost continually since 1783.

Though England had driven France from the field and from the ocean after a long war at the beginning of the eighteenth century, three new seagoing adversaries had risen against her. Austria had become a new Mediterranean power, for the Hapsburgs now reigned over large districts in Italy. Savoy became a sea power by acquiring Sardinia and for a time Sicily also. Peter the Great sent Russia toward the straits and, though he accomplished little, still from then on the young power remained vigilant at its post and the Russian general Suvarov later even succeeded in gaining victories over Bonaparte's generals.

The power whose decline at sea paid for all this was France. Her navy was cut in two by the English stroke of genius permitting Gibraltar to shut off all connection between Brest and Toulon in time of war. Even today the possession of the rock makes a situation comparable to that of a Panama Canal in English hands, dividing the two navies of America. At the siege of Toulon the French sank their own fleet.

Later they broke through a second two-year blockade of Toulon. The blockading English made repeated landings in the islands of Hyères, provisioned themselves, then returned, and set fire to Spanish galleys in the harbor of San Tropez, although it was in peacetime. Toulon has the honor to be inscribed in history as the scene of the first victory of the genius Bonaparte, who recaptured it from the English in 1793.

Along with this basic change at one of the three gates to the Mediterranean, another at the second entrance was repeatedly weighed and pondered. The Sun King reverted to the old plan for a canal at Suez. As an engineering feat, it seemed impossible, and Colbert, Louis' shrewdest minister, had the idea that the sultan should open the Red Sea to the French, allowing France to establish warehouses and begin overland transports between Suez and Alexandria.

It was a German thinker who tried to push the French king in this direction. Leibnitz, the great universal genius, had thought of a means to divert Louis XIV from his depredations on the Rhine. When Louis happened to be at outs with the Turks again, Leibnitz advised him to take Egypt. The letter from the world-famous philosopher was answered by Colbert with an invitation to Paris. But the distraction of great men is evident in the fact that Leibnitz never got an audience with the king, who understood the importance of the matter very well indeed. And so the idea of leading France into Egypt had to wait a hundred and thirty years for Napoleon, who began his adventure without knowledge of the earlier scheme.

In the great struggle between France and England it is symbolic that the latter captured one entrance to the Mediterranean, whereas the former neglected to open or occupy the other. Without these two occurrences, the positive one at Gibraltar, the negative one at Suez, the history of the Mediterranean would have taken a different course.

IX

The two alien nations that pushed to the Mediterranean in the eighteenth century, Austria and Russia, alternately threatened and courted the Turks, and their intrigues ended by strengthening Turkey. The Austrians, like the Turks, did not become a seafaring nation. The Russians were somewhat more apt.

The Hapsburgs, who had inherited and married into, rather than conquered, their scattered possessions, could well afford to lose a few. No nationalist passion, no common history or language held these peoples together, and their fidelity to the ruling house was problematical, so that the history of this patchwork state has no focus; at best it has brilliant passages in the defense against the Turks.

And, in fact, Austria's share in the Mediterranean, never necessary, was lost as easily as it was won. When a few able businessmen in

Trieste tried to form an East India Company after the pattern of the great seafaring states, it disappeared after a dozen years "through lack of interest on the part of the Vienna government." In the same way the port of Fiume passed from them to the Hungarians. The only survival of the Austrian colonial effort is the Maria Theresa dollar, a silver dollar that still passes current on the Red Sea and in Abyssinia. Long after the Hapsburgs' six hundred years of dominion had ended in 1918, the Socialist Republic of Austria still stamped the picture of the empress on silver. The Negroes in the eastern Sudan to this day pay their debts with a woman's portrait that is scarcely allowed to be shown on the wall in Vienna.

Her competitor, Catherine II of Russia, had far greater Mediterranean plans. She dreamed of a Byzantine empire, and to be on the safe side called her grandsons Constantine and Alexander. At first she wanted to divide up Turkey with Austria and roused the Greeks for a war of liberation against the Turks. Even old Voltaire recorded his enthusiasm. Soon afterward she allied herself with England. The world saw the burlesque spectacle of a Russian navy manned by British officers sailing from the Baltic to Asia Minor and annihilating the Turkish fleet here in 1770. We do not know in what language these Britons communicated with the Russian sailors or what flag they dipped to the Rock of Gibraltar as they passed through; all we know is the mutual scorn of these amazing allies.

Catherine, who loved to toy with universal schemes—for instance, suddenly demanding Corsica for the Russians—made peace, cruelly leaving in the lurch the Greeks whom she had encouraged. Their liberation was thus delayed by half a century. But one great aim she did accomplish: Russia was in the Mediterranean at last. The northern coast of the Black Sea was ceded to her; Sevastopol and Odessa were founded at the end of the eighteenth century. When Russian warships also received free passage through the straits, however, the English were alarmed; they spent more than thirty years eliminating this threat.

Nevertheless, the Russian success became a world success. About 1800 the trade and commerce of Constantinople revived after an interval of centuries. The Mediterranean no longer ceased at the straits, and the Bosporus became a greater seaport than ever before. The fact that this took place under the Crescent troubled nobody, for the envoys of the great powers had long since become men of might at Constantinople, which they regarded as a sort of colony. English, Russians, Austrians, foreigners all, dominated the official overlord of the Mediterranean. On the other hand, the countries whose coasts were washed by the sea, the old powers, had declined. France still wielded great influence but was making no headway in Louis XV's plan for Egypt. Spain had long since ceased to be a great power, and Italy had yet to become one.

But Italy was happy, or seemed to be, whereas formerly she had been powerful but constantly convulsed. Perhaps in no country did the rococo spirit flourish so freely among the people as it did here, and the great gentry relished the charm of the eighteenth century to the full. The Pope was an enlightened prince, neither bellicose nor fanatical now, and in quick succession the Vatican did two things that proved the change of the times: it dissolved the Jesuit order, and it invited Protestants to the jubilee. With this invitation the celebrated Roman carnival became international.

Three cities—ancient, medieval, and Renaissance—were built one on top of another in Rome. The town superimposed an ornamentation in character with the Italian music of the time upon its eighteenth-century structure of manners and ideas. The people who had once made pilgrimage to the capital of conscience now traveled to the capital of pleasure. Never was Rome gayer or more overcrowded than in the rococo age; she grew rich when she was powerless. Only one city could excel her, and that was not Paris but Venice.

"Everything about me here," Goethe wrote from Venice in 1786, "is a great and respectable work of concerted human strength, a splendid monument not to a ruler but to a people. And though its lagoons are gradually filling up, noxious vapors are floating over the marshes, its trade is weakened, and its power has declined, still the whole situation and nature of the Republic will not be one moment the less attractive for that. The effect here is of an old family that is still active, although the great day of its blossoming and fruition is over."

In Venice, the rococo capital, money was still sought after but was acquired rather by opportunity than by energy, and everywhere it was used for the enjoyment of life, not for investment. Where could it be squandered more merrily than here? Musicians, actors, soothsayers, magicians, rope dancers, lion tamers, with a sprinkling of clerics joining in their amusements—all wended their way along the canals and across the squares, chattering, gossiping and laughing aloud half the day and all night, indeed at every hour. A proverb said: "In the morning a bit of Mass, in the afternoon a little game, in the evening a woman." There were more gambling, more coffee drinking, more ice eating, more philosophizing about life, more smiling here than anywhere in the world.

It was not the state banquets given here for the princes and kings of the world, not the magnificent garden parties in the fancifully trimmed parks with their waterworks and statues that marked the mood of the times; it was the lanes, the *trattorias,* the cafés; the rear entrances to Goldoni's theater; the dark rooms of the seamstresses and bawds; the women who understood love and who dominated Venice. No one could quite tell the difference now between courtesans and good society, except that the former were usually the wittier. Most of the women combined Titian blondness with dark eyes and became symbols of Venice, at once glittering and mournful. The sovereign melancholy of the city, the melancholy of its shadowy canals and abrupt palaces, of its rotten and crumbling piles, of its seaweed smell, clutches every Venetian lady in the midst of her smiles, giving her a charm such as no cool, wise Parisienne possesses.

A philosopher, statesman, or man of the world coming to the carnival would not have recognized any of the remnants of the old aristocracy. All classes were on show in the same style of cloak, shawl, and cocked hat, and went to the theater and the ball at midnight, again in the richest colors. A whole city masqueraded for months on end, still conducting its regular business—all in a way so unparalleled and so compelling that it drew people from every quarter of the world when they could perfectly well have danced and played in

much larger capitals. When a doge died in February, 1789, it was
kept secret as long as possible so as not to interfere with the carnival.

Venice now produced her most famous son since Titian; he was
capable of everything and nothing and enchanted the world while
he mocked and cheated it. His father's Spanish blood seems to have
made him the Don Juan he was. Imprisoned at thirty, escaping
across the lead roofs a year later, ennobled by his own authority,
traveling through Europe, coming home at fifty, banished again at
sixty, in the end it was he after all who immortalized the senators,
the literati, and the panders and, above all, the women of Venice,
from nun to duchess. He perpetuated the whole carnival, indeed,
when he set out to banish boredom in a lonely castle at the age of
seventy by writing his memoirs.

The great mockers of the Mediterranean, Aristophanes, Ovid,
Aretino, were joined now by Casanova. He left behind new testimony to the abundant life that the Mediterranean awakens in its
best men and women. True, only a connoisseur of love can understand the truthfulness of his memoirs, which, like Marco Polo's,
have been called exaggerated and boastful; young people trying to
learn from them will understand as little as they would of Ovid.
And old gentlemen, seeking consolation in the printed page for
their loss, are also a comical audience. The book, written by one of
the men who knew most in all history about love, is really for the
man of maturity and for a few favored women. It is much more
truthful than the petty bourgeois supposes, much more philosophical
than the scholar believes. It is like a sailboat crossing the bay on a
bright, windy morning, with a fresh breeze stirring the blue water.
To understand the Mediterranean, it is as necessary to know Casanova as it is to know Cleopatra or the temple of Paestum or the
Venus de Milo or the Golden Horn at Constantinople.

Nostalgia was what made Casanova's book so beautiful, for it
was written in the cold north, where an ironic whim of chance still
holds it fast. The world even now knows but a part of it, for the rest
lies in the safe of a prudish Leipzig publisher, whose forefathers
once bought it.

X

AMONG ALL THE ISLANDS of the Mediterranean, perhaps Corsica is the most beautiful. Even on the map it is more harmonious than the others: a richly indented leaf lying exactly north and south, with stem pointing northward, its shape has a balance equaled only by that of Crete, which points east and west. Its size too strikes a happy medium. Larger than most of the others, it is still just small enough so that one can see the ocean both east and west from the high mountains in the middle, as one can from the elevated center of the Peloponnesus.

Visiting the island, we see all the moods of a fascinating woman: on the coast it is gentle and sunny; in the interior, wild and untamable. All the trees of the Mediterranean are gathered here in a small space; the evergreen mountain forest seems immemorially ancient, moist, and shady like a tropical jungle; but along the coast are fruitful gardens like those of Sicily. Hence we have in a small area the extremes of temperatures that produce passionate human beings.

The special peculiarity of Corsica, or one at any rate less pronounced elsewhere in the Mediterranean, is a scent so strong that one smells it from a boat near shore. It is the smell of underbrush, called maqui—a mixture of myrtle, blackthorn, laurel, thyme, rosemary, broom, and other herbs. In the zone of moderate elevation it covers the mountains and blossoms almost the year round. A Corsican, rowed home asleep like Odysseus, could recognize his homeland by the perfume.

Along the coast are the peasant winegrowers and fishermen; in the little medieval towns are the shippers and merchants. Here is the home of money and compromise with the world. In the interior, however, even today, live taciturn men and resolute women dominated by two ideas: morality and patriotism. To protect their own families and their own island is their one thought; neither money nor power can lure them upon the sea. Blood vengeance is the burning passion today as in the old times, and the family is held sacred as it is in central Spain. Hence comes a deep devotion to their little fatherland. They are indifferent to the fact that they must fetch most of their food by boat from the mainland, for the island has little but wine and olives, fruit and vegetables. It exports wood.

These unyielding children of another age send to the mainland for farm and forest workers by the season; meanwhile they themselves, like their fathers, can go in search of game and birds or fish for trout and eels in the mountain brooks. A poor winegrower will meet the stranger with all the pride and hospitality of a king; but if he hears that a man has been received by a family numbered among his enemies, he will withdraw. With such habits of independence, such aversion to labor, and such passionate family partisanship, politics flourish as they do in Scotland. There the Highlands have produced a race of somewhat similar temperament; only these are people of the north, subject to fog and cold and their consequences.

This pride and dislike of foreigners (which is far more likely to survive in islands than anywhere on the mainland) has always set the Corsicans against any foreign government. They could not abide either the Carthaginians or the Romans, who fought over the island; and when it became a Roman province they offered the political exiles more comfortable asylum than the powers at Rome can have intended—to the younger Seneca, for instance.

Every nation that invaded the Mediterranean in the first thousand years after Christ tried to take Corsica because of its ideal location, which allows every kind of ambush and piracy between Nice, Genoa, Leghorn, and Rome. The Vandals, living up to their name, came and ravaged the primeval forests to build a fleet; Goths and Lombards landed and looted; Byzantium, the new master, made itself utterly odious by high taxation. Then for three hundred years Corsica passed from the hands of the Moors to those of the Franks, from the Tuscan counts back to the Saracens.

At last, in the eleventh century, their will to freedom was victorious over the power of the surrounding seafarers. In the north of the island a sort of republic was established, with elections and an enormous number of officials, so that every fifth or tenth Corsican belonged to the government. It did not long endure, and once more the struggles of the mainland powers confused the status of the defenseless island. Pisa and then Genoa became master of Corsica. Later there was a count of Corsica by grace of France and at the same time another appointed by the king of Aragon. Naval battles were fought along the coasts, and fortifications were built. For a time the Bank of San Giorgio ruled the north, toward Genoa, on its own account, and the Sforzas came from Milan. The banks' mercenaries were victorious after long fighting, and new counts with resounding long titles proclaimed themselves lords of the island.

Against all these conquerors the Corsicans could do nothing but vent their fury, their love of freedom, by perpetual guerrilla fighting and endless murders and assassinations.

The cruelty of the Genoese bank and its mercenaries was the worst the Corsicans ever suffered. In revenge, they created an utter anarchy that never ceased in the interior of the island, since the external struggles never came to an end. The allied French and Turks fought the Germans and Spaniards on the island for three years, about 1550, and no one could have said where the Corsicans stood. Under a new and prolonged Genoese government in the eighteenth century, an Italian priest who studied the island estimated that over a period of twenty years there were more than a thousand vendetta murders annually.

A German adventurer, Baron Theodor von Neuhof, tried to exploit one of the many Corsican revolts against Genoa. After the fashion of the modern German "tourists," he gradually transported men and arms to the island in order to "liberate" the Corsicans, promising them the help of Europe. The island was his prize. The peasants, fishermen, hunters, and warriors, needing guns and bullets, fell in with his humor, and the baron had himself operatically crowned King Theodore I of Corsica. At his coronation he wore a red cloak, Turkish trousers, and a Spanish plumed hat. A few months later he thought it safer to depart, then came back with British assistance, and finally vanished, disgracing the German name in Corsica forever.

Great figures from the old families, notably the celebrated Pasquale di Paoli, made their appearance here during the continual struggles that filled the next thirty years. Hatred for Genoa was greater than hatred for France, yet it was a dreadful day in 1768 when the Corsicans learned that the Genoese merchants had sold the island to the French. Corsican resistance, led by Paoli, lasted a year.

His strongest supporter in the council was Carlo Buonaparte, a lawyer and deputy. By the summer of 1769 the resistance was broken, and the French moved in. During those very weeks Buonaparte's wife brought into the world her second son, whom the father venomously entered in the French register. The register is still on exhibit at his house. The son was baptized with the not uncommon name of Napolione.

XI

IT REMAINS ONE OF THE PARADOXES of history that the most celebrated son of the Mediterranean knew nothing of navigation. He was brought up on the coast, and like the best of the Corsicans, he remained devoted to the land, just as his gloomy birthplace, on a little square three minutes' walk from the harbor, turns its face to the mountains and its back to the sea. In Corsica's war-torn history we find heroes of every sort and masterpieces of defense in the dense mountain forests, but not one great sailor.

In early antiquity, under Greeks and Carthaginians, there were still seagoing strategists. But Caesar, who happened to be born into the nation that held dominant sea power after the last victories over Carthage, was never a great admiral. Still less was Augustus. Even Alexander, born close to the Mediterranean, was no naval hero, nor were any of the Byzantine emperors, not even their famous generals. Neither Mohammed II nor Solyman was a seaman; nor was Ferdinand or his grandson Charles V, who won so many victories. Agrippa, Don John of Austria, Andrea Doria are a few exceptions.

The strangers who invaded the Mediterranean were still less of seafaring heroes. How indeed could the Arabs in their deserts, the Vandals and Goths in their primeval forests have learned navigation? Only the Normans came from another ocean, and they won successes as great as the seafaring nations of Dutch and English after them. But these heroes were not begotten by the Mediterranean. Though it produced great generals and discovered the type of the *condottiere,* though it developed outstanding cosmographers and great navigators who explored their own and foreign coasts, the Mediterranean left the real naval battles to the pirates. They were successful in petty warfare because great battles of whole fleets were no longer expected.

Thus Napoleon's ignorance of navigation kept up the tradition of the heroes of the Mediterranean and of his native Corsica as well. The only disaster was that his head was full of universal schemes that could be realized only by sea and chiefly in the Mediterranean. In fact, he cherished an unhappy love for the sea that mothered him. The great vision of his conquests lay here, whereas in his struggle with England he saw before him merely a narrow strait of water dividing him from his plan.

Napoleon, who was almost always victorious on land but never at sea, nevertheless directed all his universal plans toward the Mediterranean during his greatest days as general and consul. He actually dreamed then of reviving the Roman Empire, of having Italy, Spain, and Egypt obedient to France. This was his Caesarist period. During his Alexandrine phase he strove toward India because it was English, but he knew he could get there only by way of the Mediterranean, which he meant to dominate for that reason. In the interim he had what we may call his Carolingian period, from about 1803 to 1810, during which he became altogether the European mainlander, arranging his coronation in medieval fashion and once saying, almost insanely, to a confidant: "I am Charlemagne!" All these prototypes were alive deep down in his soul. Paoli, who was the first to recognize his potentialities, said to him: "You belong among the men of Plutarch." As a realist, of course, he adapted himself to circumstances every day of his life. But above and beyond were ideal visions of world fame and history. Napoleon's career is inconceivable without his constant remembrance of great predecessors.

When the twenty-seven-year-old General Bonaparte took the arms and ideas of the revolution to Italy, the people received him as a liberator from the Austrian yoke. All Europe welcomed the great new ideas; even Spain soon joined in. Only absolutist Russia and liberal England forthwith excluded themselves—the czar because he would have lost his throne by such ideas, England because she was more interested in her empire than in the freedom of Europe. England's opposition to the new France began even before Bonaparte. In 1793 a British squadron entered Toulon, whose frightened burgesses had summoned it to their aid against the Jacobins, just as some of the Russians around 1920 did against the Bolsheviks. Bonaparte drove out the English, and soon they also lost Corsica, which they had occupied.

Once Bonaparte had beaten the Austrians in Italy, that country fell easily into his hands. The Italy of the rococo was far more outworn than even royalist France. Almost without resistance the Pope let the papal state be taken away from him and a republic be set up in Rome—the first since Augustus, that is, in eighteen centuries, with the exception of a few brief interludes. And the aristocrats who had ruled Venice for eight centuries retired almost without a murmur; the people bemoaned their passing far less than that of the four bronze horses, first stolen by Constantinople from Greece, then by Venice from Constantinople, now by Bonaparte from Venice.

In return, however, he brought to the Italians the new ideals of the revolution. People did not notice at first that they were merely trading one master for another. Genoa, Lombardy, and all the districts became republics with ancient Roman names and insignia, all of them satrapies of France, all practically without resistance. The kings of Piedmont and Naples, the Hapsburgs of Tuscany had to abdicate; only in Sicily did the Bourbons maintain themselves with English help. By the turn of a hand Italy had been transformed into a block of republics. But to the young conqueror these were mere bridges across the Mediterranean, for even then he was writing to the Directory that Corfu, Zante, and Cephalonia were more valuable than all Italy, as was Malta, "the mart of Europe."

His Mediterranean plans were already directed against England, which guarded India as her most precious possession after the loss of America. He seems to have realized at the start of his career the impossibility of taking the island of Britain and actually to have bent his thoughts upon India. This was more fantastic about 1800 than it is today, with the Suez Canal and aviation bringing the world close together. When the British navy vacated the Mediterranean to blockade the Spaniards at Cádiz, he decided his moment had come and set sail for Egypt.

He told one of his intimates that he would stay there six months or six years, depending on whether France or the Orient needed him. When his four hundred sailing vessels put to sea from the roadstead of Toulon, he knew nothing definitely except that three British captains on the decks of their vessels were at that moment straining their eyes through spyglasses to find an enemy who was supposed to be heading for Sicily. A storm, delaying by a day his departure from Toulon, probably saved him from Nelson. "That devil has the devil's own luck!" Nelson cursed, damning himself and the enemy. Bonaparte spent the four weeks' voyage mostly in bed. He could not stand being at sea—which proves how alien the watery element was to him.

No fleet like this had ever sailed the Mediterranean, for there was a university on board, traveling eastward, along with the two thousand guns. A hundred and seventy-five learned civilians with hundreds of books and instruments, whom the sailors called "the donkeys," were patronized and interrogated by the commander in chief. When he was read to, he chose Plutarch, Homer, or the campaigns of Alexander, and the Koran was brought out along with the Bible, under the heading "politics." Sometimes he would hold sessions of the academy on board and listen to two opponents argue a theme. At the same time the apparatus of scholarship was meant to serve his glory, after the fashion devised by Alexander before him.

Taken as a whole, Napoleon's Egyptian campaign was the folly of a brilliant and startlingly successful young man. The Directors perhaps gave him the necessary funds simply to get rid of him.

But the Englishman, Nelson, was the greater sailor, and when he attacked at Abukir Bay, near the mouth of the Nile, General Bonaparte was dependent on his naval officers. He could not fight for himself. Though Napoleon as a young general joined in the fighting only a few times, he personally directed sixty battles from his tent or from the very front line. But he was never visible on a ship in battle, because he did not know the sailor's trade.

If we run over in our minds the endless series of battles that have fixed the destinies of nations on the Mediterranean, we are amazed to see how seldom they took place on the ocean. For most of the naval battles were not decisive, and their sum was perhaps less significant than the terrors and depredations of the pirates. Only four Mediterranean naval battles in three thousand years really made history:

In 480 B.C. the Greeks defeated the Persians at Salamis; in 41 B.C. Octavian's vessels beat those of Antony and Cleopatra at Actium; in A.D. 1571 the united Spaniards and Venetians defeated the Turks at Lepanto; and in 1798 Nelson beat General Bonaparte at Abukir Bay. All four battles took place between the beginning of August and the beginning of October, the first three on the Greek coast, very close together. We have only vague or uncertain portraits of three of the victors, Themistocles, Agrippa, and Don John of Austria. Three of the four Mediterranean naval heroes were commoners born. Themistocles aside, they all fought for lords and masters who knew nothing of seafaring. None of them fell in these battles. All four mixed in politics, the Greek and the Roman at the heads of their states, the others in a more private capacity.

All four men, probably even the Greek, had much to do with women and were at times guided by them. All four were involved in intrigues throughout their lives and were very quick to take offense. At the same time they were all fond of splendor, concerned for honors and deportment. They all seem to have had something of the poet in them. All four won their victories in youth; only Nelson was forty but had already made a considerable name. He was the only one later killed in battle. Themistocles was banished by the Athenians a few years after his victory and died among the Persian enemy.

If we compare the lasting values of their victories, the Greek is still the most important. The Roman was merely defeating another Roman who would have ruled as well as he; the Spaniard accomplished nothing politically; the Englishman allowed his country's deadly foe to escape and did not really annihilate the enemy navy until seven years afterward. Themistocles was the greatest, if for no other reason, because he first carried on a long political campaign to procure the building of the navy, then supervised the actual work; obviously he was not only a great admiral but a genius.

XII

If at this point we look upon the Mediterranean, teeming with ships, the old seventeenth and eighteenth century drawings make the galleys seem more like festive barges than like warships. They usually curved up at bow and stern, with the mast in the middle accordingly lower at the step; the sails are extravagantly curved; a splendid tent with rugs rises on the poop. Even before 1700 there were gunboats up to 1,600 tons, picturesque even so.

Smaller sailing ships seemed like a veritable swarm of butterflies, flitting and dancing. Forward, four small sails sometimes continued diagonally upward, then two square ones of differing sizes directly over them; in the middle, one big triangular sail; and aft a still bigger one. As the wind blew upon this fantastic combination, it seemed to lend spirit to a swaying body, driving it on toward an uncertain fate.

When Nelson won his great victory that August day at Abukir Bay, the French adventurer was cut off from home; in sober truth he was lost. At the same time he learned that the English had recaptured Malta, which he had taken away; had occupied Minorca, Sardinia, and Sicily; and that the respect they inspired was beginning to exceed the terror attached to his name. When he celebrated his thirtieth birthday at Cairo, Bonaparte was threatened by a tremendous coalition including almost all the great states, even Turkey and Russia. He was playing then for his highest stakes. In nihilistic mood he wrote to his brother, with the morbid sensibility of Werther, that nothing really gave him pleasure any more: "I have exhausted everything."

In his humiliation, Napoleon went to Syria, found himself stopped by English forces at Acre, and did not recover his prestige until he faced and defeated an English and Turkish army on solid land in Egypt. Soon afterward, secretly leaving his army, he knew that he was betraying it. His was a gloomy return; two small vessels instead of four hundred, sailing with darkened lights right through the English fleet, a seven weeks' voyage to Fréjus. Men in like situations, returning home as fugitives, have often been tried and shot.

But it was Bonaparte's good fortune that the enemies of France had meanwhile been victorious, reconquering half of Italy. His country needed the one man who had hitherto always been victorious on land. It welcomed him—indeed, it received him as a dictator. Bonaparte carried out his *coup d'état* in November, 1799, as if symbolically to end the era of the revolution along with the rococo century. He did it at his weakest moment, simply because he felt stronger than his rivals. Another few months, and he won everything back by the victory at Marengo, driving out of Italy the English whom he could not master at sea.

When Bonaparte took countries and provinces in payment for his victories by the Treaty of Amiens in 1802, he had to sit passively by as Egypt became Turkish again. He even had to be glad it did not remain English. At the same time he suffered in the Mediterranean a moral defeat greater than any before or after. To gain security for French commerce he made treaties with the pirates at Tunis and Algiers, paying outright tribute as everyone before him had done. Certainly these pirates must have been the only power for whose friendship Napoleon ever paid out money. This was his one great defeat until Moscow—for the next fifteen years—and it proves again that he could not deal with the sea.

Even the new navy he built in all haste was not first-class and was under the old royal admirals—simply because he could not inspect and decide things for himself. The second great war broke out over a new dispute in the Mediterranean: the English wanted to keep Malta instead of giving it back to the Knights of Saint John. Napoleon said to the English ambassador: "I would rather see you on Montmartre than in Malta. It is the fulcrum of the Mediterranean." The idea of bases was as sharp in his mind as it had been in Cromwell's. Still he remained impotent, and if we think of him at Boulogne, inspecting the vessels to invade England, his utterances give the impression of a chagrined man with an uneasy conscience, who does not believe in his own success. Nelson's victory over the French at Trafalgar, which is not in the Mediterranean, destroyed forever Napoleon's plan for an invasion and his Mediterranean plans as well. Here, as at Abukir Bay, Nelson was on board, and Napoleon was not. Nelson fell, but the emperor at Paris turned pale.

Now that the battle has been studied for a century and more, there can be no doubt that the victory on that October day was a matter not of luck but of superior tradition and training, along with brilliant leadership. In five hours the French navy was almost annihilated, for of thirty-three vessels seventeen fell into enemy hands. Once again this battle showed Napoleon's inadequate authority at sea; an admiral who was supposed to be replaced by another at the last moment did not wait for disgrace but put out of Cádiz on his own account—something no one on land would have dared to do.

The celebrated sentence that has come down to posterity from this battle did not originate with Nelson in the form we know. Instead, sure of the magic of his own name, he wrote: "Nelson confides that every man will do his duty." One of his officers asked whether he would not rather say "England" than "Nelson"; and the word "confides" was hard to signal with flags. And so the famous command began: "England expects . . ." Since Nelson fell in this battle, it was natural to make him the national hero. The Londoners have mounted him so high that his face, atop the column, is beyond recognition.

Six weeks after his defeat Napoleon replied in his own element, on land at Austerlitz. Ashore he made good what had become impossible with no navy at sea. He occupied the Adriatic coast, snatched almost everything from Austria in that quarter, and made his relatives kings in Italy. But the most powerful man of his time could do nothing to prevent the Russian navy from going through the straits to the Ionian Islands. He could do nothing to prevent the British fleet from appearing outside Constantinople in 1807 and coming within a hair of forcing the sultan to surrender; he was saved only by the personal misgivings of an admiral who could not radio home for instructions.

XIII

AT THE SAME TIME (1806) and for the same reason, the English occupied a small Mediterranean island that had been held desirable ever since antiquity, but more for its beauty than for its strategic situation. Capri, which rises steep and forbidding as viewed from Naples, offers an idyllic surprise on the south side, for here the flowers have the luminous mountain colors that we ordinarily see only in the high Alps in summer. Where jagged cliffs stand out to shield soft valleys against the sea wind, a gentian-blue shrub grows low, woody, almost insignificant. But its blue blossoms, the size of lilacs, shine out upon the world as warmly as a human heart. The deep hue of the Mediterranean itself seems to have spread. Through the thirsty bright green of the stones, viburnum shrubs cascade down, and yellow spurge. Rosemary and barberry grow rank to an unheard-of size, and the myrtle reaches the height of a man, its white blossoms giving off their bittersweet scent as if to warn all brides. Sunny slopes are covered with a gigantic variety of sedum with yellow and lilac starflowers as big as your hand. Asters, broom, and heath crowd into the sun with tropical abundance, growing stronger than the juniper, which crouches against the rock lest the sea wind break it. Among them blossom quiet, lilac anemones, taking the shade of the fantastic wild fennel bushes or the stiffly graceful pink candlestick lilies.

The island's grottoes are named after their colors, blue, green, red, white. Only a master hand can shoot the skiff through the narrow entrance just at the moment when the waves recede, and only habitués can circumnavigate the reefs and crags in these watery caves.

Really they should be called rainbow grottoes, for all of them are alive with a play of color such as one never sees except in spectroscopic experiments. Just as all the flowers on the rocks above have the radiant, luminous hues of the Alps, so the colors are all refracted in the cavities below. Here, remote from the sun, the magic light wavers in the depths; everything dissolves in an opal gleam that soothes the eye of him who almost sacrilegiously penetrates such secret recesses.

The English fleet abandoned Capri within two years, but the English poets and lovers have kept returning, happy to find a base here not for their guns but for their imaginations.

Meanwhile Napoleon had become a ruler who possessed almost the whole of Europe, but not the Mediterranean. His blockade of England was continually riddled by way of the islands and Gibraltar. The idea of beating England in India, since she could not be beaten in England and the Mediterranean, was bound to be revived now more actively than ever. How great is the similarity with 1940! The great outfits intended to accompany Napoleon's army from Dalmatia to the Euphrates he characterized later, in exile, as chimerical; but at the time they were close to becoming a reality. The revolution in Spain and increasing friction with the czar set all at naught.

One victorious campaign followed another, and Austria was compelled by a new peace to cede her last towns on the sea. France now felt herself mistress of the Adriatic. Yet Napoleon's fleet was beaten again, at Leszno, and this time by the Austrians, who had been a Mediterranean power for a much shorter period and much less successfully than the French. At the same time the English managed to make their shrewdest treaty, surrendering everything to the Turks in return for a promise to close the straits for a hundred years. In this way the Russians, who had been there but twice, were kept out of the Mediterranean.

When the fallen son of the Mediterranean was on his romantic little isle of Elba, looking over its mellow bays back toward France, he received secret messages from Italian patriots offering him the crown of a united Italy. People had a strong feeling that this Frenchman was fundamentally an Italian and this emperor fundamentally a revolutionary. They were wrong on both counts: he had long since forgotten both these elements in his origin. Spellbound, he kept his eyes on Paris.

When the Congress of Vienna tried to rebuild the old instead of creating something new, the potentates of the Holy Alliance were so Christian in sentiment that they excluded the Turks from the negotiations because of their religion, the Greeks and Serbs because of their desire for liberty. England acquired the Ionian Islands along with Malta and from 1815 on dominated the Mediterranean by her bases in the west, east, and center. The house of Hapsburg spread out over half Italy but was confiding enough to entrust its navy to the Venetians, who now passed for Austrian subjects. In Piedmont, Naples, everywhere the kings came back, and everywhere national aspirations were ignored.

Along with the kings, the pirates also were perpetuated. Nobody in Europe dared lay hands on these African adventurers. The only ones who attacked boldly, forcibly winning release from the disgraceful tribute, were the Americans with their young navy.

XIV

THE ENTRANCE OF the United States into the Mediterranean had important consequences. Three hundred years after Columbus (a son of the Mediterranean) went to America, the Americans came back into the Mediterranean. Of course they were predominantly of English descent, but they came with purposes quite different from those of their forefathers and cousins. Indeed their opposition to England was the very key to their success. Benjamin Franklin said of the pirates: "If Algiers did not already exist, the English would found it." Almost at the same time Lord Sheffield said in the Upper House at London: "It is not in the interest of the great powers to protect the Americans."

During the first three decades of their existence the United States too had to pay tribute to the pirates. The great distances made heavy armament and convoying impossible. Their very considerable trade with the Levant compelled them in 1785 and 1787 to make treaties with Algiers and Morocco, and even so several of their ships were seized. Within the next thirty years the United States paid two or three million dollars in tribute, bribes, and ransoms.

The moral indignation expressed in many European writings after 1800 remained ineffectual for twenty years. England needed the pirates for her blockade of Napoleon and had already forced Portugal to come to terms with them. Thus they were able to reach the Atlantic and help starve out France. Then as always, the Europeans hated each other far more than they hated the pirates, and consequently even America could do nothing in this wretched war of one little corner of Africa against all Europe. The treaties of the great powers with the robber states were so humiliating that no one dared publish them, and it is only now that we can read the documents. Under the heading "gifts" there are not, for instance, music boxes and glass beads, but repeater watches, jewelry, liqueurs, fruit, delicacies. Once the Venetians sent costly brocades, and the dey rejected them, demanding war materials. France furnished parts of cannon and sent over engineers to cast guns. Once when the Swedes failed to pay promptly the pirates seized seven valuable ships and demanded punitive interest on the payment.

The business was by no means left in Oriental disorder; a special ministry at Algiers administered gifts and loot. An Arabic register covering sixty-five years looks like the lists of a tax office and sometimes of a pawnshop as well, showing the shares due to everyone who helped during or after an attack—from the minister to the weigh-master and the priest who had prayed for the success of the voyage and even the auctioneer in the slave market. The auctioning of goods suffered from the fact that a vessel usually carried only one or two kinds of cargo, so that some fine morning in Algiers the price of gentlemen's English woolens, silk stockings, or china teacups might suddenly drop.

American action in this region begins with a queer incident. In 1800 Captain Bainbridge, commanding the frigate *George Wash-*

ington, was sent to Algiers to deliver the tribute. The dey then "commanded" him to carry an Algerian envoy and his numerous suite, with presents worth half a million dollars, to the sultan at Constantinople, who was in a bad humor with his pirate vassal. Under threat of having his ship sunk Bainbridge complied. He passed the straits without a permit, which would have cost delay and blackmail, by the simple ruse of firing enough honorary salutes to create a smoke screen and then quickly getting out of range. Then he pulled down the Algerian flag and entered the harbor flying the Stars and Stripes, which the Turks had never beheld. Making friends with the grand admiral, who was the sultan's brother, he got a pardon for the straits commander whom he had tricked, put in a good word for the Algerian ruler, laid the basis for diplomatic relations with the United States, and was in due time complimented by President Washington.

But this was only a prelude. In 1803, a squadron under Commodore Preble was sent against Tripoli. On the way he captured a Moroccan raider with an American brig it had just taken and forced the Moorish sultan to give up several other American prizes. At Tripoli this expedition fared not so well. The 36-gun *Philadelphia* ran aground, Captain Bainbridge and his crew became prisoners, and the pirates quickly floated and repaired the vessel and added it to their own navy. A few months later Lieutenant Stephen Decatur performed his brilliant feat of slipping into the fortified harbor, burning the *Philadelphia,* and escaping without the loss of a man. In 1805, American forces under Commodore Barron attacked Derna by sea and land, which terrified the pirate ruler into giving up all claim for tribute in future—for which complaisance he received a cash *douceur* of $60,000. Finally, in 1815, a strong squadron under Bainbridge and Decatur appeared before Algiers and within two days an equally favorable result was obtained.

Even today the long shores of Algiers and Morocco are difficult to take. "A base at this point in Africa will come hard to the English," Napoleon had predicted. Meanwhile, however, the British

Lord Exmouth had obtained exact maps of the new coast fortification, and he ventured out with only five ships of the line. Then followed negotiations in the harbor, submission of terms, refusal, flag signals. A sudden and withering bombardment from near at hand killed thousands. The dey was wounded and later murdered by conspirators. Still the success was but half complete; the tribute went on, being paid by the smaller countries as late as 1844. Even eight years after this victory a new dey managed to repulse the British Admiral Neal. When Neal warned the dey of his strong fleet, the pirate replied: "Nimrod was the strongest of mortals, and yet he perished from the sting of a fly."

In the end this very potentate was to fall because of a fly brush. The grain his predecessors had supplied to the young French republic about 1797 was to be paid for at last by the king of France. This matter was the subject of a long dispute. At the congratulatory reception for the Feast of the Ramadan in 1827 the dey accused the French consul of conspiring against him, and the consul defended himself. The dey, an old man by then, sitting crosslegged on his divan, hit at the consul with his fly brush. This was the signal for France. A large fleet blockaded Algiers for three years. Their losses increased at such a rate that the dey, who at first had put a price of a hundred dollars on each French head, soon reduced his reward to ten and finally promised no more than a public citation.

When Algiers was taken at last in 1830, obviously the impression created was much stronger than that of our modern war news. The romance of the pirates had occupied young people and novelists too long not to be dramatic and moving when it finally reached its end. The traits of the noble robber were recounted. Stories were told of how the pirates of Morocco had long spared Portugal because she had once received a shipwrecked female relative of the sultan; how every man wounded in battle got enough of the booty to live on for the rest of his life; how French officers found a volume of Corneille along with a French artillery manual in a captured pirate battery.

Perhaps this romantic prejudice was the reason why the last

dey was allowed not only to live after the capture of the city, but to depart for Naples with much money and fifty-two wives. Thence he moved quite cozily to Paris to modernize his harem. The last Bourbon, under whom Algiers had been taken, was deposed and sent abroad a few weeks afterward; the rulers, so different in race and tradition, died one after the other in exile. Both were fat, but the wild corsair had fought for three years and to the last gasp, whereas the legitimate king, Charles X, was merely ridiculous.

With the conquest of Algiers a third great color reappeared on the map of the Mediterranean. France was once more a sea and colonial power, the strongest next to the Turks. Constantly obstructed by England, she had established her African empire in Algiers, Morocco, and Tunis by 1845. It was a great school for the French officers and engineers, the best of whom from now on were trained in Africa. Fighting the mountaineers on waterless coasts, against hostile natives, the French accomplished wonders.

Just one obstacle prevented them from becoming a great colonial nation in the long run. Their country was too beautiful, too rich, too comfortable; not many people were ready to leave it. Thousands of foreigners, especially Italians and Spaniards, had to be recruited to populate and till the new colonies. No wonder their native lands later laid claim to a country their children had helped build up. Confinement, fog, love of adventure kept urging the Englishman out of his country and across the sea. None of these motives drew the Frenchman abroad, narrow confines least of all. French civilization is older than English civilization, and so the French people matured earlier and became, if not weary, at any rate conservative and unwilling to leave their land, their cities, their homes.

But even without this factor the fertility of France would have been reason enough to hold anyone there. That is why the Englishman is the most and the Frenchman the least traveled of Europeans. The money he is so fond of the Frenchman does not try to amass by perils and exploits in far countries. He prefers 10,000 francs in Paris to 100,000 in Tunis. And if he actually does acquire his fortune abroad, he is ready to drop his work before he grows gray, for he would rather enjoy his later years than work. He and the Italian are no longer young enough to vie with men of younger nations as colonizers.

XV

THE GENIUS OF THE GREEK PEOPLE IS INDESTRUCTIBLE. Landscape and history combine to revivify the Greeks again and again after long periods of decline. The hundred islands and peninsulas are still the same as they were in antiquity. The people still show the same volatility of spirit, cheerfulness of heart, craftiness in action, imagination.

At present they have no great poets and philosophers, no great navies and armies. They have been beaten and are ruled by the barbarians, as so often before. But they have not aged yet. Their adroitness as traders and diplomats is still great, and they have a capacity for assimilating the social ideas of our time and transforming them into revolution.

It seems incredible how all the centuries of Byzantine and Turkish rule have passed over them, and how like they are to their classical forebears, from whom so many new blendings divide them. Even today we find among the people of Thessaly heads that might, in appearance, come from some ancient vase, and the quick, clear minds of the city dwellers are unchanged. Their spirit has not grown more melancholy in two thousand years. Going for a stroll in modern Athens, we still see them standing by twos in the middle of the roadway, arguing the corruption of a judge or the sophistry of a professor or the elegance of a lady's shoe. The Greeks stand there in the nineteen-forties as they did in the comedies of Aristophanes, oblivious of the fact that the auto has been invented meanwhile and is loudly trying to honk them out of the way.

Napoleon was the first who thought of liberating them, but he had too much to do in the north and west and dropped his plans. About 1800 the Greeks also felt themselves deceived and abandoned by England and Russia. Attempted uprisings ended in fearful massacres by their overlords the Turks. But this people's urge for freedom kept them forever forming secret societies and attempting assassinations. Scholars and journalists led priests from Argos, bandits from the mountains of Epirus, herdsmen from Delphi in rebellions against which the power of the Janizaries lacked nothing but the support of the great powers.

Finally, about 1820, a constellation of forces arose in which a number of European rivals became "Panhellenic" for quite different reasons: it was the watchword of the time. We shall probably be hearing the slogan again in the next few years. True, the English government wanted to keep Turkey for another century, protecting their treaty of 1809 in regard to the straits. But sympathy for the gathering Greek rebels was stirred among the English people by the stories of Turkish atrocities and among the educated classes by the name Hellas. The Russian czar, on his part, having the right to protect the Christians in Turkey, followed his fathers in wanting Constantinople, or at least the straits. France, whose interests were in north Africa and soon also in Syria, gave a helping hand simply to avoid letting the others have all the glory. Only Hapsburg, then represented by Metternich, was, as always, against any sort of popular emancipation.

In this propitious situation the Greeks abroad were rich and national-spirited enough to help their brothers. The Phanariots, literally "people at the lighthouse," in Constantinople, were, along with the Armenians, the sultan's great bankers and financiers. In Alexandria and Marseille, Genoa and Venice, Odessa and Moscow there were also many very rich Greeks. Both the men who assumed leadership, in fact, came from Russian service. Capodistrias, who looked like an English Metternich, had been the czar's foreign minister, and Ypsilanti, who had lost an arm fighting Napoleon, was a Russian general. These men represented the connection with their orthodox coreligionists.

But the help of Europe did not come because of religion, for no one there belonged to the Greek sect. It was the result of the humanism of the times. Greeks in Paris, applauded by all the scholars, were shaping the modern Greek tongue. A society of Friends of the Muses were studying in Athens and in an academy at Corfu.

Greek-aid societies were formed in Germany, and the king of Prussia, always timorous, contributed his $6,000 anonymously. How much more precious were the $500 that Voss, the translator of Homer, who was a poor man, gave with the notation: "A small contribution toward a great debt for the education received from Hellas"! The best minds of Europe wrote on behalf of Greek liberty because they knew Greece was the home of culture, and not for the Mediterranean alone.

When Lord Byron went out to join the fight, all Europe understood why. He spent his last days at Missolonghi, inadequately outfitted, disappointed by petty interests, and finally stricken with fever; and this too seemed a parable of nineteenth century genius sacrificing itself for Greece. Romantic Greece culminated with Byron's death. His death represented, as it were, expiation of the deed of another lord, who had taken the marble frieze of the Panathenaea from the Parthenon to London a few years before.

Once again the Greek islands took an active part in events, for every sort of helper and messenger, spy and fugitive could hide in this sea of a thousand retreats, the source of many legends. For a little while partisanship was pushed into the background. A bishop in Morea worked side by side with a bandit who had become a major in the British service. Even the monks of Mount Athos were moved by national sentiments. A national assembly declared the country independent after the first success in 1822, and such was the fury of the Turks that the sultan caused the all-too-innocent Greek patriarch to be hanged from the portal of his own church in Constantinople. Pogroms against Christians shocked the world, and the horrors of Chios were immortalized by the master hand of Delacroix.

But the Greeks, soon beaten, after all, by Egyptian Turks, would have been lost if Canning, "the Spartacus of Downing Street," who loved liberty and heard the voice of the people, had not become British prime minister. At the same time a young czar ascended the throne. Their navies cooperated with the French, winning a decisive victory in Navarino Bay that assured Greece momentary freedom. Also it was, or at least seemed, highly important to the relations between England and Turkey. The English government, foreseeing a Russo-Turkish war, was scared by its own daring, and the king spoke of an "unfortunate occurrence."

When the czar's troops took Adrianople, Constantinople seemed in grave peril. The jealous great powers stepped in to preserve Turkey, "the sick man," on their usual principle; but they had to surrender sovereignty over parts of the Balkans to the czar. Bulgaria and Rumania became half independent. The two, and afterward their families, quarreled over the crown of Serbia. Only the Greeks became wholly independent, though not within their natural borders. The straits were opened up to merchant ships. Now at last the Black Sea really belonged to the Mediterranean.

Again as in antiquity, Greek party struggles, ingratitude, and fratricidal war followed the victory. Capodistrias was murdered, and a seventeen-year-old Bavarian prince, thoroughly unsuited for the office, became king. He had to keep a couple of thousand Bavarian soldiers to protect him from his new people until an army revolt imposed on him a new constitution. The interest of Europe in Greece had long since evaporated, and Athens was again regarded as a dirty village with a few old temples.

Turkey, until then the greatest Mediterranean empire despite all her inner impotence, had suffered the decisive blow; as in all autocracies, it came from within. A little tobacco merchant from Albania, bold, sly, and eager to learn, had made his way to the top in Cairo. One day he invited some five hundred Mamelukes to the castle and had them all killed; as many more were slaughtered elsewhere. Like so many Mediterranean rulers, Mehemet Ali followed up his initial crime by modernizing himself into an enlightened despot, who remained momentarily a pasha obedient to the sultan. But obviously he intended, like Saladin, to make himself an independent monarch.

This upstart understood Egypt and reverted to the policy of the pharaohs by advancing up the Nile into the Sudan to get gold and slaves. His campaigns were led (a rare thing in history) by a highly gifted son with a genius for generalship. So Ibrahim Pasha has often been called an adopted child—as if the greatest generals had not descended from petty commoners.

Ibrahim was eventually beaten in Greece, where he led the Egyptian troops, but only after great victories. He died almost simultaneously with his aged father, whose magnificent successes would have been almost unthinkable without him. These struggles of father and son with the sultan, which led to the conquest of Syria and further, depended entirely on the chess game of the European powers. The great imperial dream of the tobacco merchant was a failure not because of the strength of his adversary but because of the guile of a few far-distant diplomats.

France and England fought for dominance of the Mediterranean in a sort of blockade warfare, each supporting one of the two Mohammedan princes. The tension in Europe was so great that even Paris was fortified at the spot from which the besieged cannonaded in 1871 and where today one strolls through open parks. England was eventually victorious, forcing the French and Russians in 1841 to sign the old straits treaty, which forbade all warships to pass through the Dardanelles. Thus England, possessing the key of Gibraltar, was safe from any large attack by France. The straits were closed, Suez an isthmus, the Black Sea a Russian lake, and England had free communication with India.

The personal destinies of the two interesting Egyptians remained without influence on the Mediterranean. There they failed. Ibrahim's defeat at Navarino was fortunate, for it was a disgrace to Europe that the Greeks should be subject to the Turks. The battle freed them, and Victor Hugo wrote: "Greece is free! Six years are avenged by a single day!"

XVI

AFTER THE FALL OF NAPOLEON in 1815 a strange confusion had arisen in European minds, similar to that produced by the slogans of the various present-day "isms." Everyone was talking about nationalism and liberalism. The post-Napoleonic reactionaries had fought so

long against national independence that they now lumped the two
ideas together, damning them both.

The peculiar political situation in Greece produced a paradoxical
exception in which the great reactionary powers united to fight for
Greek freedom. England, remaining aloof from the Holy Alliance
—as America did from the League of Nations a hundred years after
—had reason to be more liberal in the Mediterranean than elsewhere, for idealistic liberation also meant bases. Malta and Cyprus
had just become English, and today they are once more beyond
price.

The uprising of Spain, too, was decided by powers that did not
touch on the Mediterranean at all. After the fall of Napoleon the
expelled Bourbon, Ferdinand VII, had returned. He was a man
whose vices showed on his face—the son of the great cocotte immortalized by Goya, he was one of the kings whom the people had
forgotten to behead. His only virtue was that his vicious court made
the work of liberation easier for the South Americans and helped
Bolivar.

When, after repeated uprisings, the powers intervened to protect this spurious Bourbon—he was never the true son of his father—
Spanish affairs developed just as we have seen them doing with
our own eyes. An authoritarian state, France this time marched in
to put down the liberals and looted the country for six years. The
jubilant bourgeoisie accepted all this at the hands of the same France
that had preached revolution to their fathers. Then came the return
of the Spanish royalists and the priests, horrible revenge upon the
revolutionists, with England as a passive onlooker.

In Italy too the great powers for decades resisted the people's
efforts for liberty and unity. No one in the world is more patriotic
than the common man in Italy; but since his rulers and statesmen
are only sometimes patriots, armies in Italy have usually been worse
led than the insurgent bands. As a result Italy has had the most dictators and revolutions of any Mediterranean country.

As late as 1820 the map of Italy still bore seven colors, and the
largest two pieces belonged to foreign rulers, the Hapsburgs in the
north and the Bourbons in the south. The only native Italian was

the king of Sardinia (Savoy), along with the Pope, who now was always an Italian. How could the people help rising in a body against the foreign rulers who possessed four-fifths of its soil?

In Sicily a wretched Bourbon king, another Ferdinand, reigned longer than most rulers in history—sixty-six years. Austria could bring a certain amount of education to the north of Italy, and the atrocities of Spain found no imitation here. But the Austrians, and particularly the Hapsburgs, with all their talent for handling people, nevertheless lacked the passion and daring that go to make the true colonizer. The Austrian nobles amused themselves in Italy, the imperial house installed dukes and grand dukes in order to give them beautiful castles and fashionable courts, the greatest connoisseurs of art came over the Alps, and everyone spoke the wonderful language of the country. But for half a century Austria gave no new privileges, no improvement in social status to these foreign, subject stocks. She treated a civilized nation far older than herself with an occasionally indulgent arrogance instead of energy and love. Lombardy, people used to say, had been put to sleep by the Austrian bakers' poppy seeds. In Tuscany a minister used to reiterate the slogan: "The world runs by itself!"

But in the course of the uprisings by the subject people the Hapsburgs grew alarmed. They welcomed the cowardly King Ferdinand of Naples, who had sworn in his first terror to grant a new constitution; under their protection he forswore all his oaths. Then Metternich sent an Austrian army to Naples to put down the revolution and ordered the soldiers to stick olive branches in the muskets as they marched in—a tragicomic symbol that would fit all the false liberators of our day. These soldiers remained for six years in the foreign kingdom. From this time, 1821, dates the hatred of the Italians for the Austrians, whom they called jailers. The whole nation, having tasted freedom for a moment under General Bonaparte, now desired a republic.

Only in Piedmont, where the house of Savoy, under the title of kings of Sardinia, ruled the northwest corner of upper Italy, between Nice, Aosta, and La Spezia, did they dream of becoming kings over all Italy. Half a century later they actually did, and they are there today. All the four kings who have ruled Savoy and Italy during the past hundred years have been decent and weak. Charles Albert has the look of an epicure too irresolute for action. Victor Emanuel II looks down upon the streets of Italy from a hundred monuments with the face of a top sergeant; Humbert and Victor Emanuel III, the son and grandson of the preceding, were all honorable and inadequate.

At this time, about 1830, the Sardinian court was rather more progressive than others. The established monarchs were in such terror of Napoleon that the powers in the Holy Alliance supported every king on principle against any demand of the people. Even a great mind like Chateaubriand, once banished by Napoleon, and playing just then at being a French statesman, proposed installing several Bourbons as kings in America.

So any revolution that would accept a king with limited powers had better prospects than if it insisted on being a republic. The republican form of government failed in Prussia, Austria, and Hungary in the year 1848 but succeeded in France temporarily and was half successful in Greece and Italy. Such government was easier and much more interesting in these two Mediterranean countries, because there it was striving for popular rights and national union simultaneously, whereas in the great nations, long since united, the people merely wanted a constitution. The same liberal ideas led to the overthrow of the king in Paris and to union under a king in Athens and Rome. Since the movement of 1848 soon led to a new empire in France as well, no lasting republic actually resulted from the revolutionary turmoil. As late as 1900 Europe had but two republics, Switzerland and France, as against some forty principalities.

Italy's fate was more complicated, for she was subject not to one but to several oppressors, and this not during a mere four centuries, as in the case of the Greeks, but during fourteen. Whether they were called Ostrogoths, as about the year 500, Hohenstaufens, as about 1200, or Austrians and Bourbons, as about 1800, they were always foreign conquerors, seizing the country for its beauty and its location. The subjects, the soldiers and taxpayers, the Italian people had remained the same. Individual provinces did gain their liberty, ruling themselves through native families; this happened repeatedly in Milan, Venice, Florence, and Rome. But still there was never any attempt at national union such as the Western powers had accomplished. Now at last, with the Greeks and the Balkan nations, with the French gaining freedom in their July revolution, the spirit of the age tossed up the Italians too. It was a matter of forty years, from 1830 to 1870; and success came only in three ten-year stages. As in Greece, the help of foreign arms and victories was essential; it was actually the French in 1859 and the Germans in 1870 who won Italian unity—the same peoples whose princes had previously held the land in subjection. And, finally, success came only through the bravery and devotion of three true Italians, two of them sons of the common people.

These three, springing from the agitation and longing of the people, led the nation to liberty and union but were dependent on the aid of foreign arms. Great as revolutionists, daring as conspirators and rebels, the Italians had not enough discipline as an army to expel the enemy. In this way their liberation is distinguished from that of the Swiss, who had disposed of the Hapsburgs without help five hundred years before.

Mazzini, Cavour, Garibaldi, the last true heroes so far produced by the Mediterranean, all came from the north, from Genoa, Turin, and Nice; they must have been of very mixed blood. Born between 1805 and 1810, growing up in the stuffy atmosphere of the reaction, and thus driven to rebellion, the three represent certain characteristics of their people: Mazzini, intellect, literary interests, emotionalism; Cavour, adroitness, knowledge of men, diplomacy; Garibaldi, romanticism and adventurousness. How rich the genius of a people must be to inspire three men so completely different with the same pure devotion! All three were conspirators by nature, and only the form of their illicit activity varied according to temperament and background: one wrote, another talked, a third pulled the trigger when he wanted to overthrow the mighty.

Mazzini's handsome head, thin mouth, and high forehead reveal the poet within the idealist. Sickly as a child, repelled by the family profession of medicine, he was the most lovable and open-handed of the three. Believing wholeheartedly in the victory of the good, he awoke in his first prison to a sense of his own apostolic mission. He was filled with classical ideas that are said to have come from his mother, and he wanted liberty above all, which meant a republic. He took part with a clear conscience in a number of conspiracies aimed at the overthrow of the foreign kings and also—for he was very much the freethinker—of the Pope.

Often hunted and twice condemned to death, he often had to flee abroad. He started newspapers in the towns where he took refuge, in order to rally the best minds. He was constantly writing and conferring, indifferent to money, and usually poor. He buried himself for years in one room in Switzerland. In Paris, London, and Tessin he learned to know the interdependence of politics, and early ventured the leap to internationalism. Long before there was a united Italy, which he lived to see in his old age, young Mazzini strove for a united Europe, and propagated the idea in brilliant manifestoes. He opened his arms so wide that he even wrote a general essay "On the Duties of Man."

At the same time he was no prisoner of rigid dogma but at suitable moments would publicly urge the king of Sardinia or the Pope to unite Italy, although his dreams were republican. He even had a post in the government of a short-lived "Republic of Rome" but retired from it with the impatience of an idealist suddenly tossed into practical politics. To a certain extent Mazzini shared with Luther his purely intellectual, prophetic drive to action but was his superior by far in constancy.

Cavour, whose square, bright, clear face might have been that of a mathematician, all intelligence and acuteness, but brightened by irony, was descended from a long line of counts, but obviously got his quick understanding, as Bismarck did, from his mother—a commoner of Geneva Huguenot extraction. From his father he inherited a natural allegiance to the kings of his country, Piedmont, and he would never have conspired against them. But he was completely liberal in his thinking, declined to become an officer, and learned from the Paris revolution the lesson that even a kingdom could be liberal. Altogether practical, eagerly studying the new steamboats, railroads, and factories, working successfully on his father's estate, he waited for the right moment to join in action. At the age of thirty-seven in Turin, he began his first venture into journalism, "Il Risorgimento," which gave its name to the whole age. By a single article he led the hesitating king to declare war on Austria in 1848.

The impression of the Paris and Vienna revolutions gripped all Italy. At first everything seemed propitious. Naples, Rome, and Venice were taken by the people; Mazzini and his fellow exiles returned. The finest scene took place in Venice. Manin, the last doge, arrested by the Austrian police and now freed by the multitude, came from the gloomy prison in the palace of the Doges directly into the magnificent council chamber to resume his office. Before this, when the foreign overlords spoke of moderating their measures, he had said something that oppressed peoples might well repeat today: "We do not want Austria to be more humane; we want her to be gone." Manin's fine, serious face looks like the best type of a businesslike American, only paler and sadder.

But after a few weeks all hopes withered. Poor equipment, the hesitation of the Pope, the mutual mistrust of the princes led to swift and crushing defeat. The king of Sardinia abdicated, the revolution was easily throttled everywhere, the princes came back, and the exiles fled again, among them Mazzini and the doge Manin. The latter had held out like one of Plutarch's heroes. When the Austrians besieged Venice, with cholera and starvation and to make matters worse even by dropping bombs from balloons inflated with hot air from a stove suspended beneath them—thus staging the first air raids with devastating effect—he ventured at peril of his life to propose on his own account the surrender of the city. He did not escape until the last moment, and as an old man supported himself in Paris by teaching languages.

But Cavour was not discouraged. Under the new young king for ten years he guided first little Piedmont, then big Italy, showing himself as much a master of diplomacy as the great Italian Popes. The skill with which he lured Napoleon III to help him against

Austria on behalf of a united Italy after the Crimean war and finally
held the wavering emperor to his promise on a summer carriage
ride (they say with the help of some lovely women from Torino)
shows the true Italian art of sublime tact. He even dared to promise
Nice and Savoy to the French as the price—the same territories that
the Italians now want back. Eventually keeping this promise after
the victory, he earned the patriots' hatred. At the same time he was
secretly in touch with the groups of political conspirators in the
country, who all wanted a republic and mistrusted the royal minister. No means of extortion was too base for this utterly honorable
man so long as Italy was his goal. For instance, he threatened to
publish in America the promises of the still irresolute Napoleon.
The emperor finally did march in 1859, and very quickly defeated
the Austrians at Magenta and Solferino, then stopped in the midst
of his victorious course, sought the friendship of the vanquished,
and promptly came to terms with the young emperor Francis
Joseph. He took only Lombardy for Italy and left Venice to the
Hapsburgs.

Cavour, who was bound to feel cheated, forgot all etiquette and
caution and made a terrible scene with his own king when the
monarch, on his own responsibility, gave half the prize of victory
to his ally Napoleon. When passion once does flare up in a diplomat
and courtier like Cavour, it is as beautiful to look upon as a forest
lake, apparently always tranquil but sometimes wildly tossed by a
sudden wind. Two years afterward he had an equally violent collision with another leader and died shortly afterward.

This other leader was Garibaldi, a romantic hero of liberty, who
knew the Mediterranean better and had sailed more of it than most
Italians. As a boy on the coast, like Columbus, he had helped his
father, a small merchant; had run away to sea to escape ecclesiastical
discipline; and become involved as a sailor with Mazzini's revolutionists. Condemned to death at an early age, he fled to South America and flung himself into the Brazilian and Uruguayan revolutions. Prison, torture, release, another war; then the capture of
Porto Alegre, where he found a woman of his race who fulfilled
his dreams.

Garibaldi was a man more strongly attracted by battle the world over than by a political idea; nevertheless he was not venal, like the *condottieri,* but proud and avid of glory. He was a man who once, running out of ammunition, literally burned his boat behind him and fled, and on another occasion, being wounded in the morning, stayed all day in the saddle. The first time was for the republic of Uruguay; the second time for the republic of Rome. If Mazzini loved liberty above all, and Cavour worshiped Italy, Garibaldi's first love was adventure. He gave a romantic touch to everything he experienced, even the love and death of his wife, yet he had about him nothing of the actor, at least not until his old age.

We see him in his early forties fleeing after the defeat of Piedmont, working in a New York candle factory, later on a "tramp" merchant ship, when not long before he had been commanding an Italian regiment. Ten years later he was a general again on the same battlefields, and immediately afterward he married a countess, whom he promptly deserted. The following year, 1860, after the victory over Austria, he took ship at Genoa with a thousand volunteers, the celebrated "Mille," using a hundred ruses to deceive the enemy. He landed in Sicily a couple of days later, defeated the troops of the Bourbon king with his handful of men, and found himself dictator over a conquered Sicily and Naples within a few weeks. Then of his own free will he turned over all his conquests to the new king of Italy. He rode into Naples as an adjutant behind the king; not long before he had marched into that town as a liberator. The following day he went to Caprera, a small, lonely island northeast of Sardinia, where he owned a tiny farm, and there he dug ditches, wrote poetry, or dreamed.

The splendid conquest of southern Italy remained Garibaldi's national achievement, for it was a necessary condition of union, yet in the political chess game of the time Cavour could not venture to attempt it. The king wrote a letter to Garibaldi at Palermo solemnly forbidding him to advance on Naples but enclosing a note that ordered him not to obey. In the succeeding struggles as well this bold adventurer was constantly embarrassing the established powers that needed and used him. For all kings' fear of revolutions is so great that they are unwilling to work with revolutionists even for their own ends. The two national heroes, Cavour and Garibaldi, who are now celebrated together, could neither stomach nor trust each other.

Garibaldi always went on fighting just when a truce was politically essential. He was accordingly removed from the scene of action and "accompanied" by his countrymen to his little island. Running away from there at the age of sixty, he beat his way through the fleet, for though he loved an idyllic existence, he could not stand being forced to it. On the other hand when the supreme command ordered him to cease fighting in a subsequent battle, he replied with the one famous word, *Obbedisco* ("I obey"), and turned on his heel. After all the fighting in Italy was over, he tried his hand at new adventures, joining the French to fight the Germans. Coming back, he declined a very large gift of honor so long as the party hostile to him should be in power, began to regulate the Tiber at Rome, and married a third wife, this time a woman by whom he had had children long before. And so he lived completely according to his nature up to the age of seventy-five. Even then he retained the firm carriage, the ecstatically bright eyes in the square, bearded face. Garibaldi's greatest adversary was not Austria, not the Bourbons, not Cavour: it was the Pope. He was not fighting the Father of Christendom, however, but a particular person, a born fighter like himself, a man of steel. Since the latter was neither romantic nor generally so emotional as Garibaldi, we are bound to call the Pope superior to the adventurer as a ruler. He was a born dictator, which Garibaldi certainly was not.

Pius IX meant to become an officer like Cavour and, like him, actually became a statesman—not, however, because he had a similar aversion to arms but because an epileptic tendency prevented him from active service. Also like Cavour, he sprang from a long line of counts. Cured of his epilepsy but still unfit for soldiering, he did not become a priest until his late twenties. By his late thirties he was an archbishop, and at forty-five he was chosen Pope. Then he enjoyed the longest reign of any Pope, thirty-two years. He behaved like a complete autocrat, and in the course of his pontificate he broke with the oldest traditions. His uncommonly handsome head with its energetic chin, strong nose, and large, dark eyes resembled the faces of certain *condottieri* from his native Romagna, except that a voluptuous mouth and a sensually animated expression marked him as a favorite with women and thus in a sense as softer. In the course of the thirty-two years his features and his heart grew ever harder.

When he came into power in 1846, amid the great reaction, he decided to be a liberal Pope, half from conviction, half from ambition. Beginning with a great political amnesty, he talked of reforms, and appointed laymen to the administration of Rome and the papal state. When the revolution two years later literally knocked on the bronze portals of the Vatican, he, like many another frightened sovereign, agreed to a constitution with two chambers, one of which he would appoint. But what was he to do with the troops in northern Italy, setting out against Austria? As Catholics they demanded his blessing, and as Italians, doubly so. Now he grew afraid of his own rashness, like most of the liberal princes; nor did he wish to fall out with the Catholic Hapsburgs. He gave the troops his blessing "as far as the frontier"—the most ludicrous way in which any priest ever entrusted an army to God. Four weeks later he took refuge in neutrality.

Rome, enthusiastically nationalist, already seeing itself as the head of a united Italy, was indignant; so indeed was the whole peninsula. The rebellion forced him to dismiss the Swiss guards and to accept a civilian bodyguard. In other words, within a few days he was a prisoner. Donning the simple priestly cowl he had worn in his youth, he fled with friends to the king of Naples. The Pope had left Rome! Were the Middle Ages and Avignon coming back? Had Turks, had foreign conquerors driven him out? It was Catholic Romans; they did not drive him away, but neither did they hold him back. Rome became a republic, the whole papal state and all church property were secularized, and Mazzini took over the government—a freethinker and a European where the successor of Peter had just held sway.

What followed was a comedy of two lifeguards quarreling over who should jump into the water, leaving the drowning man without help. Napoleon III, who wanted to be crowned like his uncle, insisted on taking the Pope back himself, thus putting him under obligation. He forbade this privilege to the Austrians, who had their own special reasons for restoring the papal state as an obstacle in the center of an Italy striving for union. Garibaldi swore, *"Roma o morte!"* and led his hosts to Rome. There followed battles of red-trousered French against red-shirted Italians, a siege of Rome like those by the Vandals and Charles V, heroic deeds by the Garibaldians. But they were alone and had to withdraw; their leader made a fantastic escape to America. The republic of Rome, which had existed for five months, about as long as Rienzi's in the thirteenth century, was at an end; but the Pope, harassed by his helpers, did not return until a year later. Would he show mercy as supreme shepherd of souls?

In the eighteen months of his banishment he had reverted passionately to his inborn autocratic instincts. The pride of this dictator who had been forced to flee in disguise in the dark of night demanded revenge. Besides, in his exile he had leagued himself with the Jesuits, whose philosophy suited him to perfection. Expulsions, arrests, tortures piled up in Rome now to such a degree that Austrian officers had to stay the hands of cruel priests. At the same time the citizens were impoverished and the priests enriched until Antonelli, the secretary of state, who was born poor, could die leaving twenty-five million dollars.

The result was a popular hatred of the Vatican such as had never been known since the Byzantine struggles. As the nationalist movement increased in the fifties, the papal state was also damned as a political obstacle. The idea of secularizing the papacy was discussed all over Europe, and an Italian professor of theology wrote an anonymous pamphlet in the spirit of Cavour. The papal state crumbled away; after the French victories over Austria it lost two-thirds of its possessions. When the accession of Venice swelled the union in 1866 and the world was waiting to see Rome instead of Florence at last the natural capital of the new kingdom, only Napoleon III protected the papal state with his troops and the Pope with his authority.

During those years old Pius' self-assurance, his authoritarian defiance, kept reaching new heights. Just as he became antiliberal and cruel following his flight, he succeeded after the reduction of his state in taking full revenge on a wicked world through the feeling of his infallibility. He demanded for the church a paramount influence on education and civilization and combated the rights of man, popular rights, liberty of conscience, and science. A picture of the great council that he summoned to Saint Peter's and compared in his own words to the Council of Trent shows him on the throne of Saint Peter, far away from the exalted delegates.

Here Pius established the papal absolutism that contradicted all custom, for hitherto the councils had been autonomous and unanimity had been required of them. Now he demanded to be recognized as infallible. There was great excitement in America, which had sent 113 delegates. A fourth of all 600 votes was privately against the proposal, and the Pope simply ignored them. The priests spoke of Gregory VII. In July, 1870, at a solemn session of the council at Saint Peter's, Pius proclaimed his own infallibility in all questions of faith and morals. Lightning blazed and thunder crashed as he spoke. The priests recalled Exodus XIX. Only the Franco-Prussian War, declared a few days earlier, diverted the attention of the world. Pius, however, felt that he was at the summit of his powers: at seventy-eight he was infallible and more powerful than all the kings.

Six weeks later the battle of Sedan smashed Napoleon's empire. This was a new stroke of luck for Italy, which had already let the foreigners win two victories for her. Starting from Florence, the king immediately crossed the borders of the little papal state. A sham capture of Rome was staged, though the French troops had withdrawn weeks before. Actually the king's troops marched into Rome at their ease, as they had done in 1859 and 1866 in Milan and Venice, because foreign arms had been victorious.

Two months after his supreme moment, the infallible Pope was suddenly a prisoner. True, he still had his dignity, his liberty, his

bodyguard, three palaces, and money was offered to him. He refused liberty and money, for with all the defiance of an affronted
dictator he preferred to have the world think him a prisoner. A
new legend came into being: in Catholic foreign countries dealers
sold bundles of the straw upon which the Holy Father had to sleep.
Actually he went on living in his palace with its twenty courtyards
and its superb gardens. Nearly eighty, he would seldom have gone
outside in any case.

This was a great moment in the Mediterranean. The successor
of Peter had been elevated once more into the purely spiritual power
that his earliest predecessors had possessed. The mad insistence that
the high priest must have land, troops, police, taxes, and courts was
at an end. If Italy was to stand united before the world at last, the
papal state must give way. Either emperors or Popes had ruled
at Rome. When they tried to rule together, there was either war or
flight. So long as the kings were chief priests—as the Pharaohs,
certain Roman emperors, and the caliphs had been—the symbols of
power were gathered in a single hand. Pius IX was too old, too
despotic, too infallible to see the victory implied in his defeat. His
successor Leo XIII saw it and won veneration for the Holy See
throughout the world. At last the Mediterranean had a solid, united
kingdom at its center, with one language and one government.
The king was too much of a gentleman to take Corsica during the
breakdown of France, although young Clemenceau's party offered
it to him. He would have liked to take Tunis, but the threatening
English navy prevented him. The natural extension of the new
kingdom was bound to be in north Africa.

A new power, steam, had thrown all shipping into a bustle of
activity. It may be mentioned that the Austrian general Tegethoff
used armored ships on the high seas for the first time at Vis, in
1866, to defeat the Italians. Now the nations that built the steam-
ships were free nations—or at least most of them were. Communication everywhere was speeded up, amplified, and fought over
from all sides. The Mediterranean, so long forsaken, began to stir
again. What it needed for the new world commerce was a new

entrance. The gate that had been shut for over a thousand years was to be burst open.

The crucial moment for the liberation of this inland sea was at hand; the hour of freedom approached.

XVII

FIVE TIMES IN TWO THOUSAND YEARS the lords of Egypt had vanquished the Isthmus of Suez, giving the Mediterranean a third, man-made opening along with the two natural ones at Gibraltar and the Dardanelles. All five of these passages, the products of human planning and building, were made long before the great discoveries. The channeling and its results in the south were therefore more important than the natural openings to east and west could have been. The Dardanelles, after all, merely led into another land-locked body of water, the Black Sea, and in those days Gibraltar was considered the end of the world. The Atlantic was unknown.

The canal system of Ramses the Great, mentioned at the beginning of this volume, connected the Mediterranean with the Red Sea so cleverly, by way of the Nile and a canal in the delta, that vessels were only four days going from one sea to the other. When, in 612 B.C., seven centuries later, the Pharaoh Necho started to restore the canal, grown impassable long since, 120,000 slave laborers perished in the desert heat. But this was not what disturbed the Pharaoh. An oracle ordered him to desist because his canal would open the road to Egypt for a conqueror. The politician priests may have given him this advice in the form of an oracle for social reasons or perhaps actually from considerations of foreign policy. Certain it is that King Darius conquered the land ninety years later and actually restored the canal system. The Ptolemies returned to and extended the old canals, but soon allowed them to decay. When Cleopatra tried to save her fleeing navy from the Romans, most of the vessels could not get through.

The Romans later developed the land route from Alexandria to Suez as a link with the Indian Ocean. Finally Trajan, about

A.D. 100, built a canal system like that of ancient Egypt; part of it still runs through the city of Cairo under the name of Khalik.

Another five hundred years and Amru, the Arab conqueror of Egypt, restored the waterways, long since silted up. This was not intended to ship Egyptian grain to Europe, however, but, on the contrary, to bring it home to the harbor of Mecca. Once more a successor feared the consequences, and one of the next caliphs had the canal put out of commission lest the rebels from Arabia should thus be able to reach Egypt as the Persians had done. This restoration took place in the year 767. A waterway between the two oceans had been attempted and proved possible again and again in the course of two thousand years.

But no one had ventured to think of piercing the narrow Isthmus of Suez, with its lakes. This was a new idea. Finally the men of the Renaissance, daring to do anything because they put the elements above God and man above the elements, decided that even this was possible. Leonardo da Vinci had made brilliant drawings for canals, and hydraulic tools were being perfected. Here again the Venetians pioneered. Their search for profit led them out upon the great ocean. When we learn that they contemplated piercing Suez not after but just before Columbus, we realize afresh that countries are discovered and great inventions produced when the times demand them.

The Mediterranean was ripe for expansion. Perhaps the engineers would have succeeded in their task under Venetian auspices if the Turks had not conquered Egypt and the eastern Mediterranean. That fact, together with the great discoveries, caused the power of Venice to fade. But the problem was so very much alive at this time that a Portuguese viceroy of the East Indies, about 1500, had the almost insane notion of diverting the Nile near the island of Philae, close above the First Cataract, by a canal going directly eastward through the desert to the Red Sea. The operation would have destroyed the delta.

But nothing actually happened until Napoleon came. Definitely constructive by nature, with a classical love of glory, he picked up the projects of the Pharaohs. He had a survey made to learn the width and height of the isthmus to be pierced, as well as the levels of the two oceans. These surveys were decisive not by their result but by the stimulus that the report provided for the best minds of Europe. From that time on the question was constantly discussed. Nevertheless it was about 1860, just eleven hundred years after the second, intentional destruction of the canal for fear of Arab invasion, before the sixth attempt finally brought the decision on a great scale and for all time.

There had been five fabulous-sounding attempts, all of them silted up, five centuries apart; and various other plans were made but not carried out.

The struggle for the Suez Canal was not a petty battle but a symbolic one, and this in a double sense. Two kinds of men and two kinds of powers were contending, and although the leader of one group was victorious among the men, the power he served was finally defeated among the nations. The Frenchman de Lesseps built the canal, but in the end England took possession of it.

The first men who went out to put the hyphen between the two parts of the Old World, as they said, were true idealists; they allied themselves with experienced engineers. They built up all the emotional drive and all the body of information that finally led to success. What they lacked was a cynical energy. Their great drawback was their faith in mankind.

Enfantin, a young engineer, the son of a Paris banker, was an enthusiastic pupil of Count Saint-Simon. In his early youth he was imprisoned and then banished for daring to speak of a peaceable humanity that would use modern inventions for happiness instead of warfare. He tried to help found a sort of priestly socialism. In one picture, fringed with long black hair and beard, he looks like a savage imagined by Rousseau; in another, smooth-shaven, he has a handsome mouth that seems to enjoy life, but the fiery eyes still speak of fine plans. Underneath the picture are the words: *Chef Suprême de la Réligion Saint-Simonienne.*

This group of men regarded the building of a canal as a gift to humanity. When Enfantin and his friends went to Egypt in 1833 they might equally well have been going to Panama, for both canals were being much talked of at the time. A saying of Goethe's just before his death was making the rounds even before it saw print; Humboldt quoted it to encourage one of the later engineers. The eighty-year-old Goethe praised the canal projects as a means to the understanding of nations, as a humanitarian conquest of the globe. He said he would like to live another fifty years so as to see the canals of Suez and Panama. Forty and eighty years later the two canals were finished.

In their plans the young Frenchmen followed the surveys of Napoleon's experts in 1799; but they began quite without money—studying, calculating, drafting. Artisans, technicians, authors, all lived as laborers on the desert edge. Motives of idealism were all that held them. No one was paid; many fell ill, and fifteen men died from effects of the climate.

Linant, a Frenchman of practical experience, established connections with the ruler of the country. For old Mehemet Ali, governing Egypt practically independently, was likewise ambitious to accomplish something great. He wanted the engineers to build a great dam across the Nile near the Pyramids, as if dramatically to prove the nonsense of those gigantic chunks by accomplishing a sensible engineering feat close beside them. Politics prevented him from going on, and the friends of humanity went home without results. But it was their passion, their reports and writings that spread the idea through Europe. Before they knew it, their magnificent humanitarian plan took on political significance. The moment the statesmen of the great powers stepped in, their fine and noble motives were done for. England at first was indifferent, trusting to the Napoleonic surveys, which showed a difference in water level between the two seas. This would have required the building of locks and have made the whole thing almost impossible. According to the surveys the Red Sea was thirty-two feet higher than the Mediterranean. In those early railroading days, English public opinion was steered toward a line from Alexandria to Suez by way of Cairo.

England had long been the letter carrier between continents. All the mail from India and eastern Asia went from Suez to Cairo by dromedaries speeding the seventy miles through the desert in twelve

hours. An omnibus with twelve seats took travelers in a day's run to
the point where paddle-wheel steamers plied the Nile; then horses
drew boats along the canal to Alexandria. There the first liners
waited to take the English mail to Marseille. Even when Austrian
steamers began plying between Alexandria and Trieste in 1850, they
were not allowed to carry the India mail.

English complacency about the canal, however, was really
founded on a French mistake. Napoleon's engineers had calculated
wrong. The levels of the two seas were the same, and the canal could
be built without locks, and therefore comparatively easily and
cheaply. When the hydraulic engineers discovered the mistake their
predecessors had made half a century before, the English government was as horrified as the Vatican had been when the earth was
displaced from the center of the universe. So the canal *was* possible:
the empire trembled. Might not future combinations at Suez make
English transit difficult and facilitate an enemy's passage? "The
Suez Canal," Bismarck said, "is the cord in the neck of the British
Empire that connects the spine with the brain." England, being
more immediately concerned with her empire than with the welfare
of humanity, at once began to work against the building of the
canal.

But the problem still lay between a matter of humanity and a
political chess game. Humboldt drew the canal to the attention of
an Austrian engineer, Negrelli, whose face betrayed evidence of his
Italian and German ancestry. He was an outstanding man with great
construction jobs on the Rhine and in Switzerland already to his
credit. He studied the question on the spot and made the first definite sketch. Enfantin, the French idealist, recognized a master hand
and deferred to Negrelli in a noble-minded letter. Two Swiss bankers of the Dufour family grew enthusiastic over the project, and
made it possible to obtain $40,000 so that a commission for study
could carry out its work. Stephenson, whose father had invented the
locomotive, was a member of this commission. The correspondence
of all these men displays generosity and high-mindedness; their
faces betray such intellectuality that we imagine ourselves trans-

ported to the world of Rousseau, where the useful is done for the sake of the moral consequences.

But at the same time international politics took a hand, depressing the whole to their own lower level. Mehemet Ali scented a profit; he was willing to pay a high price to the foreign engineers, but he wanted to be the builder. His second successor in the government was a gifted young man of European upbringing, who was ready to allow certain privileges to the Europeans. The three-power commission favored Negrelli's project but vacillated in its estimates of the cost. There was talk of twelve million dollars, and eventually ten times the sum was spent. The Europeans' labor in the desert was full of tragic and comic incidents. In order to use a ship supplied by the state, they had to give money to the crew and a gold watch to the captain.

For twenty years the project had been studied by the most selfless men, great experts among them, and still it did not advance. Idealism could not break the isthmus; the Mediterranean remained closed.

But the young master of Egypt, as a child, had had a French riding master who soon became his mentor. He was the son of the then powerful French consul general, on whose influence Mehemet Ali had been dependent in the years of his rise and to whom he was grateful now. The younger generation became friends as their fathers had been. When Saïd came to the throne, he immediately summoned his teacher and friend de Lesseps.

XVIII

THE DE LESSEPSES were an old French noble family combining many-sided cultivation with the traditions of high government functionaries. Ferdinand de Lesseps (1805-1894) also had instinct and experience in handling orientals, for he was brought up in Cairo, returned later as consul, and, of course, knew about the studies made by his countrymen. Hunter, horseman, businessman, stylist, propagandist, scholar, he combined many traits of the man of the world. The only one he completely lacked was a knowledge of mechanics: he was almost everything else, but he was no engineer. This was the man who built the Suez Canal.

He had proved his intrepidity during the plague at Cairo and in a revolt at Barcelona. His energy had attracted notice everywhere, and as he combined with it a truly Oriental adroitness, he seemed to be destined for a great career as a minister in Paris; for this was the sort of man who had often successfully guided France. But he was sent to Rome on a delicate mission, to bring back the fugitive Pope Pius IX, and a sudden upheaval in the Paris government made him politically impossible. Resigning, he spent several years in the country, resolved never again to enter government service. He seems to have studied widely during those years.

When his pupil, now a monarch, summoned him to Cairo, de Lesseps was forty-nine, Saïd, thirty-two. Rich, retired from office, ambitious, widowed, free in every sense, de Lesseps resolved to turn this stroke of luck into a life career. Traveling through the country with the master of Egypt, he made it plain what the canal would mean to the world and to Egypt but pointed out that it would have to be attacked in a very different way. At a camp in the Libyan desert he presented his plans to Saïd. He had adopted almost all of them from Negrelli, whom he praised highly and whom he advised Saïd to engage.

He spoke of the commission, on the other hand, as something past, like the canals of Ramses and Darius, the Ptolemies and the Arabs. He spoke not as a discoverer but as an entrepreneur. He never laid claim to the plans, which he admitted he had bought. His young listener, as wily and as ambitious as de Lesseps himself, trusted the foreign Christian further than he did his own Mohammedan advisers. He offered no objection to the two aims de Lesseps had in view—to put the canal under French control and to build it himself. Three weeks after de Lesseps landed at Alexandria he had in his pocket the priceless permission to found a company for the building of the canal.

Going to Europe, he met with a cool reception in Paris, a hostile one in London. Every factor in England was against him. The government had its ambassadors point out to the grand vizier at Constantinople how dangerous such an undertaking might be in the hands of the upstart family at Cairo, which would thus grow ripe to secede and drop into the hands of France. The sultan refused the concession. The London bankers called the project a fraud, the government warned people against subscribing for stock, and the celebrated Palmerston described the plan as one of the many "bubble schemes." (Just to make sure, however, he also occupied the island of Perim in the Bab el Mandeb.) Only Gladstone recognized the true significance. Engineers said the canal would never be built, because the Mediterranean mud would silt it up.

De Lesseps joined battle with press and stock exchange, wrote pamphlets, delivered lectures, started a magazine, and dared to say, in the very midst of the Crimean war, that the Suez Canal would be more important than the Dardanelles. He was looking for fifty million dollars, and he found it, the larger part in France, some twenty million from his friend Saïd, the master of Egypt.

Finally he confronted the powers with an accomplished fact. He announced the establishment of the Suez Canal Company, but appointed to his commission none of the original idealists except Negrelli, who immediately gratified de Lesseps by dying. The canal was to belong to the company for ninety-nine years and thereafter to Egypt, that is, in about 1968. De Lesseps was the president. He had fifty millions and was one of the greatest entrepreneurs, but for the time being he wanted not profit but construction; his motives were humanitarian and French at the same time. Ambition above all was his motive for action. In 1859, amid great solemnities, he turned the first shovelful of earth. Thus he divided Africa from Asia and by the same motion joined Asia to Europe.

He had two pieces of good luck during the ten-year struggle for the construction. The first was Eugénie, by birth a Spanish countess and a relative of de Lesseps' mother. Now that she was empress in Paris, perhaps he flattered her with tales of Columbus and Queen Isabella. In any case Napoleon III, who often took his wife's advice, came out for de Lesseps at a moment of crisis when England was once more trying to interrupt the work. The second piece of good

luck was Disraeli, who realized the full historic importance of the
canal, now well along. Out of it he tried to win for England what
France was trying to win for herself.

A brilliant executive energy filled de Lesseps (who passed into
his sixties during the ten-year task) because he understood business,
the purchase of materials, the deploying of the army of workmen,
the whims of the sultan, of the pasha, of Empress Eugénie. He succeeded, furthermore, in facing down all opposition. Everything that
could possibly be contrived to endanger the hero of a novel was piled
up here. Thousands of fellahin died in the desert, and the pasha
refused to draft more. Then followed the lack of drinking water, at
first brought daily by 1,600 camels to the 30,000 workmen, until de

Lesseps built a special fresh-water canal for the laborers. The shares
fell from 500 to 180, and danger of complete bankruptcy threatened
the company. The discovery of unexpectedly hard rock and gypsum
cliffs and the failure of all-important machines made progress more
difficult. Sudden surprises in the number of tides, sudden lack of
coal, threats by the investors, the workmen, the desert, the sea—all
combined to produce a struggle of ten years with men and elements.

Today the figures seem as remote as if we were reading of some
ancient battle. Yet even now, seventy years after its completion, the
Suez Canal amazes engineers, not because it is so long, wide, and
deep but because it cuts through the desert. The scene of action was
what dismayed the builders, as it enchants the passenger, who can
travel through the canal in thirteen hours.

The necessary amount of human labor was reduced one-fourth
by the five lakes that could be used in the 100 miles or so of the canal.
The width also seems small, running from 325 feet in sandy parts
to 190 feet in rock. Everybody has seen some garden that was at least
190 feet long; most of the rivers we know are much wider. The canal
can be crossed in a skiff with 36 strokes of the oars, and with its 25
to 30 feet of depth it is only twice as deep as many swimming pools.
The height of the hills seems equally trifling, never more than 30
or 40 feet. All this reminds us of an ordinary tunnel. But it took
place eighty years ago, and in the desert, which consists of alluvial
deposits and sometimes rock. The loose sand that blows over the
canal in shifting magic figures is like the peach complexion of a
young girl, who has a hard skeleton under that delicate skin. It was
Goethe who said that nature is "always covered with something
soft."

The whole oft-imperiled work was held together by the energy
of a man almost entirely without the idealistic impulse of the
pioneers. Once again it was evident that will power and intelligence
are what count in battling with the elements far more than the imagination that had lent wings to the originators. The work of ten
years was accomplished by a man who bombarded no cities, oppressed no nation, led none to victory, and destroyed nothing but a
hundred-yard strip of desert sand and hills. What he made was

planned and done to outlive all the realms that generals and kings around him were snatching. His enemy was the elements, and their resistance was like that of an animal under the surgeon's knife, because they did not know what was happening to them.

At last the moment of release arrived: the ever-increasing pressure of both seas slackened. They had been within earshot of each other's roar; now freed at both ends of the bridge of land, they mingled with the water of the five lakes that they had left behind them immemorial ages ago. One March day in 1869 the first waters of the Mediterranean poured southward; five months later those of the Red Sea went north. The day came when the last shovelful was turned, and seldom can any human being have known greater satisfaction than this, when the gray-green waters of the Red Sea met and merged with the blue of the Mediterranean. Even today both currents can be recognized by their color at the ends of the canal.

A great celebration was held, with kings and emperors coming to sail through the canal. The bands played, bright buoys gleamed, flags fluttered, lighthouses pointed skyward. Desert and sea announced in yellow and blue a new form of marriage that had begun with a separation.

The beautiful Empress Eugénie, in her gay hoop skirts, leaned back in a smart boat, holding a parasol in her gloved hand, and thinking perhaps that the work could never have come to pass without her. The builder beside her, full of youthful vigor at sixty, may have been thinking that brilliance and beauty should have been joined and that he would have made this woman far happier than the sickly Napoleon, whose family by the way was not nearly so old as de Lesseps' own. The first vessel to pay the canal toll flew the British flag.

A year later Napoleon was overthrown and in captivity, and Eugénie had fled the country. Twenty years more, and a great scandal robbed old de Lesseps of the peace of his declining years. Within a few years he had flung himself with the old energy into the second task that the world now demanded of him. Instead of playing the great political role that was offered him, he still kept his eyes on the elements: Panama was the second goal that the seventy-four-year-old set himself.

But now, though his will was fresh, his mind had grown old. He was obstinate and insisted on his own solutions. The success of his first canal endangered the second, for he was unwilling to listen to the objections of the experts. He wanted to build Panama without locks because he had built Suez without locks; he was like an old man who tries to treat a young second wife just as he once treated the first. Questions of money, always easy to twist against the entrepreneur in such vast undertakings, were reinforced by political enmities. And in a few years the greatest enterpriser of his time lost fame and fortune. It is possible that he had some share in the guilt of the embezzlements his opponents uncovered; of fraud he was never convicted. His son took it all upon himself, and the aged man pretended to understand nothing of the trial, which was kept from him. De Lesseps died in his ninetieth year a ruined man.

The value and success of his work had surpassed all estimates. If we compare the year 1870 with 1935 in round figures, the annual shipping through the Suez Canal began with 400,000 tons and rose to 30,000,000. Five hundred vessels rose to six million. The dividends on one $120 share in this "fraud" rose from $23 to $500.

Disraeli succeeded at a single magnificent blow in turning this French achievement into an English one. For his world-political objectives, the originator of the Indian imperial title kept needing more and more new stages between England and India; above all, Egypt.

He got the gifted and frivolous khedive Ismail Pasha to plant cotton in the delta and to seize more and more territory as far as Aden on the upper Nile, under English guidance, so that it could be the more easily taken away from him. Thus Egypt got deeper and deeper into debt, and when this, along with his pleasures, had ruined the khedive, England, with Rothschild's help, bought the Suez Canal shares from him at a princely price. Disraeli asked no one's permission, certainly not parliament's, and his intermediary at Cairo closed the deal in the record time of ten days. The British government could now demand ten seats on the board of directors of the canal: thus it has had the deciding voice in Mediterranean history down to the most recent times.

True English courage in confessing oneself mistaken led the *Times,* which had denounced the canal for years, to admit soon after: "This country will furnish the dividends that the shareholder will receive. May they be the compensation of our error!" This sentence, typical of the best English tradition, existed along with the equal English pedantry by which the British government mails continued for twenty years to be unloaded at Alexandria, hurriedly transported overland to Suez, and there put back aboard the same ship.

Four years after de Lesseps's death, his statue towered above the end of the long quay where his canal begins, at Port Saïd. The traveler leaving Europe and approaching the all-important cleft between Africa and Asia sees this figure first. De Lesseps has become the prototype of all those who have since built great canals and dams, thus raising man in world commerce above the powers of the elements. Nobody now remembers the accusations that once shrieked through the world. The scandal is forgotten, the canal remains.

XIX

A SHIP MOVING THROUGH THE DESERT: such is the miraculous sight apparently seen by an observer on land as he watches the huge seagoing vessels travel with infinite care and deliberation through the Suez Canal. But if he is on board, the impression, particularly at night, cannot be compared with anything else in the universe. The narrowness of the canal, apparently half filled by the vessel itself, the slow pace and the solemn wilderness round about create the effect of a dead landscape, through which he glides, guided by an experienced captain and leader—like Dante and Vergil at night in purgatory.

But soon signs of the electrical century make their appearance. The lighthouse at Port Saïd swings its three beams of light. Light signals are exchanged by vessels and boats. Stars float upward and stop at a moderate height, so that one dreams that the belt of Orion must have sunk into our sphere. A little boat pulls noiselessly near; a figure mounts the deck, the bridge—the canal pilot, a smart gentleman with gray hair. The anchors rattle up. Then a brilliant gleam shoots across the water. It is the canal headlight, which rules the night like the eye of Cyclops. Everything seems noiseless; the ship appears to hold her breath, so slowly does she glide through the canal, never exceeding five miles an hour. Only the Suez boats that carry travelers send their steam whirling through the funnel of light, like a horse puffing clouds on a cold day. The glaringly illuminated strip of water narrows quickly, and the Cyclops light trickles across the fine sand on both sides.

Suddenly another Cyclops appears in the desert; the huge blue light comes slowly nearer. The two lights dazzle each other like cars on the highway, until neither can see; but what we cannot see we hear. A loud shouting and screaming begin in Arabic, with its abundant *ah* sounds. Since two vessels cannot pass, one of them must lie up according to certain rules at a wide turnout. A couple of sailors put over in a boat, and the huge vessel is moored to shore by a single cable, as if she were a park rowboat. Shouts are heard, followed by curses and orders to stop. Down goes the anchor. The ship pauses in the midst of the desert, in the midst of the night. A floating edifice with a thousand lights glides slowly past; the two giants are not twenty feet apart. Up comes the anchor, engines are started; cables cast off, sailors spring into action; the journey continues.

Morning reveals the whole desert, always more infinite than the sea. For what can be more finite than the sharp line of the sea horizon? Only in the fog does it seem boundless; the desert always is. The play of colors, from green to deep blue, orange, olive, the shifting shadows animate the desert far more than the sea, for all forms here are blown by the wind. Every shape gives the effect of a revelation. A few camels being led to the canal yonder seem like slowly moving sacred beasts of the Egyptians. Every creature becomes a symbol. Far away in the direction of the Nile delta a bright lilac cloud floats past the spyglass; those are flamingos. Motionless on a post in the Bitter Lake sits a black cormorant, the bird of wisdom.

Above a bay two kites wing in spirals one above the other, hunting fish. Far away a lonely palm appears; there it stands in the desert—a veiled woman and the desert; a group of kneeling camels and the desert; all black on the golden-yellow sand against the opal of the sky.

Suddenly a human head appears in the canal. We see it holding back to let the ship go first. It is a swimming Arab from Asia, walking through the desert, who has now tied his bundle around his head and neck to swim where his forefathers walked undisturbed. When he reappears later behind the vessel and scrambles ashore, he takes his bundle on his back, continuing his journey into the Egyptian desert, into Africa. He seems like a prophet.

All at once the ship begins to go faster. A village with a few minarets heaves in sight; a black group of twenty Arabs is seen on the beach, bowing toward the morning sun. They are praying beside the twenty resting camels. This is Suez; here the Red Sea begins, and in four more days the ship, which left Genoa four days ago, will be plowing the Indian Ocean.

The Mediterranean has gained a new entrance. Having lost its importance as the center of humanity through the great geographical discoveries, it was neglected for almost four hundred years. Now new trade routes open up, roads along which Phoenicians and Greeks, Arabs and Venetians once carried their goods. The old seaports, once powerful, then half asleep, wake again to a brisker life. The commercial genius of the Greeks is revived; Constantinople, the Peiraeus, Smyrna receive commerce from all the world; Alexandria has become again what it was before and under the Romans. Foreign flags appear from America and Japan.

The children of the Mediterranean, once scattered over the earth, are coming home now. Everyone prefers to save the time and oil of a 5,000-mile voyage around Africa. In a wondrous way the old mother has once more become the center in whose house all the children and grandchildren meet. They bring back news of far lands, goods, ideas, inventions. An inland sea whose coasts were once crowded with strangers has become an open ocean, from which the natives set forth, to return again or carry the language and civilization of their forefathers to distant continents. Everyone here is seeking a port, a roadstead, a shipyard, a coast, an island, a colony.

The Mediterranean has awakened to new life.

BOOK FIVE

THE FIGHT WITH THE STRANGER

"Soldiers of the Army of the Mediterranean! The Roman legions that you have sometimes rivaled, but never equaled, fought Carthage on this very Sea. Soldiers, Europe is watching you!"

NAPOLEON

AT THE LIGHTHOUSE

In September *the grapes redden, and many turn black. They are as sweet on the island as in the Provence to which it belongs; the wine is bright red, light, and pure.*

With his wife and three children the lighthouse-keeper goes out to his little well-tended vineyard—yesterday, today, tomorrow. In three days the vintage will be done. At first the children were glad no one saw how much they were eating as they picked. But by the second day they have more than enough and begin to amuse themselves by betting who can pick the most and how heavy the basket that each one is filling will be. Their mother is busy and serious. She calculates that the sale will not bring much, for this is a good wine year, and a hundredweight of grapes fetches a fourth less than last year. When the gardener is also a merchant, he is by no means pleased to have all his neighbors share in the blessing of the soil.

As the tall keeper stands beside the vine, he towers above it; his wife is just barely tall enough, and the children stand on tiptoe to pick the topmost clusters. Most, however, hang low, so that it is often necessary to blow or wipe the dust off a bunch. The keeper, looking upon his loved ones with the taciturn devoutness of a sailor, silently offers up his thanks to God. He watches the bigger boy lugging his basket along and carefully setting it down; then he hears the girl calling her brother because her basket is getting too heavy. Finally the youngest goes running from one to another, bringing his father a big bunch that he says is the biggest in the world. Finally he races over to his mother to blow his nose on her apron.

For thousands of years now this idyl has recurred every autumn on the Mediterranean coast—first dimly as a legend, then among the Greeks as a sort of divine worship, among the Romans in organized form, finally as an industry and a business.

Today it is an export question, regulated by large associations. But the commercial houses that ship the casks from Marseille, Genoa, and Naples hear nothing but rumbling columns of figures and the rattle of typewriters. They scarcely know what goes on in a vineyard at all. The clustered grapes interest no one except the fruiterers, of whom there are few; the real business is compassed in casks and bottles. But the idyl is in the vineyard, and never lovelier than at the time of the vintage.

The keeper puts a sort of rope harness on his donkey; he hangs a heavy basket on one side while the boy keeps the balance by holding the rope fast on the other side. The second basket goes on, and the donkey, led by the boy, plods slowly along the rows of heavily laden vines. Then it goes by the road to the village on the coast side. Here the beast's load is put aboard a small steamer and shipped to the mainland, where trucks stand waiting to take the grapes to Toulon.

Why is this scene more in character with the Mediterranean than with any other spot in the world? Have not California, Chile, the Bay of Biscay, France herself the finest of grapes? Do not Bordeaux and Burgundy produce the choicer wines?

Yet all the wines that grow around the Mediterranean, like all the Mediterranean peoples, are mysteriously akin and alike. The tart wine of Avignon, growing not far from the island where the lighthouse stands; the bittersweet sherry of Andalusia; slow-dripping Malaga; fresh Tuscan and all its cousins in central Italy; pink Capri; the darker Falerno from the volcanic soil; fiery Marsala; the dangerous wine of the Aegean islands; the honey-sweet vintages of Cyprus—with all their differences, they hint at a family feeling that transmits the heritage of character belonging to the Mediterranean; they all possess and induce a gentle restlessness without dizziness, a mental briskness without drunkenness. The wine and the people of the Mediterranean are sunny and moderate.

Those who are gathering the grapes here think only of what is near at hand, not of distant wines. Even the donkey merely wonders how much further it will be before the baskets are unloaded and he can trot home with a lighter step, the boy on his back squeezing his ribs with eager heels. The boy, pummeling and shouting, is delighted as the animal begins to run, and his little brother laughs to see him come pelting up.

Going back to the lighthouse that evening, the keeper methodi-

cally and almost unconsciously tested the instruments, pressed them, tapped them, squinted at them. Finally he skimmed over the day's log sheets. Then he turned to his book, leafed through what he had read last, and thought to himself:

. . . Well, it's a good thing the ocean wasn't absolutely abandoned, as you might have thought from the title. What troubles and battles in times like ours, which, people say, are more peaceful! He describes Corsica quite well, but there isn't enough about our Hyères Islands. That business about the indecisive naval battle is right, but there are a hundred other stories of real and near pirates who used to hide in the coves here, whom the author probably never heard of. I've read more than this about Lepanto, too. And all the things that have happened around Marseille and Toulon! In fact, there's too little about France in general; evidently the man is more familiar with Italy. I could tell him lots of things. Really an author should always be older than his reader. Well, from now on I hope there'll be more figures and less philosophy, fewer stories about kings, more about naval bases and exports. Let's see . . .

I

Thousands of generations of fish have known man in his ship on the Mediterranean. Perhaps the ancestor of the dolphin whose back we see from the deck of a steamer, flashing from the blue into the glare of a southern noon, noticed the first dug-out tree trunk near him and belligerently leapt at it to upset it. Then his grandson saw the plank boat of Odysseus and saw a shark try to destroy it. The rowing vessels of the Phoenicians swept past long dolphin generations; these men were the first who tried to fool the fishes by putting a fish mouth at the bow of the boat. The fish would no doubt have laughed at this if they could.

One morning in the days of the Romans a new kind of sail appeared in the Mediterranean. Diagonal sails still called lateen (*i.e.,* Latin) bellied out from three masts. Next came the Arabs, the first to use explosives, throwing a sort of bomb by hand or machine; it all went hissing into the sea. For some thousand years oars and sails propelled Mediterranean shipping.

Then about 1840 came the first steamer with paddle wheels.

Again the so-called experts, who are doing so much harm even now, mistook the magic value of the new invention. When the first iron vessel was to be built in England, about 1780, they said iron was too heavy to float and would deflect the compass needle. Owners of forest land and lumber dealers were especially patriotic; they circulated songs and poems about the "Wooden Walls of Old England." But it turned out that the iron vessels weighed less than the wooden, that the compass could be adjusted, and (some decades later) that steel offered yet greater advantages.

When the engine was installed in the first steamship, people did not quite trust it; the smokestack poked its nose out between the sails. Between the masts the black cylinder peered out comically; or five low red smokestacks would cower at irregular intervals among six tall masts; the mild ludicrousness of the spectacle was increased by the easygoing paddle wheels. In colored engravings

these vessels look like old maids in shawls and preposterous hats, sweeping through a ballroom to the secret amusement of the crowd.

The silhouette changed with the progress of mechanics, just as it has in the development of automobiles: a hundred years ago an American invented the screw propeller, the way for which had been cleared by work in other nations. This was one of the greatest inventions in shipbuilding, no less brilliant than the first oar and the first steamer. It too was originally derided by all the experts. When people finally ventured to trust steam alone, without sail power, the ancient Greek wind gods, still to be seen on the tower at Athens, had their darkest day. Feeling themselves despised, they began to take fearful revenge upon mortal arrogance by capsizing and sending to the bottom many of the proud, sail-less vessels.

But at the same time men contrived to make the engines smaller and smaller and correspondingly more powerful, thus increasing the capacity of steamers. As late as 1890 only one per cent exceeded 8,000 tons burden; the figures swiftly grew, and now ships of 80,000 tons have been built. About 1880 there were still roughly equal numbers of sailing and steam vessels; but then the former declined as fast as the horse-drawn carriage. Only a few rich eccentrics now cruise the Mediterranean in their sailing yachts, all of which, however, have Diesel motors—as if the last hansom cabs at the edge of Central Park in New York were to install little auxiliary motors. But the great old sailing vessels on which naval cadets learn navigation look the same today as they did a hundred years ago.

The speed of steamers has not kept pace with their size; in a hundred years they have come to travel less than three times as fast. Tea was brought from China to England by the fastest clipper in thirteen weeks, and today the passage still takes five.

The Suez Canal was what caused the Mediterranean vessels to grow, and this quite literally. Up to 1870 Mediterranean shipping had remained a sort of inland-navigation enterprise; the natives sailed as the Phoenicians and Greeks had done, from one coast to another, and very few left their own sea to venture on the great ocean. When the Suez Canal opened up the south coast, everyone hoped to sail swiftly and seize a share in the eastern trade, and so great vessels were built. The English were already plying with their largest craft. And the ancient ports that had been cosmopolitan harbors because the world ended at Gibraltar now awoke to new and splendid life, becoming great seaports in the spirit of the twentieth century: Marseille, founded twenty-five centuries before, and along with it Naples, Genoa, Algiers, Barcelona. More and more new vessels were built at more and more new shipyards. They soon had a capacity of more than ten million tons.

At these ports, former junction points of Roman and later highway systems, the new railroads now went straight to the docks. The first transfer of Oriental goods from steamer to car was as much of an event in the history of mankind as the first Egyptian canal system. About 1900 a sickly or merely pampered traveler—perhaps without changing his slippers—was able for the first time to enter a sleeping car at Paris, board ship with one stride across the tracks at Brindisi, and not disembark until Shanghai. The Mediterranean now was a mere brief waterway in a long voyage around the world.

All at once the smokestacks ceased to smoke. Without sails or oars the vessel seemed to move by some invisible force, like an automobile. And so fuel oil, which did not become general until after the First World War, also changed the aspect of the Mediterranean ports. Once the spectators, in summer clothes, had leaned on the rail of the fashionable passenger decks, looking down at a scene from inferno. They saw two long, gray-black lines of coal passers moving along two swaying planks from the dock to the open holes in the steamer's belly, dumping their coal from grayish-yellow sacks, and then returning at the same dragging gait to the giant mountain of coal on the other side. Shrouded in dust, with a deafening roar, this would go on for four, eight, ten hours. It was a sight from the old days of slavery.

Now modern engineering has laid beneath the desert two pipe lines from the oil wells of Iraq. The oil flows from the towers into the pipe, then out again at the Syrian port a thousand miles away, into a huge pool from which smaller lines are hooked up to the tanks of the great vessels. The oil is pumped in automatically. If we take the long view, the engineering advantages of greater thermal efficiency, four-fifths less time, and nine-tenths less labor, are not so important as the social advantages. The substitution of oil for coal is an event on a level with modern plant management, or the protection of women and children. When English housewives in the fourteenth century protested against the first mechanical use of coal, because it soiled their laundry, their natural reaction was finally overpowered by necessity alone. Today a vessel may sweep through the Mediterranean as white as a swan, and the sailors who empty their buckets across the decks in the morning have only dust to wash down.

Between the first appearance of steam and of oil a third event came to change the aspect of the coasts. Anyone approaching a harbor from the sea at night fifty years or so ago was guided only by the slowly swinging beacon. As he came nearer, a dim and dusky row of lamps flickered from the dock.

Electric light completely transformed the appearance of all coasts and ports; indeed the difference between the old days and the new was greater there, seen from the sea, than on the shore.

America received the creative power of light from Europe, and twice sent it back, in marvelous form, to the old home of her sons, by way of Jefferson and Edison. No achievement of America can be compared with the deeds of these two men. Anyone who has ever taken a motorboat ride on some summer night in a Mediterranean gulf and seen the lovely sweep of the coast suddenly extinguished by a short circuit, heard the shouting in the dark, then slowly accustomed his eyes to the starlight as he recaptured the mountain silhouette he sought, and finally seen the whole gulf with its fiery, festive line blaze up again in a flash half an hour later— anyone who has had that experience will realize that in man's struggle with the elements no moment since Archimedes and the Arab compass has exalted the dwellers on the Mediterranean so much as the kindling of electric light.

And it was here in the bay of Genoa and La Spezia that a man of the Mediterranean first perfected the radio. Marconi and de Lesseps and the developers of steam power and oil burning were men whose present-day accomplishments would amaze Themistocles, Caesar, and Napoleon, and make them regret what they had missed in life.

Yet neither oil nor light nor the radio has changed the face of nature on the twentieth century Mediterranean so much as the airplane has, in war and peace.

Previously navigation had been the only connection between west and east; it depended on landings at the ports. Today one can get from Paris to Bagdad without touching the Mediterranean in a tenth of the time. The most distant shores have been brought within mere hours of each other.

Now that planes are carrying not only passengers but also, to an

increasing extent, cargoes, the Suez link for which modern humanity struggled so hard has lost part of its value. The Mediterranean is
beginning to lose again the world importance it recaptured for half
a century.

And the present war shows the corresponding extent to which
navies have lost importance. The naval bases and harbors even now
are losing ground as against the air bases and airports. Rhodes,
Cyprus, Suez, even Gibraltar no longer decide the fate of the Old
World. Before our very eyes the Mediterranean is becoming a lake
again.

II

MANY AN AMERICAN, reading the history of modern Europe and its
wars from afar, shakes his head. Is he reading of fools or children,
fighting with each other over a ball or an apple? The Balkans—
that mere scrap to the north of Greece, four times fought over in
the sixty years between the Crimean war and the First World War,
that corner with neither civilization nor tradition to offer—*have* cost
hundreds of thousands of human lives. Was it some fanatical religious dispute, a social revolution, intolerable thraldom?

It was a little of all of these, but the uprising of the Macedonians,
the Serbians' will to freedom, the desire for independence among
the Bulgarians, the irredentism of the Rumanians were not so elemental in their causes, nor were they necessarily bound to bring
about world upheavals. After the Greek revolution the more savage
forms of oppression had decreased. Parliaments, self-government,
native churches had been established as a sort of half liberty in the
spirit of the new century. These Balkan peoples, having no great
past behind them like the Greeks and the Swiss, interested no one;
the quarreling over a strip of land in a tongue-twisting province
might have remained a faint rumor, like something imported from
Tibet or Uruguay in the days when the world was not yet striving
for unity.

All these wars, the Crimean war from 1854 to 1856, the second
Russo-Turkish war of 1876-1878, the Balkan wars of 1912 and 1913

ended with short-lived boundary changes in the Balkans that interest only the scholar even now, less than a century later. The Congress of Berlin, which half undid the conquests of Turkey, left behind nothing genuinely memorable. This wild, mountainous, yeasty
peninsula, which in our day makes the most noise in the Mediterranean and produces the least of lasting value, this home of closely
related races and peoples (who lived once as nomads, later as soldiers, but consisted mostly of illiterate peasants and wily lawyers),
is far less interesting, with all its frontier and power struggles, than
the history of a single city in Italy or southern France. These Monte-
negrin and Albanian victories or defeats meant little to humanity.

No doubt there were idealists and fighters for freedom even
there, but they were seldom leaders and never carried decisive
weight. The princely families that killed each other and broke up
their countries into hostile parties with their followings were not
worth the lives of their subjects. It would therefore be senseless to
list their battles and peace treaties. These struggles always brought
them to the Mediterranean; or they might be wanting possession of
such ports as Durazzo, Salonika, Constanta. Of all this, the only
significant thing was the struggle for Constantinople and the straits,
which did not change their Turkish masters for four hundred years
after 1450.

The historical factor behind all these struggles was the battle of
the last three great autocracies, trying directly or through protégés
to displace one another in the Balkans. Their spirit floated on high
like that of the Homeric gods over the warriors of Troy. Only these
were no gods—they were three decayed old bodies, Russia, Austria,
and Turkey, all three governed for several centuries in almost un-
altered medieval forms by the same ruling houses. They simply
contradicted the ideas of the great revolutions. The Romanovs,
Hapsburgs, Osmanlis dragged themselves and their millions of subjects onward through the modern era by their own weight and
inertia, paying no heed to what was going on in the west or in united
Italy.

All three bordered on the Mediterranean—the realm of the czars
through its dominion over the Black Sea, the Hapsburg empire at

Trieste and Fiume; the Turkish empire still ruled almost half the circuit of the coasts, for as late as 1912, Syria, Egypt, and Lebanon were still the sultan's territory. He had lost only the coast from Morocco to Tunis. Even in the twentieth century the sultan formally ruled from Adrianople to Erzurum, from Constanta to Aswan, from Bagdad to the Libyan desert. But all this was long since decayed and corrupt; no strong navy, no rich treasury, no governing spirit held the empire together. It was army and religion alone, or in other words force and fanaticism, that served to sustain the state. The situation was just as it had been under Mohammed and his successors.

The Hapsburgs, on the other hand, embracing eight countries, had subjects in the Balkans who wore the fez, and Reformed successors of the Hussites in Bohemia, and in the Tyrol Madonnas were set up at crossroads. They never succeeded in managing their subject nationalities, because they allowed only Germans and Hungarians to rule, keeping down the other six stocks. The Russian czars, never satisfied with their giant realm, kept their eyes fixed on the straits, although these were no threat to anyone. They also played protector of the Balkan nations, which were related to them by race and Orthodox religion. They kept fomenting revolt in the hope of riding to Constantinople on the wave. While the Western nations were occupied with great social problems and with the conquest of Africa, the three ingrained reactionary empires were in a state of constant friction and shifting alliance. In the process they butchered their subjects, who had no passions and no self-interest to inspire them. Meanwhile the will to freedom existed only in the half-despised, half-pampered Balkan nations.

In these four Balkan wars there were neither great emperors nor great generals or statesmen. Among Emperor Francis Joseph, the last two czars, and Sultan Abdul-Hamid, some were weak and some treacherous despots. All of them had too much land and still wanted more. Instead of modernizing at home, their governments intrigued abroad. The kaiser and the czar hated each other too much to attack Turkey jointly and divide her up as they dreamed of doing. A series of conspiracies entangled their empires, stirred up wars, and convulsed the nations even in peacetime. If we must pick out one Balkan nation, however, as distinguishing itself beyond the others by bravery and devotion, it is the Serbs, the basic stock of what are called South Slavs—Yugoslavs—today.

Among the Balkan princes the least powerful seems to have been the most interesting. Nikita of Montenegro, soldier, banker, and poet, as dashing as the heroes of Viennese operetta, had the knack of getting money from all the great powers and marrying his beautiful daughters off at great courts. One of them is queen of Italy today.

The Russians have had the least and the Turks the most to do with the Mediterranean; since from it, and, except perhaps in the case of Frederic Chopin, never from the east, keenness and vivacity have always sprung, the Russians remained, with the exception of a few thousand intellectuals, a dull peasant people that hymned and died for the czar. The Turks, on the other hand, continued for thirty years to rise up in unending revolt in Syria, Egypt, Albania, Arabia, Crete. These revolts were successful only in the Balkans, where the Russians and the Austrians took turns at playing godfather to new petty kingdoms. These protectors would not have allowed a republic to any of these peoples, who might, by contagion, have risen against the old emperors. Thus Bulgarians, Rumanians, and Serbs were given kings, whom they kept through the First World War after the rest of Europe had reorganized. The petty monarchs stayed in power longer than their patrons, for Russia and Austria broke up into republics.

The Balkan wars that introduced the First World War led first to a weakening of Turkey, then to a quarrel among the conspirators over the Turkish loot, and, more than anything, to tension among the great powers at Constantinople, which speeded the outbreak of the war. A succession of treaties first closed the straits to all vessels, next opened them to all, then opened them conditionally, and finally they became one of the two great Mediterranean war aims in the First World War. For he who had the straits and Suez was better off than he who held Reims or Warsaw. It was the Mediterranean that produced the decisive alliances, Italy with the Allies, Turkey with Germany.

World wars are decided on the sea, or at least through the sea.

III

BEFORE THE THREE rotten old empires crumbled in the First World War, each of them made a few desperate motions to save itself against the spirit of the times, like an accused criminal attempting one last perjured statement. The Hapsburg emperor tried to check the threatened defection of his outlying peoples by a few language decrees. The czar and the sultan, under revolutionary pressure in 1905 and 1908, granted shadow constitutions, both of them dishonest and inadequate. Emperor and sultan were much too old to give up what they had been accustomed to, and the czar never could make up his mind. Among such indications of decadence, the Hapsburg crown prince shot himself over a love affair, and members of the Russian as well as the Spanish ruling family were so-called "bleeders," who bled to death from the slightest wound—a symbolic warning to a royal house.

It did not occur to anyone that an outworn state must build up from within, as the government of Lloyd George did in the British Empire, a model of English evolution. The czar, who actually dared not change anything, lost his crown and his life in the revolution. The Austrian emperor handed on a dying empire to his successor, and despite all his guile the sultan was finally deposed. His brother, whom he had been holding prisoner, was fetched out in his place to serve for another decade as a puppet, or rather a ball of fat adorned with medals. He had spent his life at a villa on the east side of the Bosporus, looking across at his brother's palace. In a comical reversal of roles the former sultan was compelled to gaze back at his palace, toward the west side, where he had governed for three decades.

The Young Turkish leaders were at once violent and constructive, like the Soviet Russians after them. In the midst of their strug-

gles they enacted a decree that took not a thousand human but a
thousand animal lives and is among the most awful things that ever
happened on the Mediterranean, rich though it has been in battles,
epidemics, and earthquakes. One day the pariah dogs that had ruled
the streets of Contantinople for centuries were all loaded on a boat
and turned loose to devour each other on a deserted island in the
Sea of Marmara. When people returned a few weeks later nothing
was to be seen but bones. The great city was none the cleaner for this,
since the dogs had done the work of the street-cleaning department.
This was the first fascist action in Europe, sanctioning a new moral
code that would establish order through cruelty.

When the Turkish empire, the greatest Mediterranean power,
began to break up at the beginning of the present century, Italy and
France stepped forward as natural heirs. England, much stronger
than either of the two, but imperiled in her Mediterranean operations if the two should join, succeeded in keeping them apart. Two
true statesmen in Paris and Rome should have recognized that an
understanding between the "Latin sisters" was possible and that
only united could they ever be strong enough to fight the dangerous
foreigners. But matters in the European family have always gone
as they do in many homes: the quarrels of the sisters, the jealousies
of the brothers were too strong for them to unite against an outsider.

England's taking up of the struggle for the Mediterranean in a
new world situation is the basic theme of Mediterranean history in
our century and at the same time one of the main themes in English
history.

For a moment it seemed as if the two Latin powers would join
or at least come to terms. As in most families, this came about
through misfortune, when the two were worsted almost simultaneously in the great race for Africa. Italy, which had established herself on the Red Sea, wanted northeast Africa as a bulwark against
the rising colonial empire of France in the northwest. But when she
took the field against the Abyssinians in 1896, she sustained a crushing defeat at the hands of their warlike ruler.

Three years later France, pushing toward the Nile from the west, was beaten without a shot. Captain Marchand, one of the finest figures among the African colonials, had to haul down the flag he had raised at Fashoda (now Kodok), a Negro village on the upper Nile, because the English general Kitchener civilly requested him to leave room for the Union Jack. The great war between England and France that was then avoided still seems to smolder half alive today, forty years later.

The French withdrawal led first to a peaceable partition of Africa into two zones, then to the Entente, and finally to the brotherhood in arms of the First World War. This shift decided Mediterranean leadership for half a century: France agreed to support English interests with her navy, and in return England offered protection of the French north coast. Italy found herself shut out. She kept trying for forty years to penetrate the Anglo-French friendship, which dominated the Mediterranean through the two largest navies.

Once she seemed to succeed. After years of conferences among the great powers, France and Spain divided up Morocco. Spain took Fez, France Marrakech, under a protectorate. Tangier was internationalized, so that no one should build fortifications opposite Gibraltar. Thus two Mediterranean powers had assumed a formal protectorate over the third.

Thereupon Italy, under Giolitti's keen leadership, seized the opportunity for reprisal and invaded Tripoli to seize that Turkish province, now called Libya, during the prostration of a Turkey in the grip of rebellion. At that time Austria and Germany, united in the Triple Alliance, also let Italy occupy the island of Rhodes and the Dodecanese.

Since Libya is between French Tunis and half-English Egypt, and the above-mentioned islands are in the extreme east, off the southwestern coast of Asia Minor, it seemed as though Italy were turning entirely to the eastern Mediterranean and France entirely to the western. But England, with no Mediterranean territory, succeeded in being all over the Mediterranean. Thus north Africa, Turkish but a moment before, was already divided up by the time Turkey chose the German side in 1914, to perish of the alliance in the end. The First World War, whose causes and results in the

Mediterranean were so momentous, produced no naval battles on the high seas because all the powers there were marching together and acting together except for Turkey, whose navy could not get out, and Austria, also in a rat trap on the narrow Adriatic coast. The only shooting in the Mediterranean, with the exception of the sea battle of Otranto in 1917, was in the very first days, when two brilliantly commanded German warships beat their way with all sorts of adventures through the middle of the enemy fleets and requested admittance to the Dardanelles.

They could not demand it, for Turkey was still neutral at the time. But the leaders of the Young Turks, who were in power there, had been educated at German military academies, and their teachers and their fighting forces were trained by German army men. And so a few resolute men set aside the sultan and parliament and in a few days' time established the alliance with Germany by letting the German warships pass through. This was a bold stroke, like that of two young people in love, whose runaway marriage confronts the two sets of parents with an accomplished fact. The tempestuous union ended four years later in bankruptcy and divorce.

It did not decide the war, but it considerably prolonged it. Allied with Turkey, the Entente could have supported Russia and beaten the Central Powers more quickly. The German-Turkish alliance was the result neither of historical amiability nor of popular feelings, even in the most immediate past. For although German generals had drilled the Turkish army during the preceding years, English admirals had trained the Turkish navy and English engineers fortified the Dardanelles. The German construction of the Bagdad railway was only partially recognized by the Turkish government and was always supplemented by English construction plans. The Turkish alliance with Germany, then, was the wish of only a handful of revolutionary officers, who survived the subsequent defeat but briefly. These men, particularly Talaat Pasha and Enver, were typical predecessors of the present-day dictators.

At this time the strongest sea power on earth was defeated by the weakest. The Turks, who had never been sailors, hurled back the English at the Dardanelles again and again, finally forcing them to withdraw permanently. The narrowness of the straits, where the two continents approach until they are as close together as the banks of the Potomac, made them impregnable—at least, before the perfection of the airplane. Here again we see how certain favorably situated points on the sea can be defended with no navy against a strong fleet. On this account the Russians failed for several centuries to break through here from the north, and so did the Venetians from the south.

These battles at the Dardanelles and Gallipoli, in which the Turks defended ancient Byzantium, made plain the nonsense of any European war by the resources of a European armament industry. The English had developed the straits for the Turks and armed them with German Krupp cannon. These now killed the advancing English, blew one of the greatest warships of the time out of the water, and saved the capital. The two sieges of the isthmus failed not because of Churchill's plans but because the plans were inefficiently supported. During the bombardment in March of 1915, many people's thoughts all over the world went back some thousands of years to Troy. Another nation from afar had gone there, only a few miles inland, to spend ten long years taking the fortress. The remnants of those walls lay mute and lonely among blossoming trees, and the present author visited them during the great naval battle.

The guns thundered far away, and the people in the metropolis shivered as a faint echo seemed to travel the length of the Sea of Marmara to Constantinople, though this was but a trick of the ear. From the Black Sea the Russian navy was trying to force the Bosporus. A great defeat seemed to be in preparation.

At this time the Russians had binding promises of Constantinople from the English, who had balked them of the city in all the negotiations through the centuries. "I'm not looking for land, I'm looking for water," Peter the Great had cried, and his successors had dreamed of Saint Sophia's dome. Once again Constantinople was the supreme prize at stake; it held, and the war went on. But the Turks and Germans could not carry their victory into the Mediterranean, and when they tried to attack the Suez Canal through Palestine, they were beaten off.

The makers of English policy had foreseen everything correctly except in Greece. To reach the gate of the Dardanelles and at the same time to combat the Turks in Asia Minor, the Entente had to make sure of Greece. A kindly king in Athens opposed an outstanding minister until the minister overthrew the king, to whose power he succeeded. King Constantine as crown prince had taken large pieces of territory, or rather ordered their taking, and, being a pupil and admirer of the German army, as well as a brother-in-law of the German emperor, he seemed unwilling to let the English prescribe his attitude. The Allies, however, needed an ally instead of a neutral and therefore compelled his abdication in defiance of all international law. Venizelos, an Odysseuslike character, quick, crafty, indomitable, a typical son of Crete, gambled for high stakes. Secretly leaving Athens, he joined the invading troops in Northern Greece, of which he became the unofficial ruler. In many ways the tragedy of the Greek royal house reminds us of its legendary predecessors; only it had no Sophocles to record it. When the League of Nations high commissioner later reported upon the episode, he, a Frenchman, said he was in haste to end this inglorious page of history.

The second pair of straits also proved impregnable in the First World War; only here the English were on the defensive. A German-Turkish army made its way through the desert from Jerusalem to the Suez Canal, where Moses is said to have led the Jews in the opposite direction. But the English had occupied Egypt at the very beginning of the war, installed a khedive pleasing to them, and soon declared him independent—of the Turks, of course, not of the English. Like the Turks at the Dardanelles, the English had to hold the Suez Canal at any price, for in the one case the fall of the city would have permitted the junction of the enemy, and in the other it would have cut the communication line of the Allies. Both of these siege operations and their future prospects have since been affected by the airplane, which at that time appeared only sporadically.

England's victory in Palestine and Syria was possible solely be-

cause the Arabs joined her side in the middle of the war. The struggles between the two Arab pretenders, Hussein Pasha and ibn-Saud,
which we cannot detail here, showed that both were religious and
therefore hostile to the Young Turks at Constantinople, who, as
pupils of Europe, departed from the religious foundations of the
Turkish empire. The Arab revolutionists were no less modern than
the Turkish, but as true sons of Arabia they still combined the two
weapons of Mohammed, military science and faith.

For a hundred years the Wahabi, puritans of a sort, located in
Syria, had been striving for a purification of the old religion, which
they also defended by force of arms. Apparently they were repeating the old paradox of the Christian sects, which had so often fought
each other in the Mediterranean instead of joining to fight the
Mohammedans. Very similarly now Mohammedans joined with
Western Christian peoples to destroy their coreligionists at Istanbul.

Apparently religious fanaticism when joined with nationalism
will make men blind.

IV

No MEDITERRANEAN UPHEAVAL of equal importance had taken place
in five centuries. From the time the Turks first took Constantinople,
they conquered half of all the Mediterranean shores and hinterlands
with swiftly growing success: the whole east and south were Turkish. When Byzantium, under the name of Constantinople, fell for
a third time, at the end of 1918, its dominion in Asia and Africa
collapsed. Faced with such events, we are merely surprised that we
do not actually hear the crash.

If the other coast countries had of late changed masters, these
changes had affected only small sections, and never for more than
a short time. But here a world collapsed, more significantly than in
the case of the other three empires. Russia and Germany merely
altered their form of government; the stature of the countries
changed but little. Though Austria fell apart, the fragments remained in the hands of the native peoples. Turkey, however, was
divided by three great foreign powers into six countries, whose sov-

ereignty remained partial for the time being; only one-seventh was
Turkish. Thus the influence of the Western powers became paramount in the eastern Mediterranean. It still is.

No new government attracted the admiration of the world immediately after the First World War so much as Turkey under
Kemal Pasha, who towers above the dictators of our day. By energy
and threats he succeeded first in shaking a vile treaty imposed on
the Turks at Paris, then in smashing it by his victories. The idea of
saving the central part of a crashing whole was as great as the energy
with which he carried it out. Kemal, whom the present author, like
many others of that epoch, describes from personal acquaintance,
had a blue, dreamy gaze that betrayed a touch of the poet such as
one finds more often in naval officers than in generals. His impressive head contrasted violently with such crafty types as the kings of
Iraq and Arabia.

The fact that he took twentieth century Oriental women out of
their harem existence would be enough in itself to immortalize him.
This is a deed far more revolutionary than anything achieved for
women's suffrage in the West. Out of heavily veiled beings who
might show neither mouth nor neck nor head, Kemal made girls
who competed in public swimming races. In the course of a few
years he overthrew several centuries. The women of a nation of fifteen million were brought from their hiding places into the light of
the new century. At the same time the new, enlightened despot and
lawgiver, resembling Mohammed in his solicitude for health, forbade early marriage, which had been common to the age of twelve
years among girls, and also polygamy.

Kemal gradually surrendered his dictatorial powers in favor of
a parliament that received and developed its actual rights only
slowly, in step with the political education of an enslaved people.
The thing that proved his courageous genius above all was the fact
that he deposed the caliph without putting himself in his place. This
is not to be compared with deposing the Pope, if one of our modern
anti-Christian conquerors should decide to do so. The caliphate had
indeed followed as quickly upon Mohammed as the papacy upon
Jesus and Paul, but the movement had always been connected with

the temporal power of Islam. It had never become involved in such conflicts as racked the West in the Middle Ages. For in Islam emperor and Pope were one person, and the caliph merely shifted a few times from one capital to another with the dynasties.

Kemal Atatürk knew the history of his country and the soul of his people, for during his career as an officer he had studied more widely than his Young Turkish contemporaries, who ruled the dying greater Turkey in the interim. Kemal knew that the whole structure of Islam would tremble if the caliphate ceased to be. He knew that the Mohammedans in Mecca and India would lose their ancient security, yet he dared to say that the time was past: "It is enough that we should all be brothers in the Faith." And so he by no means put aside his religion along with the fez (which he abolished for himself and his people), although some of his utterances were highly atheistic. He did confiscate church property and made the priests state functionaries, but he did not persecute priests as the Russians were doing then and the Germans did afterward. He closed no mosques. He introduced the Roman alphabet and made gray-haired people learn to read and write.

How truly he apprehended the age is shown by the uprising of the intellectuals when the Arabian king Hussein dared to bestow upon himself the caliphate abolished by Kemal. At great congresses like the medieval councils the theologians argued at Cairo and Mecca about who was to appoint the new caliph, but to this day they have picked none. The Oriental nimbus had vanished with the arrival of automobile and radio, and the new Mohammedan kings in western Asia and Egypt no longer differ from the last ruling Western monarchs, except that perhaps they are rather wilier and more brunette. The caliphate cannot be restored any more than Turkey, whereas the papacy continued to exist after losing its tiny territory and has not been changed by the subsequent acquisition of a few streets and squares.

This revolution was possible to Kemal with his Turkish soldiers. Nothing better could have happened to him than that the Greek king Constantine, recalled from banishment in 1922, should try to make good what his minister Venizelos had not succeeded in getting him to do six years before. Now, after the expulsion of Venizelos, after the restoration of the monarchy and a hearty welcome from the perpetually fickle Greek people, Constantine thought young Turkey weak enough to be overrun, so that he could seize the ancient Greek possessions in Asia Minor. Poor preparation on his side, good preparation by the enemy, thoughtless confidence in English aid, a hasty advance without communications to the rear—all this led to a terrible defeat, conflagration and atrocities in Smyrna, an inglorious return to Athens, a new abdication. The honest but weak king died sadly in a foreign land. But his adversary, Kemal, had showed a completely exhausted Europe that the modern motorized Turks in khaki and helmet still had the same aggressive strength as their predecessors, the turbaned Janizaries on their wild horses, slashing with crooked sabers at the infidel.

These great victories of his new little country enabled Kemal to gain the annulment of the Paris treaties four years after their signing. With this came not only full recognition from the great powers but the dismantling of the fortifications at the straits and also sovereignty over them, exact regulations concerning free passage, and the possession of two outlying islands.

Following Lenin's lead in moving the capital to the interior of the country, he depopulated Istanbul. In situation and beauty of architecture it is still the same splendid Byzantium, but the Bridge of Nations that connects, as in old times, Galata with Pera (Begogin) no longer trembles under the crowd of people and carriages, and the bazaar no longer holds all the treasures of Orient.

In lieu of this the little new Turkey, embracing what amounts to Asia Minor, has everything it needs to live on, and cannot be starved out like Italy or Greece; it need fear no foreign dictatorship or blockade, and so far it has been able to choose freely between England and Russia. The friendship with Russia established by Kemal, the treaties that connected him with Persia and Afghanistan soon made him a champion of the oppressed peoples in Irak and Iran, a leader of the Balkan league, a new friend of Greece.

The disaster to Constantine resulted in an experiment unknown to history on such a scale. Half a million Turks living in northern

Greece were exchanged for about half a million Greeks who had been in Asia Minor. Anyone who has ever been driven from his garden, though it be to go to the home of his forefathers, can realize with feeling how many tragic destinies are bound up in this resettlement of a million human beings. Yet at the same time, with all the infinite sufferings of these people, thousands also became freer and more secure. Anyone who has witnessed it cannot help concluding that the experiment was a success.

Where climate and vegetation are as similar as they are at Smyrna and Salonika, a violent exchange such as this after great convulsions is nevertheless felt as a cure, painful though it be. Kemal and Venizelos, once more in power at Athens, acted as politicians but also as friends of humanity, and their example showed how, under favorable circumstances, human beings may be transplanted in case of extreme necessity without dying.

V

AT THE ISTHMUS OF GIBRALTAR, where lions and elephants used to walk from Africa to Europe thousands of years ago, a long, shallow arm of water appeared, dividing the continents. Where the Isthmus of Suez had so recently joined Africa to Asia, man created the waterway. Now people are studying the possibility of artificially restoring the Isthmus of Gibraltar, though under water. De Lesseps, a true wizard, capable of making black into white, and also of trying to turn white into black, was the first to propose it. Since then French and Spanish engineers have worked out schemes that once again had nothing to hinder them but the jealousy of the governments.

For as an engineering matter a tunnel under the Straits of Gibraltar could be built with no great difficulty. The sea is not deep here as it is in the channel between England and France; it nowhere reaches 1,300 feet, so that the giant tube could be more easily built and more solidly protected against the water pressure. Of approximately thirty-two miles of tunnel, only about eighteen would be under water. The tunnel would begin in Spain, west of Gibraltar rock, and end on Spanish territory at the far side near Ceuta; Spain would become a sentry on the Mediterranean, like England at the Suez Canal and Istanbul at the Dardanelles. France would send her goods direct to and from Africa as far as the western equatorial ports and thus be linked with South America by a single transshipment. Silk would be shipped from Lyon, put on a boat at Dakar, and turned over to the ladies at Rio. The meat of Argentine cattle would reach the Paris restaurants by the same route.

This communication underneath Gibraltar represents but one part of the long-planned trans-Sahara railway, a vision most expressive of French genius. France ends at the Congo, people have been saying in Paris during the last few decades. And this expression was much truer than Baldwin's dictum that the frontier of England was on the Rhine.

The Atlas is the basis of a colonial empire embodying a third of all Africa. It alone concerns us here, since it faces on the Mediterranean. Its long and eventful history from 1830 to 1930 speaks well for the glory of France. The fact that the world talks so much more of the British than of the French Empire is due not to greater talent but merely to heavier settlement by the conquering nation. For underpopulated France the colonial empire was the homeland and source of some two million colored soldiers, but there was always space enough to feed and employ all the white French at home. There were always many times more white Englishmen than white Frenchmen in the colonies and dominions. Since their settling of Canada the French have grown more easygoing; only a few hundred thousand emigrated to north Africa, and the Italians multiplied to such an extent that they were quickly and easily naturalized in French Tunis.

If we regard the steppes and the desert in the south as an ocean, the long, high mountain chain whose foothills reach from western Morocco (that is, the Atlantic) to the Libyan frontier has something insular about it. Belonging to the Mediterranean in every way, even biologically, and not to Africa, this extensive territory might be called more Spanish, even more Provençal, than reminiscent of

Egypt. If the northernmost tip of Tunis reaches the latitude of Cartagena and Syracuse, this is an indication of the Mediterranean climate in those provinces, and we can more easily understand how Cathaginians, Romans and Vandals, Arabs and Turks could feel so thoroughly at home here for more than two thousand years.

The conglomerate peoples whom these Atlas Mountains poured out for a century against the conquering French, and whom we can call Berbers only in a very general way, have retained their bellicose vigor, and in decades of battles under bold leaders they have tried and strengthened the courage and military skill of the French. For a century, we may say, north Africa formed the great military academy of France. It was only the conquest of Morocco, not completed until 1926, that gave France an outlet to the Atlantic independent of both England and Spain and thus established sea communications with her central African colonies.

But as early as the First World War the plan of having what were then a million colored Frenchmen protect forty million whites was successfully tried. The fighting power of the Moroccans and Senegalese was known and feared in the Champagne campaign. Whole armies could travel back and forth, for the western Mediterranean belonged to the Allies, Spain was neutral, and German submarines seldom dared venture in.

The effectiveness of the native armies led to an increase in their privileges. France far more than England depends on her colonial troops for the very safety of the mother country, and so the colored French were treated very differently from the colored British. French officers danced with Algerian Mohammedan women, the governor invited them to his residence, and the undersecretary of state in Paris was a colored man. These things could never have happened in London. We may call this greater tolerance on the part of the French or a greater necessity; in any case, one pattern of behavior seems to breed the other.

The rights accorded by the French to their sixty millions in Africa and Indo-China are exemplary and show at its best the freedom from prejudice that distinguishes Paris from London at almost every point. A French colonial officer who had served his country

for twenty-five years on three continents was the man who finally
saved France on the day of the Battle of the Marne—General Gallieni, who sent the troops from Paris to the front in the famous
taxicabs. And in Marshal Lyautey they produced the greatest colonizer of our time; he was inspired wholly by humanitarian ideas
and was the first conqueror who dared to say that colonies today
are justified only by the white physician and engineer.

The work that Lyautey had begun with his teacher and friend,
Gallieni, in Tonkin and Madagascar he expanded in Morocco, by
energy and especially by fifteen years of patience into a model of
modern colonial enterprise. Here in the extreme western corner of
the Mediterranean, the French initiated colonization in the spirit
of a new age. Instead of terrorizing and subjugating the natives,
which was resorted to only in cases of most extreme resistance,
Lyautey was able to manage the Moroccans by stealing nothing
from them and offering them whatever French culture possessed.

The seaports and towns, roads and canals built there will always
reflect glory on France. Lyautey did it all under the motto: "No
discouragement—smile!" Thus he gave the signal for the other
rapidly expanding colonies of France, which Georges Mandel, one
of the bravest of Frenchmen, finally prepared so splendidly for war.

In our century the weakness of Spain has been a prerequisite
for the colonial strength of France. Threatened by the English rock
that rises at the crucial point in the middle of her south coast, Spain,
exceedingly decadent in her last days as a monarchy, had to be
satisfied with a small strip in the partition of Morocco, and her only
revenge for the loss of Gibraltar was the port of Ceuta. The long,
open tongue of land that goes out from there into the narrow strait
can easily be bombarded, but on the other hand Gibraltar can be
shelled from the hill behind the port.

For a long time the Spaniards have owned three islands that
mean more than all their ports. The Balearics, once English for
seventy years, then French for seven, represent bases of the first
order in modern warfare, for they are exactly in the middle between
Marseille and Algiers. When Primo de Rivera, the Spanish dictator,
in 1926 gave his model, Mussolini, the right to land there in case of

war so as to stop French transports, this was no mere alliance; it was perhaps high treason. Accordingly the succeeding republic at once denounced the treaty.

What the French succeeded in doing in the Spanish area of the western Mediterranean they have never quite managed in the east. In Syria, where they took over part of the Turkish heritage, the Arabs fought them for twenty years. Although connected for centuries by church and commerce, they never seem to have been popular in Beyrouth and Damascus. Perhaps they overreached themselves when they tried to shut off Syria from the sea with a chain of four miniature republics instead of making it a strong power with a long coast line. Indeed, there were moments when France, exhausted by the First World War, was ready to exchange or even surrender Syria, which had been given to her in time of peace. It was another sign of weariness when the French left their war materials lying in Alexandretta and turned them over to the Young Turks.

For that reason, too, the risings in Syria were incessant. The Arabs, like the rest of the world, could feel that France after her victory was declining as a world power. True, Faisal, who at first proclaimed Syria as his kingdom, had to give way. But he soon found himself summoned to rule Iraq, and his brother made himself independent in the fertile Syrian plain, both of them depending upon English assistance. If the oil had not been flowing into the new pipe lines, French capital might have withdrawn altogether.

Yet the wealth, location, and beauty of the country would justify a boom that might have been expected to be greater, not smaller, than that in Morocco. Lebanon still presents the same magnificent spectacle. The hundred-year-old cedars still tower skyward there, and the groves in the high mountains are still peopled with bears, as in the time of Solomon. Down in the plain Damascus has retained its splendor from Arabic days, except that the women, no longer veiled, show off their Paris stockings and prefer imported silver fox to the bearskins on sale, which very likely are not from Lebanon at all.

VI

THE DECISIVE STRUGGLE that was preparing in the Mediterranean during the thirties was based on the conflict between Italy and England. Neither Spain nor Yugoslavia nor Turkey was vital; even France was little more than an adjunct of England. In order to understand the Italian aspiration, we shall do well to compare a few economic statistics covering the Mediterranean Sea in the thirties.

Italy is the most heavily populated and most important country on the Mediterranean, for France, lying on two oceans, with a short Mediterranean coast line, cannot be counted in her entirety. Spain has twenty-five, Jugoslavia, Egypt, and the new Turkey each four-teen million inhabitants; Italy has forty-five million. Egypt, because of her unique situation as a narrow river valley between two deserts, cannot be compared in density of population. In Spain, Greece, and Palestine there are 130 or 140 persons to the square mile, in Turkey 53, in France 197, but in Italy 359, and if we count out uninhabitable stretches, as many as 540.

Of the fourteen countries fronting on the Mediterranean in the thirties, only such thinly settled ones as Turkey, Tunis, Algiers, and Spain could feed themselves. France could support herself com-pletely, though only a small part belonged to the Mediterranean. Most of these countries had an excess of wine and olive oil, which they exported, and enough meat and wool. Spain, France, and Yugoslavia lived independently on their own agriculture and raw materials. Most of them, however, lacked petroleum and cotton.

France had the most of everything, Italy the least. France not only possessed all she needed except oil and rubber but had so much iron ore that she turned only one-fifth of it into steel, whereas Italy made four times as much steel as she produced of iron ore. France could keep eighty per cent of her own wine. In Italy, on the other hand, long, rough stretches were barren, and only Lombardy and Sicily could be called rich. Since France had everything but always wanted to live the most comfortable life, she imported almost as much as she exported, while in Italy the ratio was as three to two. Per capita France imported more than twice as much as Italy, *although* she was so rich and *because* she was so rich. Italy, on the other hand, lacked coal, ore, wood, and grain, and yet, taking the Mediterranean in the narrower sense, she housed a third of all its population.

Nothing was more natural than that this overpopulated country, poor in raw materials, should try to expand. Nature pointed toward Africa.

In addition there was history, in a double shape. As in old royal families, the sonorous name of Rome provided even the remotest descendant with romantic aspirations toward rivaling his fathers. A nation whose frontiers were eighty per cent seacoast strove to cross the ocean. But there it had been disappointed after the First World War, receiving almost nothing on the sea. If Austria had disappeared from the Adriatic, Serbia had taken her place. The competition was so keen that even during the First World War the Serbs in exile held demonstrations against the promises made to the ally, Italy, on her entrance into the war. This was why d'Annunzio, the first fascist, came forward immediately after the First World War and occupied Fiume by a poetic surprise attack, enjoying the highest esthetic pleasures in the process. When someone asked him afterward whether he did not compare himself with Lord Byron, he was offended. It was not until later that the Italians snatched bays, ports, and islands in the eastern Adriatic from the Yugoslavs by treaties and by force and further strengthened themselves by a protectorate over Albania.

Not communism, whose efforts had already faded away in Italy, but the disappointments of the Paris peace created fascism. Mussolini, who had been a soldier in the war, was well aware of his countrymen's dubious value as soldiers. In ten great battles they were never able to beat their Austrian adversary, and subsequently the advancing Germans forced them into a catastrophic retreat. This weakness was taken into account at the peace conference. Italy was by no means cheated in the peace but instead was rewarded far more highly than she could have expected after three years of lost battles. She received two large provinces in the north. But, being given very little on the sea, she forgot her naval inactivity as well as her military defeats and declared she had been cheated because the Yugoslavs, who had fought and suffered far more, were also rewarded. A poor and overpopulated country has four recourses: emigration, industrialization, colonies, birth control. The most natural, emigration, had long made things easier for Italy. For many years almost a million people emigrated, to the advantage of their prosperity and at no cost to their souls. At present ten million Italians are living abroad, eight million in America. When the latter half closed her gates in 1927, the excess poured into underpopulated France. The emigration also profited the mother country in the shape of great sums of money, for the emigrants sent home above a hundred million dollars every year and at the same time increased exports through their connections.

But a nationalist movement like fascism cannot promote any such natural solution, and still less birth control. Dictators live by huge numbers, which form their stake, and which they, like gamblers, must keep increasing. Above all they live on soldiers, whose replacements must keep on coming into the world. Whereas fascism, then, limited emigration and raised the birth rate by bounties, it was forever complaining about lack of space, and so, along with a great process of industrialization, it had only the fourth recourse left, the colonies.

It has been discovered that the Italian in foreign countries quickly adapts himself and proves his worth, whereas in his own colonies he is usually a failure. As a colonizer he lacks tenacity, self-sacrifice, patience, exactness—in fact, almost everything but imagination. As human beings the Italians are far too interesting and anarchical to be great empire builders. And they are too much southerners to treat the Negro properly. They still despise him as the old slave traders did, and as a result they had a bad name in east Africa before the First World War. During the war itself, they were driven to the coast by incessant native risings, a circumstance that never confronted the French and English. It was only a decade later, in 1928, that the Senusi were finally subdued in Libya.

Libya was the name Mussolini gave to the territory between Tunis and Egypt, in memory of the Roman province. Libya cannot be compared with either. It is largely steppe and desert and is fertile only at a few points on the coast. This is not Italy's fault, not even that of nature. It is the fault of the Turks, who allowed this country, so fertile in antiquity, to run down until a century may be needed to make good the omissions of four centuries. When fascism proclaimed "expansion or explosion," there was no other territory left on the opposite coast. The strategical situation was not favorable unless the Italians finally succeeded in breaking the Anglo-French alliance, for Libya lies between the two. It would also be possible to build a road through the Sahara as far as Timbuktu and Darfur in order to reach the English Sudan and Lake Chad.

Thus Libya could be no more than a gate to southward and a base for war, particularly since it has but one natural fort, Tobruk. Libya lacks what the English have to the east and the French to the west: half a continent, the substance and the connection between the two great oceans that Africa affords. Italy held scattered individual bits of east Africa, mostly infertile, not unified by any plan, either social or imperialistic.

How was fascism to attain its objective of producing a powerful Italy ruling the Mediterranean alone or at least predominantly? Industrialization was a task set by the century for all countries, at once furthered and facilitated by invention. Italy could only repeat the process, which she did. But if she checked emigration, constantly sighed for the lost children on whose remittances she lived, if she kept people at home and rewarded them for multiplying to the detriment of the country, only the last road was open to her: to place her people in great habitable colonies and to fetch grain and raw materials from there.

This was feasible by one policy alone: alliance with England.

Mussolini, whom the world has brushed aside as the brutal dictator he often actually has been, is in fact neither hangman nor general nor visionary but a diplomat. He continues the great school of Italian diplomacy that began in the prime of Venice, made the dictators of the Renaissance successful, and ended for the time being with Crispi and Giolitti.

He succeeded for a decade in conciliating or at least quieting his adversaries by a neatly constructed system of treaties. By favorable agreements with Kemal the Turk, with Venizelos the Greek, with Arabs and Spaniards and South Slavs, he secured his position in every quarter at least so long as peace lasted. And still he lost the game.

The tragedy of Mussolini is threefold. First the law of dictatorships keeps involving him against his will in new wars, since his inflammatory methods forbid him ever to call a halt. Furthermore he is a man who saw the truth in 1915 when he, more than anyone else, placed his nation at England's side in the war; and yet, afterward he forgot or surrendered this basic insight. In addition there is a third element, and that is the knowledge of his people's nature. No one is more skeptical of the Italians than their leader, and the present author has heard him speak enviously of the Germans, who are such splendid, warlike, and obedient material to work with. For twenty years he tried to make the Italians act like the Prussians, knowing beforehand that it was impossible. This is why he finally leagued himself with Prussian efficiency, not seeing that it was bound to throttle him.

His political line was by no means straight; repeatedly he tried to go with England, and England with him. By tradition, history, and literature the English people are more deeply akin to Italy than to France; England has nearly always fought against France, almost never against Italy. When the Washington Conference stabilized the naval ratio of America and England on one side, France and Italy on the other, at about five to two, Mussolini began to be anti-French. He reminded his people of Nice, Corsica, and Tunis and was praised and rewarded for this by England. In 1925 the two spheres of influence in Abyssinia were united, which strengthened Abyssinia against France in the Red Sea. It was no accident that the conservative Churchill was an admirer of Mussolini.

Three years later the friendship of the English ceased, partly because Italy was growing too strong for their liking, partly because the Labour Government in England had to combat the Italian dictatorship. Here again a system of violence at home broke up the successful foreign policy of a statesman. Mussolini paid for his anti-social government with the loss of his prestige, first as party leader, then in world politics, and this not in England alone.

The two rivals were still able and willing then to reach an understanding. England announced in 1929 that she would reduce her position in Malta and that she had reason to shift more of her sea power to the great oceans. English statesmanship under Balfour had shown how an empire may be rebuilt if the spirit of the age demands it. These statesmen seemed to realize that in the Mediterranean, too, other nations must be allowed to spread out so long as a limit could be set and some control exercised.

Mussolini, on the other hand, knew and still knows perfectly well that the Roman Empire is a catchword for the crowd and that Rome is no longer the center of the world, nor is Paris. The capitals today are Washington, Berlin, and perhaps London. Accordingly, with his anti-French sentiments and in view of the declining French power in Europe, he could reach an understanding only with London or Berlin.

Mussolini called Italy an island in the Mediterranean and urged his people to think of themselves as islanders. The Mediterranean, he said, is for France a trench between mother country and colony, for England a shortening of the sea route, but it is Italy's living space. Whereas Giolitti denied his people's right to call the Mediterranean *mare nostrum,* since it must be accessible to all nations, a decade later Mussolini exclaimed: "The Mediterranean for the Mediterraneans!" This correct and simple theory had been defended by the Greeks against the invading Persians, by the Romans against the Teutons and Arabs, then by Pope Julius II against the advancing Germans and French, by Venetians and Spaniards against English and Dutch. It was still defensible.

But it depended on just one condition: in order to maintain this claim, the most populous country on the Mediterranean, the land with the longest coast line, the heir of old Rome must be as strong, young, and warlike as Rome, and in addition it must be a seafaring

nation. The Italians, however, were not, as has sometimes been
stated, too immature, but far too mature. As Marshal MacMahon
said, they had lost every battle and won every war; that is, for centuries they had been better diplomats and negotiators than warriors
and sailors. Theirs was the talent of the later Byzantines, who also
usually let others win their victories for them and flourished long
after their warlike vigor was gone. The Italian nation's belief
that, with the disintegration of Turkey and the weariness of France,
it was superior to all others in the Mediterranean was no doubt
justified, but it carried no impact. In the long run nobody can be
a leader by defensive tactics unless he has a long record of strength
behind him.

Montesquieu summed up the whole situation two hundred
years ago with brilliant malice: "The balance of power in Europe
is maintained by the industry of the northern nations and the idleness of the southern nations."

But in order to deal with the uncanny stranger who began to
haunt the Mediterranean, though he did not dwell there, a people
needed a spirit of aggression, self-sacrifice, system, and an ambition
for dominion, or else it had to get along with the stranger. This
was not possible in alliance with France, because England would
then have doubled her opposing forces. In alliance with England
it was possible.

Of course Mussolini looked for points of support everywhere.
He found them in the Dodecanese and Rhodes in the east, Spain
in the west, and Abyssinia in the south. He waged an inglorious
war with tanks and planes against naked Negroes carrying spears,
and after an easy victory he built on their dead bodies a structure
that the world regarded as a parody of the British Empire. He thus
acquired a country whose opening up would cost a whole generation enormous sums even if he did not lose it in a subsequent war.
His important success here was not the military triumph over the
Negroes but the diplomatic victory over England. If, despite this
crisis, he was still adroit enough after his victory to reach a sort
of understanding with England in the so-called Easter treaties of

1938, the English desire for this understanding was thereby made plain.

The fact that Mussolini still chose the German rather than the English alliance, although he could not stomach either the Germans or their leader, shows the fascination exerted upon an autocrat by the Gorgon spectacle of gigantic armaments. His downfall will soon prove his decision wrong, even if England, the uncanny stranger in the Mediterranean, should not be victorious.

VII

THE STRANGER WAS UNCANNY because he was not seeking and occupying land, like all earlier interlopers. Goths and Vandals, Arabs, Turks, and Berbers had invaded the Mediterranean to pluck the fruits along its shores and to establish in the Middle Ages dominions that embraced all Spain, half of France, all of Italy and Greece for centuries. Along with their weapons they brought their religion, their customs, their methods, their vessels. They all came to stay, even those who afterward had to withdraw. As long as the Mediterranean was the center of the world, it irresistibly attracted the people from the outlying fringes, from Darius to Mithridates, from Charlemagne to Charles V, from Peter the Great to Alexander II, from Richard Coeur de Lion to Francis I, from Omar to Solyman. All were striving toward this brighter sphere, the sunnier skies, the blue sea, the silver-kissed isles, as if happiness dwelt there.

The English were the first and (except for the Dutch episode) the only ones who came like rich and distinguished travelers in a yacht, courteously dipping their flag to every port and ship, only stopping at a few islands to reserve a place by leaving a hat or umbrella. Then they vanished again without asserting any claims. Afterward their fleets arrived to occupy the reserved seats, but even the navy seemed to be out merely for a sail. During their Mediterranean stay the English have barely fired a shot—only three times in 240 years: at Abukir Bay in 1799, Alexandria in 1882, and the Dardanelles in 1917.

Between stops on its cruise, the English yacht had to guard the inlet and outlet of the great inland sea at Gibraltar and Suez.

The point then was to direct eastern commerce overland from Asia to England, and at the same time prevent the two French fleets from uniting. Against this barricade France finally built the Canal du Midi, which joins the Atlantic and the Mediterranean by way of the Garonne and will take warships from Toulon to Brest. France was the last remaining rival for England to fear after the destruction of the Spanish Armada, an antagonism that has rather rusted in the last forty years. The French conquest of Algiers increased English caution more than ever.

The liberation of Italy, which in itself was popular with the English, like everything Italian, could not but seem, when completed, a possible threat to the English Mediterranean power. Italy had won her wars of unification only by foreign arms. But was it not possible, the English asked themselves, that she might prove successful at sea, as the Saracens, Venetians, and Genoese had once done from those same shores? Might she not threaten with a formidable navy after a few decades? Stronger bases for the British sea route were necessary, and the most important was at the new canal, the majority of whose stock Disraeli had bought up so neatly.

That the Suez Canal was completed simultaneously with Italian liberation was mere chance; but it was no accident that the great powers also began simultaneously to divide up Africa. A piece of territory like this will sometimes become a sudden craze, like a style in hats or novels, and everyone is determined to have a share. The English, making sure of the new canal and the road to India, conquered the Sudan at the same time. The canal had increased the self-esteem of the Egyptians and also their hatred of foreigners, and the revolutions of the eighties in the delta and on the upper Nile were connected with these events. The revolt of Mohammed Ahmed, who took the Sudan away from the English for fifteen years, and that of the fellah Arabi were fundamentally more than welcome to them.

At such moments as these British statesmanship shows its masterly skill. Instead of recoiling from an unexpected enemy, the English are strengthened by him and thus joined in magnificent unity, as we have just been observing in the Second World War. Those were great strokes of good fortune in the history of the empire when the English had the privilege of liberating Egypt from its popular leader and therefore of bombarding Alexandria, and later when they had to avenge the death of General Gordon and conquer the whole Sudan. On both occasions the English could say that they had been regretfully compelled to make an extended stay. France lost her influence in Egypt, though there were still a great many Frenchmen there, and Italy never had any influence then or later. The Italians, though triply superior in numbers, were mostly poor people and laborers, whereas the English were rich men and masters.

Churchill put the whole problem in words a few years ago with true British casualness. For 230 years, he said, England had possessed control of the Mediterranean, and she had never asked whether her warships had the right to enter or leave the great sea.

The occupation of Egypt, which has now lasted just sixty years, also ended Turkey's influence there and made possible the great conception that Lord Curzon was to formulate as the Cape Suez and Cape Singapore triangle. It was by no means only the 8,000-mile shortening of the route to India or the cotton in the delta and on the Blue Nile. We may say that the occupation of Egypt meant the securing to England of half the African continent. At the beginning of the First World War she strengthened her position by suspending the neutrality of the canal, which she took under her protection—that is, occupied—along with the Nile Valley.

The advantages to Egypt, on the other hand, were more to Egyptian self-esteem than to Egyptian liberty. In 1914 a more complaisant khedive was installed, and after the First World War a grandson of Mehemet Ali was made king; subsequently he and Egypt were accorded various rights. But English soldiers, guns, and planes have never left Egypt, and the British high commissioner is still the most powerful man in Cairo, though he no longer bears the title. The eyes of the Cairoans, as they watch British troops drilling in the huge barrack yard on the Nile, are as moody as ever. When prime minister MacDonald asked the popular leader Zaghlul Pasha to what limits he wanted the British troops withdrawn, he replied, "To London."

Now that England has the all-important southeastern corner of the Mediterranean in her hands, Gibraltar has taken on new meaning: instead of a barrier it has become the control station of the empire route, a function that once belonged to Cape Town. But in time of war Gibraltar bars the enemy's way on the west, and Suez blocks his path on the south, so at need the English can bring their troops and goods from India around the Cape without running into danger in the Mediterranean. Thus so long as Gibraltar and Suez are not taken they form a personal union, as it were, much as certain kings formerly doubled their power by union with a second inherited country. Suez too was basically an inheritance, for the French had planned the canal.

Between the occupation of Gibraltar and of Egypt, in 1704 and 1882, England took possession of two islands on two important dates, considerably strengthening her position in the Mediterranean: she occupied Malta and Cyprus.

Malta fell to England in 1800, under Napoleon, and since he himself called it the heart of the Mediterranean, this represents a French defeat that is having its effect again today, as well as adding one more to Napoleon's list of failures at sea. Architecturally and linguistically the history of the Mediterranean can be traced in this little island. From slabs with strange marks that must have been made by prehistoric aborigines down to the alleged dwelling of the Apostle Paul, Norman towers, and the rich baroque palaces of the Knights of Saint John, we find here examples of every sort to show the marvelously colorful history of the Mediterranean. If we look at it with half-closed eyes, as one does to catch the outlines of a landscape at sunset, it seems like a fairy tale.

Listening to the talk of the Maltese, we hear a mixture of South Italian and Arabic, with some fragments of French. As remote descendants of many races, living easily and lazily in the enervating sirocco, they seem to have grown useless since the occupation. They

live mostly by the export of lace and wine. But their forebears led an adventurous and luxurious life here. The central location of Malta, about a thousand miles from Gibraltar, Port Saïd, and Cyprus, has always made it desirable. From such an island as this one may conquer the world or be conquered by it; it is like a capricious woman. The island is regarded by experts as the strongest sea fortress in the world, stronger than Gibraltar or Pearl Harbor, because it has no land frontier to defend and can turn everything to its own protection.

Cyprus, which the English occupied in 1878, ostensibly to protect the Turks from the Russians, once again through Disraeli's acumen, became another temporarily prolonged stay and was not definitely taken over until 1914. This largest island east of Sicily has running through its center mountain ranges where all the mountaineer peoples of the Mediterranean have dwelt. Indeed we see the debris of history lying about here everywhere, overgrown and beautified by nature. The British governor lives on the slopes of Olympus in summer; the sweet Cyprian wine served at his table is a symbol of the contact between the Greeks and Venetians and his own seamen here on furlough.

Cyprus and Malta, the only English colonies in Europe, are remnants of an outworn concept of the state, completely anti-British in sentiment, the more so since ninety per cent of all the inhabitants are Greeks in the former and Italians in the latter. In Cyprus rebellions kept on into the nineteen-thirties. Experts suggested that both islands be given up as useless, and instead both have been fortified more strongly than ever in the last decade. In the harbor of Famagusta, a fishing village, the gun barrels now peer from the Venetian ruins.

From Cyprus the distance by air to Syria is counted in minutes —the first time in history that distances have gone by minutes. Here on the east coast of the Mediterranean the dissolution of Turkey has produced a new situation for England and a new strategy as well. Before the First World War England merely had her fleet here. Afterward she acquired great bases and strategic points. In the Mediterranean the great result of the First World War has been that England dominated the eastern sea from the Libyan frontier to Haifa and assured herself, in the shape of French Syria, a sort of buffer state against the new Turkey on the north.

But the disintegration of old Turkey, which brought England such strong positions in the East, necessarily created a new adversary, the rising power of Arabia, which refused to be downed. Here English policy has adhered with varying success to different ruling houses. Since England sought no colonies there, she was usually able to outmatch the passionate wooing of Italy, which hoped to rule, or at least to participate. A century before, in 1839, England had taken the southeast corner of Arabia in charge at Aden, and later the island of Perim. After the First World War she opened up the land route to India, in the footsteps of Alexander the Great, by way of Iran and Iraq to the Persian Gulf and finally even included the third element, the air, in peacetime traffic and wartime defense. She transformed the oldest city of the Orient, Bagdad, into the newest, the junction point of the great air lines.

Yes, the Tales of a Thousand and One Nights are over, and Scheherazade goes on:

And when the thousand and second night fell, the loud-speaker in the market place at Mecca carried the speech of ibn-Saud to the crowd, the armored cars rolled through Medina, planes roared over Bagdad, the rocket boats hissed along the Bosporus, the Persian oil was pumped from the pipe at Acre. And here at Damascus the girls in the stadium were doing gymnastics in shorts. But still, as the sun went down, they all turned their faces toward Mecca, and those whose arms were free flung them up and prayed as their fathers did: "Allah is Allah and Mohammed is his prophet."

VIII

THE ARABS AND THE TURKS held firm far more than a thousand years against the assault of the Christians, finally surviving even the collapse of the caliphate. The power and unity of Islam thus proved themselves in a magnificent fashion that was unknown to a Christianity torn by many sects in the same thousand years. That was why Christianity never conquered the Orient. After the First World War the Arabs quarreled among themselves no less than the Allies, but they never allowed the basis of their religion to be shaken. When ibn-Saud, as head of a puritan faction in Islam, came in conflict with Hussein, political causes produced political results. When he became king of Hejaz in 1925, he carefully avoided deciding the question of the caliphate on his own account, as his adversary Hussein had done. These movements are not yet settled, but would they still be movements if they were?

The Holy Places at Jerusalem were far less likely to remain un-

disputed than Mecca. For a time during the First World War there
was some thought of turning over Jerusalem to the Pope, as in
the days of the medieval kingdom. It was the Vatican that strove
for this and England that prevented it, because she wanted to hold
the western as well as the eastern side of the Suez Canal. This purpose begot the Jewish state.

This magnificent idea was by no means the worse because of a
second motive in the background. On the contrary, if the power that
was to establish the state for the Jews derived a political profit from
the step, the guarantee was better than if a few humanitarians had
wrestled for an emotional resolution. And the intention expressed
by Mr. Balfour as a cabinet minister (he was not yet Lord Balfour)
was entirely honest. Actually, in true English fashion, it was no
more than a short letter written to Lord Rothschild saying that
"His Majesty's Government views with favour the establishment
in Palestine of a national home for the Jewish people, and will use
their best endeavours to facilitate the achievement of that object."
But "nothing shall be done which may prejudice the civil and
religious rights of existing non-Jewish communities. . . ."

Balfour and the Jews who had thought this out were not the
first to do so, but it was they who succeeded in realizing older ideas
at the right moment by the right means. In the nineties the Zionist
movement had found in Theodor Herzl a leader who was a prophetic spirit. The glamor and the emotional aura of the first inventor and discoverer surround him. A man of letters without
power or money, armed with nothing but his faith and his ability,
he abruptly returned from bourgeois Vienna, from the civilization
and music of a peaceable time and country to the rocky heights
and desert places from which his forefathers had been driven out
almost two thousand years before. A journalist, he went from
Austria to the Mediterranean, determined to lead his coreligionists
thither.

But in the course of thirty years only a few followed him, for
neither the Turks, owners of Palestine, nor the great powers gave
any guarantees to the immigrants. The history of these first establishments has all the magic fascination that surrounds American

or South African pioneers; the great story will always give strength
to Jewry against days of persecution to come.

The second and much greater movement, which began in
1919, also looked back emotionally to the time of the forefathers.
But here the religious element was much smaller, and Zionism
today is determined by nation first and only secondarily by religion.
There are as many infidel Jews in Palestine as there are infidel Jews
or Christians in the rest of the world. This second period of the
Jewish state took a far more stormy course than the first because of
its achievements and difficulties. When the first Jews came to the
new British protectorate, they were welcomed as cousins and assured of the deepest sympathy in a fiery letter from the Arab king
Faisal, which even stated that on this soil the two peoples could
live and flourish only in mutual contact.

But soon the thing happened that has always started anti-Semitism all over the world: the intelligence, industry, perseverance,
and talent of the Jews were too great for the liking of their neighbors, and they rebelled because this energetic new competition condemned them to unaccustomed labor or starvation in this half-Arab
country. The English were alarmed at what they should have foreseen. The complaints of the Arabs turned to threats, the threats to
fighting, there were rebellions in the country, and the army had
to intervene. All the carefully nurtured sympathies of the Arabs
for England were suddenly in jeopardy.

The English, who, in contrast to most other nations, confess their
mistakes almost with a passion, sent a commission to Jerusalem, and
the commission flatly declared that this was a matter of right opposing right. MacDonald called the whole thing a great history
of double dealing, condemning the government for having made
impossible promises, and Churchill pointed out in vain that the
Jews had never been promised all of Palestine but only the establishment of a national home in that country. The government halted
a large part of the Jewish immigration and made plans for partition.
Then they discarded them again, and the risings were renewed.
Murders and guerrilla warfare followed. The work of the Jews
was endangered and sometimes destroyed.

For what they had created on this Mediterranean coast during the first years had great stature. Detractors tried to minimize it by pointing out that the Jews had got a great deal of money from all over the world—as if all colonies had not been financed at first by the mother country or a company! No one who has not seen Palestine before and after the Jewish immigration can realize their achievement. From eight per cent of the population in 1919 they grew to forty-five per cent twenty years later. Instead of 50,000 there are now 500,000 Jews living in the home of their fathers. The transformation of this hard and dry region, where neither milk nor honey flows, the establishment of cities, ports, railroads, power lines, prove to the world and to the Jews themselves that they have an unrecognized talent—colonization.

But most amazing of all, this nation that was said to be made up of merchants, doctors, scholars, alien to nature, became within a few years a nation of farmers, and these were not the growing children alone, but men and women who had led the city life of lawyers and bankers in Western capitals. Ancient instincts that had been checked in the Jews by the restriction of their rights in Europe awoke again. As the commercial Phoenicians became agricultural Carthaginians, so it was with the Jews. A great abundance of life poured out over the people, who hitherto had simply prayed at the Wailing Wall in the home of their forefathers.

The pace of the age, the struggles and martyrdoms, the quickness of the Jewish temperament soon created a new legend, and before long there was no talk of King Solomon and the destruction of the temple but only of the lemon crop, electrification, and the new shipyard at Haifa. To the amazement of a mistrustful world, good order and punctuality were the rule in the new communities, and the relationship to the older Christian settlers was not bad either. The tenacity and optimism of the Jew pulled him through the grave crisis that followed the first prosperity of the new colony.

Indeed something that no one had expected happened: the Jews ventured upon the sea, becoming able sailors, and a new blue and white flag made its appearance on the Mediterranean. This did not, of course, solve the Jewish question, for of the fifteen million only a fraction were able or willing to live in Palestine. But a beginning had been made, and a people that had been hounded through nations and ages had a home again in spirit and in fact.

This is an event unique in the life of the Mediterranean. All the other peoples have disappeared—that is, have mingled and been transformed, and only their soil has remained as nature created it and civilization transformed it. Egyptians and Phoenicians, Greeks and Romans, Gauls and Goths, Saracens and Normans have been remade on their own or conquered soil. Only the Jews lost their land in earlier days, and for that very reason they preserved their peculiarities while abroad. Their return to the land of their forefathers completed the circle. It has the sound of a great legend.

IX

THE SEAPORTS OF THE MEDITERRANEAN goggled with cannon mouths in the summer sun of the year 1939. The conflict between England and Italy, and it alone, made war inevitable here—that and the alliance with the Germans. Actually the decision about the Mediterranean depended on a single man. If Mussolini had joined the Western powers, as he had twenty-five years before, the Mediterranean might have been quieter than in the First World War; for in the existing state of alliances and interests the new, small Turkey could not take the German side this time. And without an ally the Germans could not carry on a naval war in the south. Since, furthermore, long stretches of the eastern coast were now under English and French control, the outbreak of a war would simply have neutralized the Mediterranean, so long as Italy would content herself with the large concessions that England was undoubtedly ready to make.

But Mussolini, who had at first despised his German imitator, was more and more spellbound by the sight of the gigantic German war machine; in a coming war he counted on the defeat of France and perhaps England and believed that he could then expand by his own naval victories, at least at the expense of France.

Brotherhood in arms with the Germans had been tried out in the preceding years on the battlefields of the Spanish Civil War. In the end it was perhaps mostly the similar systems of dictatorship that decided Mussolini's conduct of his foreign affairs. He knew that the history of Italy, the character of the Italians, and the shifting of the center of the world made a new Roman empire impossible. In his decision to fight against England, nevertheless, a natural affinity drew the adventurer to his like, whereas he despised the established world of democracy as old-fashioned.

Mussolini had driven a refractory people to astonishing accomplishments. He had actually built the largest submarine fleet in the Mediterranean and a good battle fleet. But lack of money and raw materials, of obedience and enthusiasm—in other words, the nature of Italy and of the Italians—limited the extent of his armaments and prevented him from coming anywhere near the German figures. It was, as he once said privately, his bad luck not to govern a people such as the Germans. In 1936 Italy had two warships (and two were being built), as against three old French craft and an average of six (out of fifteen) English ships in the Mediterranean.

It must be said that Italy had the advantage of living on the scene of battle, so to speak, whereas England had only a few hastily established shipyards in the eastern Mediterranean. England and France, on the other hand, had the advantage of deriving the sources of their power from outside and being able to replenish them from the Atlantic. At Suez England could cut off the Italians from any communication with Abyssinia, and at Gibraltar she could break the flow of raw materials. The long, unprotected coasts have no deeply indented river mouths such as are common in the north. The terminals of the railways are open to the sea, and the great cities lie close to it. By sea and air Italy is exposed to any foe whose machines are stronger or more numerous than her own.

Much had been accomplished in Italy. In Sicily, whose people like to call it the bridgehead of the empire, the harbor of Syracuse had been developed, and the harbor of Messina, one of the greatest natural harbors in the world, with a capacity of a thousand vessels, had been improved. In the south of Sardinia Cagliari was built up;

French Corsica, only eight miles or a few minutes away, could easily be bombarded from the northern tip. La Spezia, uncommonly well situated, as if in a river valley, had been developed into the greatest shipyard in Italy, perhaps in the whole Mediterranean, and the poets from Dante to d'Annunzio who had sung there would have been far more pleased with this nationalist spectacle than would their English colleague Shelley, who had never dreamed of machines in that bay.

Adriatic defense was the most strongly developed. There the last adversaries, the South Slavs, had been almost entirely displaced; their ships could be bottled up. Here nature is kind to Italy, because Dalmatia, with its precipitous coast, has only a narrow fringe on the sea, with few passes into the bare mountains. Race, on the other hand, speaks for the South Slavs, who have lived here for more than a thousand years. Since the eastern coast of the Adriatic—its rear, so to speak—has but few ports and little importance, the Italians today, as in the time of Venice, have only to fortify the ends, at north and south.

In the north after the First World War, Trieste, Pola, and Venice were not developed into great naval harbors like La Spezia. Rich Trieste, so beautifully planned by the Austrians, lies forsaken. The commercial firms housed in the old palaces have closed up, and the city has no hinterland. Zara, on the other hand, in the latitude of La Spezia, is in the midst of the Yugoslav territory, as menacing as Gibraltar in Spain but threatened in its turn by outlying Yugoslav islands. Fiume was once famous for d'Annunzio's adventure; it has become, as he himself scornfully remarked in his old age, a dull commercial city. It is quite without military significance.

Further south, in the middle of the Adriatic coast, the Yugoslav port of Spalato (or Split) the ancient Spalatum, the residence of the retired emperor Diocletian, is hard to protect, the more so since the Italians have forcibly appropriated and fortified the outlying island of Lagosta. Its very name indicates the abundance of lobsters. At the Straits of Otranto the mouth of the Adriatic is completely in Italian hands. Taranto and Brindisi are fortified for airports and naval bases. In the distance lies the island of Saseno, which

Italy took from the Albanians even before the occupation and where no mortal outside the navy is allowed to set foot. Opposite is Valona, north of it Durazzo. All are armed with heavy batteries and safeguarded in every way. The Italians could never lose the Adriatic in war; they might lose it partially in peace after a great defeat.

Italy has also prepared against French and Turkish sea attacks, obviously calculating her own offensive as part of the scheme. The rocky little island of Pantelleria has been fortified as a stronghold against French Tunis and also against any fleet moving from west to east. The fortifications are said to be on a great scale—said to, for there are no pictures. Lying between Tunis and Sicily, this island controls both parts of the all-important water route, which can be reached by air in a matter of minutes, by sea in a few hours. Along with the still smaller island of Lampedusa (where none but criminals used to live), it has been called by a French seaman the navel of the Mediterranean. The position of these rocks, between Cape Bon, Marsala, and Malta, makes them priceless, and we are surprised only that no seafaring nation had ever made greater use of them before. Today they are retaliating for this tardy violation of their solitude; the craters will suddenly spit hot springs into the midst of the bustling engineers.

Against the Turks and the English, allied to Turkey in the eastern Mediterranean by treaty, the Italians have built up so powerful a system for naval fighting that an English general described all the shipping of the Aegean as under Italian control. Heavily armed little Lero, south of Samos, is openly threatening, like Gibraltar and Zara. Its guns point simultaneously at the Turkish coasts and English Cyprus. It belongs to the Dodecanese, which ought to consist, according to its Greek name, of twelve islands but actually numbers forty. This archipelago was taken—that is, "temporarily occupied"—by democratic Italy under Giolitti. Fascism has developed it.

Mussolini has turned Rhodes, the most famous of the islands, into a center of Italian culture, establishing a university, taking advantage of the beautiful climate for sanitariums, and everywhere continuing the tradition of Venice. When Solyman the Magnificent rode in after defeating the Knights Templars, he had the gate closed behind him, giving rise to the legend that he who opened it would lose Rhodes. Then followed four centuries of Turkish maladministration. Finally Mussolini had the gates broken open amid great celebration and sent his commandant through in the lead.

His large-scale naval and air armaments were calculated for a short, quick war: this alone could secure Italy against annihilation by a blockade. As the war drags on, the country becomes dependent on Germany, which, however, can send little but coal and arms. Italy has profited more by the new air arm than England, since her planes could bombard all the Mediterranean coasts from her far-flung mainland and also from Sicily, Sardinia, Pantelleria, and Lero. Accordingly Mussolini trained his young people to be aviators, and let them try their skill in Spain and Abyssinia.

In a long war, on the other hand, he must fear lack of oil and grain and also the bombardment of his coasts, ports, and shipyards; but above all, he must fear the character of his people, which tires quickly and has no love of war.

As early as the Spanish Civil War the Italian troops were a failure. The collapse of the Spanish republic, cheated and abandoned, represented a defeat of socialism like that of 1905 in Russia and 1932 in Germany. Instead of cynically calling the Spanish war "the fascist dress rehearsal," we should regard it as the source of the French collapse and the English defeats of 1940.

Particularly in the summer of 1936 the seas around Gibraltar were more of a battleground than they had been in a hundred years. With Franco there was a real pirate in the Mediterranean again. But although he torpedoed English vessels and stole French ones, neither of the two governments intervened.

In September, 1937, twenty-three Americans fell in a battalion fighting for the republic. These were the first victims of the Second World War, although it did not break out in America until four years later. Robert Merriman, a professor at a California college, was wounded six times in an assault while defending a Spanish cathedral. He perhaps deserves to be called the first American hero of the present war.

X

THE COASTS OF THE MEDITERRANEAN goggled with cannon mouths in the summer sun of the year 1939.

Three of Italy's adversaries were greatly inferior to her. The Greeks, the seafaring nation par excellence in antiquity, have long since ceased to compete in that way. Even today sixty per cent of all the Greeks live by trading and shipping, a figure attained by no other people on earth. But their merchant fleet of almost two million tons had no navy to protect it, and so the whole archipelago that is their life, and that produced their genius, lies open to any hostile action. The islands of the Dodecanese were ninety per cent Greek by population under the Turkish flag, and they still are today under the Italian flag. All the movements in the Aegean today are as vigorously Greek as ever; but the Greeks lack the power to protect themselves.

Even the Corinth Canal, the only accomplishment of the modern Greeks at sea, has remained almost without influence on their shipping. Caesar and Hadrian thought of piercing this isthmus, only four miles wide. When the canal was at length finished in 1893, it cost but ten million dollars. Being very narrow, it affords passage to small vessels only, and even these often bump the high walls. To be a pilot at Corinth is the most thankless occupation in the Mediterranean. Strategically the canal is worthless, for it saves only the short voyage around the Peloponnesus.

The entire defense of Greece depends on her alliance with England, the protector of Greece since the return of the royal family. This was the third time a banished Greek king had returned in the course of a decade. In the interim Venizelos sought alliance with an Italy not yet tied to Germany, and thus the natural ally of Greece. Greece and Italy could easily have agreed upon the few points in dispute. However, England has built naval and air bases at Crete and elsewhere on the Greek mainland and islands—bases perhaps more useful to her than to the Greeks. The Ionian Islands, along the west coast, are all too familiar to the English, who held them from

1850 to 1864 and only released them then in return for the right to use Greek ports.

The Turks, too, are by treaty allies of England in case of war. Kemal Atatürk could take no other line, for the conflicts of Italy with Turkey are greater than those with Greece. Here in miniature we have Byzantium opposing Rome again, except that in our day Istanbul has a far more powerful neighbor to the north. There was thus a sort of paradoxical friendship between the two former great antagonists, England and Russia, through the mediation of a Turkey allied to both. In 1936 the powers jointly agreed to the new demand of Turkey that she be allowed to fortify the straits, in return for the assurance that all types of vessel might pass through except submarines, with certain restrictions as to time. Today the tiers of guns raise their barrels above the straits again as they did during the First World War.

Spain, which has had to follow a policy that wavered between England and Italy since the end of her civil war, may have accomplished her most recent armament on the basis of secret treaties with Mussolini. It has been truly said that if Gibraltar is the key to the Mediterranean, Tangier is the lock. But Tangier is international, for England will allow no power to fortify itself opposite Gibraltar. From Ceuta, on the other hand, it is possible to shell the English rock. All the debates, conferences, and protocols that have occupied diplomats for thirty years with the neutralizing of this momentous entrance might be blown sky high some fine day, along with all possible harbors, by a few hours' cannonade. It is hard to estimate, too, what the armored Balearics might accomplish against British or French vessels if Spain should some day march openly on France.

In the last decade France has armed far more heavily in the Mediterranean than is generally supposed by the critics of Paris democracy. She has had to, because she is the only nation of the Mediterranean, indeed on earth, whose national defense depends on her colonies. "The great French family," as the elegant phrase expressed the dependence of forty million white Frenchmen on sixty million of the colored races, was therefore bound to receive rapidly increasing rights. The colored men were rather tempted than forced into military service, so that in the end there were an estimated two million colored soldiers. Since the French in the latest past have wanted not conquest but preservation of what they have, their armament in the Mediterranean has been limited to the defense of the European and African coasts, and to the necessary protection of transport ships from Africa.

Accordingly, at all the naval conferences France has vied with Italy alone, never with England. As the alliance with England had been established for some forty years, French misgivings about the cleavage of their navy by Gibraltar were quieted. The colored troops could also go north by the Atlantic now that France had secured Morocco, the northwest corner of Africa. Practically speaking, there would be much lost by this route. The best solution was the trans-Sahara railway, which was to start from the port of Oran at the west of Algiers and for which Secretary of War Maginot drew up plans in 1929. Rich, but never free with money, France did not raise the necessary billion dollars, and air lines and caterpillar trucks were no adequate substitute.

The railway projected by Spain from Irun to Algeciras, with tracks of the French gauge, would likewise have permitted transportation without vessels by way of the intended tunnel under Gibraltar and a spur to southeastward. By modern engineering standards these tremendous projects are far easier to carry through than the Suez Canal was; similar undertakings are an accomplished fact in America. The desert soil of the Sahara is so hard in some places that railroad ties can be laid directly upon it. This would link Senegal and the Sudan with the Mediterranean. Even with no tunnel the Negroes could be on the Rhine a week after leaving the Congo.

This was far more in accordance with the French nature than real seafaring; for the Frenchman resembles the German in that centuries of frontier warfare have made him a soldier rather than a sailor. All the more impressive was the way in which France succeeded within a decade in arming herself at sea, that is, against Italy. Every barrier against Italy was popular, and every budget item for that purpose was accepted; French contempt for the Italians merely grew under Italian threats.

The fortification of north Africa was as difficult as trade with it was easy (Algiers is the second largest customer of France), for the coast of north Africa has very few natural harbors. This, after all, is why the pirates held it so long. France has built up the three great harbors, Oran, Algiers, and Bizerte, at such pains and expense that the pirates would have passed by in horror. There is no trace of them now. But another relic has been in the harbor of Oran for thirty years—thirty-five ships of the old czarist Black Sea fleet, left there during the First World War. Now, half eaten away with rust, they look utterly fantastic, like an old crown popping up in a gathering of laborers. Communist agitators carried on their activities among the thirty-five imperial vessels as if the background inspired them.

But no power in the Mediterranean, all bristling with cannon, carries such decisive weight as the one that is not washed by it. The uncanny stranger, who seems only to be strolling here, as it were, is the one who sets all in motion, partly provoking, partly influencing the armaments of the others. England, which has nothing here but a few islands and a few protectorates, is nevertheless at home in the west, the middle, and the east, which none of the true Mediterranean peoples can say of itself.

Even he who has seen the rock of Gibraltar must depend on occasional accounts of it. The fortifications are like statesmen, whose actions their contemporaries see but whose needs and motives do not transpire, from secret documents, until the men are dead. What is actually taking place on these islands and rocks, in the ports, and along the shores of the Mediterranean, we shall learn only from the eventual victor after the holocaust. A former governor, Godley, writes that the narrow rock of Gibraltar, three miles long by a mile wide, makes a poor target. At most a lucky bomb might hit it by accident. In itself the limestone can easily be shattered, but planes can scarcely operate; there is no room for an airport, and the enemy would have to fly low, a thing made difficult by the nearness of the rock and the everlasting east wind. It is possible to cannonade from Ceuta, but only the heaviest long-range guns would have any effect.

There are said to be four thousand cannon built into the galleries of Gibraltar and bombproof cisterns each holding forty tons of water; six divisions at war strength can be housed in the casemates. Much that we see reminds us of a battleship—forts one above another, sunken towers, invisible holes filled with munitions, concealed antiaircraft guns. The secrets are so well guarded that special armorers are always confined to cleaning certain sections lest they become familiar with the whole. Even so, the layman has a sense of insecurity, because superior means of destruction have in the past always been discovered and successfully applied against all fortresses.

Malta, the center of the Mediterranean, has lost importance in the last ten years because of the development of the airplane. The Italians called it the mousetrap and said they could destroy its harbors from Sicily in an hour. England did not build up this air base without long hesitation, and even now its value is disputed by experts. Nevertheless English bombers might some day take off from Malta to scatter death and destruction on Sicily to northward and Libya to southward within the same hour.

England's weapon in the east of the Mediterranean is far more strongly developed. Since the First World War she has built up on a tremendous scale the Haifa-Cyprus-Alexandria triangle, a strategic area for sea warfare. This barrier proves that people in London count on the possibility of being unable to maintain the route of the British Empire through the Suez Canal against unknown combinations. About 1935 the fleet was withdrawn eastward into the triangle—into the inland sea, that is, and away from the open Atlantic. In ceasing to regard Malta as the focal point of her defense, England returned to the days before the Suez Canal: she staked everything on the navy itself, but at the same time hoped, if worst came to worst, to escape with part of the navy through the canal. She also began to ship bulk goods around the Cape and has thus prepared against the new world war two methods by two routes. She planned for herself protection in the Mediterranean by the navy. And lacking a navy out in the Atlantic, she still hoped to keep Italian ships penned up in the Mediterranean by the guns of Gibraltar. It takes no expert to imagine a hundred other possibilities between these two.

England counts, then, on the possibility of losing the Suez Canal and still remaining master of her empire, which alone is important to her. She has not fortified the canal; she is simply watching it; she can control it even though she may not use it herself for troop transports to Europe. As long as a decade ago the English navy began to describe the Suez Canal as superfluous, since England did not intend to get her arms from the Mediterranean but only to send them through it, and she could even do without this. Extensive construction was carried on in east African harbors to take care of that possibility.

Protection of Egypt as the gate to Africa, on the other hand, has remained so important that in 1935 England began to fortify Alexandria rapidly, while Malta declined in importance. There were also fortifications in Lemnos, Crete, and Cyprus, and treaties with Greece and Turkey. The most important point has become Haifa, now the third strongest fortress in the Mediterranean. This is the end of the pipe line from Iran—the source of oil, the power without which all the ships and planes would become immobile.

From Haifa English armaments reach deep into western Asia. Railroads connecting Jerusalem with Medina, a veritable army camp at Amman in Trans-Jordan, the airlines to Bagdad and Iran, pipe lines to the Mosul oil field, development of the port of Aqaba and two outlying islands in the Red Sea—all this together makes a gigantic bulwark connecting with and safeguarding India. A project has even been discussed for a new canal from the Mediterranean to the Red Sea, running over English territory from Acre through Palestine by way of Jaffa. But with the ports and locks, it would of necessity cost twenty times as much as the Suez Canal, since it would have to be cut through largely rocky subsoil, and it would take eight years to build.

Perhaps the English are less afraid of the expense than of the risk that an enemy might turn their work against them, like the Pharaoh who stopped his canal on the Nile for that reason. Even so, it was a century before Darius, king of the Persians, defeated Egypt.

XI

THE COASTS OF THE MEDITERRANEAN frowned with forts and bases in the summer sun of the year 1939. Trade and travel went on, the sea was alive with ships, and the people, native and foreign, traveled on it and above it.

The great steamers of the P. & O. Line brought the products of India and China on the long voyage through the Suez Canal—the same products that, centuries before, had gone around the Cape and even earlier by the old land roads through Persia and Asia Minor to the ancient ports. White-clad ladies, going for a pleasure trip without disembarking, lay on the fashionable decks of the "Lloyd Triestino," sipping their iced lemonades, and swinging high-heeled shoes. On cheap freighters scholars journeyed to isles and shores, studying primitive prehistoric forms on the slopes of Stromboli or species of palms in Tetuán or baroque palaces at Rhodes or coins at Alexandria or the new plantations outside the city of Tel Aviv.

Journalists and exporters crossed the Mediterranean by plane to carry reports or business from east to west. On all the coasts transmitters sent out their broadcasts, each trying in its own way to stir the spirit of the dwellers on distant shores. On one of these magically blue August days the present author, bent on studies for this book, flew from Corsica to Tunis and sketched the plan for *The Mediterranean* seven thousand feet above the blue Mediterranean itself.

But amid all the bustle of world commerce, while 120 million souls were enjoying life along these shores or struggling for new and better conditions, people on every coast heard the roar of motors overhead; a spyglass or simply a practiced ear would tell them that these were war planes. At the same time, on many a morning as they surveyed the familiar outline of the bay, small flat ships or great tall ships would glide along the horizon like enormous gray whales rising from the blue surface: warships and more warships.

During those summer weeks the Mediterranean was in such a state of uneasiness and preparation as never before. Never before had every city, coast, and nation alike been either afraid or ecstatic. The last naval battle fought in the First World War had taken place off in the extreme northeastern corner, at the straits; but even the three or four naval battles of the nineteenth century, in the Adriatic, at Navarino, and at Alexandria, had been episodes. The fleets of the other countries had lain quietly in port. When foreign conquerors in earlier periods came into the Mediterranean, they might seize an island or a coast, and the other nations would hear of it like news from some distant sea. The voyages of the Venetians against Constantinople, of the crusaders against the Turks, of the Normans against the Greek islands, indeed all the struggles that had taken place in the Mediterranean had been confined to small parts.

But now, in August, 1939, the ships and planes, the ports and shipyards of every nation were astir; they could all feel that a war was ahead in the north and that its beginning would send Italy too into action, thus putting the whole Mediterranean on the defensive. Actually the destiny of the ocean depended then on the decision of a single man. If he and all his arms remained quiet, no one was inclined to break the peace at sea. If he burst loose with his vessels, all the navies would rise up to fight him off or attack him.

In the radiant blue of those August days the tension rose to the breaking point. All the denizens of the Mediterranean were waiting for the first shot.

AT THE LIGHTHOUSE

AT THE FIRST SHOT *all the beacons on the Mediterranean went out. These warning, helping, consoling friends of the mariner, calling out silently with their three slow-circling beams to tell where shallows and reefs were to be feared, where breakwaters could be found at need, were put out. Their darkness symbolized this war of all against all.*

The keeper of the lighthouse in the Hyères Islands too had been ordered to put out his lights but to stay there and guard the lighthouse so that he could give warning in case of attack. Now that his years of quiet service were suddenly at an end, a new and nerve-fraying duty began, with no formalities and no set hours. This man who had performed a useful and sensible office, giving warning in fog and storm to many a ship that he knew nothing of, found himself suddenly thrust into dull vacancy, from which there was nothing useful to be got. He was too old to be a soldier, and his sons were too young. Besides, he was needed here and could not leave the lighthouse even though its light was out.

On September 1, 1939, staring out into the darkness from his little white house toward the spot where the beacon had always circled, he felt as if his best friend had died. But at the same time his heart was filled with a general bitterness and a secret dread lest France suffer defeat in this war. Above all, it was the fleet, the neighboring city of Toulon, with its ships, that quickened his pulse. His fatherland was at war, and no one could tell whether German submarines might not be in the Mediterranean already. Any night the coast, his island, the lighthouse itself might suddenly be bombarded, his little house blown to pieces.

Thus it was with double anxiety that the keeper listened several times a day to his radio, the best on the island; it gave him news from distant stations that few inland could get. Every day he sat listening, hearing word of a quaking world. But nothing agitated the old seaman so much as the war news he heard from his own sea and the countries around it:

One of the first Mediterranean reports of 1940 read: "Cellar being built for the Pope at Rome; gas masks distributed in the Vatican."

Late in May the angry speeches and accusations grew louder, artificially in Italy, quite naturally in France, which did not threaten, wanted no conquest, but was filled with contempt for the Italian soldiers. Hearing the roar of the approaching collapse in early June, the seaman was shaken to the core. For a few days he saw and heard nothing but the fate of Paris. The sea seemed empty to him; he turned his back on it and sat outside the little white house for hours at a time, his elbows on his knees, and stared into space.

On June 10 he heard that Mussolini had entered the war, without explanation, without fire, without passion. At any moment one of his submarines might shell Toulon or the lighthouse. This danger made the seaman firmer, colder, more patient. Then he heard that on the day after Italy's entrance Roosevelt said that Mussolini had stabbed his neighbor in the back. With a moody growl he agreed.

The Mediterranean was still quiet. In France everything seemed uncertain during early July. Where was Weygand? What was he doing with his Syrian army? Who was this de Gaulle who was trying to found a new France from London? Where was the navy? Would England and France actually open fire on each other?

On the third of July he heard that it had happened. The English had seized French warships in Alexandria. A naval battle between the two fleets had taken place in Oran Bay. Tremendous losses of battleships, cruisers, destroyers followed; all the airplane carriers were said to have been taken. The seaman had often anchored in Oran Bay; vividly he could see every bend in the coast, and he imagined himself aboard a cruiser. Gloom weighed upon his spirit; he could not hate the English; he could only be angry with his own government.

At the end of July his spirits flared up: at last the English had caught the Italians and sent the first destroyer to the bottom. This was the first naval battle between the two fated powers in the Mediterranean, the central nation and the stranger. But still nothing was decided. The seaman was on fire as he heard the radio announcer say that an Australian cruiser had destroyed the Italian ship "Colleoni" off Crete. Reverses followed in the middle of September: Marshal Graziani invaded Egypt from Libya and made a considerable advance with his first thrust. But although ships and planes were assisting, no Italian victory was reported.

Late October: Italy invaded Greece. The seaman had no confidence in Italian strength. What would England do? Would the great naval battle come at last? November 11: the English fleet surprised the Italian fleet in the harbor of Taranto; three battleships were gravely damaged. The English waited twenty-four hours at sea off the coast, but no one came out to avenge the defeat. When they went back to Alexandria, English dominance in the Mediterranean seemed assured. It was a great date in history, a fearful day for the pride of the Italians, who had labored for fifteen years on their navy.

Meanwhile the Greeks had not been idle: in late November they expelled the Italians and pushed forward to the Albanian ports, to Valona. The seaman, who knew all these harbors, felt his heart beat higher at the report. Where were the English? his tense eyes seemed to ask as he looked out to sea, as if to bring a new naval battle nearer with his spyglass. But he heard only the invisible voice: again the English had challenged the Italians near Sardinia, but the Italians had remained quietly in port. If only the French fleet were active now! If it could only have taken part, perhaps have assumed the lead! With bitterness in his heart the seaman switched off the radio.

In mid-December came new hope: General Wavell drove Marshal Graziani out of Egypt and pursued him into Libya as far as Bengasi. At Christmas, as the seaman sat quietly with his family, while the boy squeaked out a tune on his fiddle, the old man reflected that this fearful year in the Mediterranean had seen victory over Italy.

But 1941 began badly: the Germans were there! In mid-January an English airplane carrier was so severely damaged that she could barely reach Malta—the first victory of the Luftwaffe over a war-

ship. With it began a new era in naval warfare. Revenge followed swiftly: in mid-February an English fleet sailed into the bay of Genoa, shelling and destroying. But even now no Italian battleship ventured out.

Late March: a third naval battle, this time off Cape Matapan. Another English victory without losses, with the Italians losing several ships. Where now, after half a year, was Mussolini's proud new navy, with which he had regulated his nation's young people, the Mediterranean, the whole world? Four of his eight great warships were at the bottom of the sea, and six of his twenty-two cruisers were destroyed.

But then the iron strength of the Germans arrived to turn back destiny. In three weeks it subjugated Yugoslavia and Greece. The Piraeus was not a Greek harbor any more. At the same time the English were pushed out of Bengasi again and as far back as Tobruk by early May. Complete command of the land and probably of the water as well had passed to the Germans. A second stranger had appeared on the Mediterranean. The great duel of the two alien powers in the Mediterranean was ready to begin.

Not since the French and Germans had fought each other four centuries before in Italy had the dwellers on the coast watched a great war between two interlopers. And in a thousand years at sea there had been only one struggle between two strangers to the Mediterranean: the Arabs and Normans were the last intruders whose ships had sent one another to the bottom. Then Nelson's victory over Napoleon at Abukir Bay in 1799 was the last great Mediterranean naval battle, a hundred and forty-one years before the new duel in Oran Bay.

The most amazing thing was that the two fleets that had worked together and played into each other's hands for forty years suddenly began to shell each other. The consequences of this unnatural hostility were frightful. Italy had gained a stranger as an ally in the Mediterranean; England had lost a native ally. In the course of this new, unequal partition, Crete fell into German hands. The first invasion by air ended in victory. A heavy defeat to the English; four cruisers and six destroyers gone. The seamen knew the Cretan har-

bors as he knew the hundred bays of Greece. Was it true, then? Were the Germans invincible?

At last, in mid-July, France appeared once more in the Mediterranean, and with her came new hope. In a few summer weeks de Gaulle and England recaptured Syria, which Weygand had surrendered.

The heart of the lighthouse-keeping seaman was completely bound up with the Italian defeats. He beamed as he told his wife the news of the Italians' being thrown back in Greece and Libya. Every remote possibility of a revolution excited him; his prayers were directed toward the collapse of a people that was supposed, not by its own wish indeed but by the will of its leader, to emerge from the war as master of the Mediterranean.

. . . How it all repeats itself, he thought as he sat one Sunday under the old olive tree on the rock. It was November, 1941. . . . The fat book that has taken me from Odysseus down through the ages shows that the fortunes of our ocean are repeated over and over again. How often Italy has been great and then small again! So has France. We've been shown our mistakes with a rod of iron. Everybody feels it and realizes it; even Pierre agreed yesterday.

. . . But over yonder, where they think themselves victors, people are weary and downhearted. Someday Italy will rise up against the man who chained it to the hated Germans. Then we may talk differently about Nice and Corsica from the way the Roman radio has been doing today. Someday an order will come from Toulon, and I shall go over to the tower and turn on the light again. That day I will take the boy along and show him how to run the lighthouse. Then I'll send him to bed, and I shan't be reading a book all night long. I shall be watching the beacon turn, so that the ships will know that France is still on the Mediterranean. . . .

Sunk in these thoughts the seaman looked across the sunlit water. During the past two years he had aged greatly. The elasticity of the tanned skin, the carriage of the sinewy body were still there; anyone who had seen him now getting up and going with his long, slow strides to the outer edge of the rock would have thought him still young enough to steer a ship; and still he had aged.

But the olive tree stood unshaken, apparently no older than ever. It had probably survived some three centuries. In this half wilderness it had once sprouted out of a seed brought from shore by the west wind; high above the precipitous abyss it had struck root in cracks between the limestone ribs, splitting them slightly in the course of time, to find nourishment below and room above. Now the trunk, cracked a hundred ways, its grayish wood stained green with moss, leaned steeply over the high cliff.

The green olive tree, the gray rock, the blue surface mirroring the sun, the seaman looking across the expanse—this was the Mediterranean. And yonder lay the other island of Hyères, sparkling and silvery-blue, like a floating phantom, girdled by cypress shadows, almost uninhabited, a bit of paradise. The coast swept north and south in soft curves broken by hills gentle or abrupt, as if endless rows of spectators were standing on the shore to watch the great god and his magic doings out yonder.

Long before Odysseus this wondrous sea lay thus in the lavish sun, concealing the lurking storms that might break out at any moment. So it lies, its depths peopled with fish great and small, its surface sailed and fought over by man, a strangely irregular element that no one in tens of centuries has ever tamed, though all have courted its favor. Generative point and center of great ideas and bold deeds, source of men's wisdom, beauty, and faith: an ageless dwelling of invisible gods who live in the depths below and atop the clouds overhead.

Steady-eyed, the gray-haired seaman looked down at the surface. He was the descendant of an ancient race of seafarers, ancestor of generations to come who would all gaze aggressively at distant coasts. They would be born to new adventures, sprung from the fancy of their hearts and the magic of the waves in the never-ending struggle of man with the elements.

Imperturbably he reviewed the thousands upon thousands of human bodies that had gone to the bottom from capsized ships since Phoenician times and turned into mud and water: an army of the dead whose living strength had once plied oars, set sails, manned

*guns. All these beings had been annihilated by the merciless ele-
ment that seemed now so smiling, innocent, and blue.*

*Suddenly two seagulls in quick succession whizzed obliquely
close over the lighthouse keeper's head, flying from the coast straight
into the sun.*

APPENDIX

Abbasides. Dynasty of caliphs, ruled 750-1258. Founded by a great-grandson of Mohammed's uncle. Caliphate persisted nominally in Egypt to 1517.

Abdul-Hamid II (1842-1918). Turkish Sultan. Deposed and exiled by the Young Turks in 1909.

Achaeans. Ancient Greek tribe. Migrated from Thessaly into the Peloponnesus. Homer calls the Greeks collectively Achaeans.

Acragas. Greek name for Agrigentum, in Sicily. Now Girgenti.

Acre. City in Palestine. Headquarters of Ptolemaic rule over Palestine. Point where pilgrims to the Holy Land landed. Changed hands several times during the crusades. The Order of the Teutonic Knights was founded here in 1190.

Actium. Peninsula in Greek Acarnania, now called Azio, also La Punta. In ancient times a famous temple of Apollo. Decisive battle between Octavian (Augustus) and Antony, 31 B.C.

Adria. Town in the alluvial region of the Po. Also called Atria, Hadria in antiquity. Formerly 7½, now 13 miles from the sea.

Aegina. Greek island.

Aeneas. Greek legendary figure. Son of Anchises and of Aphrodite. Hector calls him, in Homer's *Odyssey,* Troy's bravest hero. After the destruction of Troy, Aeneas saved the god's statue, his old father, and his son and took them with him westward. Hero of Vergil's *Aeneid.*

Aeschylus (525-456 B.C.). Greek tragedian. Fought in battles of Marathon, Salamis, Plataea. Used two, later three, actors. *The Persians, The Seven against Thebes, The Oresteia.*

Agathocles (361-289 B.C.). Son of a potter, later tyrant of Syracuse. Won dictatorial power in 317 B.C. and assumed the title of king in 306 B.C. One of the richest and most powerful rulers of his time.

Agde. French town (dept. Hérault), founded by Greek settlers about 720 B.C. Conquered by Arabs about A.D. 725. Destroyed A.D. 737 by Charles Martel.

Agora. Rallying place of army and people in ancient Greece, later market place.

Agrippa (properly Herodes Julius A.). King of Judaea A.D. 41-44, a supporter of pharisaical Judaism.

Agrippa, Marcus Vipsanius (63-12 B.C.). Roman general and politician. Commanded the fleet of Augustus at Actium. Son-in-law of Augustus.

Aiguesmortes (in ancient times Aquae Mortuae). French town (dept. Gard). From here Louis IX started his two crusades, in 1248 and 1270.

Alamanni. Germanic tribe. First traced on the upper Main.

Alani. Iranian equestrian tribe. Lived in southern Russia and the Caucasus under the Roman emperors, later in Pannonia. Some of them joined the West Goths in invading Gaul and Spain. The Ossetes in the central Caucasus are probably descended from the Alani.

Alaric (about 370-410). King of the Visigoths. Laid waste Thrace, Macedonia, Greece. Ordered the sack of Rome.

Albertus Magnus (Albert, Count of Bollstädt) (1193-1280). Dominican and pioneer Aristotelian. Teacher of Thomas Aquinas.

Albizzi. One of the leading families of old Florence. Guelphs.

Alexander II (Nikolaevich). Emperor of Russia 1855-1881. Called the "Reform Czar." Killed by Terrorists' bombs.

Alexander III. Pope 1159-1181. Legate to the Diet of Besançon in 1157, when the imperial crown was declared a fief of the church.

Alexander VI. Pope 1492-1503. Divided America between Spain and Portugal in 1493. Father of Cesare and Lucrezia Borgia.

Alexius I (1048-1118). Byzantine Emperor 1081-1118. Allied with Venice against Robert Guiscard. In 1097 the leaders of the First Crusade took an oath of allegiance to him covering any future conquests in Asia.

Alfonso the Wise (1221-1284). King of Castile and León 1252-1282. Chosen as German Emperor in 1257, but never went there. Wrested Cadiz from the Moors. Most learned prince of his century; ordered the writing of the first general history of Spain. Employed Jewish scholars to translate the Bible into Spanish.

Ambron. Greek founder of Sinope.

Ambrose, Saint (about 340-397). Bishop of Milan. Son of the Roman prefect of Gaul. Religious teacher. His *De Officiis Ministrorum* served as a manual of ethics for centuries. Perfected early Christian hymnology, the Ambrosian chant.

Ambrosia. Mythical food of the Greek gods, giving them immortality.

Amenophis IV (1375-1358 B.C.). Egyptian king. Attempted to introduce exclusive worship of Aten. Therefore called himself Akhenaten. New capital Akhetaton, now Tell el-Amarna. Father-in-law of Tutankhamen.

Amiens, capital of the French *arrondissement* of Amiens. Former capital of Picardy.

Ammon. Chief Egyptian deity of Thebes (Karnak).

Amos. Hebrew prophet, fl. about 750 B.C.

Amru. Arabian general. Originally an opponent of Mohammed. Conquered Egypt 640-642. Died 664.

Anaxagoras (about 500-428 B.C.). Greek philosopher. Accused of atheism shortly before the outbreak of the Peloponnesian War. First to maintain the infinite divisibility of space and matter.

Andronicus (properly Livius Andronicus). Greek from Tarentum, brought to Rome as a prisoner of war; established Roman literature as an art about 240 B.C.

Andros. The northernmost island of the Cyclades.

Angles. Germanic people from the coast of the North Sea. Together with Jutes and Saxons they established the Anglo-Saxon kingdom in Britain, which was called England after them.

Anjou. Old French province; capital, Angers. French noble family that occupied the thrones of England, Naples, and Hungary. After 1480, title of duke of Anjou was borne by French princes of the blood royal.

Antiochus the Great, King of Syria (224-187 B.C.). His struggle with Rome is known as the Antiochian War. Hannibal fled to him at the end of his life. Antiochus refused Hannibal's advice, and was defeated by the Romans.

Antipater. Macedonian general, viceroy of Macedonia during Alexander the Great's Persian campaign. Later regent. Died 318 B.C.

Antonelli (1806-1876). Cardinal secretary of state to Pius IX. Was president of the new *Consulta di stato* and a liberal ministry in 1848.

Antoninus Pius. Roman emperor A.D. 138-161. His family came from Gaul. Adopted by Hadrian on condition that he in turn should adopt the later Marcus Aurelius. His daughter was Marcus Aurelius' wife.

Apulia. Most southeasterly of the historic regions of Italy.

Aquileia. Ancient Italian metropolis, later belonged to Venice. Of military importance to Rome from the time of Caesar. Destroyed by Alaric in 410, the Huns in 452, Theodoric the Great in 489, the Lombards in 568.

Arcadia. District in the Peloponnesus; scene of Hellenistic and Roman pastoral poetry.

Archimedes of Syracuse (290/80-212 B.C.). Physicist, mathematician. Syracuse was able to withstand the Romans for two years by means of the engines of war he invented. Discovered the "Archimedean principle," the laws of the lever, the center of gravity, the concave mirror, and much else.

Aretino, Pietro (1492-1557). Italian author and publicist, feared and highly paid because of his sharp tongue. A friend of Titian and other great artists of the time.

Argolis. Eastern peninsula of the Peloponnesus.

Arion. Greek poet and musician. Inventor of the dithyramb. Legend tells he was captured by pirates who wanted to kill him. As a last favor he asked to be allowed to play his instrument for a last time. They agreed. Suddenly Arion jumped into the ocean, and a dolphin carried him on its back to shore alive.

Ariosto, Ludovico (1474-1533). Italian poet. He was brought up at the court of the d'Estes, whom he glorified in his *Orlando Furioso*.

Aristides. Athenian general and statesman. Traditionally called the "Just." Helped in the formation of the Attic naval league. Died about 468 B.C.

Arles. French town (dept. Bouches du Rhône), one of Emperor Constantine's capitals.

Arminius (17/16 B.C.-A.D. 21). Prince of the Cherusci. Officer of the Cheruscan troops in Roman service. Acquired Roman citizenship and knighthood. In his native Germany he lured a Roman army into ambush in the Teutoburger Wald, and annihilated it. Murdered by his own relatives.

Astarte. Greek name for the chief Western Asiatic goddess, Ashera.

Ataulf. King of the Visigoths. Murdered at Barcelona in 415. Brother-in-law of Alaric I.

Athos. Peninsula and mountain in Chalcidice. Xerxes had a canal cut through the neck of the peninsula. Anchorites have been settled on the mountain since the eighth century. There are now twenty monasteries of different nationalities.

Avignon. Capital of the French department of Vaucluse. Seat of the Popes 1309-1377.

Baal. Male deity of the Western Semites. Not a proper name; signifies "Lord." Therefore used generally in connection with a place name.

Bab el Zaka. Arabian name for Strait of Gibraltar.

Bajazet. Osmanli Sultan, 1389-1403. Son of Murad I. Called "Lightning." Subdued all the Balkan states in three years. Besieged Constantinople for ten years. Taken prisoner by Timur; died in captivity.

Baldwin I (1058-1118). King of Jerusalem. Brother of Godefroy of Bouillon, on whose death he became King of Jerusalem.

Barca. North African town of the Cyrenaica.

Beatrice Portinari. Wife of the rich banker Simone de' Bardi. Dante, who made her immortal, loved her from the time he was nine. Named his daughter after her. She died in 1290.

Beccaria, di, Cesare Bonesana (1738-1794). Italian jurist and writer; wrote against torture and the death penalty. His *Dei delitti e delle pene* was translated into twenty-two languages.

Belisarius (about 500-565). General under Justinian I. Destroyed the Vandal kingdom in Africa 533-534. Fought two campaigns against the Ostrogoths in Italy.

Bellini, Gentile (1427-1507). Italian painter, brother-in-law of Mantegna. Painted the portrait of Sultan Mohammed II.

Bellini, Giovanni (1430-1516). Italian painter, brother of Gentile, teacher of Giorgione, Palma, Titian. Experimented with the new oil paints. "Pietà," "Coronation of Mary," "Sacred Conversations."

Berenice. Daughter of the Jewish king Agrippa. Mistress of Vespasian's son Titus.

Bessarion, Johannes. Cardinal and titular patriarch of Constantinople. A

Platonist, advocated the union of the Greek and Roman churches. Bequeathed his collection of manuscripts to the library of St. Mark's in Venice.

Blondel. Legendary minstrel of Richard Coeur de Lion. Is said to have recognized the king, who was imprisoned in the castle of Duerrnstein, by a song known only to the two of them.

Boeotia. Region of Greece between Parnassus and the Gulf of Euboea.

Botticelli, Sandro (1444/45-1510). Italian painter, pupil of Filippo Lippi. Originally a goldsmith. "Birth of Venus."

Bramante (properly Donato d'Agnolo) (1444-1514). Italian architect and painter. Began the new Saint Peter's at Rome in 1506.

Brennus. Senonian general who beat the Romans at the Allia and captured Rome. In weighing out the ransom he used false weights, which he justified with the now traditional phrase, *"Vae victis."*

Brunelleschi, Filippo (1377-1446). Italian architect and sculptor, originally a goldsmith. Creator of the early Renaissance style in architecture. Introduced perspective in painting. Also active as an engineer, builder of fortifications, and mechanician.

Bucentaur. General term for ceremonial vessels of rulers and states on the Mediterranean. Now applied almost exclusively to the ceremonial barge of the Republic of Venice.

Buffon, de, Georges Louis Leclerc, Comte (1707-1788). French naturalist. Famous for his work *Histoire naturelle.*

Buonaparte, Carlo (1746-1785). Father of Napoleon I, jurist, fought against France in the Corsican wars of liberation. Later submitted, even getting his title of nobility confirmed.

Burano. Town belonging to Venice.

Caligula, Caius Caesar (A.D. 12-41). Roman emperor 37-41.

Calypso. Homer mentions Calypso, in the *Odyssey,* as the daughter of Atlas. The nymph Calypso owns the mythical island of Ogygia. Odysseus' ship was wrecked near her island, and for seven years he was Calypso's prisoner.

Canaan. District of the Holy Land, probably on both sides of the Jordan.

Canossa. Mountain castle in northern Italy. The meeting between the German Emperor Henry IV and Pope Gregory VII took place here in 1077.

Cape Bon. Northeastern extremity of Tunisia.

Cape Matapan. Southern point of the Peloponnesus.

Cape Spartel. Northwestern point of Africa, at the Strait of Gibraltar.

Capodistrias, Giovanni Anton, Count (1776-1831). Greek statesman. First in Russian service; regent of the Greek Republic from 1827. Assassinated.

Carlos, Don (1545-1568). Eldest son of Philip II of Spain.

Carpenter, William Benjamin (1813-1885). English naturalist; deep sea explorer of the Mediterranean and the North Sea.

Carrara. Italian town, famous for its valuable marble quarries.

Castiglione, Baldassare, Count (1478-1529). Italian writer and diplomat. In his *Book of the Courtier* he depicts the ideal of the courts of his day. Portrait by Raphael.

Catherine of Siena (1347-1380). Patron saint of the Dominican Order. Venerated for her visions, her care of the sick, and her political talent. Induced Pope Gregory II to return from Avignon to Rome.

Cavour, di Camillo Benso, Count (1810-1861). Italian statesman who brought about the national unification of Italy.

Cephalonia. Largest Ionian island, near the entrance to the Gulf of Patras.

Chaeronea. Ancient Greek city in western Boeotia, home of Plutarch. Philip II of Macedonia defeated Athens and Thebes here in 338 B.C.; Sulla defeated one of King Mithridates' generals in 86 B.C.

Chalcedon. Ancient city at the entrance of the Bosporus, near modern Scutari, across from Constantinople.

Chalkis. Main town on the island of Euboea, Greece. Many ancient colonies were founded from here.

Charles Albert. King of Sardinia 1831-1849. Early champion of the movement for Italian unity. Abdicated after his defeats at Custozza and Novara.

Charles V (1500-1558). Holy Roman emperor 1519-1556; also King of Spain. Carried on wars against France, the Turks, the Algerian and Tunisian pirates, German Protestants. Conquered Mexico, Peru. Abdicated, 1555.

Charles X (1757-1836). King of France, younger brother of Louis XVI. In 1824 succeeded Louis XVIII on the throne. Overthrown in 1830. Just before this he had begun the conquest of Algiers.

Charybdis. A current, mentioned by Homer, in the western Mediterranean, three times daily threatening the ships passing there.

Chioggia. City in the Italian province of Venice, at the southern end of the lagoons.

Chios. Greek Aegean island, near Smyrna. Scene of Turkish massacres during the Greek War of Liberation.

Chrysostom, John, Saint (about 347-407). Patriarch of Constantinople.

Cilicia. District of southern Asia Minor.

Cimbri. Germanic people, originally settled on peninsula of Jutland. Migrated through Gaul to Spain, from there through Gaul to Italy. Sustained a crushing defeat at the hands of Marius at Vercellae.

Claudius (Tiberius Claudius Nero Germanicus). Roman emperor A.D. 41-54. Was looked down upon by Augustus and Tiberius, and kept out of politics. During his reign Britain was systematically conquered.

Clement VI. Pope 1342-1352. Took up his residence at Avignon, which he bought in 1348 from Queen Joanna of Sicily.

Clovis I (466-511). Merovingian king of the Franks. Subjugated the Alamanni from the Main to the Alps. Conquered the kingdom of the Visigoths. Embraced Christianity.

Cluny. City in the French department of Saône-et-Loire. Source of the great Benedictine reform movement, whose aim was the deepening of monastic life and faithful adherence to the Pope.

Cnossus. Town in ancient Crete, south of Herakleion.

Colbert, Jean Baptiste, Marquis de Seignelay (1619-1683). A commoner by birth. Directed the economic policy of Louis XIV for two decades.

Colleoni, Bartolommeo (1400-1475). Italian condottiere. Celebrated equestrian statue by Andrea del Verrocchio at Venice.

Commodus, Lucius Aelius Aurelius. Roman emperor A.D. 180-192, known as the "athlete on the imperial throne."

Comnenus family. Byzantine imperial dynasty 1057-1059, 1081-1185 in Byzantium; 1204-1462 in Trebizond. The final flowering of the Byzantine empire occurred under their rule.

Conrad II. German emperor 1024-1039. Tried to bring about the union of Germany with Italy by marriages between German and Italian royal houses and the filling of Italian bishoprics with Germans.

Constantine I (the Great). Roman emperor 306-337. Prepared the way for the development of Christianity into a state religion. Transferred his residence from Rome to Byzantium, which was named Constantinople in 330. Successfully fought the Goths.

Copernicus, Nikolaus (1473-1543). Polish mathematician, astronomer, physician, canon of Frauenburg. Founder of the heliocentric system. *De orbium coelestium revolutionibus.*

Corcyra. Greek name for Corfu.

Cornaro, Catherine (1454-1510). Member of a Venetian family; queen of Cyprus.

Correggio, Antonio (1484/94-1534). Italian painter. Father of baroque painting. Frescoes of "The Assumption of Mary" in the cathedral at Parma.

Corsica. Mediterranean island. The Etruscans, Phocaeans, Carthaginians, Romans, Vandals, Byzantines, Franks, Saracens, Pisans, Genoese, successively ruled the island. Has belonged almost continuously to France since 1768.

Cortes, Hernando (1485-1547). Spanish conqueror of Mexico. Destroyed his boats before beginning his march into the interior.

Cosenza. Southern Italian city at the mouth of the Busento. Alaric, king of the Visigoths, is said to have been buried in the river near this city.

Council of Constance (1414-1418). Ended the papal schism and made some reforms in the church. Sanctioned burning of John Huss.

Council of Florence, 1438-1439. Attempted union of Roman and Greek Churches.

Crassus, Marcus Licinius (115/114-53 B.C.). Roman profiteer, one of the triumvirs. Made an enormous fortune by buying the property of those proscribed under Sulla. Defeated Spartacus. His biography written by Plutarch.

Crete. Largest Greek island. A mixture of races here produced the Minoan civilization. This influenced the Mycenean civilization of Greece. Romans, Byzantines, Saracens, Venetians, and Turks have held the island.

Crillon, Duc de (1717-1796). French general, later in Spanish service. Captured Minorca, tried vainly to take Gibraltar.

Crispi, Francesco (1819-1901). Italian Prime Minister, supporter of the Italian-German-Austrian alliance.

Cyme. Ancient city in Asia Minor.

Damarete. Wife of tyrant Gelon of Syracuse (485-478 B.C.). Named after her is the Damareteion (10-drachma coin).

Delos. Island in the Aegean Sea. In antiquity celebrated for the worship of Apollo, who was supposed to have been born there, as was Artemis. Holy district in ancient times where nobody should be born or die. Later most important slave market (up to 10,000 slaves sold in one single day).

Democritus (born about 460 B.C.). Greek philosopher. Atomistic theories. Causality laws, etc.

Deucalion. Son of Zeus and Pyrrha, father of all Greeks. Legend: When Zeus decided to drown men because of their sins, he ordered Deucalion to build an ark, and Deucalion survived the flood.

Dias, Bartolomeu (about 1450-1500). Portuguese navigator. The first to circumnavigate the southern tip of Africa, which he called Stormy Cape. The king changed the name to Cape of Good Hope.

Diocletian. Roman emperor (284-305). Established absolute monarchy. Reformed the administration of the empire. Introduced maximum prices as a safeguard against famine. Persecuted Christians. Abdicated 305; died 313.

Dionysus. Greek god. Probably originally a god of fertility, later god of wine.

Dionysius I (430-367 B.C.). Tyrant of Syracuse. A commoner by birth, opponent of democracy. Distinguished himself as an officer, and extended his power as far as the Adriatic. Plato stayed with him for some time.

Dionysius II. Son of the preceding. Tyrant of Syracuse. Brought Plato to his court.

Djerba. Island on the Syrtis Minor.

Dnieper. The ancient Borysthenes. The largest river in European Russia except the Volga.

Dodecanese. Twelve islands in the southeastern Aegean Sea. Rhodes, Patmos, etc. Formerly Turkish possession; since 1912 Italian.

Domitian. Roman emperor 81-96. Son of Vespasian. Had himself addressed as "Lord and God."

Donatello (about 1386-1466). Italian sculptor. Chief master of the early Renaissance. Friend of Brunelleschi. "David" (at Florence), the first bronze nude since antiquity; equestrian statue of Gattamelata at Padua.

Dordogne. River (and department) of southwestern France. Prehistoric excavations.

Doria, Andrea. Genoese admiral and statesman. Charles V appointed him supreme admiral of the sea, and bestowed on him the princedom of Melfi and the principality of Tunis. First fought for Francis I of France.

Doria family. One of the oldest Genoese noble families.

Draco. Athenian lawgiver. Undertook the first codification of existing penal law.

Durazzo. Albanian seaport, ancient Greek Epidamnus, Roman Dyrrachium. Founded by Corcyra (Corfu). The starting point of the Via Egnatia, which ran to Thessalonica and thence to Byzantium.

Edrisi, Abu Abdallah Muhammed El (about 1100-1166 A.D.). Famous Arabian geographer. Lived at King Roger II's court in Sicily.

Eleatics. Philosophical school of Elea, founded about 540 B.C.

Elis. Westernmost region of the Peloponnesus in antiquity.

Elizabeth. Queen of England 1558-1603. Daughter of Henry VIII.

Emanuel (the Fortunate, the Great). King of Portugal 1496-1521. Summoned scholars and artists to his court, equipped voyages of discovery (Vasco da Gama, sea route to the East Indies; Cabral, Brazil). Father-in-law of Charles V. Famous code of laws.

Empedocles (490-430 B.C.). Greek philosopher. Called the inventor of oratory by Aristotle. Is said to have committed suicide by jumping into the crater of Etna.

Enfantin, Barthélemy (1796-1864), leading disciple of Saint-Simonianism. Drew up a plan for the construction of the Suez Canal. Founder and later director of the French Paris-Lyon-Mediterranean railroad line.

Enver Pasha (1881-1922). Turkish statesman and general. Leader of the Young Turks. In 1911 Turkish Commander against the Italians in Tripoli. Turkish commander-in-chief during the First World War.

Ephesus. City in Ionia, Asia Minor.

Erasmus of Rotterdam (1465/6-1536). Humanist. Introduced the pronunciation of Greek now current. Praise of Folly, Adagia.

Eratosthenes (about 275-195 B.C.). Greek scholar of the Alexandrian school. Head of the Alexandrian Library. Carried out the first real surveying;

established the first scientific system of geography; founder of scientific chronology.

Erechtheum. Second largest temple on the Acropolis of Athens. Built 420-408 B.C.

Essenes. Members of a Jewish community first in evidence about 150 B.C. Rejected war, confining themselves to peaceable trades. Held all property in common, rejected marriage, and simply adopted children.

Este, d', Isabella (1474-1539). Wife of the Duke of Mantua. Both were strongly under the influence of Castiglione's *Book of the Courtier*. Connected with all the great minds of the time, such as Raphael, Mantegna, Giulio Romano.

Etruscans. Ancient people of Etruria. Masters of a large part of the Italian peninsula before the Romans.

Euboea. Second largest island of Greece in the Aegean Sea. From 146 B.C. in Roman (and later Byzantine) hands; in 1205 under Lombardian, in 1366 under Venetian rule; from 1470 to 1829, Turkish possession.

Eudoxia, Augusta (about 401-460). Daughter of the Athenian sophist Leontius and wife of the Eastern Roman Emperor Theodosius II.

Eugénie (1826-1920). Empress of the French. Daughter of a Spanish Count and a Scotswoman; wife of Napoleon III.

Exmouth, Edward Pellew, first Viscount (1757-1833). English admiral, successfully attacked Algiers in 1816.

Fatimids. Mohammedan dynasty, 909-1171, who traced their origin to the youngest daughter of the prophet Mohammed.

Faustina. Wife of Marcus Aurelius. Died A.D. 176.

Ferdinand I (1423-1494). Illegitimate son of Alfonso the Magnanimous of Aragon, who in 1458 left him the kingdom of Naples, including all southern Italy and Sicily. He patronized the arts, oppressed his subjects, treacherously massacred Angevin leaders, and impoverished the people by futile wars.

Ferdinand II (the Catholic) (1452-1516). United Castile and Aragon by his marriage to Isabella of Castile. Conquered Granada, the last stronghold of the Moors. Acquired Naples and Navarre. Forwarded the discovery of America. Introduced the Inquisition, persecuted the Jews and Moors.

Ferdinand VII (1784-1835). King of Spain 1824-1833. Summoned Napoleon into the country in 1808. Spiteful, narrow-minded. Reintroduced torture and the Inquisition, and hanged the Liberals who had spent years fighting for him.

Firenzuola, Agnolo (1493-1545). Italian writer. *Of the Beauty of Women*.

Flavii. Roman plebeian family, frequently prominent under the Empire after the rise of the Flavian dynasty founded by Vespasian.

Francis I (1494-1547). King of France. Four wars for the possession of Naples, Milan, hegemony of Europe.

Francis Joseph I (1830-1916). Emperor of Austria 1848-1916. Lost Lombardy and Venetia in 1859. Lost Austro-Prussian War in 1866. Annexation of Bosnia and Herzegovina in 1908.

Francis of Assisi, Saint (1182-1226). Founder of the Order of Franciscans.

Franco, Francisco. Spanish general. Leader of the rebellion against the Spanish Republic in 1936. Dictator with German and Italian help. Piracy in the Mediterranean.

Franks. West Germanic tribe. Collective name for several tribes on the lower Rhine. The name means "wild" or "noble."

Frederick II (the Great) (1712-86). King of Prussia 1740-1786.

Frederick II of Hohenstaufen (1194-1250). King of Jerusalem and Sicily. German Emperor 1212-1250.

Fréjus. Seat of government of the French department of Var.

Frisians. Germanic tribe, originally settled along the coast of the North Sea north of the Zuider Zee.

Fuggers. Rich merchant family in Augsburg, who successfully did business everywhere. As bankers to crowned heads they were made counts and elevated to the nobility.

Gallieni, Joseph Simon (1849-1916). French general, author, and explorer. French colonial achievements in Indo-China; Madagascar his contribution. Saved Paris in the Marne battle, during the First World War.

Garamantes. Ancient name for nomadic tribes in the Sahara, probably the Berbers.

Gascony. Old French district in the western foothills of the Pyrenees.

Gattamelata, Erasmo de' Narni (about 1370-1443). Venetian condottiere. Son of a baker. Taken into the Venetian nobility after a victorious war against Milan. Statue by Donatello, Padua, 1453.

Gaza. Harbor town of southern Palestine. Once one of the main towns of the Philistines.

Gemistus, Georgius (Plethon) (about 1375-1450/2). One of the leading scholars in the Byzantine Empire. His lectures at Florence induced Cosmo de' Medici to establish the Platonic Academy.

Genghis Khan (about 1155-1227). Mongolian prince, founder of an empire. Invaded China, Korea, reached the Caspian Sea, the Crimea.

Genseric. King of the Vandals from A.D. 428. Crossed over from Spain to Africa, dominated the Mediterranean, sacked Rome in 455, annihilated the Roman navy in 461 and 468. Died in 477.

Ghibellines. Name, derived from the German *Waiblinger,* for the Italian adherents of the Germans, particularly of the Hohenstaufen emperors.

Ghirlandaio (1449-1494). Italian painter. Maintained a famous studio in Florence, exerting great influence on the painters there. "Madonna and Saints" (Uffizi, Florence), "Visitation" (Louvre, Paris).

Gideon. One of the judges of the Israelites. Defeated the Midianites, who had crossed the Jordan and were looting the country.

Giolitti, Giovanni (1842-1928). Italian prime minister, before 1914. Also 1920-1921.

Giorgione (about 1478-1510). Italian painter. Pupil of Giovanni Bellini. "Three Philosophers," "Sleeping Venus" (Dresden).

Godefroy de Bouillon (about 1060-1100). One of the leaders of the crusade of 1096, "Defender and Baron of the Holy Sepulcher."

Gordon, Charles George (1833-1885). British general. In 1877 governor of the Sudan.

Gozzoli, Benozzo (1420-1497). Italian painter, assisted Ghiberti in making the two bronze doors of the Baptistry in Florence. Assisted Fra Angelico da Fiesole.

Gracchus, Caius Sempronius (153-121 B.C.). Roman tribune of the people. Accomplished the distribution of grain at special prices to the poor, broke the influence of the senators in the jury courts.

Gracchus, Tiberius Sempronius, the Elder (162-133 B.C.). Roman tribune of the people, social reformer. Assassinated by the partisans of the large landowners.

Grado. City of northeastern Italy, on the Adriatic.

Gregory VII. Pope 1073-1085. Forbade lay investiture. Maintained that the Bishop of Rome, as successor of the Apostle Peter, could dispose of all earthly possessions as well as of heaven. This brought him into conflict with the German Emperor Henry IV (Canossa, 1077). Effected a reconciliation with the Normans.

Gregory XI. Pope 1370-1378. Returned from Avignon to Rome to prevent the loss of the ecclesiastical state.

Guelphs. Name, derived from the German *Welfen,* for the Italian opponents of the German emperors.

Guiscard, Robert (about 1015-1085). Duke of the Normans 1060-1085. Founded the powerful Norman kingdom in southern Italy, conquered and sacked Rome in order to "liberate" the Pope.

Gustavus Adolphus (1594-1632). King of Sweden from 1611. To assure himself command of the Baltic he intervened in the Thirty Years' War. He was a combination of gifted general and shrewd businessman. He overstrained Sweden, thus bringing about her eventual decline.

Hadrian. Roman emperor A.D. 117-138. Abandoned the policy of conquest for the Roman Empire, restricting himself to defense. Athens was his favorite city; he was the first Roman Emperor to wear the beard affected by Greek philosophers. Built his own tomb, now called Castle of Sant' Angelo.

Hafiz (after 1320-1389). Nickname of Persian poet Shams-ed-din Muhammed.

Hanno the Great. Carthaginian general, aristocrat, opponent of Hamilcar. Subjugated Theveste.

Harun-al-Rashid (765-809). Abbasid caliph. Made Basra the center of the Mohammedan world. Famous for his love of justice, and chivalry. *The Thousand and One Nights* deal with him.

Hasdrubal. Brother of Hannibal, who left him behind in Spain as chief in command.

Hawkins, Sir Richard (1562-1622). English sailor, fought the Spanish Armada and Algerian pirates in the Mediterranean. Went on voyages to Africa and the West Indies.

Helike. Town in ancient Achaia. Famous for its cult of Poseidon. In a catastrophe, about 373 B.C., devoured by the ocean.

Hellenic League (often called the Attic or Delian League). Established 478 B.C. by Cimon and Aristides. Directed against Persia. It enabled Athens to free herself of dependence on Sparta, and establish her own hegemony at sea.

Hellespont. Ancient name of the Dardanelles.

Henry II. German Emperor 1002-1024. Supported Pope Benedict VIII against the Greeks in southern Italy.

Henry IV. Holy Roman Emperor 1056-1106. Undertook three expeditions to Italy.

Henry the Navigator, Infante of Portugal (1394-1460). Distinguished himself at the capture of Ceuta in 1415. Grand Master of the Order of Christ, established against the Moors. Started the first school of navigation in the world. Sent out expeditions of discovery, laid the foundations for the Portuguese colonial empire.

Herculaneum. Ancient seaport on the Bay of Naples. Buried, along with Pompeii and Stabiae, by an eruption of Vesuvius in A.D. 79.

Hermes. Greek deity. Messenger of the gods, inventor of the lyre.

Hero of Alexandria (flourished between 150 and 100 B.C.). Greek mathematician and physicist, inventor of various devices and machines.

Herod (about 62 B.C.-A.D. 4). Governor, later tetrarch, of Galilee. Appointed King of Judaea by Rome, united all the Jewish territories under his rule, splendidly enlarged the Temple at Jerusalem.

Herodotus (500/490-about 424). The earliest Greek historian. The "Father of History." Traveled extensively.

Herzl, Theodor (1860-1904). Founder of modern Zionism.

Hesiod. Greek poet of the 8-7 century B.C. *Theogonia,* etc.

Hiero (died 467/66 B.C.). Tyrant of Syracuse. Transplanted the inhabitants of Naxos and Catania to Leontini, occupying Catania with a thousand mercenaries. Broke the sea power of the Etruscans in the naval battle of Cyme. Called Pindar and Aeschylus to his court.

Hillel the Elder. Jewish scholar. Flourished in Jerusalem about 30 B.C.-A.D. 10. The seven rules for interpretation of the Torah are attributed to him. Famous for his gentleness and love of peace.

Himera. Ancient Greek colony in Sicily, at the Himera River. Destroyed by Hannibal.

Himilco. Carthaginian navigator who sailed around the west coast of Europe and discovered the British Isles.

Hiram I. King of Tyre (970-936 B.C.). Sent building materials to King David and King Solomon, for the palaces and temple. With Hiram's help Solomon tried to start sea trade in his inland state.

Hittites. People of eastern Asia Minor. Founded a great empire in the old Orient between Egypt and Assyria.

Hohenstaufen. Swabian royal house, which occupied the German throne 1138-1254.

Holbein, Hans, the Younger (1497/98-1543). German painter who attained the highest distinction in England. Great master of portraiture, in the service of Henry VIII. "Kratzer the Astronomer" (Louvre), "Henry VIII" (Rome).

Holy Alliance. League uniting Alexander I of Russia, the emperor of Austria, and the king of Prussia. Concluded at Paris in 1815. Later joined by all the Christian sovereigns of Europe except the Pope and the Prince Regent of England. Ostensibly aimed at the preservation of peace, religion, justice. Became a mere cloak for reactionary outrages.

Honorius. Roman Emperor A.D. 395-423. First emperor in the West after division of the Empire.

Horuk (1473-1518). Pirate. First Turkish ruler in Algiers, whose sheik had called for his help against Spain. He eliminated the sheik, and made himself ruler.

Humboldt, von, Alexander (1769-1859). German natural scientist who explored South America from 1799 to 1804. *Voyages aux régions equinoctiales du nouveau continent; Cosmos.*

Hyksos. Bedouins from Canaan who ruled Egypt from 1700 to 1550 B.C.

Hyphasis. Ancient name of a river in northwest India.

Ibn Saud, Abdul Aziz. Modern Arabian ruler.

Ibrahim Pasha (1789-1848). Son of Mehemet Ali. Egyptian general and viceroy. Led Egyptian troops to Greece in 1824.

Ictinus. Greek architect of the second half of the fifth century B.C. He and Callicrates together built the Parthenon (448-432).

Illyria. Name given by Greeks and Romans to the east coast of the Adriatic from Istria to Albania. Subjugated by·Augustus (35-33). Later possession of Ostrogoths, Byzantines, Turks, and Austria.

Indo-Germans. Peoples speaking Indo-Germanic languages—Indians, Slavs, Germans, Greeks, Romans, Celts, etc.

Innocent III. Pope 1198-1216. Guardian of Frederick II of Hohenstaufen. The first to maintain the principle that the Pope was the vicar of God— instead of Peter's alone—on earth, and therefore entitled to all temporal and spiritual power.

Isaac Angelus II. Byzantine emperor 1185-1195, 1203-1204. Dethroned by his brother in 1195, restored by the crusaders.

Isaiah. Hebrew prophet (between 750 and 700 B.C.).

Isocrates (436-338 B.C.). Greek orator, teacher of rhetoric. Urged the union of Greece in order to put up a strong defense against Macedon.

Isthmian Games. Ancient Greek national festival games on the Isthmus of Corinth. Celebrated in the first and third year of each Olympiad.

Ithaca. One of the Ionian islands. Whether the one we know is identical with the home of Odysseus is questionable.

Janizaries. Turkish troops, started in 1329 with a membership made up of captives who had been converted to Islam, later reinforced with Christian subjects. Distinguished by special fighting power and cruelty.

Jeremiah. Old Testament prophet. Accused of blasphemy when he proclaimed the downfall of the state and imprisoned as guilty of high treason when he prophesied the conquest of Jerusalem.

Jerez de la Frontera. City in the Spanish province of Cadiz. The Arabs under Tarik defeated the Visigoths here in 711.

Joanna the Mad (1479-1554). Queen of Castile. Mother of Charles V.

John XII. Pope 955-963. The first pope to give up his baptismal name and assume a new one as pope. Summoned the German emperor Otto I to Italy, and was later deposed by him.

Josephus, Flavius (37-about A.D. 103). Jewish historian. Fought Rome during the Jewish uprising. Afterwards got into the good graces of Vespasian by prophesying the imperial crown. *History of the Jewish War.*

Josiah. King of Judah 639-609 B.C. Reestablished the political independence of Judah.

Juba I (died 46 B.C.). King of Numidia. A follower of Pompey against Caesar.

Juba II (died A.D. 23). King of Numidia. Son of Juba I; husband of the daughter of Antonius and Cleopatra. Augustus gave him Mauretania as a kingdom.

Jugurtha. King of Numidia (about 160-104 B.C.). The struggle of Rome against him was called the Jugurthine War (111-106).

Julius II. Pope 1503-1513. Patron of Bramante, Michelangelo, Raphael. Began the new St. Peter's, consolidated and enlarged the church state.

Justinian I. Byzantine Emperor 527-565. Cleared the west of the Empire (Africa, Sardinia, Corsica, Italy, Sicily, parts of the Spanish coast) of Vandals and Goths. Sought to combine the powers of emperor and pope.

Jutes. The Germans originally settled in Jutland; migrated to England.

Kabyles. North African tribe, living in the Atlas Mountains.

Khurasan. District in Persia.

Knox, John (probably 1505-1572). Disciple of Calvin, translator of the Bible, reformer of Scotland.

Kush. Hebrew name for Abyssinia.

Laconia. District of the southeastern Peloponnesus. Ancient Sparta was located here.

Larissa. Town in Thessaly.

Latin League. A loose confederation of Italian cities. The best known was Alba Longa, later Rome.

Latins. Ancient inhabitants of Latium. According to Roman tradition, Aeneas named the people after a king, Latinus. The capital was Alba Longa.

League of Cambrai. Formed against Venice in 1580 by the Pope, Emperor Maximilian I of Germany, and Louis XII of France.

Leibnitz, von, Gottfried Wilhelm (1646-1716). German philosopher, mathematician, physicist, mechanician, jurist, political writer, historical and linguistic scholar. Suggested to Louis XIV the building of the Suez Canal. Planned to establish an Academy of Civilized Nations to guide the future, which Leibnitz saw as a combination of science, technology, and pure Christianity.

Lemnos. Largest island in the north Aegean.

Leo VI (the Wise, the Philosopher). Byzantine emperor 886-911. During his reign Thessalonica was taken by Mohammedan pirates.

Leo I (the Great). Pope 440-461. Canonized. The primacy of the pope became clear during his reign.

Leo X. Pope 1513-1521. Son of Lorenzo de' Medici. Michelangelo, Raphael, etc., worked at his court.

Leo XIII. Pope 1878-1903. Opened the papal archives to historical studies. His chief aims, the reestablishment of the church state and the reincorporation of the Greek Church, he did not achieve.

Lepanto. Town in Aetolia. On October 7, 1571, Don John of Austria, with an Italian and Spanish fleet, won here a naval victory over the Turks.

Leucothea. In Greek mythology, a sea goddess (nymph), the daughter of Cadmus.

Leukas. One of the Ionian islands.

Levi Ben Gerson (1288-1344). Jewish philosopher, interpreter of the Bible, mathematician, and astronomer, from southern France.

Libya. Earliest name for Africa so far as it was known to the Greeks. (West of the Nile to the Atlantic Ocean.)

Ligurians. Ancient people living in the region between the Cévennes Mountains, the Po River plains, and the Rhine and Rhone rivers.

Limes. Fortified boundary of the Romans; for instance, the Limes Germanicus, the boundary between the empire and the Germans.

Linant de Bellefonds, Maurice Adolphe (1800-1883). Chief engineer in the building of the Suez Canal.

Lipari Islands. Group north of Sicily.

Livia Drusilla (58 B.C.-A.D. 29). Roman empress, wife of Augustus.

Lombards. Germanic people, settled in historic times on the lower Elbe. Invaded Italy. Lombardy is named after them. The Lombardic language was absorbed into Italian about A.D. 1000.

Loyola, de, Ignatius (1491-1556). Spanish officer, founder of the Jesuit order. *Exercitia spiritualia*. Canonized 1622.

Lucullus, Lucius Licinius (about 117-57 B.C.). Roman general, distinguished himself as administrator and soldier. After his period of service he became famous for the luxury of his life. Introduced the cultivated sweet-cherry tree into Europe from Pontus.

Luini, Bernardino (about 1480/85-1532). Italian painter. Frescoes of the Ambrosiana (Milan), "Decapitation of John the Baptist" (Florence).

Lusignan, de, Guy. Descended from an old family in Poitou. King of Jerusalem, lost the throne, and took over Cyprus in 1193.

Lyautey, Hubert (1854-1934). French general, 1916-1917. Secretary of War until 1925. Resident General of Morocco.

Lysippus. Greek sculptor of the fourth century B.C., court sculptor to Alexander the Great.

Maccabees. Family of Jewish heroes who freed the Jews of Syria. Flourished chiefly 160-60 B.C. Aristobulus assumed the title of king. Mariamne was the wife of Herod the Great, who had all male children of her family killed to assure himself of the throne.

Maeander (today Menderes). River in Asia Minor.

Maecenas, Gaius (died 8 B.C.). Roman knight and financier. A confidant of Augustus. Patron of Horace, Vergil, Propertius. His name has become a common noun.

Magenta. City in northern Italy. The French and Piedmontese defeated the Austrians here on June 4, 1859.

Mahdi, The (Mohammed Ahmed) (1848-1885), Rebellion of. Defeated by Kitchener at Omdurman.

Maimonides. Jewish physician and philosopher. Born at Córdoba in 1135, expelled as a Jew. Led a wandering life, became personal physician to Sultan Saladin. Died 1204.

Mamelukes. Originally Turkish slaves, used in the Egyptian army at the time of the Ayubites (1171-1250). Attained influence, formed a ruling dynasty (1250-1517).

Manin, Ludovico (1726-1802). Last doge of Venice.

Manuel I (Comnenus). Emperor at Constantinople 1143-1180, steered the empire through the perils of a marauding expedition by the Normans in 1147 and the second crusade (1147-1148).

Marbod. King of the Marcomanni. Founded a powerful empire, the center of a league of tribes, about 9 B.C. in the region of modern Bohemia. It was destroyed by Arminius. Marbod fled to the Romans.

Marchand, Jean Baptiste. French soldier and explorer. Figured in the Fashoda incident; forced back with his French troops from the Sudan by Kitchener, 1898.

Marcus Aurelius. Roman emperor A.D. 161-180. "A philosopher on the imperial throne." *Meditations.*

Marduk. Deity of Babylon about 4000 B.C.; later chief national deity.

Margaret of Parma (1522-1586). Daughter of Charles V; Stadholder of the Netherlands 1559-1567.

Marius, Caius (156-86 B.C.). Roman general. Uncle of Julius Caesar. Annihilated Teutons at Aix-en-Provence in 102 and the Cimri at Vercellae in 101.

Marlborough, John Churchill, Duke of (1650-1722). English statesman and general. One of the leaders in the War of the Spanish Succession. The victor of Hoechstadt in 1704, Oudenarde in 1708, Malplaquet in 1709.

Marmara, Sea of. Inland sea between the Bosporus and the Dardanelles.

Marranos. Contemptuous Spanish term for baptized Jews and Moors.

Marsala. Harbor town in western Sicily. Garibaldi disembarked here with his volunteers May 11, 1860.

Martin V. Pope 1417-1431. Restored papal sovereignty in Rome and the Papal State. King Alfonso of Aragon set up an opposition pope when Martin failed to support his pretensions in Naples.

Massinissa (died 149/8 B.C.). King of the Massyli in Numidia. Went over from the Carthaginians to the Romans in the Second Punic War, and partly caused the Third Punic War.

Mecca. Arabian city, holy place of Islam.

Medici. Florentine patrician family, bankers. Assumed the leadership of the people against the great families in the fourteenth century, actually ruled the city in the beginning of the fifteenth century. Charles V made their territory a duchy.

Medici, de' Cosmo. Chief of Florentine Republic 1434-64, patron of Brunelleschi, Donatello. Founder of the Platonic Academy. Laid the groundwork for the Bibliotheca Laurentiana. Gathered the most important humanists around him.

Mehemet Ali (1769-1849). Founder of the present Egyptian dynasty.

Meloria. Island in the Ligurian Sea. In 1241 King Enzio here defeated the Genoese navy, and in 1284 the Genoese defeated the Pisans.

Messalina, Valeria. Third wife of the Roman Emperor Claudius, who had her killed; she was probably better than her reputation.

Messina. City at the northern tip of Sicily.

Michael VIII (Palaeologus). Byzantine emperor 1259-1282. Founder of the last Byzantine dynasty, the Palaeologi. Aided by the Genoese, captured Constantinople in 1261.

Michelangelo Buonarroti (1475-1564). Italian sculptor, painter, architect, and poet. The Tombs of the Medici (Florence), paintings on the ceiling of the Sistine Chapel in Rome, designs for the completion of St. Peter's, Rome.

Miletus. Ancient Greek city in western Asia Minor.

Miltiades. Athenian general, tyrant of the Thracian Chersonese. The victory of Marathon in 490 B.C. was his work.

Misenum. Naval station for the Tyrrhenian fleet in southern Italy under Augustus. The city was destroyed by the Saracens A.D. 890.

Missolonghi. City on the Gulf of Patras. Chief bulwark of the Greeks in the war of independence. Lord Byron died here. When it became impossible for the city to hold out longer, the defenders blew themselves up along with the inrushing besiegers.

Mithras. Ancient Indo-Iranian deity, whose cult spread from Persia throughout the entire Roman Empire in the time of the early emperors. Women were excluded from the cult.

Mithridates Eupator (the Great). King of Pontus, born about 131 B.C.; reigned 120 to 63 B.C.

Mocenigo. Venetian family that produced seven doges.

Mona Lisa. Wife of Francesco del Giocondo, Florence. Made famous by Leonardo's portrait (Louvre).

Montpellier. Capital of French department of Herault. Founded by fugitives from Magelone, destroyed by Charles Martel. Famous medieval university.

Morosini, Francesco (1618-1694). Venetian admiral and doge. Made Captain General against the Turks in 1668, conquered Athens in 1684. Hero of Crete.

Murano. City near Venice, famous for its glass industry.

Murcia. City and province of southeastern Spain.

Mycenae. Town in the Greek province of Argolis. In Greek mythology founded by Perseus. Capital of King Agamemnon, about 1600-1500 B.C.

Mylae. Ancient city near Messenia in Sicily. Naval victory of the Romans over Carthage in 260 B.C., victory of Agrippa over Sextus Pompeius in 36 B.C.

Myron. Attic sculptor in the first half of the fifth century B.C.

Narses. General under Justinian I. Defeated the Ostrogoths near Taginae in Italy A.D. 552.

Naucratis. Ancient Greek town in Egypt. Center of Greco-Egyptian trade before the foundation of Alexandria.

Nausicaa. Daughter of Alcinous, king of the Phaeacians, in the *Odyssey*.

Navarino. Greek bay in Messenia. Scene of defeat of the Turkish-Egyptian fleet in 1827.

Nebuchadnezzar II. King of Babylon 605-562 B.C. Destroyed Jerusalem in 586. On inscriptions he mentioned only his peaceful accomplishments, the construction of canals, etc. The so-called Hanging Gardens of Semiramis were built by him for his wife.

Necho. Pharaoh 609-595 B.C., tried to connect the Nile and the Red Sea by a canal. Sent out Phoenician sailors who circumnavigated Africa.

Negrelli, Alois Ritter von Moldelbe (1799-1858). Austrian engineer. His surveys proved the possibility of building the Suez Canal without locks.

Nerva, Marcus Cocceius. Roman emperor A.D. 96-98.

Neuhof, Theodor, Baron (1686-1756). German adventurer who made himself King of Corsica and ruled there for nine months.

Newton, Charles Thomas, Sir. English archaeologist (1816-1894). English consul in Rhodes and Rome. Brought valuable discoveries of ancient sculpture to London. *Travels and Discoveries in the Levant.*

Nicaea. Ancient city near the present Turkish Isnik. Famous for the first and seventh Ecumenical Councils (A.D. 325, 787), which were held there.

Nikita. King of Montenegro.

Normans (also called Vikings). German-Scandinavian warrior tribe. From the eighth to the eleventh century, pirates; then founders and conquerors of colonies.

Ogygia. Mythological island in the Mediterranean, possibly Malta. The island of the nymph Calypso in Homer's *Odyssey*.

Olympia. Shrine of Zeus and Hera at Elis. Scene of the Greek national festival, the Olympic Games.

Olympus, Mount. Near the Thessalian-Macedonian border. The palace of the gods in Greek mythology.

Omar I. (582-644). Second successor of Mohammed. Founded Basra and Kufa, introduced the reckoning of time from the Hejira.

Orion. Famous mythological hunter. Loved by Eos because of his beauty. Killed by Artemis.

Osiris. Egyptian god of the Nile and of flood.

Ostia. Seaport of ancient Rome, at the mouth of the Tiber.

Ostrogoths. One of the Gothic tribes. In the fourth century B.C. they founded a great empire on the Black Sea. Under Theodoric the Great they were dominant in northern and central Italy. His empire included Italy, Sicily, Dalmatia, Slavonia, the Alps, and Provence.

Othman (1259-1326). Founder of the Ottoman Empire, which was named after him.

Otto I (the Great). German emperor 936-973. Undertook three expeditions to Italy.

Otto II. Son of Otto I. German emperor 973-983. Advanced as far as Tarentum, defeated the Saracens at Colonne in Calabria in 982.

Palma, Il Vecchio (about 1480-1528). Italian painter. Supposedly a pupil of Giovanni Bellini. Represented the Venetian Renaissance at its height. "Santa conversazione" (Louvre).

Palmerston, Henry John Temple, Viscount (1784-1865). English statesman. Called "Lord Firebrand" because of his temperament.

Pamirs, The. Plateau of central Asia, known as the "Roof of the World."

Panathenaea. Chief festival of Athena. Celebrated at midsummer in ancient Athens. Oil from sacred olive trees was distributed as the prize in the contests held on this occasion.

Pantelleria. Volcanic island near Sicily. Today a naval base.

Paoli, di, Pasquale (1725-1807). Fighter for Corsican freedom. Directed rebellion against the Genoese and against France when the Genoese sold the island to her.

Paphlagonia. Anciently a mountain district in northern Asia Minor.

Parnassus. Mountain in Phocis, Greece. Mythological residence of Apollo and the Muses.

Paros. Greek island of the Cyclades group.

Pelasgians. Regarded by the ancient Greeks as the original inhabitants of Greece.

Pepin the Short. King of the Franks 752-768. Established the church state proper by the so-called Donation of Pepin.

Père Joseph (properly François Leclerc de Tremblay) (1577-1638). French Capuchin, confidant of Richelieu, known as the "Gray Eminence."

Pergamum. Ancient city in Mysia.

Perugino (properly Pietro Vannucci) (about 1450-1523). Italian painter. The most important painter in Umbria before Raphael. "Madonna Enthroned with Saints" (Florence).

Peruzzi. Florentine family, of great political and economic influence, particularly in the thirteenth and fourteenth centuries.

Peter the Great. Russian Czar (1682-1725). Founded St. Petersburg. Father of Russian aspirations in the Baltic and Black Sea. Issued ordinance in 1722 providing that each ruler should choose his own successor. Sought to modernize Russia.

Petrarch, Francesco (1304-1374). Italian poet, scholar, pioneer of Humanism. *Rerum vulgarium fragmenta.*

Phaeacians. Mythological nation of seafarers inhabiting the island of Scheria, which probably is Corfu.

Phanariots. Inhabitants of the Phanar, a section of Constantinople. Once largely Greeks who belonged to the old Byzantine Empire. In a broader sense, a sort of aristocracy of birth and office. The Phanariots took an active part in the Greek War of Liberation in 1821.

Pharos. Island off Alexandria, at whose eastern tip Ptolemy II built a lighthouse that was considered one of the wonders of the world. Completed in 280-279 B.C.

Pharsalus. Town on the edge of the Thessalian plain. A decisive battle between Caesar and Pompey took place here in 48 B.C.

Phigalia. Town in Arcadia with the celebrated Temple of Apollo, supposedly built by Ictinus.

Philip II. King of Spain 1556-1598. Son of Charles V, central figure of the Counter Reformation, which he tried to carry through in the Netherlands. His navy, the Armada, which he sent against England in 1558, was destroyed; in the Mediterranean he fought against Islam.

Philip V (died 179 B.C.). King of Macedonia. Made alliances against Rome with Hannibal, later with Antiochus III of Syria. Defeated in 197 at Cynoscephalae.

Philip the Arab. Roman emperor 244-249. Born in an Arabian village.

Philip the Fair. King of France 1285-1314.

Philippi. Ancient city of Thrace, named for Philip II of Macedon. Antony and Octavian (Augustus) defeated Brutus and Cassius here in 42 B.C.

Philistines. Nation in Palestine, which is named after them.

Philo of Alexandria (30/20 B.C.-A.D. 54). Jewish Hellenistic philosopher.

Phocaea. Ancient town of Asia Minor. A trade center of great importance; mother town of many colonies (Marseille, etc.).

Phoenicia. Ancient name of the long, narrow strip of land at the center of the Syrian Mediterranean coast.

Phryne. Greek hetaira, who is said to have served as Praxiteles's model for the Aphrodite of Cnidus.

Pico della Mirandola, Giovanni Francesco (1463-1494), Italian humanist, philosopher. Invited the scholars of the world to come to Rome at his expense in 1496 in order to argue nine hundred of his theses. The Pope forbade this disputation. *De dignitate hominis.*

Pietro della Vigna (1190-1249). Judge of the court, head of the imperial chancellery, confidant of Frederick II of Hohenstaufen. His eyes were put out for embezzlement.

Pindar. Greek lyricist (about 518-after 446 B.C.). *Odes.*

Piraeus. Port of Athens.

Pius V. Pope 1566-1572. With Venice and Philip II of Spain he formed the league that was victorious against the Turks at Lepanto.

Pius IX. Pope 1846-1878. During his pontificate the church state as a temporal power came to an end. After the king of Italy moved to the Quirinal, the Pope regarded himself as a prisoner in the Vatican. Convoked Vatican Council, 1870, which decreed papal infallibility.

Poitiers. Capital of the French department of Vienne. Charles Martel defeated the Arabs here A.D. 732.

Pollio, Asinius (76 B.C.-A.D. 5). Roman teacher of rhetoric and writer. Wrote a history of the civil war between Caesar and Pompey, established the first public library in Rome.

Pontus. Northeastern coast region of ancient Asia Minor.

Porto Alegre. Capital of the Brazilian state of Rio Grande do Sul.

Posidonius (born about 130 B.C.). Greek philosopher. Calculated the size of the earth, discovered the dependence of the tides on the moon, calculated the distance from sun to earth.

Praxiteles (about 400-330 B.C.). Greek sculptor. He and Scopas were the most celebrated sculptors in marble about the middle of the fourth century.

Preveza. Port in northwestern Greece. The Turks here defeated the united navies of Venice, Spain, and the Pope in 1538.

Priam. King of Troy, father of Paris and Hector. Killed by the Greeks at the taking of Troy.

Propertius. Roman writer of elegies, about the middle of the first century B.C. Belonged to the circle around Maecenas; friend of Vergil.

Propontis. Ancient name for the Sea of Marmara.

Protagoras (about 485-415 B.C.). Greek philosopher. Traveled all over Greece. Charged with atheism in Athens. Taught the subjectivity of sense perceptions.

Ptolemies. Members of the Macedonian dynasty that ruled Egypt from the time of Alexander the Great (323-30 B.C.).

Ptolemy I (died 283 B.C.). Friend and general of Alexander the Great, upon whose death he received the sovereignty of Egypt. Established his residence at Alexandria.

Ptolemy II (285-246 B.C.). Son of Ptolemy I. Made Alexandria the center of the civilization of his day.

Puteoli. Ancient city near Naples. The port of Cumae, one of the leading ocean cities of Italy. Modern Pozzuoli.

Pydna. Ancient seaport of Macedonia. In 168 B.C. the Romans under Aemilius Paulus here defeated King Perseus of Macedon.

Pyrrhus (319-272 B.C.). King of Epirus. Fought against Rome with the Tarentines, against Carthage with the Syracusans. His victory over the Romans at Ausculum was so dearly bought that he is said to have exclaimed, "One more such victory, and we are lost."

Pythagoras (died 497/6 B.C.). Greek philosopher of Samos. Established in Italy a society rather like a religious order for the cultivation of science and morality. The society, which quickly spread, was finally suppressed.

Rameses II (the Great) (1292-1225 B.C.). Egyptian Pharaoh. Long wars with Hittites; retained possession of Palestine. Regarded as a peerless king.

Raphael Santi (1483-1520). Italian painter, represented the Renaissance at its height. Pope Leo employed him to direct the building of St. Peter's and to preserve the ancient monuments.

Renan, Ernest (1823-1892). French Orientalist. *Life of Jesus.*

Richard III. King of England 1483-1485.

Rienzi, Cola di (1313-1354). Roman Humanist, politician. Son of an innkeeper, became a notary, proclaimed the sovereignty of the Roman people in 1347, issued a proclamation for the unification of Italy.

Roger II. King of Sicily 1130-1354. United the Norman dominions of southern Italy into one state. Tried to extend the Sicilian power over the Mediterranean.

Rooke, Sir George (1650-1709). British admiral who hoisted the British flag at Gibraltar in 1704 on his own responsibility, occupying the rock in the name of Queen Anne.

Roxolana. Probably a Russian by birth, slave of Solyman the Magnificent, over whom she had great influence.

Rubicon. Small river in northeastern Italy. By crossing this river Caesar opened the civil war in 49 B.C. The ancient course of the river was different from what it is today.

Ruyter, de, Michel Adriaanszoon (1607-1679). Dutch admiral. Defeated the English in the Four Days' Battle in 1666, fought in the Mediterranean in 1675 with a small fleet at Agasta and Stromboli.

Saint John, Order of the Hospital of. Oldest religious chivalric order. Founded in 1070 by merchants from Amalfi. After their conquest of Rhodes they were called Knights of Rhodes; after receiving Malta in fee, Knights of Malta.

Saint Bernard, Great and Little. Important passes over the western Alps.

Saint Theresa of Spain (1515-1582). Chief representative of Spanish mysticism.

Saint-Raphaël. French city on the Mediterranean, department of Var, near Fréjus.

Saladin (1137-1193). Sultan of Egypt and Syria. Established the Ayubite dynasty in Egypt in 1171, inflicted a shattering defeat on a Christian army in 1187. His conquest of Jerusalem led to the third crusade.

Salamis. Greek island in the Gulf of Aegina. The Greek fleet defeated the Persians here in 480 B.C.

Salerno. City in southern Italy. In the early Middle Ages a Lombard possession, then Norman. Famous for its medical faculty, which became the model for all European medical schools.

Salza, von, Hermann. Master of the Teutonic Order 1210-1239. Moved the Order from Palestine to the Occident. The most faithful friend of Frederick II of Hohenstaufen.

Samaria. City in central Palestine. Herod the Great received it as a gift from Augustus.

Samos. Greek island in the Aegean Sea. The art of casting bronze was discovered here about 600 B.C. Athens conquered the island in 365 B.C., expelled the population, and resettled the island.

Samson. One of the judges of Israel, a national hero from the tribe of Dan.

San Lazzaro. Lagoon island, southeast of Venice.

Santorin. Southernmost of the Cyclades group.

Saracens. In ancient times name for the Arabs of the Northwestern Arabian desert and the Sinai peninsula. Later extended to cover all Arabs and peoples of Arabic culture.

Sardinia. Second largest island of Italy. A grain center of the Carthaginians, since 238 B.C. under Roman rule. Occupied by the Vandals A.D. 458-533. Inhabitants Sardes.

Savonarola, Girolamo (1452-1498). Italian preacher and ecclesiastical-political reformer in Florence. An opponent of the Medicis. Hanged as a heretic.

Scutari. Suburb of Constantinople on the Asiatic side of the strait. Also, a city on the Yugoslavian coast.

Scylla. In Homer's *Odyssey,* a six-headed monster living in a cave opposite Charybdis.

Scythians. Inhabitants of the South Russian steppes in ancient times; nomads.

Seleucia. City of northern Syria, port of Antioch. Several other cities of this name in western Asia, all dating from Hellenistic times.

Selim the Drunkard. Turkish Sultan 1566-1574. Interested chiefly in poetry and wine. The conquest of Cyprus was the sole result of his initiative.

Selinunte. Westernmost Greek colony in Sicily.

Seljuks. Turkish ruling family, whose progenitor, Seljuk, came from western Turkestan. Several dynasties in Persia, Mesopotamia, Syria, Asia Minor, during the eleventh and twelfth centuries.

Semite. Descendant of Shem, the son of Noah. Includes peoples of western Asia, northern and eastern Africa. There is no such thing as a Semitic race.

Seneca, Lucius Annaeus (the Elder). Latin teacher of rhetoric, born in Spain, came to Rome in the middle of the first century B.C., and wrote from A.D. 38 to 41.

Seneca, Lucius Annaeus (the Younger) (died A.D. 65). Son of Seneca the Elder. Philosopher, writer, tutor of Nero. His tragedies and ethical writings were widely read during the Middle Ages. *Phaedra, Medea, Epistolae morales ad Lucilium.*

Sète (formerly Cette). French fortified harbor town on the Mediterranean. (Department of Hérault.)

Sforza, Catarina (1463-1509). Wife of Girolamo Riario, a son of Pope Sixtus IV. *"Femina, quasi virago, crudelissima e di grande animo."*

Sforza, Ludovico (called *Il Moro*) (1451-1508). Duke of Milan.

Shaw, John (1773-1823). American naval officer, commander in the recapture of Mobile, Alabama.

Sidon. Ancient harbor town of the Phoenicians, today Saïda. Conquered by Alexander the Great in 333 B.C., and in 33 B.C. by the Romans.

Sierra Nevada. Highest mountains in Spain, in the southern part of the country.

Sinan (probably 1489-1587). Turkish architect to Solyman the Great and Selim I and II. Some three hundred buildings are attributed to him, among them the Princes' Mosque in Constantinople.

Sinope. Ancient city, originally an Assyrian settlement, then a Milesian colony on the Black Sea. Modern Sinop.

Smyrna. Town of Asiatic Turkey, founded by Aeolians.

Solferino. Town in the Italian province of Mantua. In 1859 the French and Piedmontese defeated the Austrians here.

Solyman the Magnificent. Turkish Sultan 1520-1566. Conquered almost all of Hungary, besieged Vienna. His fleets ruled the Mediterranean as far as Spain, the Red Sea, and part of the Indian Ocean. The greatest extension of the Empire came in his reign. Wrote poems, *Divan of Sultan Soliman the Great.*

Spezia, La. Italian town and naval base in Liguria.

Spina. City at the southern mouth of the Po.

Spinola. Genoese family. Ghibellines. One of the four greatest Genoese houses.

Stilicho, Flavius (about A.D. 365-408). Roman general, statesman. Son of a Vandal. Defeated Alaric and the Ostrogoth Radagaisus in Italy.

Strabo (about 63 B.C.-A.D. 20). Greek geographer. Traveled extensively. *Geography.*

Stromboli. One of the Lipari Islands. Volcano.

Sulla, Lucius Cornelius (138-78 B.C.). Roman general, statesman, dictator with unlimited tenure, notorious for his proscriptions. The first Roman general to reach the Euphrates.

Sunium. Foothills at the southern tip of Attica. Fortified in ancient times.

Sybaris. Greek colony in southern Italy, founded by Achaeans about 706 B.C. Destroyed at the end of the sixth century. The word "sybarite" has come into use as a common noun.

Sylvester II. Pope 999-1003. One of the greatest scholars of his time, which led people in the Middle Ages to believe he had made a compact with the devil. Wrote on mathematics and logic.

Syracuse. Province and city in Sicily, founded by Corinth in the second half of the eighth century B.C.

Syrtes. Two gulfs on the North African shore of the Mediterranean.

Tacitus, Cornelius (after A.D. 50-after 116). Roman consul, viceroy of Asia, historian. *Germania, Histories, Annals.*

Tacitus, Marcus Claudius. Roman emperor 275/6. Successor of Aurelian. Killed by his soldiers.

Talaat Pasha, Mehmed (1874-1921). Leader of the Young Turks. Assassinated 1921.

Tarik. A freedman, Arabian general, crossed to Spain in A.D. 711, inflicted a decisive defeat on the Visigoths at Jerez de la Frontera. To cover his crossing he built a castle, Jebel-al-Tarik, now Gibraltar.

Tarquinius. Etruscan family name. Two kings of ancient Rome: Tarquinius Priscus (616-579 B.C.) and Tarquinius Superbus (534-510 B.C.).

Tartessus. Ancient town on the southwest coast of Spain, near modern Cadiz. Famous for its silver and tin markets.

Tasso, Torquato (1544-1595). Italian poet. *La Gerusalemme Liberata.*

Tel Aviv. Greatest modern Jewish city in Palestine. Founded by Zionists.

Telemachus. Son of Odysseus and Penelope.

Templars. Religious order of knights, founded about 1119 for the protection of the pilgrims going to the Holy Land. Headquarters in Jerusalem, then in Cyprus. Disbanded in 1312.

Tenedos. Turkish island in the Aegean Sea, fort barring the entrance to the Dardanelles.

Teraphim. A sort of household gods of the earliest Israelites, represented in human form, later regarded as idols.

Tertullian, Quintus Septimius Florens (after 150-about 222). Oldest Latin church writer, creator of the Latin liturgical language, among the founders of the old Catholic doctrine.

Teutoburger Wald. In the upper Ems territory, where the Roman general Varus was defeated by the German Arminius, A.D. 9.

Teutons. German or Celtic-Helvetic people, crushingly defeated by Marius at Aquae Sextiae in 102 B.C.

Thales of Miletus. Greek philosopher (about 600 B.C.).

Themistocles (about 525-459 B.C.). Athenian general and statesman. Developed the Piraeus into a naval harbor; victor of Salamis.

Theodora (about 508-548). Consort of Justinian I.

Theodoric the Great. King of the Ostrogoths 471-526 B.C. Defeated and killed Odoacer. His dominion extended over Italy, Sicily, Dalmatia, part of Pannonia, Noricum Mediterraneanse, Rhaetia.

Theodosius the Great. Roman emperor 379-395. The last ruler over the Roman Empire in its entirety. Welcomed the Goths into the commonwealth as allies, required them to do military service.

Theodosius II. Eastern Roman emperor 408-450. Grandson of Theodosius I.

Theseus. Athenian national hero. Originator of the joint settlement of Attica, founder of popular rule.

Thessaly. Province in northern Greece.

Thomas Aquinas, Saint (1225/26-1274). Church father, called the Angelic Doctor. *Summa theologiae.*

Thrace. Southeastern part of the Balkan Peninsula.

Thucydides (about 460-400 B.C.). Greek historian, chronicler of the Peloponnesian War.

Thule. According to the account of Pytheas of Massilia, the place where the sun sets, the unattainable north of the inhabited earth, hence Ultima Thule.

Tiberius, Claudius Nero. Roman emperor A.D. 14-37. Stepson of Augustus. Applied the law of lese majesty; misanthropic, retired to Capri A.D. 26.

Ticino. Tributary of the Po. On its bank Hannibal defeated the Romans in 218 B.C.

Tintoretto (properly Jacopo Robusti) (1518-1594). Italian painter, pupil of Titian. "The Smithy of Vulcan" (Venice).

Titus, Flavius Vespasianus, Roman emperor 79-81 A.D., destroyed Jerusalem in 70. Consecrated the Colosseum at Rome, begun by his father, Vespasian. Arch of Titus, Baths of Titus in Rome.

Torquemada, de, Tomás (1420-1498). Spanish inquisitor general.

Toscanelli, Paolo del Pozzo (1397-1482). Italian physicist, astronomer. Influenced Columbus' plan of discovery.

Trajan, Marcus Ulpius. Roman emperor 98-117, the first provincial to occupy the throne. The Roman Empire reached its greatest extent during his reign. Tacitus, Juvenal, Pliny the Younger, Plutarch lived in his day. Trajan's Column in Rome.

Trebizond. Port on the Black Sea. Founded by Greeks from Sinope in the seventh century B.C.

Tribonian (died A.D. 545). Eastern Roman jurist. President of the commission that revised the legislation of Justinian.

Trierarch. Athenian commander of a trireme for a term of one year. He was responsible for equipment and maintenance.

Tuscany. Historic section of Italy whose capital is Florence. Region of ancient Etruria, which was called Tuscia in the Middle Ages.

Tyrrhenians. Greek name for the Etruscans.

Uganda. British protectorate in east Africa.

Umberto I. King of Italy 1878-1900. Son of Victor Emanuel II, father of Victor Emanuel III. Assassinated.

Urban II. Pope 1088-1099. Relied on the Normans for his authority; began the crusading movement.

Valencia. Former kingdom on the east coast of Spain. A modern Spanish province and city.

Valens, Flavius. Eastern Roman Emperor 364-78. Allowed the Visigoths, harassed by Huns, to settle in Thrace. Was killed by them. Their fleet dominated the Mediterranean. Emperor Justinian annihilated them.

Valette, de la, Jean, Grand Master of the Knights of St. John 1557-1568. Founded the city bearing his name in Malta.

Vandals. Eastern Germanic people originally settled in Silesia and Poland. Emigrated to Spain, Africa, where they conquered Carthage. Their empire included the Roman province of Africa, the Balearics, the Pityusae, and Corsica.

Vicenza. Town in upper Italy. Residence of Longobardian kings in the early Middle Ages.

Victor Emmanuel II. King of Italy 1861-1878 (King of Sardinia from 1849). Called "Il Re Galantuomo" because of his honorable nature.

Vikings. Name for Normans.

Villehardouin, de, Geoffroi (about 1150-1213). French historian. Joined in the fourth crusade, which he chronicled in his *Histoire de la conquête de Constantinople*.

Visconti. Lombardic noble family, can be traced back to 1075, ruled Milan 1277-1447. Ducal title hereditary from 1395.

Vistula. Chief river of Poland. Rises in the Yablunka Mountains, empties into the Baltic.

Viterbo. City and province of Italy, originally the Roman colony Vicus Elbii.

Voss, Johann Heinrich (1751-1826). German philologist and writer, translator of classical literature—Homer, Horace, Hesiod, Aristophanes.

Wallenstein, von, Albrecht (1583-1634). General in the Thirty Years' War on the imperial side. Made an immense fortune by purchasing the estates of the rebels.

Yahweh (Jehovah). Name of the God of Israel. Interpreted as, "I am."

Ypsilanti, Alexander, the Younger (1792-1828). Leader in the Greek War of Liberation. Born in Constantinople, brought up in Russia, stirred up the rebellion of the Greeks in the Danube principalities in 1821.

Ypsilanti, Demetrius (1793-1832). Brother of Alexander Ypsilanti, took complete command of the troops in eastern Greece in 1828.

Zaghlul Pasha (1860-1927). Anti-British prime minister of Egypt.

Zara. City on the Dalmatian coast, became a Roman colony under Augustus, taken by Venice in the beginning of the thirteenth century, has belonged to Italy since 1920.

Zarathustra. Ancient Iranian religious reformer. His dates cannot be determined.

Zephyrus. West wind. Son of Astraeus and Eos, in Greek mythology.

Zrinyi, Miklos, Count (1508-1566). Hungarian general. Famous for his heroic defense of Szigetvar against Solyman II. Was gravely wounded, taken prisoner, and killed.

INDEX

A

INDEX

The
MEDITERRANEAN
Region